NATURE IN THE NEW WORLD

NATURE
IN THE
NEW WORLD

From Christopher Columbus
to Gonzalo Fernández de Oviedo

BY

ANTONELLO GERBI

TRANSLATED BY

JEREMY MOYLE

 UNIVERSITY OF PITTSBURGH PRESS

Originally published as *La natura delle Indie Nove: Da Cristoforo Colombo a Gonzalo Fernández de Oviedo,* copyright © 1975 Riccardo Ricciardi Editore, Milan

Published by the University of Pittsburgh Press, Pittsburgh, Pa., 15260

Library of Congress Cataloging-in-Publication Data

Gerbi, Antonello, 1904–1976
    Nature in the New World.

    Translation of: La natura delle Indie nove.
    Bibliography: p. 425
    Includes index.
    1. America—Discovery and exploration—Spanish.
    2. Natural history—America—Early works to 1735.
    3. America–Early works to 1600.   I Title.
    E123.G3713   1986   970.01′6   85-22563
    ISBN 0-8229-3516-3 (alk. paper)

This book was supported by translation and publication grants from the National Endowment for the Humanities. Additional assistance for the translation was provided by the Banca Commerciale Italiana, Banque Sudameris, and Dr. Anthony A. Benis.

Contents

Contents

Translator's Preface

ANTONELLO GERBI died on 26 July 1976, shortly after the publication of the Italian edition of this work. His disappearance robbed the field of intellectual history of one of its most outstanding practitioners, and the present translator of a much valued adviser, companion, and friend. In preparing the English translation of this his last work I was thus unable to enjoy the constant and close collaboration with the author that had aided me so much when working on the translation of his *Dispute*. I was however extremely fortunate in finding a most competent substitute in his son, Sandro, who carried out much painstaking research in various libraries on both sides of the Atlantic in response to my numerous queries regarding points of bibliographical or historical detail. The generosity of the National Endowment for the Humanities also enabled me to consult Antonio Alatorre, of the Colégio de México, the Spanish translator of Gerbi's work, and Daymond Turner, of the University of North Carolina, Charlotte, the renowned Oviedo expert. The fourth member of the team whose joint experience and wisdom I unashamedly exploited was Jeremy Lawrance, of Magdalen College, Oxford, and the University of Manchester, who read the manuscript, checked my translations from Spanish and Latin, and made many useful suggestions concerning matters relating to the world of Renaissance Spain. I should like to take the opportunity of expressing my gratitude to this distinguished quadrumvirate, both for the warm welcome they accorded me whenever I visited them and for their unstinting help in professional matters.

The Italian edition of this work gives all quotations in the original language. As these are numerous and often lengthy, and as the languages primarily concerned—Spanish and Latin—are less accessible to English-speaking readers than to their Italian counterparts, I have preferred to put all quotations into English. The translations are my own, unless otherwise indicated. The reader wishing to consult the original language versions may of course refer either to the Italian or Spanish editions of this work, or to the primary sources named in each case.

One of the most difficult problems facing the translator is the extent to which he may legitimately "improve on" the original. He is constantly tempted to second-guess the author, to emerge momentarily from behind the mask of enforced anonymity and put in his own two pennyworth, to set the record straight. I have manfully resisted that temptation, even, for instance, when Gerbi takes Brogan's word for it that the English are now far too polite to refer to their nearest continental neighbors as "frogs." The work now submitted to the reader is therefore a straightforward translation of the highly innovative study presented to the Italian-speaking public in 1975, rather than an annotated or updated edition incorporating subsequent research on the same subject. When the time is ripe for this latter undertaking we may perhaps hope to see a new edition of the *Natura* from the same hand that recently produced the superb new Italian edition of the *Dispute of the New World,* Sandro Gerbi. Such minor modifications as I have made are therefore purely editorial: the addition of a slightly fuller bibliographical reference or the correction of some figure or the spelling of some name that may have gone astray. Attention is not of course drawn to these admendments in the text, as such interpolations could be distracting to the reader. In this connection I should however mention that I have inserted references to the works of Thomas D. Goodrich, Murdo J. MacLeod, P. Revelli, and William M. Sherman, as notes found among Gerbi's papers after his death showed that he planned to mention these authors in any future edition of the *Natura*.

The severest test of the translator's vow of anonymity arose, curiously enough, in connection with Oviedo's own foray into that same field, his translation of a work of Italian devotional literature. Here Gerbi's reference (chap. XV, sec. 6, end) to "an extremely rare, indeed unfindable" work, about which "nothing can be said with certainty until the Italian text has been compared with the supposed Spanish translation," proved altogether too much of a challenge. A visit to the British Museum, together with information supplied by Antonio Alatorre and Sandro Gerbi, revealed the actual situation to be as follows. Oviedo's source was not in fact Fra Cherubino da Siena, as Gerbi (and Daymond Turner) conjectured, but one "Pietro da Lucca," in other words, Pietro Bernardini, canon regular of San Frediano da Lucca, professor of sacred theology, and author of the *Fundamento della vita cristiana* and other works of devotion. The work actually translated by Oviedo, the *Regule della vita spirituale et secreta teologia,* ran into at least five editions. A copy of the 1504 edition is to be found at Harvard, while the British Museum possesses both a copy of the 1538 edition and—most fortuitously—a copy of Oviedo's *Regla de la vida espiritual.* Having personally perused and compared these two last-named volumes I can vouch for the fact that they are indeed the same work. The purchaser of the sale item mentioned by Gerbi (chap. XV, n. 104) was Eugenio Asensio, who gave some details of it in his article "El erasmismo y las corrientes espirituales afines," *Revista de Filología Española,* 36 (1952), 98–99.

Oviedo is the main subject of the present work, and in view of the frequency of reference to his various works the following somewhat abbreviated citation system has been adopted in the footnotes. All references to the *Historia General y Natural* (abbreviated to *Hist.*) contain two pairs of numerals, separated by a colon. The first pair, one Roman and one Arabic, refer to the *book* number and *chapter* number; the second pair, again one Roman and one Arabic, refer to the *volume* number and *page* number. All references are to the Amador de los Ríos edition, unless the letters "PT" appear after the colon, in which case the volume and page numbers refer to the Pérez de Tudela edition. The letter "a" or "b" following the page number indicates the first or second column on that page. Some books of the *Historia* have a preface or "prohemio," indicated as "proh." Citations from the *Sumario* (*Sum.*) refer to the Miranda edition, those from the *Quinquagenas* (*Qu.*) to the Fuente edition, and those from the *Claribalte* to the 1519 edition.

The only other works for which abbreviations have been adopted are Peter Martyr d'Anghiera's *De Orbe Novo decades* (*Dec.*; see chap. VIII, n. 1) and the *Colección . . . España* (*CDIE*), the *Colección . . . Archivo de Indias* (*CDII*), and the *Coleccion . . . Ultramar* (*CDIU*), full details of which are given in the bibliography. The journals most frequently cited are abbreviated in the footnotes as follows: *Cuadernos Americanos* (*CA*), *Hispanic American Historical Review* (*HAHR*), *Journal of the History of Ideas* (*JHI*), *Revista de Historia de América* (*RHA*), and *Revista de Indias* (*RI*).

J.M.

PART 1

From Columbus to Verrazzano

❦ I ❦

Introduction

1. THE INFERIORITY OF AMERICA ACCORDING TO BUFFON

THIS study of Oviedo and the earliest chroniclers of American nature grew out of my research on the "weakness of America," in other words the thesis that the American continent is in some way inferior—and, to be more specific, immature—in relation to the Old World, and that animal life in America suffers from degeneration and arrested development. Hegel is the most famous exponent of this thesis, which was first formulated in scientific terms by Buffon.

It is of course true that chroniclers and travelers had referred to relatively weak or inferior aspects of American nature long before Buffon, indeed almost from the time of Europe's first contacts with the New World, but the criticism and condemnation had remained incidental and episodic and had not been built up into a curse on the whole continent. These sporadic observations were to provide the eighteenth-century critics of America and the Americans with their material but not their arguments, with data but not with physical and geographical theories.

It should also be remembered that the historians of antiquity and the early naturalists of America had no concept of evolution. Following the biblical and Aristotelian tradition, they believed in the fixity of the species, nature as immobility, or as variety fully unfolded in space, unmarked by "the silent and unending march of time." But when Buffon and his supporters and adversaries spoke of the "immaturity" and "degeneration" of the Americas, they were using concepts that implied an evolutionary system of nature; they were immersing nature in history and implying a development cut off at birth or an exhaustion through old age. Nature is brought to life, made fluid and changeable. The terms applied to America thus assume a new tone and coloring; and—negative as they may be— they leave some hope for the future, or at the very least, in insisting on an irreversible degeneration, cast a ray of light on the continent's remotest past.

But in another sense—the aspect on which Buffon most prided himself and which some historians count as his greatest achievement—his thesis is less original than he thought. Without referring to the inferiority or superiority of either continent, Buffon on more than one occasion boldly claims to have been

3

the first person to note the radical difference between the fauna of South America and that of the the Old World.[1] And Brunetière (following in the footsteps of Perrier) took Buffon's claim a step further when he stated categorically that between 1757 and 1764, with his study of the animals of the Americas, Buffon founded zoological geography as he went along.[2]

The claim is admissible only in the sense that Buffon was perhaps the first naturalist and biologist to study the animal species in their geographical environment, as phenomena of the physical world and not as unalterable and impassive prototypes that came forth perfect from the hands of the Creator, from Noah's Ark or the feral couplings of their forebears. What Buffon founds, in my opinion—although I am open to contradiction by the competent experts—is geographical zoology.

2. PRECURSORS OF ZOOLOGICAL GEOGRAPHY

But zoological geography, which tackles this problem from the other end, setting out from the study of the earth and examining the distribution of the animals throughout its various parts, although it may only have assumed scientific shape toward the middle of the nineteenth century (as late as 1881 Samuel Butler doubted its existence)[3] comes into being as curiosity, necessity, incidental observation, as problem and the dawning of a fragmentary solution, long before Buffon. Aristotle, on the basis of a remark that made a deep impression on Columbus (the presence of elephants in Asia and Africa), had said that the same latitudes had the same fauna,[4] a thesis which is the precise opposite to Buffon's "discovery." And history of science textbooks name as precursors or initiators of zoological geography the historian Poseidonius of Rhodes (130–50 B.C.), Basil the Great, bishop of Caesarea (360 A.D.), and the great Arab geographer al-Idrisi (1153).

Julius Solinus, writing in the third century A.D., can already be found distributing the zoological curiosities and monstrosities among the various countries he describes. In connection with Italy he deals with snakes and wolves (chap.

---

1. Observing, for instance, that "the most important and most general fact, the fact least known to all naturalists before me . . . is that the animals of the southern parts of the old continent are not found in the new, and that reciprocally those of South America are not found at all in the old continent" (*Histoire naturelle* . . . [Paris, 1749–1804], VII, 129, Suppléments, quoted by P. Flourens, *Histoire des travaux et des idées de Buffon*, 2d ed. [Paris,1850], p. 143. Elsewhere Buffon repeats that "this general fact, which it seems was not even suspected" is so important that it must be corroborated with all possible proof ("Animaux de l'ancien continent," in *Oeuvres complètes* [Paris, 1826–28], XV, 407–08). And later he was to announce complacently: "I have demonstrated this truth by such a great number of examples that it can no longer be called into question" ("Époques de la nature," 1779, in *Oeuvres complètes*, V, 221). Cf. A. Gerbi, *The Dispute of the New World* (Pittsburgh, 1973), p. 565ff.
2. *Manuel de l'histoire de la littérature française* (Paris, 1898), p. 375. Cf. E. Perrier, *La philosophie zoologique avant Darwin* (Paris, 1884), p 63: "Buffon deserved to be considered the founder of zoological geography."
3. "The same question arises in respect of the distribution of many plants and animals; the reason of the limits which some of them cannot pass, being, indeed, perfectly clear, but as regards perhaps the greater number of them, undiscoverable" (S. Butler, *Alps and Sanctuaries* [London and Toronto, 1931], p. 135).
4. Samuel Eliot Morison, *Admiral of the Ocean Sea* (Boston, 1942), I, 369.

VIII, pp. 292–94);[5] Pontus gets the beaver (XIX, 333) Hyrcania the tigers and panthers (XXI, 342–43), Scythia the deer (XXII, 346); the bison and aurochs go to Hercynia (XXIII, 348), the elephant to Mauretania (XXVIII, 363), the bear to Numidia (XXIX, 366), the dragons to Ethiopia (XXXII, 384), the phoenix to Arabia (XXXVI, 400), and so on.

3. "Similar" and "different" animals

But these almost emblematic pairings, like the moralistic allegories of the *Physiologus,* could not be used to deduce any comparison, any distributive criterion. Empirical and picturesque, these semi-legendary sitings fell into no logical category. It is thus a significant step foward—indeed a crucial one for the future application of the thesis to the American species—when Marco Polo, following perhaps in the distant footsteps of Herodotus,[6] introduces the crude, practical, and fruitful categorical distinction between animals *like* ours and *other than* ours.

Marco Polo tells us quite specifically which animals in the kingdoms he visited are *similar* to ours and which altogether *different* and proper to those countries: "Throughout India their birds are different from ours";[7] in Madagascar too there are "birds very different from ours" (p. 290), and in Choilu "there are beasts that are different from the others . . . peacocks and hens that are bigger and more beautiful than ours, and everything they have is different from ours, and none of their fruits are like ours" (p. 279); in Zanzibar "all their beasts are different from all others in the world" (p. 292), and so on, without the difference being any cause of condemnation or rejection. Indeed in most cases this discovery prompts admiration: the Madagascans "have such different animals and birds that it is quite a marvel" (p. 291). He makes frequent mention of leopards, "leofants," "leocorns," and unicorns, featherless and hairy chickens, men with tails and men with dog's heads; of lions that "are very large and very dangerous," so that if someone were unwisely "to sleep outside at night, he would be staightaway eaten" (pp. 191–92); and in general of "many very fine wild animals" (p. 161).

This constant reference to *our* animal and vegetable species, as if to an unvarying paradigm, contains an implicit and categorical Europeocentrism that is of crucial importance both because of the value judgments which it prompts and dictates and because it leads on to the assimilation and absorption in an undifferentiated exoticism of whatever is *different* from what we know, of a

5. Gaius Julius Solinus, *Collectanea rerum memorabilium,* in *Antiquitatum variarum autores* (Lyons, 1560), pp. 252–454. Solinus in fact announces in his preface that "keeping the divisions of the globe" he has interlarded the geographical description with items of ethnographical and zoological information: "In among this we have described the characteristics of the men and other animals" (p. 257). Oviedo was familiar with Solinus (*Hist.,* XXXII, 4: III, 238). Cf. M. T. Hodgen, *Early Anthropology in the Sixteenth and Seventeenth Centuries* (Philadelphia, 1971), pp. 41–44.
6. Hodgen, op. cit., pp. 25–26.
7. *I Viaggi* (Florence, 1863), p. 262.

generic "differentness" in which the specific characteristics of each single exotic thing become confused and submerged. But these are the dangers inherent in research: "We have no other guide to truth and reason than the example and idea of the opinions and customs of the country where we are."[8]

And in fact this basic alternative, so very simple and easily reversible, is extremely fruitful. Saying that a new—generally animal or plant—species is "like in Europe" or "like in Spain," or like "in our country" (or else, as Columbus does, to comment that some of the native women do up their hair "just the way the women of Castile do") means accepting it within one's own mental horizon, appropriating it to the known and familiar world, recognizing that it possesses the normality, traditionality, and rationality of the animals and plants of our own climes. It means, therefore, automatically extending the knowledge that we have of the nature of our own world to the nature of every part of the world—thus to the New World too, and as it were being happily reassured to recognize the species to which we are accustomed, which we can trust, of which we do not need to be wary. The exotic becomes familiar.[9] It is a spontaneous movement, an instinctive reaction. "The first impulse was to rediscover the Old World in the New."[10] Thus it is not just a matter of the Old World casting itself upon the New: it is the home world taking peaceful possession of the overseas discoveries.

When Fernando Columbus talks of "well-built houses . . . with the tops woven with very fine works of foliage, like the gardens seen in Valencia," he draws spiritually closer to the natives of Borinquén; and even more so when he describes the ornaments which other primitive peoples "wear on a string around their necks, like we have an Agnus Dei, or other relic."[11] The European's religion is fused and confused with the savage's superstition.

In the same way, when de Thou is talking about Mexico almost a century later (1604) and describes its fabrics, tooled leather, poplars, and vines as being "like" those of China, Flanders, and Castile, he immediately renders these exotic curiosities familiar to the reader: "There is no amazement, no mental upheaval. The known world expands, and it turns out that in the major part of the New World,

8. Montaigne, "Des cannibales," in *Essais*, I, xxi (Pléiade ed., Paris, 1933), p. 213.

9. J. H. Elliott, *The Old World and the New, 1492-1650* (Cambridge, 1970), p. 19, referring to the reports of Hernán Cortés and Bernal Díaz del Castillo. Magnaghi had already stressed that it had been a good thing for many explorers that they were *not* scientists and were thus less inhibited by current doctrine and more receptive to the newness of the things of America: "It was a blessing if one was not too learned, if one was unencumbered with the sort of medieval learning that Columbus possessed, and could thus feel less bound by traditions to which one had often, and in vain, to subordinate the results of the new discoveries" (*Amerigo Vespucci*, 2d ed. [Rome, 1926], p. 143). On the "assimilationist" approach, cf. Michèle Duchet, "Monde civilisé et monde sauvage . . ." in *Au siècle des lumières* (Paris and Moscow, 1970), p. 9. And on the two methods, positive and negative, of describing and assimilating or rejecting novelties, see Hodgen, op. cit., pp. 196–201. Darwin again was to exploit the convenient and synthetic contrast or analogy; see Nora Barlow, ed., *Charles Darwin and the Voyage of the Beagle* (New York, 1946), pp 8, 54, 56, 70, etc.

10. G. Gusdorf, *Les principes de la pensée au siècle des lumières* (Paris, 1971), p. 140.

11. Fernando Columbus, *Vita di Cristoforo Colombo* (London, 1867), pp. 144, 298, 318; cf. p. 326 and passim.

the level of civilization is already that of the Old World."[12] Recognition is already an act of conquest and subjugation. Had not the protoplast Adam, by naming the animals, set the seal on man's superiority over the entire fauna? He had "carried out a sort of exorcism, a first taking of possession."[13]

Nor did it end there. When the newly discovered peoples began to be discussed, the similarities—whether real or fanciful—with European customs were used as "proof" in support of monogenetic or diffusionist theses and strict temporal and causal links; or rather, as Hodgen puts it, "cultural similarities were clothed with documentary import."[14] And this process was facilitated by the fact that, as Foucault noted, "the sciences of the sixteenth century were obsessed . . . by the notion of Similitude."[15] The tacit assumption that Euro-Asiatic civilization was chronologically anterior to American civilization was tantamount to anointing the New World with all the promise of youthfulness.

4. MEANING OF "DIFFERENTNESS"

It is another attitude altogether that prompts a writer to state, "This species is different from those we know." Such an observation is the first step in a quest that leads beyond the known world, advancing into the unknown and opening the way to ever bolder intuitions and inferences. It postulates another world beyond the known one and thus immediately poses the problem of the possible relationship between the two. It demands a new definition and hence a whole new logic of the things of nature. It opens a breach in the old and unquestioned oneness of nature, but in so doing allows the new species to creep between the cracks and crevices of that shattered unity. It is understandable that in early geographical maps the drawings of the animals typical of each area should stress the differences rather than the similarities, the new rather than the familiar—and hence the bigger animals rather than the insects and snails.[16] To recognize and point out the "differentness" of a species is thus, as we said, not just the first but the decisive step in capturing the new reality, taming it, and bringing it within our own mental framework.

One might mention in passing that such recognition denies and rejects the vision of a closed and fully known world, a nature always and everywhere the same, and suggests new ways—by analogy, subsumption, dependence on a third term—of recovering in some way the lost unity. The nagging question then

---

12. A. Stegmann, "L'Amérique de Du Bartas et de De Thou," in *La découverte de l'Amérique* (Paris, 1968), p. 308.
13. Giorgio Vigolo, "Palinuro," *Corriere della Sera,* 11 December 1972.
14. Hodgen, op. cit., pp. 309–13.
15. H. V. White, "Foucault Decoded: Notes from Underground," *History and Theory,* 12 (1973), 1, 34; cf. p. 46 (comparisons and metaphors).
16. W. George, *Animals and Maps* (London, 1969), pp. 25, 187.

immediately presents itself: if this species is different from Europe's, is it "better" or "worse"? Is is taller or shorter? Stronger or weaker? More useful or less useful? Thus arise all those further extrapolations and deductions that are to culminate in the "dispute." One innocent little question unleashes an irresistible tide of century upon century of diatribe, calumny, and panegyric.

If we then consider the fact that almost all the travelers avail themselves of both approaches (for Oviedo, see below, chap. XVIII, sec. 17), saying that some aspects of the nature of the Indies are like ours and others are different, we find that the distinction we have sought to analyze (the like is the known, the unlike the new) leads us back to the trite observation that the advancement of knowledge is invariably characterized by an alternating rhythm, reflecting the observation of affinities and peculiarities, uniform and unusual features. Buffon gives it as common knowledge that "we can only judge by comparing" and that "our knowledge is based . . . entirely on the relationships which things bear to those which are like them and those which differ from them."[17] Scientific observation knows no other method than the observation of generic similarities and specific differences.

5. THE NEW WORLD AND THE OLD

Thus one must reject not only the claims of Perrier and Brunetière but those other theses—much repeated in our own times—maintaining that the discovery of America presented Europe with a problem of truly tremendous implications: "whether or not American reality shares the same nature as all other things and creatures,"[18] a problem supposedly amounting to nothing less than "the greatest threat that has ever darkened the horizon of the European mind"[19] and which Europe answered by postulating a priori the identity of Europe and America and then seeking to confirm the same identity a posteriori through descriptions and travel journals.

This whole construction is somewhat artificial. The discovery of America unquestionably acted as a powerful stimulus to naturalistic and anthropological enquiries. The effect on European philosophical thought was felt more slowly, beginning only toward the end of the sixteenth century, with Montaigne and Bruno.[20] The philosophy of humanism was in fact already perfectly capable of accommodating the new geographical discoveries, which, in their inmost essence, belonged to the same spiritual current: the enlargement of the physical

17. "Discours sur la nature des animaux" in *Oeuvres*, X, 115, quoted by F. Tinland, *L'homme sauvage* (Paris, 1968), p. 23.
18. Edmundo O'Gorman, "Trayectoria de América," in *Fundamentos de la historia de América* (Mexico, 1942?), p. 86.
19. Ibid., p. 89.
20. Elliott has rightly commented on "the apparent slowness of Europe in making the mental adjustments required to incorporate America into its field of vision" (op. cit., p. 81) and on the fact that "the European reading public displayed no overwhelming interest in the newly-discovered world of America" (ibid., p. 12; see also p. 14).

world beyond the Ocean was immediately paralleled with the expansion of the historical horizon resulting from the rediscovery of classical antiquity. The ingenious O'Gorman, who refers to the "profound fundamental cowardice"[21] of Renaissance thinkers and would like to put humanism—as a "negative" era for philosophy—in brackets, inserting America and its discovery in a presumed "underground" stream running from the scholastics to Descartes,[22] paradoxically robs himself of the basic concept for understanding the assimilation of America in the European conscience—what he is pleased to call the "Philosophical Conquest of America."[23]

The truth of the matter is that the first questions posed by the New World, far from being "so many more threats to the convictions and systems of the Old World,"[24] repeated doubts and queries that were already fully familiar to Europe's tormented conscience.

6. The Indian and the salvation of the heathen

The greatest problem, the problem of the nature and quality of the Indian, emerged spontaneously in the shape of the problem of his "soul" and possible salvation, his dutiful and perhaps obligatory baptism—in other words, as a recent and specific instance of the age-old question of the "salvation of the heathen."[25] Saint Thomas Aquinas had conceded that if the pagan had never heard of the Christian faith, his paganism was not a sin (while the aggressive heathenness of the Saracen *was* a sin). And Dante, after touching on the problem in the *Inferno* (IV, 40–42) and *Purgatorio* (III, 40–45), tackled this formidable question once again in the third and culminating section of the *Divine Comedy*, with trembling conscience and holy dread, with supreme precision and verbal splendor:

> "For 'Here's a man,' thou saidst, 'born of some breed
> On Indus' bank, where there is none to tell
> Of Christ, and none to write, and none to read;
> He lives, so far as we can see, quite well,
> Rightly disposed, in conduct not amiss,
> Blameless in word and deed; yet infidel
> And unbaptized he dies; come, tell me this:
> Where is the justice that condemns the man
> For unbelief? What fault is it of his?"
> (*Paradiso*, XIX, 70–78, tr. Dorothy L. Sayers)

21. O'Gorman, *Fundamentos*, p. 21.
22. Ibid., pp. 27–28.
23. Ibid., pp. 81, 105.
24. Ibid., p. 26; cf. ibid., p. 86.
25. On whom see L. Capéran, *Le problème du salut des infidèles* (Paris, 1912), and, for the most conspicuous specific instance, A.-H. Chroust, "Utrum Aristoteles sit salvatus," *JHI*, 6 (1945), 231–38. On Virgil, see the classic work by D. Comparetti, *Virgilio nel Medio Evo* (Livorno, 1872), esp. I, 290–92.

Dante's contemporary, Marco Polo, wrote ingenuously of one of the incarnations of Buddha: "If he had been baptized a Christian, he would have been a great saint with God" (p. 274).

And barely ten years before Columbus set sail from Palos, Pulci's Astarotte, "the new spirit of the age" (De Sanctis), answered Dante's question—as repeated to him by Rinaldo—asserting that the salvation of the antipodeans was a certainty, an absolute certainty, indeed so certain that only an "ignoramus" would doubt it. "If that had been the case your Redeemer would have shown a preference for this part, and Adam would have been shaped up here for you, and He Himself crucified for love of you. You should know that everyone is saved by the cross" (*Morgante Maggiore,* XXV, 233 et seq.).

Once the Americas had been discovered, the problem of the salvation of their natives was debated in Valladolid and by the Council of Trent, with greater or lesser indulgence but without any of the solutions proffered casting doubt on their potential for salvation.[26] Later this same problem instigated Father Lafitau's original and fruitful idea of comparing the American natives to the pagans of antiquity.[27]

7. The physical nature of the Americas

The problem of nature in the Americas was tackled and debated with equal candor and good sense. The first descriptions are impressively sincere and circumspect, revealing a marked concern for objective accuracy. Humboldt already noted that if one looked carefully at the original works of the early historians of the conquest one could not but be amazed at finding the seeds of so many physical truths in a Spanish author of the sixteenth century.[28] The exaggerations which fed the twofold legend of America the *weak* and America the *strong* were almost without exception later developments. Nor is there any justification— either in respect of the earliest reporters, the Columbuses and the Oviedos, or the later ones—for O'Gorman's statement that all the chroniclers do their best to confirm that nature is identical in the Americas and the Old World. "They can be summed up," writes the Mexican, "in a single phrase: 'nothing to report.'"[29] And, even more outrageously, "The sum of the arguments of the chroniclers on this problem comes down to a stubborn insistence on the fact that, although it may be a question of a 'New World,' it is not a world that is new."[30] According

---

26. Copious details in F. Mateos, "Ecos de América en Trento," *RI,* 22 (1945), 581–600. On the problem in the Council of Trent and in the seventeenth century see H. Busson, *La pensée religieuse française de Charron à Pascal* (Paris, 1933), pp. 414–17. Cf. also R. Romeo, *Le scoperte americane nella coscienza italiana del Cinquecento,* 2d ed. (Milan and Naples, 1971), pp. 35–37.

27. See S. Zavala, *América en el espíritu francés del siglo XVIII* (Mexico, 1949), pp. 176–77.

28. *Kosmos,* cited by Elliott, op. cit., pp 5–6.

29. *Fundamentos,* p. 98.

30. Ibid., p. 104.

to O'Gorman, Father Acosta was the first to insist on the autonomous individuality of America, as something new and unprecedented.[31]

Leaving aside the vagueness of the terms used and the resulting ambiguity of O'Gorman's thesis, which at one point denies that the chroniclers recognize America as a world that is new (which is obviously absurd) and elsewhere denies that they consider its nature to be essentially different from nature in Europe (which is obvious and banal: none of the chroniclers doubts that America was created by God, like the Old World, and that nature is *one* throughout the world), the important point is that the reports always stress what is *new* about the New World, not what is the same as the Old World. From Mellin de Saint-Gelais (1556) to Fray Tomás de Mercado (1571), it is endlessly repeated that in the Indies *everything* is different from the Old World.[32] Marmontel was to observe wittily that "the old world . . . was so astonished at the discovery of the new that it could not be persuaded that the latter resembled it."[33]

It was only natural that it should be so, and it takes no more than a glance at the texts to discover that if one really wants to sum them up in a single phrase it would tend rather to be a very reasonable and sensible "here we have something new." And they contain absolutely no "stubborn insistence," but if anything a patient and careful enquiry into the characteristics proper to the newly discovered regions.

Oviedo is for a number of reasons the greatest of the early historians of nature in America. For a clearer understanding of his originality, let us consider the intellectual perspective of those who preceded him as describers and interpreters of the physical reality of the New World.

31. Ibid., pp. 100–01. P. R. Cutright, in *The Great Naturalists Explore South America* (New York, 1940), asserts with even more remarkable naivety and ignorance that "in the accounts of these and other expeditions made by the conquerors there is little mention of the fauna and flora of the regions they explored, and such descriptions as were written are, for the most part, fantastical [Raleigh is given as an example!]. It was not until the close of the eighteenth century that a naturalist, in the true sense of the word, visited South America."
32. On the former (and others), see Gerbi, *Dispute*, pp. 565–66; on the latter see Elliott, op. cit., p. 21.
33. J. F. Marmontel, *Les Incas* (Paris, 1777), p. 3.

❧ II ❧

Christopher Columbus

1. First reactions to American nature

CHRISTOPHER Columbus had things other than nature to occupy his mind. His indifference to some of the most astonishing aspects of the Americas, such as the new constellations to be seen in the American heavens, has been remarked on more than once.[1] The flora and fauna of America do, however, immediately attract his attention and even manage to distract him momentarily from the search for gold, producing reactions in him that already contain in microcosm all the later attitudes of the European in America.

It is now more than a century since Humboldt congratulated Columbus on being as shrewd an observer of nature as he was intrepid a sailor;[2] in the Admiral's *Journal* and reports he found already "formulated all the problems that occupied the attention of the scientists in the second half of the fifteenth century and throughout the sixteenth century."[3] Thus it seems all the more curious that Alfonso Reyes should complain that Columbus left us "no real impression of American nature and life,"[4] and that Iglesia likewise should insist that "in

---

1. For example by Samuel Eliot Morison, *Admiral of the Ocean Sea,* I, 353, and throughout the article by L. Olschki, "What Columbus Saw on Landing in the West Indies," *Proceedings of the American Philosophical Society,* 84, no. 5 (July 1941), 653. J. Wasserman, in his *Christoph Columbus, der Don Quichote des Ozeans* (Berlin, 1930), p. 102, also criticizes Columbus's descriptions as generic and flat, prosaic and commercial. But Hugues gets closer to the truth when he writes that "although ignorant of botany . . . Columbus is led solely by his feeling for nature to pay careful attention to anything that presents a novel aspect" (*L'opera scientifica di Cristoforo Colombo* [Turin, 1892], p. 102). See also G. E. Nunn, *The Geographical Conceptions of Columbus* (New York, 1924); C. Verlinden, *Kolumbus: Vision und Ausdauer* (Göttingen, 1962), and *Origines de la civilisation atlantique* (Neuchâtel, 1966), p. 450.

2. Alexander von Humboldt, *Examen critique de l'histoire de la géographie du Nouveau Monde* (Paris, 1836–39), III, 21–25, 148n, 228–30; *Cosmos* (Madrid, 1874), II, 52–54. C. Jane too recognizes Columbus's "keen appreciation of natural beauty" (*The Voyages of Christopher Columbus* [London, 1930], Introduction, p. 11). Morison actually finds that "Columbus's appreciation of the beauties of nature was equal to that of eighteenth-century romancers" (*The European Discovery of America: The Southern Voyages* [New York, 1974], p. 128). But Elliott, with more balanced judgment, comments that "Columbus . . . shows at times a remarkable gift for realistic observation, although at other times the idealised landscape of the European imagination interposes itself between him and the American scene" (op. cit., p. 19).

3. *Cosmos,* II, p. 260. Fernando had already gone to great lengths to praise the way his father diligently "set down day by day in minute detail whatever happened on the voyage," the winds, the distances covered, the sails and currents used, the birds and fish seen on the way, etc. (*Vita di Cristoforo Colombo,* pp. 58–59).

4. A. Reyes, "El presagio de América," in *Ultima Tule* (Mexico, 1942), p. 62.

Columbus there is never any disinterested description," and only an *"alleged feeling for nature."*[5]

The important point, in actual fact, is to remember Columbus's expectations, the disappointments he suffered, and the precise aims with which he was writing. His reactions to American nature are never coldly scientific observations, but genuine "reactions," sometimes emotional and enthusiastic, sometimes full of repressed and disguised disappointment. On the one hand, having failed to find in the Antilles the dreamed-of paradise gleaming with gold, he is overcome with doubts and misgivings that will later provide support for numerous denigrators of the continent. On the other hand, and more importantly, he feels joyfully at one with nature in the tropics, revels in the eternally springlike climate, experiences a sensation of perfect happiness and exhilaration, finds himself at peace with his tormented spirit and the dumbly hostile world, and gives vent to an enthusiasm that will echo down through the centuries, all the way to Humboldt and Jacquemont.[6] The weather is always like May. The beauty of one area persuades him to baptize it *Jardines,* "the gardens." Not only nightingales sing, but a thousand other little birds, and innumerable species of palms sway gently in the breeze. The natives are possibly exempt from Original Sin, pure as Adam. If pearls, as Pliny says, are born from the dew falling into oysters, there must certainly be vast numbers of pearls in the Indies, since the dew is abundant!

Small wonder that subsequent observers, failing to rediscover all these paradisal virtues in the Indies, realistically underlined other shortcomings, which were then used to back up the thesis of the inferiority of the American continent.

2. The Journal of the First Voyage

As a record of Columbus's first voyage, and hence of his earliest impressions, we have an unparalleled document: his diary or *Journal,* possibly the oldest "diary" in literary history, that by virtue of its very nature (although probably kept for purposes of nautical calculation) unfolds the miracle of the discovery with the steady rhythm of each passing day.

The authenticity of the *Journal*—"one of the most extraordinary monuments of the human mind"[7]—can no longer be seriously doubted. But the form in

5. R. Iglesia, *El hombre Colón* (Mexico, 1944), pp. 34, 41. For Iglesia, Columbus is merely a Genoese "businessman" with an overlay of Castilian mysticism. In some curious way he fails to grasp the actual historical novelty of Columbus, his tenacity as an explorer, his longing for greatness and discovery that make him typically modern and quite different in thought, action, and results from so many other medieval merchants and mystics.

6. See Gerbi, *Dispute.* "It might be expected that the natural beauty of the West Indian islands, seen for the first time in such ideal conditions, would make an exceptionally strong appeal to a man with the poetic temper of Columbus" (Jane, op. cit., pp. 68–69). Cf. J. Pérez de Tudela's comment: "Columbus was, once again, its [the Indian adventure's] inspired inventor; it was he who first described, in terms of poetic rapture, the bewitching and perfumed beauty of the tropics" ("Visión de la découverte du Nouveau Monde chez les chroniqueurs espagnols," in *La découverte de l'Amérique,* p. 275).

7. J. H. Mariéjol, *Pierre Martyr d'Anghera* (Paris, 1887), p. 203. On the various versions of the *Journal,* see E. Jos, "El libro del primer viaje," *RI,* 10 (1950), 719–51 (see esp. pp. 723–25; on Jane's version, pp. 732–41). It subsequently

which it has come down to us, Las Casas's transcription-cum-summary, adds another posthumous layer to the veils drawn spontaneously by the Admiral himself. Columbus, in fact, far from having any scientific objective in drafting the *Journal,* is predominantly concerned with justifying his enterprise in the eyes of Queen Isabella, with his elation at his first success, and his commitment to proving geographical and cosmographical theses that will justify a new and better-equipped expedition to the rich lands of far eastern Asia.

The descriptive limitations imposed on him by the fact that he was addressing himself to Her Sovereign Majesty (which also account, according to some scholars, for his idealization of the sexual customs of the natives and his insistence on the possibility of their conversion to Christianity) play a minor part in comparison with the limitations resulting from his own passion and illusions and rapturous longing, completely inimical to detached observation of such a singular nature. Columbus *wants* to show that the islands discovered are delightful of climate and bursting with prodigious riches, so that the Spaniards will be able to live as well as they did in Spain, and better: they are overflowing with gold, or at least near to the places where the gold comes from and the spices grow, and the natives are so artless in bartering and so cowardly in battle that with the wiles of honest trading or the violence of arms, they can easily be persuaded to part with whatever one wants from them.[8]

The cowardice and weakness of the Indians, which were to form the refrain of so many diatribes right through to de Pauw and beyond, can be traced back to Columbus's well-meaning propaganda. To stir up the ambitions of the Catholic Kings without frightening them into their all too familiar prudence, the Admiral generalizes the legitimate terror of the natives of the Antilles—already the persistent target of the ferocious Caribs—at finding themselves invaded by this new breed of creatures coming from the sea, men or demons or whatever they may be, armour-plated, bearded, thundering and smoking, pale of countenance, and holding out fistfuls of multicolored glass beads, flashing and glowing in the sunlight. (But when, barely eight years later, Columbus wants to assert his claims and exalt his services to the crown he is to boast of having conquered the Indies "from a *warlike* and numerous people," from a "savage and *warlike* people, that make their home in mountain and forest.")[9]

This theme of the unwarlike weakness of the natives fitted in so perfectly with Las Casas's humanitarian thesis that he in turn, when transcribing Columbus's

---

became quite usual for sailors to keep journals. And Bacon would marvel that people kept diaries for sea journeys, where there was nothing to see but the sea and the sky, whereas generally speaking they were not kept for land journeys "wherein so much is to be observed" ("Of travel," *Essays Civil and Moral,* XVIII [1597]. In point of fact Columbus's journal describes events on both land and sea.

8. They give away everything they have for a few glass beads or tortoiseshell fragments "and I think they would do the same with spices and gold if they had any" (3 December). Time and again, in fact, Columbus emphasizes the natives' readiness to indulge in barter.

9. Letter of 1500, in *Relaciones y Cartas* (Madrid, 1892), pp. 320, 325.

diary, certainly omitted nothing that would enfeeble the Indian. It is likely, if anything, that he left out or summarized passages that did not suit his book, or that he found secondary to his chosen twofold purpose, to exalt the memory of Columbus and protect the Indian population.[10]

Let us now—with the due reservation called for by the prejudices on the part of author and editor of the text, bearing in mind that Columbus seems to have been an assiduous reader of and firm believer in Marco Polo, whose book, as Morison so imaginatively put it, he had "in his head, if not in his hand,"[11] and not forgetting that the Journal remained unpublished until 1825, and that of the early historians only Andrés Bernáldez, Fernando Columbus, and Las Casas seem to have been acquainted with it, and of recent historians only Muñoz,[12]— let us now turn again to this little book that enshrines the earliest observations made by a European on nature in America.

3. MEAGER FAUNA, EXUBERANT FLORA

On the first island he touched on that fateful day, 12 October 1492, Columbus found "no beast of any sort . . . save parrots." At first sight, America's fauna seems meager in the extreme. Two days later, noting the splendor of the fresh green vegetation, like Castile in April or May (14 October), Columbus settles on the contrast—meager fauna, exuberant flora—that is to be repeated down through the centuries. The comparative formula is then reiterated, with few variations, time and again: the new islands, even in the winter months, are as luxuriant and fruitful as the lands of Europe in the best season.

This initial amazement is followed by a vague feeling that such a climate and such a land must produce creatures and plants of extraordinary powers. Terrestrial creatures may be said to be entirely absent. "I saw no animals on land of

10. Humboldt found changes in Columbus's journal made by Las Casas (see for example *Examen critique,* II, 47, 340–41) and lacunae (ibid., III, 103*n*), but he is exaggerating when he calls it a "cold and laconic extract," a paraphrase in the friar's "insipid" and "boring" style (ibid., and III, 227–30). On the text of the Journal, see also Jane, op. cit., pp. 59–60.

11. "Texts and Translations of the Journal of Columbus's First Voyage," *HAHR,* 19 (1939), 239. It is of course true that Humboldt always remained skeptical about Columbus's knowledge of Marco Polo, as he never mentions him by name (see *Examen critique,* I, 63–64*n*, II, 350, III, 200–01, IV, 245; and *Cosmos,* II, 250). But more recent scholars tend to think that Columbus not only read Marco Polo's *Viaggi* shortly before 1492 (Morison, *Admiral of the Ocean Sea,* pp. 64–69, 315; Olschki, "What Columbus Saw," p. 653; E. Jos, "La génesis colombina del descubrimiento," *RHA,* 14 [1942], esp. 32–33, 43*n*, 45*n*) but that it, in conjunction with the Toscanelli map, had a considerable effect on his thinking (G. H. Blanke, *Amerika im englischen Schrifttum des 16. und 17. Jahrhunderts* [Bochum, 1962], pp. 14, 16; Morison, *Admiral of the Ocean Sea,* pp. 64–65). See also D. B. Quinn, *England and the Discovery of America, 1481–1620* (New York, 1974), pp. 106–07.

12. For Bernáldez, see B. Sánchez Alonso, *Historia de la historiografía española* (Madrid, 1941), I, 401. It is uncertain whether Herrera was acquainted with the Journal. Justin Winsor, *Narrative and Critical History of America* (Boston and New York, 1866–89), II, 46 (citing "portions in German in *Das Ausland,* 1867, I") and H. Vignaud, *Histoire critique de la grande entreprise de Christophe Colomb* (Paris, 1911), I, 18–20, and II, 259–61, assert that he was. Morison, "Texts and Translations," p. 236, disagrees. Despite some instances of similar phraseology, that could easily be due to affinities of theme and background and to the tenacious idiomatic usages of the period and setting, Oviedo seems to have been unacquainted with the Journal. This adds considerable significance to certain coincidences of attitude to which we shall be referring later.

any sort, save parrots and lizards. A boy told me that he saw a large snake. I saw no sheep or goats or any other animals. . . . if there had been any I could not have failed to see some" (16 October). The insistent repetition contains a note of wonder: though he looks everywhere about him and listens carefully to the crew's stories, the Admiral can find barely a trace of any animal on land.

But the fish are a constant surprise, "fish so *different* from ours, that it is truly wonderful," multicolored and speckled like cockerels, and of such beautiful colors "that everyone marvels at them and takes great delight in them." Myriads of birds warble overhead and flocks of parrots hide the sun, "birds big and small of so many sorts and so different from ours, that one is left marveling" (21 October).[13]

As for the trees, they are startling in their variety and *newness*. "Many trees very *different* from ours . . . and with branches so varied in shape that it is the most astonishing thing in the world, how great a difference there is between one kind and another" (16 October). Their beauty rivals their novelty; they are as green as Andalusia in May, but "the trees are all as *different* from ours as day is from night: and likewise the fruit and the herbs and the stones and everything else." Even if some trees were "similar in nature to others existing in Castile, yet there was a very great difference, and there were so many other sorts of trees that nobody could enumerate them nor compare them with those of Castile" (17 October).[14]

Faced with such exuberance, Columbus is overcome with three separate emotions: enthusiasm for the *newness* of the flora of the Antilles, admiration for its exceptional beauty, and annoyance at being prevented by lack of time and botanical knowledge from appraising its medicinal powers and nutritional value. From the purely cognitive point of view, American nature is different and surprising, "unlike." From the aesthetic-hedonistic viewpoint, it is beautiful and pleasing, euphoric. From the practical point of view, it *must be* very useful and very good, but Columbus does not know. Before all else, he is in a hurry to find gold: "There may be a lot of things of which I know nothing, because I am reluctant to linger here, being anxious to explore numerous islands with a view to finding gold" (15 October).[15] Moreover he cannot even distinguish among these various generic "trees" and candidly confesses and regrets it. "I believe the islands contain many herbs and many trees which will be worth a great amount in Spain for dyes and as medicinal spices, but I do not recognize them and I much regret that" (19 October). "There are trees of a thousand sorts, all with their

13. More "birds of many kinds *different* from those in Spain, except partridges and nightingales that sang, and geese" are mentioned on 6 November.

14. The Admiral mentions his amazement at trees " different from ours" again on 28 October.

15. Again on 27 November he says: "I do not linger in any port because I would like to see as many lands as possible"; and in the letter to D. Luis de Santángel, of 15 February 1493, he states picturesquely that "this voyage was taken at such a dash."

various fruits, and all marvelously scented. It makes me the saddest man in the world not to know them, because I am quite certain that all are valuable" (21 October).[16]

Firmly convinced that he has reached the eastern tip of Asia, Columbus—still under the influence of Toscanelli's undiscriminating and glowing prophecies[17]—never doubts that all those trees could be identified with precious plants of the Indies and Moluccas if one had the expert knowledge; but he himself does not dare to state as much—and rightly, because one would search vainly for Asiatic prototyes for many American herbs and plants.[18]

But his glance dwells lovingly on every detail of the islands, whose mere existence is sufficient to realize his lifetime's dream and guarantee his immortal glory, quite apart from the splendor of high offices for himself and his descendants. His pen, at times so dry and energetic, now becomes a brush whose delicate strokes caress the tiny islands, on which fortune would subsequently smile so little. With a sort of lover's awkwardness he seeks to wax poetic, and produces a flood of warbling nightingales, blossoming springtimes, May meadows, and Andalusian nights.

4. CUBA: DIFFERENCES FROM AND AFFINITIES WITH EUROPE

The wonder and surprise continue in the broad and beautiful island of Cuba. There Columbus runs into an absurd natural prodigy, "dogs that never barked," and—the antiphrasis renders the extraordinary contrast very well—"tame wild birds" in the natives' houses, and even "large snails, but tasteless, and *not like those of Spain*" (29 October).[19] A whole fauna completely different from Europe's. The flora too is distinctive: there is much cotton, there are "mames," which "are like carrots, and taste like chestnuts" (but which are, according to Las Casas, actually potatoes) and green beans and kidney beans *"very different from ours."*

As the days pass, however, the eye becomes accustomed, nature becomes more familiar, and the first impression of violent contrast with the animals and plants of Europe gives way to a vague but significant awareness of the affinities and similarities. The sailors find "an animal that looked like a badger" and catch a fish, among many others, "which looked just like a pig" (16 November). The Admiral notices "large mice . . . and huge crabs," and in the sky he sees lots of birds and detects a heady scent of spices (17 November). Instead of the exotic

---

16. Columbus mentions similar regrets on 23 October.

17. C. De Lollis, *Colombo nella leggenda e nella storia* (Lanciano, 1931), pp. 110–11.

18. Thus Humboldt is exaggerating when he stresses Columbus's "naive credulity" in rediscovering "in the New World everything his memory can recall of East Asia" *(Examen critique,* IV, 245n).* The feature that best supports Humboldt's thesis is Columbus's insistence on recognizing all sorts of spices in the Caribbean islands.

19. More "huge snails" were found on 16 November, and on the same day pearl-bearing oysters were brought up, though without pearls in them.

and ill-defined trees, he recognizes "oaks and strawberry trees" and a multitude of noble pines straight as spindles, which he can already see sawn up into planks for caravels or raised as masts "for the largest ships in Spain." The forest becomes a fleet. The virgin timber of the American woods is already raw material, merchandise for the mother country, a source of incalculable riches and naval might. The sovereigns will be able to "build as many vessels as might be wished there" (25 November).[20] Two days later, the vision takes more concrete and specific shape: the king and queen will very easily be able to subjugate the new islands, convert the inhabitants, and build cities and fortresses there; and to ensure their lasting dominion over the islands they would be well advised not to allow "any foreigner, except Catholic Christians, to trade or set foot here" (27 November). The foreigner Columbus had only set foot in America six weeks earlier and he was already jealous—in Spain's interest—of any other "immigrant." The barely discovered paradise is immediately annexed in spirit to the crown of Castile.[21]

Columbus's attitude to nature, which, as we have seen, is strictly subordinated to his ambitions and his political dream, is now about to be reversed. Nature in the West Indies is no longer radically different from Spain's. It is now similar, now almost identical, and more beautiful.[22]

5. HAITI: THE "SPANISH" ISLAND

By the time the source of the precious metal is eventually located in Haiti— the Admiral having abandoned Cuba after a fruitless quest for the mines—the change is finally complete. Haiti is the *isla Española,* the "Spanish Island."[23] It is Spain, it belongs to Spain and resembles Spain in every way. There is no further need to glorify the newness of the plants and animals: the nuggets and the gold-bearing sands are as beautiful a novelty as one could wish. It now becomes preferable to depict the island as a welcoming and familiar dwelling-place, where acclimatization is no problem and where one can live as in the mother country. Columbus reaches the coast of Haiti on 5 December, and on 6 December he immediately notes that the trees are smaller than in the other islands (less wild

---

20. This *topos*—trees being turned into ships—is little more than a metaphor. There are instances of ships being transformed into nymphs in Virgil (*Aeneid,* IX, 77ff) and Ovid (*Metamorphoses,* XIV, 530ff). In Ariosto (*Orlando Furioso,* XXXIX, 26–28) we have the miracle of "branches" cast into the water "all of a sudden becoming ships." And need one mention the "firs" driven into the sea by Jason? (V. Monti, *Al signor di Montgolfier*). See also the letter from John Day to Columbus (1497–98) on Cabot's expedition: "they found big trees from which masts of ships are made" (Samuel Eliot Morison, *The European Discovery of America: The Northern Voyages* [New York, 1971], p. 207; cf. ibid., p. 215).

21. Such promptitude had already struck Humboldt, *Examen critique,* III, 259–60.

22. The climate is so healthy that not a single member of the expedition suffered so much as a headache or had to spend a day in bed, save one old man, who suffered from "the stone"—but this was an infirmity "that had afflicted him all his life," for which the local climate cannot be blamed, Columbus implies, going on to add trumphantly, "and he straightaway got better within two days" (27 November 1492: was the Cuban climate really so good for the kidneys?).

23. Andrés Bernáldez was to repeat that Haiti was to the other islands as gold was to silver. On the later but no less fervent enthusiasm of Alonso de Zuazo (1518) see Elliott, op. cit., p. 20.

exuberance) "and many of them are similar in nature to those in Spain, such as holm-oaks and strawberry trees and others, and this is also true of the plants." He sails further along the coast and confirms his finding "that the whole of that land is very hilly, but has no large trees, only holm-oaks and strawberry trees, *just like the land of Castile*" (7 December). He sees crops "like barley" growing in the fields and broad valleys and countryside and very high mountains, "all resembling Castile." He tries fishing with nets, "and before he reached the shore a skate, *like those of Spain,* jumped right into the boat. Up until then he had seen no fish which resembled those of Castile." The passage goes on and concludes with a sort of hymn of joy exulting in the refrain "Castile". "The sailors went fishing and caught some more skate, and sole and other fish *like those of Castile.* He went a little way into that country, which is all cultivated, and heard a nightingale sing, and other birds *like those of Castile. . . .* He found myrtle and other trees and plants *like those of Castile,* and the land and the mountains resemble Castile too" (7 December). Even the rain and the cold are *"like October in Castile";* and near the port of San Nicolas there are two very beautiful plateaux "almost *resembling the lands of Castile,* and indeed these are superior, wherefore he named this island Hispaniola, the Spanish Island" (9 December).

And so it goes on. Once the enthusiasm of a headstrong visionary like Columbus is aroused the rhapsodies fall thick and fast, unrestrained by any formula, and the equation, already bold enough, becomes a mere stepping-stone to hyperbole. Haiti is like Castile? No, Haiti is better than Castile. Its waters contain fish like those of Spain (11 and 13 December) and mastic like that which makes Chios rich—although the Haitian mastic stubbornly refuses to set, which the sailors ascribe to the inopportune season or the waters (10 and 11 December)—and "young women as fair of skin as any that could be found in Spain." But there are also lands of such beauty "that the fairest and best lands in Castile could not compare with these,"[24] and orchards groaning with fruit, rich meadows and broad good roads, nocturnal melodies of nightingales, fragrant breezes and choruses of crickets and frogs and sweet-smelling spices and cotton; and the as yet

---

24. And a few days later: "In all Castile there is no land that can stand comparison with it for beauty and goodness. All this island and the island of Tortuga are as cultivated as the plain of Cordova" (16 December). There are further comparisons, of climate and vegetation, on 19 and 21 December. The crews are equally enthusiastic: "All affirmed that it was quite impossible for any other region to be more beautiful" (F. Columbus, *Vita di Cristoforo Colombo,* pp. 91–92).

Filson Young (*Christopher Columbus and the New World of His Discovery* [London, 1911], cited by Iglesia, *El hombre Colón,* p. 32), noted that "Columbus . . . has but two methods of comparison: either a thing is like Spain, or it is not like Spain," but he did not explore the far-reaching implications of those conventional abbreviations. In fact he considers them puerile defects and pictures Columbus, the shrewd and wary Genoese, like Alice in Wonderland, "wandering, still a child at heart, in the wonders of the enchanted world to which he had come" (cited in *El hombre Colón,* p. 33). Enrique Rioja goes too far the other way, extolling the accuracy, exactitude, perspicacity, and clarity of Columbus's observations of nature, noting however that he is led by his "preconceived notion that the same species exist here as in Spain" to apply "names known and currently used in the peninsula to species that were previously totally unknown," thus committing some "obvious errors" ("Apostillas de un naturalista a la relación del primer viaje del Almirante de la Mar Océana," *CA,* 6 [1945], 137–48, esp. p. 144).

unfound gold will be found: "They found no gold but it is not surprising that it was not found in such a short time" (13 December).[25]

The potatoes there are as thick as a man's leg, and the trees "so heavily leaved that their foliage is no longer green, but a verdant dark color." The fields are just waiting to be sown with corn, the pastures to be grazed by any sort of cattle and then "everything in the world that man could desire" will flourish in these gardens, fields, and pastures (16 December). Even the natives are more Spanish than the Spanish, in the Admiral's eyes, and he insists that they be treated absolutely fairly, because "he considers them already Christians and subjects of the sovereigns of Castile, *more than the peoples of Castile*" (21 December). They are gentle and softly spoken and always laugh when they speak (25 December), "not like the others who seem to be threatening when they speak"; and they give away gold and parrots and cotton cloth without a second thought.

When the *Santa Maria* goes aground they help to salvage the cargo and "not a leather thong or a plank or a nail was missing"—something which would not have happened "anywhere in Castile"—and indeed they do their best to console the Admiral, offering him everything they have (25 and 26 December). True, they daub their bodies black, red, and other colors, but the Admiral learns that "they do this to protect themselves in some degree against the sun" (24 December and see also 13 January 1493—a first attempt to provide a rationalistic explanation of the rites and customs of the primitives and the first hint of the savages' delicate constitution, which would later be one of Las Casas's most frequent arguments). In short, there is no comparison with Cuba and the Cubans: "There is as great a difference between them and between that island and this in everything, as there is between night and day" (24 December).[26] Gold itself finally arrives in abundance, indeed is "infinite." The Admiral, smothering his exaltation with impatience, was already on 27 December "thinking to make haste for the return to Castile with all possible dispatch."

25. Humboldt points out that Columbus lays greater emphasis on the beauty of nature than on precious metals, which would have increased the importance of the lands discovered, and draws the conclusion that the Admiral was first and foremost a lover of the beauties of nature (cf. Fernando Columbus's comment on "the Admiral being enamored of its [Cuba's] beauty," *Vita de Cristoforo Colombo*, p. 83) and sentimentally enthusiastic about the landscape (*Examen critique*, III, 230n). R. Bacchelli, in a more balanced and cautious judgment, sees Columbus as "a refined and delicate observer and lover of the beauties of nature," etc. ("L'Ammiraglio dell'Oceano," in *Nel fiume della storia* [Milan, 1945], p. 26). Columbus is described as a "landscape painter" by P. Henríquez Ureña in his article "Paisajes y retratos," *La Nacion* (Buenos Aires), 31 May 1936. "Columbus was a poet, a great poet of nature," according to C. Pereyra, *Historia de la América española* (Madrid, 1920), I, 19, 151. Olschki, "What Columbus Saw," pp. 634–40ff, stresses somewhat more accurately that Columbus is much more interested in the natives than in physical nature and nautical or geographical questions. On the nightingale "hallucination," see Olschki, *Storia letteraria delle scoperte geografiche* (Florence, 1937), pp. 11–21.

26. The difference between Cuba and Hispaniola ("Hispaniola is a marvel") is also underlined in the two letters to D. Luis de Santángel (15 February 1493) and Rafael Sánchez (4 March 1493), in which Columbus summarizes his report (see especially *Relaciones y cartas*, pp. 187, 198). In these letters he repeats some of the comments we have noted, but in the absence of any strict chronological order they fail to show how his wonderment developed and grew with each passing day.

6. THE RETURN: HALLUCINATIONS AND MYSTICISM

The return journey and the subsequent expeditions, from which nothing has survived in the way of original reports barring a few letters, produce no new observations in the field of science or natural philosophy. From the ship they see the usual frigate birds and petrels and in the sea tuna fish, a shark, and sargasso, almost always mentioned at the end of the daily observations, as a normal occurrence. In the so-called *lettera rarissima* of 7 July 1503, relating to the fourth voyage, Columbus mentions numerous species of animals seen on the mainland, many "and very different from ours": two fierce "pigs," a wild beast "that resembles a marsh cat, except that it is much bigger and has a face like a man's," big woolly chickens, "lions, stags, roebuck," and so forth.[27] But there is no recurrence of that lucid balance between dream and greed, that alternation of enquiry and exploitation which had given free reign to the Admiral's contemplative spirit and tender curiosity when he visited the first islands.

The reality of gold, the alchemist's image of the sun,[28] steals the scene, its dazzling glow overshadowing the charming landscape, the leafy plants, the meek natives. Legend and greed combine to prevent the study of nature. The temperature of the mental climate rises and rapidly approaches a state of delirium. In Jamaica gold is gathered in lumps as big as beans, not like in Haiti where there were only grains as big as seeds of corn. . . . In the province of Avan there are men born with tails. Another island to the east is populated solely by women, the unfailing Amazons (6 and 13 January). . . . Three mermaids rise up out of the ocean, "clear out of the sea," but they are not so beautiful as they are painted, as "somehow [the reader is left to imagine how] their faces looked like men's." Creatures from the ancient myths invade the newly discovered lands and seas. Reality is already being transformed into a confused, hallucinatory vision. And the Admiral is impatient, tremendously impatient, to return and tell his sovereigns and the world—in the formula of exaggerated pride that was later to prove modest—that "he had found what he was looking for" (9 January 1493).[29]

The storm makes him repent of this excess of conceit. He fears that his immense longing to bring back such great news is itself a sin and that God will

---

27. Ibid., pp. 375–76. Slightly exaggerated, but elegant as always, are the comments of Alfonso Reyes on Columbus's visions and hallucinations ("El presagio de América," pp. 62–64). De Lollis underlines Columbus's concern with exalting his enterprise, but concludes that "his verbosity is so great [in the journal, albeit *summarized* by Las Casas!] and so little imprinted with the reality of the things that passed before his eyes as to render it impossible for the Catholic Kings then or the reader of today to gain even an approximate idea of what Columbus was describing and what impression it made on him" (op. cit., p. 109).

28. Michel Mollat, "Soleil et navigation au temps des découvertes," in *Le soleil à la Renaissance* (Brussels, 1965), p. 93.

29. His wild and fanciful hope of liberating the Holy Sepulcher with the gold from the Indies also eventually found partial and unexpected fulfilment. The American metals strengthened Spain's empire and thus weakened the Muslims' pride and the expansion of Islam (Elliott, op. cit., p. 88).

punish him, not allowing him to reach Europe: "Any little gnat could interrupt and prevent it." He makes vows of pilgrimages and candles and masses and fasts, orders the crew to do the same, and promises a sailor that he will personally pay his expenses when he makes the pious pilgrimage to the Holy Virgin of Loreto (14 February 1493 and 3 March 1493). He is no longer the man who claimed (22 December 1492) that he did not like to weigh anchor on a Sunday "solely out of piety and not on account of any superstition." Meanwhile, he lets the sailors believe that it is "some act of devotion," that is, some sort of spell, when he has a barrel thrown into the sea with an account of his expedition sealed inside (14 February 1493). The mystical streak in his complex character comes to the fore, pompous and overweening.[30] His system for measuring the ship's speed by counting his heartbeats[31] takes on an almost symbolic trueness. The ship's course follows the throbbing pulse of his trembling organism. Its speed through the salt waters of the ocean matches the even tempo of the pulses of blood pumped into his arteries by the life-giving muscle. The "heart" prevails over the "head." And already the religious solemnity of his adoration of nature begins to degenerate into the "melancholic and chimerical exaltation" of his later years.[32]

By the time of the second voyage the candor and surprise of that initial revelation are in conflict with his stubborn determination to prove a desperate geographical thesis: that the Antilles are identical with the extreme part of Asia. The early enthusiasm is stifled by ridiculous efforts to patch up his shattered dream—the dream dissolved by an irrepressible and immense reality—with the aid of legal documents and sworn statements, and finally submerged by a re-gurgitation of biblical memories and Christian mythologies, casting over the land of a new continent the childishly inadequate image of the ancient Garden of Eden.

30. For a possible justification of Columbus's mystical enthusiasm, to be found in the "shift" from geographical to metaphysical "next world," cf. the comment by M. Mahn-Lot: "Seen from the standpoint of his contemporaries, the rapture of a person like Columbus, self-styled revealer of the 'new earth and the new heavens' foretold by Isaiah and then by the Apocalypse, no longer seems so extraordinary" (review, in *Annales*, 19, no. 6 [Nov.–Dec. 1964], of W. G. L. Randles's "Le nouveau monde, l'autre monde et la pluralité des mondes," in *Actas do Congreso Internacional de História dos Descobrimentos* [Lisbon, 1961]). On American nature as seen by Columbus, see also the book by the photographer Bradley Smith (*Columbus in the New World* [New York, 1962]), who photographed the scenery and the peoples of the four voyages.

31. Frederick J. Pohl, *Amerigo Vespucci, Pilot Major* (New York, 1944), p. 62.

32. Humboldt, *Cosmos*, II, 51. Already in the closing lines of the *Journal*, at once so proud and so humble, Columbus feels himself an instrument of Divine Providence; everyone said his enterprise "was a joke," but he trusts in God " that it will be the greatest honor of Christianity." (The word "joke" crops up several more times in his writings, for example in the letter of 7 July 1503, *Relaciones y Cartes*, p. 380, to describe how his project was viewed.) Terán finds Columbus "Italian," i.e., clearheaded and practical *before* the discovery, "Spanish," i.e., mystical and inspired, *after* the discovery (*La nascita dell'America spagnola* [Bari, 1931], pp. 18–19). But Jos, "La génesis colombina," p. 24, is forced to the conclusion "that already on [Columbus's] first voyage his brain had ceased functioning normally." On his religiosity and mysticism, see also Iglesia, *El hombre Colón*, p. 40f, and Pedro de Leturia, "Ideales político-religiosos de Colón en su carta institucional del mayorazgo," *RI*, 11 (1951), 679–704.

❧ III ❧

Doctor Alvarez Chanca

O N E of the members of the Admiral's second expedition was a doctor from Seville, Alvarez Chanca. And from Hispaniola, Dr. Chanca wrote a letter-cum-report to the cathedral chapter of Seville which was read and used by Andrés Bernáldez but subsequently remained unpublished right up to the beginning of the last century, when Navarrete published it. In view of its date, late 1493 or early 1494,[1] of the rarity of other authentic accounts of the second voyage (which was in fact, as we know, the first voyage of reconnaissance and colonization of the new lands discovered accidentally on the 1492 voyage), and in view above all of the fact that Dr. Chanca emerges from this brief document as a shrewd, lively, and accurate observer, this forerunner of the literature of American nature, written on the spot and not in Spain, by a man of science rather than a soldier or man of letters, deserves greater attention than it has so far received.[2]

1. ENTHUSIASM FOR THE FLORA

Dr. Chanca is an enthusiastic admirer of the American flora. He never tires of extolling its prodigious variety, its astonishing difference and novelty when compared with Europe's: "In this island [Mariagalante] the woods were amazingly thick, and there was such a variety of totally unknown trees that one

---

1. On the date of Chanca's letter, see Humboldt, *Examen critique,* II, 111n.
2. Nothing is known about Chanca. However I have not seen the work by Aurelio Tió, *Dr. Diego Alvarez Chanca: Estudio biográfico* (Puerto Rico, 1966), 450 pp. (!), reviewed in *HAHR,* 49, no. 1 (February 1969), 132–33; and in *RI,* 27, (1967), 267–69, by S. Arana-Soto ("Puerto Rico rinde homenaje al Dr. Chanca"), according to whom it is "the first work in the world on the subject" (p. 268). Fernández de Navarrete, *Colección de los viages y descubrimientos que hicieron por mar las españoles desde fines del siglo XV* (Madrid, 1825–37), I, 69n, supposes it is the same Diego Alvarez Chanca who published in Seville, in 1514, a *Commentum in parabolas divi Arnaldi de Villanova.* On his office, performed "with great diligence and charity," and on his salary, see Columbus's *Memorial* of 30 January 1494, in Navarrete, op. cit., I, 382–83. Cf. also P. Henríquez Ureña, *La cultura y las letras coloniales en Santo Domingo* (Buenos Aires, 1936), pp. 18, 20; L. Olschki, "The Columbian Nomenclature of the Lesser Antilles," *The Geographical Review,* 33 (1943), 398, 402. But in another study ("What Columbus Saw," pp. 642–43) Olschki expresses the curious view that Chanca shows "little interest in the geographical, nautical and natural aspects of the country" and that "his whole attention is directed to their [the islands'] inhabitants"! Equally unjustified, I feel, is Cecil Jane's description of Chanca as "that businesslike careerist" (op. cit., pp. 87–88). On the cathedral chapter of Seville (to whom Chanca addressed his letter), "one of the most prestigious corporations of the time," presided over by Fr. Diego de Deza, Columbus's protector, see M. de la Puente y Olea, *Los trabajos geográficos de la Casa de Contratación* (Seville, 1900), p. 211.

could only marvel at those with fruit, those with flowers, while everything was green."[3] This dense verdure in midwinter sends the good doctor into raptures. Mariagalante, island of marvels, was "all mountainous, very beautiful and green right down to the water, which was a joy to see, because at that time of year in our land there is hardly anything green" (ibid.).

But when he finds that the same is true of all the other islands (with the sole exception of one "most of which is treeless," p. 356) Chanca concludes cautiously: "I *suspect* that the grass never dries up throughout the year. *I do not think* that there is any winter in this island [Hispaniola] nor in the others, because lots of birds' nests are found at Christmas-time, some with nestlings and some with eggs" (p. 358).

The forest of Haiti is so "thick that a rabbit could barely make its way through it; it is so green that there is no season at all when fire could burn it." The land is so fertile and generous that vegetables grow "more there in eight days than in twenty in Spain" (p. 368). The comparative criterion looms up again irresistibly; but the good doctor of Seville treats it with due discretion. He finds a tree "whose leaves have the finest scent of cloves that I ever saw [*sic*] and it was like a laurel, except that it was not as big; so I think," he concludes, "that it was of the laurel species" (p. 349). He comes across another tree that has no fruit on it but which he thinks must bear nutmegs, "and I say that I think so because the taste and scent of the bark is like nutmegs" (p. 370). He also finds linaloe, "although it is not of the sort that we have hitherto seen in our parts [Spain]; nevertheless there can be no doubt that it is one of the species of aloes which we doctors use." And referring to the cinnamon, finally, he admits that "it is not as fine as that seen back home," but he immediately adds a comment that foreshadows Father Acosta's gentle irony a century later: "We do not know if perchance this is caused by not knowing the right time to pick it or whether perchance the land produces it no better" (p. 370). Human or telluric shortcoming? Faulty technique or a failing of the soil?

So Dr. Chanca knows that nature is one in the two worlds, and he knows that the obvious and astonishing differences between the plants of one and the other world are differences of genus and species. His expert herbalist's eye catches both the affinities and the peculiarities of the simples of the Antilles, and more than once he tells us about their effect on the human body—fruits that burn the mouth (pp. 349–50), and others that have a bitter taste (but probably because the specimens gathered were rotten, p. 370)—and even more often he defines trees in terms of their usefulness: there are wool trees (somewhat thorny, "but one can probably find some means of gathering the wool"), cotton trees, wax trees, turpentine trees, and so forth.

---

3. Navarrete, op. cit., I, 349. Citations of Dr. Chanca in the text refer to this edition.

2. LESSER INTEREST IN THE FAUNA

Chanca is less interested in the animals. He remarks on the absence of quadrupeds and wild animals (p. 358); notes a few species of rabbits and edible lizards (iguanas?); a great abundance of fish, "more wholesome than Spain's," always provided it is eaten fresh, because in this warm damp climate it goes off easily (p. 368); and the great variety of birds, including "two parrots that were very large and very *different from any previously seen*" (p. 350). Generally speaking there are no domestic birds, but in one island "there were some ducks in the houses," which he describes with loving care, "most of them as white as snow but some black, very beautiful, with smooth tufts on their heads, bigger than Spanish ducks, though smaller than geese" (p. 359).

3. CURIOSITY ABOUT THE NATIVES

Chanca shows the same curiosity about the natives, but here his tone becomes superior and almost scornful. The good physician is obviously much more at home with a plant or with a beast than with these horrendous, wild, and yet unarguably human specimens. He almost sounds like some modern-day health inspector when he is describing their insalubrious and "bestially" built houses, "so covered with grass or damp that I am amazed how they live" (p. 363). As soon as he comes across huts that are a little better built, but still of grass, he notes that "the people seemed more civilized" (p. 352). He readily admits that these people, completely beardless, may be fiercely jealous (pp. 356, 364).[4] And he is amazed that they possess so many stone instruments, "for it is astonishing that they can be made without iron" (p. 370). At one point he sees that the natives fight with sharp darts and cheerfully compares the instruments used to fire them with the crossbows used by the boys in Spain to shoot their small arrows. The natives, he notes, "fire their missiles a great distance with considerable accuracy" (p. 367).

But the medical man once again gets the better of the ethnographer when it comes to tattooing or the native's eating habits. He laughs like Pascarella at the "silly idiot with his head / Painted like some infant's toy" (*La scoperta de l'America*, sonnet 29), and considers his diet nothing short of bestial: the Caribs "came with their eyes and eyebrows smeared with soot, which I think they did to show off, and they were even more dreadful like that" (p. 356). This first impression does not last, however. "Their way of dressing up, male and female, is to paint themselves—some black, others white and red, with such faces that to look at them you cannot help laughing; their heads are partly shaven and partly with locks of hair, in so many ways as to defy description. In conclusion,

---

4. For a contrary view, see Michele de Cuneo, below, chap. V, sec. 5.

whatever we in Spain might consider typical of a madman is here regarded by the best of the Indians as highly desirable" (p. 369).

The grotesque and idiotic image of these faces daubed in the cause of elegance comes to mind again when we see them pressed greedily to the earth "consuming whatever snakes and lizards and spiders and worms can be found on the ground; so that they seem to be more bestial than any beast on earth" (p. 371).[5]

January 1494, at the latest. The Dominicans have not yet arrived, nor the jurists, nor the *encomenderos,* and already the Indian is likened to an animal. Aristotle does not come into it yet, nor does the theory of natural slavery. The native's chronic hunger, his inevitable "filthy eating habits,"[6] remove him far from civilized humanity in the eyes of the facetious and forgetful doctor, who had himself suffered the pangs of hunger on board during the crossing and would not perhaps have turned up his nose at a nice snake and lizard stew, in those fearful days when "it was prudent to restrain ourselves, so that whatever weather might lie ahead we woud be able to keep ourselves alive" (p. 368).

4. FERNÁNDEZ DE SANTAELLA

It was only a few years later that another learned Sevillian was admiring the singular novelty of American nature, if Master Rodrigo Fernández de Santaella, founder of the University of Seville (died 1509), really wrote the book that is ascribed to him by León Pinelo, *De ignotis arborum atque animalium apud indios speciebus, et de moribus Indorum,* and if this promising title is not a deceptive description of the content of the work.[7]

5. The passage is also cited by Elliott, op. cit., p. 42, who sees it as an example of the facility with which the Europeans went from idealization of the native to the opposite extreme, once they came into personal contact with him.

6. Cf. the comment by Columbus's son Fernando in his *Vita di Cristoforo Colombo:* "The Indians in general eat much filth" (exemplified, p. 89; see however pp. 155, 158).

7. Puente y Olea, op. cit., p. 211, citing P. Picatoste, *Apuntes para una biblioteca científica española del siglo XVI* (Madrid, 1891), p. 211.

❧ IV ❧

Nicolò Scillacio

NICOLÒ Scillacio too was a doctor, but his affinities with Chanca go no further than this shared profession. First and foremost, Scillacio, a Sicilian and doctor and teacher at the University of Pavia, never set foot in America. He did however visit Spain as a young man and was later in Barcelona where he studied a "novelty" of pathology, the so-called Gallic disease, and he was always a great friend of the Spanish. Secondly, Scillacio wrote his epistle to Ludovico il Moro, *De insulis meridiani atque Indici maris nuper inventis* (13 December 1494),[1] not in Castilian but in Latin, thus showing that he addressed himself to quite a different audience.

1. SECONDHAND INFORMATION AND GROSS BLUNDERS

But most of all — as an obvious corollary of the above — he confines himself to repetition and dissemination, contributing nothing of his own. He gets his information from Spaniards, from the obscure William (Guillén) Coma and, perhaps indirectly, Pedro Margarite, and possibly from others, but he is careful to add nothing whatsoever thereto. And when he is recounting marvels and prodigies, such as a certain rock astonishingly rich in gold, he covers himself by adding, "I would be ashamed to write this, unless it were received from a trustworthy source" (p. 92, lines 16–17). His maxim is a passive and slavish prudence: "I have not dared to alter or add anything, beyond what I have heard or learned."[2]

In fact Scillacio did add a few contributions of his own in the form of geographical blunders[3] and fanciful notions of cosmography, identifying the lands

1. Published, apparently, at Pavia in 1494 (C. Merkel, *L'opuscolo "De insulis nuper inventis" del messinese Nicolò Scillacio* . . . [Milan, 1901], pp. 7, 117) or in 1495, it was reprinted in an edition of 102 copies by Lenox in New York in 1859, with the translation by J. Mulligan, and in the *Raccolta Colombiana*, pt. 3, vol. 2, pp. 83–94, which is the text from which I quote, although criticized on a number of occasions by Merkel, op. cit., pp. 9–10, *79n41, 82n80.* I do not know why Magnaghi, *Vespucci* (1926), p. 83, says that Scillacio had "translated Columbus's second voyage into Latin."

2. Cited by A. Ronchini, *Intorno a un rarissimo opuscolo di Nicolò Scillacio* . . . (Modena, 1846), p. 8, which is practically the only source of biographical information. See also, once again by Ronchini, *Nicolò Scillacio e la sua relazione sulla scoperta del Nuovo Continente* (Modena, 1875), which however seems to be quite simply a reprint of the 1846 work (Merkel, op. cit., p. *71n1*).

3. "Preconceived opinions" and "gross errors" are also mentioned by G. Berchet in a note to his edition of Scillacio in *Raccolta Colombina*, pt. 3, vol. 2, p. 83. Attention is once again drawn to "further embellishments by the mediocre mind of Scillacio" (and to his meager intelligence) by the wise and scrupulous Merkel, op. cit., pp. vii, 28, 67.

and islands discovered on the other side of the Atlantic with Ethiopia, Arabia, India, and the kingdom of Saba (biblical Sheba) and imagining that Columbus circumnavigated Africa, thus creating a mystery surrounding the second voyage that defeated even Humboldt.[4]

The truth of the matter is that deep down Scillacio was not tremendously interested in plants and animals and only dealt with them spasmodically and sketchily, certainly not in any systematic fashion. This shows, as has been rightly pointed out, that "the original author of the Relation reworked by Scillacio was a person with little curiosity for the things of nature, even though they had attracted the attention of a man such as Michele da Cuneo who was anything but a scholar and who did not really attach much importance to the strictly scientific aspect of the voyage."[5]

2. AMAZEMENT AND ADMIRATION

The general impression is one of awe and amazement. What he says of *one* island is valid for all the Antilles, even if he does not know exactly where that particular island is, whether in Arabia or India! "I would not be wrong in calling this island *Felix,* whether it were part of Arabia or India" (p. 91, lines 18–19). And regarding the gold to be found there: "It is wonderful to relate and incredible to hear, how rich the region is with blessed gifts" (p. 92, lines 12–13).

When dealing with Guadeloupe, Scillacio already comes up against the bewildering problem of the great rivers, which was to torment Peter Martyr a little later (see below, chap. VIII, sec. 14). Do they perhaps come from vast snowfields? No, but from abundant springs, and they make the land they irrigate highly fertile. The trees have "branches bowed down with wild apples," and every type of seed flourishes prodigiously in those islands. "The seeds never come to any harm: they never dread darnel, vetch, or wild oats" (p. 87, lines 12–13).[6] One can thus plant anything one likes there, "for the soil rejoices, even in the gardens that are closer to the city, and never reject anything that you throw in it; it accepts nothing without giving it back much more abundantly and with

---

4. To Ronchini, who had sent him "the most noteworthy parts of Scillacio," Humboldt wrote, in some perplexity (1846), "How was it that Scillacio failed to learn from his correspondents that Columbus sailed southwest from Cadiz?"–concluding sadly and skeptically, "The history of the discoveries gets most regrettably confused by the history of opinions" (Ronchini, *Un rarissimo opusculo,* pp. 13–14). Ronchini recalls apologetically that "Ethiopia" was then equivalent to "Africa" (see also Vespucci, in Magnaghi, *Vespucci* [1926], pp. 100–01), but he admits that Scillacio used "tainted sources" (*Un rarissimo opusculo,* p. 13). Scillacio's mistake, and his supposed subsequent withdrawal of the copies of his work, is adduced by Merkel as an explanation of its rarity (op. cit., pp. 7, 16–67, 81n68; cf. p. 42).

But it may perhaps be worth recalling a fact that is pure coincidence, yet not unintriguing, namely that it was the great classical geographer Scylax of Caria who, on the orders of Darius I, circumnavigated India, crossed the Red Sea and concluded his journey at the Isthmus of Suez. Scillacio's ramblings retrace, in reverse, the voyages of the ancient Greek. He, of course, was from Messina, possibly originating from the Squillace in Calabria from which the poet and viceroy of Peru, Prince Esquilache, took his title. *Habent sua fata cognomina?*

5. Merkel, op. cit., pp. 41, 43, 45, 61. On Michele de Cuneo, the first person to attempt to "systematize" the nature of the Indies, see below, chap. V.

6. On the fecundity of the land in general, and the greater or lesser yield of the various seeds, see Michele de Cuneo, below, chap. V. sec. 2, and Columbus's "Memorandum" (to Torres), cited in Merkel, op. cit., p. 113n219.

great increase" (p. 91, lines 13–15). And the harvest is sufficient for twenty years![7]

There is an extraordinary abundance of fragrant and medicinal plants, "whence they gather huge heaps, a ceaseless income for the merchants" (p. 91, lines 25–26). And no less extraordinary is the tastiness of the fruit (a feature that would be repeated in even more lyrical terms by Peter Martyr—see below, chap. VIII, sec. 16, end—and Oviedo,—see Appendix C). Scillacio takes particular delight in certain "*asses*[8] . . . very similar to turnips in shape, unless the peppers develop a little too much." When cooked these vegetables change taste and "if you mix an almond sauce with them, you will taste nothing more delicious, you can devour nothing more appetising" (p. 87, lines 2–3). They are also good for the sick, the doctor assures us. "Their seeds, abundant and of varied flavors, have been taken over to Spain, lest they should be lacking in our part of the world" (p. 87, lines 7–8).

The animal population of the islands includes hares, snakes, big lizards, birds and lot of parrots, and also, of course, the usual meek, mute, and edible dogs. "There are ever so many dogs, however, though none that bark, and no madness" (p. 88, lines 2–3), obvious signs of a tame and feeble nature. The sea, in turn, is full of excellent fish with abundant therapeutic virtues. "It abounds in fish of delicious flavor, which, once they have been tested by the doctors [the Galenic Scillacio seems to feel that his profession is entitled to the privilege of sampling this unusual food], are served to improve the health of the sick" (p. 91, lines 34–35).[9] Other fish, "of vast body, the size of an ox, are devoured by them, when the feet have been removed, and have a flavor like veal; if you once taste them [the incorrigible glutton interpolates] you will give up other edible fish" (p. 91, lines 35–36).[10]

3. NATIVES AND CANNIBALS

As far as the men are concerned there is a clear contrast between the unwarlike natives and the savage cannibals who "wage unceasing war on the Indians, who are meek and fearful, for culinary purposes" (p. 86, lines 26–27).[11] They use

---

7. The "propaganda" aspect of the work (or the relation on which it is based) is well brought out by Merkel, op. cit., p. 63.

8. The "asses" are doubtless the same plants that Chanca calls *ajes,* and Ramón Pane, in his description of Haiti (which is strickly ethnographical and thus outside our present theme), *agi,* "certain roots, like coleseed [rape], and others like radishes" (Fernando Columbus, *Historia della vita e dei fatti di Cristoforo Colombo* [Milan, 1930], chap. 61, II, 53). Merkel, op. cit., p. 35, says they are very much like rapes, only somewhat bigger, like melons, and stresses the way the gluttonous Scillacio drools over them. They must in fact have been yams or sweet potatoes.

9. Merkel points out that Chanca and Michele de Cuneo also have some good words for the fish found in the West Indies (op. cit., p. 114n230).

10. Ibid., p. 62.

11. Merkel (op. cit., pp. 30, 37, 39) notes that the cannibals, the most "sensational" discovery of the second voyage, are a subject of particular interest to the "credulous" Scillacio ("exaggerations", says Magnaghi, *Vespucci* [1926], p. 36n) while "Columbus's companions, Michele de Cuneo and Chanca, expatiate about them without laying any particular emphasis on the matter" and thus provide us with "valuable details," while Don Fernando and Las Casas "talk about them as little as possible," the latter (with good reason) even doubting their cannibalism (and their custom

sharpened weapons and canoes, and they have the cruel habit of fattening up the captured children like capons, after castrating them (p. 87, lines 37–38).[12] It will be no easy task to induce them to accept our laws and customs (p. 87, lines 42–43).

The Indians, on the other hand, "have easygoing ways: all things are held in common, with no suspicion, no shameful 'this is mine, this is yours,'" and so on (p. 92, lines 42–43). Although obviously classical in derivation, the phrase is an almost verbatim anticipation of Rousseau's famous reference to "the first person to enclose a piece of land and take it into his head to say 'this is mine.'"[13]

But the coincidence should not really be overemphasized. Absence of private property is a myth typical of the "golden age": it gleams forth like an unprecedented marvel in the newly discovered Antilles and casts its glow down through the centuries beyond Jean-Jacques, to Proudhon and Marx.

As to their physical aspect, the natives are beardless, "bare-chinned through lack of hair," and long-lived: "They live to a very advanced age" (p. 93, line 12). The womenfolk are modest, a touch lascivious, but do not let the Spaniards go too far. "They are sensuous of gesture, a little wanton in their gait; they play with us, and flirt rather boldly, so long as nothing more improper occurs, for they get annoyed if you take the game too far" (p. 93, lines 18–19). And unfortunately the Spaniards do tend to take it too far—every Spaniard grabbed himself three or four native girls, Bernáldez writes, and Scillacio actually says it was five, "for the sake of offspring, I imagine," which leads to all sorts of problems: "Uncontrolled lust for the wives of the Indians was the cause of war and the incentive for hate" (p. 89, lines 37–38).[14] Always the *cunnus teterrima belli causa.* . . .

---

of castration) and naively wondering whether the baskets of human bones that were found were not quite simply "remains of ancestors"! Elsewhere Las Casas, "if he could not excuse it, derived some satisfcation from the fact that cannibalism had also had its devotees in ancient Ireland" (Elliott, op. cit., p. 34).

12.　Michele da Cuneo also mentions the castration of the youths taken prisoner, but he is not sure if this is done to fatten them up for subsequent consumption or to ensure that "they will not mix with their wives" (Merkel, op. cit., p. 89*nl46* and p. 93*nl54;* on Chanca's opinion, ibid., p. 92*nl52*). Fernando Columbus is in no doubt: the natives are castrated "to fatten them up, almost the way we are accustomed to fattening capons, so that they will be tastier" (*Vita di Cristoforo Colombo*, p. 144), and Las Casas says the same (Merkel, p. 33 and p. 95*nl60*).

13.　*Discours sur l'origine de l'inégalité*, pt. 2, opening lines; see Merkel's comments on this passage, op. cit., p. 58.

14.　On the lasciviousness of the Christians see also Merkel, op. cit., pp. 48, 60, 103*nnl92–93*.

❧ V ❧

Michele da Cuneo

1. First Systemization of Nature in the Indies

N O less realistic, indeed at times quite bluntly and cheerfully coarse, is Michele da Cuneo, a native of Savona, who sailed with the second expedition and told its story in a letter (to Gerolamo Annari) dated 15–28 October 1495. With his unqualified devotion to the Admiral and the frankness of his impressions, Michele da Cuneo seems to give us a rough foretaste of the so much later account which Bernal Díaz del Castillo wrote (in 1568) glorifying Cortés and the conquest of Mexico. But his simplicity, or rather inexpertise, does not prevent him attempting what is the first methodical systemization of the whole nature of the Indies, beginning with the plants and going on through the animals to conclude with the men. His letter, therefore, rather than Peter Martyr's *Decades,* can fairly claim "the privilege of being the first example of a general history of the Indies."[1]

While Columbus's observations are often highly vivid, but isolated, almost incidental, "told off" like a measure of the passing days, Michele's scrutiny, "in order to reply specifically to the things you have asked of me,"[2] unstintingly reveals the whole living world and seeks to summarize its salient characteristics.

Michele is quite open with himself about the pecuniary objective of the enterprise. He recalls, for example, the twenty-nine days spent "in terrible weather, eating badly and drinking worse," and not even "decently clothed"; but he immediately adds, by way of cynical consolation, "but our greed for the said gold kept us all strong and lusty," even if shortly thereafter he has to admit, disenchanted, that despite their protracted search "never a single grain of gold was found by anyone" (p. 56). When the Indians were asked about the metal they either replied evasively or simply "said they did not know it and had never seen it" (p. 69). As for the other great mirage, pearls (no spices were found), the eager

---

1. A. M. Salas, *Tres cronistas de Indias* (Mexico and Buenos Aires, 1959), p. 15.

2. L. Firpo, ed., *Prime relazioni di navigatori italiani sulla scoperta dell'America: Colombo, Vespucci, Verrazzano* (Turin, 1966), p. 50. (Citations in the text refer to this edition.) Merkel, op. cit., p. 68, compares Chanca and Michele da Cuneo with Columbus's *Journal,* and finds the latter "all in all richer in substantial information and precise facts."

explorers found extensive oyster beds, true, and collected five or six boatloads of oysters, "all of which we opened and [their disappointment perhaps balanced by this gastronomic delight] we found not a single pearl, but they were very good to eat" (p. 71). And the disappointment continues, alas, in the restful island of Jamaica: "We found nothing better there than in the others" (p. 72).

2. Plants, fruits, and other products

Michele gives a rather vague description of the plants, but for each we are told what fruit it produces and whether it is good to eat or whether instead it produces a "fruit, to our taste, fit only for pigs," or perhaps that "the inhabitants eat it, but to our taste it is not very good" (p. 57). All this tasting, testing, and experimenting is evidence of the sailor's curiosity and is in fact an attempt to answer the primary question, whether these fruits are like Europe's or different from Europe's (see above, chap. I, sec. 4);[3] but it represents the first step toward a methodically empirical investigation, that in Oviedo was to attain a high degree of scientific seriousness.

Michele describes another fruit as "not good to eat, because it is very bitter" (p. 58)—we can almost see him pulling a face—while yet another is delightedly reported to be "in every way good to eat, and rapidly digested, tasting like a peach only better still." Green vegetables are abundant, indeed "infinite," but not as good as Europe's; and a certain "melic" (apparently maize) is said to be "not very good for us—it tastes like acorns," while another fruit, flat like a cake and with a chestnut skin, is specified as "tasting like an acorn and being excellent food for pigs" (p. 61).

There are trees that exude a liquid that "burns like wax, as we experienced ourselves," and certain other fibers are used for making fishing nets (p. 60). Michele's utilitarianism never fails him, and does not stop there. All sorts of seeds were brought back from the Indies and sown in Spain to determine which did well there and which did not—another practical attempt to achieve a factual rather than merely conceptual assimilation of the nature of the Indies to the nature of the Old World.

3. Animals: Scarce or numerous

The account of the animals is brief and to the point. Michele da Cuneo provides one of the very earliest statements of the thesis of the scarceness of the American fauna. "There are very few animals in these islands," especially quadrupeds and land animals; these few include the subsequently notorious "nonbark-

---

3. There are also fairly frequent comparisons between the native huts and "our hunting lodges" (Firpo, p. 53), between a great river and the Guadalquivir (p. 54), between the olive complexion of the inhabitants and that of the Canary Islanders (p. 63), between manioc and Europe's turnips (p. 62), while certain "huge . . . and very tasty" conches are "as big as calves' heads" (p. 71).

ing dogs" and three species of rabbit, some as big as hares, but others "much smaller than ours" (p. 62). For this reason animals were brought from Spain and many prospered there, "particularly the pigs," precisely because of the stated abundance of acorns (p. 62). None is reported to have degenerated there. There are vast numbers of birds, including infinite numbers of parrots—"these I ate often," but their meat is not very good (p. 62); the pigeons however are excellent, and the swallows and sparrows, and so forth. The fish likewise are abundant, of both known and unknown form, but "very good," and the turtles "infinite" and "huge," "excellent to eat," while a "sea toad" is found to be "not to our taste, though the Indians eat it" (p. 63).

4. Realistic portrait of the natives

The portrayal of the natives, both Indians and cannibals, is likewise entirely unidealized, though it includes numerous features that are to be repeated *ad nauseam* by America's explorers and denigrators. The men are few and thinly spread over an immense country; they are "great sodomites"; they make their women work ("the men busy themselves solely with fishing and eating") and they are not worth much as slaves: "In our opinion they are not laborers, and are very much afraid of the cold, and are also short-lived" (p. 74). They also "have very little in the way of beard" and "shave their hair and beards" (p. 64); all speak the same language (an obvious and lasting error, but avoided by Vespucci—see below, chap. VI, sec. 8); and, as reported by Dr. Chanca, "have filthy eating habits," that is, devour "all sorts of nasty and poisonous animals," like large snakes (even the famished Michele ate them when there was nothing else "and they seemed very good") and dogs ("that are not very good"), grass snakes, lizards, spiders, crabs, and so forth.

Michele has no faith at all in the vaunted "goodness" of the savages, and when Columbus presents him with an island of at least thirty thousand souls, he loses no time in bringing it under the plough: "And I cut down trees and planted the cross and the *gallows too* and in God's name I baptized it Bella Saonese," in honor of his native Savona (p. 72). Right at the end of the letter, on the other hand, Michele da Cuneo offers us one of the very first personifications of the sententious West Indian cacique, an individual whom Columbus had forbidden to go back ashore, "saying that he wanted to use him to discover the land and then he would let him go. Then the said king, pointing heavenward, replied that God was in Heaven and rendered justice to all men, and that he called for justice before him in due time." And Michele admiringly concludes: "In our view he was a very astute man" (p. 76). Astute, that is to say crafty, capable of invoking the supreme Deity to protect his own immediate interests.

The cannibals, on the other hand, greedily gobble up the Indians "like we do kids"; they have knives, clubs, bows, and other weapons, share their women between all of them (excepting sisters), and worship an idol whose priest, all dressed in white, sits silently in the temple "and the first female that enters the temple, he lies with her" and all the other women kiss her devotedly "because the said saint has deigned to have commerce with her" (p. 65).

5. CURIOSITY ABOUT THE NATIVES' SEXUAL CUSTOMS

With the same interest in sexual topics Michele tells us about the castration of young men (perhaps to fatten them up for eventual consumption?);[4] and to fill his reader in on "the women situation" in the Indies he recounts how on an island near "Santa Maria la Galante" they captured "twelve very beautiful and very fat females" aged fifteen or sixteen (p. 50), well endowed with "tactile gifts": "The women have very round, firm, and well made breasts" (p. 63).

In conclusion, yes, the natives "live like veritable animals" and "copulate openly whenever they feel like doing so," but they are not jealous,[5] indeed (a characteristic that is to become almost proverbial and an ill omen for the future) "in my opinion they are a cold people, not very lustful, possibly because they eat poorly" (an ingenious dietary explanation that is at least as valid as Buffon's so much later and more complicated explanations).

Michele da Cuneo even manages to come up with a rational explanation for their practise of sodomy: the meek-mannered Indians have contracted "this accursed vice" from the savage cannibals, who, "while subjugating the Indians and eating them" subjected them "also . . . to that excess as a mark of scorn, the habit then proceeding" and, he conjectures, "growing from one to the other" (p. 65). They acquired a taste for it, in fact. . . .

With the same jovially forthright realism Michele also goes on to tell us about an adventure of his with a beautiful female cannibal, another gift from the Admiral after a skirmish. He takes his Briseis off to his quarters, and since she was "naked as was their custom" he "conceived a desire to take pleasure with her." The fierce savage defended herself stoutly with her fingernails. But our bold Michele, "to cut a long story short," then took a rope-end to her and so set about her that she raised "unheard-of screams, such as you would not believe. Finally we came to an agreement and I can tell you that she actually seemed to have been brought up in a school for harlots" (p. 52). Michele leers delightedly.[6]

4. See above, chap. IV, sec. 3. On Michele's delight in relating scabrous details see Magnaghi, *Vespucci* (1926), p. 91n.

5. For a conflicting opinion see Dr. Chanca, above, chap. III, sec. 3.

6. *La scoperta de l'America,* sonnet 36. The chaste Merkel, op. cit., p. 95n 160, modestly skips the whole episode, "because he [Michele] recounts the pleasure that he took of this woman in a form not so much dishonest as downright bestial," and treats us to a quick little sermon on the future cruelties of the conquest and the turpitude of . . . Michele da Cuneo!

❧ VI ❧

Amerigo Vespucci

1. COLUMBUS AND VESPUCCI

THE contrast between Columbus the visionary and Vespucci the realist is a cliché of Americanist literature. With the added twist of the now familiar series of events that led to the New World being given the name of the Florentine rather than the Genoese,[1] the theme lends itself to such obvious and prolific variations on the ironies of men's destinies, on geniuses cheated of their due glory and astuteness or downright fraud triumphing over innocence that it is small wonder it should have prospered and be prospering still in the immense congeries of writings on the subject.

The contrast is real enough, for that matter; and even if it were not buttressed by biographical antitheses — between Columbus in disgrace and Vespucci held in the highest esteem — or posthumous circumstances such as those relating to the baptism of the continent, it would suffice to mark a distinct difference between their respective attitudes to the enigma of the new lands. But the distinction between visionary and realist fails to go to the root of the matter. It is normally the practical man, the businessman, the person who goes straight for results, that is considered the realist, while the man beset by theoretical doubts, the seeker after truths of no immediate use, the resolver of abstract problems, is looked on as the visionary. In point of fact this psychological assumption introduces a source of serious error into the assessment of these first two supreme navigators. Columbus is a visionary, true, but precisely because he was predominantly concerned with practical pursuits and passions, the thirst for glory, the desire for riches, the longed-for redemption of the Holy Sepulchre and, ultimately, his obsession with justifying his claims, showing that his promises had been kept and making sure of the rewards agreed. Vespucci is a realist because despite his

---

1. Cf. Edward Gibbon, for example (1789): the Florentine is found guilty of having "unworthily occupied or rather stolen" one of the four parts of the globe, but "posterity is just; and each generation repeats that Columbus discovered *America,* without recollecting the obscure name of Amerigo *Vespucci*" (*The English Essays* [Oxford, 1972], p. 373). But Robertson had already protested, in even more scathing terms, that "the bold pretensions of a fortunate impostor have robbed the discoverer of the New World of a distinction which belonged to him," etc. (*History of America* [London, 1777], I, 150).

merchant origins he is always motivated first and foremost by scientific curiosity. Vespucci, confronted with the nature of the New World, becomes grave and thoughtful, enquiring and humble, reactions which could not be more different from Columbus's noisy claims and triumphant and mystical discoveries.

Vespucci is as cautious as Columbus is rash. Vespucci is the Pilot, Columbus the Admiral. Vespucci is the Florentine, brought up in the most cultivated society of the Renaissance and endowed with a healthy dose of ironic skepticism. In Columbus, constantly on the move and self-taught, the traits of the Genoese—the notorious Genoese shopkeeper—keep adamantly resurfacing. While Columbus deduces his route speculatively from medieval texts, and cannot believe his own eyes when a world other than the one he was seeking looms up unexpectedly before him, Vespucci remarks in passing and almost sotto voce that rationally speaking, experience is worth a lot more than theory,[2] and that the inhabitability of the tropics, denied by most "philosophers," must therefore, after his voyage, be accepted as a fact.[3] While Columbus wallows in his own religious fantasies and deliberately encourages those of his sailors, Vespucci dubs himself a follower of Saint Thomas, and slow to believe.[4]

2. The three authentic letters

Modern criticism has reduced Vespucci's literary stock-in-trade concerning his voyages to three letters, addressed to his principal and friend Lorenzo di Pier Francesco de' Medici, the first dictated from Seville on 18 July 1500, the second from Cape Verde on 4 July 1501 and the third from Lisbon in 1502—letters that were certainly known to his contemporaries but published only in 1745, 1827, and 1789 respectively.[5] The first describes the voyage undertaken on behalf of the king of Spain, the second and third the voyages for the king of Portugal. The first is possibly more naive in the storytelling, while the other two reveal a more explicit ambition for future glory,[6] with overtones that seem to echo Dante's noble aspiration to live on "amongst those who will call these present times ancient."[7] But in substance the three letters can be considered a single work, the first coherent and deliberate description of the physical nature and inhabitants of

---

2. See letter from Seville, 18 July 1500, in A. M. Bandini, *Vita e lettere di Amerigo Vespucci* (Florence, 1745), p. 73. In a passage quoted by Humboldt (*Examen critique*, V, 27), Amerigo (or his forger?) counters Pliny's authority with experience. The Latin naturalist did not know one in a thousand of the products of America, and this considerably detracts from his work.

3. Bandini, op. cit., p. 73; cf. ibid., p. 101.

4. "I am one of St. Thomas's people, slow to believe, letting time do its work" (letter from Lisbon, 1502, in F. Bartolozzi, *Ricerche storico-critiche circa alle scoperte d'Amerigo Vespucci . . .* [Florence, 1789], p. 235).

5. A modern, annotated translation of the three authentic letters may be found in Pohl, op. cit., pp. 76–90, 126–36; cf. ibid., p. 235. On Vespucci's relations with Lorenzo di Pier Francesco de' Medici, see the letter published by E. H. Gombrich, *Symbolic Images* (London, 1972), pp. 80–81; and cf. pp. 43 and 65 of that work.

6. Pohl, op. cit., p. 127 in letter of 4 July 1501; Bartolozzi, op. cit., p. 170.

7. *Paradiso*, XVII, 118–20.

the Brazilian coast and the region to which Vespucci himself gave the name Venezuela, as he had seen a whole city of houses built on the water there.[8]

It is quite true that Amerigo's gaze is normally turned to the skies—"I many times went without sleep at night, contemplating the movement of the stars of the other pole"[9]—admiring the new constellations that reminded him, as they would later remind so many others, of Dante's famous lines,[10] or intent on measuring the distance between the planets and the moon so that he can fix his longitude almost exactly. True, also, that his mind is mainly occupied with cosmographic and cartographical concerns, with the dividing line fixed by the pope between Spanish and Portuguese possessions and with the pattern of currents that helps him to determine the shape of his new world. But the minerals, plants, and living creatures do not escape his calm attention.

3. THE NEWNESS OF THE AMERICAS

Nature in the New World is new and surprising. Vespucci notes the fact without hyperbole. The precious stones found there are of little-known species and only dubiously identified by the jewelers.[11] The spices are unusual and of questionable quality: "We saw crystal, and infinite flavors and odors of spices and herbs, *but unknown ones.*"[12] All the plants and fruits are different from those that thrive in the old hemisphere.[13] And the wild animals are of so many different species that it is difficult to see how they could all have fitted into Noah's Ark (another soft hint of skepticism),[14] and certainly they are unlike those found in Spain.[15]

As for the men, they are different in that they go about naked, are beardless

---

8. "Houses with their foundations in the sea, like Venice" (Bandini, op. cit., p. 80; cf. ibid., p. 19).

9. Ibid., p. 69.

10. *Purgatorio,* I, 22–27. Vespucci also says that "they are ever hidden from those of the North" (Bartolozzi, op. cit., p. 170), obviously recalling Dante's "oh widowed world of the North, for ever deprived of the sight of them." The stars of the South are "manifold and very much larger and brighter than those of our pole" (pseudo-Vespucci, in Bandini, op. cit., p. 53; cf. pp. 56 and 113: "stars . . . unknown to us," bigger than one thinks).

11. "Some jewellers *say* it is beryl . . . other stones, that seemed very fine to us" (ibid., pp. 83–84).

12. Bartolozzi, op. cit., p. 179.

13. "None of those trees, nor their fruit, matched the same ones on our side" (Bandini, p. 68); "many other fruits, all unlike ours" (ibid., p. 76).

14. St. Augustine had already taken it upon himself to calculate the exact displacement of Noah's Ark and produce other ingenious subterfuges aimed at refuting those who "say that . . . the ark was not big enough to contain so many kinds of animals of each sex, seven of every clean one, and two of every unclean one" (*De Civitate Dei,* XV, 27). The doubts mentioned in passing and half-jokingly by Vespucci were to be a source of much soul-searching for Father Acosta (*Historia natural y moral de las Indias* [Seville, 1590], IV, 6), as would later be recalled by Robert Burton (*Anatomy of Melancholy* [1621; New York, 1938], p. 415), Father Feijoo (*Solución del gran problema histórico sobre la población de la América* . . .), Father Sánchez Labrador (J. Rey Pastor, *La ciencia y la técnica en el descubrimiento de América* [Buenos Aires, 1942], p. 143), and the Mexican Jesuit Francisco Xavier Alejo de Orrio (1763). The religious writers were particularly concerned about the occasion offered by the existence of this singular American fauna, that had not been part of Noah's cargo, for indiscreet conjectures on the plurality of creation, for dangerous suppositions regarding preadamitical species and heretical questionings of biblical chronology. And it was in fact this same disintegratory quality of the fauna of the Antarctic archipelagoes that earned it a place in Diderot (*Supplément au voyage de Bougainville* [1772; Pléiade ed., Paris, 1935], p. 755).

15. Bartolozzi, op. cit., p. 172.

and without shame,[16] and in that they have different ideas, customs, and food; but they are not deformed or monstrous, as Europeans imagined the "antipodeans": they are well built and well proportioned, agile, numerous, and long-lived. They are indubitably men, and Vespucci becomes so interested in them that he tends to skimp the rest of the description or treat it almost as mere background and setting for his cannibals. Man, however primitive, was still the worthiest and most interesting subject of study for the disciple of the humanists.[17]

The Brazilian forest is a dense tangle of beautiful and fragrant trees, and from its depths innumerable multicolored birds warble sweet melodies.[18] Many of the birds are splendidly polychromatic,[19] others ugly as sin[20] (there is no affected idealization in Vespucci); and snakes of fearsome proportions slither along the ground.[21] But the plants are all evergreen, never losing their leaves, and the whole year round they bear fruit and give forth delicate aromas.[22]

4. The Earthly Paradise

Vespucci is so carried away by all the luxuriant vegetation, the perfumed air, the tastes of fruit and root that twice he says he feels he is in an Earthly Paradise[23] or close to the Earthly Paradise;[24] the pseudo-Vespucci too was to declare that "if there is any Earthly Paradise anywhere in the world it must without doubt be not very far from here."[25] Charles VIII had used the same terms, very shortly before (1495), to describe the splendid gardens of Naples: "All they seem to lack is Adam and Eve [whose part would be played, after a fashion, by the American natives] to become an Earthly Paradise."[26]

Columbus too had concluded that the land of Paria was situated somewhere in the vicinity of the Earthly Paradise. The two expressions, although literally identical, are however entirely different in meaning. First of all it is one thing to say "this is Paradise" and quite another thing to say "this is like being in Paradise,"[27] but quite apart from that the literary sources of the two expressions

16. If one were to recount "how shameless they are, it would mean embarking on an indecent topic, and it is better to pass over it in silence" (Bandini, op. cit., p. 76).

17. "With regard to the details of the places visited [on the second voyage], and the return route followed, he provides no details at all. The account appears to be aimed solely at informing his Medici master about the customs of the natives," while the natives to the north of the Equator had already been described by Columbus and others (Magnaghi, *Vespucci* [1926], p. 181).

18. Bandini, op. cit., p. 67; Bartolozzi, op. cit., p. 171.

19. Bandini, op. cit., p. 76.

20. Ibid., p. 67.

21. Ibid., p. 77.

22. Cf. ibid., op. cit., pp. 65 and 83 (trees "all aromatic"); Bartolozzi, op. cit., p. 171. Abundant and high quality brazilwood: Bandini, op. cit., pp. 80–81; Bartolozzi, op. cit., p. 179. Healthiness of the air and earth: ibid., p. 178.

23. Bandini, op. cit., p. 68.

24. Bartolozzi, op. cit., p. 171.

25. Bandini, op. cit., p. 113.

26. Terry Comito, "Renaissance Gardens and the Discovery of Paradise," *JHI,* 32 (1971), 483–506, with learned analysis of the meaning of the metaphor and its implications.

27. Pohl, op. cit., p. 221. On his interest in nature and landscape, see Morison, *Southern Voyages,* p. 284.

are quite different. Columbus is thinking of the Bible, Vespucci of the *Divine Comedy.* There is an obvious—to my mind—mnemonic relationship between that fragrant forest and the "ancient wood" crowning Mount Purgatory, the "divine forest dense and verdant" in which the "little birds" practiced "their every art," the paradisal forest that Matilda herself identifies as the Garden of Eden: "They who in olden times sang of the golden age and its happy state perchance dreamed in Parnassus of this place. Here the root of man's race was innocent; here spring is everlasting, and every kind of fruit."[28] When Dante had entered the forest he had immediately become aware, like Amerigo two centuries later, of the pervading, penetrating fragrance, "emanating from the soil on every side."[29]

Shortly before, Vespucci had recalled that the skies of the Southern Hemisphere were lit with beautiful and glittering constellations, never known to the Northern Hemisphere. And Dante, in the canto preceding that of the Earthly Paradise, had seen and admired "stars brighter and bigger than their wont."[30] And the "four holy lights," "never yet seen save by the first people," Vespucci had, as we already know, recognized in the Southern Cross, shining out over the savages of the tropics.

5. Other echoes

Other echoes are likely, if not certain. Possibly that furious and powerful adverse current, so much more threatening than the whirlpools of the columns of Hercules and Scylla—"mere duckponds" in comparison—that terrifies the explorer and his companions and from which they flee northward in consternation,[31] has a precedent in the "whirlwind" that—precisely in the Southern Hemisphere lit by "the stars of the other pole"—falls on the vessel of Dante's Ulysses, envelops it, capsizes it, and plunges it down into the ocean depths.[32] And perhaps also Lethe and Eunoë, those two sluggish and diverging rivers like Euphrates and Tigris, that well up "almost like friends" from a spring in Eden,[33] continue in the broad and lazy current of those two gigantic rivers (Amazon and Pará?) that issue forth from the mysterious, impenetrable Brazilian forest, flowing one eastward and the other northward, "creating fresh water in the ocean."[34]

Vespucci, recalling at one moment a line from Petrarch[35] and a moment later the pagan and Dantesque fables of Antaeus and Penthesilea,[36] carries across the Atlantic a lay, unbiased mind, a mind at times not altogether respectful toward

---

28. *Purgatorio,* XXVIII, 2, 25, 140ff.
29. Ibid., XXVIII, 6.
30. Ibid., XXVII, 89–90.
31. Bandini, op. cit., p. 68.
32. *Inferno,* XXVI, 90–142. The Ulysses canto is quoted by the pseudo-Vespucci: Bandini, op. cit., p. 4.
33. *Purgatorio,* XXXIII, 112–14.
34. Pohl, op. cit., p. 77; Bandini, op. cit., pp. 66–67, 75.
35. Bartolozzi, op. cit., p. 176.
36. Bandini, op. cit., p. 81.

the Old and New Testaments (Noah and Saint Thomas), but devoted to the vernacular classics, to the value of experience and the altogether modern eagerness to measure, describe, and explore the world: "We went for the purpose of discovery . . . and not to seek any profit."[37]

Las Casas was to call him "astute and eloquent," Ramusio to praise his "singular intellect" and "very fine mind," and Humboldt, closer to our own times, would conclude his lengthy study by pronouncing him frank and truthful.[38]

6. The animals and the natives

When Vespucci mentions the animals, which are all "of the forest" (in other words, wild),[39] because the natives "do not keep dogs," he settles for describing them with familiar names—lions, stags, bears, rabbits, panthers, wildcats, wolves, and monkeys[40]; but their number and quality are already sufficient to convince him that this land is no island, but the mainland, a continent.[41] And this realization in turn increases his interest in the natives who, as the numerous population of such a land,[42] cannot be dismissed as some quaint islanders, almost accidental phenomena, but must be seen and studied as an essential variety of the human species—despite the majority of philosophers denying their existence.[43] Their very numbers increase their scientific worthiness. The natives, rather than the gold and spices, the natives and not the plants or animals, surprising as they may be, the savages, the naked men, the cannibals—here we have the most notable feature of the New World.

Vespucci was certainly no sentimentalist, nor even a "humanitarian." He coolly records the slaughters perpetrated, the burning and sacking of villages[44] on the Venezuelan coast. The West Indians, he states bluntly (as did Columbus

---

37. Bartolozzi, op. cit., p. 178.
38. Humboldt, *Examen critique*, V, 8; cf. ibid. for Las Casas, III, 14, and IV, 45; for Ramusio, IV, 147, and V, 189.
39. Bartolozzi, op. cit., pp. 172, 174; Bandini, op. cit., p. 83.
40. Bandini, op. cit., pp. 73–77; Bartolozzi, op. cit., p. 172.
41. Bandini, op. cit., p. 77; cf. Peter Martyr, below, chap. VII, sec. 14.
42. Bandini, op. cit., pp. 73–79; Bartolozzi, op. cit., p. 172.
43. "But as for the fables about the existence of Antipodeans, it is totally unreasonable to attach any credence thereto" (St. Augustine, *De Civitate Dei*, XVI, 9). Before Augustine, Lactantius (*Divinae Institutiones*, chap. 24) had denied not only their existence but the very possibility thereof, earning himself the scorn, in company with Augustine, of La Peyrère (see A. de León Pinelo, *El Paraíso en el Nuevo Mundo* [Lima, 1943], I, 35–36) and the savage criticism of Father Feijoo (*Españoles americanos*, secs. 18–20). Dante's Ulysses too, following the traditional teaching, hungered after "experience, beyond the sun, of the world without people" (*Inferno*, XXVI, 117).
    This opinion of Dante's ("that the sea is empty and without men") is recalled, and in fact precisely in relation to the Ulysses episode (wrongly cited as "Inferno, XVIII") in the introduction to the *Quatuor Navigationes* attributed to Vespucci (Humboldt, *Examen critique*, III, 15n). And, according to a reviewer of Elliott's book in the *Times Literary Supplement* of 6 August 1971, Bartolomeo Vespucci, Amerigo's nephew, a professor of astronomy at Padua, "stoutly maintained, in a textbook he edited in 1508, that the torrid zone was uninhabitable and life below the equator impossible." For abundant citations from ancient and modern sources, see G. Atkinson, *Les nouveaux horizons de la Renaissance française* (Paris, 1935), pp. 255–61. Pascal too was to heap scorn on Pope Zachary for excommunicating anyone that believed in the antipodes: the king of Spain was quite right to listen to Columbus, who had been there, rather than the pope! (*Lettres Provinciales*, XVIII [Paris, 1926], II, 273–74).
44. Bandini, op. cit., pp. 77–78.

before him), are shy and stupid, and one can do whatever one wants with them. And in fact when the first voyage looks like ending with a heavy deficit, Amerigo has no hesitation in carrying off some of the natives by force and embarking no less than 232 of them, whose subsequent sale as slaves in Castile (less 32 that died on board ship) make it possible to close the expedition's accounts with a modest profit.[45]

7. LIFE AMONG THE CANNIBALS

But his curiosity, especially on the second voyage, impels him into an act of audacity worthy of the most self-sacrificing ethnologist or anthropologist. Filled, like Ulysses of old, with a desire to know the customs and usages of these peoples, and animated solely by peaceful intentions and a curiosity about the world—"we signaled back to them that we were peace-loving people and we were journeying about to see the world"[46]—Vespucci goes ashore and for twenty-seven days shares the cannibals' lives.[47] He becomes a savage to understand the savages. And if he does not become a cannibal, neither does he for a moment act the missionary, nor seek to do business with them. His journey, he repeats, is a journey of exploration, not in search of riches or trading possibilities.[48]

The savages have neither laws nor religion. They know nothing of the immortality of the soul, nor of private property. Everything is owned communally, and they have no political boundaries at all. They get married without formality, taking more than one wife, but are very jealous of their women. The women, even when pregnant, eat everything and wash themselves right up to the time they give birth, their deliveries being easy and painless.[49] They all live in long rows of huts and sleep in cotton nets slung in midair (hammocks), without blankets. They feed on fish, shellfish, fruit, and the meat of birds and animals, frequently including human flesh.[50] They decorate themselves with bones and colored pebbles, piercing their cheeks and lips in horrendous shapes.

45. Ibid., pp. 82–84. The slave trade, especially as regards female slaves, lasted considerably longer in Florence than elsewhere, in fact almost to the end of the sixteenth century (G. Biagi, "La vita privata dei fiorentini," in *Fiorenza, fior che sempre rinnovella* [Florence, 1925], pp. 75–78).

46. Bandini, op. cit., p. 80.

47. Bartolozzi, op. cit., pp. 172ff. On the first voyage he had spent a whole day with the cannibals, but had returned to the ships at nightfall (Bandini, op. cit., p. 75).

48. Bartolozzi, op. cit., p. 178. Some ten years later his fellow-citizen Machiavelli would delight in "slumming it" with the country people, chatting with the "passers-by," asking them "news of their home towns" and noting "various tastes and fancies of men" (letter to Vettori, 10 December 1513). But it need hardly be pointed out that Machiavelli's approach is characterized by altogether different feelings of bitterness, disdain, and arrogant spiritual violence.

49. The pseudo-Vespucci would add that they were exceedingly lascivious, indeed downright lustful: "we could hardly fight them off"; but they were not ugly, and even after having several children they still had breasts, bellies and "those parts that one cannot decently name not unlike those of virgins" (Bandini, op. cit., pp. 13–15, 24, 108–09).

50. On cannibalism, see Bandini, op. cit., p. 74; Bartolozzi, op. cit., pp. 174, 176–77. The pseudo-Vespucci adds with casual brutality that they marvel "to hear us say that we do not eat up our enemies" (Bandini, p. 18); he reports that they castrate the boy prisoners for the purpose of eating them (ibid., p. 36) and that father eats son and son father, just like that, just however it turns out! (p. 109).

The description continues, with a naturalist's objectivity, telling us of their customs in war, their savagery with their defeated foes, the bloody sacrificial ceremonies when they become possessed with diabolical frenzy, and the technique they have thriftily adopted of smoking human flesh for consumption at a later date. Vespucci, frankly disgusted, rebukes them without success and buys ten of the victims marked down for slaughter, both males and females, to secure their escape from this awful fate. The slave-trader, for once, ransoms the innocent.

8. WAR AND LANGUAGES

But what most intrigues and puzzles him is this frenzy for war, in a people that share everything and thus are not driven to do battle out of greed for dominion or possession. He is still unsatisfied with the savages' own explanation, that the war began in far-off times, and that they are seeking to avenge their ancestors.[51] This profitable slaughter, with its alimentary and economic corollary—dead enemies are eaten and prisoners bound into slavery—has such subhuman characteristics that Amerigo, ready and willing as he is to see the man in the cannibal, just cannot comprehend it and remains perplexed.[52]

Whether or not it predates Peter Martyr's first *Decade* (see below, chap. VIII, n. 10), Vespucci's letter therefore represents a marked advance on the view propounded by the Milanese writer. Peter Martyr attributed the savages' wars to territorial rather than pecuniary ambitions. Vespucci even rules out that motive, introducing the notion of primitive war, quite alien to the schemes of our own civilization, of war as a way of life, spontaneous and unmotivated, the "heroic" and natural war that would later be discussed by Hobbes and Vico.

The same shrewdly enquiring spirit and anxiety to "understand" these primitive peoples are revealed in Vespucci's interest in their widely differing languages. It is all very well for European scholars to insist that there are not more than seventy-seven different tongues in the whole world. Vespucci does away with this traditional philological boundary too, and notes that twenty natives speak seven different languages, that he has personally heard no less than forty spoken, and that in the whole world there must therefore be more than a thousand.[53] Pigafetta was later to embark on a methodical study of the native languages, but Vespucci can still be credited with having discovered the almost incredible multiplicity of primitive idioms and of having broadened, to a dizzy-

---

51. Bartolozzi, op. cit., pp. 176–77.

52. This uncertainty is echoed and intensified in the pseudo-Vespucci of the *Mundus Novus*—in the *jocundus interpres* or "jovial translator" who supposedly put the letter into Latin—who describes the natives at one point as "good-natured and friendly people" and elsewhere as savage cannibals (A. Magnaghi, *Amerigo Vespucci* [Rome, 1924], I, 77–78).

53. Bandini, op. cit., pp. 77, 81, 83; and the pseudo-Vespucci, ibid., pp. 11–12.

ing degree, not only the known world, but the philological measure of our babelic humanity.[54]

9. THE EPISODE OF THE GIANTS

The only episode that leaves us more incredulous than amazed is the story of the giants encountered in what seems to have been the island of Curaçao. There Vespucci and ten of his companions run into seven women, so tall that the smallest is a handspan and a half taller than any of the Europeans present. These ladies are terrified, and one of them offers refreshments to the visitors. They in turn plot to carry off a couple of the younger women and make a present to the king of these phenomena of nature, since they are indubitably taller than the average man. But at that point thirty-six male giants appear on the scene, so tall that every one of them is bigger kneeling down than Vespucci standing up, and armed with bows and arrows and paddles. Some of Vespucci's companions give themselves up for dead. Others assure the giants of their good intentions, and all return in good order and embark safely.

The episode is so picturesque and unlikely[55] that the forger of the *Quatuor Navigationes* attributed to Amerigo lifted the whole passage and added further details. But if it is not an insertion we must perhaps explain it as the result of one of the malarial attacks that Vespucci suffered on his return, before drafting his letter.[56] And in fact, quite apart from seeming totally out of place in an account that is always notable for its objectivity, the admission of such a grave imprudence is inconsistent with Vespucci's boast of having completed his voyages with a

54. There is no mistaking the Vicoan tendency in this discovery of Vespucci too.

55. See Navarrete, op. cit., III, 7; Magnaghi, op. cit. (1926), pp. 98–99; Bandini, op. cit., pp. 79–80. Giants were never seen again on that island. The unusually precise numbers of *seven* women and *thirty-six* men also seem to suggest some vague allegorical meaning. In the closing cantos of *Purgatory,* where Dante is describing the Earthly Paradise and which we know from various other sources to have been familiar to the Florentine Vespucci, Dante admires *seven* women, followed by "twenty-four elders," they in turn followed by another seven, making thirty-one (*Purgatory,* XXIX, 83, 134–43), plus four animals (*Purgatory,* XXIX, 92), and finally Beatrice (*Purgatory,* XXX, 32)—in all *thirty-six* figures whose allegorical significance can be found in any commentary. Four of those seven fair women correspond ("here we are nymphs, and in heaven we are stars," *Purgatory,* XXXI, 106) to the four southern stars (*Purgatory,* I, 23–27) explicitly recalled by Amerigo. The other three come forward "dancing their angelic caribo" (*Purgatory,* XXXI, 132). The exact meaning of that surprising word "caribo" is unknown; possibly it indicates some sort of song or roundelay. According to Oviedo "this name Caribe [inhabitant of the Caribbean Sea] means only bold or daring or plucky" (*Historia,* XXI, 6; II, 133b).

The sacred tree of Paradise is so large that "it would be a source of wonder to the *Indians* in their forests, for its height" (*Purgatory,* XXXII, 41–42). And when the symbolic chariot is "transformed," Dante sees looming over it a wild and fantastic apparition: "Seated upon it, as secure as a fortress crowning a hill, I saw a shameless harlot, darting looks around her; and as if to ensure that no-one carried her away, I saw a *giant* standing beside her; and from time to time they kissed one another" (*Purgatory,* XXXII, 148–53).

The recollection of this whole episode in the *Purgatory* could, in fact, have provided the visual and verbal prompting for the unlikely episode in Vespucci's letter. Olschki, *Storia letteraria,* has shown how frequent it was for travelers (including Marco Polo and Columbus), when relating what they had seen, "unconsciously to deform their recollections under the influence of literary sources with which they were familiar" (G. Levi della Vida, in the "Correspondence" section of *Modern Language Notes* [March 1945], p. 210).

56. Bandini, op. cit., p. 84.

minimum loss of human life. From the first voyage he brought back fifty-five of fifty-seven members of his crew (two were killed by Indians); from the second — which he knew when he set out would be quite dangerous[57] — he brought back all his men unharmed.[58] Neither in Vespucci's time or since, I believe, have such stunning geographical results been obtained with such slight losses.[59]

10. VESPUCCI'S HUMANITY AND SHREWDNESS

Vespucci clearly did not look on the lives of his men as "expendable" in the uncaring and easygoing way almost all the other captains and conquistadors did. He did not, of course, have precise authority as commandant or captain over his men, and thus he certainly had no power to impose the severe penalties with which discipline was — with difficulty — maintained among the crews. But he was indubitably the leading personality, the moral if not the technical or military leader of the fleet. And at least in this ambiguous role the Florentine trader and cosmographer showed himself as thrifty with European lives, as reluctant to indulge in pointless sacrifice and bravado, as he was happy when he could save the lives of the natives (above, sec. 7).

Vespucci, in short, was well endowed with that simple humanity that so often goes hand in hand with the resolute firmness and realistic vision of the scientist and merchant. Caution is the first step to perspicacity. And Vespucci's perspicacity in dealing with the things of this world, his organizational gifts and practical good sense are well illustrated — better than in the happy outcome of his voyages and in the modest success of his affairs in general (he died a poor man) — in the answer he gave to Cardinal Jiménez de Cisneros's question on how to derive the greatest profit from the export trade to the West Indies. In today's terminology, Vespucci replied that trade with the Indies was rather complex and that many of the articles needed in the Indies could be bought elsewhere, in Portugal or the Canaries, more easily than in Spain. His suggested solution was therefore either an export tax combined with unrestricted free trade, or fiscal participation in a commercial monopoly, without any capital outlay from treasury funds, and with duplicate accounting for checking purposes.[60]

Neither the Spanish nor the Portuguese government adopted either system. It is quite probable that some of the worst consequences of their extreme and shortsighted exclusivism would have been avoided if one or other of the shrewd Florentine's suggestions had been heeded.

---

57. Bartolozzi, op. cit., p. 169.

58. Pohl, op. cit., p. 125.

59. Almost three centuries later James Cook returned from his three-year-long second voyage having lost only one man out of his crew of 112 — which must have been a source of immense admiration to "those who accepted as inevitable a heavy death-roll on a long voyage" (*Times Literary Supplement*, 30 November 1946).

60. Letter from Seville, dated 9 December 1508, to the cardinal archbishop of Toledo, Jiménez de Cisneros, in *Cartas de Indias*, ed. Ministerio de Fomento (Madrid, 1877), pp. 11–13 and fasc. C; translated in Pohl, op. cit., pp. 231–33.

❧ VII ❧

The Pseudo-Vespucci

1. FLAWS AND CRUDITIES

AFTER Magnaghi's studies, the authenticity of the reports attributed to Amerigo Vespucci—the *Mundus Novus* (August 1504) and the letter to Pier Soderini known in various reprints and translations as the *Quatuor Navigationes* (September 1504)—is generally rejected. They were drafted by some unknown and not very talented scholar in the early sixteenth century on the basis of the Florentine's few and sober original letters, and rushed into print to exploit the momentary thirst for information on the New World and the eternal hunger for tales of marvels and fantasy. The crudeness of the author's Latin, the naivety of some of his chronological patchwork, and his general tone, half boastful and half puerile, betray a man of little learning. Perhaps he also wanted to exalt Florence and Amerigo's *four* voyages to compare with Genoa and Columbus's *four* voyages. He certainly had no hesitation in spicing his story with scandalous and obscene details—for instance that the savages when they defecate "do everything not to be seen" whereas they urinate without restraint, even "while standing talking to us," and are quite unembarrassed[1]—anything, in fact, to add zest and piquancy to his work, which would richly deserve Vico's stinging definition: "tales of travelers seeking to make their books marketable with monstrous details."[2] In short his work is something more akin to a popular adventure story than a deliberate and calculated scientific forgery.

Oviedo, who did in fact know and admire "the learned Amerigo, who was a great seafarer and a learned cosmographer,"[3] does not appear ever to have used the reports attributed to him, which in 1513 were already viewed with skepticism

---

1. Bandini, op. cit., p. 12.
2. Giambattista Vico, *La Scienza Nuova* (Bari, 1911–16), I, 174. Magnaghi (*Vespucci* [1926], p. 28) describes the work as "crammed with contradictions and crude errors."
3. *Hist.*, XX, I: II, 9b. Humboldt's statement that "Oviedo nowhere mentions Amerigo Vespucci" (*Examen critique*, IV, 278) is explained by the fact that he was only acquainted with the first nineteen books of Oviedo's *Historia* (I, 134*n*), the others having remained unpublished until 1851–55. Thus the argument that Humboldt deduced (IV, 133–34, and V, 188–89) from Oviedo's supposed "silence" on the priority of the discovery of the South American continent ceases to apply.

by the scholarly world.[4] Oviedo, who was scrupulous about citing his sources and refers to numerous other chroniclers of the period, never mentions any of Vespucci's writings and only quotes him in connection with the latitude of Cape St. Augustine. Nor is it likely that he deliberately ignores them out of any pro-Columbian and therefore anti-Vespuccian sentiments (the long-lasting quarrels between the supporters of the two explorers are well known)[5] since, as we have seen, he recalls the Florentine with profound respect. One might at most conjecture that he was displeased at the pseudo-Vespucci's insistence on speaking of a *new* world, in reference to the lands that Oviedo claimed to have been known to and owned by the mythical prehistoric monarchs of Spain; and he might well have been even more offended by the gross inaccuracies in what claimed to be an original description of the nature and natives of America.

Meanwhile the glory of the name of America, spreading throughout the civilized world, cast a reflected glow on the writings attributed to the first legitimate bearer of that name. The growing fame of the continent lent greater credence to Amerigo's accounts. What better source of information on the new lands than the reports by the person who had—albeit involuntarily—given them their name? The *Mundus Novus* and the *Letter of Amerigo Vespucci on the Islands Newly Discovered in Four of His Voyages* were therefore read avidly, reprinted, and translated: they raced across Europe, and traces of them are found in Thomas More, Erasmus, and the French poets of the Pléiade. At the end of the eighteenth century Jefferson was still using them in his polemic against Buffon.

2. ENTHUSIASM FOR AMERICA

If they are therefore of no value whatsoever as a "source" for the knowledge of nature in America, they do have a value, indeed considerable value, for the history of the legend of the New World. In outline, in fact, the pseudo-Vespuccian account depicts America as splendidly new, bursting with life, luxuriant and well-stocked with men and animals. "That land is well filled with people and everywhere well stocked with many different animals, very little like ours, except lions, bears, stags, pigs, kids and does, and even they have some deformity distinguishing them from ours." It is entirely lacking in domestic animals, but this deficiency is balanced by an extraordinary quantity of other beasts, which are however all wild and "difficult for me to describe." With this prudently naive device the reporter manages to avoid telling us what animals he is alluding to, and with equally reticent vagueness he extols the miraculous

---

4. Pohl, op. cit., pp. 178, 231. A partial rehabilitation of the authenticity of the *Mundus Novus* was attempted by Luis de Matos, "Un aspect de la question vespuccienne: l'auteur du 'Mundus Novus'," in *Charles-Quint et son temps* (Paris, 1959), pp. 157–66. And Morison, *Southern Voyages,* pp. 304–14, calls for a review of all the sources, particularly since most of those published are riddled with mistakes.

5. On Oviedo's presumed anti-Vespuccianism, Bartolozzi, op. cit., pp. 25–27, 162. See above, chap. VI, sec. 1.

abundance of birds of all colors.[6] No further particulars are given us regarding the creatures of another region (possibly Marayo): "The island contains vast numbers of animals of all sorts, who all drink dirty water"—as a "distinguishing feature" the fact that the creatures in question drink dirty water is not a great help![7]

When he does attempt to be specific the pseudo-Vespucci leaves us almost equally disappointed. "Gigantic mice" and "lizards with forked tails"[8] belong to that same semimythical fauna that numbers among its most illustrious examples the iguanas (?) as big as goats, cunning, sharp-clawed, and of loathsome aspect, that would have seemed veritable serpents (or dragons?) if it were not that they lacked wings![9]

3. GIANTS MALE AND FEMALE

The human population could not, of course, fail to include the giants and giantesses. Here, as we have seen, the fake Vespucci takes his cue from the real one, but in rewriting the episode he cannot resist touching it up, embellishing it with crude virtuoso flourishes. Five giantesses (not seven), three young and two old, are so terrified at the sight of the minuscule Europeans that they are frozen to the spot, almost like damsels of today transfixed at the sight of a mouse. The giant ladies are taller than the strapping figure of Francesco Albizzi, but "better proportioned than we are." The Spaniards contemplate kidnapping the three stalwart maidens and carrying them off to Castile. But at this point there appear on the scene no less than thirty-six burly fellows, still bigger than the besieged females, and they too are "handsome and well built, so that they were a pleasure to behold," and moreover armed with bows and arrows, staves and long clublike sticks. . . .

The tables are turned, the Europeans quickly realize they are in for a hiding and, after a brief powwow, scoot off with their tails between their legs ("we found some excuse to leave the hut"), making rapidly for the ships. Some distance behind them come the three dozen naked rascals, chattering among themselves, and when they see the Europeans embark they wade into the sea and loose off a shower of arrows after them. To which the Spaniards reply with a couple of cannonades, and the giants take to the nearby hills and the Spaniards to

6. Navarrete, op. cit., III, 237. Comparison with the corresponding passages in Vespucci's original letters (Pohl, op. cit., pp. 78, 83) reveals the forger's tendency toward exaggeration and astonishment: it is the forger who added the "very little like ours" and the "some deformity," the vague and qualifying expressions, etc.

7. Navarrete, op. cit., III, 259. Humboldt had already noted the extreme imprecision, the "desperate vagueness" (*Examen critique,* IV, 168), "the intentional or fortuitous terseness of the narrator" (p. 192), apart from his flagrant errors and chronological blunders (pp. 273, 283).

8. Navarrete, op. cit., III, 288; Bandini, op. cit., p. 60. Of the animals "few are similar to ours . . . and those still have a certain dissimilarity" (Bandini, op. cit., p. 26, and cf. p. 111).

9. Navarrete, op. cit., III, 230–31; Bandini, op. cit., p. 22.

the open sea.[10] As a story it has its charm, but it is hard to believe that it could have been written or read as an authentic or reliable document.

4. THE SODDEN TROPICS

The descriptions of the physical nature of the land are equally conventional and generic and probably borrowed at least in part from other accounts, where they are not taken from the letters of the authentic Amerigo, of course. The new lands are very agreeable and fruitful, full of trees "which are green in all seasons and never lose their leaves."[11] The eternal greenness of the tropics, already noted by the real Vespucci, is described again in another passage which also refers to their extreme wetness, not in fact mentioned by Amerigo himself. "We found the same land to be entirely waterlogged, and indeed crossed by great rivers, but it still revealed itself to be very green, and filled with tall and very high trees. . . . Furthermore when we sought a way into it and as we kept turning around about it, as we said before we found it so flooded by the waters of the rivers everywhere that there was no place anywhere that was not sodden with the deep waters."[12] These hasty brush strokes were to provide the original prompting for the so much later construction of the "submerged" continent, sodden or rotting, or at least improperly dried out.

Emerging from these marshes the sailor sees a village built on piles, "situated over the water, like in Venice."[13] When describing American nature the story-teller stresses its generic difference from the nature of the Old World, but when he comes to describing America's men and their usages and their artifacts he frequently resorts to comparisons and parallels with the things familiar to his readers. It is a small and perfectly justifiable literary expedient: against the backcloth of a surprising and fearsome nature, as captivating as it is new, he brings on peoples that are not so very different that they cannot be imagined, portrayed, and recognized at least as men, not so different and monstrous as to be incapable of arousing the interest of other men. Many of the pseudo-Vespucci's animals are vague or impossible to imagine, but the group of twenty bell-shaped huts springing out of the water "like in Venice" forms a quite distinct and so to speak recognizable picture.

---

10. See above, chap. VI, sec. 9; Navarrete, op. cit., III, 260–62; Bandini, op. cit., pp. 41–43. Mutual fright is a stock motif of comedy: disregarding the classics, it can be found in Ruzzante (*La Moschetta*) and on innumerable occasions in the Commedia dell'Arte. The genius of Mozart (or Emanuel Schikaneder or Carl Ludwig Giesecke, pseudonym of the naturalist Metzler?) exploited it hilariously and poetically in the meeting of Papageno and Monostatos (*Magic Flute*, act I, scene 2, no. 6).

11. Navarrete, op. cit., III, 237–38; Bandini, op. cit., pp. 1–7, 38, 60, 111–12, 113.

12. Navarrete, op. cit., III, 248–49.

13. Ibid., p. 225; here again Amerigo's brief passing reference (cf. Bandini, op. cit., pp. 19, 80) is embellished with picturesque detail.

5. THE NATIVES' EPICUREANISM

No less graphically depicted are those Indians who have red skins *like lions,* their entire bodies hairless, and ugly of feature, "having flat faces like the Tartars."[14] Their religious notions are quite simply nonexistent, so that they cannot even be said to be like the Moors or the Jews. They observe some *barbarian* rites[15]—and behave barbarously[16]—but in fact they are worse unbelievers than the gentiles or pagans and as to their life-style might be called Epicureans.[17]

They are, however, rather curious Epicureans, despising the gold and precious stones "which we in Europe hold to be riches";[18] they do not trade but give away freely and are always greedily asking their friends for things; they eat only when they get hungry, and then barbarously[19] and are amazed at the Spaniards not devouring their enemies either alive or dead[20] they offer the Spaniards their wives for the night "with all generosity," while those fun-loving native women, like Potiphar's wife, "so shamelessly importuned us that we were scarcely able to resist them"[21] (cf. above, chap. V, sec. 5, and chap. VI, n. 49). Every rule has its exceptions: "A woman of the hills," some revengeful or jealous Amazon, comes up behind a young Christian surrounded by a circle of female savages touching him and "marveling to behold him," but this pitiless lady deals him such a blow that "she stretched him out dead."[22]

These vivid hues and puppetlike details come straight out of the world of popular prints and balladmongers. While Vespucci's Christian name was— unknown to him—spreading across the immensity of the Indies, a small and almost entirely fanciful pamphlet was circulating throughout Europe under the false authority of his name. A doubly spurious fame thus came to be attached to the Florentine, who really deserved a glory more genuine and more genuinely his own. Tommaso Campanella did not know how right he was when he wrote:

> "A un nuovo mondo dai nome, Americo,
> nato nel mondo de' scrittori illustri
> che, vie più che gli altri, adorni e illustri
> Nè pur poeta hai della tua gloria amico."[23]

---

14. Navarrete, op. cit., III, 212.
15. Ibid., p. 222.
16. Ibid., p. 154.
17. Ibid., pp. 218–19.
18. Ibid., p. 220.
19. Ibid., p. 215.
20. Ibid., pp. 224–25.
21. Ibid., p. 233.
22. Bandini, op. cit., p. 50.
23. "Agli italiani che attendono a poetar con le favole greche," Madrigale 3, *Poesie* (Bari, 1915), p. 86: "You gave a new world its name, Americo, You, a scion of that world of famous writers Which you have adorned and made illustrious even more than the others; And yet no poet have you to befriend your glory."

❧ VIII ❧

Peter Martyr

1. LIFE AND CHARACTER

CONSIDERABLY different from Columbus's attitude is that of Peter Martyr, "the Livy of American historiography,"[1] the Milanese humanist at the court of the Catholic Kings whose letters and pamphlets to princes, bishops, and scholars first spread the news of the transoceanic discoveries throughout civilized Europe.[2] Peter Martyr has nothing of Columbus's mystical temperament: the

1. De Lollis, op. cit., p. 159; T. Celotti, in the introduction to the 1958 edition of his (partial) translation of Martyr's *De Orbe Novo*, p. 22. Yes, but only because he wrote "Decades"! "He claims as his model no less a work than the classic example of Livy's *History*," recalls Giuseppe Pennesi, "Pietro Martire d'Anghiera e le sue relazioni sulle scoperte oceaniche," in *Raccolta Colombiana*, pt. V, vol. 2, p. 73n4. Martyr's reputation thus benefited from the same sort of spurious sorcery of titles that was to cause Galiani (as an author of *Dialogues*), as it had already caused Pontano (as author of Lucianesque and philosophizing colloquies), to be absurdly compared with Plato!

For citations of Martyr's works I have, unless otherwise indicated, quoted from the Cologne edition of 1574 that contains the first three *Decades de Orbe Novo* (out of eight published), the *De insulis nuper inventis*, (which subsequently, "slightly touched up," became the fourth Decade) and the *De Babylonica legatione* (an annotated translation of which has been brought out by Luis García y García, *Una embajada de los Reyes Católicos a Egipto* [Valladolid, 1947]); for the Decades subsequent to the fourth I have quoted from the translation by J. Torres Asensio, reprinted in Buenos Aires, 1944 (with introduction by Luis H. Arocena and bibliographical essay by Joseph H. Sinclair); in each case the reference to the Decade and chapter is followed by the page number of the edition in question. I. Ciampi (*Storia moderna* [Imola, 1881–84], II, 375), says that the Hakluyt edition (Paris, 1587), is actually the best and most accurate. Now, however, we have the very fine, complete, and annotated French translation of the *De Orbe Novo* by Paul Gaffarel (Paris, 1907) and the Spanish translation by A. Millares Carlo (Buenos Aires, 1964), which includes a study and appendices by Edmundo O'Gorman.

2. Peter Martyr d'Anghiera was born in Arona although he often describes himself as of "Milanese" origins (with greater justification than "Arrigo Beyle") and in his will refers to himself as "a native of Milan, born in the township of Arona." The year in question was 1447 according to Sánchez Alonso, 1455 according to Prescott, and 1459 according to Almagià; Fueter says 1457, and would seem to be right, because Martyr himself writes that he is embarking on his seventieth year on 2 February 1526 (*Dec.*, VII, 8, p. 614). He was in Rome, under the protection of Pomponius Laetus, in 1478, and in August 1487 left the city for the court of Spain, where, save for one diplomatic mission to Cairo (from summer 1501 to August 1502, traveling via southern France, northern Italy, Venice, Zara, and Crete) he remained until his death in 1526. He took part in or at least witnessed the war in Granada ("I was present at the war") after which he wanted to go off home to Italy; but the wars devastating the peninsula at that time and the insistence and promises of the Catholic Kings eventually persuaded him to stay in Spain.

His journey into Egypt is echoed at various points in the *Decades;* the fruit found in the Indies reminds him of something similar he ate in Alexandria (*Dec.*, II, 3, p. 131), and the natives of Paria wrap themselves in cotton cloaks "after the fashion of the Turks" (*Dec.*, II, 7, p. 183). There are references to the island of Crete (*Dec.*, III, 8, p. 206), to the broma (shipworm) that is also found in the two ports of Alexandria (*Dec.*, III, 4, p. 254), and to the multitude of fish in the Nile (*Dec.*, VIII, 7, p. 606); and perhaps he is also recalling this trip when he accurately describes the books of the Mexicans covered with hieroglyphics after the manner of the ancient Egyptians (*De insulis nuper inventis*, p. 355; *Dec.*, V, 10, p. 470; cf. W. H. Prescott, *History of the Conquest of Mexico and History of the Conquest of Peru* [New York, 1936], pp. 59n, 199n.

influence of his beloved teacher, the paganizing Pomponius Laetus; his familiarity with the Latin classics; and the very environment of the court, in which he always seems to have been thoroughly at home, obtaining important offices, honorary missions, and substantial benefices—everything combined to produce in him an unbiased and contented observer, lukewarm in his defence of Spanish interests and coolly grateful to Providence for having so greatly enlarged the circle of believers in Jesus Christ.[3]

2. ENTHUSIASM AND PRIVILEGED INFORMATION

But Peter Martyr is a true son of the Renaissance and a good man of letters. He has the sense of measure, of what is elegant and fitting, a taste for the pleasing and agreeable rather than the enormous and fearsome. His enthusiasm, however, bursts out spontaneously when he describes the broad immensity of the New World opening up before the Europeans, its richness, variety, and infinite possibilities. In it he sees more than a confirmation of the classical legends and a boundless sphere of action for sixteenth-century man. The New World is for Peter Martyr almost what the Messiah was for the first Christians: a confirmation of the ancient prophecies and a promise of future life. Peter Martyr is delighted to be in Spain, where news of the discoveries arrives more promptly and abundantly, where he can tremble at the sight of the fearsome savages, glaring like chained lions, and admire the multicolored parrots and samples of spices; where he can actually touch and weigh in his hands the gold nuggets of nine and even twenty ounces, drool at the sight of a pearl of more than one hundred ounces, and keep in his house for a few days—and measure with awe—the enormous femur,

---

Later on, the question of whether the Aztec characters were hieroglyphics was amply discussed by Father Kircher and various other authors, whose opinions are reported by Eguiara y Eguren in the third of his *Prólogos a la Biblioteca mexicana* (1755; Mexico, 1944), pp. 69–70, 94–96. Sigüenza y Góngora, followed by Eguiara, concluded that they were genuine hieroglyphics and indeed that they proved "the Mexicans to have descended from the Egyptians." Heeren reexamined the problem on the basis of the material brought back from Mexico by Alexander von Humboldt (see also the work by his brother Wilhelm von Humboldt, *Über die Aufgaben des Geschichtschreibers* [Leipzig, 1821], pp. 16–17), and made a careful comparison between the Egyptians' hieroglyphics and the Aztecs' ideograms, showing up the substantial differences (*Ideen über die Politik* [Göttingen, 1826], V, 39–42).

Among the letters of the *Opus epistolarum* relating to the Indies (letters 123–24, 130, 134–36, 141, 143, 145, 153, 157, 159, 165, 168, 169, 177, 180, 450, 537, 689), some of which were recast in the *Decades* (which are themselves, especially the early ones, not unlike *epistulae*—Salas, op. cit., pp. 26, 27, 49) and reprinted separately on various occasions (including the *Raccolta Colombiana*, pt. III, vol. 2), one can find further elements essential for determining Peter Martyr's attitude to American nature: "the geographical letters in the *Opus Epistolarum* . . . do not duplicate the *De Orbe Novo*," writes Mariéjol, op. cit., p. 191*n*.

The last Decades, which refer almost exclusively to the undertakings of Cortés, derive mainly from the conquistador's reports (on which see below, chap. X); and being written in Martyr's old age, they contain lapses of memory (recognized by the author—*Dec.*, VII, 6, p. 529; *Dec.*, VIII, 8, p. 614), and were never revised by the author for publication (T. Celotti, *Mondo Nuovo* [Milan, 1930], pp. 12, 76; Celotti's selection omits completely the last four Decades).

3. See below, sec. 19. Motifs of a pagan or classical timbre seem to come to him more spontaneously and more easily than those of Christian nature. Prescott noted that Martyr's account of the death of Prince Don Juan, comforted by his reading of Aristotle, was "in more of a classic than a Christian vein" (*History of the Reign of Ferdinand and Isabella* [Philadelphia, 1872], II, 357*n*24).

corroded with age, of a Mexican giant;[4] where he can personally question Christopher Columbus, the Pinzóns, Enciso, Oviedo,[5] the Vespuccis, Cabot, and Colmenares; where he can also, in the Council of the Indies, listen to the daily reading of a host of idiotic and boastful accounts of self-styled discoverers of the already discovered;[6] and where he can shut himself up in a little room with the archbishop of Burgos, Fonseca, and pore over heaps of maps and portolanos and a solid sphere of the globe, to make his reports to the pope more complete and exact.[7]

In his own home, on an open terrace, he has a young Mexican dress up in various costumes and perform the war dances and symbolic dances of his country and ceremonial mimes and a simulated religious ecstasy. And in the inner rooms he organizes meetings of veterans of the Indies to discuss problems of New World geography; he listens attentively to the various reports on the miraculous phosphoresence of the firefly; he shows the cardinal of Aragon a dessicated marsupial brought back by Vicente Yáñez (1499–1500), insisting that he admire it from every angle, and introduces Cortés's secretary, Juan Ribera, to the papal legate, to the Venetian ambassador and a Milanese nobleman, all panting to hear and see the great novelties;[8] and derives equal pleasure from the pilots' opposing theories and the Italian visitors' admiration and amazement.

3. PRIDE IN THE RICHNESS OF HIS MATERIAL

These individual pleasures are merged and sublimated in the reaction that sets the tone of all his writing, his pride and delight in the richness of the material offered to him and the admiration, amazement, and delight that it will arouse in his readers. "I feel my spirits rejoice when I am addressing some experienced persons from amongst those returning from that province." He does not write to make dry "history" but to give pleasure to his correspondents, to provoke their wonder and joy (the *Decades* have been aptly described as epistolary, incidental, and fragmentary in character—see above, n. 2), and for his part he is certain of

4. *Dec.*, I, 2, p. 19 (the Indians); I, 2, p. 26 (nine-ounce nuggets); I, 4, p. 49 (twenty-ounce nuggets); I, 8, p. 94 (the pearl); V, 9, p. 457 (the bone). See also the curious warning to Cardinal Ascanio Sforza, to whom he sends specimens of spices, that he should take care, because they burn the tongue (*Dec.*, I, 2, p. 27). He also received specimens of spices from the Moluccas and distributed them among various people, keeping a few for His Holiness (*Dec.*, V, 7, p. 437). Others he bites into and tastes himself (*Dec.*, VIII, I, pp. 500–01).

5. "Many people have told me astonishing things about these matters, including a certain Gonzalo Fernando de Oviedo, who is one of those royal magistrates known by the Spaniards as *veedor* [inspector], and who boasts of having been ashore in this land longer than any of the others" (*Dec.*, III, 5, p. 260). Cf. D. Turner, "Biblioteca Ovetense," *Papers of the Bibliographical Society of America*, 57 (1963), p. 161, no. 5, and below, chap. XVII, sec. 15.

6. Decade IV, preface.

7. *Decades*, passim, especially I, 6, p. 73 (Columbus); I, 9, p. 96 (the Pinzóns); II, 6, p. 174 (Enciso); II, 10, p. 199 (maps and globe); III, 5, p. 258 (Giovanni Vespucci, nephew and successor of Amerigo as pilot and cartographer); III, 5, p. 264 (Oviedo); III, 6, p. 268 (Cabot); III, 10, p. 323 (Colmenares); etc. Concerning these maps, on one of which Columbus supposedly collaborated and on another Vespucci, see Pennesi, op. cit., p. 75, and Pohl, op. cit., pp. 191–92.

8. *Dec.*, V, 10, pp. 467–68 (dances); III, 10, pp. 326–27 (discussion between Morales and Oviedo); V, 10, p. 462 (Ribera and the Italians); VII, 9, p. 534 (cucuyo). Further discussions and "comparisons" between veterans of the Indies: ibid., VII, 2, pp. 506–07.

the immortality promised him, indeed guaranteed him by the rich material of his oceanic decades.[9] And Pomponius Laetus himself, who years earlier had discouraged him from taking himself off to the fanatical and semibarbarous Spain, is now tongue-tied and almost tearful with emotion.[10] The hallucinatory sense of wonder and solemn excitement that attended the discovery of the Pacific are expressed by Martyr in tones that made a deep impression on Leo X and that Keats alone would be able to emulate.[11] The presentiment and conviction of a new era, of a new and powerful impulse given to the progress of the human race, of a rebirth and triumphal march, are as explicit and joyful in the court humanist as in the letter of Gargantua to Pantagruel. And in truth the first founding of the Abbey of Thélème is celebrated through the pen of Peter Martyr, in the Islands of the Antilles.

4. Rediscovery of the golden age

We live in marvelous times: "Every day there sprout, germinate, take root, mature, and are gathered in richer harvests than those preceding. Antiquity's reports of the exploits of Saturn or Hercules, or any other of that sort of hero, pale into insignificance."[12] But the fairest of the new prodigies, the most aus-

9. Pennesi, op. cit., pp. 35, 41. This deeply felt enthusiasm overcame his reluctance to publish the *Decades*, the manuscript of which was apparently purloined from him by Lucio Marineo Siculo—or according to some people by Íñigo López de Mendoza, count of Tendilla (Pennesi, op. cit., pp. 53–61). Cf. Mariéjol, op. cit., p. 193; Ciampi, *Storia moderna*, III, 374.

10. Epist. 152 to Pomponius Laetus, cited in E. de Vedia, ed., *Historiadores primitivos de Indias* (Madrid, 1858), I, v–vi. Some of his letters are dated as early as 1493.

The first Decade, which from internal evidence (see pp. 51, 102, etc.) would seem to have been already finished in 1501, was reworked and summarized by the Spanish humanist Hernán Pérez de Oliva in his *Ystoria de Colón* (see the important article by L. Olschki, "Hernán Pérez de Oliva's *Ystoria de Colón*," *HAHR*, 23 [May 1943], 165–96); and it was published, apparently without the author's consent (see preceding note), in a Venetian-Italian summary sent by Angelo Trevisan to Domenico Malipiero in Venice, in 1504 *(Libretto de tutta la navigazione de' re di Spagna),* reprinted in 1507 and published in a Latin translation in 1508; subsequently reprinted by J. B. Thacher in his *Columbus* (New York, 1903), I, 457–85, and by Lawrence C. Wroth (Paris, 1929); the original Latin text was eventually published in 1511.

The first three Decades were published together, with the author's permission, in 1516; the *De Insulis* also in 1516 (so Palau says, but this cannot be true) or in 1521 in Basel; reprinted, Basel, 1532; Paris, 1532; Cologne, 1532; Strasbourg, 1534 (in German); Antwerp, 1536; Basel, 1537 and 1555; London, 1555 (in English); Basel, 1582 (in German). All eight Decades were published in 1530, the first three or four being reprinted in Basel in 1533 and Cologne in 1574, and all eight in Paris in 1578 and Madrid 1892. Old translations (partial): into French, Paris, 1532 and 1533; into Italian, Venice, 1534 and 1563; into German, Strasbourg, 1534; into English, London, 1555 (containing the first use— following a Scottish document of 1548–49— of the word *colony* in English: see the dictionaries and H. M. Jones, *Ideas in America* [Cambridge, Mass., 1944], p. 46), 1577, and 1597; and 1612, 1620, 1626, and 1812 (these four in full); London, 1885 (Decades I–III); Birmingham, 1885 (Decade IV); Westminster, 1895 (Decades I–III); into Dutch, Antwerp, 1563 (partial). Modern translations of the *Decades* include those into Castilian, 1892 (reprinted, Buenos Aires, 1944); into French, 1907 (partially published in 1892–93, 1897, 1898, 1900, 1902); into English, 1912; into Italian, 1930 (incomplete). According to the bibliographer Nicolás Antonio, Martyr compiled a summary of Pliny's *Natural History,* which was also published (H. Harrisse, *Bibliotheca Americana Vetustissima* [New York and Paris, 1866], p. 126).

11. *Dec.,* III, 1, p. 210; Mariéjol, op. cit., p. 194; Keats, *On First Looking into Chapman's Homer.* Thus to my mind there is little justification for Jane's sneering dismissal of him as an "inveterate gossip," someone who "prided himself on his talent for composing appreciative obituary notices" (op. cit., pp. 5, 126).

12. *Dec.,* III, 4, p. 255. See also the beginning of the following book: "Our fruitful New World daily and unceasingly procreates and brings forth fresh things" (ibid., and cf. below, sec. 16). Rabelais (*Pantagruel,* chap. VIII) lays particular emphasis on the rebirth of good studies. Peter Martyr's enthusiasm is more universal and actually sweeps away the prodigies of antiquity. On his pride and joy in the richness of the material, see Mariéjol, op. cit., pp. 191, 235.

picious and promising of the discoveries (for him as for his contemporary Scillacio—see above, chap. IV, sec. 3) is the rediscovery of the golden age, of
primitive innocence and happiness among the naked savages of the Indies. O
blessed inhabitants of Hispaniola, "if they could but acquire religion [a stylistic
interpolation, and incompatible with everything that follows], since naked, without weights or measures, and most of all without the fatal curse of money, living
in the golden age, without laws, without false judges, without books, they lead a
life content by nature, with never a care for the future." The letter is dated May
1494. The first image of America is reflected in the mirror of humanism. And in
that shining mirror it glows and sparkles like the dream of the poets of antiquity,
like the realization of an ideal state, intact, in which nature is the only rule, and
spontaneity repeals the law.[13] It is of course true that although they know no
thirst for gain these peoples are driven by territorial ambition to wage ceaseless
war on one another; but Peter Martyr cannot believe that the golden age was
altogether immune from that plague either.[14]

5. The natives' communism, eloquence, and bravery

Two features characterize the blessed condition of the natives: one, relating to
their social organization, is the common ownership of goods; the other, an
individual trait, is their wisdom and personal bravery. Both characteristics had
been neglected or contradicted by Columbus, with his talk of cowardly and
imbecile natives, and it is Peter Martyr, irresistibly drawn to the idyllic and borne
forward on the crest of the wave of an age-old tradition,[15] who first records them

---

13. In his opening pages Peter Martyr had described how the natives found by Columbus "all, that is to say the
people of either sex, go through their entire lives naked, content with a state of nature" (*Dec.*, I, 1, p. 5). And the title of
the first edition of the three Decades, (Alcalá, 1516) promises to reveal to the reader, among other things, "the golden
age, naked people, free of the curse of money" (title reproduced by J. H. Sinclair in the Torres Asensio translation of
the *Decades*, p. xxvii).

It was precisely this sort of information that most whetted the curiosity of his correspondents. Roman friends and
Italian princes, Martyr relates, were so insistent in pressing him to write that he would have to have had his pen
permanently in his hand: "Indeed they were lost in amazement when they heard that new lands had been discovered,
and about unknown peoples leading their lives naked and content with what nature gave them; and they were filled with
a burning desire to be informed of everything" (*Dec.*, I, 10, p. 112).

It therefore seems to me inexact to say, as Menéndez Pelayo does, that Martyr dwells "*malevolently* and curiously on
the rites and customs and superstitions of the natives, wherever they most strongly contrast with the habits of the Old
World" ("De los historiadores de Colón," 1892, in *Obras completas*, XII, 84). If anything, I would say that Martyr
notes the *affinity* between the Indian superstitions and those of the Old World; and in the contrast of customs there is a
nostalgia for primitivism, quite without malice toward either Old or New World.

14. "In no way do we think that the Golden Age lived immune from that plague" (*Dec.*, I, 2, p. 22). Epist. 133, of
1493, already says that Columbus "found the men content with a state of nature, naked, feeding on natural foods, and
root bread," etc. (in *Raccolta Colombiana*, pt. III, vol. 2, p. 40). But he quickly adds (Epist. 134, p. 41) that there are
continual struggles and wars among the natives, "and indeed there are disputes of Thine and Mine, among them, just
as with us." Vespucci (see above chap. VI, sec. 8) wrote that the natives did not fight out of greed for booty, nor to
extend their domains, but only out of a spirit of atavistic vendetta: "They fight not for the purpose of ruling or extending
their dominions or on account of any other inordinate cupidity, but solely on account of longstanding enmity implanted
in them long ago" (Navarrete, op. cit., III, 214).

15. Abundant documentation is G. Costa, *La leggenda dei secoli d'oro nella letteratura italiana* (Bari, 1972). On
Martyr, see especially p. 75. On "mine" and "thine," p. 81 (Bembo), p. 128 (Campanella), p. 147 (Chiabrera) and

and etches them into history; and for centuries they remain the basis for a hundred utopias and a hundred portraits of the noble savage.[16]

Among the Cuban natives "it is recognized . . . that the land is the property of all, like the sun and the sea, and Thine and Mine, seeds of all evil, are unknown amongst them. They are indeed easily content, since in that ample land there are many more fields than are needed. Theirs is the golden age; there are neither ditches nor walls nor hedges to separate the farms. They live in gardens open to all. Without laws, without books, without judges, but by their own nature they cultivate the right. They judge that man to be bad and wicked who delights in doing injury to others."[17]

Peter Martyr obviously applauds this naive and healthy criterion. And his sympathy shows through clearly when he gives us some of the little speeches addressed to the Spaniards by the natives, in which the primitive's raw common sense contrasts favorably with the European's prejudices, giving us another foretaste of a literary form that was to reach perfection in the *Lettres persanes* and an attitude that would be echoed with greater emphasis by the dashing heroes of the romantic dramas, rebuking the powerful for their acts of tyranny.

In the *Decades* we already have an elderly native lecturing Columbus on the punishment of souls in the next world, which the powerful admiral would do well to heed and consequently "make an enemy of no-one"; and Columbus finds himself forced to admire "such wisdom on the part of naked man."[18] And we find an even more perfect example of a character by now familiar to us in the young son of the cacique Comogro, who treats the Christians to a speech full of elegance and wisdom, admonishing them for their evil lust for gold, mentioning other peoples who set more store by the craftsman's work and the usefulness of

---

passim. See also Scillacio, above, chap. IV, sec. 3, and Ronsard, in R. Le Moine, *L'Amérique et les poètes français de la Renaissance* (Ottawa, 1972), p. 202, ("all their goods are common property, without quarrels over 'thine' and 'mine'"); and Giordano Bruno, *Spaccio de la bestia trionfante*, III ("that wretch" that extinguished the Golden Age, "the one that discovered 'thine' and 'mine'," ed. Gentile [Bari, 1927], II, 148).

16. As early as 1547 the stern Sepúlveda would feel the need to warn against those who imagined that the Indians lived in a peaceful and poetic golden age: "And do not think that before the coming of the Christians they lived a life of ease and in the Saturnian peace of the poets," because in fact they engaged in ceaseless warfare and with such savagery that even victory could not assuage them, only cannibalism—a savagery repellent (Sepúlveda insists) in people that are *not* courageous like the Scythians, but craven and cowardly! (*Democrates alter* [Mexico, 1941], pp. 104–06).

17. *Dec.*, I, 3, p. 45. Again in the last Decade, written in 1525–26, Peter Martyr returns to the description of the paradisal nature of his beloved Jamaica (*Dec.*, VIII, 3, pp. 579–80; eulogies of Jamaica, of which he was appointed abbot in 1524, can also be found in the *Opus Epistolarum*, epist. 800 [1524], p. 70, and epist. 831 [1525], p. 73). Further comments on the peace-loving communism of the natives, *Dec.*, II, 3, p. 145; on their ignorance of money, weights, and measures, III, 3, p. 229; on their scorn for gold and their willingness to barter it away, "because the things that is most prized is invariably that which is unusual," *Dec.*, III, 1, p. 207, cf. I, 1, p. 5.

When talking about the Mexicans, Martyr waxes enthusiastic about the use of the cocoa bean as money, because this frees its possessors from avarice, inasmuch as it cannot be hoarded or buried—thus anticipating the numerous more modern advocates (Silvio Gesell and the "Social Credit" movement) of a coinage that would lose its value if not spent rapidly (*Dec.*, V, 4, p. 393, and VIII, 4, p. 587, also quoted by Prescott, *Mexico and Peru*, p. 84).

18. *Dec.*, I, 3, p. 44. See also above, chap. V, sec. 4. For an outstanding eighteenth-century example of the same literary genre see the speech by the ninety-year-old Tahitian in Diderot, op. cit., p. 760ff. And for the now traditional eloquence of the savages, Gerbi, *Dispute,* pp. 204, 259–60, etc.

the artifact than the metal itself, mere "lumps of earth." Among these people of the south, he tells them, "gold is no less abundant than iron amongst us"—this plenitude of iron (Martyr explains to us) being easily deduced by the Darien native from the Christians' use of the metal for their swords and javelins. Once again the Spanish captains have to admire the speech of the naked youth. Then Prince Comogro goes on to say, with measured pauses and an orator's persuasive gestures, that although they do not thirst for gold, his peoples do wage war "out of ambition, for the sake of dominion," and he exhorts the Christians to attack his enemies. The Christians will get the gold and the Comograns their revenge and security. The young man showed no little skill, as we can see, in weaving together economic and political arguments and almost succeeded in making mercenaries of the Christians. When he fell silent, in fact, "our men, in truth, began watering at the mouth, with their great hopes of gold."[19]

These natives, so cherished in the imagination, have already ceased to be the same Indians that Columbus had described, for his own practical and religious ends, as cringing subjects, foolish bargainers, unwarlike warriors, and easy material for sensational conversions. Ten years later (1502) the Admiral was still telling his son Fernando that his task was now completed, since he had shown "that the path [to the Indies] was easy and navigable and its usefulness obvious, *and the peoples very tame and unarmed*."[20]

Peter Martyr, although he despises the Spanish plebs,[21] shows a more human sympathy toward the American natives (earning himself, among other things, Las Casas's undying admiration).[22] In the great debate as to whether they are to be considered free or slaves by nature (or because of their cruelty, asocial behavior, cannibalism, or other vices), Martyr takes no sides.[23] But his humanity and Renaissance spirit keep him open-minded, benevolent, and understanding, as demonstrated by the anecdote of the naive and simple Indians, "good men," who are persuaded by the Spaniards that leaves of paper can be made to talk.[24]

---

19. *Dec.*, II, 3, pp. 150–52. Further examples of the savages' oratorical powers: III, 2, pp. 224–25. Note also how carefully Martyr transcribes and translates the words of a cacique (III, 8, p. 289) and recounts the catechetical and moral dialogues between Gil González and the cacique Nicaragua (VI, 4–5, pp. 481–84). In his rehash of the first Decade (see above, n. 10) Pérez de Oliva succeeds only in diluting the original when he reproduces the cacique's speeches in amplified and rhetorically beautified versions (Olschki, "Ystoria de Colón," p. 194).

Elsewhere Peter Martyr himself shows greater appreciation for the craftsman's skill than for the value of the metal; and he responds ecstatically, as Albrecht Dürer would do a few years later, to the outstanding artistic beauty of the Mexicans' goldwork and other artifacts (*De Insulis*, pp. 358–59; cf. *Dec.*, I, 3, p. 32; V, 2, p. 367; V, 3, pp. 388, 394; V, 10, p. 426; VIII, 4, p. 585. His approach in this connection was already noted and approved by Prescott, *Mexico and Peru*, p. 329n. See also Gaffarel's translation of the Decades, p. 389, with references to Oviedo, Gómara, and Las Casas.

20. Fernando Columbus, *Vita di Cristoforo Colombo*, p. 283, my italics.

21. Mariéjol, op. cit., p. 189.

22. Cf. Salas, op. cit., pp. 228–29, who rightly contrasts it to Oviedo's suspicious criticism.

23. Pennesi, op. cit., pp. 100–01.

24. *Dec.*, III, 8, pp. 299–300. Cf. Oviedo, *Sumario*, chap. 10, pp. 131–32; *Historia*, I, 27a: III, 137b. "This is the way they very cleverly deceive the poor islanders," and Martyr finds that "one has to laugh." There is however no

He finds the Indians interesting as curious specimens of nature and exciting as paradigms of innocent virtue, but when they are victims of the Spaniards they also earn his heartfelt sympathy, and when they are victorious over the invaders his impartial praise.

At such times the ethnographer assumes the stance of historian, and a passion for justice fires him as he pityingly recounts how "the naked wretches were easily put to flight by our weapons"[25] or tells of the savage hounds used to exterminate them;[26] when—delighting in the dramatic contrast—he portrays them as aggressive, bold, and courageous in battle; and when, with toga-clad solemnity, he describes how "both men and women fought fiercely to regain their liberty," and how, naked and armed only with arrows and wooden swords, they overcame the invaders;[27] when, finally, with an image half biblical and half "romantic," he represents them as captives in Hispaniola, desperately homesick, fleeing toward the north coast of the island where the winds of their homeland blew and the familiar constellations shone in the sky, and there, throwing their arms wide, with their mouths panting to catch their native breezes, languishing and slowly falling senseless to the earth of their insufferable exile.[28]

Again in 1525 he assured his friend Gaspare Contarini, ambassador of the Venetian Republic and later cardinal, that "between the Spanish island [Santo Domingo] and Jamaica, which is not very large, there used to be, when they were discovered by Columbus, a million souls and more," but now "on account of the cruel treatment by the Spaniards" (who forced "those poor unaccustomed men" to dig for gold), on account of the despair driving them to their deaths, or because the mothers "killed their own children," there are almost none left.[29]

Salas goes so far as to say that on the question of the Indian and the problem arising out of his contact with the Europeans, Peter Martyr "saw everything or almost everything, years before Oviedo and Las Casas"[30]—which, as we shall

---

malice on the narrator's part. (In his account of the humiliation of Montezuma, Martyr's tone is similarly ambiguous, so that Prescott feels that "one may doubt whether pity or contempt predominates in Martyr's notice of this event"— *Mexico and Peru*, p. 348n). Elsewhere the strange customs of the natives, which they themselves look on as extremely elegant, just as the Ethiopian thinks black is more beautiful than white, merely prompt him to a general reflection on the madness of men and the vanity of human aspirations (*De insulis*, pp. 353–54).

25. *Dec.*, II, 4, p. 157. It was reported that 1,200,000 perished from the ill-treatment they received in the Spanish mines (VII, 2, p. 503). On the flouting of the excellent laws for the protection of the natives (see Gerbi, *Dispute*, pp. 76–79) because "those that are mild as lambs at home become ravenous wolves as soon as they arrive there" (tropicalization of the white men, noted already in 1524–25!), see *Dec.*, VII, 4, pp. 516–17.

26. *Dec.*, III, 1, pp. 208–09; III, 2, pp. 223–24. See below, chap. XIX, sec. 12.

27. *De insulis*, pp. 342, 363.

28. *Dec.*, VII, 1, p. 500.

29. Report by Gaspare Contarini, on return from his embassy to Charles V, read to the Senate on 15 November 1525, in E. Alberi, ed., *Relazioni degli ambasciatori veneti al Senato*, ser. I, vol. II (Florence, 1840), p. 50. Of Peter Martyr he says that "he is Milanese, a member of the Council of the Indies, and also has the task of writing the history of those lands and those voyages" (ibid.). Peter Martyr mentions Contarini several times, e.g., when he is describing the arrival of booty and treasure from Mexico: "I took the Venetian ambassador and many nobles to look at them" (*Opus Epistolarum*, epist. 778 [1523], p. 67).

30. "And what he says," Salas goes on maliciously, "shows how he avoids the repetition and weightiness of the other two, for all their blustering" (op. cit., p. 52).

see more clearly when we come to deal with Oviedo, is undoubtedly exaggerated praise. But it should be equally clear that one cannot dismiss Peter Martyr simply as a "journalist" (Menéndez Pelayo, Fueter, Olschki), an inquisitive epistoler with a preference for the striking and sensational events (Sánchez Alonso), "a slave to novelty" (Iglesia), a talented newspaperman and reporter,[31] or a "diligent correspondent."[32]

6. NO "JOURNALIST" BUT AN INQUISITIVE HUMANIST

It has to be admitted that he is an avid and insatiable information-seeker. When he finds himself in Cairo, waiting for the date to be fixed for his audience with the sultan, he does not waste his time: "Lest I should allow any time to slip through my hands in vain, as they say, when the occasion arose I looked into the nature of the region, the customs of the inhabitants, the governing of slaves, and other things, which are in my view worthy of mention."[33] And when he finds himself in Spain he is impatient to "interview" anyone returning from the Indies to the peninsula and the court.[34] Like Coleridge's good Hermit, "he loves to talk with marineres / That come from a far countree." He sifts through what he learns in order to eliminate the matters of lesser import, and without further ado, without bothering too much about elegance of style, he hands on the rest of the information to his readers. He always has this public in mind and makes due allowance for their tastes and preferences; he is constantly fearful of boring them and apologizes for the inevitable repetition and the digressions he can never resist.[35]

But these are the formal, external qualities of the journalist, or rather of anyone sitting down to draft a report on the basis of varying and prolix sources. Oviedo was to follow the same pattern, although in his case the avowed objective was to tell the truth and the whole truth (not only the part that might interest the reader) and although it is also true that he failed to live up to his intention not to repeat himself and not to expatiate on well-known topics, and thus often fell prey to verbosity. From this point of view Peter Martyr is a more expert writer. In 1522 the emperor's secretary, Maximilianus Transylvanus, on summarizing the

31. Mariéjol, op. cit., pp. 173–74, 198, 219.

32. Salas, op. cit., pp. 21, 26, 48.

33. De Babylonica legatione, III, p. 403.

34. "Nobody . . . ever returned to the court without being enticed to come and lay before me, both orally and in writing, whatever they had found out" (Dec., II, 7, p. 176). See below, sec. 15. And he is ever ready to reopen his "new world," whose doors he had closed only shortly before! (Dec., III, 1, p. 205). His material is like the hydra, growing seven new heads for each one cut off (Dec., V, 10, p. 459). The ocean is more prolific than "the sow of Albano, that farrowed thirty piglets at one go, so they say" (Dec., VII, 1, p. 498; VIII, 2, p. 631).

35. "I just assemble those things which in my judgment I deem likely to give satisfaction to lovers of history"; longwindedness "I think better left out" because "I do not want to bore my readers with details" (Dec., III, 1, p. 208); "I will not say any more [about these lakes] lest by dwelling too long on the same subject we should become boring" (III, 8, p. 291); "it would be tedious rather than pleasant to relate" (De insulis, p. 360). Cf. also Dec., V, 6, p. 421, and V, 7, p. 429; Mariéjol, op. cit., p. 203; and Salas, op. cit., pp. 28–29.

exploits of the Castilians from the discovery of America to Cortés's conquests, concluded, by way of bibliographical note, that on this whole subject "Peter Martyr has written many very great and very true things, in an elegant manner." [36] The raciness of his style, the vivacity and briskness of the *Decades* delighted Pope Leo X, who read them aloud after dinner, to the great joy of the cardinals and his sister, [37] and subsequently entertained generations of scholars and enquiring minds, right down to Humboldt, Menéndez Pelayo, and Eduard Fueter.

7. SELF-CENSURE AND RELIGIOSITY

In censoring his own work Martyr cuts out not only material that he fears may be boring but anything excessively cruel or corrupting. [38]

But when he has copious botanical details to recount, the epistoler sets aside his fear of being boring. He recognizes that the envious will probably ridicule him and tell him that he gets too bogged down in minutiae; all the same, he reminds the pope and himself, Pliny and the other learned men mixed all sorts of things up together to teach posterity about the whole universe, the shapes of the lands, the customs of the peoples, and the nature of things. To those who deride his labors, Martyr replies with derision for their "misguided zeal." [39]

All these deliberately imposed (or occasionally forgotten) limitations in any case fade into the background compared with the unconscious filtration of the news from the Indies through Martyr's classical mentality, a mentality acutely and humanistically receptive to the variety of the world. The Christian world recedes from his intellectual horizon as soon as he approaches the newly discovered islands. Martyr is sincerely religious, sometimes (as in defending the

---

36. "Relación . . . de cómo . . . fueron descubiertas . . . las islas Molucas," etc. (5 October 1522), in Navarrete, op. cit., IV, 252.

37. *Dec.*, III, 9, p. 309. In the *Opus epistolarum*, epist. 562, addressed to Leo X on 26 December 1515, Martyr tells how after dinner, "with brow serene," the pope read out the *Decades* to his sister and the cardinals until they had heard all they wanted to (Humboldt, *Examen critique*, II, 289–90, citing the 1670 edition, p. 310, of the *Opus Epistolarum*, but it must in fact be epist. 560, op. cit., p. 58: "The pope himself, since it was the feast of St. Michael, read out to his sister and convive and numerous cardinals the writings that had issued from my study concerning the new world, with great praises of me because I had taken it upon myself to describe that province, lest such remarkable discoveries should sink into the rapacious jaws of oblivion"; see also epist. 612, p. 59). Vespucci was to issue a similar invitation to a postprandial reading (in the letter to Lorenzo di Pierfrancesco de Medici, 18 July 1500, quoted in Bandini, op. cit., pp. 64–65): "And if I am a little too longwinded, set about reading it when there is more time, or as fruit, after the table has been cleared." The discovery of the Indies served up as dessert!

38. He omits the details of bloody events so as not to offend His Holiness's ears (*Dec.*, II, 9, pp. 188–89). Other cruel deeds "let me deal with briefly, since they are all horrid and not at all pleasant" (*De insulis*, p. 361). The sufferings of the slaves in the mines of Haiti "I shudder to relate. Let us dismiss this matter" (*Dec.*, III, 8, p. 295). And he skips the description of the "incenses and perfumes of these lands . . . since they are more suited to the effemination of minds than to good behavior" (*De insulis*, p. 340; cf. on other odors and fumigations that are an indication of effeminacy, *Dec.*, III, 4, p. 254; VII, 3, p. 512; VII, 6, p. 530; VII, 9, p. 549; VIII, 7, p. 601). A further instance of reticence, out of compassion toward Columbus or respect for the sovereigns of Spain, occurs when he describes the Admiral's return with his men from Jamaica to Hispaniola: "What may have become of them thereafter, I never learned" (*Dec.*, III, 4, p. 249, apparently written around 1514–15!).

39. *Dec.*, III, 9, pp. 302–03.

Inquisition) almost naively so, and he does not want to have anything to do with philosophical misgivings or Erasmian doubts,[40] Lutheran novelties (in fact in 1522 he already foresees that they will lead to lots of trouble), or More-ish resistance movements; he believes in legends, prodigies, and miracles, and dedicates the various Decades to different popes.[41]

8. THE INDIES AND CLASSICAL ANTIQUITY

But memories of the classical world—and not only the recently rejuvenated memories of the golden age—dominate his thoughts. In the humanist's mind they seem to take on a new lease of life, as if rediscovering their own element, in anything but alien surroundings. To the eyes of Peter Martyr the Indies and their peoples provide miraculous confirmation of the traditions and myths of the Greeks and Romans. They carry on and accompany the rebirth of antiquity. Peter Martyr always remains the same ingenuous scholar who, on visiting Candia, "grows indignant at the inhabitants of the island, who know the names of neither Pasiphae or Theseus and are ignorant of the history of Saturn and Jupiter."[42] Poor benighted people! To the humanist's eyes they are worse than illiterate.

The investigation of American nature, including the native, is still wholly within the spirit of humanism, striving after a better knowledge of the world. It accompanies (and sometimes serves to support or bolster up) the exploits of the discoverers and conquistadors. But deep down it is much more revolutionary, much more "progressive" than those commercial or political undertakings. Those great deeds are in fact a repetition or continuation of what had always been done in Europe; they follow on from the trend of events in the closing centuries of the Middle Ages and are aimed, more or less consciously, at balancing or blunting revolutionary developments in the Old World, the advance of Islam and the resultant blocking of the path to the East, or the Lutheran reform robbing the church of half Europe. But the first careful describers of American nature, at least up until Oviedo, expand man's understanding of the natural kingdoms, foster new sciences and fresh researches and, within the compass of their intellectual effort, also include the native (whom most of the conquistadors consider merely as object, prey, or instrument)—raising him up to human dignity even while most savagely denouncing his vices and limitations.[43]

---

40. Although he did use the young Alfonso de Valdés as secretary and scribe (M. Bataillon, *Erasmo y España* [Mexico, 1950], I, 121–22, 130–31). Cf. Pennesi, op. cit., p. 31 and n. 6, pp. 41–42n5. On his perennial anti-Semitism see the *De Babylonica legatione*, pp. 426–27, 429, 437, and Pennesi, op. cit., p. 24.

41. Mariéjol, op. cit., passim, esp. pp. 164, 184–86, 195; except Decade VII, which is dedicated (1524) to the duke of Milan, Francesco Maria Sforza Visconti (Pennesi, op. cit., p. 98).

42. Mariéjol, op. cit., pp. 52–53.

43. The Mexican Luis Villoro (*Los grandes momentos del indigenismo en México* [Mexico, 1950], pp. 15–88) saw this discrepancy between the conquistadors' and missionaries' view of the native and the view of him held by the "freely enquiring humanists" as the focal point of the long drawn-out tragedy of the native (R. M. Morse, "Toward a Theory of Spanish American Government," *JHI*, 15, no. 1 [January 1954], 73–74).

9. Critical skepticism: The Amazons

The biblical reminiscences and fantasies of someone like Columbus leave Peter Martyr quite unmoved. So the Admiral identified Hispaniola with Ophir? "Could be, but I do not believe it," sniffs Peter Martyr. "It may be so, or it may not: it is not up to me to judge; but in my view he is well wide of the mark."[44] He also doubts that the Indies are in fact Asia and leaves the responsibility for this thesis squarely on Columbus's shoulders.[45] The Admiral thought he had found the Earthly Paradise in Paria; Peter Martyr repeats Columbus's conjectures, and suddenly breaks off: "Enough of all this, since to my mind it is no more than a fable. Let us revert . . . to history."[46] Enough of fairy tales, let's get back to serious matters.

But when Columbus tells him about the Amazons, it is another matter. Martyr would like to believe in them, and yet he remains skeptical, suggesting a curious compromise interpretation of his own. Yes, there is an island where men and women are excellent archers and where the women manfully resist the outrages of the men from overseas. "This must doubtless explain the belief that there are islands in that ocean peopled solely by women: and of this I was convinced by that same Admiral Columbus."[47] But are they real Amazons? . . . It is not enough that they live singly "having no commerce with men. *Some think* they live in the Amazonian style: those of more considered views think they are cenobite virgins, rejoicing in retreat, as with us, and like the vestals found in many places among the ancients, or sacred to the Great Mother." The Amazons are nuns![48] "Rumour has it, however," that there are others who cut off their right breasts, and entertain men. But Peter Martyr's view is unwavering: "I deem it a fable."[49]

The only argument that could induce him to believe in the American Amazons is not Columbus's testimony, which is rejected in other instances, but their inherent likelihood, since the ancients attested to their existence.[50] In this case antiquity is

---

44. *Dec.*, I, 4, p. 55.

45. Pennesi, op. cit., p. 34.

46. *Dec.*, I, 6, p. 77. "The interminable extent of the coastline of Paria, the social state of the inhabitants, and the similarity of certain animals to some European species" had been for Columbus "a major argument for that land being a continent" (Pennesi, op. cit., p. 70).

47. *Dec.*, III, 9, p. 307. Cf. the reference to the island of Madanina "inhabited solely by women" (I, 2, p. 16).

48. It is perhaps worth recalling that this is the thesis of de Gandía, who thought he was the first to identify the Amazons of South America with the Inca Virgins of the Sun!

49. *De insulis*, pp. 337–38. Of the Amazons of Madanina he had written with similar skepticism that "it is *believed* that the cannibals . . . go to visit these women, just as of old it was related that the Thracians crossed the sea to the Amazons of Lesbos. . . . *This is what they say:* I am merely repeating it" (*Dec.*, I, 2, pp. 16–17). And he confirms his skepticism, despite the testimony of the Imperial Secretary Alfonso Argollo (*Dec.*, VII, 8, p. 543), and of the ostiary of the Imperial chamber, Santiago Cañizares (*Dec.*, VII, 9, p. 554). Likewise, of a Mexican region inhabited solely by women: *Dec.*, V, 10, p. 469. I would thus not list Martyr, as Leonard does in an article containing some subtle observations on belief in the Amazons, as one of those who accepted and broadcast the legend (I. A. Leonard, "Conquerors and Amazons in Mexico," *HAHR*, 24 [1944], 561–79); cf. Hodgen, op. cit., pp. 30–31.

50. A skeptic on the subject of monsters and prodigies (rejecting for instance as idiotic the stories of men with tails—*Dec.*, VII, 2, p. 508), Peter Martyr was inclined to be more credulous "with data [such as the reports of the Amazons] that appear to present analogies with the fables of antiquity" (Eduard Fueter, *Geschichte der neueren*

called in as criterion for the truth of American nature. But usually, and with more typical procedure, American nature serves as a criterion for the truth of the ancient traditions. Martyr argues as a cultured European and is delighted to find the facts and features of the New World confirming and explaining the classical world. While Oviedo, as we shall see, frequently invokes Pliny's testimony to make the nature he sees before his eyes more credible to his readers, Peter Martyr, who never went to the Indies, uses the data from the Indies to make the classical texts more acceptable and comprehensible. America acts as marginal gloss for the texts of Graeco-Roman literature. The world discovered by Columbus unexpectedly illuminates the codices rediscovered by the humanists.

10. AMERICA AS LIVING PROOF OF THE GRAECO-ROMAN FABLES

The natives' superstitions, for example, remind Peter Martyr of the Myrmidons, Corinth, and the ancients' tutelary deities. And he goes on: "Well, illustrious prince, after this will you wonder at the spirit of Apollo that once provoked the wild frenzy of the Sybils? You thought that superstitious antiquity had perished."[51] But no, antiquity is alive and flourishing in America.[52] There are fish so huge that "the things told about the dolphins of Baiae or Arion bear no comparison with the deeds of this fish";[53] and caciques, that divide up Hispaniola between them, "just as we read that *fabled* Aeneas divided Latium up among various people."[54] And native women that are naked, fair-skinned, beautiful, and savage, so that "when people see them they think they have seen the most shapely dryads, or native water-nymphs, of whom the ancients told *fables*."[55] The Ciguana Indians advance into battle daubed with war paint, "like the Thracians and Agathyrses." With their long dark hair made to stand on end "in a thousand curious fashions" they resemble "specters emerging from the caverns of the underworld."[56] On the coasts of Maya and Cubagua the Spanish glimpse monsters that could be Tritons.[57] And the huge trees of the gulf of Uraba, in whose branches the natives build houses and shelters, lend credence to Pliny's description of the trees in India: "So I am no longer amazed, if we have

---

Historiographie [Munich and Berlin, 1936], p. 296). Similar examples of events of antiquity (victories of small armies over large ones) lending credibility to Cortés's fabulous exploits: *Dec.*, V, 1, p. 353.

51. *Dec.*, I, 9, p. 110. These native superstitions, Martyr writes elsewhere, are far superior to Lucian's *True History*, "insofar as these are actually in use among men (even though they are childish), while that was merely a story made up for amusement" (*Dec.*, I, 9, p. 102). The Indians' mythologies are also compared to the childish fables of Greek mythology (*Dec.*, VII, 3, p. 511), and the superstitions regarding a cave on Hispaniola to the beliefs of "rude antiquity" in the fabled Demogorgon (*Dec.*, VII, 8, p. 541).

52. There is a curious expression used by Fernando Columbus, when (at Cateva) he speaks of "a great lump of plaster, that seemed to be worked of stone and mortar; and the Admiral ordered that a piece be taken as a memento of that antiquity" (*Vita di Cristoforo Colombo*, p. 305).

53. *Dec.*, III, 8, p. 292.

54. *Dec.*, I, 2, p. 22.

55. *Dec.*, I, 5, p. 59.

56. *Dec.*, I, 7, pp. 80–81.

57. *Dec.*, VIII, 7, p. 605. The Cantabrian Sea apparently contains mermaids.

believed what Pliny and other authors wrote concerning the trees in India, which were said to be so high that one could not shoot an arrow over them."[58]

This comparative method is so original and so fruitful that it will still seem a great discovery two centuries later, when Lafitau and Fontenelle apply it once again to the American savages, when Vico systematizes it[59] and Galiani sums it up lucidly in the Martyr-like formula: "If one wants to discover the truth amongst what is said to have happened in far-off times, there is no simpler way than to look at the present-day customs of the illiterate peoples in far-off lands, the remoteness of place having the same effect as diversity of time."[60]

11. The limitations of Martyr's approach

The coherence of Peter Martyr's approach is clearly seen in its limitations and corollaries. There are prodigies of antiquity in which the Christian must not and cannot believe. He will therefore refuse to believe in analogous prodigies in the Indies. Antiquity thus serves as a middle term for a critical argument that derives deductions applicable to the natural world of the Indies from a Christian premise. In the Indies, in the island of Boiuca, alias Agnaneo, the Fountain of Youth has supposedly been discovered. Almost everyone at the court of Spain believes in it. But not Peter Martyr. As a Christian, he refuses to acknowledge that nature can have such power, believing that God has reserved to himself the prerogative of restoring youth, "just as he alone can look into the hearts of men."

Speaking as a humanist, however, he sets aside the criterion of God as limit on the miraculous power of nature; and as far as he himself is concerned denies the Faustian miracle of the fountain, "unless we were perchance to believe the Colchian fable of Jason's rejuvenation or the leaves of the Erythrean Sibyl."[61] If one could believe in the sibyl, the Fountain of Youth too would be credible. Unbelief in the fables of the ancients serves as a curb on belief in the fables of the moderns.

Years later, toward 1524–1525, having received further corroborating testimony, Martyr takes another look at the problem of the fountain and this time ends up admitting that it is possible. But he admits it (be it noted) not on the basis of the healing remedies of Medea, nor the miracles of Circe (his refusal to believe in these prodigies remains unchanged), but on the basis of the power of nature, now become almost God-like. Examples of dumb animals—eagles

---

58. *Dec.*, II, 4, p. 158.
59. In actual fact Peter Martyr "does not spell it out [the unity of the origins of myth]" (F. Esteve Barba, *Historiografía indiana* [Madrid, 1964], p. 55).
60. *Della moneta* (1751), I, 1 (Bari, 1915), p. 11. Cf. F. Nicolini, "G. B. Vico e F. Galiani," *Giornale Storico della Letteratura Italiana*, 71 (1918), 150.
61. *Dec.*, II, 10, pp. 202–03; Salas, op. cit., p. 44. Fontenelle (*Histoire des Oracles*, 1687) attacked the ancients' faith in their oracles in order to undermine the Christians' belief in miracles, etc., using antiquity as a middle term to pass from rationalistic premises to a critique of the Christian faith. Peter Martyr criticizes the belief in Indian prodigies from a classical-Christian viewpoint.

regaining their youth, snakes sloughing their skins, stags and crows instinctively protecting themselves against natural poisons—force him to believe that nature can do as much for her supreme creation, man.[62] Was it advancing old age that made him more credulous, more anxious to believe? Or must we interpret the new attitude as an empirical criterion replacing the literary criterion, the boundless liberty of nature bursting the bonds of authority, America now become a law unto itself, no longer judged by the yardstick of the classics?

Certainly for the bulk of his life Peter Martyr really lived in the classical world—"I had butterflies in my stomach," he writes, recalling his boyhood reading of the sufferings of Achemenides in Virgil[63]—and he is constantly immersed therein. It comes naturally to him to translate all dates into the Romans' ides, nones, and calends; to call the *adelantados'* sergeants "decurions"; to compare the Indian Catharina with the Roman Clelia and Pedrarias' wife with Ipsicrateia or Artemisia, and the undertow at Veragua with the roaring of Scylla; to give the Sallustian name Fulvia (Catilina's accuser) to the Indian woman who betrayed the five caciques' plot to her lover, Vasco Núñez de Balboa;[64] to describe certain savages as bigger than the Germans and Pannonians and nomads like the Scythians, or to contrast another tribe's way of settling disputes with the custom of matching champions from the opposing armies "as the Romans often did, and many others, according to the ancients"; to describe the Christians as being tormented by ferocious bats "as if by Harpies," and compare Balboa on his Darien peak to Hannibal in the Alps (and shortly afterward to Elisha and Hercules); or else, more generally, to admire certain pearls as worthy of Cleopatra, or to say a Darien tiger is more dangerous than the Caledonian boar or the Nemean lion, and so on.[65]

But in nearly all these cases, and innumerable others it would be superfluous to mention, we are really dealing with almost conventional expressions, scholarly

---

62. *Dec.*, VII, 7, pp. 535–39.

63. *Dec.*, II, 10, p. 203. Achemenides (*Aeneid*, III, 614, 691) is also mentioned in *Dec.*, III, 4, p. 249. A further indication of his classicism, and simultaneously of the way he shrugs off the dross of classicism on coming into contact with the New World, can be seen at the point where he justifies his use of the term *Admiral* rather than the more orthodox—from a strictly literary point of view—*archithalassus* or *navarchus* or *pontarchus*, and in his frequent references to caravels and bergantines, using the modern terms (*Dec.*, II, 7, p. 184).

He is always at pains to call everything by its correct name and often gives translations from official Latin into the current vernacular, e.g., giving the Italian and Spanish terms for the shipworm that attacked Columbus's ships (*Dec.*, III, 4, p. 245, and V, 7, p. 437). On a wood resistant to shipworm, whose existence was denied by Oviedo (*Hist.*, XV, 4; I, 457b), see *Dec.*, III, 6, p. 275; V, 9, p. 453; VII, 10, p. 561; and VIII, 6, p. 599; on an antishipworm pitch, III, 8, p. 299.

64. *Dec.*, II, 5, p. 164. Another spontaneous if inappropriate classical reference is noted by Celotti, op. cit., pp. 291–92, in *Dec.*, III, 4, p. 254.

65. *Dec.*, I, 2, p. 23 (Catharina); I, 9, p. 97 (Scythians); I, 10, p. 114, and II, 4, p. 156 (bats); II, 2, p. 136 (Scylla—cf. III, 6, p. 272); II, 6, p. 172 (duels); II, 7, p. 181 (Pedrarias); III, 1, p. 210 (Balboa—cf. III, 3, p. 236); III, 1, p. 216 (Cleopatra—cf. III, 2, p. 219 and III, 7, p. 278); III, 2, p. 221 (tiger). Other examples on pp. 209, 240, 278, 279, 281, 288, 302, 303, 305, 308, 309, etc. Two more harpies appear in *Dec.*, VII, 10, p. 563. In the fifth Decade, Cortés is compared to Caesar in Gaul and his companions to the Greeks in the Persian wars (*Dec.*, V, 1, p. 352). The Argonauts' enterprise was a mere trifle compared with Magellan's (*Dec.*, IV, 7, p. 438; see below, chap. XVIII, sec. 10). But Celotti (op. cit., p. 249) detects a "hint of subtle mockery" in the comparison of Balboa with Hannibal.

formulas lacking any specific meaning. We must in fact confess that when we see how casually Peter Martyr uses them we begin to wonder whether we might not perhaps have attached too much weight to other comparisons of his, in which we thought we glimpsed a thought or almost a philosophy. Dante had expressed himself in much the same way when he described the transformations suffered by the thieves as more astonishing than those narrated by the ancient poets: "Let Lucan now fall silent. . . . Let Ovid cease to speak of Cadmus and Arethusa."[66] But for the fourteenth-century Florentine the classical myths are overshadowed by the seething images of his own fantasy; for the sixteenth-century Milanese, by the factual data and eyewitness accounts of the very latest geographical discovery. For Peter Martyr, America is the visible complement of that "venerable antiquity" that he was not lucky enough to experience.[67]

12. EXPERIMENTAL EMPIRICISM

Certainly, when he is confronted with an obvious contradiction between the beliefs of the ancients and the reports of the moderns, he judges without bias, and usually judges well. On the basis of the newly acquired experience of the Indies he resolutely refuses to attach any credibility to the two notorious theses of classical geography, the uninhabitability of the tropics and the nonexistence of the antipodeans—although these theories had been upheld by very learned men and even saints: "It is not given to any one man to know all things."[68]

He is already an empiricist, as Oviedo will be. To convince himself of the hardness of an American stone attached to a wooden handle, brought back for him by Columbus himself, he brings it down with all his might on some iron bars, and dents them, without the stone suffering the slightest scratch.[69]

When travelers returning from the Indies give him an explanation of the origin of pearls that conflicts with Aristotle's and Pliny's accounts, he does his utmost to reconcile the opposing authorities: the Darien pearls are probably different from the pearls of India, Arabia, Ethiopia, and Taprobane that were known to those famous scholars of antiquity, "and their opinions should not be totally discarded."[70] When they tell him about a black sea and fish that sing and lull people to sleep like sirens, he does not of course believe it, but he is equally reluctant to rule it out completely. If there is a Red Sea, why could there not be a

66. *Inferno,* XXV, 11, 94ff. "Charon, for that matter, had already found a place in the Christian Dante's Hell" (B. Croce, *Poesia antica e moderna* [Bari, 1943], p. 409).

67. *Dec.,* III, 3, pp. 236–67.

68. *Dec.,* III, 1, p. 217. Cf. also III, 6, p. 269; the close of the preface, not numbered; VII, 6, p. 530; and above, sec. 2.

69. *Dec.,* V, 4, p. 395. For some other very hard stones, that almost ruin hammer and anvil and blacksmith before they are broken, see VII, 7, p. 540.

70. *Dec.,* III, 10, p. 313–15. A further instance of historical criticism is Martyr's suspension of his amazement at the incredible number of garments, six thousand, owned by Montezuma, when he sees an example of these "garments": a simple square veil, like the robe the pope throws over his shoulders when he is combing his hair, to avoid getting hairs and other dirt on his pontifical vestments (*Dec.,* V., 3, p. 380, and V, 10, p. 464).

black sea? Are there not certain newts that speak and do not frogs sing under water? Let everyone believe whatever they want to; certainly, however, nature is capable of great things.[71]

13. GEOGRAPHICAL PROBLEMS TACKLED

Whenever a new scientific problem comes up he is always ready to discuss it, scrutinize it, to toil away over it with a seriousness that may be naive but is certainly not characteristic of a mere "journalist." Here again he sometimes seems to forget his fear of boring the reader—or possibly relies on the reader's interest being as lively and sustained as his own—and plunges into complex questions of natural philosophy, climatology and geography, the pearl-bearing oysters, the gulfweed, the Caribbean currents, the origin of gold-bearing seams, the day "lost" when one goes round the world from east to west,[72] the artificial creation of giants,[73] the snows of the torrid zone and the heat of the northern regions,[74] or the reasons for the size of the rivers in America.

14. THE ORIGIN OF THE GREAT RIVERS

This last enquiry is typical. On receiving the very first reports Martyr is skeptical about the enormous size of the Marañón and suspects that the Pinzóns are telling him fairy stories; but when he goes on to ask them whether it might not be a branch of the sea they reply no, absolutely not, since it is fresh water. Martyr reflects that there are other fairly sizeable rivers, and that nature is (as usual) all powerful, and ends up admitting it: "We shall cease to be amazed." But he is not altogether convinced. "We shall understand these things more fully eventually."[75]

The problem becomes even more baffling with the discovery of the Pacific. The land separating the North Sea and the South Sea turns out to be no broader than six days' march. How can such mighty rivers as the Marañón and so many others descend from this slender strip of land? The question was perfectly reason-

71. *Dec.*, V, 9, p. 453. For a similar argument used in favor of the possibility of finding spices outside the Spice Islands see *Dec.*, V, 10, p. 465–66, and VII, 6, p. 529–30; on a miraculous tree, VII, 1, p. 499; on a fountain of pitch, VII, 7, p. 540.

72. *Dec.*, III, 5, p. 257, and Epist. 77, cited by Humboldt, *Examen critique*, I, 300. Martyr is very proud of having been the first to resolve—in consultation with the Venetian ambassador Gaspare Contarini—the problem of the day lost by the *Victoria* in going round the world from East to West (*Dec.*, V, 7, pp. 440–41; cf. Celotti, op. cit., p. 75). But see below, chap. XI, sec. 3.

In the *Opus Epistolarum* too Peter Martyr never misses an opportunity of drawing attention to some unusual natural phenomenon: a comet, an earthquake, a hail of aerolites, or even the variation in the level of the Mediterranean that he noted himself in Valencia, having gone there for this precise scientific purpose (Celotti, op. cit., pp. 49–50). But Celotti exaggerates when he describes Peter Martyr in his biography as "the very epitome of the enquiring mind," a person who delved "with real passion into every question of interest to science" (p. 75).

73. *Dec.*, VII, 3, pp. 513–14.

74. *Dec.*, I, 6, pp. 71–72.

75. *Dec.*, I, 9, p. 99. His problems were complicated by a certain confusion between the information relating to the Orinoco and that relating to the Marañón. On this question see also Mariéjol, op. cit., pp. 214–15.

able, before anything was known of the continent's sudden vast expansion south of Panama. And Peter Martyr cast around in vain for the answer. Do they really exist, those lofty mountains described by Columbus? And even if they do, where do the waters come from? Whence do they rain down, descend, or break forth? It is a fact that nowhere else in the world is there such a thin strip of land between two vast oceans: "Nowhere else do we read of two seas of this sort separated by such a narrow land, if what the inhabitants say is true." Perhaps the earth, squeezed between so much sea, absorbs a little of this water and casts it back with the rivers. Or perhaps the water falls silently from the air, as Peter Martyr saw it drip from the walls of caves in Spain, in a cavern near Granada and another near Valladolid?

Springs of such origin are certainly possible; but they are of modest dimensions, drop-by-drop secretions, a slow weeping of the caverns and not majestic currents, like those of the American rivers. A more reasonable supposition would be the frequency of torrential rains, these lands being situated beneath the equinox and between two limitless seas.

Arriving at this last plausible conjecture Peter Martyr halts and concludes provisionally: "However it may be, most Holy Father, I am unable to disbelieve so many men who have visited those lands; and I can only repeat those things, although very many of them seem unlikely." He cannot ignore the unanimous reports, although the phenomenon reported seems absurd. But he will feel free to present his own arguments sometimes, so that scholars will not look on him as a simpleton, believing the first thing he is told; "lest the famous men of learning . . . judge us therefore to be so foolish as to accept without question anything that happens to be recounted to us." The European's critical mind struggles to come to grips with a nature that proves unexpected and surprising, but which it must somehow be possible to grasp with our concepts, to measure with our science.

Peter Martyr ponders the question again and comes up with another hypothesis: that the waters come from several rivers flowing together into reservoir-lakes high in the mountains, where they join forces and come pouring down. At this point the writer begins to worry that his efforts may be misunderstood. Possibly someone will laugh at him, pointing out that even in the Old World we have the Po and other great rivers, and that there is nothing to be amazed at (a sort of precursor of O'Gorman, who will tell us that there is nothing new in America). No, Martyr replies to his imaginary adversary: the case is different. American nature is original.

The rivers of the New World are short, not like the Po. This glaring factual error is rapidly followed by an accurate guess at the true situation: "There are however those who believe the land to be very broad elsewhere, although it is narrow here."[76] And the conjecture is swiftly developed and reinforced. "In the

76. *Dec.*, II, 9, pp. 195–98.

area of Uraba and Veragua, the seas are separated by only a small isthmus. The area washed by the River Marañón, however, must be deemed to form part of a broad region."[77] And getting even warmer: "The reason that the Marañón is so huge is that it flows from far off to the sea, through watery lands."[78] As the true shape of the continent was gradually revealed, its apparent paradoxes dissolved with the legends, and its characteristics became explicable within the framework of the traditional physical geography of the Europeans. As the material knowledge of the Americas grew richer, so it became easier for this knowledge to take its place within the patterns of western scientific thought.

Before he leaves the subject, however, Peter Martyr hints at another possible reason, though eventually rejecting it as unacceptable: could these great rivers perhaps be fed, like Alphaeus, from remote subterranean caverns? But his conclusion is categorical: this we know, this we do not know, yet. We shall learn the truth one day.[79]

The truth is in fact discovered very shortly afterward. When he finally learns of the vastness of the Marañón River basin, Peter Martyr rejoices: so he had seen aright. He had "prophesied" the reality of things. There is therefore no longer anything stypefying about the once "portentous" Marañón. In this comprehensive explanation—the truth intuited and proved—his mind finds solace and satisfaction.[80]

15. MARVELS OF THE FLORA AND FAUNA

The plants and animals interest Peter Martyr rather less than the natives, treasures, and hydrographical enigmas of the Indies. On one occasion he even seems to lose patience with them: "And now enough of quadrupeds, birds, insects, trees, grasses, essences and other things of this sort. Let us turn our attention to the doings of the men and their way of life."[81] The ethnographer in him gets the better of the naturalist. Thus I would hardly call him "superior to Aristotle, Theophrastus, Columella, and Pliny in describing the things of nature."[82] But his curiosity is ever vigilant and grows with each Decade; his sense of landscape inspires him to some elegant descriptions,[83] and he was certainly brought abundant information on the animals and trees by pilots and officials, discoverers and merchants, all of whom normally called on him "on their return

---

77. *Dec.*, III, 4, p. 252.
78. *Dec.*, III, 5, p. 265.
79. *Dec.*, II, 9, pp. 198–99; *Dec.*, III, 9, p. 305. The origin of rivers and the way they worked in general was one of the most taxing problems for the medieval geographers (Pohl, op. cit., p. 5), and later for Scillacio (see above, chap. IV, sec. 2). On the conviction that the truth would eventually be revealed, cf. the passage quoted above, n. 75.
80. *Dec.*, V, 9, p. 450.
81. *Dec.*, VIII, 7 (end).
82. Hakluyt's words, quoted by Ciampi, *Storia moderna,* III, 300–01. Cf. idem, "Le fonti storiche del rinascimento: Pietro Martire d'Anghiera," *Nuova Antologia,* yr. 10, vol. 30 (1875), 717–44.
83. See Mariéjol, op. cit., pp. 226–27.

from the Ocean";[84] and he must have been sorely tempted to recount the extraordinary properties and characteristics of the transoceanic flora and fauna.

He frequently gives in to this temptation, regaling the reader with stories of the astonishing creatures encountered in the Indies. There is the cacique's pet fish that answers to its name and carries ten men on its back;[85] another that can be used to catch other fish,[86] and various other sea monsters.[87] There are the famous nonbarking puppies, ugly as sin, with foxlike snouts, but edible;[88] great beasts in Cuba "whose horrendous roaring could be heard by night" from the ships;[89] a marsupial, an animal "known to none of the writers, to my knowledge," which — exceptionally — he saw with his own eyes (though dead);[90] toads that are engendered, in Darien, from the drops of water from a certain marsh used for sprinkling on the floors of the rooms, "just as in various places I myself saw drops of water becoming fleas in summer."[91] And time and again he refers to the splendid parrots, vampire bats, and fierce crocodiles;[92] and in Darien "in addition to tigers and lions" and other well-known animals, "many monsters."

But he only once actually describes one of these creatures, a real paradox of nature: it has a proboscis, but is not an elephant; it has the dimensions and color of an ox, but is not an ox; the hooves of a horse, but is not a horse; ears bigger than those of any other animal, but not however as big and drooping as those of the pachyderms. . . .[93] This delight in the recounting of marvels and propounding of riddles is glimpsed again when Martyr models another scene of animal life before our very eyes in the form of the strange great beast "that resembles a large long-tailed ape," that leaps and almost flies from branch to branch, which has lost one arm by the time it is captured but still succeeds in latching onto a savage wild pig with the other and almost strangling it. "This and other monsters, that land nourishes."[94]

84. "This man [Andrés Morales] came to me, as those returning from the Ocean usually do" (*Dec.*, III, 7, p. 277).

85. *Dec.*, III, 8, pp. 292–93, after a fine description of the manatee.

86. *Dec.*, I, 3, pp. 38–39. He was at first doubtful about this and was ridiculed in Rome when his report reached there, but the phenomenon was in fact subsequently confirmed (*Dec.*, VII, 8, p. 542).

87. *Dec.*, I, 10, p. 114 (alligators?); II, 1, p. 127; III, 8, p. 289 (sharks).

88. *Dec.*, I, 3, p. 40; *De insulis*, p. 345. Cf. *Dec.*, I, 1, p. 8, where those same quadrupeds, the only ones found by Columbus, are called rabbits, "three sorts of rabbits," with greater zoological accuracy than the later chroniclers, who called them "dogs," because they were actually *hutias*, which are rodents. Epist. 133 of the *Opus Epistolarum* already notes quite accurately that "the island begets nothing in the way of quadrupeds, apart from huge lizards, harmless however [nature the ever-benign] and a certain sort of small rabbit, not unlike our rats" (p. 40). Cf. *Dec.*, VII, 9, p. 553.

89. *Opus Epistolarum*, epist. 164 (1495), p. 49.

90. *Dec.*, I, 9, p. 100; II, 9, p. 192.

91. *Dec.*, III, 6, p. 273. Celotti (op. cit., p. 308) claims that this was due to the "numerous toads' eggs contained in that stagnant water." Cf. Gerbi, *Dispute*, p. 10.

92. *Dec.*, I, 8, p. 91; III, 6, p. 274. On the bloodsucking bats, see also *Dec.*, VIII, 7, pp. 604–05.

93. *Dec.*, II, 9, p. 192; most likely a *danta* or tapir. On the wild animals of Panama, leopards, tigers, lions, etc., see also *Dec.*, V, 9, p. 450.

94. *Dec.*, III, 4, p. 244 (in Cariai).

16. NATURE VARIED AND BENIGN

The aspect he principally stresses, however, is the benign quality of nature in the New World, a benignness in harmony with the innocent and blessed life of the natives. Although some of the animals are manifestly dangerous and cannot really be identified with the "meek wild beasts" of the golden age;[95] although there are sea monsters in the habit of emerging from the sea and sinking their teeth into the odd unwary Christian, poisonous bats as big as turtledoves, and even among the trees some whose shade is lethal, others whose fruits turn to worms, and still others whose leaves cause painful bruises;[96] by and large life is soft in these islands and supposed continent. Creatures from the Old World acclimatize very well: Hispaniola produces not only gold and spices but "even good horses, things that used not to be bred before in the island, but which the Spaniards brought there, and now come to perfection."[97]

The almost incredible variety of species and their *diversity* from those known in the Old World make life in the Indies soft, pleasant, and surprising. Nature is richer and more powerful than in the Old World and brings forth creatures that the European cannot even imagine. West Indian trees are different from Europe's, but their fruit is edible.[98] In Paria there are all sorts of animals, reptiles, insects, and even quadrupeds "unlike ours . . . of all shapes, manifold and unnumbered."[99] And all are meek, except the lions, tigroids, and crocodiles. And these "tigroids," are they really tigers? One Ledesma of Seville, who once ate their meat, found it as good as beef. . . . But how do they know it is a tiger, if they have never seen one? "When they are asked what makes them think it is a tiger, if they never saw a tiger, they answer that their judgment is based on its spots, its fierceness and agility, and other clues given in various writers"; in other words from the circumstantial evidence. And Peter Martyr is left with his customary doubts: "We can only take their word for it."[100] Criticism of the summary zoological definitions has begun.

95. Costa, op. cit., p. 166 (Metastasio).

96. *Dec.*, II, 1, p. 122; III, 6, p. 275; VIII, 7, p. 601. Cf. below, chap. IX, sec. 7. But on the other hand the leaves of the *jaruma* tree cure all wounds and reattach limbs severed by a saber blow (*Dec.*, VII, 1, p. 499).

97. Contarini, op. cit., p. 51. "Wheat is the only thing that does not do well, because on account of the fatness [humidity?] of the ground it grows so tall and soft that it never ripens" (ibid.).

98. *Opus Epistolarum*, epist. 133, p. 40.

99. In the *Opus Epistolarum*, however, Martyr argues that the land of Paria must be a continent "because their woods are everywhere full of *our* animals, like stags, wild boar, and others of that sort, and among the birds, of geese, ducks, and peacocks, but not multicolored ones" (epist. 168, falsely dated 1496, p. 50).

100. *Dec.*, III, 2, pp. 222–23. A little further on he reports again that "they also claim that the land is infested with crocodiles and lions and tigers . . . and they write that in the homes of their allies they found the skins of lions and tigers that they had killed" (*Dec.*, III, 6, p. 274). In Campeche, apart from various birds, there were found "wolves, lions, tigers, foxes, and wild quadrupeds, like boar, stags, and hares" (*De insulis*, p. 332; and the same in Mexico: *Dec.*, V, 8, p. 447). In the *Opus Epistolarum* there is also reference to three "tigers" captured by Cortés, one of which escapes, wreaks havoc, and is thrown into the sea, another is killed, while the third will, it is hoped, manage to evade the pirates and reach Spain (epist. 771 [1522], p. 68), a hope which is in fact happily fulfilled (epist. 778 [1523], and epist. 809 [1525], pp. 68, 73). A prolix and picturesque description of the animals of Chiribichi (including meek lions, anteaters, and a species of malodorous monkey that defecates live snakes) is drawn up on the basis of reports by the Dominican friars (*Dec.*, VIII, 7, p. 601–08). For a further determined effort to find the right name for a natural product

Another process that makes its first appearance with Peter Martyr—albeit in embryonic form—is the critique of the critics of American nature. The travelers returning from the Indies relate enthusiastically how well all animals do there and "on the subject of growth, compare the oxen to elephants and the pigs to mules," but a more realistic perspective induces Martyr to cut these "hyperboles" down to size. Anything excessive or dictated by an obvious intent to impress is greeted with caution, skepticism, or straightforward disbelief.[101]

In the islands, however, nature is more maternal and inoffensive than ever, and there are no fierce animals whatsoever, "not any at all, not even one: all the island creatures are tame apart from the men in many of them," in other words, excepting the Carib cannibals. Having fixed this clear distinction between the islands and the mainland (the latter recognized as a continent precisely by reason of this diversity of its fauna),[102] the historian can ecstasize over the paradisal climate and amazing fecundity of the islands. Hispaniola is classically allegorized as Thetis surrounded by swarms of Nereids (the lesser islands), attending her and combing her locks.[103] The mildness of its climate makes it preferable even to Italy. The trees grow to enormous heights, the meadows are thick and luxuriant, "and our cattle are said to be born fatter there, and turn out much bigger, on account of the lush pastures."

Everything grows there with charmed, indeed impetuous, exuberant fruitfulness.[104] The fertility of the land is "incredible to hear. They insist and indeed swear on oath that the ears of corn are thicker than a man's arm."[105] And the sugarcanes, that are squeezed in twenty-eight "presses," are taller and fatter than anywhere else in the world; they too "are said to grow to the thickness of a man's arm . . . and to one and a half times the height of a man."[106] And how remark-

---

(the banana) see *Dec.*, VII, 9, p. 549. So I would not agree with Ciampi (*Storia moderna*, III, 385, and "Pietro Martire," p. 741), that Martyr failed to "study the characteristics that distinguished the new species from ours," nor would I thus rebuke him for not having "aspired to the general laws followed by nature in its works." Obviously Martyr is Martyr, not Humboldt or Darwin.

101. *Dec.*, III, 7, chap. 3, p. 282; Salas, op. cit., p. 41.

102. "The animals that we mentioned above, and many others that are not found in any of the islands, testify to this land being a continent" (*Dec.*, I, 8, p. 90). See below, n. 105, and Vespucci, above, chap. VI, sec. 6. The continent too, for that matter, has a plethora of strange and pleasing birds, "many kinds unlike ours," good to eat and sweet of song, in addition to the usual various kinds of parrots (*Dec.*, III, 9, p. 194). See the description of the tasty Mexican turkeys and fruits like and unlike European ones (*Dec.*, V, 3, pp. 390–91).

103. *Dec.*, III, 7, p. 227; III, 9, p. 305.

104. *Opus Epistolarum*, epist. 156 (1495), p. 47. See also the immediately preceding and following parts of this section of my text.

105. *Dec.*, III, 7, p. 282. Columbus's companions had in fact already found "this land [Haiti] to be the most fruitful land under the sun" (*Dec.*, I, 1, p. 11; cf. I, 3, p. 30, etc.). The region of Quiriquetana, or Ciamba, on the mainland, is also prodigiously rich in plant life. But this region, unlike the islands, "nourishes both lions and tigers, stags, roebuck, and animals of that sort" and birds, and well-built natives, who paint their bodies red and black to make themselves beautiful (*Dec.*, III, 4, p. 240).

106. *De insulis*, p. 364. Licenciado Alonso Zuazo had written to Charles V from Santo Domingo (22 January 1518): "There are also cane-fields . . . the cane is as thick as a man's wrist and twice as high as the average person" [the height of two men, instead of Peter Martyr's one and a half]. But there were no mills as yet, so the landowners had been given permission to "build mills to process the sugar, which will be a source of huge riches" (in M. Jiménez de la Espada, *Relaciones geográficas de Indias*, vol. I, *Antecedentes* [Madrid, 1881], p. xviii).

ably quickly all the European seeds thrive and bear fruit in the Indies! There is already an abundance of every sort of fruit and vegetable. "Is this not worthy of admiration, most Holy Father?"[107] European plants grow better there than in Europe ("they turn out much bigger"). The homegrown plants add a touch of the exotic to the flora of Darien.

In a couple of lines he admiringly sums up the usefulness of each plant, including the succulent pineapple, which King Ferdinand pronounced excellent (but which Peter Martyr never got to taste, because of the few specimens sent to Spain all but one were found to be rotten on arrival), and the vegetable that the natives call "the potato," which has skin the color of the earth but pure white flesh, and a taste resembling the chestnut, only somewhat sweeter.[108] While he is writing the last Decade he is actually presented with a certain quantity of these potatoes and says he would willingly have sent the Holy Father a share of this rare delight, if the distance had not been so great. The pope's portion goes to the papal legate, who devours it "greedily" and will thus in due course be able to bear witness to His Holiness of the goodness and tastiness of this New World tuber.[109]

17. THE ANIMALS ABUNDANT AND VIGOROUS

Such goodness of the earth is reflected in the animal life. To Peter Martyr the thesis of the degeneration of nature in America would have seemed a paradox. The abundance of vegetable foodstuffs makes many of the animal species better and stronger and tastier there. The herds of cattle have multiplied out of all proportion in Hispaniola, so that the island already exports large quantities of horses and sheepskins and oxhides to the mother country.[110] True, these cattle "produce meat that is insipid and indeed, so they say, lacking marrow, or if there is any, it is watery," but the Hispaniola pork is tasty, healthy, abundant, and a lot better than the European;[111] and "the young of all animals, on account of the luxuriant grass, turn out fatter than their parents, although they are fed only grass, no barley or other grain."[112]

The phenomenon interests Peter Martyr so much that he never tires of describing it, even repeating the travelers' verbal exaggerations: "They say the oxen, pigs, and horses grow better there and the animals are bigger than their forebears,

---

107. *Dec.*, II, 9, pp. 189–90. "Oh astonishing riches," Martyr's hymn of praise goes on. Cf. also V, 9, p. 454; VII, 1, p. 498; VII, 9, pp. 547–48.

108. *Dec.*, II, 9, pp. 190–91. Almost all the flora found in the islands represented species previously unknown: "They found no known trees in those islands, apart from the fir and the palm" (I, 1, p. 11). The banana, improperly called *plátano*, is a fruit that Martyr cannot identify with certainty, and so he does not know what name to give it: the Egyptians say that it is the fruit with which Adam besmirched the human race; others call it *musa*, etc. (*Dec.*, VII, 9, p. 549). In the same book and in *Dec.*, VIII, 6, pp. 597–99, there are further lengthy botanical descriptions.

109. *Dec.*, VIII, 3, p. 580. On Peter Martyr's gluttony, see Mariéjol, op. cit., p. 160.

110. *Dec.*, III, 7, p. 283.

111. *Dec.*, I, 10, p. 115; II, 1, p. 131; II, 9, p. 191; III, 7, p. 283.

112. *Dec.*, I, 10, p. 115. The bread, however, seemed "lacking in substance" to anyone used to bread made from wheat. Cf. above, n. 97.

on account of the richness of the soil."[113] He sees the animal kingdom prospering in the richness of the plant world—a view indubitably closer to the truth than that of those later naturalists, right up until the nineteenth century, for whom the characteristic trait of America was the antithesis between an exuberant flora and a stunted fauna[114]—and in this mutual harmony of living creatures detects another sign of the blessedness of nature in the New World.

18. Invitation to the pope

There is even one passage in which he almost seems to be inviting the supreme pontiff to move to such a pleasant country: "Could one wish for anything happier on earth, most Holy Father, than to live where it is granted to see and enjoy so much and so many things; what more blessed than to lead a life where you are not forced to shut yourself away in narrow chambers, in the freezing cold, or the troublesome heat?" The gold flowing in the rivers and growing like a tree in the earth ensures and guarantees the country's perfect healthiness.[115]

Up to this point the chronicler builds his case on the charms of nature, but then he suddenly remembers that he is a Christian and his interlocutor the Vicar of Christ and hastily goes on: "No dangerous animal is ever found in those parts. . . . all things are blessed, and even more blessed now, since so many thousands of men are received into your flock." And after this somewhat transparent addition he apologizes for laboring the point, resorting once again to a pagan metaphor to explain and justify his enthusiasm as a good Christian. "The fervent joy that fills my soul, when I see and hear and write these things, like a Delphic or Sybilline inspiration, makes me repeat these things so often, particularly when I realize [another obvious mental interpolation] how much it means for the expansion of our religion."[116]

19. Spain exalted

This glorification of the new lands—so vast that even without counting the Portuguese territories they are three times as big as all Europe[117]—often endows

---

113. *Dec.*, III, 6, p. 274. Cf. above, sec. 16.

114. Cf. Gerbi, *Dispute*, pp. 448–49. Martyr's thesis was accepted right up until Darwin's time. He, however, observing precisely the paltry South American fauna in the midst of such exuberant flora and, in contrast, the powerful fauna of the South African deserts, wrote: "That large animals require a luxuriant vegetation has been a general assumption which has passed from one work to another, but I do not hesitate to say that it is completely false." Large mammals can exist in regions where there is very little food, the camel being a typical example. "Among the mammalia there exists no close relation between the *bulk* of the *species* and the *quantity* of the vegetation in the countries which they inhabit" (*Voyage of a Naturalist Round the World*, chap. V [New York, 1871], I, 108–12), which is an explicit, direct contradiction of the Milanese scholar's opinion.

115. *Dec.*, III, 7, p. 284. There is an obvious hint of alchemy in this drinkable gold. "The seams of gold are like a living tree" (*Dec.*, III, 8, pp. 296–97, with awestruck description).

116. *Dec.*, III, 8, p. 294. A little further on his enthusiasm for the immensity of the new lands is extended to include, as a fourth term, the propagation of the faith: "It is enough to know that there are vast lands awaiting us, waiting to embrace our people, language, customs, and religion in the years to come" (*Dec.*, III, 9, p. 308).

117. *Dec.*, I, 10, p. 115. Cf. the "Preface": "We offer three Europes to one reputed continent." Martyr returns to the praises of the vastness of the new lands at the beginning of the sixth and seventh Decades (pp. 476, 498), and in VII, 6, p. 531 etc.

his portrayal of America with an unreal, Edenic, and theatrical[118] quality, as his eulogies fade and merge into the more general glorification of the greatness of Spain and the boldness of the Spaniards.

The riches and splendors of the Indies are the Emperor Charles's greatest acquisition; and those lands, which the ancients always insisted were empty, will in fact, with their teeming peoples, furnish him with the means to dominate the whole world. The *Decades* present the sovereign with a complete description and illustration of that region, "a land crammed with people, pleasant, rich, most blessed, a thousand islands crowned with gold and gleaming white pearls. . . . Come to embrace a new world, and do not torment us any further with our longing for you. Here, oh youthful and most illustrious King, the instruments will be prepared through which the whole world will belong to you." [119]

Trade with the New Indies grows more flourishing every day. In 1525 Martyr could write with his usual easy enthusiasm that "the stream of ships parting the ocean waves on their way to the new worlds and back is now as abundant as that of the merchants crossing the border to the fairs at Lyon, or coming in from France and Germany for the Belgian fairs at Antwerp." [120] The Americas are Spain's "great fair." To prevent the transatlantic treasures falling into the hands of pirates, Peter Martyr—supplementing his geographical description with a word of practical advice—suggested in the Council of the Indies and gained the emperor's approval for the system of armed convoys (as already practiced in fact by the Italian maritime republics).[121] The treasure-laden ships should assemble in Hispaniola from all parts of the Indies and thence, seeking safety in numbers, head for Spain, defying the enemy ambushes.[122]

Following this system, Spain's new acquisitions will be made both familiar and secure. And the Spaniards deserve this empire, having really earned it: "Not to Saturn, nor to Hercules, nor any of the ancients that sought out new shores and brought them within the realm of civilization, can our more recent Spaniards count themselves inferior." [123] Glory be to Spain therefore, glory to the sailors

---

118. Salas, op. cit., 56–57.

119. *Dec.*, "Preface," at the end. Cf. the similar invitation to the pope (above, sec. 18).

120. *Dec.*, VIII, 9, at the end.

121. On the arrangements for ships to travel in convoy, see A.P. Sereni, *The Italian Conception of International Law* (New York, 1943), p. 52.

122. *Dec.*, VII, 4, p. 521.

123. *Dec.*, I, 10, p. 119. Cf. the passage cited at the opening of sec. 4 above, which goes on: "If the tireless labors of the Spaniards lead to new discoveries, we shall bend our mind to them" (*Dec.*, III, 4, p. 255). And in fact when he learned about the feats of Cortés, Martyr once again had occasion to praise the Spaniards as superior to the Romans. The transportation of the brigantines overland from Tlaxcala to Mexico was something the Romans would have found difficult even when they were at the height of their greatness (*Dec.*, V, 8, quoted by Celotti, op. cit., p. 64).

In another passage (*Dec.*, V, 4, p. 404), Martyr somewhat curiously justifies his usual omission of less important details on the legalistic grounds (*de minimis non curat praetor*) that since he is recounting such great deeds as those performed by the Spaniards it is quite legitimate for him to leave out those minor details that the Greek and Jewish writers, having lived their lives within restricted geographical limits, would certainly have included in their histories. If a Greek had done what Magellan did, "who knows what the Greeks would have invented," given the hyperboles they

and conquistadors. Glory because they expanded the crown's dominions? . . . Because they extended the realms of the cross? . . . Yes, of course, but the writer has more immediate interests. Glory be to Spain, that "offered such ample literary material to those of great talent." Peter Martyr goes on, with a mixture of pride and modesty, describing himself as only a precursor of those mighty intellects "for whom I will have opened up the way since I myself, as you can see, did no more than put together those things, both because I have no skill at dressing things up in fine raiment, and because I never took up my pen with the intention of writing as a historian."[124] But in his heart of hearts he is well aware of his good luck. He already perceives, with extraordinary foresight, that his future fame is more firmly guaranteed by his reports on the new islands than by any of his other literary labors (see above, sec. 3). And just as he himself would be savagely criticized by Oviedo for recounting what he had *not* seen, Martyr attacks the Venetian Alvise Cadamosto for recounting, and claiming to have seen, what he read in the Milanese writer's books.[125] From generation to generation literary jealousy, the scholars' besetting sin, leaves behind it a foaming wake of polemic and rancor.

---

used to describe the Argonauts' little enterprise! (*Dec.*, V, 7, p. 438). Maximilianus Transylvanus also brought his "Relación" (1522) to a close by drawing a favorable comparison between the voyage of the *Victoria* and Jason's journey (Navarrete, op. cit., IV, 284). The theme was to be taken up again by Campanella in a famous "sonetto caudato" and in the canzone "Grecia, tre spanne di mar," that contrast the winning of the golden fleece with the so much greater enterprise of Italy "finding new worlds" and taming the oceans (*Poesie* [Bari, 1915], p. 216; see below, chap. XVIII, sec. 10).

124. He claims that his letters were never carefully composed, just "dashed off" (*Dec.*, I, 10, p. 115). So Peter Martyr too, elegant and polished writer as he is, claims like Oviedo to have written his works without frills, to have merely put down the facts and let them speak for themselves, as they had no need of embellishment or a clothing of historical solemnity. Cf. "the rough garments, in which we did no more than wrap these remarkable things, we left unornamented" (*Dec.*, III, 9, p. 303, and VIII, 1, p. 567).

125. Cadamosto is accused of having plagiarized the first three letters of the first Decade, that Peter Martyr freely allowed to be read out to the Venetian ambassadors, and of which he permitted copies to be made. However the shameless Cadamosto speaks in the first person of things "that he himself never did and that neither he nor any other Venetian ever saw." Quite possibly he also plagiarized what he wrote about the Portuguese! He certainly never sailed with Pedrarias's great fleet (which Martyr describes with due solemnity, and in which Oviedo first sailed for the Indies), because Pedrarias took great pains "to ensure that no foreigner was mixed in with the Spaniards, without the king's express command," and apart from a few Genoese that were friends of Columbus's son the only foreigner on board was Peter Martyr's fellow countryman, Francesco Cotta, and he was only accepted after considerable pressure on the part of Martyr, who had been in the service of the court no less than twenty-six years. "So much for the Venetian Cadamosto then, and all the things he claims to have seen . . ." (*Dec.*, II, 7, pp. 177–79). Humboldt claims that Martyr got Cadamosto muddled up with Angelo Trevisan (*Examen critique*, IV, 128), and Harrisse too exonerates Cadamosto (*Bibliotheca Americana*, pp. 75–76). On the real truth of the matter, and how Martyr acted "in good faith . . . but mistakenly," in accusing Cadamosto, see Celotti, op. cit., p. 219n.

❦ IX ❦

Martín Fernández de Enciso's Suma de Geographía

1. NATURE OF THE WORK

WHEN Martín Fernández de Enciso, bachelor of laws and veteran of the Indies—where he had fought under Ojeda's orders and worked on Ojeda's behalf—sat down to draft his *Suma de Geographía,* first published in Seville in 1519 (and reprinted in 1530 and 1546), he was well aware of its originality. This was no journal, or relation, no mere letter or series of letters on this or that newly discovered land. The *Suma de Geographía* is not only the first book on America printed in Spanish,[1] it is a general treatment not just of the West Indies but of the whole world; it does not refer directly to any voyage in particular and does not even mention which lands were discovered earlier and which later. The whole world is one datum, the object of the geographer's measurements and descriptions.

The whole world comes under his gaze; but the date, the dedication to the emperor, the author's own life and the wording on the title page, promising a description of "all the parts and provinces of the world, especially of the Indies," confirm that the author's prime interest is in the lands newly discovered in the West, in the hemisphere that Enciso unhesitatingly asserts to be one of the two parts which go to make up the world, "one Eastern . . . the other Western," the former divided into three parts "as our ancestors divided it up, namely: Asia, Africa, and Europe," and the latter into two parts, the first comprising the few lands discovered to the northwest of the island of Hierro (westernmost of the

---

1. Harrisse, *Bibliotheca Americana,* p. 168, following Obadiah Rich. Andrés Bernáldez, the parish priest of Los Palacios, had of course told the story of Columbus's first two voyages on the basis of the Admiral's papers and possibly the writings of Dr. Chanca (Jane, op. cit., p. 87; Sánchez Alonso, *Historiografía española,* I, 401, 446), but his *Historia* was published only in 1856. Enciso's *Suma* thus remains "the first Spanish book which gives an account of America" (*Encyclopedia Britannica,* 11th ed., XI, 625) and "a cornerstone in the history of navigational literature" (Boies Penrose, *Travel and Discovery in the Renaissance* [Cambridge, Mass., 1925], p. 95; cf. pp. 265–66, 294).

Canaries), in other words, Labrador and the "Bacallaos," the other the vast regions to the southwest of that island, the West Indies.[2]

The remarkable accuracy shown by Enciso, who was writing, we must remember, at a time when nothing was yet known of Mexico or Peru and very little of the coastline around Panama (xxix), is the fruit of an unusual combination of cultural background and broad experience. Enciso was a scholar, a man of letters and a lawyer, familiar with the classics and skilled in astronomy; and he had been in the Indies, where he had acted with varying success as lawyer, royal official, financial backer, conquistador and peacemaker, and speculator on the metal market.

2. Enciso and Balboa

Enciso was the "first conquistador to take up his pen with educational intent."[3] Partner and companion of Alonso de Ojeda, founder of Santa María de la Antigua, the first Spanish city on the American mainland, and the first person to bring food-producing plants and domestic animals to that inhospitable region,[4] Enciso had been with Balboa in Darien. He was ousted by Balboa, because he was "too great a rival to him," and embarked in a waterlogged bergantine that Balboa hoped would sink,[5] and his goods confiscated. But he regained his freedom and promptly scuttled off to Spain to complain about his wrongs, managing to persuade the king to punish Balboa. When Balboa found himself recalled to Europe he realized that if he was going to regain the sovereign's favor he would have to come up with some spectacular discovery or conquest in the very near future; and

---

2. Of the three early and complete editions of the extremely rare *Suma de Geographía* I have seen only the last (1546), "newly revised and corrected and purged of certain faults that it contained." In this edition the last ten pages (those following p. lx) are erroneously renumbered from xlix to lviii: in quoting from this 1546 edition I shall refer to these repeated pages with "bis" numbers. I have not seen the French translation apparently made by M. de la Roquette. Humboldt noted that this book had "become extremely rare" (*Examen critique*, III, 173n). J. T. Medina, in *El descubrimiento del Océano Pacífico* (Santiago de Chile, 1913–14), I, 288–89n60, says that it is "now [1914] extremely rare," and in fact cost £80 at that time; but Palau, *Manual del librero hispano-americano*, states *sub voce* that it is not so rare as is generally thought.

It has, however, been little studied. Rafael Altamira only mentions it as a "short but interesting" work ("La huella de España en el Pacífico," in *La huella de España en América* [Madrid, 1924], p. 121); and almost all the other references are equally generic, including that by Puente y Olea, op. cit., p. 101. H. H. Bancroft, "Early California Literature," in *Works,* vol. 38 (San Francisco, 1890), p. 661, merely comments that the *Suma* "gave personal observations on America." Oscar Peschel, in his *Geschichte der Erdkunde* (Munich, 1865), p. 329, credits Enciso with having been the first to attempt to calculate the distance between America and the Cape of Good Hope. His description of the West Indies is included in its entirety in J. T. Medina, *Biblioteca Hispano-Americana, 1493–1810* (Santiago de Chile, 1898–1907), I, 201–18, and in the same author's *Descripción de las Indias Occidentales por Martín Fernández de Enciso* (Santiago de Chile, 1897), printed in an edition of two hundred copies. I have quoted from this latter edition, except where otherwise stated.

3. C. Pereyra, *Las huellas de los conquistadores* (Madrid, 1929), p. 78; cf. ibid., pp. 21, 87. Enciso is erroneously listed by Guamán Poma de Ayala, *Nueva corónica y buen gobierno* (Paris, 1936), p. 374, among the conquerors of Peru. Cf. Medina, *Biblioteca,* I, 71.

4. Puente y Olea, op. cit., pp. 95, 98–99, 129, 377, 432.

5. Oviedo, *Hist.*, XXVIII, 3: PT, III, 181–82; but from the suspect brigantine he was then "passed" to a caravel. Further information in G. Benzoni, *La historia del Mondo Nuovo* (1565; Milan, 1965), pp. 42, 47–50.

sure enough, before the arrival in the Indies of his judge and executioner, Pedrarias Dávila, accompanied by Enciso as *alguacil mayor* (and Oviedo as *veedor*), Vasco Núñez de Balboa, with one supreme effort, succeeded in resting his greedy and astonished eyes on the Pacific Ocean.

Enciso was thus the instrument of Balboa's downfall and his glory. And in the *Suma de Geographía* he could weave together and purify his memories of those savage twists of fate, translating the vast and awesome spell of those new lands into clearcut images and measured phrases.

In the colophon to his work, repeated almost verbatim in the ensuing editions, Enciso acknowledges among his sources "the Historia Bactriana, the two Ptolemies, Erastothenes, Pliny, Strabo, Joseph, Anselm, the Bible, the general history, and many others," [6] but also—and doubtless for the Americas in particular—"the experience of our times, which is the mother of all things." The accumulated information and traditional wisdom collected by the classical geographers on the Old World is supplemented by the universal mother of the sciences, the experience of current times (that experience which Vespucci had already found preferable to theory), providing direct knowledge of the New World.

3. DYNASTIC AIMS AND THESES

The aims of the *Suma de Geographía* were still almost exclusively practical. It was to serve first of all as a guide to pilots and navigators and as instruction to the young and ignorant Charles V. The first aspect comes out clearly when Enciso is dealing with hurricanes—how they are formed, how they are more violent in the torrid zone, and how shipwreck can be avoided—and concludes that "the lack of acquaintance with these things has been the cause of the loss of many ships in the West Indies, that are within the torrid zone" (1546 ed., viii^r–ix^v).

As for the second, he ingratiatingly if somewhat tactlessly informs the emperor that his "tender years . . . have not allowed him a chance to read the books that speak of geography," and that for this very reason, for his instruction, so that "he may study geography" (as Boris Godunov would say), he has composed his book, writing it in Castilian so that it will be accessible to a greater number of readers.

---

6. I could suggest—though this would be pure conjecture—identifying the less well known of the authors cited as follows: "Historia Bactriana" could be a derivation of the widely known *Roman d'Alexandre* or of the *Historia de Proeliis;* the "two Ptolemies"—Ptolemy Lagida (died 283 B.C.), author of a *History of Alexander,* and the famous astronomer Claudius Ptolemy (2nd century A.D.); "Eratosthenes" of Cyrene (3rd century B.C.), author of a *Geography;* "Josephus"—Flavius, the Jewish historian; "Anselm," probably referring to the scriptural commentaries of Anselm of Laon (died 1117); the Bible is recalled by the land of Ophir, whence Solomon brought the gold for the temple (1546 ed., pp. viii^r and l-bis^r) and a long digression on sacred history from Adam to Jesus (1546 ed., pp. xliii^r–xliv^v); the "General History" is the *General estoria* of Alfonso the Wise (written ca. 1272–84), which contains copious geographical details and was widely read up until the sixteenth century (Sánchez Alonso, *Historiografía española,* I, 263–66, who also asserts, p. 266n104, that "the last work in which one can see traces of its reading is El Tostado's *Comentario sobre Eusebio* [1506–07]," whereas Enciso's *Suma* actually dates from 1519).

There is a further allusion to Charles's youth at the end of the dedication, where it is even more tactlessly stressed with the image of Alexander the Great held up as an example to the nineteen-year-old monarch, "that great Alexander of Macedon, who began his conquests at the age of seventeen years and passed away at thirty-two," and who was accustomed to say that men of noble stock and royal heart "have not to seek to live well and long, but to die honestly and gloriously."[7] And it was precisely this heroico-elegiac maxim that the young Charles was to bear in mind "for the things to come and the things past." But a few lines further on Enciso, possibly realizing that such insistence might strike the melancholy Charles as a bad omen, or else forgetting the harsh injunctions of the Macedonian ruler, expresses his hopes for the prosperity of the king and the Spanish monarchy "to whom may God grant long life and a long reign." . . .

A more interesting element in the same dedication is a politico-dynastic thesis which Peter Martyr had already sketched out and which Oviedo would later enrich and develop. Charles is the heir, not only of the Roman Empire (it was actually in that same year, 1519, that he was elected emperor of the Holy Roman Empire), but of the mythical dominions of Jason and Hercules, and those of the Goths and of King Pelayo. He has more provinces and kingdoms than any of these powerful rules had, more than Alexander, more than Rome itself, at the beginning of their conquests. He is therefore clearly predestined by heaven to rule over the whole world, including the non-Christian peoples. Let His Majesty make haste to conquer it, because it is rightfully his, and let him not be beaten to it by the king of Portugal! (1546 ed., viii^r, xlv^v). He is starting out from such an advantageous position that he must exploit it for his own glory and the glory of Spain—already the richest and most blessed peninsula of Europe (1546 ed., xxvi^r)—and for the good of the true faith. The old dream of a universal monarchy is now bolstered up with strategical or, as we would say today, geopolitical arguments, and with a hefty portion of those genealogical and hereditary claims so welcome to Charles because they gave his pretensions to dominion over the two worlds a legitimacy independent of papal donations and the costly votes of the electors (see below, chap. XVIII, sec. 11).

From this point of view the *Suma de Geographía* is an inventory of everything belonging to Charles, de facto and de jure, and the detailed program of his forthcoming conquests and annexations. It is a guidebook and memorandum on worldwide expansion. It even includes a minute world map ("a figure in flat" or,

---

7. The Macedonian is Enciso's favorite hero; he is constantly referring to him and portrays him in idealized terms (1546 ed., p. xxiv^v). For Enciso, Alexander was not even Macedonian, whatever his teacher Aristotle says, but Spanish, no less, and from Cordova, the illustrious city that also produced Avicenna, Averroes, Lucan, Seneca, "our own Juan de Mena," and of course the Great Captain "who conquered Naples" (ibid., p. xxv^v) . . . "the best city in Italy after Rome" (ibid., p. xxxii^v). But shortly before it was Milan that was "the greatest city in Italy" (ibid., p. xxxii^r)!

in modern parlance, two-dimensional) with all the lands of the universe seen and known "from authentic writings"—a map which to the jaundiced eyes of those of us who witnessed two world wars seems to be the progenitor of all those other maps where one encroaching and dominating color indicates the future boundaries, the sphere of influence, or the living space of one or another "great power." Enciso's map[8] and its explanatory text give full details of frontiers, routes, latitudes and longitudes, mountains and rivers and the provinces through which they flow, "and the quality of the people of each province and their laws or sects, and the fruits and things and metals found in each one." All that Charles has left to do is to "decide" what is most seemly for the service of God and His Majesty, "for the discovery and conquest of the lands" still held by the heathen.

4. The riches of the Indies

In the description of the Indies, however, the imperialistic aim gives way to an overwhelming interest in the lands and islands already occupied. The fauna, flora, and peoples of America represent, for Enciso, a familiar reality with its own intrinsic importance. Even the gold and the pearls, even the coveted spices take up no more of the short tract than the minimum that could not decently be denied to such conspicuous and appetizing characteristics of the New Indies. Enciso, who was avid for gold, seems to be dissatisfied when it has only ten or twelve carats (xxviii) or is mixed with silver or copper (xxiv). On the Island of Pearls he even saw one pearl, with his own eyes, "shaped like a wild pear, the best and biggest I ever saw" (xxix, cf. xxii), but he never seeks to dazzle his readers or the sovereign or the treasure-hunters with the normal eulogies of those riches. "I repeat what I was told" is his usual formula. A cacique that he took prisoner (xxv) said that "lumps of gold as big as eggs" were fished out of the Cenú River. At the springs of the Dabaine River "they say that there are great mines, but the truth of the matter is not known, beyond what the Indians say and the fact that pieces of fine gold weighing seven or eight pounds have been found in the Indians' possession" (xxviii—modest and believable figures). In Uraba there is gold "but as there has not been much looking there as yet, one does not know" (xxviii). In the islands of the South Sea "there is much gold and pearls, according to what the Indians say" (xxx). And even in Cartagena there is gold, "although not so very much, and they [the Indians] say that twenty leagues away to the southwest there is a lot of gold and that anybody who is looking for it should go there" (xxiv; cf. xvii, etc.).

The metallic gleam of the Indies was obviously already fading, although it would not be very long before Mexico and Peru revived it to burn a hundred

---

8. Puente y Olea writes: "We do not know whether it [the map] still exists" (op. cit., p. 101). But see Amando Melón, "Del portulano de Juan de la Cosa a la carta plana de Martín Fernández de Enciso." *RI*, 10 (1950), 811–15.

times brighter. And the Indians had already learned that ingenuous (and, for the purposes of discovery, extremely fruitful) trick of sending the Christians off to seek gold "a little further on," a good twenty leagues away from their own land.

In his actual dealings with the natives (who are numerous, he insists, contradicting the ancient theory of the uninhabitability of the tropics), Enciso was certainly anything but benevolent. He defended the rights of the conquistadors, firmly opposed the protests of Las Casas and the Dominicans,[9] and always upheld the legitimacy of the war against the idolators, the justice of killing them if they resisted and enslaving them if they were captured. but when he is describing their acts and customs he betrays a sort of half-felt sympathy, a reluctant propensity for kindness, an effort to be objective, and an unruffled certainty of their humanity and possession of at least some virtues.

5. THE *REQUERIMIENTO*

Enciso's comments on the *requerimiento* typify this. The *requerimiento* was, of course, the juridical summons addressed to the Indians, enjoining them to recognize the Holy Trinity, the Son's investiture of the pontiff, the pontiff's granting of the Indies to the kings of Castile and hence the legitimate sovereignty of these kings and their successors over all the Indian lands and islands; a summons which, if rejected, endowed the Spaniards' slaughters and violent conquests with the character of a just war.[10]

This extraordinary concatenation (or, to be more accurate, rigmarole) of theological and juridical arguments, of dogma and papal bulls, biblical tradition and political privilege, read out in Castilian, was supposed to be understood and accepted by the half-naked Indians. . . . And it was no less a person then Enciso himself who claimed to have invented the *requerimiento,* which was given legal form by the jurist Palacios Rubios.

Idolaters, he had said in 1513, have no right to the lands they possess. Certainly God gave Adam the whole earth so that he might enjoy the fruits thereof, but the idolators, disavowing the sole true God, committed such a sin of ingratitude that they "lost the earth." It was lost by those idolators who were

9. See the document dating from 1528, in Medina, *Descripción,* pp. viii–ix, where one of Enciso's boasts is that he served the emperior "in twice defending the Indies against the Dominicans," and where he expresses himself in favor of the Franciscans, who (we will recall) at first "worked at the court . . . against the freedom of the Indians" and persecuted the archibishop of Granada for the "spirit of tolerance and moderation exemplified by that virtuous man" (Humboldt, *Examen critique,* III, 299–300; cf. Angel Rosenblat, *La población indígena de América desde 1492 hasta la actualidad* [Buenos Aires, 1945], p. 101). For Las Casas's acquaintance with Enciso's work, see Salas, op. cit., p. 226.

10. We shall come back to the *requerimiento* when discussing Oviedo's ideas on the subject—see below, chap. XIX, secs. 21–24. E. Bullón, *El dr. Palacios Rubios* (Madrid, 1927), says absolutely nothing at all about Enciso's claims to have invented and tested the instrument. Zavala too, in *Las instituciones jurídicas en la conquista de América* (Madrid, 1945), p. 91n, gives a date of 1513 for the *requerimiento;* cf. idem, "La doctrina del dr. Palacios Rubios sobre la conquista de América," in *La "Utopía" de Tomás Moro en la Nueva España y otros estudios* (Mexico, 1937), pp. 31–43, and "Las doctrinas de Palacios Rubios y Matías de Paz," *Memoria del Colegio Nacional,* 5 (1951), 71–94, and 6 (1952), 67–159.

conquered by Joshua in just war, and lost by those other wayward sons of Adam who worship so many different gods in the Indies.

The new lay argument, that they possessed their lands "by the right of peoples," was dismissed by Enciso as "frivolous and without foundation." Their ingratitude to God deprives them of any subjective legal entitlement. To take their land away from them it was therefore unnecessary to have "any other reason than the fact that they were idolators." When the expedition of Pedrarias Dávila was being prepared, this argument "was held to be so good" that the formidable document was drafted without further ado—"the *requerimiento* was drawn up in writing"—and given to Pedrarias like some sort of "secret weapon" or magic talisman bestowing an aura of sanctity on his imminent conquests, "and off he went with it." Nor did Enciso confine himself to playing the crucial editorial role of which he was so proud. He was also the first, he claims, to test its effectiveness: "The first time this formula was used it was I myself that addressed the *requerimiento* to the caciques of the region of Catarapa, in the port of Cenú."[11]

But the inventor and first tester of that powerful ultimatum fails to mention in his memorandum what reception it was accorded by those caciques. He did in fact have good reason for omitting that detail in a review of the instrument's merits. . . . The caciques' reply had however been related by Enciso in his *Suma de Geographía,* in a passage of extraordinary frankness, a passage in which the immediate spontaneous truth of his actual experience prevails over the lawyer's vanity and the official's claims, in which the sympathy of the man inclines visibly, and with a certain scandalous delight, toward the enemy, the idolator, the rebel. The caciques reply that they find the idea of a single God fair enough but that the papal donation was a hoax: "The Pope must have been drunk when he did it, because he gave away what was not his to give; and . . . the king who asked and took this favor must have been some sort of madman, because he was asking for something belonging to someone else." Let the king come and take this "favor" for himself, let him come forward and they will stick his head on the top of a pole, "as they had done with some of their other enemies, whose heads they showed me stuck up on top of poles near that village." They were the lords of the land, and "they had no need of any other lord."

Enciso, with a sidelong glance at those macabre trophies, threatens them again with war and enslavement. But their reply remains unchanged and indeed becomes even more specific. The caciques warn "that I would be the first person to find my head on top of a pole" and immediately seek to translate their words

---

11. "Memorial que dio el bachiller Enciso de lo ejecutado por él en defensa de los reales derechos, en la materia de los Indios," in *CDII,* I, 441–50. This document is tentatively dated 1526 by Medina (*Descubrimiento,* I, 289*n64*) and probably prior to 1529 by Zavala (*Las instituciones jurídicas,* p. 92*nl*).

into acts. A scuffle ensues, two Spaniards are killed by poisoned arrows,[12] but the Indians are overcome. One of their caciques is captured, and Enciso concludes nobly: "I found him a man of much truth and a man who kept his word and a person who could see bad as bad and good as good." One can almost see Enciso offering his hand to the defeated enemy, and there is an unmistakable hint of a sigh of bitterness in the immediately following words, with which he closes the episode: "And this is more of less the way all wars are conducted there" (xxvi). . . .

6. SYMPATHY FOR THE NATIVES

One might be tempted to suspect, somewhat unkindly, that Enciso also wanted to use this story to show how perversely heretical and stubbornly heathen the Indians were (and indeed Las Casas rushed to their defense).[13] But the suspicion proves unfounded, in view of other examples of intellectual goodwill toward the natives. Enciso reveals at the very least an ironical amiability in respect of the local population, "good people, although naked" (xv). Some other Indians, that "wear their hair cut short, with tonsures like monks," are described—possibly with a hint of sarcasm toward the Spaniards—as "good people, that do no harm to those that they meet, if those others do not harm them first" (xxiii). (A positive and embryonic form of the famous saying, "Cet animal est trés méchant: quand on l'attaque il se défend").

Enciso even seeks information about the abhorred cannibals[14] and learns how they fatten up their prisoners before eating them and—a detail whose utility to Charles it is difficult to see, although he was a notorious glutton—"the most tasty morsel, so they say, is the fingers, and the lean of the man's loins" (xviii). The conjugal customs and funeral rites are described without any intention of sarcasm or ridicule, indeed with a careful attention to what the Indians do and the reasons that they give for doing it. Thus Enciso tells us at great length about the

12. One of the two Spaniards killed was Diego de Bustamante. The episode occurred in 1514 or 1515 (Medina, *Descubrimiento,* I, 148).
13. Enciso's story did in fact cause quite a scandal. It was reported by Las Casas (*Historia de las Indias,* II, 63 [Madrid, 1875], III, 6–8), López de Gómara (*Historia general de las Indias* [Saragossa, 1552], III, 19), Montaigne (*Essasis,* III, 6, ed. cit., pp. 876–77), Herrera, *Historia general de los hechos de los castellanos* (dec. II, bk. i, chap. 2), and later Washington Irving (*The Life and Voyages of Christopher Columbus* [New York and London: Putnam, n.d.], IV, 297–99), who recognizes that the natives' reply contained "something of natural logic." The Mexican patriot Fray Servando Teresa de Mier also admired the Indians' firm response: "No monarch, theologian or scholar could have given such a sound reply" (José Guerra [Mier's pseudonym], *Historia de la revolución de Nueva España* [London, 1813], I, 344n; and, with variations, in his *Escritos inéditos* [Mexico, 1944], pp. 254–56). Las Casas first of all uses the anecdote as pretext for a violent outburst against Enciso—"out of your own mouth, oh bachelor Enciso, I judge you"—but then goes on to question its authenticity, because the Indians could not possibly have understood the *requerimiento* and could not therefore have been guilty of the blasphemy against pope and king, "and thus I doubt that the Indians said these things of the pope or the king" (*Historia de las Indias,* loc, cit.). Cf. also Medina, *Descubrimiento,* I, 112n.
14. Elsewhere Enciso remains unmoved as he writes about the Scythian cannibals (1546 ed., p. xxxviiʳ) and even the "sick" crusaders following Godfrey of Bouillon "who ate the meat of the Moors they killed" (ibid., p. xviiʳ).

Indians' devotion to the Virgin Mary, whom they see first of all as a sort of helper to the Christian cacique, or as a "very beautiful woman, who came to help him with a stick, and beat them all to death," but whom in the end they recognize as *true Goddess,* "and when they saw that, they said that Saint Mary was a good cacique," . . . extending their zeal as neophytes to the point of obliging every Christian they met to recite the Ave Maria, whether he felt like it or not: "And they took me myself, and I said it to them many times and stayed with them three days." [15]

In the same way he refers good-humoredly to the way some of the Indians mangle the Spanish language (xxviii)[16] and observes amiably that the Indians of the Yucayas "are not very black" and that some of their women "are well disposed" (xxi). In Venezuela "the people are very well disposed, and there are more comely women than there are in other parts of that same land" (xxii), while in Cartagena the women and the men, all "well-disposed persons," all equally naked, fight equally bravely. "I captured a girl some eighteen or twenty years old, who was said by everybody to have killed eight Christian men" (xxiv)—but Enciso discreetly refrains from saying if and how he avenged his comrades at the expense of the bellicose maiden.

Even more unusual, for that time, is Enciso's high regard for the natives' mental capacities. We have already seen an example of this in the case of the *requerimiento.* In Santa María he admires the gaily colored cotton fabrics ("they are something to see"), and even more the astonishing garments made of woven feathers, more beautiful than any European artifact, "some like great diadems, that the women put on their heads and that reach down to their waists, like the ribbons on a bishop's mitre; and it is all so well worked, that it is a marvel to see the diversity of the colors and the work and art of it all, and as the colors are natural and proper, they stand out so well that no artificial work of the sort that is done in Europe, is so good or so agreeable to the sight" (xxiii). Finally, the closing words of the description of the West Indies contain a precise prophecy of the imminent discovery of the more advanced Mexican civilization: toward the Pacific, beyond the islands rich in gold and pearls "there is a land where, according to the Indians, there are people who have books and who write and read like us." [17]

---

15. Pp. xx–xxi. Magellan too, when attempting to convert the king of Zubu, told him that among the many advantages he would enjoy as a Christian there was the fact that he would vanquish his enemies more easily! (A. Pigafetta, *Primer viaje en torno del globo,* trans. F. R. Morcuende [Madrid, 1922], p. 103). This popularized version of *In hoc signe vinces* was therefore quite usual. The story of the Virgin-cacique is also given by Peter Martyr, who was told it personally by Enciso (*Dec.,* II, 6, published three years before the *Suma*); but the humanist addressing the pope gives a refined and embellished version that has none of the realism of the original. Edification gets the better of ethnography and Enciso's crude sketch pales into a pious tinted image.

16. See also Oviedo on the "yras" and "yrachas" (*Hist.,* XXIX, 27: III, 134a).

17. P. xxx. "To the Northwest of the end of Cuba," he had written, "there appeared a large land, which they believe to be the mainland" (p. xxi).

7. NATURE AND EXPERIENCE

If in many of these references, and particularly in certain basic attitudes, Enciso must be seen as a precursor of Oviedo, in the descriptions of animals and plants he remains a long way behind the *alcaide* of Santo Domingo. It is not that he lacks interest or the requisite graphic skills. Whenever he interrupts the details of nautical distances and compass points, capes and gulfs, whenever, so to speak, he steps ashore and observes the animals and the plants, and the men too, Enciso provides us with some lively and colorful sketches and notes. Nor does he lack the experimental spirit, the willingness to interrogate nature directly, instead of simply absorbing its voice and song. Enciso can write, as could Oviedo so much more frequently: "I put this to the test" (xxiii).

But his interest in nature is desultory, sporadic, and inclined toward the picturesque and sensational. He is never far away from the land of fable, as for instance when he is describing the mythical Amazons (1546 ed., xxxvii^v, xxxviii^v), or the Arabian phoenix (ibid., xlii^r), or the loquacious and prodigious hyena, that is female one year and male the next and has in its eyes a stone called "hyena" which, if placed under the tongue, confers prophetic powers—"and the magicians use these."[18]

This does not mean, however, that Enciso is ready to believe anything. In the island of Meroe, beyond the equinoctial line, he says curiously, "there are many monsters and men with heads of dogs, although this is not to be believed" (a little like the person who said of the evil eye, "I don't believe it myself, but it does exist"), not because the thing itself is impossible but because Christians and Moors coming from those parts say that "they heard nothing about it" (ibid., liv). In Cirenaica, on the other hand, "they say that there are men without heads, and other with heads of dogs"; however, this too "is not to be believed" (ibid., l^r).

Empiricism takes precedence over eyewitnesses, whether they exist or not. . . . For example, little faith is to be attached to the merchants who went adventuring beyond India (Marco Polo? 1546 ed., lix^v).[19]

Thus the experiment to which he refers (xxiii) relates to that legendary tree whose shade causes headaches and later a swelling of the face, and even blinds anybody who falls asleep in the shade: "All of this I have seen myself by experience." Enciso picked a few "apples" from this tree, fed them to a dog and when the dog died four hours later, had it "opened up to see the effect of the

---

18. P. 1: characteristics that come straight out of the medieval bestiaries. Cf., for example, the Cambridge Bestiary (12th century).

19. Likewise he says of England that "it was peopled by giants," conquered and driven out by the Trojan Brutus, and that there were trees there with leaves that turned into fish when they fell into the water and into birds when they fell on dry land (1546 ed., p. xxv^v). In Sicily too "there were giants" that Jove plunged into Etna (p. xxxiii^r; reminiscences of Enceladus? See also pp. xxxvii^v and xliv^r). Then in Greece there was a miraculous fountain where flaming torches were put out and unlighted torches burst into flame (p. xxxiv^v).

apple," finding that "the whole thing had turned to worms in the body" (xxiii).[20]
When questioned by Peter Martyr,[21] Enciso reported that the bite of the Darien
bats was not poisonous, as he knew by experience himself, having been bitten on
the heel once when he left it uncovered because of the heat, and that he had found
by experience that sea water and cauterization with fire cured the wounds caused
by poisoned arrows. But his experience of America also serves as an interpretative criterion for other lands. In seeking the cause of the Nile floods he
thinks that he has found the answer in the tropical rains, "as is shown clearly by
the experience in the lands of the West Indies and Castile the Golden . . . of
which I myself have had experience" (1546 ed., xlvii^v).

8. The fauna of Darien

His best descriptive effort is reserved for the fauna of Darien. With good
reason New Granada historian Fray Pedro Simón refers anyone seeking further
details on Darien to Herrera, Gómara, "and Enciso himself, who also wrote
about this and better than anybody else, having been there himself."[22] Enciso
was in fact the first to penetrate those regions and takes an obvious delight in
depicting them as swarming with savage, strange, and dangerous beasts. "There
are many tigers and lions, and other different animals and tailed cats, which are
like monkeys except that they have big tails; there are lots of pigs; there are some
animals as big as cows, and fleshy, and brown in color, which have feet and
hands like cows, heads like mules and big ears; in this country they call them
mocha cows."[23] "Some people told me that they had seen lynxes, however I
myself never saw any." What he did see were lizards (caymans? or alligators?) as
big as "bullocks" and with dorsal scales so tough that ten lances bounced off
them as if off a rock. One of them was eventually despatched—"I myself
succeeded in killing the first that was killed," he says, although in fact it was one
of his servants who stabbed it under its belly—and after Enciso and his men had
gazed awestruck at its formidable double line of teeth, it was quartered, cooked,
and eaten.

The lions and tigers too are edible. One man by himself is sufficient to kill a
lion. The tigers are bigger "and have very robust arms and great strength; but
they are heavy, run very little, and are faint of heart." On one occasion a man
became aware that a tiger was following him, "and the man just kept walking
along, and the tiger followed some three or four lance-lengths behind, for a

20. Jean Mallart was still repeating the legend in the middle of the century in the doubly aggravated version that
anyone who ate the fruit of the tree died devoured by worms and anyone who dozed off in its shade went mad (Le
Moine, op. cit., p. 146).

21. *Dec.*, II, 4.

22. Fray Pedro Simón, *Noticias historiales de las conquistas de tierra firme en las Indias Occidentales* (1626–27;
Bogotá, 1892), III, 365; cf. ibid., pp. 353, 363–65. Simón, however, seems to refer to Enciso as a historical source, as
a chronicler of the Darien achievements.

23. According to A. Cardoso ("Nuestros conocimientos en ciencias naturales durante la Epoca colonial,"
Humanidades, 11 [1925], p. 345) these were tapirs.

whole league, without daring to attack the man" (xxvii). The image thus created—of an American tiger that is not fleet of foot, as Pliny says it should be, and is cowardly, against all the rules—was of course destined to become a commonplace of New World historiography.

The iguanas, the turkeys, the little green parrots and big ones of all colors, red and blue and black and green, "beautiful to behold," the other little birds likewise green "and very pretty," the fish and the armadillos,[24] the rabbits "which enter the houses to breed," and the partridges complete this extraordinary fauna, some examples of which we rediscover, with Enciso, in other parts of Central America, such as the tigers and lions, against which stockades are built so that "they may not enter by night in amongst the houses," and the "many different birds of this land, and hens like geese with very pretty wattles" (xxiv).

Of the animals of other places in the Indies, Enciso gives somewhat summary information. Passing reference is made to some green parrots of Paria, and a yellow-breasted variety of the same, that "soon learn to speak and speak a lot" (xvii), to the prolific and contented cattle of Hispaniola (xix), and the large numbers of pigs and stags of Paria (xxiii).

9. THE EDIBLE FLORA

But when it comes to the plants Enciso is more lavish with detail, particularly as regards plants that represent a potential source of food. The potatoes (xvii, xix), the highly perfumed *piñas* ("when there is one of these in a room it fills the whole house with its smell")[25] and other fruits, the meal-producing root crops, the maize and "the bread and wine" obtained therefrom—the bread of good quality and the wine substantial and tasty—all claim the political geographer's attention. The things one can live on and the things one dies from mark the limits of his botanical curiosity. Thus Enciso notes that the Indians of the Yucayas, being accustomed to eat only fish and roots and grass shoots, "die if they are taken to other parts and given meat to eat, unless the meat is only very little" (xxi)—an original dietary observation that was later to be used by Humboldt.[26]

---

24. Enciso's description (p. xxvii) is briefer, but does not differ from Oviedo's (*Hist.*, XI, 23: 1, 411–12). Where Enciso says that it "looked like an armored horse," Oviedo more longwindedly writes that "there is none [no animal] to which they can be compared except armored horses," etc.

25. Would they have been pineapples or avocados or something else, that miraculous fruit that became yellow when ripe, and inside was "like butter, and of marvelous flavor, and leaving such a good and delicate taste that it is quite marvelous"? (1546 ed., pp. liv-bis^v).

26. "An observation that confirms what I have developed elsewhere on the lack of flexibility of the physical constitution of uncivilized man" (*Examen critique*, III, 173n). The same observation was made by François Coréal, in his *Voyages aux Indes Occidentales . . . depuis 1666 jusqu'en 1697* (Paris, 1722), I, 117, which in turn provided Jean Jacques Rousseau (*Discours sur l'inégalite*, in *Oeuvres* [Pléiade ed., Paris, 1959–69], III, 199) with a source for vegetarian and pacifist corollaries. On Coréal, already attacked by Eguiara y Eguren, op. cit., pp. 218–19, see the hostile R. Carbia, *Historia de la leyenda negra hispano-americana* (Buenos Aires, 1943), pp. 101–03.

Humboldt also quotes Enciso in connection with the Sierra Nevada de Santa Marta (*Examen critique*, IV, 295n; for the passage cited see p. xxiii), and the villages of Venezuela, which according to Enciso were the only ones "in all the West Indies" in which there had been found weights (for gold) and thus, Humboldt infers, represented "so many little

Only by way of exception does he mention other plants of varying usefulness, such as cotton, which is used to make the cloths mentioned above, and the hammocks (xvii, xxv), or the tall reeds that are used to make sticks, which are exported from Trinidad even to Spain (xvii), of the incense which is used for their religious ceremonies. The incense trees grow on a hill near the Marañón, in the depths of the equatorial forest. But the association of ideas, perhaps, or the memory of Christmas services and celebrations back among the frosts of Castile, inspire this touching and delicate description: "The trees are high and the branches like plum trees, with the incense suspended from them like ice from the roofs when it snows in winter in the mountains" (xvi). The lacework of the icicles hanging down from the eaves glitters for a moment in the tepid dampness of the Amazon forest.

10. ENCISO AND OVIEDO

How is it that Oviedo, who is so unstinting with his erudite citations, never mentions Enciso's work? Not even in book XXI, where he is describing the coastline of America in minute detail and naming pilots and geographers — Alonso de Santa Cruz, Alonso de Chávez, Diego Rivera, Antón de Alaminos, Esteban Gómez, and the first voyages of Ojeda (1501) — and "other cosmographers" and a "modern map" (which must be that of Alonso de Chávez),[27] does he mention the *Suma de Geographía,* which — albeit imperfectly — had provided the first vital description and which for a whole generation remained "a traveling companion for those sailing in the Indies."[28] Could Oviedo, who was in Seville in that very year 1519 and remained there until April 1520, possibly have missed the book that had just emerged from the presses of Jacobo Kromberger? The book which was reprinted in 1530 by that same Kromberger who would five years later be bringing out the first part of Oviedo's own *Historia?* The book by a man whom Oviedo had certainly known and who was indeed (Medina writes) "a close friend of his,"[29] although he pours scorn on his disastrous illusion that in Cenú there were "vast treasures of gold";[30] whose practical activities (1508–1509) are amply detailed in his *Historia;*[31] and whom he men-

---

centers of civilization and commerce" (ed. cit., p. xxii; *Examen critique,* IV, 306–07). Humboldt's overall view (ibid.) of the *Suma* is that it is "a very remarkable work."

W. George mentions Enciso for his accurate description of the iguana (op. cit., p. 66), the armadillo (p. 69), the tapir (pp. 74, 77), the Indian rhinoceros (p. 130) and the anteater (p. 132).

27. Cf. *Hist.,* XXI, 7 and 11: II, 139b, 150b.

28. Pereyra, *Los conquistadores,* p. 78.

29. Medina, *Descubrimiento,* I, 289. See in fact Oviedo, *Hist.,* XXIX, 17: PT, III, 277 ("he was my friend").

30. *Hist.,* XXIX, 10: PT, III, 247–48; XXIX, 33, sec. 15: PT, III, 346.

31. *Hist.,* XXVII, 4: II, 425–28; XXVIII, 3: II, 472a, 474, 477b; XXIX, I: III, 4a; XXIX, 2: III, 6a; XXIX, 5: III, 21a; XXIX, 6: III, 24a; XXIX, 10: III, 51a. Oviedo does not even mention Enciso when he is talking about the foundation of Santa María de la Antigua and the conquests of Rodrigo de Bastidas (XXI, 6: II, 134b), but he does mention and praise his founding of the city of Darien (VI, 47: PT, I, 207), and his relationship with Ojeda and Balboa — who took a severe dislike to him, see above, sec. 2 (*Hist.,* XXVII, 4: PT, III, 141–43; XXVIII, 4: PT, III, 180–82 and 185). On Enciso as conquistador see also Peter Martyr, *Dec.,* II, 1–4, 6–7; some vivid passages in Irving, op. cit., IV, 218ff, 287ff; and Medina, *Descubrimiento,* I, 33–50, 70–72, 109–10, 116, 148, 288–90, 300.

tions also as the source of one of Peter Martyr's numerous errors?[32] Even if there were no internal indications (e.g., the pineapple, below, Appendix C) it seems highly likely that Oviedo would have come across one or another of the three editions of the *Suma de Geographía* published during the years in which he was working on the same subject. "Oviedo," Turner insists, "must have owned a copy of his *Suma*."[33]

His silence is thus almost certainly intentional. His claim to be the first historian in the Indies, a claim to which he attached so much importance, was to some extent undermined by the existence, already in 1519, of a *Suma* predating his *Sumario* of 1526, whose second edition (1530) again forestalled Oviedo's *Historia* of 1535, and the third edition of which (1546) came out a year before the new and more complete edition of Oviedo's major work (1547). Moreover Enciso was a lawyer, a member of that profession detested and condemned by Oviedo, but a person who had undeniably *seen* what he recounted; he was also a man of broad education, while Oviedo secretly recognized and regretted the inadequacy of his own literary studies.

Factors such as these must have counted for a great deal in a man of Oviedo's nature, but if they are not felt to be an adequate explanation of the omission one can perhaps find other more recondite grounds for personal hostility. Neither Enciso nor Oviedo was the sort of person to forget an injury or forgo revenge for a wrong suffered. Oviedo's grudges are proverbial: suffice it to recall his unrelenting and malevolent persecution of Vasco Núñez de Balboa.[34] In 1528[35] or 1529 Enciso had Diego del Corral and his ex-companion-in-arms, Francisco Pizarro, thrown into debtors' prison;[36] and he fills his memoranda with accusations and insinuations.

No less than three times in his petition of 1528 the hidalgo Enciso bewails the fact that the governorship of Santa Marta has been given to a person "to whom the Holy Inquisition does not give offices" and whom he himself does not name, and he recalls his own services and merits and pecuniary sacrifices.[37] Now in 1524 the king had appointed Rodrigo de Bastidas governor of Santa Marta[38]

---

32. *Hist.*, XVII, 4: I, 499a. Enciso apparently recounted to Martyr "marvels of the devotion and conversion of a cacique of Cuba who was called the Commander, and of his people." But Oviedo is suspicious: "I have heard nothing at all about that . . . and I doubt it."

33. D. Turner, "Biblioteca Ovetense," p. 167, no. 53.

34. Medina, *Descubrimiento*, I, 288.

35. M. J. Quintana, "Vida de Pizarro," in *Obras Completas* (Madrid, 1897–98), II, 342.

36. Navarrete, quoted by Medina, *Descubrimiento*, I, vii. Medina notes Enciso's stubborn determination in collecting his dues and asserting his claims over sixteen years (ibid., I, 73n17; cf. I, 290).

37. Medina (*Descubrimiento*, I, 290) supposes that Enciso meant the Germans, who had been given other concessions and whom he *feared* might also be given the governorship of Santa Marta. This could easily be true. But another conjecture is perhaps admissible, particularly since in his petition Enciso speaks as if that desirable post had already been filled. Certainly it was *not* in fact awarded to the Germans. And who did get it . . . ?

See Oviedo, *Hist.*, XXV, 17: II, 316–17, on the granting of a Venezuela governorship bordering Santa Marta (ca. 1538) to the German "Fedreman" (Nikolaus Federmann), which was immediately revoked because of the protests of the cardinal of Sigüenza, a decision being taken shortly thereafter "not to allow any German to govern personally in these parts."

38. Oviedo, *Hist.*, XXVI, 2: II, 336a.

although some twenty years earlier he had been arrested by Bobadilla—that same Bobadilla who had had Columbus thrown into chains—and, together with the Admiral, he had been sent back a prisoner to Spain where their Catholic Majesties ordered him to be set free and indemnified. The cause of his arrest, according to Oviedo, was that "having made his way to this city by land as soon as he escaped from the sea, he traded for gold with the Indians along the way."[39]

But it is curious that precisely when he is recounting the career of Bastidas, Oviedo should twice remark that then, in 1508, in contrast to the situation at the time he is writing (1548), the Catholic Kings sought to populate the Indies by allowing "criminals and base persons" to go there.[40] Could Bastidas have been the person whom the Inquisition would not have employed?[41] Certainly Enciso must have known him very well, because it was with Rodrigo de Bastidas that he made his first crossing from Spain to the New World.[42]

Oviedo, however, always speaks rather favorably of Bastidas (to whom he also became related by marriage when he gave his daughter's hand in marriage to the nephew of the son of Don Rodrigo, bishop of San Juan, also bearing the same name, Don Rodrigo de Bastidas), praising him as a good colonist, a good governor, and great philanthropist.[43] "Bastidas and I were friends," he says.[44] It was actually during the time he was governor of Santa Marta that Bastidas unwisely invaded the neighboring governorship of Cartagena, which had been granted to Oviedo (who had requested it when Santa Marta, initially offered to him, had been given to Bastidas, "because I knew that it [Cartagena] was as good or better").[45] Oviedo, not normally a person to pass up the chance of a few pennies, never insisted on claiming for damages. Why? Because, he says, Bastidas's heir, the bishop of Venezuela and later of San Juan, was "so noble and reverend a person and my neighbor in this city of Santo Domingo, a person not to be vexed but served," and also because both he and Bastidas were good friends

---

39. Ibid., p. 335a. This was a serious offence. Enciso himself, during his governorship of Darien, "forbade all trafficking with natives for gold, on private account, under pain of death" (Irving, op. cit., IV, 304).

40. *Hist.*, XXVI, 2: II, 335b, 336b.

41. A further cause of suspicion is that in 1519 the governorship of the island of Trinidad was sought by a person, unnamed by Oviedo, to whom it was almost granted, "and at one time it was said that it had been given him, but since he was a *suspect* person" and there was some doubt as to whether he would keep his promises, it was eventually denied him (*Hist.*, XXVI, 1: II, 333b). Who was this "suspect person?" In 1520 Charles V appointed Rodrigo de Bastidas governor of Trinidad; but Diego Columbus objected, saying that Trinidad had been discovered by his father, and Rodrigo de Bastidas, out of deference, did not press his claim: "He did not insist in the undertaking, because he did not want to offend him" (ibid., XXVI, 2: II, 335–36).

42. Harrisse, *Bibliotheca Americana*, p. 168, citing Herrera, *Historia general*, dec. I, bk. vii, chap. 11; and Medina, *Descubrimiento*, I. 35.

43. *Hist.*, XXVI, 3: II, 344a, and see below, chap. XIX, n. 229. Irving says that Bastidas differed from the majority of the discoverers "by his kind treatment of natives" (op. cit., IV, 196, a feature that endeared him to Las Casas (Medina, *Descubrimiento*, I, 10*n31*), but that cannot have been too welcome to the stern Enciso. With regard to his origins, Irving says only that he was "a wealthy notary of Triana," the maritime suburb of Seville (op. cit., IV, 196). On his career, see Medina, *Descubrimiento*, I, 9–13.

44. Oviedo, *Hist.*, XXVI, 3: II, 338b. On Bishop Rodrigo de Bastidas, XXV, 1: II, 296b; XXV, 20: II, 323b; XXVI, 21: II, 324–28.

45. *Hist.*, XXVI, 3: II, 338a.

and loyal servants to the vicereine of the Indies, "mother of the Admiral Don Luis Colón" (Doña María de Toledo).[46]

Such scruples, like those of Bastidas toward Diego Columbus (see above, n. 41), leave us somewhat skeptical, not to say *suspicious*. . . .

46. Ibid., p. 339b.

❦ X ❦

Hernán Cortés

1. APOLOGETIC AND UTILITARIAN INTENTIONS

THE five letters in which Cortés tells the emperor the story of his discoveries and conquests take us a step backward, though not so much chronologically (they date from 1520–1526) as in the author's attitude to the new lands described. They remind us less of Peter Martyr's keen curiosity and immediate mental sympathy than of Columbus's determined efforts to convince their Catholic Majesties that they made a really good deal when they agreed to fit out his expedition. Cortés does not address himself to a readership of cultivated scholars, but to his superior and sovereign. He never forgets that his addressee is hungry for yet more lands to rule, impatiently awaiting cash donations, always suspicious, and quite capable of breaking any vassal whose loyalty he doubts for a moment. Cortés is so meticulous about recording his expenditure and the debts he has contracted, especially in the later letters,[1] that his whole story sounds like an attempt to justify a hefty bill, to persuade the client that it is not really all that much, seeming to imply that if the sovereign would just like to settle up he will have got a bargain.

The sovereign, in turn, was a man who counted the pennies, as Cortés well knew. His interest in geography was limited to finding the easiest and safest routes to the Spice Islands, and his interest in natural sciences went no further than mines and precious stones and the possibility of the expeditions living off the land, without supplies having to be sent out from Spain. The past and present glories of the Aztec empire lay beyond the mental horizon of Charles V who, as we know, lost no time in melting down the gold artifacts and astonishing sculptures, the splendid and tragic treasures freshly arrived from Mexico. Cortés knows who he is writing to, and if he mentions the cruelty and savagery of his defeated adversaries it is only to provide a better legal claim to conquest; if he makes some passing reference to the wild animals, it is because he knows they

---

1. See for example the *Cartas de Relación* (Madrid, 1940), II, 82, 116, 119, 217, 237. Unless otherwise stated I have quoted from this edition, which follows the classic Gayangos edition (*Cartas y Relaciones de Hernán Cortés al Emperador Carlos V* [Paris, 1866]).

will please the sovereign, both for the picturesque and exotic quality they give his dominions and for their cynegetic value.

Cortés is a soldier and politician to the core of his being. His account consists almost exclusively of warlike exploits and diplomatic cunning. One encounter follows the last with the monotonous frequency of duels in a chivalric epic. And every other day there is the confrontation with the natives, with the attendant persuasions and threats, the hundred times repeated paraphrase of the regulatory *requerimiento,* and the ceaseless efforts to entice messengers, caciques, warriors, or the ruler of Mexico himself into the Spaniards' armed compounds, within the orbit of Charles's empire.

When the conquistador's third letter tells Charles that the city of Temixtitán is "very beautiful" and will make a worthy capital of all the new provinces, the emperor realizes, even before Cortés spells it out, that what he means is that it is a place where the Spaniards will be "very strong and safe and very much masters of the natives and such that they cannot in any way be troubled by them."[2] The city reconstructed by the Spaniards will, within five years (five-year plans are nothing new) "be the most noble and populous city existing in the inhabited world, and with better buildings"; but most of all this new city will be "separate from the natives, because a stretch of water comes between us."[3] When Cortés describes a gulf as "the most beautiful thing in the world," he means that it forms a safe and spacious anchorage.[4]

2. EXCLUSIVELY STRATEGIC CONCERNS

This exclusive utilitarianism—almost completely stifling the bucolic hedonism that surfaces on rare occasions, as in the description of the broad, fresh, beautiful, and gentle "park" of Guastepeque, with its streams and gardens and orchards and "sweet-smelling flowers"[5]—makes it impossible for Cortés to experience the naive astonishment that overwhelmed Columbus when he came face to face with the New World, and in which Peter Martyr happily indulged from the other side of the ocean. Cortés sees things with the cold gaze of the soldier. Even the virgin forest, a stupendous and prodigious sight for every European and especially a Spaniard, the virgin forest so vividly and movingly described by Oviedo, only strikes Cortés because of the tactical difficulty of marching through it in good order, with guides forming the vanguard, and because—a revealing metaphor—"such was the thickness and height of the

---

2. Ed. cit., II, 54; in other words, beautifully capable of withstanding a siege. A province is "a very good thing" when it is well populated and endowed with thriving commerce, abundant foodstuffs, and rich owners of slaves and livestock (ibid., II, 159–60).

3. Ibid., II, 111.

4. Ibid., p. 187.

5. Ibid., I, 210–11.

trees that even if one clambered up them one could not see a cannon shot's distance."[6]

His pursuit of the secrets of the earth follows much the same lines. Cortés proclaims, "I have always wanted to be able to give Your Majesty a very detailed account of all the things of this land";[7] and he sends ten soldiers to discover the "secret" of the river that flows from the volcano Popocatépetl. But even this expedition has a practical and military purpose: the crater of the volcano provides the Spaniards with the sulphur they need to prepare emergency ammunition.[8] And generally speaking, when Cortés talks about "secrets of the earth" he means little-known paths to take the enemy in the rear, seaways that are safe from ambush by pirates, secret hideaways in the mountains or in the indentations of the coastline.[9]

The supreme secret, the most sought after by everyone, is the passage through to the South Sea, the quick, safe way to the Spice Islands. Time and again Cortés relates the efforts he has made, the expeditions he has dispatched, the ships built and launched, the information gathered, the hopes nourished; and at the end of the fifth letter he can still be found promising, like some bold medieval knight, "to discover all the Spice Islands and other islands this way . . . and even to see to it that Your Majesty does not hold the Spice Islands in pawn, like the king of Portugal, but holds them as his own, and the natives of these islands recognize him and serve him as their king and lord and natural master . . . and I agree that if I do not do as I say, Your Majesty should have me punished, as one who has failed to tell his king the truth."[10]

Apart from these special peculiarities of the countries he describes, Cortés almost never shows himself at all inclined to investigate their particular aspects and usages. Indeed he admits that the task is beyond him. To describe the marvels of Temixtitán, the rites and customs of its people and their civil arrangements, "would require spending a lot of time and being a very expert chronicler: I could not tell a hundredth part of what could be said about them."[11] And the Aztec treasures included "such marvellous things that in writing they cannot be indicated or understood, without being seen."[12] Other instances of voluntary and

6. Ibid., II, 146.

7. Ibid., I, 67.

8. Ibid., II, 113. Cf. Oviedo, below, chap. XVIII, nn. 232–34.

9. Ed. cit., II, pp. 104, 160, 187, 246 and passim. On the practical and strategic nature of Cortés's investigations, see also R. Iglesia, *Cronistas e historiadores de la conquista de México: El ciclo de Hernán Cortés* (Mexico, 1942), p. 60, and the review of a new English translation of the *Cartas* in the *Times Literary Supplement* of 2 February 1973. On Cortés being "basically a showman," see the biography by H. R. Wagner, *The Rise of Hernán Cortés* (Los Angeles, 1944), reviewed *HAHR*, 24 (1944), 619–21. See also, among the endless bibliography, the 615-page special double issue of the *RI*, 8, nos. 31–32 (1948).

10. Ed. cit., II, 244; other allusions in II, 50, 61–62, 86, 115.

11. Ibid., I, 97.

12. Ibid., II, 48. He does not even match the Venetian Contarini's feeble attempt to describe the natives' feather fabrics: "They seem to be of different colors, according to how the light falls, as one sees on a pigeon's neck" (op. cit., p. 53); Contarini also saw "some gold vases . . . very fine and very well worked" (ibid.).

involuntary abdication are not difficult to find; one curious example is the matter of the five great lords sent to him by Cuauhtémoc, whose names, however, "I will not mention here, as they are not very relevant."[13]

3. SUBSTANTIAL CONTRIBUTION TO THE KNOWLEDGE OF AMERICA

If, however, from the *formal* point of view, Cortesian historiography marks no step forward, and indeed in a certain sense a step backward, its *substantial* contribution to the knowledge of America is both vast and spectacular. For the first time Europe is given a description of a land beyond the seas that is radically different from the Antilles and the Tierra Firme: a land, first of all, whose climate is not tropical, whose fauna and flora are therefore, like the climate, considerably less unlike those familiar to the Europeans; a land that is not inhabited, like those hitherto discovered, by savages either timid or fierce, but that is instead the home of an advanced and flourishing civilization rivaling Europe in the level of perfection achieved in certain techniques; a land, finally, whose natives prove to be as pugnacious, intelligent, and even cunning as the cleverest and bravest of the Spaniards.

For the first time, in fact, America wears a countenance similar to Europe's. Cortés lists all these characteristics of Mexico one by one. Perhaps he fails to stress them forcefully enough, with the result that for centuries the features that Mexico (and later Peru) share with the archipelago and the Central American isthmus override the differences; and to the eyes of the far-off Europeans the characteristics of the West Indies and Panama extend to the lands of the Aztecs and Incas. The differences between America and Europe submerge the differences between the various parts of America, just as to the white man's inexperienced eye all Chinese and Negroes resemble one another.

4. MEXICO MATCHED WITH EUROPE . . .

Cortés, however, was obviously fully aware of Mexico's originality as compared with the lands of Central America. This awareness is expressed spontaneously in negative form: "No, the lands of Mexico are not as different from Spain as the Central American lands are." This denial of newness blends in turn with the formal shortcoming already noted in Cortés's attitude. His lack of scientific curiosity and his totally practical interest (formal shortcomings) combine with the richness of the new material, the remarkable civilization of the Mexican state, and the singular mildness of the climate and nature to persuade Cortés that Mexico is almost like Europe, that it can be attached to the other provinces of Charles's empire with no discontinuity, that it is the *New Spain*.

---

13. Ed. cit., II, 41. Iglesia has underlined Cortés's coldness and almost indifference toward things and facts that were truly astonishing (*Cronistas e historiadores*, pp. 18–22); but he gives equal emphasis (p. 23) to Cortés's rapture and amazement at what he found to be the "chimera," the "stupendous illusion" of Mexico.

Cortés is thus the first firm advocate of the equation of Europe and America, the first to believe that it was feasible to measure the New World with a European yardstick and assimilate it in every way to the Old World.[14]

When we come to Oviedo we shall see his constant objections to these convenient identifications. After what we have said at the opening of this section, let it suffice for now to note that the description of America as the equal of Europe reflected a prevailing concern for the practical aspects of conquest, for political and worldly matters; when America was described as different from Europe the prevailing spirit was a scientific concern for exact knowledge, a desire to individualize and define. In the former case Europe's fist closed greedily and possessively round America. In the latter case, the European eye contemplated America, sought out the qualities proper to it, observed it from a distance in order to see it in perspective. In Columbus we saw an alternation of these two approaches; in Peter Martyr antiquity comes in as a third term, to complicate the problem, but the accent falls on the blessed and exemplary newness of the New World. In Cortés, the conquistador, the prevailing theme is the Europeanness or actual Hispanism of America. Oviedo, we repeat was at pains to correct this over-facile equation, identifying each case in which America's nature equaled Europe's and each case in which it was immediately different.

5. . . . IN THE THREE NATURAL KINGDOMS   .

Even in his first letter (1519) Cortés reports delightedly that the land discovered is "very fat and full of beautiful vales and river-meadows, of such quality and beauty that in all Spain there can be no better. . . . This land possesses all sorts of game and animals and birds, similar to those of our nature . . . so that in the way of birds and animals there is no difference between this land and Spain and there are lions and tigers. . . ."[15] It is only natural that all the plants and vegetables of Spain should do marvelously well in such soil. One beautiful valley, "abounding in all things that can be found on earth," is described emphatically as being "very well suited for the raising of all sorts of livestock and growing each and every one of the plants of our nation."[16] If the emperor will have seeds sent out Cortés assures him that in Mexico there will shortly be

---

14. The archetypal American myth of the Amazons strikes a discordant note in this process of rapacious assimilation. What the lords of Ciguatán say about the usual island of the Amazons is simply reported without discussion or acceptance (ed. cit., II, 84). Oviedo, however, is skeptical about the reports of the island: "No Christian gives any credence to these women" (*Hist.,* XXXIII, 36: III, 447b; cf. XXV, 14: PT, III, 42–43, and below, chap. XVIII, sec. 19). In Cortés's instructions from Velázquez on 23 October 1518 it was suggested that he should discover "whereabouts these Amazons are to be found, that are somewhere near there, according to those Indians that you brought" (document reproduced in Zavala's *Las instituciones jurídicas,* p. 313). See also Leonard, op. cit., although that article is concerned mainly with the origin of the toponym "California," and the conquistadors' familiarity with the chivalric poems.

15. Ed. cit., I, 27; lions and tigers in Montezuma's menagerie—I, 109; a lion killed in a hunt—II, 170; birds like in Spain—I, 108.

16. Ibid., II, 220.

"a great abundance," bringing extensive economic and political benefits to the crown.[17]

As for plants and cattle, Mexico can compare with the best Europe can offer. As regards minerals, the earth of Mexico is no less opulent, no less generous than that of the Old World. The eternal legend of Ophir finds immediate application: "In our opinion one must believe that this land is as rich as the land whence Solomon is said to have obtained gold for the temple."[18] Finally, to parallel his delight at seeing Europe's seeds and animals growing and multiplying in Mexico, Cortés relates that cannon can be made there, and indeed that he himself has used the copper and tin (or zinc) from the Mexican mines to cast the first American artillery, "two demiculverins . . . a serpentine cannon and two sakers . . . and another demiculverin." His foundry is now in full production: "I have been making a few pieces every day."[19] If firearms can be made there, Mexico has all it needs to match mother Europe step for step!

6. The natives and Spain

Cortés obviously realizes immediately that the natives enjoy an advanced level of civilization. They do, admittedly, practise human sacrifice—"this some of us saw, and those that saw it say that it is the most terrible thing and the most terrifying sight they ever saw"—and they will therefore have to be taught Catholicism. But this will suffice because, apart from that abominable custom and the sin of sodomy, "they live a more politic and reasonable existence than any of the peoples hitherto seen in these parts."[20]

Especially in the second letter, in which he recounts his first contacts with the Aztec peoples and expresses his joy and surprise most spontaneously, there are frequent comparisons with cities and things of Spain. It is conceivable that these fleeting references are also due to haste, inadequate powers of description, or the laziness of the writer who resorts to an abbreviation familiar to his interlocutor to make himself more easily understood. But there can be no doubt about the intention and meaning of these parallels. "The city [Tlaxcala] . . . is much bigger and stronger than Granada."[21] "This city [Cholula] is . . . the most beautiful city from the outside, like those in Spain . . . there are a lot of poor people . . . who beg . . . as do the poor in Spain."[22] "The lord [of Iztapalapa] has some new houses . . . which are as good as the best in Spain."[23] In Cuzulá there are "such buildings and such good ones that they say that in Spain there could be

---

17. Ibid., pp. 109–10; cf. ibid., p. 126.
18. Ibid., I, 27–28.
19. Ibid., II, 112–13.
20. Ibid., I, 13.
21. Ibid., p. 56; cf. Oviedo, *Hist.*, XXXIII, 3: III, 272a.
22. Ed. cit., I, 65.
23. Ibid., p. 74, with the reservation "except masonry and other rich things that they use in houses in Spain, which they do not have here."

no better . . . a lodging house and fortress which is bigger and stronger and better built than the castle of Burgos."[24] "The city [of Temixtitán] is as big as Seville and Cordova."[25] "It has another square twice as big as the city of Salamanca."[26] "There are men like those known in Castile as porters for carrying heavy loads."[27] The native laborers use "some sort of sticks, that they handle just like workmen in Spain wielding spades."[28] "There are fruits of lots of sorts, including cherries and plums which resemble those of Spain."[29] "There are many sorts of cotton thread for sale . . . and it seems like the Granada Silk Exchange with its silks, although this other is in much greater quantity. They sell as many colors for painters as can be found in Spain."[30] "The main tower is higher than the tower of the cathedral in Seville,"[31] and so on.

Eventually Cortés himself tires of listing similarities and sums up: "And not to be any more longwinded in relating the things of this great city (although I would not finish so soon) I will say no more except that in their service and demeanor, the people in those parts lead almost the Spanish way of life, and with as much accord and order as there."[32] What has been said of the capital remains true for the whole country. With deliberate solemnity Cortés concludes: "Because of what I saw and understood regarding the similarity that all this land has to Spain, both in its fertility and in its size and the cold winters which it has, and in many other things that made it similar thereto, it seemed to me that it was most suitable to give this same land the name New Spain of the Ocean Sea."[33]

There are also parallels with other parts of the Old World, with Italy, or the Moorish lands. The Mexicans' system of government is similar to the oligarchies of Venice, Genoa, or Pisa,[34] and the people of the Yucatan wear "very delicate shawls painted like the Moors' *alquizales.*"[35] But Spain is always uppermost in Cortés's thoughts. The natives too are always discussed from the viewpoint of their future relationship with the Spaniards: as vassals, enemies, converts, or allies. Quite unlike the West Indians, whom Columbus described as inept and cowardly, they are quarrelsome and unruly: "Your imperial majesty must realize

---

24. Ibid., p. 85.
25. Ibid., p. 98; cf. Oviedo, *Hist.*, XXXIII, 10: III, 299b. The Venetian Contarini reports that in the capital Tenochtitlán "the water rises and falls twice every day, as it does here in Venice" (op. cit., p. 53).
26. Ed. cit., I, 99; cf. II, 11; Oviedo, *Hist.*, XXXIII, 10: III, 299b; and XXXIII, 26: III, 397a.
27. Ed. cit., I, 99; cf. Oviedo, *Hist.*, XXXIII, 10: III, 300a.
28. Ed. cit., II, 28.
29. Ibid., I, 99.
30. Ibid., p. 100; cf. Oviedo, *Hist.*, XXXIII, 10: III, 300b.
31. Ed. cit., I, 102 (the famous "Giralda"); cf. Oviedo, *Hist.*, XXXIII, 10: III, 302a.
32. Ed. cit., I, 106.
33. Ibid., p. 166; see Oviedo's geographical reservations (different latitude), *Hist.*, XXXIII, 16: III, 343b.
34. Ed. cit., I, 57; cf. Oviedo, *Hist.*, XXXIII, 3: III, 272b.
35. Ed. cit., I, 28; a further comparison with African clothes: I, 64; the Mexican temples are always called "mosques," etc. This was the term applied generically to the infidels' sanctuaries and temples. Curiously enough the first clear Moorish influences on the architecture appeared with the Spanish: the royal chapel of Cholula "follows the plan of a mosque" (P. Henríquez Ureña, *Literary Currents in Hispanic America* [Cambridge, Mass., 1945], p. 222n 45).

that these people are so turbulent that whenever they see something new or some hubbub going on they are immediately up in arms, because they are so accustomed to rebelling and rising against their masters."[36] And they are anything but obtuse imbeciles. When Cortés's orders that they be treated to a reading of the *requerimiento*—that verbose announcement drafted by the jurist Palacios Rubios as legal justification of the war against anyone refusing to accept it, of which we spoke above (chap. IX, sec. 5)—"they are people of such capacity that they understand the whole thing and know it very well."[37] And they believe the Spaniard when he assures them that he is visiting their lands as Charles's emissary, "to see them and to speak to the lords and people of the country of certain things to be carried out in his royal service and for their benefit."[38]

Indeed Cortés has such a high opinion of the Mexicans that he shrinks from treating them like the Carib savages of whom gold was asked or demanded, just like that, without further explanation. When in the name of the Emperor Charles V, Cortés has to demean himself to ask Montezuma for money, his main and typically Spanish fear is that the haughty Aztecs may form a poor opinion of a European sovereign who has been portrayed to them as all powerful and supremely just and yet sends his soldiery to plunder distant and peace-loving countries. Is this magnificent emperor so poor and so greedy for gold? With a delightful apologetic euphemism Cortés explains the situation to Montezuma: "I told him that Your Highness needed gold for certain works you were having done. . . ."[39]

When such a European excuse is offered to the first sovereign of the New World, when the conqueror puts himself on the same mental level as the conquered and offers him well-meant if clumsy excuses, another large step has been taken toward understanding, another step toward recognition of a humanity with common needs.

36. Ed. cit., II, 101. "Cortés found the Aztecs surprisingly stubborn" (Iglesia, *Cronistas e historiadores*, p. 51).
37. This illusion, or fraudulent invention, is in line with Cortés's mistrustful and generally negative attitude toward the natives, that led him to be suspected of having influenced the drafting of Sepúlveda's *Democrates alter* (on which see Gerbi, *Dispute*, p. 69): Salas, op. cit., p. 198, on the authority of Angel Losada, "Hernán Cortés en la obra del cronista Sepúlveda," *RI*, 9 (1948), 127–69. Las Casas does not, however, appear to have been acquainted with Cortés's *Cartas* (Salas, op. cit., p. 228).
38. Ed. cit., II, 167.
39. Ibid., I, 94; writing to the sovereign, however, Cortés was to say that he had sent him 60,000 gold pesos all at once "for the *need* that we knew Your Majesty had," ibid., II, 239.

❧ XI ❧

Antonio Pigafetta

1. THE REPORT UNKNOWN TO PETER MARTYR

On 8 September 1522 there arrived in Seville the wretched and glorious remnant of Magellan's great expedition—just one ship with 18 survivors, of the five ships and 237 (or more likely 265 or maybe 280)[1] men that had quit that same port on 10 August 1519; the ship dropped anchor near the wharf for which they had so long been yearning, all the guns were fired, and the following day, barefoot and in their shifts, candles in hand, they trudged to the churches to fulfil the vows they had made in their hour of peril. For the task of questioning the veterans of this first circumnavigation of the globe, collecting the journals and documents of the living and the dead and drafting the official report of the voyage, the choice fell of course on Peter Martyr.

It seems certain, however, that one of those few survivors, Francescantonio Pigafetta of Vicenza, a man somewhat more curious than his shipmates about new things and people, and anxious to secure his niche in history (as he reveals in the dedication of his work), instead of handing over his notes to the official chronicler of the Council of the Indies took them to Valladolid and offered them in personal homage to Charles V, wishing to offer the emperor's sacred majesty—as he himself writes—"not gold or silver, but things that will be highly prized by such a Lord. . . ."[2] It was indeed a stroke of luck for posterity that Pigafetta's account, instead of being recast in the humanist's Latin prose, should have thus fortuitously remained in the author's own hands, since Peter Martyr's account, sent to Pope Hadrian VI, was lost without trace, and Ramusio concluded that it must have been burnt or lost in the sack of Rome in 1527.[3]

---

1. Andrea Da Mosto, in *Raccolta Colombiana*, pt. V, vol. III, pp. 13–47, 53n2. Cf. Morison, *Southern Voyages*, pp. 352–55, 451, 462.

2. Antonio Pigafetta, *Il primo viaggio intorno al mondo*, ed. Camillo Manfroni (Milan, 1929), pp. 273–74; and Morcuende, op. cit., p. 186 (8–9 September 1522; the same words occur in the colophon to the French edition of 1525). Note that the traveler puts information above riches and spiritual wealth above economic. The *Victoria* brought back spices but no metals (see the "discharge" document in Navarrete, op. cit., IV, 247–48). On the language in which Pigafetta's account was originally drafted and the relationship between the journal delivered to Charles V and the account subsequently published, see Da Mosto, op. cit., pp. 37–47; S. Zweig, *Magellano*, (Milan, 1938), p. 284; M. Vocino, *Marinai italiani ed iberici sulle vie delle Indie* (Rome, 1955), pp. 84–86.

3. G. B. Ramusio, *Raccolta di navigationi et viaggi*, (Venice, 1550–56), I, p. 373, where he also discusses the loss

It is of course true that Peter Martyr devotes the whole of book VII of his fifth Decade to the great voyage of circumnavigation of the globe, and Pennesi has maintained that the account addressed to the pope was "decanted" into that Decade.[4] But Peter Martyr is caught between his desire to magnify the undertaking and his determination to cut down Magellan, who is unfairly described as a traitor to his king (the king of Portugal) and accused of abusing and wreaking mortal violence on the Spaniards, "under the pretext of justice" (when in fact the Spaniards had mutinied and were thus legally punished). The discovery of the strait that has borne his name down through the centuries is described as accidental, and even his heroic death on Matán, in the Philippines, is described as just punishment for his greed for spices![5]

Could Pigafetta—who was devoted to the memory of his leader—perhaps have been aware of the animosity that the chronicler of Spain bore Magellan? One might infer as much from the fact that he did not apparently give him his information (there are various fundamental discrepancies between the two accounts) and the fact that Peter Martyr never mentions Pigafetta, saying only that the eighteen survivors were "completely illiterate." So either Pigafetta pretended to be so, or Peter Martyr took his revenge for Pigafetta's reticence by lumping him with the wretched remnants of the crew, these "few and feeble persons" mentioned in the documents of the time, which list among the survivors the "supernumerary" Antonio Lombardo, or Antonio de Plegafetis.[6]

But the gentleman from Vicenza was in fact so far from being "illiterate" that between the end of 1524 and early 1525, on the basis of the journal already offered to the emperor, he drafted—at the request first of all of the marquis of

---

of a day (see above, chap. VIII, sec. 13, and below, sec. 3) and praises Pigafetta. See also Morcuende, op. cit., pp. 20–21, which cites Peter Martyr, *Opus Epistolarum,* epist. 767, 797 (cf., in fact, *Opus Epistolarum,* epist. 767 [1522], p. 66, and 797 [1524], pp. 69–70); and the *Relación del último viage al estrecho de Magallanes de la fragata de S.M. "Santa María de la Cabeza" en los años de 1785 y 1786* (Madrid, 1788), pp. 184–85n3. Pigafetta and the great voyage of the ship *Victoria* are also mentioned by Martyr's friend, Gaspare Contarini, op. cit., pp. 48, 51–52.

4. See Manfroni, op. cit., p. 35.

5. From the documents assembled in the fourth volume of Navarrete's *Colección* it emerges that the Spanish authorities, disappointed perhaps by the results of the costly expedition, showed considerable animosity toward Magellan, and opened a sort of court of inquiry, interrogating the survivors. These judicial sequels were quite a common event in the aftermath of expeditions, and in this case things were made rather worse by the fact that the leader, Magellan, was of Portuguese origin. Oviedo however defends Magellan against the suspicion, based on a misunderstanding of a statement in Pigafetta (see Manfroni, op. cit., pp. 43–44), of having already learned about the strait from a chart drawn by Martin of Bohemia (the notorious Martin Behaim, born in Nuremberg, who rates three-quarters of a column in the *Enciclopedia Italiana,* s.v.) that he found in the treasury of the king of Portugal. And who was this Martin of Bohemia? "Never was there such an authority seen or heard, written or portrayed." Credit for the discovery was due to Magellan's "spirit" much more than "to the learning of the Bohemian, because hitherto there is no record among Bohemians or Christians that any such famous cosmographer was ever born in Bohemia" (*Hist.,* XX, 2: PT, II, 229b, with a distinct echo of his hostility toward gypsies or "Bohemians"). But in actual fact—begging Oviedo's pardon—Martin Behaim was known at least by name to Pigafetta and Magellan (Morison, *Southern Voyages,* pp. 381–82). See also Quinn, *England and America,* pp. 82–84, 108–09.

6. See documents in Navarrete, op. cit., IV, 96, 248. In the ship's complement (ibid., pp. 14, 24) he is called "the said Antonio Lombardo" and in the column for "country" the entry is "Lombardy" (rather than the name of a town as in almost all the other cases). On "Byzantium which is in Lombardy," an obvious misunderstanding of "Vicenza," see Manfroni, op. cit., p. 11. In Navarrete (op. cit., IV, 369) there is a different list of sixteen of the eighteen survivors, that coincides only partly with the others cited. Pigafetta, in any case, is not on the list; by 1524, when the sixteen made their sworn statements, he was no longer in Spain.

Mantua, Federico Gonzaga (1523) and subsequently of Pope Clement VII (1524), and dedicated to the grand master of the Order of Rhodes (of which he was a member), Philippe de Villiers de l'Isle Adam-—a fuller report which, after various vicissitudes, was first printed in an abridged translation into French in 1525, and subsequently in Italian in 1536 (Venice) and 1550 (in Ramusio's collection); it was translated into English by Richard Eden (1555) and was finally published in extenso in 1800 by Carlo Amoretti, on the basis of the Italian manuscript in the Biblioteca Ambrosiana in Milan.

2. MAGELLAN'S DISCOVERY

The goal of Magellan's expedition was the Spice Islands, and thus for him America was not a target but an obstacle. It was indeed *the* obstacle, blocking the direct path to the Spice Islands. If the endeavor had been fully successful it would have relegated the newly discovered continent to a position of minor importance. From this point of view the expedition was of course a fiasco. The route discovered turned out to be not only much longer and more difficult than Vasco da Gama's, but longer also than the route across the isthmus of Panama, which was being laboriously opened up at that very time. For decades after Magellan, until Drake's famous and so much more profitable foray (1578), almost nobody followed in Magellan's wake.[7] The sale of the Moluccas to the Portuguese and the repeated catastrophes suffered by all those who were bold enough to try to imitate Magellan's exploit led to the abandonment of the tortuous Antarctic route. In Spain there even began to be doubts about the very existence of the strait and suggestions that it might have been blocked up by some cataclysm.[8] Little more than a century later Bernardo de Balbuena was writing that Magellan "discovered the *useless* path to the riches of the East."[9]

Two attempts at colonization (1529, 1539) had failed. And only much later, with the development of Peru and Chile, did the strait acquire a degree of commercial importance, though only for a strictly limited period: from 1740, when the system of the galleons was abandoned and permission was given for Cape Horn trade,[10] to 1915, when the Panama Canal was opened. Thus the geographical importance of Magellan's voyage far outweighed its practical

7. The official *Relación* of 1788 (see above, n. 3) mentions the disastrous expedition of García Jofre de Loaysa (1525–26; on whom see Oviedo, *Hist.*, XX, 4: PT, II, 237a), the unsuccessful expedition of Cabot (1526), who failed to reach the Strait of Magellan, the catastrophic enterprise of Simón de Alcazaba (1534–35, on which see Oviedo, *Hist.*, XXII, 1–3: II, 153–66), the equally unfortunate attempt by Alonso de Camargo (1539) and the voyage of Juan Ladrilleros, the first person to traverse the strait from west to east (op. cit., pp. 201–21). Cf. also Zweig, op. cit., pp. 290—91.

8. Ercilla, *La Araucana*, I, 7–8; cf. the *Relación* of 1788, pp. 220–21; Humboldt, *Examen critique*, V, 252–53; Manfroni, op. cit., pp. 64–65.

9. *El Bernardo* (1624), canto XVIII (Madrid, 1851), p. 331b. On Magellan in literature, see below, chap. XVIII, sec. 10.

10. R. Levene, *Investigaciones acerca de la historia económica del virreinato del Plata* (La Plata, 1927–28), I, 293.

results. As previously in the classic case of Columbus, a commercial illusion led to enormous scientific progress.

3. THE MOLUCCAS AND AMERICA

When Pigafetta was writing his report, however, he was still under the impression that the voyage had been an unqualified triumph. The focus of his account is therefore the Spice Islands, and the narration of the events preceding the arrival of the fleet in the Asian archipelagoes serves only as a dramatic and picturesque prelude. The older editions, in fact, are all entitled *Voyage to the Moluccas,* while the later ones, published when consideration of the *scientific* results had finally outweighed the purely utilitarian angle, are entitled *First Voyage Around the Terracqueous Globe,* or *Around the World.* For Pigafetta, then, the expedition's stopping-places in America, Brazil and Patagonia, act only as points of reference, like the wings of stage scenery, designed to make the fragrant and balmy landscape of the Moluccas recede into the farthest distance, beyond a vast unmoving ocean.

In reality they account for very few pages of his narrative, and even in those a taste for the picturesque and the surprising, the traveler's amazement and amusement, take pride of place over the spirit of scientific observation. It is not that Pigafetta lacks curiosity about the things of nature or the ability to judge their real worth. Oviedo himself, who made ample use of Pigafetta, had high praise for the "knight of Vicenza," describing him as "a speculative gentleman, anxious to understand what he saw." [11] Pigafetta notes the crops growing in the fields, the customs of the savages, and the strange appearance of some of the animals; and when he gets back to Cape Verde and finds that it is Thursday rather than Wednesday, as it should have been according to his diaries, he records his amazement and provides the correct solution to the problem: "We know not how we had erred: I had made an entry every day, without interruption, because I had never been ill. But, as was later explained, it was not a mistake; since the journey had been made continually westward, coming back to the same place like the sun, this had brought about the gain of twenty-four hours, as can be clearly seen." [12]

---

11. *Hist.,* XX, 3: II, 28b, but with the reservation, "in truth, in some of the things that this gentleman describes in his account, I have been neutral or perplexed" (ibid.). Oviedo uses Pigafetta's testimony to supplement the reports written by Maximilianus Transylvanus and the account given to him by Juan Sebastián de Elcano, who brought the last ship, the *Victoria,* back to Spain after Magellan's death—see below, chap. XVIII, sec. 10 (loc. cit. and *Quinquagenas,* pt. III, st. 6, cited by Amador de los Ríos in the Introduction ["Vida y escritos de Gonzalo Fernández de Oviedo y Valdes"] to his edition of Oviedo's *Historia* [Madrid, 1851–55], I, xlix*n13*). Moreover, "it seems clear . . . that Oviedo had some sources which are not recognizable now, and some have contended that he had access to Magellan's own papers" (Winsor, op. cit., II, 616).

Puente y Olea, op. cit., p. 200, calls Pigafetta a "curious" observer and "very cultured for his time." Even Da Mosto admits he is "generally accurate" (op. cit., p. 35) and Magnaghi calls him a "diligent and acute observer," who gives us "complete descriptions" of the natives he visited (*Enciclopedia Italiana,* s.v.).

12. Manfroni, op. cit., pp. 271–72. The crew of the *Victoria* were frankly horrified when they realized they had eaten meat on a Friday and celebrated Easter on Monday . . . (Herrera, quoted by Humboldt, *Examen critique,* I, 300*n*).

The explanation given so simply by Pigafetta, who does not claim it as his own ("as was explained"), is now generally attributed to Peter Martyr, who expounds it in the course of a whole lengthy harangue on this knotty "philosophical" problem; having described how he cross-questioned the returning sailors to see whether perhaps they had mistakenly forgotten to count a day spent in prayer, or to allow for 29 February in the leap year of 1520, he finally presents it as his own theory, thought out in long and learned conversations with his friend the Venetian ambassador, Gaspare Contarini.[13] But it was only in the last century that Phileas Fogg comes close to losing £80,000 because he overlooked the elementary truth observed by the Lombard explorer, who had taken three years rather than eighty days to circle the world.

4. CREDULITY AND SKEPTICISM

Though he can be astute enough when he is using his head and his senses to think and observe, Pigafetta can be almost completely devoid of critical capacity when he is retailing the tall stories he picks up along the way. Possibly he thought he should enliven his account, or perhaps he felt it his duty to embellish the factual report of the voyage with a halo of incredible legends that would lend it the myriad magic hues, the fabled rays of far-off lands. Whatever the intention, the fact remains that without any overt expression of incredulity this shrewd and canny Lombard tells his readers about such natural phenomena as a tree on one of the Canary Islands—where there are no springs—that is permanently enveloped in a thick fog and whose dripping branches provide the islanders and the animals, both domestic and wild, with "abundant" supplies of drinking water,[14] and about certain black crowlike birds that wait for a whale to open its mouth and then dive down its gullet and go straight on to devour its heart;[15] he also asks them to believe what he was told by his "old Maluco pilot" about an island whose inhabitants are barely a cubit tall, but have ears as long as their bodies, so that when they lie down to sleep one serves them as a mattress and the other as a blanket,[16] and the well-known tale, relayed along with others by the much-

---

13. *Dec.*, V, 7, end. Cf. Da Mosto, op. cit., p. 34; Manfroni, op. cit., pp. 20–21, 271–72; Zweig, op. cit., p. 273. The Spanish translation is somewhat more long-winded: "We could not be persuaded that we had made a mistake of a day, and I less than anybody, because I very carefully and without a break marked the days of the week and the date of the month in a journal. We soon realized that our calculation was not wrong, because having sailed always westward, following the course of the sun, on returning to the same place we had necessarily to have gained twenty-four hours over those that stayed still where they were: one need only think about it to be convinced" (Morcuende, op. cit., p. 185). On the attribution of the solution to Contarini, see G. Marinelli, "Venezia nella storia della geografia cartografica ed esploratrice," in *Atti del R. Istituto Veneto di Scienze, Lettere ed Arte*, 6th ser., vol. VII, no. 7 (1888–89), 973–74.

14. Manfroni, op. cit., p. 79.

15. Ibid., p. 148. The Spanish edition does actually contain a hint of skepticism at this point, as it goes on to comment: "The only proof they gave us of this is that the black bird can be seen eating the heart of the whale, and that the whale is found dead and without a heart."

16. Manfroni, op. cit., p. 253 (Morcuende, op. cit., p. 175). In the Transylvanus version (Navarrete, op. cit., IV, 277), their ears are so wide and long "that they had the habit of covering their whole heads with one of them." The Italian uses his ears as a sleeping-bag, while the Spaniard finds them convenient as a balaclava. . . . This is, however, an obvious echo of old and apparently ineradicable legends.

quoted "senior pilot of ours," of the Amazon women that murder all menfolk and are impregnated by the wind.[17]

At times he is prepared to go even further and vouch himself for what he relates. Thus when he watches the bodies of twenty-one members of the crew being committed to the deep he makes the curious observation that the Christian bodies "went to the bottom face upward and the Indians always face down."[18] In similar vein he talks about the "animated" and apparently apprehensive leaves of certain trees, that "flee from the touch."[19] adding a delightful detail that betrays the presence of at least some investigatory instinct: "I kept one nine days in a box. When I opened it the leaf was going round and round in the box."[20] But when he is not spying on these pedunculate leaves escaping from their brief imprisonment for a breath of air ("I believe they live on nothing except air"), when he is not leaning overboard to follow the final whirlings of the corpses in the boiling wake of the ship, Pigafetta is quite straightforward and matter-of-fact. At the end of a long account of the customs and rites of the sovereigns of China, he concludes: "All these things and many others . . . were told us by a Moor; and he said he had seen them." *Relata refero.*[21]

5. LITTLE INFORMATION ON PLANTS AND ANIMALS

His comments on the animals and the even rarer references to the plants tend likewise to be merely accessory. Little enough interested, as we have seen, in American things in general—glimpsed in passing on his way to the East—his horizon is here further limited by his overwhelming interest in the human popula-

---

17. Manfroni, op. cit., p. 258.

18. Ibid., p. 271; Morcuende, op. cit., p. 184. This legend is also repeated by Herrera: see Da Mosto, op. cit., III, n. 15.

19. Manfroni, op. cit., p. 196.

20. Ibid.; Morcuende, op. cit., p. 134. Martyr mentions these leaves that slither about like worms and, ever ingenious and full of fantasy, hypothesizes that "between the two faces of the leaf there must be compressed some vital spirit which, like a momentary gust of wind, moves the leaves" (*Dec.*, V, 7, p. 430).

21. Manfroni, op. cit., p. 265; and with more overt skepticism in the Spanish edition: "I myself have seen nothing of this whole matter that I have just related" (Morcuende, op. cit., p. 181). Oviedo, after extracting from Pigafetta's report numerous items of information about the spice trees, and other details of the Moluccas, wisely concludes: "This author says a lot of other things that he knew *by hearsay*, both of Java and of Malacca and China, which *I did not feel to be worthy of attention*" (*Hist.*, XX, 3: II, 30b). A little further on Oviedo repeats the story of the bodies in this cautious form: "And *it seemed* that the Christians sank with their faces to the heavens, and the Indians face down" (ibid., p. 31a). And he concludes by saying that he has extracted from Pigafetta's narrative whatever seemed to him to agree with history and with the other witnesses, "leaving much else out as unfit for our present purposes and *rejecting fables and conjectures*" (ibid., p. 32b; my italics).

For a long time those fables caused Pigafetta's report to be looked on with some mistrust. The authors of the abovementioned official Spanish *Relación* of the 1785–86 voyage note tartly that "Pigafetta had no more of the sailor in him than a firm belief in St. Elmo and his appearance in the form of *ignis fatuus* during storms," and that *therefore* he is fairly reliable in nautical matters, because he must have got his information from the pilots; but he is not believable when he is recounting all these "foolishnesses" and "ridiculous fables" (*Relación*, p. 185n3; cf. p. 325). On St. Elmo's fire in Coleridge's *Ancient Mariner*, see the copious documentation in J. L. Lowes, *The Road to Xanadu*, rev. ed. (London, 1930), pp. 79–87, 484–85, and for Bacchus's drunken confusion between "the golden-haired stars of St. Elmo" and "two fine flasks brimming with good wine," see Francesco Redi's dithyramb *Bacco in Toscana*. See also Morison, *Southern Voyages*, pp. 357–58, 364, 445.

tion, whether of the Brazilian forest or the Patagonian pampa. Fruit and animals only concern Pigafetta in relation to their usefulness to man.

He does however mention pineapples, "truly the nicest fruit existing" (p. 82); penguins, fat and abundant so that within the space of an hour enough are captured to provide for the crews of five ships;[22] seals, luckily slow-moving and clumsy, since "they would be very fierce if they could run" (p. 90); the guanaco ("head and ears the size of a mule's, neck and body like a camel's, legs of a deer, and the tail of a horse"), whose skin furnishes the Patagonians with shoe leather (p. 91); and flying fish, which are assiduously pursued by three other species of fish, but which when caught by man "make excellent eating" (p. 107); as well as various other animals, both edible and otherwise (p. 100).

In the Moluccas he also describes two dead (but unstuffed) birds of paradise, which the king of Bachián sent for the king of Spain;[23] and he too mentions the pigs with navels on their backs,[24] and a rarer phenomenon, a sort of bird with no anus, and another (luckier?) sort that lives solely off the droppings of other birds (pp. 81–82). But these are rarely more than passing comments, splashes of local color to enliven his canvas. Pigafetta's real originality lies in his careful observation and lively description of the appearance and mentality of the natives.

6. HUMAN INTEREST IN THE NATIVES

Pigafetta never doubts their humanity, nor does he recoil at their savage customs. On the contrary, he makes every effort to understand, justify, and rationalize them. The Brazilians are not of course Christians, but neither are they idolaters, because "they worship nothing; they live according to the usage of nature" (p. 83). They all go about naked, "shorn and beardless, because they remove their hair" (p. 85), are fairly long-lived, sleep in hammocks, and row about in long canoes with oars that look like our bakers' oven-paddles. "And thus black, naked, and shorn they look, when rowing, like inhabitants of the Stygian swamp" (p. 84). The apparently classical reference is deceptive, as Pigafetta doubtless had in mind the "people covered in mud, there in the swamp, all naked and with anger in their faces," that Dante saw where the gloomy stream of Hell "forms a marsh, whose name is Styx."[25] Pigafetta was certainly not familiar with the Greek and Latin texts.[26] Even when he speaks of the island inhabited

---

22. Manfroni, op. cit., p. 89; Morcuende, op. cit., p. 51. Pigafetta also noted that they had no wings for flying, and that they fed on fish.

23. Manfroni, op. cit., p. 230; Morcuende, op. cit., pp. 164–65; cf. Oviedo, *Hist.*, XX, 3: II, 29n; Navarrete, op. cit., IV, 84–85, 278, 282. One cannot help wondering in what state the poor little bodies of the birds sent as gifts from the Moluccas arrived in Spain. But Transylvanus, in the last of the passages cited, assures us that these angelic little creatures "never go rotten or smell badly, even when they are dead"!

24. Manfroni, op. cit., p. 86. According to a note in the Spanish edition the animal in question would have been the peccary or *tajacu*, "which has a dorsal gland that was taken to be the umbilicus" by the first people who saw it; Manfroni also states as much, p. 86n5.

25. *Inferno*, VII, 106–12.

26. His education seems to have been rudimentary and he was perhaps no more than nineteen when he left home

solely by women he makes no mention of the mythical Amazons. His comparisons are always with familiar and specific everyday realities. The natives' shaven heads remind him of monks' tonsures. The favorite pastime of the savages of the Isle of Thieves is to take their wives out in canoes, which are like *fuselere,* the punts the Venetians use for lagoon fishing, "only narrower" (p. 118).[27] And the triple crown of palm leaves adorning the great parasol-shaped hat—also of palm—worn by the young and comely queen of Zubú (in the Moluccas)—a curiously contemporary figure with her "black and white cloth covering her from head to toe and . . . her mouth and nails bright red"—this exotic headgear of the elegant Malayan ladies is defined as "resembling the pope's"! (p. 152).

The good gentleman of Vicenza is equally understanding in his approach to the cannibals, for whose peccadillo he provides a reasonable and intriguing explanation. These cannibals (he says) only eat the flesh of their enemies, and certainly not out of hunger or because they find it particularly good, but rather out of a combination of vendetta and bravado, as a defiant rite of war, a sign of rage, and savage rivalry.[28] The practice can be traced back, Pigafetta reports, to the time when a savage taken prisoner by another tribe was recognized by an old woman as the murderer of her only son. In a moment of fury the old lady fell on the man "like a mad dog," sinking her teeth into his shoulder. Subsequently he escaped and on returning to his people displayed his wound and announced that his captors had tried to eat him alive. And his own tribe, determined to match the savagery of their enemies, resolved in turn to eat them, but only after killing, quartering, and smoking them.[29]

With the same placid amusement Pigafetta relates how an attractive female savage, "a good-looking girl, boarded the flagship one day for no other reason than to settle down somewhere" (this is what the Italian text says, but the Spanish is more explicit: "to offer herself to the sailors, to get some gift"); and there, having stolen a nail more than a finger long "with great elegance and coquet-

---

for Spain. He writes in an argot that is a mixture of Italian, Venetian, and Spanish. His *Tratado de Navegación* is considered very elementary (see Amoretti in Morcuende, op. cit., pp. 17, 26, 72n); Magnaghi, in the article on Pigafetta in the *Enciclopedia Italiana,* describes it as "a compilation of very little value." Da Mosto, op. cit., pp. 35–36, has a rather higher opinion of it. But it is now thought to be a free translation of the *Regimento da Altura de Leste-Oeste* by the Portuguese cosmographer Rui Faleiro (Morison, *Southern Voyages,* p. 341).

27. A typical *fuselera,* with four oarsmen and a hunter can be admired in the charming little picture by Pietro Longhi, *La caccia in valle,* in the Galleria della Fondazione Querini Stampalia in Venice.

28. Manfroni, op. cit., pp. 84–85 and 251.

29. This was apparently told him by the pilot Giovanni Carvalhos, who spent four years in Brazil. De Pauw, who savagely attacks Pigafetta for his reports about the giants (*Recherches philosophiques sur les Américains* [Berlin, 1768–69], I, 289–90; see below, n. 33) briefly mentions his explanation of the natives' cannibalism (ibid., pp. 216–17). But he fails to mention that delightful and almost mouth-watering detail about the Benaján, in the Moluccas, namely that they "eat only the heart of a man, raw, with a little orange or lemon juice" (Manfroni, op. cit., p. 199).

tishness she thrust it through from one side to the other of the lips of her nature" (p. 87). And the bemused observer permits himself to wonder, somewhat irreverently, whether her purpose was concealment or adornment.[30]

Pigafetta then gleefully recalls some of the highly profitable bargains he struck with the natives: a basket of potatoes obtained in exchange for a ribbon or a hawk-bell, enough fish for ten people swapped for a little mirror or a pair of scissors, or other foodstuffs for playing cards: "For a king of danari, which is a playing card, I was given six chickens, and they still thought they had cheated me."[31] But here too, where there is more than a hint of mockery—just as when he is telling us about one of their "garments" of parrot feathers "with big wheels at the bottom end of the larger feathers, a ridiculous thing" (p. 85; Spanish edition, p. 48), or scoffing at them for thinking that the longboats "were the ships' offspring and that when the boats were launched from the ships into the sea this was the ships giving birth to the boats" which were then suckled by the ships (p. 87; Spanish edition, p. 49)—Pigafetta basically sympathizes with the poor wretches and describes them as good-natured simpletons, easily convertible to Christianity. If they were less ingenuous, he seems to imply, it would perhaps be harder to lead them to the true faith. . . .

7. THE PATAGONIAN GIANTS

For all this, however, Pigafetta's main contribution to American ethnography and legend lies elsewhere. After two months in the Patagonian port of San Julian, where the fleet had anchored at the end of March 1520 to take refuge from the southern winter, two months without a trace of an Indian, "one day we suddenly saw a man, of the stature of a giant, standing naked on the water's edge, dancing, singing, and throwing dust on his head" (p. 90; Spanish edition, p. 52).

The image is unforgettable, and reinforced by the copious details on the following pages it was to imprint itself indelibly on the European imagination. Three centuries of continuous research hardly sufficed to begin to erase it. "Since the voyage of the exaggerator Pigafetta, who was the first to believe he saw savages of colossal stature in the South of America, 247 years have elapsed," years of pointless and ferocious argument.[32] But in 1800 Pigafetta's editor himself, Carlo Amoretti, claimed that Pigafetta's evidence was worth more than

---

30. *Sic* only in Morcuende, op. cit., p. 50. The Italian edition adds instead, "and shortly thereafter she stole quietly away." On other cases of infibulation of the (male) genitalia, cf. Manfroni, op. cit., pp. 159, 258.

31. Manfroni, op. cit., p. 83; Morcuende, op. cit., p. 45. On p. 149 (Morcuende, p. 103) he mentions more bartering with the natives of the Moluccas, getting gold in exchange for metal, iron, and other "cheap goods"; Magellan himself eventually had to ban such shamelessly profiteering exchanges, because "they would have ruined trade for ever"! His ban was misunderstood and left the Spanish authorities very suspicious: Navarrete, op. cit., IV, 285, 288, 291–92, 294.

32. De Pauw, *Les Américains,* "Discours préliminaire."

de Pauw's and that giants must exist, do exist, or at least did exist.[33]

In point of fact Pigafetta's description is perhaps only slightly exaggerated or slightly distorted by optical illusion, and the conversion of the Patagonians into giants was a myth that emerged subsequently under the influence of the well-established traditions of biblical and classical giants. Pigafetta tells us that this first giant "was so big that we only came up to his waist" (pp. 90–91), but we do not know how tall Pigafetta was, nor the average height of his shipmates. We do know, on the other hand, that they had recently been in contact with the Brazilian natives, who were small of stature; and we might thus conclude that they were expecting more natives of the same size. We know that the Tehuelche, the now almost extinct inhabitants of Patagonia, had a median height for males of five feet seven inches to five feet eleven inches and were very strongly built, with small extremities (their lower extremities, however, being swollen by the famous clogs that earned them the name *Patacones*)[34] and elongated trunks; and we know that in those latitudes shadows fall very obliquely, and in open spaces even a modest elevation stands out surprisingly. So there is enough to make us refrain from totally rejecting the evidence of a witness like Pigafetta, who was certainly inclined to embellish and idealize whatever he actually saw (a little further on he extols the singular excellence of the squalid Straits of Magellan),[35] but is normally accurate in his descriptions and measurements.

The emperor's secretary, Maximilianus Transylvanus, who also carefully cross-questioned Captain Juan Sebastián de Elcano and the surviving sailors and immediately (1522) drafted an account of the enterprise, says only that the Patagonians were "extremely robust of body, *like* giants," and that in preparation for war they donned a garment made of skins "which was so long that it reached to the ground, making the Spaniards think that they were much bigger in body than before."[36] And Peter Martyr confines himself to saying that the Patagonians

33. Da Mosto, op. cit., p. 33*n3*, also mentions de Pauw as a denigrator of Pigafetta. See above, n. 29. The official account of the 1785–86 voyage categorically denied the existence of Patagonian giants, asserting merely that the natives of that area were tall and robust, and holding Pigafetta exclusively responsible for the legend or fable (*Relación*, pp. 324–26). On the reality of the matter and the possible causes of the illusion, see also Da Mosto, op. cit., p. 57*n6*.

34. The Genoese Pilot says the Patagonian males "are of a height of nine to ten palms, very well-built" and "wear shoes . . . filled with straw inside, to keep their feet warm" (Manfroni, op. cit., p. 300).

35. Every half a league, he says, there are "secure harbors, excellent waters, wood, though not cedar, fish, sardines, mussels and celery, an edible plant, but there are also inedible ones. . . . I believe there is no fairer and better strait in the world than this one" (ibid., p. 106).

36. Maximilianus Transylvanus, *Relación . . . de cómo y por quién y en qué tiempo fueron descubiertas y halladas las islas Molucas*, in Navarrete, op. cit., IV, 249–84 (see esp. pp. 257, 259). On the early editions of this work in Latin (Rome, 1523 and 1524, and Cologne, 1524), see also Harrisse, *Bibliotheca Americana*, p. 244ff, and Medina, *Biblioteca*, I, 92–98, who also included it in his *Colección de documentos inéditos para la historia de Chile* (Santiago de Chile, 1888–1902), I, 256–97 (in vol. II, p. 417ff, there is also Pigafetta's account, this time based on the French text). The 1788 *Relación* states incorrectly that Transylvanus's epistle is "a copy of everything that Pigafetta says" (p. 186*nl*), and that he "merely translated Pigafetta, embellishing the work with other improbabilities that his fellow-countryman [*sic*] did not dream up" (*Relación*, p. 326).

were unarmed (Pigafetta describes their bows and arrows) nomads, outlaws, and "tall in stature."[37] But Contarini already describes the Patagonians as "fierce men and much taller than us, according to the crew of the ship *Victoria*."[38]

Pigafetta is thus the real culprit (and the greatest beneficiary) of the belief in the existence of giants in the Southern Hemisphere. His description is in fact crammed with convincing detail. Behind the first giant, whose appearance and arms are carefully detailed, there immediately looms up another, and then a whole group, who at once begin to dance and sing, pointing their fingers to the sky. The rite is different from the first giant's—he humbly sprinkled his head with soil, almost as if with biblical ashes; the newcomer holds up a finger like a protesting citizen. But the real meaning of these gestures—probably to do with religious magic—remains obscure and unexplained.

The giants are soon joined by giantesses, who are certainly not idealized. Loaded down like beasts of burden, shorter but fatter than their menfolk, with "teats half a yard long" and painted faces, they are dressed like their "husbands" except that "before their nature they have a little bit of hide covering them"— and we can easily believe Pigafetta when he writes that he found them rather ugly.[39]

When Vico took them as the surviving representatives of the barbaric and heroic age, he portrayed the *Patacones* as proud and ungainly, but their main distinguishing feature is their enormous appetite: "Each of the two that we captured ate a whole bag of biscuits and downed half a bucket of water in one draught. And [Pigafetta is horror-struck at this splendid example of 'filthy eating'] they ate mice without skinning them" (p. 98; Spanish edition, p. 60). They let themselves be taught the Paternoster, which they can eventually recite "like us, though with very coarse voices" (p. 94; Spanish edition, p. 56), but are somewhat suspicious by nature and not easily captured.

Magellan would have liked to take a couple of the sturdiest specimens back with him to Spain, with their wives, to breed, but this turns out to be no simple task. The two giants are eventually captured by a trick: they are loaded down with mirrors, knives, and trinkets, and then offered two splendid iron manacles, which they eye greedily, as they love iron, but have no means of holding as their hands are full; so the Europeans offer to fix the manacles on the Patagonians'

37. *Dec.*, V, 7, p. 428.
38. Contarini, op. cit., p. 52.
39. The Spanish edition describes them as having "pendulous" teats, bodies painted red, and yellow circles around their eyes; "however," the astonished European then goes on, "their husbands seemed to be very jealous" ("these giants . . . are very jealous of their wives"—Manfroni, op. cit., p. 96). Pigafetta reacts with the same naive surprise to the natives of Giailolo, whose "women are ugly, and go about naked like the others," but whose men, who "go about naked like the other men . . . are so jealous of their wives that [an explanation of a crude Ruzzante-like realism] they did not want us to go ashore with out trouser-flaps open, because they said their women thought we were always ready" (ibid., p. 220). On the meager virility of the natives, cf. pp. 160, 308. On the "violation of the women," the cause of the natives' hostility, see Peter Martyr, cited by Zweig, op. cit., p. 252, and above, chap. IV, sec. 3 (end).

wrists to make it easier for them to carry them. The unwary giants agree, and a moment later they are firmly chained—like Manzoni's Renzo when the notary's two officers "hastily bind his wrists with certain devices known hypocritically and euphemistically as cuffs." . . . Renzo squirms free, crying out, "What treachery is this? Is this any way to treat a gentleman . . . !"[40] And the two Patagonians, realizing they have been tricked, snort like bulls and call loudly on Setebos to aid them.[41]

Setebos remained unmoved. But their cries rang out so loudly in Pigafetta's pages that almost a century later their echo could be heard in the impotent snarling and well-founded terror of Caliban: "I must obey—the monster growls in response to Prospero's commands—his art is of such power, It would control my Dam's god, Setebos, And make a vassal of him." And again in his last appearance in the play: "Oh Setebos, these be brave spirits indeed! How fine my master is! I am afraid He will chastise me."[42]

The giantesses are luckier: they manage to escape with their new consorts, their children and animals. And one of the pursuers dies from a poisoned arrow. Of the two prisoners, one, on board the *San Antonio* (which deserted and returned to Spain under the command of Esteban Gómez), died of heatstroke in the Atlantic, as the ship approached the Tropics (p. 104; Spanish edition, p. 65), while the other died of scurvy in the Pacific, after kissing the cross and receiving baptism (pp. 110–11; Spanish edition, pp. 68, 70).

8. THE NATIVE LANGUAGES

But he did not die in vain. Pigafetta had struck up a close friendship with the kidnaped giant and got him to explain the principles of the giants' medicine and the reasons they gave for the use of emetics and bloodletting; he also found out about the basic tenets of their religion, whose fundamental principle was worship of the devil (pp. 96–97; Spanish edition, pp. 58–59), and, with extraordinary patience in the long days at sea, got the giant to teach him the language of the Patagonians, managing to accumulate a small vocabulary.

It was no idle pastime. Peter Martyr had already patiently and carefully collected native words and had attempted to provide a transcription of them in Latin characters.[43] Pigafetta himself had already compiled a short dictionary of the

40. A. Manzoni, *I Promessi sposi,* chap. XV (Milan, 1934), p. 246. This trap was to be used frequently to capture natives. It was apparently used treacherously by Alonso de Ojeda to take prisoner the proud cacique Caonabó, husband of the crafty and lascivious (with the Spaniards) Anacaona. Oviedo, perhaps out of a certain chivalric diffidence, confines himself to repeating that when Caonabó was captured it was *said* that "Hojeda did not keep the promise that the cacique *said* had been made to him, or else Caonabó had not understood him" (*Hist.,* III, 1: PT, I, 56; cf. Felipe Fernández-Armesto, *Columbus and the Conquest of the Impossible* [London, 1974], p. 133).

41. Manfroni, op. cit., p. 95; Morcuende, op. cit., p. 57. Setebos or Settebotte reappears as the archfiend, pp. 97 and 109–10; Morcuende, pp. 59, 68. Setebos was the enemy of Osiris, chief of the powers of darkness in ancient Egyptian mythology.

42. *The Tempest,* act I, sc. 2; act V, sc. 1.

43. Salas, op. cit., p. 47.

Brazilians' idiom and managed to put together a much larger one of the languages of the Philippines and the Moluccas. Through these philological endeavors Pigafetta sought to draw closer in spirit to the various peoples he visited. With his enquiring mind that led him to look into their beliefs and rationalize or Europeanize their motives, with his desire to understand and be understood, with his firm and serene faith in a common humanity, and with his new instinctive wisdom, Antonio Pigafetta became a disciple of the savages, rather than their master, and thus forged the first indispensable instruments for the contacts essential to the development—with the slow passing of the centuries and exchanges more fruitful than that greedy bartering—of their halting progress toward civilization, their hoped-for inclusion in the greater family of mankind.[44]

44. Jefferson, who collected Red Indian vocabularies, deplored the fact that nobody had compiled vocabularies of the numerous Indian tribes and nations that had died out, because they would have shed much light on the origins of the Americans (*Notes on Virginia* [New York: Modern Library, n.d.], XI, 226, and *Works* [New York and London, 1904–05], III, 509–11). In 1789 he was endeavoring to assemble "all the vocabularies I can of the American Indians, as those of Asia" (*Works,* V, 444; see also *Works,* III, 320 [1787], and III, 422 [1788]). And in 1800 he wrote: "I have . . . never failed to avail myself of any opportunity which offered of getting their [Indians'] vocabularies. I have now made up a large collection" (*Works,* IX, 125); and in 1801 he was congratulating himself on having collected some thirty "tolerably full, among which the number radically different is truly wonderful," which he found difficult to explain (*Works,* IX, 171).

❧ XII ❧

Giovanni da Verrazzano

1. NORTH AMERICA AND THE REDSKINS

THE letter from Giovanni da Verrazzano to King Francis I (8 July 1524) incorporates a large stretch of the coastline of North America within the description of American nature, which had hitherto been confined to the lands discovered by the Spaniards, and thus brings into the picture details and characteristics markedly different from those observed in Central and South America. It also affirms the continentality of the Americas, previously looked on as mere appendages or breakwaters of Asia.[1]

The Florentine's report, though it remained largely unknown until recent times (despite the appearance of Hakluyt's English translation in 1582, long before it was published in France), made it more difficult to generalize and draw categorical conclusions from those early observations. Particularly from the ethnographical standpoint, it introduces us to natives — the redskins — in every way different from the indigenous population of the West Indies and of Tierra Firme.

The further north one goes, the more the whole nature of the American continent becomes familiar, friendly, and normal, so that literary echoes and classical images lend themselves readily to describing it (pp. 132–34), and each locality is promptly baptized with a French toponym. The natives are "completely naked" but well proportioned, "not very strong" but "agile and very fleet of foot" (p. 169). "They are very generous, and whatever they have, they give" (p. 174). And in contrast with the observations made regarding the West Indians, "they live a very long time and rarely fall ill. . . . they must eventually die at a ripe old age, we think" (p. 177). The followers of their chiefs are invariably spoken of by Verrazzano — in the French manner — as "gentlemen" (e.g., p. 175). Nor does a word ever pass his lips implying aversion, fear, antagonism, or condemnation.[2]

They have no religion whatsoever but they copy all the gestures that they see

---

1. Firpo, op. cit., p. 186 (all page references given here for Verrazzano's letter refer to the Firpo edition). Cf. J. Habert, "Jean de Varrazane: État de la question," in *La découverte de l'Amérique* (Paris, 1968), pp. 51–59.
2. Hodgen, op. cit., pp. 368–69.

the devout Christians making (p. 180). They are friendly and eloquent, like the man of Arcadia who on hearing the roar of a European's musket "stood as if stunned and then burst into speech, preaching like a friar, pointing his finger to heaven" (pp. 171–72); and they also possess an effective array of oratorical gestures, as evidenced on the occasion when having nothing further to barter "the men performed all the acts of disdain and rudeness that any brute creature can make, such as showing their behinds, and laughing" (p. 179).

The women are no less proud. Michele da Cuneo's cannibal lady may have finally surrendered voluptuously to the lashes, but when the French "did everything in their power" to "capture" a young native girl "aged eighteen or twenty . . . very beautiful and tall of stature," with a view to carrying her off to France, "it proved quite impossible, what with the great shrieks she gave, for us to get her back to the shore," so that they had to leave her "in the woods" (p. 169).

2. ANIMAL, VEGETABLE, AND MINERAL RICHES

The land to which that comely and noisy redskin girl was so much attached is in fact pleasing and highly fertile, rich with a thousand forest fragrances and every possible sort of tree—both known and unknown in Europe—and "sweet-smelling flowers different from ours" (p. 170). Moreover it is "suitable for every sort of crop"—wheat, wine, oil, and so forth (pp. 170, 175).

"There are animals in great numbers: stags, roebuck, lynxes, wolves, and other sorts" (p. 176), and "wild animals that are considerably more wild than in our land of Europe, on account of their being continually disturbed by the hunters" (p. 170), and then very many birds "suitable and convenient [Verrazzano seems to be tipping the sovereign a wink] for all the delightful pleasures of the chase" (p. 164). The New World is already seen as a game reserve for Francis I.

There is almost no mention of gold and spices. The old mirages of rich booty are replaced by concrete prospects of colonization. The natives, in fact, do not like gold, because it is yellow, "a color they abhor, preferring blue and red to any other" (p. 174). Nor are they interested in other metals, although some have "copper beads in their ears" (p. 179), or in silken or gilded cloths, and the little mirrors just make them laugh. All they want are hawk-bells, glass beads, "little blue crystals and other such fancy things to put in their ears or round their necks" (p. 174). The tone is mocking, but there is also a certain benevolent, condescending sympathy. Verrazzano does not, however, rule out the possibility of the newly discovered lands, given their supposed proximity to Asia, "possessing some spices or aromatic liquor or other riches, gold or some other, the earth having very much a tendency to that color" (p. 164). The landscape of America is tinged with yellow, so there must be gold in it!

3. OLD WORLD AND NEW

From every line he writes we sense that Verrazzano, like Pigafetta but unlike most of the other reporters, is of "good family," a man of cultured, classical, and humanistic upbringing. He is therefore well suited to capturing the New World, bringing it within the Old World's schemes and translating it into the Old World's images. He knows very well, as we said above, that it is "new," in the sense that it is not a geographical appendage of either Europe or Asia;[3] but he absorbs it, measures it, and "explains" it in terms of the old continent. When he wants to locate an American promontory, he tells us that it is on the same latitude as Carthage and Damascus and another place is described as being on the same parallel as Rome.[4] The natives are not very different from the Saracens or the Ethiopians. They are as nimble as the Orientals, and especially the Chinese and Mongolians (as described by Marco Polo). The hairstyles of the matrons and the married women "resemble those of the women of Egypt and Syria" (p. 174). Wild vine shoots coil round the trees "like they do in Cisalpine Gaul" (p. 170).

One striking feature in all these details is the frequency of terms of comparison drawn from the Eastern Mediterranean or adjoining regions, or those made familiar by travelers' tales. This has led to the conjecture that Verrazzano "made voyages to the Levant,"[5] but it is possibly more likely that he resorted to these comparisons because the East—both near and far—was fairly familiar both to King Francis and to the European public and was at the same time the archetypal rich and fabled land.

4. PLACE-NAMES BORROWED FROM EUROPE

As if to balance this constant likening of American features to aspects of the Old World—but at the same time in implicit affirmation of the link between the two worlds—Verrazzano doles out generous quantities of names of European regions and localities to baptize American islands, bays, and rivers (one much quoted example being Sannazzaro's Arcadia, subsequently known for centuries

---

3. Morison, *Northern Voyages*, p. 313; R. Almagià, *Gli italiani primi esploratori dell'America* (Rome, 1937), pp. 363–64. From the very earliest discoveries, obviously, the old and known world served as a term of comparison and point of reference for the distances and the positional relationships of the newly discovered lands. Columbus locates Veragua in relation to other American lands by saying it is "in the same situation in which Tortosa lies with respect to Fonte Arabia in the Iberian peninsula, or Pisa with respect to Venice in Italy" (Almagià, op. cit., p. 191).

4. One island is described (Firpo, op. cit., p. 173) as being "similar in size to the island of Rhodes" (it was this comment that led to the naming of the state of Rhode Island in 1663—see Morison, *Northern Voyages*, p. 303). And the coastline of what is now Maine boasts "beautiful ports and channels, like in the Adriatic, in Illyria and Dalmatia" (Firpo, op. cit., p. 180).

5. Morison, *Northern Voyages*, p. 285. Almagià in fact states categorically that "it is clear from a well-known letter from Bernardo Carli in Lyon dated 4 August 1524 . . . that he had traveled extensively in the near East, staying in Cairo for some time" (op. cit., p. 354; cf. further reference to the same letter on p. 368, where the date is given as 24 August); but elsewhere (p. 463) he confines himself to saying that "in his youth he *probably* undertook voyages to the near East, and perhaps to other places too."

as Acadia, or Nova Scotia),[6] and he is even more unstinting with names of more or less eminent personages, more or less deserving of this gratuitous accolade. While the Spaniards tended to name their discoveries on the basis of some local feature or used the name of the saint whose day it was, and Cabot gallantly baptized the island of St. Catherine "probably in honor of his wife,"[7] the Florentine, first among the explorers of North America, used the titles of half the court and reminiscences of his native Tuscany to sprinkle the reports and maps of his voyages with European—and predominantly French—names;[8] a symbolic taking of possession, in many cases resulting in toponyms that have lasted right up to our own times.

6. Reciprocally, Verrazzano was responsible for introducing the first native place-name (Norombega) into European cartography (Almagià, op. cit., p. 452n196).

7. Ibid., p. 326.

8. Morison, *Northern Voyages*, p. 299; Almagià, op. cit., pp. 358–61, 366–67. Cartier soon followed his example (Almagià, pp. 359, 384).

❧ XIII ❧

The Spanish Government and the Geographical Knowledge of the Indies

1. LIMITED INITIAL INTEREST

THE crown's desire for detailed information on the newly discovered lands appears to have been neither as intense nor as constant as the scientific curiosity of the cultured classes in Europe in general, and Italy in particular. Jiménez de la Espada, who studied more than fifty instructions and "capitulations" addressed to captains, pilots, and adventurers between 1501 and 1573, in the course of his research into the antecedents of the famous "Ordenanzas de poblaciones y descubrimientos" of 1573, found himself forced to conclude that there was no invariable directive on this point. Sometimes the departing explorers were asked to furnish the minutest detail of the locations, qualities, and products of the lands they were setting off to discover, other times (especially between 1523 and 1528) there were no requests for geographical descriptions at all.[1] As for the Portuguese, even in 1550 "the inquisitive Ramusio deplores the negligence of the kings of Portugal, who should have required and preserved the fresh memorials of each successful expedition."[2]

Columbus had taken it upon himself to provide information, spurred originally by his desire to justify his undertaking and subsequently by his wish to glorify it. The sovereigns read the Genoese sailor's journal with great pleasure and in great secrecy ("we ourselves and no other person whatsoever have seen something of

---

1. Jiménez de la Espada, *Relaciones geográficas*, pp. xxiii–xxvii. The discovery of America, Burdach notes, was a purely economic event, which at first, and indeed for some considerable time, had no repercussions and only later revealed its true significance (*Reformation, Renaissance, Humanismus* [Berlin, 1918], pp. 136–37). On the much livelier and more methodical interest shown by the Spanish monarchy in the second half of the sixteenth century, see Rosenblat, op. cit., p. 84.

2. Edward Gibbon, op. cit., p. 378.

the book that you left us")[3] and asked for more details, but only regarding location and route. The totally practical nature of their interest comes out even more clearly in their letter of 16 August 1494, in which they ask to know the number of islands found, their names and their distances one from another, and whether the seasonal difference mentioned by the Admiral means that there are two summers and two winters every year over there; the letter closes on a point of natural history, true enough, but one inspired solely by the court's frivolous concern for the chase and the possible enrichment of the royal aviaries: "And send us as many falcons as you can from there and specimens of all the birds that can be found and obtained there, because we want to see them all."[4]

Only in the instructions for the fourth voyage do the sovereigns ask Columbus for an exact account of the islands and their inhabitants, their riches in metals, precious stones, pearls, and spices. Prompted partially by their increasingly serious interest in the economic possibilities of the new lands, and partially by a desire to curb the Admiral's now familiar tendency to flights of fantasy, they no longer leave him free to relate his quasi-biblical conjectures or semi-hallucinatory visions, but instead ask him specific questions in the form of a sort of rudimentary questionnaire.

The idea was a good one, but it was rarely adopted in the numerous capitulations and ordinances analyzed by Jiménez de la Espada, or at most only in the abbreviated form of an injunction to write and report on everything occurring or discovered. In 1504 Juan de la Cosa was asked[5] to seek "gold and silver, and trading profits, and other metals, and pearl-seeds and pearls and precious stones and monsters and fish and birds and spices and drugs and other things of any kind of quality whatsoever"; and in a *cédula* or warrant of 1505 the governor of Hispaniola was instructed to explore the neighboring islands "to learn their secrets and the nature of the people."[6] Neither Vicente Yáñez Pinzón (1501 and 1505), Ojeda (1504), Diego Velázquez (1518) nor Magellan (1519) were even asked for the administrative formality of a "relation," and later, as we have already seen, there is complete silence up until 1528. From 1529 onward reports only seem to have been requested when the discoverer sought "some special

3. Letter from Barcelona, 5 September 1493, cited in Jiménez de la Espada, *Relaciones,* p. xx.

4. Ibid., p. xxi. On the 1494 letter, see also Almagià, op. cit., p. 152. The courts of fifteenth-century Europe sought far and wide for their hawks and falcons. Filippo Maria Visconti sent all the way to Poland and Turkey for his purchases (M. Borsa, *La caccia nel milanese* [Milan, n.d. but 1924], p. 138). But what the drafter of the sovereigns' letter probably had in mind was the exquisite chapter LXXIX of Marco Polo's *Viaggi* (ed. cit., pp. 132–35), in which the Venetian describes "how the Great Khan goes hunting," and precisely "in the region of the Ocean Sea," with ten thousand falconers and five hundred "gyrfalcons and peregrine falcons and saker falcons in great abundance"; and the limitless delight that he takes in that spectacular hunt: "And you should know that there is no lord in the world, that could have so much pleasure in this world, nor that had the power of having it, neither was, nor ever will be, to my mind." Ferdinand's passion for hunting was proverbial ("the only amusement for which he cared much was hunting," especially falconry"—Prescott, III, 409), and Charles V's even more so.

5. Document transcribed in Puente y Olea, op. cit., p. 22.

6. Ibid., p. 38.

award of revenues, vassals, and leagues of land in whatever he discovered or colonized," in which case he was of course, before being granted his request, asked to furnish His Majesty with a precise account of what he had found in that land. But even this restriction was applied only loosely, and sizeable concessions were granted to Hernando de Soto, Gabriel de Socarrás, and Francisco de Orellana "without the previous condition."[7]

2. CURIOSITY AND ZEAL OF LOCAL OFFICIALS

This relative indifference on the government's part is in strong contrast with the interest shown by local governors and conquistadors, who instructed their subordinates, captains, or lieutenants to explore, investigate, ascertain, and measure with all diligence and zeal not only the geographical locations, metals, and species, but also the people, the fruit, the plants, animals, natural phenomena, the arms and languages of the natives, and their social systems. This eager curiosity is ideally exemplified in the instructions given by Diego Velázquez to Hernán Cortés (1518), by Pedrarias Dávila to Licentiate Gaspar de Espinosa (1519), by Hernán Cortés himself to Álvaro de Saavedra Cerón (1527), by Diego López de Salcedo to Gabriel de Rojas (1527), and by the Viceroy Antonio de Mendoza to Fray Marcos de Niza (1538).[8]

Here again, then, in the field of study and reconnaissance of the new lands, government initiative clearly lagged a long way behind the enterprise shown by the Spanish adventurers and colonists of the New World. The policy of the mother country, so often shortsighted and backward in economic and administrative matters, proved no better in the scientific field, showing itself once again hesitant, cumbersome, and only grudgingly prepared to follow and ratify the lead given by the inquiries of local officials.

3. THE *CÉDULA* OF 1533 AND OVIEDO

There is, however, a notable *cédula* dated 19 December 1533 in which Charles V asks Alvarado for a full report of Guatemala, with its boundaries, cities, "the qualities and pecularities existing there," the inhabitants "including their rites and customs in particular," and the Spaniards, and where they live "and how many of them are married to Spanish women or to Indian women, and how many of them unmarried; and what ports and rivers it has, and what buildings have been erected there, and what animals and birds breed there, and of what quality they are." Jiménez de la Espada states unhesitatingly that this unusual *cédula* is the most important and interesting he found: it is "an abridgement, compendium, and preview of all those that followed, containing the essence of them. . . . Who

---

7. Jiménez de la Espada, *Relaciones geográficas*, p. xxvi.
8. All ibid., pp. xxvii–xxix.

could have dictated it?" He denies that it could have been Pedro de Esquivel, as Fermín Caballero suggested, but he puts forward no other hypothesis.[9]

For our part, we would merely recall that on 15 October 1532 the king had ordered all officials in the Indies to give Oviedo, if asked, "reports on lands, events, and other things," and that on 25 October 1533, less than two months before the order to Alvarado, Charles had written to Oviedo telling him to send forthwith to Madrid as much as he had already written of his *Historia,* sending on supplements and additions as they were finished. It would therefore seem that the appointment of Oviedo as Chronicler of the Indies (1532) coincided with a revival of geographical interest at court in the new lands, no doubt also due to the astonishing news then coming in from Peru.[10] As early as 19 July 1534 the emperor could be found writing to the bishop of Tierra Firme, Fray Tomás de Berlanga: "In view of the reports that have been sent to me of the affairs and riches of Peru, and its magnitude, I desire to be kept fully and specifically informed of the affairs of the said province."[11] The same instructions—probably *not* carried out—were repeated to Fray Vicente Valverde when he was appointed bishop of Cuzco (1536).[12] But the first descriptions of Peru were drafted spontaneously by Miguel de Estete and Cristóbal de Molina (1536, 1539).[13]

There is thus, to my mind, a degree of inaccuracy in Carbia's intriguing assertion that the interest in geography and natural history that prevailed in the first twenty years after the discoveries gave way, around 1520–1525, under Las Casas's influence, to an interest in the way the Indians were treated, in the process of conquest and pacification, pushing into the background "the preoccupation with finding out about the prodigious nature of the Indies."[14] Las Casas's preaching indubitably increased interest in the Indian problems in government circles, helping to keep these problems in the limelight and show up their complexity, their inherent dangers, and the way they were inextricably bound up with the basic ideologies of the Catholic monarchy itself. But it was always a practical interest, the government's concern for the good administration of the newly occupied lands, for the procurement of as much wealth as could possibly be extracted therefrom, with a minimum of military force and brutality. It was a "political" interest of the sort already evident in the instructions and recommendations given by Ferdinand and Isabella, and not a cognitive interest, a feature that never loomed very large in the sovereigns or their ministers, whether before or after Las Casas; although this cognitive interest seized Columbus the

---

9. Ibid., pp. xxxviii–xl.
10. For some of the very first reports on the land of Peru, ibid., p. xl and ff.
11. Ibid., p. xli.
12. Ibid., p. xlii.
13. Ibid., pp. xlii–xliv.
14. R. Carbia, *La crónica oficial de las Indias Occidentales* (La Plata, 1934), p. 75.

very moment he first set eyes on the new islands, continued in Peter Martyr, and spread rapidly throughout Europe, it was, if anything, diverted by Las Casas and focused on the problem of the Indian and thus directed exclusively toward ethnographic investigation, neglecting and indeed ignoring the fauna, the flora, the physical attributes, and natural economy of the new continent.

4. Reports Varyingly Received

A reflection of this phenomenon of diffraction—between the practical and political interest of the Spanish monarchy and the cognitive interests of its servants, both Spanish and non-Spanish, between the national objective of aggrandizement and the human aim of geographical progress—can be seen in the varying reception accorded to the reports from the Indies in Spain and the rest of Europe, a reception so much warmer and more studious and attentive in almost all the rest of Europe than in Spain itself, from whose ports the caravels and brigantines had sailed.

As late as 1627 Juan Rodríguez de León, the brother of Antonio de León Pinelo, could be heard complaining that foreigners knew and studied the Indies much better than the Spaniards themselves: "As gold and silver are the only items of the Indies that appeal, its writers are as forgotten as its history is neglected, and what should be native to Spain is a purely foreign occupation; thus other people's pens are more familiar with our conquests than our own curiosity."[15]

The relative lack of interest in the Indian discoveries on the part of the as yet unformed Spanish public opinion, in contrast with the immediately enthusiastic response of all cultivated Europe, has been noted and wondered at already on more than one occasion. Essentially it reflects the historical paradox that it should have fallen to one of the most backward countries of Western Europe to take the decisive step in the worldwide expansion of European civilization. Before it ever became the "channel" along which the treasures of the Indies flowed to stimulate the growing complexity of European industry and trade, Spain was the "instrument" of Europe's infiltration of the New World.

A relatively muted instrument, however. The bulk of the Spanish population, poor, weary, and ignorant, remained largely unstirred. The adventurers emigrated to the New World to get away from the poverty of Spain: they were as much fugitives as conquerors. And their governors, after endless hesitation and backsliding, only committed themselves to backing the caravels of Italians and Portuguese—from Columbus to Magellan—when they saw the gleam of gold reflected in the islands of the farthest West.

For decades after the *Niña* sailed back into Palos—until 1535 when Oviedo's *Historia General y Natural de las Indias* was published—the only account of

---

15. "Discurso apologético" (unpaginated) prefacing "La Biblioteca del Licenciado Antonio de Léon su hermano," i.e., León Pinelo's *Epítome de la biblioteca oriental y occidental, naútica y geográfica* (Madrid, 1629).

Columbus's voyages and discoveries printed in an edition accessible to Spaniards was to be found in Peter Martyr's Latin *Decades*. There was not even a Spanish translation of this text, a circumstance which probably induced the humanist Hernán Pérez de Oliva to compile a literary reworking of the "Ystoria de Colón" on the basis of the *Decades*,[16] a work which is in fact still unpublished today.

The *Decades of the New World* were in Latin, and despite a momentary wave of humanistic enthusiasm Latin remained much less familiar to the Spaniards of the Renaissance than to the Italians and French.[17] Mention has already been made (above, chap. VIII, n. 10) of the various editions of the *Decades* printed in Basle, Antwerp, Cologne, Paris, and Venice, and of early translations into Italian, English, and French. No edition was printed in Spain after 1530; no translation was made until the fourth centenary of the discovery of America![18] That ignorance of Latin should have impeded acquaintanceship with the New World, or rather that lack of interest in classical texts should have gone hand in hand with an indifference to the geographical discoveries is certainly no mere coincidence but further proof (if any were needed) of the basic unity of that universal spiritual reawakening that led men to seek out antiquity beyond the Dark Ages and New Lands beyond the unknown seas.

5. BELATED AWAKENING OF SPANISH INTEREST

Spain remained largely untouched by this tendency, or experienced it only secondhand.[19] The Spaniards only began to become acquainted with their new empire when Cortés and then Pizarro set out on their glorious adventures. The former's letters were printed in Spain in 1522 and 1525.[20] In 1526, to please Charles V, Oviedo published his *Sumario*, and finally in 1534 the first accounts

---

16. Olschki, *"Ystoria de Colon,"* esp. pp. 188–89.

17. Ibid., and more generally, on the limited appreciation of classical studies in Renaissance Spain, B. Croce, *La Spagna nella vita italiana durante la Rinascenza* (Bari, 1917), pp 30–31, 89, 90n4, 102, 111, 166–67, 247; E. Gothein, *Il Rinascimento nell'Italia meridionale* (Florence, 1915), pp. 203–04 and passim; L. Olschki, *Struttura spirituale e linguistica del mondo neo-latino* (Bari, 1935), p. 148; and below, chap. XVII, sec. 12. A. Morel-Fatio recalls Paolo Giovio's disdain, as expressed in his *Elogia*, for the meager and superficial humanistic culture of the upper classes in Spain (*Historiographie de Charles Quint* [Paris, 1912], p. 118). Even the very learned marquess of Santillana, Iñigo López de Mendoza (1349–1458), "was totally ignorant of Greek and almost completely wanting in Latin" (A. Farinelli, *Italia e Spagna* [Turin, 1929], I, 397).

18. The first Decade was published in Seville in 1511, without the author's knowledge and against his wishes (see above, chap. VIII, n. 10), and the first three in Alcalá in 1516. All the Spanish editions are extremely rare. Only in 1892 did Joaquín Torres Asensio publish his translation of the *Decades* in Madrid, in four volumes.

19. This is one of Croce's principal theses and is also advanced by the Catalan Pedro Bosch Gimpera, who laments: "There were times when it seemed that Spain was going to become fully part of the Renaissance, but she carefully avoided the repercussions that the Renaissance brought with it and, in a certain way, the Middle Ages were prolonged" ("Para la comprensión de España," *CA*, 7, no. 1 [1943], 169).

20. The second and third letters were published in Seville in 1522, the fourth in Toledo in 1525. It should however be noted that: (1) these editions are extremely rare, which suggests it was a very small printing; (2) Cortés's letters were immediately circulated in translations printed in Latin, Italian, German (Nuremberg, 1524; Venice, 1524) and later in French; (3) they were reprinted in Spanish only toward the middle of the eighteenth century, and the first complete edition is the one in the Biblioteca de Rivadaneyra series (Vedia, op. cit., I, 1–153; see also the bibliographical note in this same work, pp. xv–xvii).

of the conquest of Peru were published in Castilian.[21] Of the three accounts of Magellan's voyage, one was written by an Italian, Pigafetta, one by a Bruxellois, Maximilianus Transylvanus, the third by a Portuguese, Gaspar Correa.[22]

Much later again the legend of El Dorado was to arouse more lively and lasting interest among foreigners than among Spaniards,[23] and, impelled by jealousy and mistrust, the Madrid government even went so far as to try to prevent foreigners gaining any knowledge of the resources of the new Spanish colonies. In Philip II's instructions in 1573, seeking exact and complete "relations" on Spain and the Indies—instructions that marked a great step forward in the methodology of statistical and geographical enquiry—question three asked for information on the climate and weather and question twenty-seven on the native animals, birds of prey, and domestic fowl and on how the animals brought over from Spain "grow and multiply," but the accounts obtained tended to be more like lists or inventories, and in fact the questions derived directly from administrative and fiscal needs, connected with the *encomienda* system.[24]

21. On the "fanciful histories" that gained wide circulation in Europe in response to the immense interest in the new discoveries, ranging from "straightforward discoverers' letters, dished out to a curious public by publishers of all countries," to adaptations and extracts embellished with wildly exaggerated titles, see Carbia, *Crónica oficial*, pp. 81–83, with examples from 1523 (Cortés's letter printed by Kromberger in Seville), 1534 (letter from a Mexican friar, printed in Venice) and 1545 (brief fragment of Oviedo translated from the Italian and printed in Paris).

22. Much to the amazement of a reviewer in *HAHR*, 44, no. 3 (August 1964), 413.

23. V. T. Harlow, "Introduction" to Walter Raleigh, *The Discoverie of the large and bewtiful Empire of Guiana* (London, 1928), pp. lxix, xciii; Pereyra, *Los conquistadores*, p. 350; E. de Gandía, *Historia crítica de los mitos de la conquista americana* (Madrid, 1929), pp. 113–14; C. Bayle, *El dorado fantasma* (Madrid, 1930), p. 416.

24. Jiménez de la Espada, *Relaciones geográficas*, pp. xxxi, xxxv–xxxvi, li, lviii, lxx. Cf. Howard F. Cline, "The 'Relaciones Geográficas' of the Spanish Indies, 1577–1586," *HAHR*, 44, no. 3 (August 1964), 341–74, mentioning a forthcoming study by Leoncio Cabrero, "Las *Relaciones geográficas* de Nueva España: Su aportación al estudio de las ciencias americanistas."

Interlude

BEFORE looking at Oviedo's ideas on nature in the Americas it might not be amiss to take stock of the sum total of knowledge gathered and set down before the publication of his *Sumario* (1526). This is in fact the only way we can hope to assess the novelty of his contribution and see each of his observations in its true perspective. Our rapid review of the writings of all those who preceded Oviedo in settling their gaze on the physical reality of the New World was of course undertaken for that very purpose.

But now that we find ourselves on the threshold of Oviedo's great edifice we are forced to recognize that our project has failed. Any attempt to trace a line of development from Columbus to Oviedo is completely illusory, indeed misleading. The authors we have discussed do not speak the same language. Their mental interests are different, and thus the visual angles from which they view America are different too. Their intellectual backgrounds and impedimenta of knowledge are different, their scales of values worlds apart. Thus the interest that each of them brings to the things seen or (as in Peter Martyr's case) avidly gleaned is absolutely different.

Rarely do we find what we might call a "scientific" intention, an attempt at systematic description. The prevailing sentiments are of a quite different, and heteroclite, nature: personal advantage, the desire for fatter profits, pride of discovery, flattery of the powerful (or those believed to be so), a journalistic determination to "make news," display of arcane erudition, delight in storytelling, mercantile speculation, and the eternal pervasive greed for gold.

Even the natives are "used" in totally conflicting ways: at one moment pictured in a state of primitive innocence, as latter-day representatives of the mythical golden age (while in reality remaining characteristic embodiments of demands and aspirations proper to the late fifteenth and early sixteenth centuries), at the next thrust down to become the lowest, most abject specimens of the human race, "formed to live like brutes," as Dante's Ulysses put it, lacking any intellectual, moral, religious, and maybe even physical gifts, like low-grade raw material or the most simple primal matter; and at times displaying monstrous idiosyncrasies, of build or otherwise, that turn them into curious creatures of a semimythical fauna, from which the "white man" recoils in horror and consternation.

There is another obvious reason why it is impossible to relate a history of the development of the physical knowledge of America: the dozen or so most important authors do not form a chain of scholars, handing on their findings and interpretations from one to another. To all intents and purposes, in fact, apart from the odd exception (Peter Martyr again) they are completely unaware of each other.[1] They address themselves to different publics and certainly do not feel called upon to back up their descriptions—almost invariably of "things never before seen"—with precedents and corroborating testimony. They do not (it need hardly be said) read the "literature" of the subject, and even if they happen to be familiar with it they deliberately ignore it, lest it detract from their own originality. Each is his own authority, even when, by chance or of necessity, what he relates tallies with other accounts. Viewed from the distance of several centuries they look like solitary scouts or reconnaissance patrols, sailing or galloping, along diverging paths, toward the unknown heart of the continent.

And yet we remain stubbornly convinced that this fragmentary introduction was not entirely wasted. It has shown us the themes, theorems, and problems of acquaintanceship with the New World, the techniques for tackling it, so to speak, the logical obstacles that blocked the path to a knowledge of this world, the prejudices and lingering memories that conditioned this knowledge.

Nor is this all. This review may have served some purpose not only as an introduction to Oviedo's work and not only as an assessment of the contribution of these travelers to the study of American nature, but also, in taking us back beyond the systematizations of later observers—such as the great Acosta or Father Cobo or even the mythologizing Antonio de León Pinelo—as a first rough formulation, almost a rudimentary sketch, of nearly all the questions which, on an altogether different scientific level, the naturalists of the eighteenth century asked themselves.

There is almost no accusation or calumny—of the fauna, flora, or climate of the New Indies—pronounced by Buffon, de Pauw, or one of their many followers, that cannot be traced back to a legend or item of factual data found somewhere among these incunabula of Americanistics. For although, as we have just said, the early chroniclers, from Columbus to Verrazzano, were unaware of each other, by the end of the eighteenth century they were almost all well known to the scholarly world (the sole significant exception being three-quarters of Oviedo's *Historia*) and were thus able, after a lapse of more than two hundred years, to back each other up, to contradict, correct, or enrich one another, both

---

1. But Oviedo—privileged in this too—was acquainted with the writings of Columbus, Vespucci, Peter Martyr, Enciso, Cortés, and Pigafetta, as well as the reports of numerous other pilots and conquistadors.

reciprocally and in respect of the numerous "travelers" and "naturalists" of the intervening period (ca. 1556–1750).

The first diatribes, those we have recounted here, were, almost three centuries later, taken up again, given new life, distorted and pressed into the service of other often utterly alien themes, feeding the flames of what we have taken the liberty of calling "*the* dispute of the New World." They merged one with another, to a certain extent, and in the remote and misty perspective of the long passing years acted as multicolored backdrop, or perhaps as painted allegorical curtain, for the great stage of the fabled Indies.

When we remember the course run by these ideas, it will not seem paradoxical to look on this little sheaf of studies as a sort of prologue to the eighteenth-century polemic, the first wing of the diptych, to accompany that other volume which I wrote so long ago.

❦ PART 2 ❦

Gonzalo Fernández de Oviedo

❧ XIV ❧

Life and Literary Reputation

1. PUBLICATION OF THE *HISTORIA*

O V I E D O ' S literary reputation has suffered curious fluctuations. The *Sumario* was a huge and immediate success and the *Historia General y Natural de las Indias* even more so. The first part of the *Historia,* the only part published in the author's lifetime, in 1535, was reprinted (1547), translated into French (by Jean Poleur, 1555),[1] and included, in Italian, in the third part, of Giovan Battista Ramusio's classic *Raccolta de navigationi et viaggi* (Venice, 1550–1556).[2]

The success of that first part is further proved—albeit negatively—by the various explanations put forward for the nonpublication of the other parts, which Oviedo had ready for the press[3] and which circulated in manuscript form. According to an old legend, picked up by Harrisse,[4] it was because "a great conflagration destroyed the printing establishment of Francisco Fernández de Córdova, His Majesty's printer, with all its contents, including the printed parts and manuscripts of Oviedo." According to López de Gómara,[5] it was because of the clandestine opposition (1548) of Las Casas. According to Fueter,[6] it was because of the sheer bulk of the work, "which nobody wanted to print." It seems to me not unlikely that the authorities of the time, who were also to ban (17 November 1553) the recent *Historia General de las Indias* (1552) of López de Gómara, were reluctant to publish a work containing severe criticism of the

---

1. This French translation was prefaced by various laudatory sonnets, by both the author and the translator, on which see Le Moine, op. cit., pp. 69, 163, 168, 217 and notes.
2. The *Sumario* of 1526 also features in Ramusio's collection, together with the account of the "Navigation of the great river Maragnon" (Bartolommeo Gamba, *Serie dei testi di lingua italiana* [Venice, 1828], pp. 481–82), in other words, it would seem, the first five chapters of book XLIX. See Amador de los Ríos, "Vida," pp. cvi–cvii*n44.*
3. *Hist.,* VIII, 20: PT, I, 260a. In the closing lines of the work Oviedo announces (1549) that he will embark upon a fourth part (L, 30: PT, V, 417b).
4. *Bibliotheca Americana,* pp. 338–39.
5. *Anales* (1548; Oxford, 1912), p. 258, quoted by Agapito Rey, "Book XX of Oviedo's *Historia general y natural de las Indias,*" *Romanic Review,* 18 (1927), 56, and by Iglesia, *Cronistas e historiadores,* p. 133, who accept López de Gómara's version. Oviedo could have reprinted the first part of the *History,* already published in 1535, without need of a new license; but not the subsequent books, of which (according to Rey) only book XX was then published.
6. Op. cit., p. 298.

clergy and the conduct of the Spanish in the Indies, criticism that was given additional weight by the official character of Oviedo's *Historia*.

In fact, on 29 November 1563, the king ordered Andrés Gasco, "inquisitor in the City of Seville," to hand over to the Council of the Indies "with all diligence and due precaution" certain books in his possession "written in the hand of Gonzalo Fernández de Oviedo, commandant of the fortress of Santo Domingo on the island of Hispaniola, which deal with the Indies, that have not been seen or examined or authorized for publication . . . so that having been seen and examined therein [in the council] we can see that appropriate action is taken on this matter." The document was published by Medina[7] in connection with the *Crónica* of Cieza de León, which the council also expressed a desire to study.[8] At the beginning of the seventeenth century the canon Andrés Gasco left Oviedo's original (?) codices, which had at one time belonged to the Convent of Montserrat, to the Casa de Contratación. But Antonio de León Pinelo, when drafting his *Epítome,* thought (1629) that the work had been left unfinished and noted that the book dealing with Magellan had been written by Oviedo "as the twentieth book of the general [history] that he hoped to complete" and which was to be in fifty books.[9] In 1775 an almost complete version of the text was to be found in the archives of the Ministry of Grace, Justice, and the Indies,[10] and the government was apparently prepared to arrange its publication,[11] but the plan was not put into effect.

Amador de los Ríos, however, affirms that in 1556–1557 Oviedo "obtained permission to have the *Historia* published."[12] All that is really certain is that manuscript copies were used in turn by Muñoz, Prescott, and Ticknor.[13]

---

7. Archivo General de Indias, estante 139, cajón I, legajo, II, tomo 24, folio 169, in Medina, *Biblioteca,* I, 256.

8. Garcilaso, who had not yet published the *Comentarios reales,* was also suspect (see Henríquez Ureña, *Literary Currents,* p. 64). Not even government historians could escape the censor. In 1571 the position of "Cronista Mayor de las Indias," or "Chief Chronicler of the Indies," was set up (Carbia, *Crónica oficial,* p. 100). But article 119 of the ordinances of the Royal Council of the Indies (El Pardo, 25 October 1571) requires the official chronicler to lodge his work with the council "and only that which the councils think should be made public may be published or allowed to be read." J. Torre Revello, who promises to illustrate the implications of this ban on another occasion, says it is to be found in the *CDII,* XVI, 457–59 ("La expedición de don Pedro de Mendoza y las fuentes informativas de . . . Herrera," in *Contribuciones para el estudio de la historia de América: Homenaje al Dr. E. Ravignani* [Buenos Aires, 1941], p. 612n); it can also be read in Jiménez de la Espada, *Relaciones geográficas,* I, lxi, xcii, and, with slight textual modifications, in the *Recopilación de leyes de Indias,* ley I. tít, XII, lib. II. One of the first tasks of the first official chronicler, Juan López de Velasco, was to see whether the *Historia del Perú,* published in Seville in 1571 by Diego Fernández, should be suppressed, as Viceroy Francisco de Toledo demanded (see L. Hanke, "Viceroy Francisco de Toledo and the Just Titles of Spain to the Inca Empire," *The Americas,* 3 [1946–47], 11–12).

9. *Epítome,* p. 92 (and cf. p. 69).

10. Harrisse, *Bibliotheca Americana,* p. 339. An official document, published a few years later, the *Relación* of 1788, states that "this is as far as Oviedo's description goes, because his death in 1557 led to the interruption of the printing of this work which, together with others on America, is preserved in MS" (p. 209n3). On the whereabouts of various manuscripts, see L. Gómez Canedo, *Los archivos de la historia de América: Período colonial español* (México, 1961), I. 176, 191–92, 195; II, 10, 59, 72, 129.

11. Navarrete, op. cit., I, lxxv; Winsor, op. cit., II, 346.

12. "Vida," p. lxxx. It is possible that the animosity toward Oviedo shown by certain ultra-hispanophiles like Carbia (see below, chap. XVIII, n. 100) is a carry-over of those suspicions harbored by the authorities in respect of the opinions of the official historian.

13. *History of Spanish Literature* (Boston and New York, 1891), II, 42n28.

The part published was, however, sufficient to secure Oviedo's fame. Doctors and naturalists, geographers and historians from every part of the world read it, discussed it, and quoted it as an authority. In 1544 Oviedo was visited in Santo Domingo by Johan Cano, a Spaniard who had married "a legitimate daughter of Montezuma" and established himself in Mexico. With somewhat tropical immodesty and exaggeration Oviedo recommended that he read the first volume of his *Historia,* informing him that the book in question "existed already in Tuscan and French and German and Latin and Greek and Turkish and Arabic, although I wrote it in Castilian." [14]

2. ITS CIRCULATION AND REPUTATION

The works of the chroniclers and scientists of the sixteenth and ensuing centuries contain innumerable quotations and obvious derivations from Oviedo, whose *Sumario* (1526) and *Historia* gave the first scientific descriptions of rubber trees, the tobacco plant, and a multitude of medicinal extracts and edible plants. Of the plants of Peru, the earliest chroniclers (Hernando Pizarro, Jerez, Pedro Sancho de la Hoz, Estete) only mention seven species. Oviedo describes another thirty or thirty-five, including the coca and cinnamon. [15] López de Gómara, when discussing his version of the relationship between Velázquez and Cortés, described Oviedo (about 1552) as having been "the most diligent, of all those who have commemorated the affairs of the Indies, in following history," saying that although he may have been led astray on that point, his good faith was not in question—"in everything else a good man." [16]

His work can be found in the catalogues of private libraries of Elizabethan England. [17] Father Cobo, in the first half of the seventeenth century, still "at times follows Oviedo almost literally." [18]

More than one scholar, drawing on Oviedo, who had provided the first methodical description of the phenomena of the Indies, bestowed on him the

14. *Hist.,* XXXIII, 54: III, 552b. Amador de los Ríos ("Vida," p. lxii) accepts the boast as a proven fact, and it is repeated as a fact by Carbia, "La historia del descubrimiento y los fraudes del P. Las Casas," *Nosotros,* 72 (1931), 153n14, citing (irrelevantly) Medina, *Biblioteca,* I, 109–12, and the bibliography by B. Sanchéz Alonso, in whose third and last edition, entitled *Fuentes de la historia española e hispano-americana,* 3 vols. (Madrid, 1952), the *Historia* is listed as no. 3586.

But Oviedo himself implicitly contradicts it, when he writes in the last chapter of the work: "As soon as my writings reach Italy and Germany and Turkey and circulate among different peoples of the Catholic Christian republic, or penetrate the provinces possessed by the infidels in the world, they *will* be translated and written in various languages" (*Hist.,* L. 30: IV, 590–91). See also D. Turner, "Biblioteca Ovetense," no. 88, and below, chap. XV, sec. 18.

15. E. Yacovleff and F. L. Herrera, "El mundo vegetal de los antiguos peruanos," *Revista del Museo Nacional,* 3, no. 3 (1934), 269. The Argentine specialist Humberto Paoli (quoted by Rey Pastor, op. cit., pp. 125–26n) calls Oviedo "the first commentator on the plants of America," and Rey Pastor approves: "It can be stated unhesitatingly that Fernández de Oviedo was the first naturalist to present a methodical review of the most useful plants of the American flora and to make them known in Europe" (op. cit., p. 128).

16. López de Gómara, *De rebus gestis F. Cortesii,* attributed to Gómara by Iglesia, *Cronistas e historiadores,* pp. 219–23, and given in an appendix to that work, p. 279.

17. Blanke, op. cit., p. 26.

18. Yacovleff and Herrera, op. cit., p. 247.

paternity of discoveries that were not his. The illustrious William Gilbert, founder of the theory of earth magnetism (*De Magnete,* 1600) and the Jesuit Giovanni Battista Riccioli (1598–1671) believed that it was Oviedo, rather than Columbus, who first noticed magnetic variation.[19] Ferrando credited him with having predicted the Panama Canal.[20] Others, disregarding his permanent reluctance to baptize the geographical curiosities of the Indies on his own authority (see below, chap. XVIII, sec 18), gave him credit for having been the first to name the Sargasso Sea.[21]

Redi cites him in connection with the armadillo and the iguana.[22] Vico mentions him on the subject of human sacrifices. In Voltaire there are clear recollections or faint echoes of some of Oviedo's more curious items of information (for example the "cowardly" lions and the pigs with navels on their backs). And the great Humboldt, in a splendid passage extolling the scientific curiosity and restless philosophical spirit of the Spaniards of the sixteenth century, pays Oviedo the signal compliment of considering him the founder, together with Father Acosta (who is in any case considerably later), of "what is today called physical geography."[23]

3. THE ACADEMIA DE LA HISTORIA EDITION

At the beginning of the nineteenth century the Academia de la Historia of Madrid, which housed the manuscripts collected by Juan Bautista Muñoz for drafting his *Historia del Nuevo Mundo* (broken off after the publication of the

---

19. Rey Pastor, op. cit., p. 160.

20. R. Ferrando, "Fernández de Oviedo y el conocimiento del Mar del Sur," *RI,* 17 (1957), 478. Pascual de Andagoya established the characteristics of the isthmus. Oviedo recognized its importance as a shortcut to the Spice Islands (XXXIX, 30: PT, III, 334; see below, chap. XIX, sec. 39).

21. J. Gavira Martín, "Recientes investigaciones sobre el Mar de los Sargazos," *Boletín de la Real Sociedad Geográfica,* 80, nos. 1–6 (1944), cited in *RI,* 6, no. 22 (1945), p. 777.

22. Francesco Redi, *Esperienze interno a diverse cose naturali* (Florence, 1686), pp. 54. 57. The *Encyclopedia Britannica* (11th ed., I, 99a, s v "Accademics") is mistaken in stating that the Accademia dei Lincei published in Rome in 1651 "the magnificent edition of Fernández de Oviedo's *Natural History of Mexico* . . . elaborately annotated by its members." The work published by the Lincei, the *Tesoro messicano* (or *Rerum medicarum Novae Hispaniae thesaurus*), already almost completely printed in 1628, is based on the reports of Francisco Hernández of Toledo (1517–87), a doctor and botanist also mentioned by Redi (*Esperienze,* p. 22, in connection with the Maldives coconut, and, p. 94, concerning the *xocoxochitl,* or Tabasco pepper), but who, far from being easily confused with Oviedo, does not even deign to mention him; in fact, incredible as this may seem to modern scholars, he does not even seem to have known of the work of his illustrious predecessor and fellow-countryman (E. Alvarez López, "El Dr. Francisco Hernández y sus comentarios a Plinio," *RI,* 3 (1942), 251–90, end). In turn the Hernández of Toledo and Mexico should not be confused with Francisco Fernández of Cordova, conquistador in Central America, also mentioned by Redi, *Osservazioni intorno alle vipere* (Florence, 1686), p. 64.

23. Humboldt, *Cosmos,* II, 255–56, 270, 275. The commendation is also mentioned by M. Menéndez Pelayo, "Historiadores," 106n (to whom it is attributed, for the purposes of refuting it, by Henríquez Ureña, *La cultura,* p. 65) and by Rey Pastor, op. cit., pp. 27–28, 148. De Pauw had already linked Oviedo's name with Acosta's: "The news of the discovery of another hemisphere caused great astonishment in Europe. . . . Everyone wanted to see the reports . . . but Acosta and Oviedo stood out amongst the first to publish reports because they included observations on the animal kingdom" (*Défense des Recherches Philosophiques* [Berlin, 1770], p. 84). Note that De Pauw, like Humboldt, names Acosta *before* Oviedo, reversing their chronological order. A similar judgment is delivered by Enrique de Vedia: Oviedo "opened the door to the study of the natural history of America" (op. cit., I, xi). And Barros Arana considers Oviedo and Father Acosta the only naturalists of merit before Ulloa (*Obras,* vol. IV [Santiago, 1909], p. 137n).

first volume in 1793), decided to undertake the publication of the works of Las Casas and Oviedo. But the American revolutions and the renewed intensity of the attacks on the Spanish administration induced it to suspend (1 May 1821) the publication of Las Casas, with which it had apparently embarked on its work. "It was felt that in the prevailing circumstances its publication would not be appropriate or opportune, not its authorization seemly for the nation."

Thirty years later the Academia recognized that circumstances had changed and, with regard to Oviedo, referred to the recent work by Amador de los Ríos (probably the study prefacing the first volume of the new edition) to prove that it was useful to rebut foreign calumnies by bringing to light the original texts.[24]

In the end, then, the complete publication of Oviedo's *Historia* was undertaken by the Academia de la Historia three centuries after its author's death and brought to a conclusion, under the editorship of José Amador de los Ríos, between 1851 and 1855. But those four fat quarto volumes, totaling more than twenty-four hundred double-columned pages plus the one-hundred-page biography of the author, instead of refurbishing the venerable old historian's reputation seem to have been destined to bury it under their monumental weight. The *Historia,* this "most voluminous work written since the time of Adam,"[25] "is too bulky to have found many scholars prepared to read it attentively all the way through."[26]

4. Oviedo's glory in decline

In recent decades, indeed, Oviedo's glory has been in decline, with the verdicts pronounced becoming more negative and almost scornful. Menéndez Pelayo questions Oviedo's impartiality, accusing him of having a "somewhat lax moral conscience" in his views on the "outrages and excesses," of being overly concerned with banalities and given to indulging his old soldier's violent prejudices. He comes close to calling him stupid—"Oviedo was certainly not a man of great understanding, although of strong will"[27]—and makes no bones about

---

24. See the relevant documents, dating from 1821, 1851, and 1856, in the *Boletín de la Real Academia de la Historia,* 78 (1921), 277–85. Humboldt too regretted the fact that "despite the orders of Charles III most of the precious works of this historian have remained unpublished" *(Examen critique,* I, 134n). The preface to the 1851–55 edition ("Advertencia," p. vi) explains the long delay in terms of the difficulty of assembling a complete set of the manuscripts and the shortage of funds.

25. In the words of Salas, op. cit., p. 103, who also recalls how proud Oviedo was of the immense bulk of his product.

26. J. Pérez de Tudela, "Rasgos del semblante espiritual de Gonzalo Fernández de Oviedo," *RI,* 17 (1957), 430. The edition has also been accused of being "vague and incorrect" as far as Ponce de León is concerned by J. G. Shea (in Winsor, op. cit., II, 283), who finds the 1535 edition preferable.

27. "Historiadores," pp. 88–89. But in his *Historia de la poesía hispano-americana* (Santander, 1948), II, 288, Don Marcelino admits that "among the early books on America there is none as interesting as his."

Vicente de la Fuente, when he came to publish the first part of the *Quinquagenas* (Madrid, 1880), noted that "Oviedo's works were born under an evil star" (p. vi); and sure enough, his own edition got no further than the first part. On the complete ignorance regarding Oviedo's works (apart from the *Historia* and the *Sumario,* of course) on the part of scholars even in the eighteenth century, see Fuente, op. cit., pp. xii–xvi. In 1788 (5 May), however, José Rodríguez de Castro wrote to Francisco Cerdá, who in turn informed Juan Bautista Muñoz, who was collecting material for his *History of the New World,* that the Royal Library contained two Oviedo manuscripts, the *Oficios de la Casa Real de Castilla* (first and second parts) and the *Batallas y Quinquagenas* (A. Ballesteros Beretta, "Don Juan Bautista Muñoz," *RI,* 3, no. 10 [1942], p. 613). The oblivion into which Oviedo's work had fallen was finally deplored

criticizing the weakness of his Latin. This was an old charge, already leveled by Las Casas, which we shall be discussing further on, and which was effectively rebutted by Pérez de Tudela.[28] In his history of Columbus, writes Menéndez Pelayo, Oviedo made mistakes that he could easily have avoided if he had read Peter Martyr's *Decades* more carefully, "if in fact he had sufficient Latin to understand them."[29]

Other scholars (e.g., Barros Arana, Jiménez de la Espada, and Vignaud) and literary historians honor him with a word or two of hasty and generalized approval, or charitably spare him the usual bio-bibliographical notes, without really studying or evaluating him. Morel-Fatio does not consider him in his *Historiographie de Charles-Quint,* probably because Oviedo concerned himself above all with the New World. Carbia does not consider him in his monograph on *La crónica oficial de las Indias Occidentales,* because, he states, Oviedo was not an official historian, but wrote on his own initiative, without anybody having entrusted him with the task.[30] Philip Means ignores him completely in his *Biblioteca Andina.* He would never have got a mention in the large volume — more than five hundred pages — dedicated by Margaret Trabue Hodgen to *Early Anthropology in the Sixteenth and Seventeenth Century* (Philadelphia, 1971), if he were not named once, in passing, with half a dozen others, among Vico's sources (and even then he does not make it into the index!).

The extreme rarity of his works has also probably helped to hinder their study. The first editions are among the highest-priced items of early Americanist literature, and even the more recent Academia de la Historia edition costs a tidy sum.[31] It is generally only dictionaries and reference works that devote an article or a paragraph to Oviedo: there are, certainly, good essays and monographs, but not a single comprehensive work, even if Turner's bibliography generously succeeds in marshaling no less than 353 items![32]

Fueter, despite a balanced, sympathetic, and perspicacious approach, concludes that he does not consider Oviedo a historian: "His book is . . . not a historical narrative."[33] The article by Angela Valente in the *Enciclopedia Ital-*

---

by Emiliano Jos, "Centenario del Amazonas: la expedición de Orellana y sus problemas históricos," *RI,* 4, no. 11 (1943), p. 15. The odd thing is that this particular comment should have appeared in a journal published by the Instituto Gonzalo Fernández de Oviedo, which in its more than thirty years of existence has devoted to Oviedo no more than one special issue and a handful of other papers.

28. Pérez de Tudela, "Rasgos," p. 432.

29. Menéndez Pelayo, "Historiadores," p. 90.

30. *Crónica oficial,* pp. 76–78. The weakness of the argument is demonstrated by what Carbia himself writes, ibid., pp. 88, 93–94.

31. In the Maggs Bros. "Spanish America" catalogue (No. 612, London, 1935), the first edition of the *Historia,* with book XX published in 1557, is marked £550. Book XX alone, £200. The second edition, with the Francisco de Jerez chronicle (1547), is offered at £450 (and a further mutilated copy at £105). The complete 1851–55 edition has a price tag of £35. In the whole of this abundantly rich catalogue the only items with prices notably higher than those asked for the early Oviedos are the first editions of Cortés's letters. It need hardly be pointed out that today these prices would be at least quintupled.

32. Daymond Turner, *Gonzalo Fernández de Oviedo: An Annotated Bibliography* (Chapel Hill, 1966).

33. Op. cit., p. 298. "He is no historian," is the verdict of Salas too, op. cit., p. 101.

iana says that the *Historia* "has no critical quality and lacks art," and that the "valuable information" it contains "must be accepted with great caution"! And the shrewd Magnaghi rebukes him for glaring inaccuracies and errors in dates "and in the details of the voyages." [34] Henríquez Ureña goes the whole hog and writes that Oviedo "does not describe the fauna and flora of the New World any better then Las Casas." [35] Alvarez López, on the other hand, rates him above Acosta as a naturalist, but below him as a philosopher. [36] Wassermann judges him "an uncritical compiler of dubious facts." [37] It comes as no surprise that Porras Barrenechea, in a brief and pithy passage, chides him for his anti-Pizarrism and his violent temper, concluding that Oviedo's sympathy for the defeated betrays "an inferiority complex"! [38] But it is surprising that Otis H. Green, in his long history of the Castilian mind from El Cid to Calderón, despatches Oviedo so rapidly; yes, he says, the exotic material did interest him, obviously, "yet he lacked scientific imagination. His account is descriptive, factual, and dry. Some of his chapters contain but a single sentence: on leopard, or on deer." López de Gómara he finds considerably better, although he wrote a quarter of a century later. [39] In a vast anthology of Hispano-American colonial literature, Oviedo is quite simply ignored as being too "courtly and cynical." [40] And from a more recent anthology, of French poetry of the Renaissance, we learn that Oviedo "applied himself to denigrating the natives." [41]

Oviedo's sole admirers are Cesare de Lollis, who refers to him approvingly throughout his work on Columbus, [42] and more recently Ramón Iglesia, who writes thoughtfully and sympathetically on Oviedo's *Historia,* and particularly book XXXIII (the conquest of New Spain), which is the longest, but still only one of the fifty books of the *Historia.* [43] A place apart must be given to Alberto M. Salas's essay, [44] which is occasionally debatable, but in general exemplary and very shrewd.

All in all, Oviedo's fortunes have reached such a low point that the most recent

---

34. *Vespucci* (1926) pp. 85, 124, 156n2.

35. *La Cultura,* p. 65.

36. "La filosofía natural en el P. José de Acosta," *RI,* 4, no. 12 (1943), 306–08.

37. Op. cit., p. 85.

38. "Los cronistas de la conquista: Molina, Oviedo, Gómara y Las Casas," *Revista de la Universidad Católica,* 9 (1941), 240–44. In much the same vein Carlos Pereyra, after citing one of the frequent passages in which Oviedo bewails the sad end of various "adelantados" (see below, chap. XIX, sec. 5), comments with malicious superficiality: "Oviedo, who says this, had no sympathy for the great enterprises, madness when they failed, and works of genius when the achievements came up to expectations" (*Los conquistadores,* p. 101).

39. O. H. Green, *Spain and the Western Tradition: The Castilian Mind from "El Cid" to Calderón* (Madison, 1963–66), III, 28. The charge of excessive brevity can only refer to the *Sumario,* and in a summary one obviously does not go into detail!

40. Abraham Arias-Larreta, *Historia de la literatura indo-americana,* vol. 2 (Kansas City, 1970), reviewed in *HAHR,* 52 (1972), 503–06.

41. Le Moine, op. cit., p. 319.

42. De Lollis, op. cit., passim, esp. pp. 137, 140, 142, 213.

43. Iglesia, *Cronistas e historiadores,* pp. 77–93.

44. Op. cit., pp. 63–158. José Miranda, however, editor of the *Sumario,* concludes (op. cit., p. 42) that Oviedo is much superior to Peter Martyr and Las Casas, and possessed (p. 61) of a "vast and imperious . . . curiosity, of truly majestic character."

narrator of how Europe "learned" American nature (O'Gorman, *Trayectoria de América*) leaves him in utter oblivion; and the most recent authority on the cultural relationship between American and Europe (Lewis Hanke) cites him as an example of the type of European who merely notes the curiosities or deficiencies of animal nature in the New World, cats that do not caterwaul or roosters that crow less resonantly than in Spain.[45]

Nothing could be less true of Oviedo, who is the first and foremost an admirer and panegyrist of American nature. Nothing so falsifies the historical prespective of the process by which the Old World became acquainted with the New as ignoring the first official chronicler of the Indies, the patient, painstaking, and discerning historian of the physical nature of America.

5. LIFE: OVIEDO AND COLUMBUS

Gonzalo Fernández de Oviedo, hidalgo of Madrid and scion of an old Asturian family, and "mozo de cámara"[46] to the Infante Don Juan, was barely fourteen years old when he first met the Genoese Christopher Columbus at court. And he saw him and met him more than once at the camp beneath the walls of Granada, on the fateful and auspicious occasion when the great task was finally entrusted to him as the centuries-long cycle of the Reconquest reached its triumphant close and the broader cycle of overseas conquest was about to begin;[47] and he saw him again in Barcelona, triumphant, "with the first Indians brought back from those

45. See the account of the conference held in Lima on 20 August 1943, *La Prensa* (Lima), 27 August 1943. Oviedo, in his concern to call everything by its name and not to settle for analogies, observes that even the animals of the old world have changed nature in the new, that the roosters crow "less raucously than in Spain, and the cats are less noisy in their nocturnal lovemaking" (from the manuscript of the conference). See below, chap. XVIII, sec. 26.

46. Amador de los Ríos ("Vida," pp, xiii–xiv, xvi) denies that Oviedo was ever a page. But Oviedo harks back to the time when he and Diego de Rengife "were pageboys" (*Qu.*, p. 357), and he writes: "I was present, as a pageboy, at the siege of Granada" (*Hist.*, II, 7: I, 29a), and "I was a pageboy at the court" (VI, 39: I, 229–30). He describes himself as "pageboy" in 1490 in an unpublished passage of the *Quinquagenas*, pt. III, est. 22, quoted by D. Clemencín, "Ilustraciones al elogio de la reina Isabel la Católica," in *Memorias de la Real Academia de la Historia*, 6 (Madrid, 1821), p. 222; by Amador de los Ríos, "Vida," p. lxxviii; and by Humboldt, *Examen critique*, III, 303n. Amador de los Ríos's theory is accepted by the more recent biographers. Only Harrisse, somewhat curiously, supposes, in his *Christophe Colomb* [Paris, 1884], p. 97n3, that he was a page in 1490 and subsequently, in 1496, "mozo de cámara" (valet?). On the "pages" brought up at court, see *Hist.*, III, 9: I, 406.

Be it said once and for all that I have drawn on Amador de los Ríos's "Vida" for almost all the biographical details. But in view of its eulogistic tone, its slips like this one, its gaps (an especially serious one for the years 1505–14, but too little is said also for the years 1549–54), the fact that it is now more than a century old, and the fact that in the meantime great strides have been taken in the history of the geographical discoveries, the time would seem to be ripe for a new life of Oviedo, less exclusively based on his works and possibly complemented by methodical research on his sojourn and activities in Italy. Following on the extensive research by diligent Spanish scholars (Manuel Ballesteros Gaibrois, Enrique Otte, José de la Peña y Cámara, etc.) a first valiant attempt was made by Juan Pérez de Tudela Bueso in the introductory essay, "Vida y escritos de Gonzalo Fernández de Oviedo," prefacing his edition of the *Historia* (Madrid, 1955), I, vii–clxxv. I have of course tried to take account of these works. But even Medina, having paid due homage to Amador de los Ríos's biography, suggested (1898) that Oviedo could "indubitably be studied much more by exploring the Archivo de Indias, which houses numerous interesting documents relating to the first real historian of the Indies, some of which we intend to make known in our *Vasco Núñez de Balboa" (Biblioteca*, I, 149).

47. He recalls the event with deep emotion fifty-six years later, on closing his *Historia*: L, 30: IV, 591–92. Cf. VI, 46: I, 239a; IX, Proh.: I, 330b ("I saw the first admiral on many occasions); II, 7: I, 29ff.

parts in the first voyage of discovery."[48] On his return from the Indies the Admiral succeeded in arranging for his young sons to become pages to the idolized, fascinating and extremely spoiled Infante Don Juan, heir apparent to the throne of Spain. And Diego and Fernando soon became close friends of the fifteen-year-old Oviedo.[49]

6. WANDERINGS IN ITALY

The smooth course promised by these numerous portents was interrupted by a tragedy which, indirectly, was also to contribute to their fulfillment. The Infante Don Juan, a few months after marrying the daughter of the Emperor Maximilian in Burgos, amid splendid festivities,[50] died suddenly (4 October 1497). Juan del Encina intoned his solemn, despairing lament, "Triste España sin ventura." Domenico Fancelli carved (1511–1513) his magnificent funeral monument, inspired by Pollaiuolo and Desiderio da Settignano.[51] His court was scattered, and together with other faithful followers of the prince, Gonzalo Fernández de Oviedo left Spain "to wander through the world"—as he himself wrote— "roaming its various parts, a carefree youth, sometimes engaged in the wars and other times wandering from various parts and kingdoms to other regions."[52]

48. *Hist.*, II, 7: I, 29a. With exaggerated compression of time and events, Humboldt, *Examen critique*, II, 146, asserts that the impression made on Oviedo in Barcelona "was so strong that for thirty-four years he busied himself with the products and history of America." Jane however (op. cit., p. 81) points out that Oviedo was then barely fifteen years old, and that the description was written many, many years later, by which time the importance of the discovery was recognized and proclaimed, which would have colored and glorified that memory of early adolescence.

49. So says Amador de los Ríos ("Vida," p. xv) on the basis of a vague statement by Oviedo himself (*Hist.*, III, 6: I, 71a), and so Harrisse repeats (*Christophe Colomb*, p. 102n4), citing Las Casas, *Historia de las Indias*, I, 101, and II, 79. But it is known (Navarrete, op. cit., II, 17, doc. xi, cited by Vignaud, *Histoire critique*, I, 407–08n90: De Lollis, op. cit., p. 86) that Diego had already been appointed a page to Prince Don Juan on 8 May 1492. Fernando, Columbus's natural son by Beatriz Enríquez, was born on 15 August 1488 (De Lollis, op. cit., p. 76; Vignaud, op. cit., I, 638–41) and in April 1493 was therefore not even five years old. Vignaud too (I, 525n85) ignores these difficulties, and Winsor (op. cit., II, 5) and Humboldt (*Examen critique*, III, 367) only refer to Diego being appointed a page. Humboldt does however note the chronological difficulty relating to Fernando, and refers back to Navarrete, op. cit., I, 152, and III, 561, 580, 597, 601 (*Examen critique*, III, 370n). The unnamed author of the biographical study of Fernando Columbus prefacing the 1892 Madrid edition of the *Historia del Almirante* writes vaguely that Diego was a page "and this honor must also have been extended to D. Fernando . . . despite his illegitimate origins" (II, ix). Don Fernando himself, for that matter, writes: Don Diego, my brother, and I . . . served as pages to Prince Don Juan"; and he tells how in 1499 they went on to become pages to Queen Isabella (*Historia del Almirante*, chap. lxiv, ed. cit., II, 33). Columbus had written (Journal, 14 February) that his sons were "studying in Cordova," and in the "very rare" letter of 7 July he reminded the king and queen that he had "all my sons at your royal court" (*Relaciones y Cartas*, p. 380).

50. On the magnificence of the occasion, and on the three sumptuous silver and gold services, mere trifles, however, compared with the vessels made from his Peruvian plunder by "a soldier who had not so long ago we saw to be poor, and without silver nor even tin nor property," in other words Hernando Pizarro, see *Hist.*, XLVIII, 6: PT, V, 230–32.

51. A. De Bosque, *Artisti italiani in Spagna* (Milan, 1968), pp. 364, 367–68.

52. Amador de los Ríos, "Vida," p. xvii. Although he claims to have been in Africa ("all that I have seen of Europe and Africa"—*Hist.*, VI, 10: PT, I, 170a) and to have toured almost all over the world (" a great part of the world"— XLVII, 1: PT, I, 130a), there is no documented record of these journeys.

The death of a prince often produced this result. With the passing of Beatrice d'Este (8 January 1497) "everything went to rack and ruin and the court was transformed from a happy paradise into a gloomy hell. Whereupon every virtuous man was obliged to take another path, and I amongst the others, seeing so many of my hopes come to nothing . . . took myself off to Rome" (Vincenzo Calmeta, "Vita del facondo poeta volgare Seraphino Aquilano" [1504], in the *Rime* of Serafino dall'Aquila, [Bologna, 1894], I, 12).

In fact his wanderings were confined to Italy. Oviedo spent three or four years in the peninsula and Sicily: the decisive years, from the twenty-first to the twenty-fourth of his life (1499–1502), coinciding with the peak of the Italian Renaissance, the period of its most mature and triumphant achievements. The young Oviedo was first of all in Genoa, then in the Po valley, in the service of Spain and of princes like Lodovico il Moro, duke of Milan, and Giovan Francesco III, duke of Mantua. While in Genoa (where he spent four and a half months in 1499) he saw companies of German mercenaries in the pay of Messer Giovanni Adorno, Lodovico il Moro's captain general, and noted curiously that among the Germans there were quite a lot of Jews.[53] Nor did he omit, while in that city, to make the pious journey to kiss the chains of Saint John the Baptist in the Cathedral of San Lorenzo, and put them round his neck and across his chest, in the certainty that this would ensure his escape if he were ever jailed or imprisoned.[54]

That same year, 1499, also found him at the court of the duke of Milan, where he found favor and fortune, but once again a stroke of fate sent him roving. Lodovico il Moro fled before the French armies led by Trivulzio (September 1499), and the young Spaniard moved on from Milan to Mantua, to the court of Isabella Gonzaga. And there, at her prompting or behest, he soon joined the princely entourage of the youthful Cardinal Giovanni Borgia Lanzol, "the younger," Alexander VI's great-nephew and legate and a person "very well disposed toward the Spanish," whom he preferred for his household offices. Oviedo accompanied him to Milan, where he witnessed the solemn entry of Louis XII (6 October 1499), and also perhaps to Turin, then returning with him to Pavia, and by way of the Ticino and the Po to Ferrara and thence to Bologna.

Meanwhile Cesare Borgia besieged and took Imola and then Forlì and shortly afterward (Oviedo implies) poisoned his cousin's son, Cardinal Giovanni. Oviedo gives us a minute description of the cardinal's terrible death throes and tells us how he accompanied the body all the way to Rome, where it was buried in Santa Maria del Popolo on 27 January 1500.[55]

---

53. *Qu.*, p. 164 (and Pérez de Tudela, "Vida," p. xxiii).

54. And indeed, he relates, on two separate occasions he miraculously escaped confinement: *Libro del blasón* (ca. 1550–51), ms. cited by Pérez de Tudela, "Vida," pp. cviii–cix*n332*.

55. Pérez de Tudela, "Vida," pp. xxv–xxvi. Santa Maria del Popolo was in fact a church for which the Borgia family had a particular devotion. Cardinal Rodrigo Borgia, subsequently Pope Alexander VI, had had an altarpiece made for the high altar of the church by Andrea Bregno in 1473. One of its chapels contained the tombs of Alexander's son Pedro Luis, first duke of Gandía, and later Pedro Luis's half-brother, Juan, second duke of Gandía (he too probably murdered at the behest of his brother Cesare Borgia in 1497), as well as that of the celebrated Vannozza Caetani (or Cattanei), Cesare's (and Lucrezia's) mother. Santa Maria del Popolo also became, on the intercession of Agapito Gerardino, Cesare Borgia's secretary, the burial place in 1500 of Oviedo's friend Serafino dell'Aquila (Calmeta, op. cit., I, 13).

On the suspicions aroused by the death of Cardinal Giovanni ("rushed off to Rome and hastily buried without any stone to mark his grave") see M. Bellonci, *Lucrezia Borgia: La sua vita e i suoi tempi* (Milan, 1939), p. 189. Thus I find it difficult to accept the conjecture by J. de la Peña y Cámara, "Contribuciones documentales y críticas para una biografía de Gonzalo Fernández de Oviedo," *RI*, 17 (1957), p. 659, that Oviedo was already in Naples in 1499 and went

He stayed on in Rome for the Jubilee and went on from there to Naples, where he had a front-row seat for the dramatic events leading to the downfall of the Aragonese dynasty and the installation of the kings of Spain on the throne of Naples.[56]

In August 1501, finally, he accompanied ex-Queen Juana to Palermo, and together with her returned to Spain in 1502. (His stay in Italy thus coincided with the equally little known sojourn in that country of another Spaniard of much the same age who, after serving in the south under the orders of Gonzalo Fernández de Córdoba, the Great Captain, from 1498 to 1501, left in that same year, 1502, for the Indies where he would immortalize the plebeian name of Francisco Pizarro.)

Oviedo had left Spain as "mozo de cámara" and soldier of fortune, with a good but not particulary refined education behind him. He came back, after witnessing so many wars and scuffles, maneuvers and intrigues between French and Spaniards, with a heightened and pugnacious patriotism.[57] But he came back, above all, as a wholehearted disciple of humanism,[58] a lover of fine arts and culture, filled with reverence for antiquity reborn and the new literature, with his eyes avidly opened to a world expanding prodigiously in time and space.

The future historian of the Indies, if a Spaniard by birth, language, and office, is an early sixteenth-century Italian in his mentality,[59] his scientific curiosity, in his lofty concept of his office of historian, and finally in the subtle humor which not infrequently filters through and lights up the enormous farrago of his writings.

In particular, as we shall see, his attitude to the physical nature of America is what we might expect from an unprejudiced but not ingenuous observer, from a gifted "dilettante" enamored of his material, happy to rediscover nature, not only mentally, in tune with the general movement of the Renaissance, but concretely, in lands hitherto unknown; to be able to emulate Pliny and at the same time render him eternal homage in becoming himself, proudly and enthusiastically, the Pliny of the lands across the ocean.

---

from there to Rome for the Jubilee. On Cesare Borgia see also Oviedo, *Relación de lo sucedido en la prisión del rey de Francia,* in *CDIE,* XXXVIII, 454–55. Oviedo also tells us he "often" saw Lucrezia Borgia, of whose beauty and excellent wit he speaks in glowing terms (Pérez de Tudela, "Vida," p. xxvin*60*).

56. For fuller details see below, chap. XIV, sec. 2.

57. Pérez de Tudela, "Vida," p. xxvii; see also ibid., pp. xxx–xxxi, and his "Rasgos," p. 407.

58. His "humanist education," which made it possible for him to gain a better understanding of the practices and customs of primitive peoples by comparing them with the habits of the peoples of the classical era, is brought out by M. Ballesteros Gaibrois, "Fernández de Oviedo, etnólogo," *RI,* 17 (1957), 459, correcting Fueter's curious statement (op. cit., p. 293–94) that Oviedo had no contact with humanism.

59. "A good humanist and courtier" is what A. Castro calls him, in his *La realidad histórica de España* (Mexico, 1954), p. 640. "He is a typical Renaissance man," writes Ferrando, op. cit., p. 478. Cf. L. Díez del Corral, *Del viejo al nuevo mundo* (Madrid, 1963), pp. 163–64 ("a consummate European"), p. 173 (experience of vineyards in Italy), and p. 245.

7. OVIEDO IN THE INDIES

After a decade of obscurity in Spain (1502–1512) Oviedo was off on his travels again, but this time in the opposite direction; turning his back reluctantly on Italy, he took the decisive step of embarking for the Indies, for the New West across the seas.

Oviedo betook himself to these shores for the first time in 1514, with the expedition of Pedrarias Dávila and the title of "Veedor de las fundaciones de oro de la Tierra Firme" (Inspector of the Gold Mines of the Mainland),[60] after a number of years spent in the militia, on obscure literary works[61] and various abortive projects, including a plan to return to Italy to fight under the orders of the Great Captain, and in family misadventures. He was already a man in the prime of life, unlike almost all the conquistadors, who were still young men when they sailed for America.[62] His mind was already formed, even if it only matured in the Indies. The rest of his life, his six journeys back to Spain, to accuse others and defend himself, the offices he filled and the wrongs he suffered, his long years of service as commandant of the fortress of Santo Domingo, the deaths of his relatives and offspring, the slow inexorable weariness brought on by so many misfortunes and so many labors, are all submerged and reflected in his work.

60. This is the title to which Oviedo most frequently refers, and certainly the most important one. But by royal warrant dated Valladolid 9 August 1513, Oviedo, at the prompting of Lope de Conchillos (secretary to the council, and mentioned a number of times in the *Historia*), was appointed also "Escribano mayor de minas y del crimen y juzgados de Tierra Firme" (Chief Clerk of the Mines and Crime and the Tribunals of the Mainland) and "marcador del hierro de los indios y esclavos" (brander of the Indians and slaves). Amador de los Ríos recalls that from 1528 he was "treasurer of the twentieth of the receipts set aside for the ransoming of captives," citing the Muñoz collection, vol. 79, A 106).

Oviedo refers explicitly to the former title (*Hist.*, XXIX, 8: III, 34a; XXIX, 9: III, 41; and XXIX, 14: III, 67b), writing that "on behalf of Secretary Lope Conchillos, who was chief clerk in that land, I appointed the clerks of the tribunal of the governor and the mayor, and those that undertook those expeditions." As for the latter and less honorable title, neither Oviedo nor his biographers seem to attach much importance to it; but it probably provided fuel for his adversaries, starting with Las Casas and ending with Larousse.

On 4 October 1524 the king approved the sale as slaves of the Indians—and not only the Caribs—captured in the expeditions, provided the *requerimiento* had been read out to them. "For this purpose he ordered them to be branded on the thigh: and this sad task was entrusted to and taken on by—it grieves me to say—Gonzalo Fernández de Oviedo" (Medina, *Descubrimiento*, I, 163*nll*, citing "*Documentos*, pp. 493–94," i.e., vol 2 of his *Descubrimiento*, which is entitled *Documentos relativos a Nuñez de Balboa*). George Edward Ellis, "Las Casas and the Relations of the Spaniards to the Indians" (in Winsor, op. cit., II, 299–348) explains Oviedo's animosity toward Las Casas by saying (p. 314) that Oviedo "had large interest in the mines and in the enslaving of the natives." A few months later, on the death of Juan de Quincedo, "Veedor de las fundiciones del oro y Procurador de Tierra Firme" (Inspector of the Gold Foundries and Procurator of the Mainland), Oviedo was appointed (royal warrant of 2 November 1513) also to these positions. By royal warrant of 19 June 1519 he was appointed Regidor (councillor) of Nuestra Señora de la Antigua del Darién, and in 1520 he filled the office of "receptor general de la cámara e Fisco por Sus Magestades" (Collector of Taxes for their Majesties) (*Hist.*, XXIX, 14: III, 71a).

61. Including the Catálogo Real de Castilla, a history of the kings of Spain, on which he embarked at the request of King Ferdinand in 1505, and which he finished only in 1532 (Amador de los Ríos, "Vida," pp. xxi, lvii; Enrique Otte, "Aspiraciones y actividades heterogéneas de Gonzalo Fernández de Oviedo," *RI*, 18, no. 71 (1958), pp. 24*n*, 60; Pérez de Tudela, "Vida," pp. cxvii*in371*, cxxi*n388*, clxxii; "Rasgos," p. 427.

It should be noted that very shortly after his return from Italy the ex-"page" was already considered a "writer." But when he returned from the Indies for the first time and told Peter Martyr (1515) about the prodigies of gold and precious stones and the curious customs of the Indians, his fame had already declined to the point that the Milanese scholar refers to him vaguely as "a certain Gonzalo Fernández de Oviedo" and "this Oviedo" (*Dec.*, III, 5, pp. 260–61).

62. Terán, op. cit., p. 29.

This personal element is present in all his writings, which often read more like "memoirs" than history, but above all in his major work, the work he wrote on the king's instructions and for the salary of thirty thousand *maravedís* a year,[63] the work to which he devoted so much care and from which he hoped to gain that worldly and other-worldly reward that he had failed to secure through his practical activities (of which he speaks little, and almost always to bewail his economic losses and reverses), in that *Historia General y Natural de las Indias* which, despite its dedication to his Caesarean Majesty Charles V and despite the success of the first part published, was still three-quarters unpublished when its author died, on 26 June 1557, clutching the keys of the fortress of Santo Domingo, which his successor had to prize loose from the dead man's hands.[64]

8. THE MAN IN THE WORK

Oviedo the man is clearly visible in the work, with all his aspirations and failings: with his untroubled and uncomplicated faith: his Spanish patriotism — suspicious, hot-headed, and exclusive: his simple and robust good sense: an instinctive if intermittent humanity toward the Indians — not love or charity, but a principle of rational conduct, dictated as much by the requirements of the king's service as by the Christian's obligations to his neighbor; with a vast and lofty notion of his role as historian and a sufficiently elevated notion of his own importance to warrant the inclusion in the *magnum opus* of his quarrels, infirmities, and family losses, of the cattle he had to sell for a song, and the splendid pearls sacrificed — alas — at a miserable price in a moment of dire necessity.[65]

---

63. See document dating from 1532, in Gómez Canedo, op. cit., I, 147.

64. At the end of the part published (in 1552 or 1557, according to the bibliographers), i.e., of book XX, the printer added the colophon-cum-epigraph: "No more of this book was printed, because the author died" (Medina, *Biblioteca*, p. 290; Harrisse, *Bibliotheca Americana*, p. 338n2; *Hist.*, XX, 36: II, 110). According to Amador de los Ríos ("Vida," p. lxxxi), Oviedo died "in the summer of 1557," in that selfsame city of Valladolid, where Christopher Columbus had died fifty-one years earlier. But Henríquez Ureña (*La cultura*, p. 73) says that he died in Santo Domingo and that "it has mistakenly been said that he died in Valladolid." And Pérez de Tudela, on the basis of reliable documents, says the same thing ("Vida," p. clxvi). To be more specific, Oviedo died on 26 June 1557, in a room in the battlemented tower of the fortress, the *homenaje* or keep, built by Ovando, but a rather more wretched affair than that mendaciously described by "the good Oviedo" and the present-day "enlarged, elegant, and showy" building, to quote the words of an admirer of Gen. Trujillo, Luis E. Alemán, *Santo Domingo Ciudad Trujillo* (Santiago, 1943), pp. 113–14; see also Bernardo Pichardo, *Reliquias históricas de la Española*, 2d. ed., (Santiago, 1944), p. 52.

65. The pearls that he bought were some of the most beautiful that had ever been seen in the Indies, but he had to sell them at a loss "to meet certain necessities that befall me. And jewels of this sort should only be sold to someone who is looking for something like them, and not by looking for someone to buy them, like I did" (*Hist.*, XIX, Proh.: I, 587b). But elsewhere he says he suffered "a heavy loss" because he let himself be taken in regarding the quality of the pearls sold to him (XIX, 11: I, 610a). So was he swindled over the purchase or fleeced because of the forced sale? What we do know is that he possessed one round pearl of twenty-six carats, and had another pear-shaped one in Panama in 1529, and sold it in Santo Domingo "to a German of the Belçares company" (i.e., the Welsers) for 450 *castellanos* (*Hist.*, XIX, 8: I, 605b). The twenty-six carat round stone, "perfectly round . . . the size of a small bodoque [crossbow ball]," he acquired in Panama (about 1522) for 650 "good gold pesos," took back with him to Spain in 1523 (*Hist.*, XXXVII, Proh.: III, 626a) and resold to Count "Nansao" (Nassau), marquis of Cenete, the emperor's lord chamberlain, who gave it to his wife, Doña Mencía de Mendoza (*Sum.*, chap. 81, p. 267). On the large and very beautiful mother-of-pearl shells that he took back to Spain, see *Hist.*, XLII, 12: IV, 424a.

On another enormous pearl, that was in reality a piece of mother-of-pearl disguised to fool the ingenuous, see *Hist.*, XX, 1: II, 18a. On yet another, pear-shaped, that passed through the hands of Pedrarias (and was probably the stone bought by Pedrarias from Don Pedro del Puerto, who, having paid 1200 gold pesos for it, was so restless and tormented

The warmth of his domestic ties, doubtless intensified by his long absences, prompts him to praise his successive wives in fond and chivalric terms and moves him to tears at the death of his only remaining son, drowned on the way back from Chile with Almagro, his grief being soon redoubled at the death of his five-year-old grandson.[66] Decades after the death of his first wife, Margarita de Vergara, "one of the most beautiful women of her time in the Kingdom of Toledo and in our Madrid," Oviedo can be found still recalling some delightfully legendary qualities of "my Margaret," as he called her: that never in her life did she spit; and how on the unhappy night of the delivery of a stillborn child that was to leave her health so ruined that a second childbirth carried her off to her tomb, her tresses, which were a palm's breadth longer than she herself (and "she was no small woman") "turned from the color of fine gold to that of fine silver"[67] — that is, the purest white, Oviedo insists in his declining years, as white as his own hair now is or as white as the pale margins of the page he is writing on.[68]

The death of his second wife, Isabel de Aguilar, he tells us, was a blow that left him "quite desolate and beside himself"; having loved her more than himself, he was on the point "of losing his mind"—adding, however, with a curious switch from despair to epigram, another reason for his inclination to the state of

---

that he was quite unable to sleep and "did nothing but sigh, and became almost mad"—*Hist.*, XIX, 8: I, 605a; XIX, 10: III, 49b; XIX, 30: III, 153b) and thence to the king and, before being destroyed in a fire, left its glowing reflection in the poetry of Cervantes and Lope de Vega, see Medina, *Descubrimiento*, I, 188–89n17. On his trading in, and perhaps also fishing for, pearls, see Pérez de Tudela, "Vida," p. lxxviii, and Otte, "Aspiraciones y actividades," pp. 33–36. See also Manuel Luengo Muñoz. "Inventos para acrecentar la obtención de perlas en América durante el siglo XVI," *Anuario de Estudios Americanos,* 9 (1952), 51–72.

On the prices he got for the livestock sold from his "property in the town of San Juan de la Maguana," see below, chap. XVIII, sec. 22, and *Hist.*, III, 11: I, 85a; cf. III, 13: I, 91a. On his opulent house in Santa María del Darien, with its prolific orchard, which however cost him 1500 gold pesos, *Sum.,* chap. 10, p. 135; *Hist.*, VI, 1: I, 164b; XXIX, 14: III, 70a. On his fertile "estate" three and a half leagues from Santo Domingo, where maize yields one hundred and fifty times the seed sown, *Hist.*, VII, 1:I, 266b; cf IX, 18: I, 349a. On "another estate of mine, one league from this city," *Hist.*, XV, 1: I, 451b. On his profitable business deals in Nicaragua, (church vessels and vestments and slaves, gold and pearls) in 1527–29, see Otte, "Documentos inéditos sobre la estancia de Gonzalo Fernández de Oviedo en Nicaragua," *RI,* 18, nos. 73–74 (1958), 627–51.

66. *Hist.*, XLVII, 6: IV, 283 (and cf. Pérez de Tudela, "Vida," p. cxxxi). "For my sins I lost my only remaining son, drowned," Oviedo noted in his own hand in a manuscript preserved on the Biblioteca Colombina in Seville (Harrisse, *Bibliotheca Americana, Additions* [New York and Paris, 1872], p. xiii*n5*). Of the two sons that were with him when he reached the port of San Juan in Darien (24 June 1520), one, aged eight, died just two months later (*Hist.*, XXIX, 14: III, 66–67).

Oviedo was not only a friend of Almagro ("he was a great friend of mine"—*Hist.*, XLIII, 3: IV, 121a) and probably an adviser of his (1526), but also his legal agent ("apoderado") in 1535 (not in 1532, as Diego Molinari says, in his *El nacimiento del Nuevo Mundo* [Buenos Aires, 1942], pp. 153*n1,* 169*n1*). The document, entitled "Poder otorgado por el adelantado don Diego Almagro a favor de Gonzalo Hernández de Oviedo" (and Juan Téllez, Cristóbal de Mena, and Juan de Espinosa), was signed in Cuzco on 18 June 1535 and published by Medina in his *Chile,* IV, 323–25.

67. *Hist.*, VI, 39: I, 229–30. Cf. Pérez de Tudela, "Vida," pp. xxxv–xxxvi, and Castro, *España,* pp. 639–40. This idealization of his wife's saliva has some curious counterparts in the passages in which Oviedo relates the rite of the sputum of "Bogotá," with the prostrate or kneeling caciques collecting his saliva "as if it were some holy and precious thing" (*Hist.*, XXVI, 13: II, 371a; XXVI, 23: II, 390a), and of Atahualpa, whose precious saliva could not be allowed to be lost on the ground, and who therefore had "a very high-ranking woman standing permanently beside him for this purpose, who held out her hand for him to spit into" (XLVI, 10: IV, 183b). In the *Quinquagenas* of his declining years (pp. 86–87) he mentions that giants, all giants—not only tall wives—enjoy a unique privilege of immunity from catarrh: ". . . men exceeding five cubits in height do not spit."

68. Unpublished passage in the *Batallas y Quinquagenas* (1550–57), cited by Pérez de Tudela, "Vida." Cf. n. 77, below.

matrimony: "I was not accustomed to the concubines that my neighbors kept (and some of them two)."[69] And still at the age of seventy-two he speaks of his third wife, Catalina de Riva Flechas y Burguillos, whom he shortly took to comfort his widowerhood, and who lasted longest, with a warmth and ardor more reminiscent of a callow youth.[70]

In the same open way this man who had lived among arms and warfare since earliest childhood tells us how after the treacherous blow dealt him by Simón Bernal (which was at first thought to be fatal but from which he recovered "very shortly")[71] he never left home without five or six trusted men around him, "who guarded me continually with their arms," or else with his face covered, and even at home he was always anxious and wary and "afraid as any man could be."[72]

He repeatedly protests that he has forgotten the offence, as a good Christian should, and prays God to pardon the offender, but his rancor wells up again unquenched as soon as they try to reconcile him with Pedrarias "and they could not, because I was convinced that they had turned their knives on me with Pedrarias's backing and advice, and I deeply resented this."[73] And very right and proper, we might add, those of us who do not believe in fictitious peacemaking, "sham peaces," as Cardinal de Retz called them,[74] we who have read Corneille[75] and might echo Asmodé's sneer: "After that they reconciled us; we embraced and have been mortal enemies ever since. . . . "[76]

9. OLD AGE AND DEATH

Not until his declining years, when he had suffered the pangs of repeated bereavement and the pain of an illness that prevented him walking without a stick, were the glowing embers of his affection and animosity doused by the gray ash of disappointment. There is nothing of Faust in Oviedo. A quiet melancholy steals over the aging historian, white-haired and white-bearded, toothless,[77] and almost totally deaf.[78]

---

69. *Hist.*, XXIX, 14: III, 70–71. On the early conquistadors' "harems of Indian women," see Rosenblat, op. cit., pp. 102, 214.

70. *Batallas*, cited by Pérez de Tudela, "Vida," p. clxi. Cf. Amador de los Ríos, "Vida," p. xli. The marriage of their daughter Juana to Rodrigo de Bastidas (son of the *adelantado* of Santa Marta of the same name) produced numerous descendants, some called Gonzalo Fernández de Oviedo (one of whom fell on hard times in the 1600s) and finally the two poets Heredia, the Cuban and the French.

71. *Hist.*, XXIX, 17: III, 85.

72. Ibid., XXIX, 19: II, 89a, 90a.

73. Ibid., XXIX, 24: III, 121. On the Christian's duty to pardon offenses, although "as for the world, it is customary amongst men of honor to avenge affronts, and not hide them or suffer to the prejudice of one's honor," see *Qu.*, p. 43.

74. *Mémoires* (Pléiade ed., Paris, 1968), p. 54.

75. Corneille, *Le Menteur*, IV, 1, lines 1132–43: *Rodogune*, I, 5, lines 313–26.

76. Le Sage, *Le diable boiteux* (Paris, 1880), I, 25–26. Cf. Trilussa, "Er pranzo de l'alleati" in *Le Storie*, in *Poesie* (Milan, 1951), pp. 438–39.

77. *Qu.*, pt. III (unpublished), est. 22, cited by Clemencín, op. cit., VI, 222; by Amador de los Ríos, "Vida," p. lxxxviii; by Humboldt, *Examen critique*, III, 303n; and by Pérez de Tudela, "Vida," p. clx*n537*. In 1535, at the age of fifty-seven, Oviedo's hair was already white (*Hist.*, "Epístola dedicatoria," I, cxii).

78. *Hist.*, XXXII, 4: III, 239a (cf. Pérez de Tudela, "Vida," p. cxxxiii and n. 435). In the same passage Oviedo notes that he can hear music if he puts his teeth (what teeth?) "on the head of the guitar or the body of the clavichord,"

The Indies, which he had so much admired when he was in his heyday and to whose tepid clime he longed to return when the frosts of Castile began to chill his bones in middle age, cease to enchant him in the last years of his old age. He no longer makes additions or corrections to his *Historia General,* somehow discouraged after his long labors,[79] and devotes his greatest efforts to the *Batallas* and the *Quinquagenas,* to re-evoking the dreams of chivalry, the moral and religious maxims, the military ideals and noble heraldic spirit of his youth and middle age.[80]

The Indies, once an arena of unrivaled splendor and glory, become a prison. As if beneath "an irremovable banner" Oviedo remains tied to the soil of America: "And so I cannot flee the Indies, because I am old and advanced in age . . . it pleased God [that] . . . I should go wandering through the world and come to rest in these lands so foreign and removed from where I was born and am a native."[81]

When the conquistador sighs like an exile, turning his gaze back to more familiar lands, and from the depths of the virgin land he has discovered and occupied feels a reawakening hostility toward the intruder, then he becomes himself the loser, a conquistador conquered. He bends his gray head, his task finished. "Die Uhr steht still . . . Der Zeiger fällt."[82]

---

thus anticipating the modern hearing devices entailing sound transmission through the bone rather than acoustically. The discovery of the importance of bone transmission for hearing is generally ascribed to Giambattista Morgagni (1761). Oviedo mentions other scientific observations, whose originality can only be assessed by a specialized historian, e.g., the simultaneous occurrence of seaquakes and earthquakes (against Pliny's theory), *Hist.,* VI, 29: I, 215–17.

79. Pérez de Tudela, "Vida," p. clxii. There are no references in the *Historia* to events later than 1548; cf. also Pérez de Tudela, "Rasgos," p. 439.

80. Pérez de Tudela, "Rasgos," p. 441.

81. *Hist.,*XXXIV, Proh.: III, 559: cf. XXI, Proh.: II, 111–12.

82. Goethe, *Faust, Part II,* act 5.

❧ XV ❧

Oviedo and Italy

1. THE FALL OF KING FREDERICK

T H E chronicler's relations with the men, things, cities, and books of the peninsula call for closer scrutiny. We might pick up the story again with his arrival, at the age of twenty-two, at the Aragonese court of Naples (above, chap. XIV). For though, as we have seen, Oviedo traveled the length and breadth of Italy, from Milan and possibly Turin all the way down to Palermo, the most important moment, and most lasting memory, was his stay in Parthenope.

Early in 1501 France and Spain had come to an agreement—adducing various hypocritical pretexts and with prompt pontifical blessing from the Borgia pope, Alexander VI—to split the Kingdom of Naples between them, France taking the Terra di Lavoro (the province of Caserta) and Abruzzi, Spain getting Calabria and Apulia. The act was accomplished with barely more formality than Russia and Germany's pact to carve up Poland in 1939, with the sole difference, entirely favorable to the aggressors of four hundred years ago, that on that first occasion the Great Captain, chivalrous as ever, sent the king of Naples a message informing him of the impending dual invasion. "And you can take my word for that," Oviedo was later to write, "because I was there myself."[1]

The good King Frederick had no choice but to submit to the injunction addressed to him by the two greatest military powers of the time, and all those present burst into tears; it was Sunday, 4 July 1501. An anonymous commoner mockingly dramatized the sovereign's predicament in a semi-macaronic quatrain that Oviedo was to recall almost half a century later (1547–1548) in America, comparing it with the natives' epic and plaintive songs:

> "A la mia gran pena forte
> Dolorosa, aflicta et rea,
> Diviserunt vestimenta mea
> Et super ea miserunt sorte."[2]

---

1. A report can also be found in the unpublished *Batallas* (cf. Pérez de Tudela, "Vida," p. xxix*n*69). There is an echo of this scandalous collusion in the *Orlando Furioso* (XVII, 74–76), where Ariosto suggests that France and Spain would have done better to join forces for a crusade against the "foul Turk."

2. *Hist.*, V, 1: I, 129a: "To my great and grievous sorrow, / To my anguish and affliction, / They have torn apart my

The king left with his galleys and "all his artillery" for the island of Ischia— granted him for six months, the duration of the truce—this island being "a very strong thing" but to all intents and purposes besieged, by the French on the mainland and the Spanish at sea; and there, in that little island of marvels and terrors, golden sun and azure waters, miracle-working springs and devastating earthquakes, he gathered about him, as if on an enchanted isle, a little Shakespearean court. There was no Duke Prospero, of course, but the spirit of Ariel was present among the followers and retainers of the nobly proud and defeated king, surrounded as he was by the poet Sannazzaro, by children and women, by the young princes Don Alonzo and Don Cesare, and by four illustrious and most unfortunate ladies, a veritable quartet of weeping women, consisting of the repudiated queen of Hungary (Beatrice of Aragon), the exiled duchess of Milan (widowed by poisoning and bereaved of her son), the future queen of Poland, and the "Señora Escandarbeza," ex-queen of Albania.[3]

From Ischia, shortly thereafter (2–3 August 1501), "the young queen, the king's sister, went over to Sicily with a fleet which the Great Captain sent for her on the order of their Catholic Majesties," and Oviedo, as a mark of King Frederick's honor and friendship, was entrusted with the task of accompanying Queen Juana[4] first to Sicily (he was in Palermo in early August 1501) and then, in May 1502, all the way back to Spain, whence he never again returned to Italy.

2. THE DUKE OF CALABRIA

Oviedo's work retains, however, another singular mark and lasting reminder of those last few months spent in Italy at the court of his Most Serene (and most unfortunate) Highness King Frederick of Aragon. At the moment of the collapse the king's oldest son, still a boy of fourteen, Ferdinand of Aragon, marquis of Bisceglie, prince of Taranto, and, since 1496, duke of Calabria (the ritual title of the heirs to the throne of Naples), took his oath as the eventual successor to the

---

raiment / And cast lots for who shall take it." The formal surrender came with the Pact of Aversa (25 July 1501). See Luigi Volpicella, *Federico d'Aragona e la fine del Regno di Napoli nel MDI* (Naples, 1908), p. 65.

3. A. Rodríguez Villa, ed., *Crónicas del Gran Capitán* (Madrid, 1908), pp. lxii–lxiv (Oviedo texts). Chariteo (*Rime*, [Naples, 1892], II, 310) poetically imagines that there was a fifth and even greater lady, Isabella del Balzo, queen of Naples, but the invention is given the lie both by Oviedo's silence and by Volpicella, op. cit., pp. 76–77 (see, however, against this, p. 73), followed by B. Croce, *Storie e leggende napoletane* (Bari, 1948), p. 211n. Other details and dates are given in Volpicella, op. cit., pp. 67, 71, and in G. C. Speziale, *Storia militare di Taranto* (Bari, 1930), p. 59ff.

4. Juana had been left a widow, while still very young, on the death of her husband Ferdinand II of Naples ("Ferrandino"—Pérez de Tudela, "Vida," p. xxx). Her mother, Juana the Elder, sister of Ferdinand the Catholic, had traveled to Spain to seek his consent for her daughter's marriage to the duke of Calabria, but Ferdinand delayed his decision (see Oviedo text in Rodríguez Villa, op. cit., p. lxxiii, and cf. Volpicella, op. cit., pp. 15, 19). Later on she was vainly courted by emissaries of Henry VII of England (curious details in E. S. Turner, *A History of Courting* [London, 1954], pp. 56–58). On the two "sad queens," mother and daughter, see Croce, *La Spagna*, p. 140ff and "La corte delle Tristi Regine," *Archivio Storico per le Provincie Napoletane*, 19 (1894), 354–75. On the office entrusted to Oviedo by King Frederick, see Pérez de Tudela, "Vida," p. xxx.

throne in the presence of Oviedo himself[5] and ran off to shut himself up in the fortress of Taranto, where he was besieged, patiently and somewhat half-heartedly, by the troops of the Great Captain.[6] His father sailed from Ischia (6 September 1501) to take refuge in France, where he hoped to find help in recovering his kingdom; and a few months later (1 March 1502) Taranto surrendered to Gonzalo Fernández de Córdoba, with the solemn stipulation in the terms of surrender of the stronghold that the young Prince Ferdinand was to be left completely free.

The condition was not, however, observed, and instead, on the orders of the Catholic King, Prince Ferdinand was sent off a prisoner to Spain. This flagrant violation of a pact sworn on the Holy Sacrament was the subject of prolonged and vehement argument at the time. No one could actually believe that a knight as famous as the Great Captain should have failed to keep his word, and it was suspected that the real blame for this sordid business should be laid at the door of the Catholic King, anxious perhaps at the danger inherent in having the legitimate heir to the throne of Naples at liberty, particularly when his father, exiled in France, was still free and active. It was in fact a repetition in miniature of the clamorous and "horrendous" political treachery of the Spaniards in robbing their friend King Frederick of his kingdom.[7] Thus the young duke of Calabria was seen as a victim of the tortuous and suspect policy of the Catholic King and the whole sad episode as a conflict for the conscience of the Great Captain, caught between his soldier's oath and his duty of obedience to the king.

In the turbulent political situation of the times the teenage duke, dragged off a prisoner into exile, was quickly cast in the idealized role of sublime but tragic hero, much as the duc d'Enghien would be three centuries later. The Spaniards of course did everything in their power to clear the name of the Great Captain, but he himself, writing to his sovereigns on 1 May 1502, said that Don Ferdinand "desired to place himself in Your Highnesses' hands," but that he "changed his mind" at the instigation of his followers; that he, Don Gonzalo, then offered him twenty thousand ducats, later raised to twenty-five thousand and then thirty thousand, which he had no intention of really paying, "more with the idea of detaining him than giving him the money," and meanwhile playing for time; and that knowing the situation of the kingdom and the "anxiety of the French to carry off the young man," he did not let him leave, but "entertained the duke politely at his pleasure for twelve days, to prevent him leaving," until he finally received

5. Oviedo, *Quinquagenas,* passage transcribed by Cesáreo Fernández Duro, *La mujer española en Indias* (Madrid, 1902), p. 37. On these events see Volpicella, op. cit.; on the duke of Calabria in particular, pp. 29, 33, 57, 61–63, 67, 78.

6. Details in M. Capila, "Crónica general del Gran Capitán," in Rodríguez Villa, op. cit., chap. 22 (p. 83) and chap. 30 (pp. 93–94); and in the anonymous "Crónica manuscrita del Gran Capitán," III, 26 (Rodríguez Villa, op. cit., pp. 320–21).

7. B. Croce, *Storia del regno di Napoli* (Bari, 1925), p. 93.

precise instructions and resolved "not to let him go under any circumstances," which was the reason why he made the offer mentioned, given that "without going back on what had been promised to him in the terms of surrender of Taranto one could not do otherwise"; however the Catholic King must not worry, he would not have to pay a penny, because Don Frederick would not approve the agreement and would insist that his son be set free again.

The letter goes on with singular cynicism: "In my opinion it is necessary that the duke should remain in our power, and I intend to maintain and insist on this as long as I am able, until Your Highnesses instruct me otherwise," and it even explicitly recalls that "when agreement was reached with the duke over his leaving Taranto" the Great Captain gave him two hostages, who were to remain with him "until the duke was out of his provinces," and how that too had turned out to be a hollow guarantee for the duke.[8]

These candid confessions, or rather these boastful claims, which actually seem to imply that the duke's imprisonment was attributable solely to the Great Captain, reveal the extreme fragility of the Spanish historians' defenses. The arguments advanced, for instance, by the anonymous author of the "Historia del Gran Capitán," who denies that Gonzalo Fernández de Córdoba ever made such a promise, stresses the kindness supposedly shown later by the Spanish sovereigns to Duke Don Ferdinand and describes Paolo Giovio as ill-informed,[9] whereas the latter in fact produces evidence of the failure of the Spanish general to keep his word and speaks of deception and treachery, blaming the Catholic King for forcing the Great Captain to do "dishonest things."[10]

In the early years, however, the duke's imprisonment in Spain—whither, it would appear, he was enticed by a gross deception[11]—was very lenient, a typical gilded cage. Giovio himself says that in Spain the prince was placed in "a

8. "Cartas del Gran Capitán," in Rodríguez Villa, op. cit., pp. xxv–xxvii.

9. "Historia del Gran Capitán," III, 33, and X, 13, in Rodríguez Villa, op. cit., pp. 325–26, 433. Other details: ibid., II, 42, p. 110. Cf. also the passages from Giovio transcribed by B. Croce, "La grandiosa aneddotica storica di Paolo Giovio," *La Critica*, 40 (1942), 178 (subsequently reprinted in his *Poeti e scrittori del pieno e del tardo Rinascimento* [Bari, 1945]), that testify to Gonzalo's belated repentance and remorse. In his defence, see Speziale, op. cit., pp. 62–71.

10. "La vida y chrónica de Gonzalo Hernández de Cordoba," trans. Pedro Blas Torrellas (1554), pt. I, in fine, in Rodríguez Villa, op. cit., p. 501.

11. He was promised by the king and the Great Captain that he would be given the hand in marriage of the fifth (not the second, as Bacon says in his *History of the Reign of King Henry VII*, 1622, in *Works* [London, 1902], p. 585; but see ibid., p. 609) and last daughter of the Catholic Kings, Catherine of Aragon, who since 1497 or even since 1494 (Bacon) had been betrothed to the eldest son of the king of England, her junior by a year (not three, as Bacon says, op. cit., p. 609), but who was destined to die shortly afterward (1502). Catherine, three years older than the duke of Calabria, was somewhat plain and graceless, but endowed with great moral and intellectual gifts. "Extremely learned" was how she was described by no less a Latinist than Erasmus, who later (1527) dedicated to her his *Christiani matrimonii institutio* and with whose *Praeparatio ad mortem* (1534) the divorced queen consoled herself as she approached her end. Catherine also taught Latin to her daughter Mary, before she became the pupil of Luis Vives, another admirer of her learning. Her fiancé, Arthur, was also in fact "very studious and learned, beyond his years" (Bacon, op. cit., p. 611). Catherine, the first of Henry VIII's six wives, whose love of music, gentle disposition, and noble bearing throughout her misfortunes and travails are only too well known from the (partly) Shakespearean tragedy, was of course subsequently repudiated in favor of Ann Boleyn. On her classical learning, see the fine biography by G. Mattingly, *Catherine of Aragon* (London, 1971), pp. 17, 138–39, 171, 211.

free and honored prison." Peter Martyr attests to the fact that he was received at court with all due honor, describing him as "a young man worthy of the kingdom and of the royal blood, of outstanding intellectual achievements and distinguished appearance";[12] and Guicciardini confirms that he was "received with kindness" by the king of Spain, who "kept him at his side on public occasions with almost regal honors."[13] Queen Isabella did him the unusual honor of having him seated beside her.

In the first few years of his exile his education continued to be undertaken by his Neapolitan tutor, Crisostomo Colonna, to whom Galateo—who had shared with Colonna the task of instructing the prince and had in 1499 celebrated the prince's natural gifts and excellent masters in a Latin epistle wishing him prosperity—recommended (1504–1505) that due care be taken to ensure the Italian upbringing of the prince ("You received an Italian, give back an Italian, not a Spaniard");[14] and certain gentlemen were assigned to his service, one of whom was none other than Oviedo, who had already rendered faithful service to his father and uncle.[15]

But however gilded, and almost courtly, the cage remained a cage. At the age of eighteen the duke was named viceroy of Barcelona, but shortly thereafter he attempted to run off and join his sadly reduced family (ca. 1506) and King Ferdinand had him condemned to permanent imprisonment. Even this, however, was not really all that strict, if his captive "liberty" could be further limited when the Catholic King, warring with the French (1512), uncovered a plot "originating with a friar sent secretly to Ferdinand by the duke of Ferrara," supposedly involving a secret commitment on the part of the duke of Calabria, who "seemed to be forgetting the reverses of the past,"[16] to go over from Logroño to the French camp. The go-between, the Neapolitan Filippetto Coppola, son of the famous Francesco beheaded by the duke's grandfather, was quartered, and the duke of Calabria, who was obliged to witness the hanging of his servants, was imprisoned (November 1512) with no more than two servants in the fortress of Játiva, the same "Zattiva" of Ariosto's Fiammetta,[17] near the gay city of Valencia, a fortress "normally used by the Aragonese kings as a prison for persons eminent either because of their nobility or their achievements."[18]

---

12. *Opus Epistolarum,* epist. 252, cited in Prescott, *Ferdinand and Isabella,* III, 31n43; and Mariéjol, op. cit., pp. 181–82.

13. F. Guicciardini, *Storia d'Italia,* bk. V, chap. 2 (Florence, 1835), p. 189b, followed by P. Giannone, *Storia civile del regno di Napoli,* XXIX, 4 (Milan, 1844–47), IV, 413–14.

14. Croce, *La Spagna,* p. 111; but a couple of years later Colonna returned to Italy as tutor to Bona Sforza, and the duke of Calabria reverted to being "a Spanish prince, surrounded by a Spanish court" (ibid., p. 118). On Colonna, see also Croce, *Storie e leggende napoletane,* pp. 194, 203, 205–06, 208; and T. De Marinis, *La biblioteca napoletana dei Re d'Aragona,* 6 vols. (Milan and Verona, 1947–69), I, 195–204, and esp. p. 201n18.

15. Pérez de Tudela, "Vida," p. xxxiii; Salas, op. cit., p. 66.

16. "Crónica manuscrita del Gran Capitán," III, 33, in Rodríguez Villa, op. cit., p. 326.

17. *Orlando Furioso,* XXVIII, 54.

18. Guicciardini, op. cit., bk. XI, chap. 3, p. 445b, and Croce, *La Spagna,* p. 118. Alfonso d'Este's court at Ferrara was the home of the duke of Calabria's mother, the widowed Queen Isabella (Giannone, op. cit., IV, 424; Chariteo, op. cit., I, clxxvii). And to Ferrara too, according to a notarial act, went the duke in 1519 (but he was in prison!) to collect a

After all these adventures and reverses and with a further and decisive swing of the pendulum in his favor, the duke, who had learned enough from his past troubles to refuse to support and lead the *Comuneros*, was finally freed by Charles V on 13 December 1523, wedded to Germaine de Foix, widow of the Catholic King, and subsequently also appointed (1526) viceroy of Valencia "with the award of an abundant income" of twenty-eight thousand ducats and a court that from a bishop down to the last scullion totaled 218 "servants." A veritable retracing of steps, from the Tarpeian Rock to the Capitol. . . .

Here, on the viceregal throne, the duke could live "with due display," bringing to the receptive Valencia "the sumptuous ways of the Italian Renaissance" and the Provençal courts of love.[19]

He also built up a rich and splendid collection of books, magnificently bound, which included various precious codices from the famous library of the kings of Aragon, possibly brought to Spain with the permission of his Catholic Majesty, when the library was transferred there in 1504.[20] Later on, the court of this former student of music and singing[21] became the focal point of a school of musicians and composers including, apparently (according to the program of the Madrigalistas de Madrid, 1972, but I have not been able to confirm this from other sources), the famous Cristóbal de Morales and Matteo Flecha the Elder. Some of their creations and variations can be found among the fifty-five *villancicos* collected in the celebrated Uppsala Songbook (1556), so called because it was unearthed in 1809 in the library of that university.

Years earlier, when the Catholic King passed away (February 1516), many Neapolitans had hoped that in his will, to relieve his conscience,[22] he would have restored the imprisoned duke to the throne of his forebears. But all the duke inherited, alas, was a few offices in the kingdom of Naples, an apanage of fifty

bequest from Cardinal Luigi D'Aragona (De Marinis, op. cit., I, 201b). And from Ferrara, on the death of their mother in 1533, the duke summoned to his side in Valencia his sisters Giulia and Isabella (1535), who brought with them four Italian "madamas," Maria, Joanella, Beatrice, and Laura.

    On Valencia, a city famed for its "sybaritic laxity" and frivolous customs, see O. Macrí, "L'Ariosto e la letteratura spagnola," *Letterature Moderne*, 3, no. 5 (1952), p. 520. Ariosto's Ruggero, languishing and sentimental, looked "as if he were accustomed to waiting on women in Valencia" (*Orlando Furioso*, VII, 55). And Bandello writes of Valencia "that in all Catalonia there is no more lascivious and wanton city" (*Novelle* [Milan, 1934], I, 496). On Valencia in 1494–95, see De Bosque, op. cit., p. 158; in 1502, ibid., pp. 24–25, 57ff; at the end of the century, see G. Botero, *Le relationi universali* (Venice, 1602), p. 6: its inhabitants are generally despised, because they are "almost steeped in pleasure . . . worthless in battle . . . because of their delicacy they are called 'Peniti' by the other Spaniards . . . there is no city in Europe where the women of ill repute are more esteemed: a truly shameful thing."

    19. De Marinis, op. cit., I, 195–204; V. Castañeda "Don Fernando de Aragón, duque de Calabria," *Revista de Archivos, Bibliotecas y Museos*, 25 (1911), p. 272.

    20. De Marinis, I, 195–204. Since 1825 the remnants of the collection have been in the University Library of Valencia. Many were sold, "as it was thought that being in manuscript and in the Tuscan tongue they were worthless" (ibid., p. 202a; cf. Castañeda, p. 277n, and De Bosque, op. cit., pp. 285–95).

    21. Croce, *Storie e leggende napoletane*, p. 209.

    22. Croce, *Regno di Napoli*, p. 96; cf. idem, *La Spagna*, pp. 109–10. In the act of surrender of Taranto the Great Captain supposedly promised the duke "that the Catholic Kings, his uncle and aunt, would cherish him in the place of a real son, and would give him so great a part in their kingdoms that he would never miss that kingdom" ("Crónica manuscrita del Gran Capitán," III, 33, in Rodríguez Villa, op. cit., p. 326).

thousand ducats and, some years afterward (1526), as we have seen—and not through any deathbed remorse but as a result of Charles V's shrewd calculation, carefully disguised to look like the duke's reward for declining to put himself at the head of the rebellion of the "Flemings" (*Comuneros*)—the aforementioned Germaine, left a widow again by her second husband, John, marquis of Brandenburg, governor of Valencia. She was a rich widow, certainly, still attractive, free-spending and passably merry. Moreover, so it is said, she had always been enamored of the duke,[23] but by then she was barren, so that the marriage sealed the extinction of the illustrious legitimate dynasty of the Aragonese of Naples.[24]

This match too was to provoke considerable comment and insinuation from the pamphleteers. According to Varillas the marriage was arranged because Germaine spent money like water and the duke had only two concerns in life, to steer clear of anything that looked difficult and to enjoy himself as much as possible, so that their union did not involve the least political danger. According to Bayle, the marriage amounted to a loss of rank for the widowed queen, in spite of the punctilious ceremonial and solemn etiquette with which it was celebrated.[25]

The prince, however, was no longer allowed to leave Spain, where, being left a widower by Germaine in 1536, he contracted a further marriage, this time with an illustrious lady of Valencia, Mencía de Mendoza, marchioness of Cenete,[26] equally famous for her culture and her girth.[27] But with Germaine he had already acquired the abandoned monastery of San Sebastián[28] in the Huerta de Valencia, which he then rebuilt and named San Miguel de los Reyes, subsequently bequeathing his books to it. In the rich city of Valencia, for almost a quarter of a century, he carried out his viceregal functions with great dignity, careful gener-

---

23. Castañeda, op. cit., p. 271.

24. Guicciardini, op. cit., bk. XV, chap. 1, p. 602b; Prescott, *Ferdinand and Isabella*, pt. II, chap. 24, ed. cit., III, 404*n* and 419–20*n71*. The Catholic King had made an agreement, on marrying Germana, to leave her the kingdom of Naples when he died, but subsequently (Germana's only son lived no more than a few hours) he left it instead to his daughter Joanna the Mad.

Similarly the Catholic King had ordained in his will that the duke should be set free, with a title and income that would allow him to live like a prince. But the fulfillment of this provision was put off until 1523 on various pretexts, of the sort that can always be found to oppress the unfortunate (Juan de Mariana, *De rebus Hispaniae*, book XXX, chap. 27, p. 637, cited in P. Bayle, "Réponse aux questions d'un provincial," in his *Oeuvres diverses* [The Hague, 1737], III, 687b).

25. Bayle, op. cit., pp. 683–88.

26. Castañeda, op. cit., p. 279; "Crónicas del Gran Capitán," III, 33, in Rodríguez Villa, op. cit., p. 326. See above, chap. XIV, n. 65. Thus it is easy to understand the mistake made by Giannone (op. cit.,, IV, 424) when he says that Ferdinand the Catholic gave him "to wife the barren Mencía de Mendoza, so that he would have no issue." Ferdinand had died back in 1516; and Charles's distrustful intention, that the duke should have no heirs, had in fact already been realized by marrying him to Germana, "horse-trading in the marriage market being such a frequently used political instrument with him," as we are aptly reminded by Ramón Carande, "Carlos V: Viajes, cartas y deudas," in *Charles-Quint et son temps*, p. 219.

27. Morel-Fatio, *Historiographie*, p. 57.

28. Croce, *Storie e leggende napoletane*, p. 212; *La Spagna*, pp. 118–19. A footnote adds: "The society that gathered round the duke of Calabria in Valencia and life in that society are described in Luis Milán's *Libro intitulato el Cortesano* (reprinted in the *Colección de libros raros o curiosos*, vol. VII, Madrid, 1874)." On this work see also R. Palmieri, "Di una imitazione spagnuola del *Cortigiano* (*El Cortesano* di Luis Milán)," *Il Conciliatore*, 2 (1915), 471–93.

osity, and strict justice and love for the arts;[29] and in that city he ended his
earthly life in 1550,[30] expiring among the old-gold brocades of the great bed of
the sovereigns of Naples. Ten thousand requiem masses were celebrated for the
repose of his soul.

In Bandello's *Novelle* (1554) Ferdinand appears in his role of viceroy and
"lieutenant-general" and governor, ordering the decapitation of the proud and
"lovely" Violante and her slave-girl Giannicca, who have been found guilty of
mercilessly slaughtering the former's seducer.[31] And another of Bandello's tales
features as protagonist that same duchess of Amalfi (Giovanna Piccolomini?)
whose story—told to Bandello by Cesare Fieramosca, brother of Ettore, and
filtering down through Belleforest and Painter—was eventually to be taken up
again in John Webster's fiery and bloodthirsty *Duchess of Malfi* (ca. 1614),
whose list of characters does in fact open with a certain "Ferdinando, duke of
Calabria," son of a certain Henry of Aragon and twin brother of the duchess,
tortured to point of madness, but who cannot possibly be identified (and not only
for reasons of chronological and dynastic incompatibility) with the pale historical
creature we are here discussing.

To the real life, unhappy, and much "used" duke of Calabria, Oviedo—from
the time that he was assigned to his service by Ferdinand the Catholic (1502)—
always remained bound as if to some great and worthy lord, so much so that
when he came to publish his first work, the chivalric romance *Claribalte,* in
Valencia in 1519, he dedicated it to the same Don Ferdinand, at that time still
shut up in the nearby castle of Játiva, expressing the hope that in reading this
ballad the duke might for a few moments be able to forget his many misfortunes,
and with the wish, barely veiled, that one day the prince might be permitted to
remount the throne of his forebears, the throne to which he had aspired ever
since, as a youth, he had replied to his tutor Colonna: "I wish to live with a
scepter in my hand."[32]

The same wish, and almost an exhortation to return to his fatherland and rule
over Naples, had already been addressed to him (post 1504) by another faithful
follower, the gentle Jacopo Sannazzaro, who had accompanied the dispossessed
King Frederick, "our lord and master," into exile in France and attended him
until his death in 1504. In the fourth *Ecloga Piscatoria* (composed after 1505)
Sannazzaro had boldly and audaciously prophesied: "For the time will come for

29. Various of Charles V's letters on affairs relating to the government of Valencia can be found in M. Foronda y
Aguilera, *Estancias y viajes de Carlos V* (Madrid, 1914), pp. 513, 522, 525–27, 534, 539, 541, 543, 567.

30. Prescott, *Ferdinand and Isabella,* III, 31; and Pérez de Tudela, "Vida," p. lxv. On the funeral rites see De
Marinis, op. cit., I, 201–02n22. On his death and will, Castañeda, op. cit., pp. 279–86.

31. *Novelle,* ed. cit., I, 506–07; cf. ibid., I, 319–32. A certain Doña Violante, wife of Don Luis Margarite, and
therefore not "of humble lineage," "of humble stock," "of poor and low-born parents," "of low-born blood," as
Bandello insists on describing his heroine, was one of the great ladies of the court of Valencia (Castañeda, op. cit.,
pp. 272–73).

32. Croce, *Storie e leggende napoletane,* pp. 205–06, 210–11.

me when I shall sing of the return of the scepter of Naples and the defeat of kings by your spear."[33]

And in that same span of years the Catalan Chariteo, in his short poem *Pascha* (composed between autumn 1503 and 1509), professed himself certain that Ferdinand, "that clear diamond of unbreakable virtue," would remount the throne as the sun came out again when the clouds dissolved.[34] Thus Oviedo was merely reechoing, belatedly, the desires and hopes of the Neapolitan friends and supporters of the captive prince.

A few years later Oviedo was to learn from the mouth of the duke of Calabria himself all the details of the meeting between the emperor Charles V and his prisoner, King Francis of France—details that Oviedo would include in the little book in which he recounted King Francis's imprisonment. And ten years later again, in 1535, when Oviedo was already installed in Santo Domingo as commandant of the fortress, he still kept in touch with the duke of Calabria's court, and from one of his ex-colleagues, one of the duke's courtiers, he received the news of the Turkish evacuation of Hungary.[35]

Oviedo's hopes of seeing Italy again were to prove as vain as the duke of Calabria's dynastic ambitions. Relatively little is known about the next ten years or so of Oviedo's existence except that he married and lost his wife and was obliged to adapt to life as a notary public and secretary to the Inquisition. But he obviously remained on the lookout for some way of emerging from that humdrum obscurity, and when in 1512 the Great Captain began preparing to take an army back to Italy to do battle there again our nostalgic hero was fired with noble enthusiasm. Oviedo, though only recently remarried and possibly already a father, signed on as "one of the leading secretaries."[36] For this expedition, which would have taken him back to his beloved Italy and in a privileged position, under the immediate orders of the greatest captain of the age, Oviedo, in his own words, "spent what little he had." Unfortunately, "after we had been in Cordova some months, while the troops were gathering and the quartermasters had already left for Malaga," news came from Italy that induced the king to disband the already mobilized army, sell the ships and supplies, and abandon the expedition.

Once again, just as after the death of Prince Don Juan and his sad experiences

---

33. Quoted by Prescott, *Ferdinand and Isabella*, III, 31–32n43, and by M. Scherillo, *Le origini e lo svolgimento della letteratura italiana* (Milan, 1926), II, 230, and paraphrased by Gothein, op. cit., pp. 308–09. Cf. Croce, *Storie e leggende napoletane*, p. 216.

34. *Pascha*, V, 163–84, in Chariteo's *Rime*, ed. cit., II, 411–12; cf. I, clxxvii, and Croce, *La Spagna*, p. 109.

35. On his exact function and other biographical details cf. Pérez de Tudela, "Vida," pp. xl–xlii. See also *CDIE*, XXXVIII, 488.

36. See his *Relación de lo sucedido en la prisión del rey de Francia*, pp. 419, 488. The duke is mentioned once again in the *Historia*, eating "cooked frogs" in Vitoria (1524) with the Lord Chancellor Mercurino de Gattinara (*Hist.*, XII, 10: PT, II, 67a); and in another passage there is a fleeting reference linking (possibly with some remote mental echo) "Calabria and the land of Taranto, in the kingdom of Naples" (*Hist.*, XXI, 5: PT, II, 319).

in the courts of Italy, Oviedo found himself unemployed, penniless, and—to complete the analogy—a member of a group dispersing in various directions, "each going his own way." The Great Captain, disappointed and impoverished, retired to Loja; of the rest, some "went home, some left for the war in Africa, some for the war in Navarre, some for Italy, and others for the Indies [and here we seem to hear one last sigh for the country just previously named]; and I, for my sins, was one of the latter."

3. OVIEDO AND CHRISTOPHER COLUMBUS

Despite this disappointment, Italy remains ever present in Oviedo's writings. Columbus, the Ligurian, "from the province of Liguria, which is in Italy," is his supreme hero, from beginning to end of the *Historia*.[37] Oviedo guards his glory jealously and sees him as the culminating point of a strict historical perspective. All the other discoverers and conquerors of the Indies are worthy of fame only to the extent that they recognize as "tutor and example" the Admiral who taught them all the way, provided the first incentive, and strengthened their resolve.[38] Oviedo pronounces a particularly solemn eulogy: in everything regarding the Indies the person of Columbus invariably precedes all others because he was the "cause of everything that is known in these parts, and he taught it and discovered it for all those who enjoy it."[39] The prize he deserves, for the treasures Spain has derived from the Indies (and—the ritual formula—for "having brought the Catholic faith to these parts and all these natives"), is a statue of solid gold like those described in the fables told by the historians of antiquity.[40]

But despite all this Oviedo acquired the reputation of being an anti-Columbian with many of the early biographers of the Admiral, merely because he repeated—without accepting ("I hold it to be false")—the legend of the Portuguese pilot, which was still held to be true by Sassetti (1582),[41] at least repeated by Francis Bacon in the seventeenth century,[42] believed by Feijoo in the eighteenth century,[43] and even echoed in our own century in Vignaud's well-known theories. This reputation was reinforced by his identifying the West Indies with the mythical Hesperides, which in no way detracts, says Oviedo, from Columbus's glory, in fact adds to it.[44] Fernando Columbus's attacks and Las Casas's animosity (the latter motivated by factors that have nothing to do

37. *Hist.*, II, 2: I, 12a.
38. Ibid., XXI, 5: II, 128b; XXI, 7: II, 135–36 (dating from 1537—in 1536 Don Luis Columbus had had his privileges confirmed by the emperor).
39. Ibid., I, IV, 8: PT, I, 108a.
40. Ibid., VI, 8: PT, I, 167.
41. Perhaps on the strength of Oviedo? "Although a Castilian, under the pretext of defending him, writes that he stole the discovery of that world from a Portuguese pilot" (*Lettere* [Florence, 1855], pp. 195–97, 309).
42. *History*, p. 597 (Bacon's pilot is Spanish, however).
43. *Solución*, par. 10.
44. *Hist.*, II, 3: PT, pp. 17–20.

with Columbus), representing as they did the reactions of two of the most important sources for the Admiral's biography, helped to earn Oviedo this undeserved reputation.

Humboldt actually refers to a "mutual hatred" between Fernando Columbus and Oviedo;[45] following Ramusio, he calls Oviedo a "malicious historian" for the pilot "calumny"[46] and describes him bluntly as an "enemy of the Admiral."[47] But elsewhere he frankly admits his surprise that the faithful Oviedo should always be considered a "detractor" of Columbus and an "enemy" of his family, as he continued until his dying day to defend the Admiral's deeds, services, and rights,[48] and expressed his wish to be buried in the Cathedral of Santo Domingo, near Columbus's tomb (see below, chap. XVII, sec. 25).

Harrisse, in turn, emphasized Oviedo's impartiality toward Columbus and his unceasing admiration for the Ligurian.[49] Jos, finally, demonstrated conclusively the reason for Fernando Columbus's animosity: as a former companion and friend of Oviedo and feeling sure, after the high praise bestowed in the *Sumario,* that Oviedo would also glorify the discoverer in the promised *Historia,* he was disappointed and annoyed to find that it contained the thesis that the Antilles had belonged to the ancient kings of Spain and thus to see the crown's lawyers presented with a formidable argument at the precise moment (1535) when "the ruinously lengthy lawsuits of his family were at their most critical juncture."[50]

In point of fact it is true that the Admiral's son vehemently contests the thesis of the Hesperides, but only a few pages earlier he had himself repeated the tale of the Portuguese pilot who supposedly gave Columbus his information,[51] quoting none other than Oviedo, mentioning the story merely as a "curiosity" but without contradicting it, and indeed comparing it with others.[52] Oviedo, for his part, is lavish in his praise of Columbus's son.[53] For certain details of the Admiral's third voyage he prefers the account that he obtained directly from Fernando to the version of the pilot Hernán Pérez Mateos, a resident in Santo Domingo;[54] and in the long-lasting question of the lawsuits he always takes the side of the

45. *Examen critique,* III, 302*n;* cf. ibid., V, 189.
46. Ibid., IV, 149.
47. Ibid., V, 189.
48. Ibid., IV, 132–33.
49. *Christophe Colomb,* pp. 106–07.
50. E. Jos, "Fernando Colón y la *Historia del Almirante,*" *RHA,* 9 (1940), 19. For an "authoritative assessment of Oviedo as a source on Columbus" (Pérez de Tudela, "Vida," p. xliin*121*) see A. Ballesteros Beretta, *Cristóbal Colón y el descubrimiento de América* (Barcelona, 1945), I, 29–34. It is however generally acknowledged today that Oviedo was the first to recognize Columbus's greatness and historical importance. See H. M. Jones, *O Strange New World* (New York, 1964), p. 400, quoting L. Bredner, "Columbus in Sixteenth-Century Poetry," in *Essays Honoring L. C. Wroth* (Portland, Maine, 1951), pp. 15–30. Pérez de Tudela, in his review of E. O'Gorman's *La idea del descubrimiento de América* (Mexico, 1951), in *RI,* 12, no. 47 (1952), 147–50, stresses how Oviedo remains indifferent to and almost unaware of Columbus's illusion that he had reached Asia.
51. Fernando Columbus, *Historia del Almirante,* I, 47–48; *Vita e fatti,* pp. 31–36.
52. Vignaud, *Histoire Critique,* II, 216*n423.*
53. *Hist.,* III, 6: PT, I, 62a.
54. Ibid., III, 3: PT, I, 59a; XIX, 1: PT, II, 189–90.

Columbuses and welcomes the finding in their favor,[55] because he never wavers in his conviction that the Genoese sailor discovered America and therefore fully deserved the reward promised to him and to his descendants. Moreover, through some mysterious design of Providence his discovery was legitimized *a priori* and thus validated, not invalidated, by the ancient hereditary right under which the Indies had belonged from time immemorial to the crown of Spain.

4. KNOWLEDGE OF ITALIAN LANGUAGE AND LITERATURE

Oviedo himself tells us how enthusiastically he learned "Tuscan" and read and bought books in Italian that he took with him to the Indies and which still half a century after their purchase he cherished as a precious reminder of his youth and instrument of spiritual improvement. "I roamed throughout Italy, doing everything I could to learn and read and understand the Tuscan language, looking for books in that language, of which I have some that have been in my company for more than fifty-five years, as it has been my desire that with their aid I should not altogether waste my time."[56]

How much he read and revered them is evident from the abundance of quotation in the *Historia*. There are relatively few traces of Spanish literature (see also below, n. 158): the occasional ballad and "our famous poet" Juan de Mena;[57] the *Vocabulista* of Antonio de Nebrija;[58] a few of the early chroniclers;[59] often El Tostado and some of the more recent historians, such as Pedro de Mejía[60] and Maximilianus Transylvanus,[61] Charles V's secretary and publisher of Magellan's voyage; and a few contemporary polemicists and polygraphs like Pedro

---

55. Ibid., XVIII, 20: PT, II, 152.

56. *Qu.*, III, est. 23 (unpublished part), cited by Amador de los Ríos, "Vida," p. xviii*n22;* and by Pérez de Tudela, "Vida," p. xxxi. These books must have been among the very first Italian incunabula taken to the New World (cf. E. W. Palm, *Los monumentos arquitectónicos de la Española* [Ciudad Trujillo, 1955], I, 109). Oviedo mentions the difficulty of protecting his books from the voracious *cucarachas* and is delighted to note that they cannot "in any way at all" get into a pine box that he ordered in Madrid in 1535, "for the transportation of certain books" (*Qu.*, p. 241).

57. *Hist.*, XXXV, 2: III, 590a; XXXVIII, Proh.: III, 635a; cf. XXV, 9: II, 297b. Bernardo del Carpio and El Cid Ruy Díaz, the heroes of so many ballads, are mentioned in *Hist.*, XXV, 19: II, 323a; Fernán González and El Cid again, ibid., XXV, 22: II, 330b, and El Cid alone, XXIX, 21: III, 113a. The "ballad of King Ramiro," L, 10, par. 27: PT, V, 344b.

58. *Hist.*, VI, 27: I, 212b. Further praise of Lebrija (or Nebrija), thanks to whom "the Latin language has flourished in Spain," ibid., XXVI, 5: II, 343b, where Oviedo regrets that his son should have associated himself with the plot of the traitors who assassinated Rodrigo de Bastidas.

59. Ibid., II, 5: PT, I, 24a; VI, 49: I, 248–49; XXV, 4: II, 280b (*Crónica de D. Juan II*); XXIX, 21: III, 102b (*Crónica del Conde Fernán González*, quoted indirectly); XLVII, 5: PT, V, 146.

60. Of whom, however, he cites mainly the *Silva de varia lección* (Seville, 1542—*Hist.*, VI, 322ff: I, 219ff), whence he comes up with various curious little tidbits, including reference to "a man called 'Colan the fish,' native of the city of Catania in Sicily" (*Hist.*, VI, 38: II, 227a). Mejía was a good friend of Oviedo, but one who reminded him of his past afflictions (*Hist.*, VI, 39: PT, I, 198a); and it was he who, in Seville in 1548, passed on to him the long report by Alonso de Montemayor, on whom see below, chap. XIX, sec. 4 (XLIX, 10 and 14: PT, V, 286b, 291b, 299). In the *Silva*, Mejía compares the savages' marriage customs with those of the ancient Romans (Hodgen, op. cit., pp. 336–37).

61. *Hist.*, XX, 1: II, 9b, 15b. On Transylvanus, cf. Sánchez Alonso, *Historiografía española*, I, 440.

Ciruelo.[62] Traces of other European literatures are almost entirely absent, and quotations from biblical or classical Greek or Latin sources (almost certainly taken from anthologies or Italian or Spanish translations) are much flaunted but not particularly abundant.[63] The poets, historians, and scholars of Italy, however, are quoted by Oviedo with obvious delight, in a sort of deliberate display of culture and refinement.

5. THE FOURTEENTH-CENTURY POETS

Petrarch, the idol of the humanists, appears to be his favorite author. Oviedo mentions the canzone "Italia mia . . .";[64] the sonnets "Una candida cerva sopra l'erba,"[65] "La gola, il sonno e l'oziose piume" (which contains the famous line, "Povera e nuda vai, filosofia"),[66] and "Giunto Alessandro a la famosa tomba";[67] the *Triumph of Love*[68] and the *Triumph of Fame;*[69] the *De Remediis utriusque fortunae;*[70] the "dialogues" regarding the traitor, detested by the very people that

---

62. Of Pedro Ciruelo, a prolific theologian and polemicist, Oviedo cites (*Hist.*, VI, 47: I, 244a) the *Reprobación de las supersticiones y hechicherías* (Salamanca, 1539), "which went through numerous editions" (*Enciclopedia Espasa*, s.v.). This work is cited in the *Quinquagenas* too (p. xxv). When, however, in connection with astrological terms, he mentions "the very learned and very excellent Master Ciruelo, who wrote so well, as is well known in our Spain" (*Hist.*, XXI, 5: II, 126b), he is probably referring to his *Commentarius in Sphaeram mundi Johannis de Sacro Bosco* (Paris, 1498; Florence, 1537), in which Ciruelo also recalls the discovery of America and the arrival in Spain of the first natives (cf. Maggs Brothers Catalogue No. 743, item 3).

63. First and foremost Pliny (possibly read in Italian—see below, chap. XIX, n. 240); then Ptolemy, Titus Livy, Cicero, Julius Caesar, Virgil, Marcus Varro, Seneca, Columella, Theophrastus, Ovid, Martial, Fabius Pictor, and Polybius (secondhand from Leonardo Aretino—*Hist.*, XXVII, 6: II, 491b), Vegetius, Valerius Maximus, Justin, Strabo, Julius Solinus, Diogenes Laertius, Sallust, Aristotle, Thucydides, Plutarch, Homer, Xenophon, Plato, the pseudo-Dares Phrygius and Dictys Cretensis, the "History of Rhodes," Appian of Alexandria, Flavius Josephus, Julius Frontinus, Herodian, Lactantius, Suetonius, Vitruvius, Quintus Curtius, Diodorus Siculus, Albertus Magnus, Paolus Orosius, St. Gregory, Eusebius, St. Jerome, Athanasius, St. Hilary, the Bible, St. Augustine, Isidore, Avicenna, and Aben Ruiz are among the ancient and medieval authors quoted, often, as we have said, at second hand.

But "more attention should be paid to the numerous unstudied medieval anthologies of classical works. It is not always realized to what extent authors in the Middle Ages depended on such collections rather than on the complete classical texts. It was one of the differentiating features of the Renaissance that it went to the original texts" (B. L. Ullmann, "Trends in Greek and Latin Studies," *Studies in Philology*, 42 [1945], p. 411). From this point of view, as in certain other ways (see below, chap. XIX, secs. 1–3), Oviedo is still very "medieval."

64. *Hist.*, XXXIII, 21: III, 365a; possibly recalled earlier, in the *Claribalte* (see below, chap. XVI, sec. 8).

65. *Hist.*, VI, 8: I, 178a.

66. Ibid., VI, 51: I, 258a.

67. Ibid., XXXI, Proh.: III, 184a.

68. Ibid., VI, 8: I, 182a; XXV, 11: II, 304b: " . . . the knights of the Round Table, about whom there are so many fables written and papers filled with dreams, as Petrarch says." In fact: "Here we have those that fill our papers with dreams, Lancelot, Tristan and the other wanderers" (*Triumph of Love*, lines 79–80). The same quote occurs in the *Quinquagenas*, p. 232 (on which see Farinelli, *Italia e Spagna*, I, 50); see also *Hist.*, XLIX, 1: IV, 381a.

69. *Hist.*, VI, Proh.: I, 162b ("Nestor who knew so much and lived so long"); XXIX, 21: III, 109b; XXXIII, 13: III, 324a.

70. Ibid., XLI, 3: IV, 33b. Oviedo refers to this particular work as "De próspera e adversa fortuna," an abbreviation of the title under which the Spanish translation was published in Valladolid in 1510. Cf. A. Bonilla y San Martín, "Erasmo en España," *Revue hispanique*, 17 (1907), 433, and n. 2, who quotes A. Farinelli, *Sulla fortuna del Petrarca in Ispagna nel Quattrocento* (Turin, 1904), p. 2 (subsequently reprinted in *Italia e Spagna*, I, 19–20). It is therefore incorrect to say, as does the learned E. W. Palm, *Monumentos arquitectónicos*, I, 30, that Oviedo cites only Petrarch's sonnets in the *Historia*.

use him,[71] and regarding an "evil and unchaste woman."[72] Oviedo invokes Petrarch's authority to fix the years of Gregory the Great's pontificate[73] and repeats his opinion on the vanity of alchemy as zealously as any disciple.[74] He admires him as poet, moralist, and historian. His lasting familiarity with Petrarch is confirmed in the frequency with which the Tuscan is quoted in Oviedo's final work, the belated and only partially published *Quinquagenas*. He takes particular delight in the *Triumphs,* which provide him with quotations, items of information, images, and moral maxims; but the *Canzoniere* too, and some of the prose works, supply him with elegant turns of phrase and erudite affectations.

In the published part of the *Quinquagenas* Oviedo quotes the *Triumph of Love* with particular frequency, the *Triumph of Fame* and the *Triumph of Chastity* somewhat less so. It is curious to note that never, in any of the major works, does he cite the *Triumph of Death,* the *Triumph of Time,* or the *Triumph of Divinity.*[75]

Oviedo almost always translates the lines he quotes, but more than once he professes himself—justifiably—dissatisfied with his translation. In respect of the lines quoted on page 77 of the *Quinquagenas* he observes that "these lines do not sound the same in Spanish as they do in Tuscan, in which they are very excellent"; and referring to the lines translated on p. 537 he adds, "in Tuscan they sound very good," and proceeds to paraphrase them again in prose. In the same place Oviedo also cites an elegant "commentator" on the *Triumph of Love,* possibly referring to Illicinio (Bernardo Lapini, or Bernardo da Monte Illicinio di Siena), who provided the commentary of the "most moral triumphs" in the edition (Venice; Stagnino, 1513; Gamba, op. cit., no. 601) that also contains the *Canzoniere* with Filelfo's commentary: Oviedo was in fact familiar with and quotes from this commentary (see below, sec. 6). Farinelli (*Italia e Spagna,* I, 61*n*.2) already noted that the *Quinquagenas* contained "expressions peculiar to Petrarch's *Triumphs.*"

From the *Canzoniere* the *Quinquagenas* recall, on pp. 248 and 250–51, the line "Forse ch'ogni huom che legge non se intende" (line 46 of the obscure canzone CV, "Mai non vo' più cantar com'io soleva"), and no less than three times, on pp. 38, 231, and 238, though somewhat mangled, the famous line, "La

---

71. *Hist.,* XXVI, 5: II, 343–44. This would not be the dialogues *De contemptu mundi,* could be the *Eclogae,* or more probably the already mentioned *De remediis utriusque fortunae.*

72. *Hist.,* XXVII, 6: II, 438a.

73. "Francisco Petrarca, in the *Summa* that he wrote on the lives of the Supreme Pontiffs, says that Gregory . . . " (*Hist.,* V, Proh.: I, 124b). This is the *Chronica delle vite de Pontifici et Imperatori romani,* existing in various printed editions dated 1478 (Florence), 1507 (Venice), 1526, 1534, etc., and which was for a long time (and still by Turner, "Biblioteca Ovetense," no. 91) attributed to Petrarch (cf. Gamba, op. cit., p. 161, nos. 639–41; Rauschburg Catalogue No. 5, item 362).

74. *Hist.,* XXVIII, 6: II, 493a.

75. *Triumph of Love: Qu.,* pp. 38, 77, 200, 232, 488–89, 527, 536; *Triumph of Fame:* Qu., pp. 225, 323; *Triumph of Chastity: Qu.,* p. 337. Las Casas too quotes the *Triumphs* as a source of historical data, regarding a city "in the seigniory of Pisa" that was depopulated by a plague of ants (*Historia de las Indias,* bk. III, chap. 128, ed. cit., III, 248).

vita al fine, e 'l dì loda la sera" (line 31 of canzone XXIII, "Nel dolce tempo della prima etade").

Of the prose works, apart from a maxim that I have not been able to locate ("Malascaczia il vicio chi ha facto il calo," attributed to Petrarch in the *Quinquagenas,* p. 34), Oviedo twice (*Quinquagenas,* pp. 335 and 447) mentions—in reference to Trajan and Saint Ignatius respectively—the apocryphal *Lives of the Roman Emperors and Popes.* Oviedo's words, "a summary and brief account of popes and emperors, written by Francisco Petrarca," correspond exactly to the colophon of the Florentine edition (ca. 1500): ". . . Lives of Popes and Emperors of Rome by Messer Franciesco Petrarca . . . composed . . . with assiduous diligence and brevity" (Gamba, op. cit., no. 639). Finally there is a Petrarchan flavor, though it is not in fact from Petrarch, in the line that "a poet said in a sonnet, 'who will be faithful to me if I betray myself,' " which Oviedo, as usual, translates into Castilian (*Quinquagenas,* p. 29).

Of Dante, the "famous" [76] but certainly less familiar poet, and less accessible to a foreigner, Oviedo knows at least the *Inferno* and the *Paradiso.* He mentions, in fact, in the *Historia* [77] and the *Quinquagenas,* [78] the episode of Guido da Montefeltro, Justinian's words on the peace of Augustus, [79] the opening of the *Divine Comedy,* [80] and twice Canto III of the *Inferno.* [81] And he repeatedly mentions the famous commentary by Cristoforo Landino. [82]

Of Boccaccio's works Oviedo has read the *Life of Dante* [83] and more than once cites the tract on "Illustrious Women" (*De claris mulieribus*), [84] but not the

76. *Hist.,* VI, 48: I, 242a. Oviedo also draws inspiration from Dante's terza rima and Petrarch's *Triumphs* in composing his *Quinquagenas* (Pérez de Tudela, "Vida," p. clxiv*n549*). Columbus's companion and Oviedo's friend the Erasmian Diego Méndez de Segura, a resident of Santo Domingo, possessed a copy of Dante and bequeathed it in 1536 to his children (J. Caillet-Bois, "Un olvidado erasmista de América: Diego Méndez de Segura," *Humanidades,* 30 [1944–45], 59–66). On the problem of Dante's meager influence in Spain after 1515 (because he was suspected of unorthodoxy?), cf. W. P. Friederich, "The Unsolved Problem of Dante's Influence in Spain, 1515–1865," *Hispanic Review,* 14 (1946), 160–64, and the bibliography mentioned there.

77. *Inferno,* XXVII, 67, quoted in *Hist.,* XXVII, 4: II, 425a.

78. *Inferno,* XXVII, 118, in *Qu.,* p. 217.

79. *Paradiso,* VI, 80–81, quoted in *Hist.,* XII, Proh.: I, 388a.

80. *Hist.,* XXIX, 33, par. 31; III, 167b.

81. "Abandon hope . . . " (*Inferno,* III, 9), in *Qu.,* p. 170; lines 76–78 in *Qu.,* p. 141, where he adds that "the commentator Peponforo Landi [*sic,* certainly meaning Cristoforo Landino] tells us what this boatman and the River Lethe are." Dante is *not* quoted respecting Minos, *Qu.,* pp. 505–06.

82. *Hist.,* VI, 48: I, 242b; VIII, 6: I, 298; XXIX, 25: III, 124b; see below, chap. XVI, sec. 8. Oviedo could well have owned a copy of the famous edition (Gamba, op. cit., no. 315) printed in Florence in 1481 containing the *Divine Comedy* with the commentary by Landino, the life of Dante named in the third of the passages mentioned, and illustrations attributed to Sandro Botticelli. The *Quinquagenas* too refer to Landino's commentary, apropos of Charon and Acheron (p. 141), the cruelty of Ezzelino da Padova, *Inferno* XII (p. 167), and Canto XXXII of the *Inferno* (p. 171); cf. Farinelli, *Italia e Spagna,* II, 392.

83. *Hist.,* VI, 48: I, 242a, referring to the dream of Dante's mother, recounted and interpreted by Boccaccio at the beginning and end respectively of his life of Dante. Even in the 1500s the *Life of Dante* was "known to very few persons outside Italy" (Farinelli, *Italia e Spagna,* I, 101–02).

84. *Hist.,* V, 3: I, 135a; VI, 49: I, 215b. According to D. Turner, "Biblioteca Ovetense," p. 163, Oviedo used the anonymous Spanish translation published in Seville in 1528.

Decameron, which he probably lumped with the chivalric poems and romances as frivolous and morally unworthy reading.[85] Yet in the albeit moralistic *Quinquagenas* we find quoted, much to our surprise, not only the usual "Illustrious Women" but the scurrilous "Labyrinth of Love" or *Corbaccio*—which he had translated in 1525[86]—and for no less a maxim than this: "Chi due bocche bacia, l'una convien che puzza" ("If you kiss two mouths, one must needs smell bad").[87]

Oviedo also refers at least twice to a popular Florentine proverb ("Tutto il mondo è come casa nostra"—"The whole wide world is just like home").[88] At one point he quotes it to support his conviction that nature is one and the same in Europe and America and teaches the Indians the arts that Theseus (according to Plutarch) taught the Athenians, and then he refers to it again when commenting on the fact that there are poor people begging in the squares and houses and markets of New Spain, just as there are in Old Spain. In each case it is the voice of Florentine folk wisdom that Oviedo hears when he is tackling the problem of the analogies between Old World and New. And we have already seen (above, sec. 1) how Oviedo drew another parallel between the bitter popular quatrain on the fall of King Frederick of Naples and the songs of the West Indian natives.[89]

---

85. On Oviedo's moralistic aversion for books of mere fantasy (although he wrote one himself, the *Claribalte,* published in 1519), see below, chap. XVI, sec. 3. Possibly Oviedo looked on the *Decameron* as one of those profane and romantic books whose importation into the Indies was repeatedly banned, from 1531 onward, by the Spanish monarchs. And it is known that up until the sixteenth century Boccaccio's minor works were much better known in Spain than the *Decameron,* which was the last of his books to influence Castilian literature (C. B. Bourland, "Boccaccio and the Decameron in Castilian and Catalan Literature," *Revue Hispanique,* 12 [1905], 1–232, esp. pp. 10–11; and A. Farinelli, "Boccaccio in Ispagna," in *Italia e Spagna,* I, 91–386, esp. p. 381). The *Decameron* was published in Spanish in Seville in 1496 (Farinelli, *Italia e Spagna,* I, 379). It was not, however, until 1559 that the work was banned by the Inquisition (Bourland, op. cit., p. 59), and then only in the Castilian text (unless expurgated), not in the Italian (M. Menéndez Pelayo, *Historia de los heterodoxos españoles* [Buenos Aires, 1945], V, 476*nl*). On the fifteenth-century Spaniards' almost total unfamiliarity with Dante, Boccaccio, and Petrarch, cf. A. Giannini, "Impressioni italiane di viaggiatori nei secoli XVI e XVII," *Revue Hispanique,* 55 (1922), 68, citing A. Farinelli, "Appunti su Dante in Ispagna nell'età media," *Giornale Storico della Letteratura Italiana,* 45 (1905), suppl. 8, pp. 40–41; but cf. Percopo, op. cit., p. clxxxiii ff.

86. Cf. Pérez de Tudela, "Vida," p. xlix. The translation, which remained unpublished at the time and is never mentioned by Oviedo, is possibly the anonymous one published in Seville in 1546. Cf. A. López de Meneses, "Gonzalo Fernández de Oviedo, traductor del *Corbaccio,*" in *Revista de la Biblioteca, Archivo y Museo del Ayuntamiento de Madrid* (Madrid, 1935), and in *Clio,* 10 (1942), 144; M. Maticorena Estrada, "Una traducción desconocida de Fernández de Oviedo," *Estudios Americanos,* 13, nos. 67–68 (1957), 299–300; *RHA,* 45 (June 1958), bibliography item no. 17631, pp. 305–06; Otte, "Aspiraciones y actividades," p. 43*n*89. Farinelli (*Italia e Spagna,* I, 50*n,* 329*n*) finds indications of a familiarity with the *Corbaccio* in the *Quinquagenas* and explains (I, 264ff) how that salacious little work could pass for an edifying and almost ascetic tract. D. Turner, "Biblioteca Ovetense," p. 163, no. 18, says that Oviedo must have owned the Spanish version of the *Corbaccio* (*El Laberinto de Amor* [Seville, 1546]) and that the translation, though usually attributed to Canon Diego López de Ayala, could even have been Oviedo's own work.

87. *Qu.,* pp. 206, 460. One of Oviedo's spiritual masters, St. Antoninus of Florence, counseled against reading Boccaccio's *Corbaccio,* the "Hundred Stories and the fables of the paladins" (V. Zabughin, *Storia del Rinascimento cristiano in Italia* [Milan, 1924], p. 119).

88. *Hist.,* VI, 49: I, 253a; XXXIII, 4: III, 278b. On the Tuscan language, "the best of the Italian vernaculars," cf. *Qu.,* cited by Pérez de Tudela, "Vida," p. clxiv*n549.*

89. Both in the *Hist.,* (II, 9: I, 40a) and in the *Quinquagenas* (p. 230), Oviedo recalls another Italian proverb, "It takes more than a white tablecloth to spread the table," and, in the latter work, somewhat curiously, the Sicilian song that says "a word to the wise suffices" (*Qu.,* p. 397). Oviedo makes abundant use of Spanish proverbs, on which I shall have more to say later.

6. HISTORIANS AND HUMANISTS OF THE FIFTEENTH CENTURY

The fifteenth-century authors mentioned by Oviedo include the humanist Francesco Filelfo (not "Philadelpho"), in respect of his commentary on Petrarch,[90] and the *Historia Bohemica* of Aeneas Silvius Piccolomini, a "native of Siena," quoted regarding the bloodthirsty heretic Zisca, who left instructions in his will that a drum be made out of his heart so that he could continue to terrorize his enemies from beyond the grave.[91] But he is particularly fond of quoting Leonardo Aretino, the founder of humanist historiography (Fueter) and Saint Antoninus of Florence, whose writings included a universal history which provided Oviedo with details on the peoples of the East.

Of the works of Leonardo Aretino (Leonardo Bruni), "a conscientious and elegant historian," Oviedo refers several times to a universal chronicle ("compendium of chronicles" or "compendium of histories" or "tract") which he calls "El Aquila volante,"[92] and also reveals a familiarity with the *Punic War*[93] and the classic *Florentine History*,[94] which latter probably had an influence on certain formal aspects of his own writing of history.

Of the saintly archbishop of Florence, whose religious writings were so widely circulated in sixteenth-century Spain and Mexico,[95] Oviedo was familiar with the crude anthology of tales from all over the world known as the *Antonio,* which provided him, as we shall shortly see, with a rich fund of comparative and other material: not only stories of two-headed monsters, that he parallels with the case of the Siamese twins born in Santo Domingo,[96] and all sorts of ideas on Genghiz Khan and the Tartars,[97] that he matches with what he has learned and related

90. *Hist.*, VI, 8: I, 178a. On this commentary, which the irascible Filelfo undertook reluctantly, on the instructions of his master, Filippo Maria Visconti, but which was several times reprinted, cf. G. Voigt, *Il Risorgimento dell'antichità classica* (Florence, 1888), I, 513–14.
91. *Hist.*, VI, 30: I, 217a. *The History of Bohemia* was "translated into Spanish by Comendador Hernán Núñez de Toledo and printed in Seville in 1509" (F. Picatoste, *Los españoles en Italia* [Madrid, 1887], p. 190).
92. *Hist.*, V, II: I, 157b; XXVII, 5: II, 434b; XXXI, Proh.: III, 185b; XXXII, 4: III, 238a; XXXIII, 29: III, 413a. The *Libro intitolato Aquila Volante* (Venice, 1506, 1508, 1549, etc.) "is a popular history going up to the time of Boniface VIII, interspersed with quotes from Dante." The first person to attribute it to Bruni seems to have been the printer Alessandro Paganini (Hoepli catalogue, 8–9 April 1932, item 80; Rauschburg catalogue No. 5, item 78). Apart from some of Boccaccio's works Bruni was the only Italian author represented in the library of Isabella the Catholic (Prescott, *Ferdinand and Isabella*, II, 185n) and was "idolized by the Spanish humanists" (Farinelli, *Italia e Spagna*, I, 356).
93. *Hist., XXVIII, 6: II, 491b; XXXIV, Proh.: III, 558a.*
94. Ibid., XXXIII, 37: III, 457a.
95. R. Ricard, "Reflexiones acerca de la evangelización de Méjico por los misioneros españoles en el siglo XVI," *RI*, 5, no. 15 (1944), 11. The Florentine archbishop is cited several times in the "Dos cartas al Rey contra los moros de las Filipinas" of Licentiate Melchor de Ávalos (1585), in *Cuerpo de documentos del siglo XVI sobre los derechos de España en las Filipinas*, ed. L. Hanke and A. Millares Carlo (Mexico, 1943), pp. 75, 80–81, 86, 90, 96, 105; and named as an authority by Sarmiento de Gamboa (cited by R. Porras Barrenechea, "El pensamiento de Vitoria en el Perú," *Mercurio Peruano*, 27 [1946], p. 480).
96. *Hist.*, VI, 11: I, 195–98.
97. Ibid., XXIX, 20: PT, III, 287a; XXIX, 27: III, 134b; XXXII, 2: III, 224a; XXXII, 3: III, 232a. Note that Oviedo draws on an Italian author even for information regarding the Tartars, while relations between Tartars and Castilians had existed since the fourteenth century (Molinari, op. cit., p. 26n). Even then the Tartars were idealized and called upon to play the role later assigned to the Indians, and more generally to the Noble Savage. In various

regarding the Indians, but also the resolutions of the Council of Constance on the cult of images, as taught to the natives of Nicaragua,[98] and the historical example of the Sicilian Vespers, when Italian Christians massacred French Christians.[99] Some of Oviedo's most inspired observations on comparative ethnography, both between Far Eastern and Far Western races and between the primitive nations' savagery and that of the civilized peoples, can thus be traced back to the Florentine saint. And even in later years, right up to the end, Oviedo continues to use Saint Antoninus as a basic reference work.[100]

Another fifteenth-century religious writer, Fra Cherubino da Siena, mentioned once in the *Quinquagenas,* is probably the author of the book that Oviedo translated and had published in Seville in 1548[101] under the title *Regla de la vida spiritual y secreta teologia.*

Fra Cherubino is a pious writer and a good man of letters (he appears on the list of language authorities approved by the Accademia della Crusca) but, to our taste at least, arid, casuistic, and bigoted. Certainly by the mid-sixteenth century, after Erasmus and Luther, his formalism and little numbered rules must have seemed somewhat too shallow and ingenuous, which might well explain the very limited success of the Spanish translation rather more accurately than the factors mentioned and bewailed by Oviedo, namely the public's addiction to light reading in preference to books which will "improve the soul."[102]

In its time, however, Fra Cherubino's little tract, or rather manual, was a best seller. Published in Florence in 1477, it was reprinted in Modena, Lucca, and Florence in 1482, again in Florence in 1483 (twice), in Ferrara, Parma, Florence,

---

seventeenth-century utopias one notes how features drawn from Garcilaso become mixed up with others taken from travels in Tartary (cf. G. Atkinson, *The Extraordinary Voyage in French Literature Before 1700* [New York, 1920], passim). See below, chap. XVIII, sec. 12.

98. *Hist.,* XLII, 3: PT, IV, 382a; L, 10, par. 30: PT, V, 348a.

99. Ibid., XXXIII, 37: III, 456b. St. Antoninus's *Chronicon* or *Summa historialis* was first published in Nuremberg in 1484 (3 vols). Turner, "Biblioteca Ovetense," p. 163, no. 6, conjectures that Oviedo "probably knew this work in one of the later printings, such as that by Nicholas Wolff at Lyon, 1512." On St. Antoninus, cf. Zabughin, op. cit., pp. 117–26; Voigt, op. cit., I, 376–78; on his theses (unknown to Oviedo) regarding the just causes for waging war on pagans and infidels, see J. Höffner, *Christentum und Menschenwürde: Das Anliegen der spanischen Kolonialethik im goldenen Zeitalter* (Trier, 1947), p. 55ff. Oviedo also quotes him in the *Historia* (II, 1: I, 11b).

100. He quotes him for the attribution of the Stabat Mater to St. Gregory (*Qu.,* p. 297), on the cause of Trajan's death (*Qu.,* p. 335), and on the Jews baptized in Spain (609 A.D.) and expelled from France (*Qu.,* p. 280). If the *Supplementa Chronicarum* really were the work of St. Antoninus, as is mistakenly stated by the editor of the *Quinquagenas* (Fuente, op. cit., p. xxxi), the preceding list would also have to include these references: *Qu.,* p. 144 (on the viper of the Visconti), p. 335 (on Trajan), p. 338 (on Virgil's bomb), p. 533 (on St. Jerome). In the *Historia,* the *Supplementa Chronicarum* are cited for various items of information on ancient history (V, 3: I, 137; VI, 44: I, 236b; VI, 49: I, 246b, 251, 252a, 253a; XX, 13: II, 56b) and biblical history (III, 5: I, 68a). But Vignaud notes: "*Supplementum Chronicarum.* Bergomensis (Jacobi). A famous work, printed and translated several times, which served as a model for the famous Nuremberg Chronicle" (*Histoire critique,* II, 299n69). Fueter, op. cit., p. 181, mentions Jacopo da Bergamo, in fact "Frater Jacobus Philippus Foresta von Bergamo," as a crude compiler of the same sort as St. Antoninus; and he describes his *Supplementum* (1st ed., Venice, 1483) as "a book affected by humanism only in certain details" (op. cit., pp. 184–85).

101. See also J. A. Alvarez Baena, *Hijos de Madrid* (Madrid, 1789–91), II, 359; Medina, *Biblioteca,* I, 231, "a theological tract attributed to Oviedo"; Menéndez Pelayo, *Poesía hispanoamericana,* I, 288, who thinks it is original; Oviedo, *Libro de la cámara real* (Madrid, 1870), pp. 138–39; Pérez de Tudela, "Vida," pp. cxxxvii–cxxviii, clxxiii.

102. The printer, then, made little or nothing out of it: Amador de los Ríos, "Vida," p. lxxiii*n32.*

and Bologna in 1487, and again in Bologna in 1489 (twice), and over the next few years (1490–1494) several times more in Florence and Venice.[103] So it is hardly surprising that it should have caught Oviedo's eye while he was in Italy. But nothing can be said with certainty until the Italian text has been compared with the supposed Spanish translation, which is unfortunately extremely rare, indeed unfindable.[104]

7. CONTEMPORARY GEOGRAPHERS, HISTORIANS, AND MEN OF LETTERS

Oviedo also knew the writings on the Indies of the Bolognese scholar, Lodovico de Varthema,[105] whose *Itinerario* was first published in Rome in 1510. He mentions in passing an item of geographical information reported by Amerigo Vespucci,[106] and is of course familiar with the *Decades* of Peter Martyr of Anghiera,[107] which began to appear in Seville in 1511. He makes extensive use of the report on Magellan's voyage by "Micer Antonio Pigafecta Vicentino,"[108] admires Sebastian Cabot as a cosmographer,—but finds numerous errors in his maps and despises him as a captain[109]—and severely criticizes the obscure Sicilian historian Fray Bernardo Gentil[110] and the more illustrious Lucio

103. G. Sbaraglia, *Supplementum et Castigatio ad Scriptores Trium Ordinum S. Francisci* (Rome, 1908–36), I, 203–04. An elegant reprint was published in Imola in the late nineteenth century by I. Galeati e Figlio: *Regole della Vita Spirituale di Frate Cherubino da Siena del secolo XV,* ed. Francesco Zambrini (Imola, 1878), including biographical details (see pp. xix–xxvii). See also Gamba, op. cit., no. 286.

104. There is no trace of the work in the Italian and American libraries I have visited. In the Estanislao Rodríguez catalogue No. 65 (Madrid, 1935), item no. 94 was offered at 500 pesetas: "Fernández de Oviedo y Valdes (Gonzalo).—*Regla de la vida espiritual y secreta Theología.* (At the end:) Printed in the most noble city of Seville, by Dominico Robertis, on 18 February 1548. In octavo, parchment, frontispiece engraved, in two colors, gothic script. 101 numbered pages, and 3 containing the table [of contents]. This work . . . is so rare that references have usually been based on a note by Nicolás Antonio, who did not even manage to see it for himself, since he did not mention the number of pages. In our view it is the sole surviving copy." [On the eventual purchaser of this item and the apparent original of Oviedo's translation see Translator's Preface to the current work.]

105. *Hist.,* VIII, 1, par. 10: I, 292a.

106. Ibid., XX, 1: II, 9b. The "Florentine master" praised as a great expert in geographical and astronomical terms (XXI, 5: II, 126b) is almost certainly Vespucci.

107. As we shall see (below, chap. XVII, sec. 12), Peter Martyr is one of his favorite targets because he reports at second hand.

108. *Hist.,* XX, 1–2: II, 15, 21–31; but always with a hint of critical skepticism (cf. Ferrando, op. cit., p. 476; and above, chap. XI, sec. 3). Pigafetta's report to the grand master of the Knights of Rhodes, Villiers de l'Isle Adam ("Miçer Phelipo Villiers Ledislan" as Oviedo calls him), possibly drafted originally in French, was first published in Paris, ca. 1525; the first Italian edition dates from 1534 or 1536. On "the ship *Pancalvo,* out of Genoa, that went to the Strait of Magellan and had passed almost the whole Strait," met by Alonso de Cabrera in the Rio de la Plata (1537), see *Hist.,* XXIII, 12: II, 191a; XXIII, 13: II, 197a.

109. See *Hist.,* XXI, 2–3: II, 114–15; XXIII, 2: II, 169–70; XXXIII, 53: III, 544a; XLV, 2: IV, 140a. Oviedo praises Cabot, "of Venetian origin and brought up in the island of England," his voyage to Rio de la Plata and his navigational charts, but always with a slightly disdainful tone, possibly due to the fact that Cabot had fallen into disgrace in Spain, been banished to Oran (1530) and then, against the wishes of Charles V, gone over to the service of England (1549).

110. *Hist.,* XXXIV, 3: III, 562. J. B. Muñoz stated that he had been unable to read anything written by Bernardo Gentil and that everything he knew about him had come out of three letters from Marineo (*Historia del Nuevo Mundo* [Madrid, 1793], I, xiv). Meager details in Harrisse, *Bibliotheca Americana,* p. 370n7 (with reference to Muñoz); A. Farinelli, *Divagazioni erudite* (Turin, 1925), pp. 276–77; P. Verrua, *Umanisti ed altri "studiosi viri" italiani e stranieri di qua e di là dalle Alpi e dal mare* [Geneva, 1924], pp. 1, 3, 116, 133, with reference to other writings of the same author. I have not seen the article by J. de la Peña y Cámara, "Un cronista desconocido de Carlos V: El humanista siciliano Fray Bernardo Gentil, O.P.," *Hispania* (Madrid), 4 (1944), 536–68, nor the book by M. A. Coniglione, *Bernardo Gentile, O.P., Umanista siciliano* (Catania, 1948), both mentioned by D. Turner, "Biblioteca Ovetense," p. 179, no. 5.

Marineo Siculo.[111] He cites Aristotle secondhand from Theophilus of Ferrara,[112] uses Calepino's dictionary,[113] and has studied the Milanese Cesare Cesariano's commentary on Vitruvius (1521).[114]

Travelers, geographers, and scientists must all have been familiar to him, but he is also acquainted with the works of some of his closer contemporaries in the field of scholarship and letters. In Italy Oviedo met Serafino dell'Aquila, a tedious Petrarchist and mediocre euphuist, whose works nevertheless provided Oviedo with a couple of lines that suited his book,[115] the first of which, "Per troppo variar natura è bella" ("It is nature's richness of variation that makes it beautiful") balances and contradicts the Florentine proverb on the oneness of nature.[116]

---

111. *Hist.*, XXXIX, 30: III, 145. Marineo Siculo (1445–1533) lived from 1484 onward in Spain, and from 1496 at court. Oviedo quite correctly accuses him of being "ill-informed," of having "dreamed up" what he wrote about the Indies, and of having departed from the truth in "certain private genealogies." Fueter (op. cit., p. 224) in fact says that the *De rebus Hispaniae memorabilibus* (Alcalá, 1530, cited by Oviedo) is a compilation based on the inventions of Annius of Viterbo, the principal aim of which is to "identify Roman ancestors for the Spanish grandees." In an extract in Spanish from this work (*Sumario de la sereníssima vida y herojcos hechos de los Cattólicos Reyes*, etc. [Seville, 1545]; cf. Dolphin Books Catalog of Latin American Books, no. 388), Columbus is called Pedro Colón! On Marineo, see also Prescott, *Ferdinand and Isabella*, II, 190–93; J. Amador de los Ríos, *Historia crítica de la literatura española* (Madrid, 1861–65), VII, 198 and passim; and esp. G. Cirot, *Les histoires générales d'Espagne entre Alphonse X et Philippe II, 1284–1556* (Paris and Bordeaux, 1904), pp. 77–89; and C. Lynn, *A College Professor of the Renaissance: Lucius Marineo Siculo Among the Spanish Humanists* (Chicago, 1937), pp. 52–53, 255, which cites A. Mongitore, *Biblioteca Sicula* (Palermo, 1707–24), I, 107, which lists him only as a poet. See below, chap. XVII, sec. 17.

112. "Everything that is said here can be found in the compendium of Fr. Theophilus de Ferrariis, Cremonensis, *Vitae regularis sacri ordinis predicatorum,* following what Aristotle wrote: *De admirandis in natura auditis*" (*Hist.*, II, 3: I, 14b). Fra' Teofilo de Ferrariis, born in Cremona in 1431, taught at the Dominican monastery in Venice. An enthusiastic follower of scholasticism, he edited and published St. Thomas's commentary on Aristotle and brought out a work of his own entitled *Propositiones ex omnibus libris Aristotelis collectae* (1493), on which see F. Papi, *Antropologia e civiltà nel pensiero di Giordano Bruno* (Florence, 1968), pp. 207–08.

Fernando Columbus, quarreling with Oviedo, hints that the latter, "who does not seem to have understood Greek," misunderstood what he read in Theophilus of Ferrara about the transoceanic island discovered by the Carthaginians (*Historia del Almirante,* I, 49–50). Two centuries later Voltaire was to amuse himself with the equivocation: "America has been found in Plato. The Carthaginians have been given credit for it; and this anecdote is based on reference to a book of Aristotle's that he didn't write" (*Dictionnaire philosophique,* s.v. "Population" [Paris, 1879], XX, 254).

113. *Hist.*, II, 3: I, 17b; and *Qu.*, pp. 17, 155, 462, 480.

114. *Hist.*, XXXV, Proh.: III, 581a; and perhaps also XXVII, 5: II, 434b: "that treatise that they call *Cesariano,* chapter XV." Oviedo cites his "learned commentary" also in *Qu.*, p. 23. On Cesariano as architect, cf. A. Venturi, *L'architettura del Quattrocento* (Milan, 1924), II, 774–802; *Enciclopedia Italiana,* s.v.; F. Leoni, "Il Cesariano e l'architettura del Rinascimento in Lombardia," *Arte Lombarda,* 1 (1955), 90–97; P. Verzone, "Cesare Cesariano," *Arte Lombarda,* 16 (1971), 203–10, which issue also contains C. H. Krinsky, "Cesariano and the Renaissance Without Rome" (pp. 211–18) and S. Gatti, "L'attività milanese del Cesariano dal 1512–13 al 1519" (pp. 219–30).

115. *Hist.*, XII, 5: I, 391b; XVII, 19: I, 539a. The same sonnet, "composed by a modern poet that I met and spoke with in Italy, called Serafin del Aguila," is also quoted in the *Relación de lo sucedido en la prisión del Rey de Francia,* p. 458.

116. On which see above, n. 88; see below, Appendix A. Serafino dell'Aquila was in Mantua and Milan between 1495 and 1499 and then made his way down to Rome (1499), where he died in August 1500 (A. Gaspary, *Storia della letteratura italiana* [Turin, 1900–14], vol. II, pt. I, pp. 314–15). Oviedo recalls that he was "mourned as a great poet." And G. Rossi, "Serafino Aquilano e i suoi sonetti: Un'edizione delle Rime di Serafino Aquilano sfuggita ai bibliografi," in *Varietà letterarie* (Bologna, 1912), pp. 113–33, mentions that his *Rime* went through more than twenty editions between 1502 and 1516. In one of D'Annunzio's sonnets, "Le Città del Silenzio, Urbino," in *Le Laudi* (Milan, 1904), II, 138, he is described as "a second Orpheus." And Reichenbach (*Enciclopedia Italiana,* s.v.) notes that "few men enjoyed such great and universal renown in their own time." Oviedo mentions in fact that "he was held in much esteem at that time." See also P. Monnier, *Le Quattrocento* (Paris, 1908), II, 403–04, and the decidedly negative

We have Oviedo's own word for it that he was on friendly terms with Pontano and Sannazzaro. On his visit to Naples in 1499 (or 1500?) he saw Pontano, then eighty or more years old, conversing with various other "learned gentlemen," including Sannazzaro, and he heard Pontano, in connection with some problem of interpretation, quip amiably, "We would do better to ask Messer Jacopo de Sannazzaro about that land of Arcadia, since, as he knew the language of its shepherds and mixed it with Tuscan, he will also be able to tell us what they think there of our Italian language"; at which everyone laughed, including Sannazzaro himself, "a learned and noble gentleman," who took no more offense at the barb than if his own father had spoken the words, "because in truth Sannazzaro and everyone loved and revered Pontano as a father, and he was looked on as a very learned man in that city." [117] And again in Naples, in the following year 1500, he was assured by Pontano, "who at that time was held to be one of the most well read and learned men in Italy," that Pliny dedicated his *Natural History* to Domitian. [118]

8. The Venetian scholars and cosmographers: Bembo, Fracastoro, and Ramusio

Oviedo had much closer and more significant ties, however, with the Venetian scholars and men of letters. I am not completely convinced, despite the conjectures advanced, [119] that Oviedo ever met either the writings or the person of Andrea Navagero, the friend and collaborator, as we know, of Ramusio and Aldo Manuzio, and intimate acquaintance of Peter Martyr and Fracastoro (actual author of the *Naugerius*), although, since he was Venetian ambassador in Spain, Oviedo *could* have met him in Toledo in 1525.

It was actually from Toledo that Navagero replied to Ramusio's request for all the latest publications on the discoveries of the New Indies; and precisely on 11 September 1525, while Oviedo was hastily drafting his *Sumario,* Navagero wrote to Ramusio, "Of the things *of the Indies* there is nothing to be found in print here; but in time I shall send you so many things that I shall weary you." [120] It almost sounds as if Navagero knew of impending appearance, only a few months later, of Oviedo's *Sumario,* the same *Sumario* that was in fact promptly translated and

judgment of both Pércopo, op. cit., I, cclxvii–ccliv, and Croce, "Serafino Aquilano," in *Quaderni della Critica,* 17–18 (1950), 42–46.

117. *Qu.,* pp. 486–87, already cited by Amador de los Ríos, "Vida," p. xviii. As readers of Massimo d'Azeglio's *Disfida di Barletta* (Florence, 1850) will recall, Ettore Fieramosca too was paternally welcomed by Pontano (p. 20).

118. *Hist.,* II, 1: I, 10–11. Landino's translation in fact begins with the preface "to the Emperor Domitian." Oviedo, however, follows the opinion of those who say that it is dedicated to Titus, as in fact it is. Vincent de Beauvais, quoted by St. Antoninus of Florence, and Oviedo in the dedication of the *Sumario* (p. 77), say that it is dedicated to Vespasian, an understandable error in view of the dedication: "C. Plinius Secundus Vespasiano Caesari suo s."

119. A. López de Meneses, "Andrea Navagero, traductor de G. F. de Oviedo," *RI,* 18, no. 71 (1958), 63–71, esp. 66–67. Cf. Pérez de Tudela, "Vida," p. c, n. 304.

120. M. Fiorini, "Qualche cenno sopra Girolamo Fracastoro," *Rivista Geografica Italiana,* 7 (1900), 444n, citing Tommaso Porcacchi, ed., *Lettere di XIII Huomini Illustri* (Venice 1584).

published by Ramusio himself (1534), the same *Sumario* whose publication, in the spring of 1526, was promptly followed by a further letter from Navagero to Ramusio telling him that the person with whom he had hoped to send the Spanish books "on the things of the Indies" had postponed his journey and that he would be sending them as soon as a suitable occasion arose.

Thus the publication of the *Sumario*, if not perhaps the mere news of its preparation, marks the beginning of a new phase in Oviedo's ties with Italy: a phase of reciprocal action and influence, no longer just of Italy on Oviedo, but mutual, between Oviedo in his quality as an expert on the Indies and a group of very eminent scholars and writers spread among Venice, Padua, and Verona, who revealed a lively curiosity and indeed keen scientific interest in the physical phenomena and surprising peoples of the New World. In addition to Ramusio the group included the eminent Veronese doctor and didactic poet Gerolamo Fracastoro and the famous scholar, diplomat, and historian, Cardinal Pietro Bembo.

It was the latter, for example, who thanked Ramusio for sending him Oviedo's *Sumario* "translated so well and so elegantly," saying that he could not have been more grateful to him "if you had given me a fine two-hundred-scudi horse," and who in his *Venetian History* included an extensive digression to take account of the information that he had read in Oviedo.[121] If it could be said that "no work of that remote era contains within such a limited space such a complete and accurate picture of the work of the conquistadors of that time as the picture offered to us by the Venetian chronicler,"[122] this is due to the fact that in the sixth book of his *History*, written between 1534 and 1538,[123] Bembo follows and faithfully summarizes Oviedo's *Sumario*. Fired with enthusiasm by his recent and highly prized acquisition, he interrupts the history of Venice that he is drafting, with no other literary or stylistic excuse than the potential threat to the republic implicit in the transatlantic discoveries, and interpolates therein, or rather—as he puts it— grafts on, a brisk recapitulation of the early American voyages and discoveries, a colorfully descriptive section that stands out sharply against the gray Ciceronian prose of the rest.

The autonomous nature of this inserted fragment was recognized and underscored by the French publisher who—totally ignoring the whole of the rest of the *Venetian History*, even in the foreword to the reader—printed it in 1556 under the title *History of the New World Discovered by the Portuguese*, "written by Mr. Pietro Bembo." Bembo himself, for that matter, recognized his indebtedness,

121. Letter of 21 January 1535, in Porcacchi, *Lettere di XIII Huomini Illustri* (Venice, 1560), p. 657.

122. S. Günther, "Il cardinal Pietro Bembo e la geografia," in *Atti del Congresso internazionale di scienze storiche* (1903; Rome, 1904), X, 55–68, esp. p. 62.

123. C. Lagomaggiore, "L'*Istoria viniziana* di M. Pietro Bembo", in *Nuovo Archivio Veneto*, new ser., yr. 4, vol. 7 (1904), 5–31, 334–72; 8 (1904), 162–80, 317–46; 9 (1905), 33–113, 308–40; cf. esp. vol. 7, pp. 358, 364–66. I myself am inclined toward the later date (1538), because on 19 December 1538 Bembo was writing from Padua to Carlo Gualteruzzi in Rome asking him to send, "for the purpose of my history," a copy of the famous bull in which Alexander VI had shared out the new lands between Spain and Portugal; for the text of Bembo's letter see V. Cian, "Pietro Bembo (Quarantun anni dopo)," *Giornale Storico della Letteratura Italiana*, 88 (1926), 244n.

writing to Oviedo in person; and the two kept up an amicable correspondence for years. In 1546 Bembo was still impatiently urging that Oviedo, back in Spain, should send to the press the "new and fine work, which will doubtless give very, very much pleasure."[124]

Oviedo himself several times boasts about having corresponded with the "very learned and very reverend Cardinal Bembo,"[125] calling him "a person of great letters and merit[126] and possessed of a most elegant Latin style.[127] And to Bembo he wrote a letter (20 January 1543) containing the description of the discovery of the "River of the Amazons," written just one month after that memorable day (Monday, 20 December 1542), when he had witnessed the arrival in Santo Domingo of the adventurous Captain Francisco de Orellana with a handful of his companions. Oviedo's letter, translated into Italian and included in Ramusio's collection, gave Europe its first complete account of that historic journey, which finally determined the shape and size of the South American continent. Thus it was through the collaboration of Oviedo, Bembo, and Ramusio that the discovery of the real physiognomy of South America became known to the Old World.

There is, however, another and possibly greater claim to glory, in the field of geographical history, linking Oviedo and his Italian friends. On the basis of the geographical data supplied by Oviedo, Ramusio published a map of the New World which not only was one of the finest of that century but included a feature which was at that time a sensational innovation, although nowadays commonplace: the division of the world into two hemispheres, one for the Old and one for the New World.[128] The significance of this arrangement need hardly be stressed: for the first time the American continent was accorded a geographical dignity equal to that of the Old World; it was no longer looked on as a mere appendage of Asia, a scattering of islands lost in the ocean, but a truly New World, fully entitled, in cartographical representation, to half the terracqueous globe. It can truly be said that with Oviedo's and Ramusio's map the world was, for the first time, divided into two hemispheres.[129]

124. *Lettere inedite del Cardinale Pietro Bembo e di scrittori del secolo XVI*, ed. G. Spezi (Rome, 1862), pp. 70–71 (to Ramusio; in the following letter, undated, to Girolamo Quirino, Bembo writes: "I have received the letters on the Spaniards' voyage to the New World"—ibid., p. 73); Lagomaggiore, op. cit., IX, 41–43. The "work" so impatiently awaited must have been the imminent edition of the *Historia*, first published in 1535. See also the two letters from Bembo to Ramusio, 29 October 1541 and 27 December 1543, appearing as documents no. 14 and 15 in C. Castellani, "Pietro Bembo bibliotecario della libreria di San Marco in Venezia (1530–1543)," *Atti del Reale Istituto Veneto de Scienze, Lettere, ed Arti*, 7th ser., vol. 54 (1895–96), 862–98.

125. *Hist.*, XXIX, 30: III, 152a. Cf. also Pérez de Tudela, "Vida," p. cxlv*n483*, and E. Asensio, "La carta de Gonzalo Fernández de Oviedo al cardenal Bembo sobre la navegación del Amazonas," *RI*, 9 (1949), 569–78.

126. *Hist.*, XLVII, 9: IV, 294a.

127. Ibid., L, 30: IV, 590a.

128. S. Grande, "Le relazioni geografiche fra P. Bembo, G. Fracastoro, G. B. Ramusio, G. Gastaldi," *Memorie della Società geografica italiana*, 12 (1905), 185, and idem, *Notizie sulla vita e sulle opere di Giacomo Gastaldi, cosmografo piemontese del secolo XVI* (Turin, 1902), p. 21, which do however acknowledge one or two crude precursors. On the ideological and reciprocal link between this division and Oviedo's lofty concept of the Indies, cf. J. Z. Vázquez, "El indio americano y su circunstancia en la obra de Gonzalo Fernández de Oviedo," *RI*, 17, nos. 69–70 (1957), 485, 487.

129. Cf. however Enciso, above, chap. IX, sec. 1. On other contributions by Oviedo to Renaissance cartography,

In addition to his links with Ramusio, Oviedo maintained a particularly active literary relationship with the latter's great friend Fracastoro, well known for his abiding interest in the New World, his conversations with Sebastian Cabot, and the "American" inspiration of his poem *Syphilis*.[130] "Noble friends" wrote to Oviedo from Italy to tell him that his opinion (stated at the close of the *Sumario*) on the distance from Panama to the Spice Islands was not generally accepted. And in fact Fracastoro, prompted by Ramusio, had written to introduce himself to Oviedo, the illustrious historian who "to his immortal glory, from such a remote and unknown land, spreads information to all the rest of mankind, weaving thereby such a worthy History that none more beautiful or pleasing ever perhaps saw the light of day,"[131] and had put to Oviedo various knotty problems pertaining to science, astronomy, cosmography, and natural history.

Oviedo was obviously more than flattered and wrote back to say that on the first point he deferred to the judgment of the "very wise and learned gentleman Hieronimo Fracastoro, Doctor of Verona," and thanking Giovan Battista Ramusio both for having defended him against the accusations even before he had met him and for having been so kind as to give him an account of a great argument that had arisen in the school of Padua "between eminent scientists and nobles and other persons," regarding the distance between Panama and the Moluccas, in other words, regarding the true dimensions of the globe; and finally for having at the same time asked him to develop his own thesis more fully.[132]

This argument gave rise to a lasting friendship between Ramusio and Oviedo which in turn bore further scientific fruit. Ramusio, as we have seen, included Oviedo's writings in his *Raccolta*, and this classical seal of approval assured them of circulation throughout Europe. From Venice the Italian geographer wrote in 1540 to Santo Domingo to tell the Castilian historian about an eclipse of the sun, but the letter, with such a span of ocean to cover, arrived ten or twelve days after the date on which the sun was due to disappear.[133]

Already by 1540 Oviedo had received from Ramusio the *Tabula* of Olaus Magnus, published in Venice in 1539, and was amazed to learn from it that Labrador was "joined to and one land with Europe, leaving Iceland and Scotland and England and many other notable islands surrounded by land,"[134] with the

---

cf. in particular S. Grande, *Le carte d'America di Giacomo Gastaldi* (Turin, 1905), esp. pp. 54–61 and 83; and idem, "Le relazioni geografiche," pp. 93–197, esp. p. 148.

130. C. L. Sanford, *The Quest for Paradise* (Urbana, 1961), pp. 41–47. Cf. Turner, "Biblioteca Ovetense," p. 179, no. 4. Oviedo maintained that syphilis originated in America, and when he was still in Italy he made fun of those who called it the "French evil" or the "Neapolitan evil," when it should more properly have been described as "the evil of the Indies" (*Hist.*, II, 14: PT, I, 52–55; cf. below, chap. XIX, n. 319).

131. Undated letter, quoted by Grande, "Le relazioni geografiche," p. 159, referring to Fracastoro's *Carmina*, I, 40.

132. *Hist.*, XXXIX, 30: III, 150–51. On Ramusio, cf. also Pérez de Tudela, "Vida," p. cxlv*n*482, and D. Turner, "Biblioteca Ovetense," p. 175.

133. *Hist.*, XXXIII, 53: III, 543b.

134. Ibid., XXXVIII, sole chapter; III, 636–37. From Olaus Magnus he also learned that the arctic zone was inhabited, contrary to Pliny's opinion (*Hist.*, XXI, 5: II, 127b).

significant and singularly relevant geopolitical consequence that "all the world
. . . is one same land and coast, without the sea dividing it," and half or more of
this single world continent belongs to "the crown and royal scepter of Castile
and Leon."[135] With due solemnity Oviedo expressed his repeated thanks to
Ramusio, "who, not without putting me under a perpetual obligation, has desired
that here in this New World I should know and see painted and described the
account of those northern lands."[136] And in turn he sent Ramusio a gift of an
iguana—an animal in exchange for a book, a typical product of the New World's
nature in exchange for a product of Old World technology. Unfortunately Oviedo
let himself be persuaded "that these animals ate nothing but earth," so that he
sent it off with "a hundredweight of earth in a barrel, so that it should not be short
of it at sea," and waited to find out whether it had arrived safely. But when he got
to Spain in 1546 he discovered from the person that had transported the animal
that it had died at sea.[137]

There is also an even more curious episode that illustrates the role played by
Venice at that time as a clearinghouse for information on the discoveries.[138] The
viceroy of Mexico, Antonio de Mendoza, sent his brother, Don Diego de Mendoza—the Spanish ambassador in Venice[139]—a copy of one of his reports to the
emperor on the origins of Temistitán. The Mexican report came into Ramusio's
hands[140] and—bouncing back again from Europe—was in due course received
from this his "very close friend" by the commandant of Santo Domingo, who
hastened to complete the triangle by writing to Viceroy Mendoza in person, to
ask for confirmation and further details.[141] Scientific collaboration, a lofty sign

135. Ibid., XXXVIII, sole chapter; III, 640. On the world of which more than half belongs to Spain, since the
Americas are bigger than Asia, Africa, and Europe put together, see also *Hist.*, XXI, 7: II, 136a. The geopolitical
school of Mackinder and Hanshofer attaches great importance to landmass continuity as the basis of a state's power.
The strategic importance of the North Pole, in these times of aerial armadas, is highlighted by an azimuthal projection
map, that "inevitably makes Eurasia and North America an almost continuous continental landmass ['one same land,"
in Oviedo's words], the landmass of future domination" (H. W. Weigert, *Generals and Geographers: The Twilight of
Geopolitics* [New York, 1942], p. 195).
136. *Hist.*, XXI, Proh.: II, 112. Possibly only someone who has worked for years in exile can understand Oviedo's
joy and gratitude on receiving a brand new book, fresh from the press, on a subject that passionately interested him.
137. *Hist.*, XII, 7: I, 396b.
138. Cf. P. Sardella, *Nouvelles et spéculations à Venise au début du XVIème siècle* (Paris, 1948).
139. Don Diego Hurtado de Mendoza was a devotee of the classics and a book collector (cf. E. Gebhart,
"L'histoire d'une bibliothèque espagnole," in *De Panurge à Sancho Pança* [Paris, 1911], pp. 315–19). But he lives
above all in Titian's marvellous full-length portrait (1541), now in the Pitti. The following year, 1542, Titian also
painted his mistress, and Aretino wrote a sonnet on the picture (letter of 19 August 1542 in Aretino, *Il secondo libro
delle lettere* [Bari, 1916], II, 244–45). See also E. Spivakosky, *Son of the Alhambra: Don Diego Hurtado y de
Mendoza, 1504–1575* (Austin and London, 1970). On his brother, see A. Aiton, *Antonio de Mendoza* (Durham, N.C.,
1927).
140. In the *Discorso sopra varii viaggi per li quali sono state condotte et si potrian condurre le spetierie* (in his
Navigationi et viaggi, ed. cit., I, 402ʳ) Ramusio mentions various reports from Viceroy Antonio de Mendoza, and also
"his letters written in 1541, from Mexico," which Ramusio saw "when in Flanders, at the emperor's court."
141. *Hist.*, XXXIII, 50 and 52–53: III, 531, 539. The first passage (chap. 50) is really a full-scale refutation, point
by point, of what the viceroy had reported to his brother the ambassador. With notable critical acumen Oviedo derides
the legend that "Guatezuma," Montezuma's father, was conceived by a virgin priestess of the temple of Orchilobos: "I
find it a bit hard to swallow the story of Rhea, the Vestal virgin. Bad women always make it their business to seek
excuses to cover up and gild over their crimes and wantonness; and I say gild over, because not only do they cover them
up, but make them out to be a miracle." The viceroy replied with affectionate deference (chap. 52) and Oviedo
answered (chap. 53) in the same respectful tone and with copious additional information.

of civilized times and spiritual forces triumphing over immense distances, brought the New World within the intellectual orbit of the Old and refreshed and strengthened Oviedo's old and more recent links with the culture, lands, and people of Italy.

9. THE COMPANY SET UP WITH RAMUSIO AND PRIULI

This trading of information between the two hemispheres had however already been preceded by an exchange of goods. And Oviedo's relations with Ramusio were not merely literary and scientific, as has always been believed, but financial and commercial too. We have already seen that Oviedo was no stranger to buying and selling (see above, chap. XIV, n. 65, and Pérez Tudela, "Vida," p. cxxv) nor, if things turned out that way, to the minor sharp practices of the business world (below, chap. XIX, sec. 32).

Nor should we forget—in further proof of his mercantile mind—that Oviedo always took an interest in the prices of things. He never tires of telling us how much he has to pay for grapes and wine, even if the people who do best out of the whole trade are in fact the tavern-keepers, "who make more from it than the Florentine merchants out of their brocades and gold cloth."[142] We learn what alligator eggs are fetching,[143] how much cows and yearling calves are worth,[144] the cost of corn in Mexico,[145] and the exorbitant prices at which Governor Felipe Gutiérrez sold victuals to the hungry population—although Oviedo defends him because there is no law saying a governor has to lose on a deal.[146]

Food is not the only item for which Oviedo gives us the market reports. A sheet of paper can cost as much as one gold *castellano,* and a needle the same;[147] clothes and fabrics cost ten times as much as in Seville (and yet years later there were people who found it advantageous to send clothes from Nombre de Dios to be sold in Seville!).[148] Chinese porcelain fetches astronomical prices in Giloló,[149] and even hurricane damage is assessed in terms of hard cash.[150]

He shows the same shrewd interest in the Indians' cocoa-bean money, informing us that the services of a prostitute cost eight to ten beans. He even goes on to

142. *Hist.*, VIII, 24: PT, I, 236b. "But never did the industrious Florentines weave such beautiful silk or such fine gold" as the garments with which Oberto would have liked to drape the fair limbs of Olimpia! (*Orlando Furioso,* XI, 74–75).
143. *Sum.*, p. 199.
144. *Hist.*, XXVI, 2: PT, III, 64b and 65b.
145. Ibid., XXXIII, 40: PT, IV, 186b.
146. Ibid., XXVIII, 4: PT, III, 190.
147. Ibid., XXXI, 6: PT, III, 388a; XXXIX, Proh.: PT, IV, 338a.
148. Ibid., XXVI, 2: PT, III, 65b.
149. Ibid., XX, 34: PT, III, 296a.
150. Ibid., L, 27: PT, V, 408b.

explain how this money too, like doubloons and ducats, can be forged—and a cunning way of detecting the forgery![151] Oviedo's attention is not however confined to this vegetable and edible currency, but also embraces metallic coinage in general, the money that flows from the Indies to Spain and on from Spain to other countries, never to return, because—as Oviedo explains, anticipating the formulation of Gresham's Law (1558)—"as it is the best coin circulating in the world, once it falls into the hands of foreigners it never comes back, or if it does get back to Spain, it is in debased form, with less karats and with the emperor's arms and stamp altered."[152]

But even more curious and significant is the story of the crafty native from the Moluccas who on his arrival in Spain first of all enquired about the monetary system, the relationship between ducats, *reales*, and *maravedis*, and then asked the price in *maravedis* of pepper and other spices in the various cities of Spain, from Seville to Valladolid, until the authorities became aware of this veritable "industrial espionage" and he was forbidden to accompany his compatriots back to the Moluccas.[153]

It will therefore come as no surprise to learn that at least once Oviedo gave in to temptation and decided to try his hand at the big stuff, intercontinental trading. For this, however, he needed a partner in Europe and a financial backer. He found the former in Giovan Battista Ramusio and the latter in the Venetian nobleman Antonio Priuli, of the same illustrious family as the diarist Gerolamo, Lorenzo, who was ambassador to Charles V in 1523 (died 1557), and various wealthy bankers,—the family that was later to provide the republic with three doges and the church with five cardinals.

On 24 May 1538 the notary Don Pietro de Bartoli presented himself at the proud fifteenth-century palace of the Priuli at San Severo, which still today rears up fortresslike on the corner formed by two canals, its trefoiled four-light windows, sextuple gothic arches, and marble balcony forming a marked contrast with the naked red-brick walls. There he was welcomed by the master of the house, Messer Antonio Priuli, procurator of Saint Mark. And there he found already waiting for him Giovan Battista Ramusio, secretary to the Venetian Senate, who, in the presence of the required witnesses, translated word for word

151. Ibid., VIII, 30: PT, I, 268b; XLII, 1: PT, IV, 364. On the use of cocoa beans as coinage, already in pre-Columbian times and right up to the middle of the twentieth century, see copious details in M. J. MacLeod, *Spanish Central America: A Socioeconomic History, 1520–1720* (Berkeley, 1973), pp. 32–33, 68–79, 386, 440n19, 466n1. In his very last letters (see below, chap. XVII, sec. 26) Oviedo is still giving the current prices of numerous articles: see the references given in Enrique Otte, "Una carta inédita de Gonzalo Fernández de Oviedo," *RI*, 16, no. 65 (1956), 440n, plus pars. 5, 8, 11, 24, 31, 47, 54; and idem, "Gonzalo Fernández de Oviedo an Kaiser Karl V über die Zustände in Santo Domingo," *Spanische Forschungen der Görresgesellschaft*, 1st ser., II (1928), 166–67.

152. *Hist.*, XXIX, 30: PT, III, 336a; see also below, sec. 18. Again in the letter to the sovereigns dated 9 December 1537 he calls for the base gold to be taken out of circulation and dispatched to Spain, notwithstanding those "two or three satraps" who "want to keep the good gold, as soon as they can lay their hands on it, and to settle their debts with the bad gold" (in *CDII*, I, 541; cf. III, 81–82).

153. *Hist.*, XX, 21: PT, II, 238a.

an instrument drawn up by Oviedo, commandant of the fortress of Santo Domingo in Hispaniola, historian to His Imperial Majesty, announcing the formation of a company between Oviedo and a person to be designated by him on the one side, and Ramusio and Priuli on the other.

The four-member company is to last six years, from 1 January 1538 to the end of 1543. The capital is set at 400 gold ducats (equal to 150,000 *maravedis*[154] divided into four equal shares of 100 ducats each. Oviedo, not having named the fourth partner, accepts responsibility for half the capital, but the *whole* of the capital is advanced by Priuli, without interest, on the sole condition that he is to be reimbursed before any other payments are made, out of the proceeds from the first cargo sent to the Indies. In the event—God forbid—of shipwreck, Priuli is to be reimbursed "as is only honest" by the other three members within one year, after collection and deduction of any insurance. Everything left over, that is to say the profit from the first expedition, will remain as the company's capital, which Oviedo will be able to use to send further consignments from the Indies to Spain or to other parts of the Indies.

Our friend Oviedo, in other words, without forking out a cent, guarantees himself 50 percent of the company's profits and a free hand to do as he likes with the first cash surplus, which, as it derives from the sale in America of goods bought in Venice, obviously comes into his hands. Furthermore since the "coin" current in the Indies is "bad"[155] the company entrusts the commandant with the responsibility of exchanging it and debiting it, as he sees fit "to the risk, cost, and damage of all the parties." Moreover, further purchases and sales will be carried out "in accordance with the instructions of the said commandant," whose papers, backed by his oath, will be taken on trust. Oviedo is therefore the controlling partner in the business. Finally (although this clause is not very clear) if the initial capital should be not 400 but 300 ducats "as was the first arrangement" (was there already an existing company?) the part falling to Oviedo "in respect of what he mentioned in his letter" will not be reduced.

The ship—belonging to the duke of Ferrara (Ercole II)—that will carry the goods to Messina and thence to Cadiz, is ready and waiting in Venice; in Cadiz the goods will be delivered to an agent of the two Venetians. The same person will forward them to Oviedo and will sell the "liquors and sugars"[156] and anything else sent to him from the Indies on behalf of the company.

---

154. A little further on there is a sort of codicil specifying that the ducats are to be Venetian ducats (not gold ones) of six *lire* and four *soldi,* worth 320½ *maravedis* each, rather than 375, thus making 128,200 *maravedis* in all.

155. A few months earlier Oviedo had advised the sovereigns that "this [coinage] in circulation here is extremely bad, and the only people that favor it are the swindlers, who want everything to be like they are" (letter of 9 December 1537 in *CDII,* I, 529–42, and III, 70–82, cited also by Pérez de Tudela, "Vida," p. cxxxi*n423*).

156. Santo Domingo and other West Indian islands were big sugar producers. And the sugar was also exported "in liquor," i.e., in the form of syrup: see Aretino, *Il secondo libro,* I, 83, p. 423, for a letter of 7 August 1538, expressing

Next come clauses relating to chartering, insurance, bookkeeping, possible further purchases, final liquidation (after payment of the proceeds into the bank), possible continuation of the company or increase in capital, and finally a statement by Oviedo, signed before two witnesses in Santo Domingo on 20 December 1537, in which he gives his solemn oath to stand by the agreement, pledging as collateral all his property, fixing a penalty of 2,000 ducats for any shortcoming, and expressly renouncing right of appeal to any privileged court. A similar ritual undertaking is given by Priuli and Ramusio at the end of the instrument.

We do not know how things went for this unusual transatlantic company, indeed whether they went at all and how they ended up. Certainly the document we have summarized[157] demonstrates the extent of the esteem and trust enjoyed by Oviedo in Venice, not only as a source of unusual items of information but as a partner in an obviously risky enterprise, whose outcome moreover depended almost entirely on his wisdom and integrity.

10. LASTING INTEREST IN ITALIAN WRITERS

As the years go by and his sojourn in the peninsula fades further into the past, Oviedo's interest in Italian literature and history does not in fact fade gradually away but remains intact, manifesting itself in an obvious effort to keep in touch, to read Italian books old and new and draw on them for points of doctrine and moral lessons. In the *Quinquagenas,* apart from frequently citing Petrarch and other authors mentioned in the *History*—and considerably more frequently than the chronicles and ballads of Old Spain[158]—Oviedo shows off his Italian and

---

thanks for a gift of sugar "in lumps, powder, slabs, and liquor." L. Messedaglia, "Aspetti della realtà storica in Merlin Cocai," *Atti del R. Istituto Veneto di Scienze, Lettere ed Arti,* 93 (1939), pt. 2, p. 145*n,* recalls how "Venice was for centuries the main trading center for sugar in Europe." Oviedo himself had recently written (1535) in the preface to the *Historia* (PT, I, 8b): "On their way back to Europe the ships take cargoes of sugar, . . . to keep it supplied." And further on, when he comes to describe one by one the twenty-four sugar plantations on Santo Domingo, he repeats that before sugar was produced there "the ships used to return empty to Spain, and now they go back loaded with it and with bigger cargoes than they bring over here, and *with greater profit*" (which is perhaps where the idea for his speculation first occurs to him? *Hist.,* IV, 8: PT, I, 107b). Even "the foam and molasses from it [the sugar]," which are usually given to the Negroes or thrown away in Santo Domingo, "would make the fortune of another great province" (*Hist.,* IV, 8: PT, I, 110b; cf. III, 11: PT, I, 79a).

157. The original act is not to be found in the *Archivio dei Frari.* Apparently it was lost in the fire in the lower chancery, which contained the archives of the notary Bartoli, in 1570. I have used the copy to be found in a miscellaneous codex in the Ambrosiana (S. 99 Sup.), from which I have transcribed the complete text given below in Appendix B. The document was brought to my attention by Almagià, op. cit., pp. 449–50*n177;* see, however, P. Revelli, *Terre d'America e archivi d'Italia* (Milan, 1926), pp. 69–70, no. 6. Almagià, possibly because he was writing under the Fascist government, says it is "certain" that the act "was not drawn up without the agreement of the two governments"(?) But Prof. Gaetano Cozzi tells me that "contracts between private persons did not need government approval."

158. Almost the only Spanish authors Oviedo cites are historians and chroniclers: the *Historia del rey don Pedro* (*Qu.,* p. 205), the *Historia del rey don Juan II de Castilla* (*Qu.,* p. 41–42), the *Historia General de España* (*Qu.,* p. 280), El Abulense (*Qu.,* pp. 410, 508), Andrés Bernal (*Qu.,* p. 408), and Hernando del Pulgar (*Qu.,* p. 408). The only poets quoted are once again the Petrarchist Juan de Mena (*Qu.,* pp. 61, 107) and the little known Alonso de Zamora (*Qu.,* p. 78); moral works, the *Fortalitium fidei,* the *Tratado . . . de las supersticiones y hechizerías* (Logrono, 1529) of Martín de Castañega (*Qu.,* p. 474), and, a number of times, though not always very appositely, the

Renaissance culture. He does not seem to have been familiar with either Ariosto or Machiavelli,[159] but he quotes the historical works of the better-known humanists: Aeneas Silvius Piccolomini's *History of Bohemia* comes up again,[160] together with Platina on Gregory V and Emperor Otto I,[161] an interpretation of Giorgio Mérula on Trajan's death,[162] the famous *Suplementum Cronicarum* of Foresti "Bergomensis,"[163] and Paolo Giovio on the Turkish conquests.[164] He is acquainted with Andrea Fulvio's guide to Rome (*Antiquaria orbis,* 1513, incorrectly quoted as *De Antiquitatibus orbis*), which he apparently uses as a source of information on the Lutheran schism.[165] He quotes from the Italian edition of the *Vite degli Imperatori Romani* by the "learned gentleman Johan Baptista Ignaçio."[166] But it is more interesting to note that he admires the "grace and elegant style" of the writings of Pietro Aretino,[167] recalling him as the scourge of the vices of the Roman Curia.[168]

---

great Luis Vives (*Qu.*, pp. 9, 235, 466), in addition to various current works of devotion and hagiography, including the *Life of Christ* by that same Carthusian Ludolfo of Saxony (*Qu.*, pp. 23, 44, 52, 92–93, 290, 301, 418) who had been "Isabella's favorite writer" (Juan de Lozoya, *Los orígenes del Imperio; La España de Ferdinando e Isabel* [Madrid, 1939], p. 89). A writer on agricultural matters, Gabriel Alonso de Herrera, is mentioned three times (*Hist.*, VII, 1: I, 264b; *Qu.*, pp. 7, 306).

More noteworthy are the traces of early popular literature, such as the *Libro del baladro del sabio Merlín,* translated from Italian at the end of the fifteenth century (*Qu.*, pp. 534–35, but see below, chap. XVI, sec. 3), and, as the old man's stubborn memory takes him all the way back to the refrains of his youth and childhood, a lovers' ditty and a rhyming proverb also from the turn of the century (*Qu.*, pp. 71, 311), an "old and true ballad" (*Qu.*, p. 449), and the rhymes he was given to learn as school assignments (*Qu.*, p. 90). See above, chap. XV, sec. 4.

159. But he does of course deplore, as *frivolous* reading, the stories of Guerin Mesquino and Roland (*Qu.*, p. 191).
160. *Qu.*, pp. 157, 277. Cf. below chap. XVI, sec. 3.
161. *Qu.*, p. 282.
162. Ibid., p. 337.
163. Turner, "Biblioteca Ovetense," p. 167, no. 54.
164. *Qu.*, p. 105. The editor cites the *Historiae sui temporis;* but from the context ("it is clear from the account of Bishop Paolo Giovio") it would appear more likely to be a question of the *Commentari delle cose de' Turchi* (Venice, 1531).
165. *Qu.*, pp. 133, 136.
166. *Hist.*, XXXII, 4: II, 239b; and in *Qu.*, p. 460, calling him a "learned Historian." "Ignaçio" is the Venetian Giambattista Cipelli, known as Egnazio (1478–1553), a friend of Bembo and Erasmus, editor of the Manuzio classics, object of Charles V's odium, and author (1516) of the *De Caesaribus.* Oviedo, writing between 1540 and 1548, says that the history in question was written (or rather translated) "not long ago . . . in Tuscan." And in 1555 (or thereabouts) he cites it as the "treatise . . . on the emperors," in other words by the Italian title. But cf. Turner, "Biblioteca Ovetense," p. 167, no. 43, and p. 176, no. 108.
167. *Hist.*, XLIX, Proh.: IV, 380b. D. Turner, "Biblioteca Ovetense," p. 162, no. 9, gives as source the *Coloquio de las Damas,* n.p., 1548, but Oviedo seems to quote from the Italian. The very rare *Coloquio* (Brera Library, SS. III, 55) is a straightforward translation, somewhat cleaned up and watered down, as is admitted by the translator, Fernand Xuárez, "a citizen and native of Seville," of the third of Aretino's *Sei giornate* (Bari, 1969), pp. 93–140. Nanna is given the name Lucrezia. Cuts, occasional insertions, and opportunistic or moralistic circumlocutions do nothing to improve on the original. I can find no trace of the passage quoted by Oviedo.

In the *Quinquagenas,* Oviedo twice quotes Aretino, "a modern author and indeed still living, I believe" (*Qu.*, p. 373; Aretino in fact died in 1556) who, "in the treatise that he wrote in Tuscan on 'la Paçia' says that in Italy, in the city of Norci, on the day when they meet in council, they make an announcement banning all scholars from the town" (*Qu.*, p. 214). But I have not been able to locate the source of the quotation, known also to Farinelli (*Italia e Spagna*, II, 175), in either the *Dello specchio delle opere di Dio,* or in the *Parafrasi dei sette salmi penitenziali,* or in the *Dell'umanità del Figliolo di Dio.* The name "Paçia" could make one think of the *Passione di Gesù;* but that work is only the final part of the above mentioned *Umanità.* No matter: the "fact" was, or became, proverbial. Sassetti twice (op. cit., pp. 330, 357) mentions in passing that the people of Norci "refuse to have scholars in their council."

168. In the unpublished *Batallas:* passage quoted by Pérez de Tudela, "Vida," p. xxvii; cf. idem., "Rasgos," p. 407.

He contradicts—on the basis of a verbal report received directly from an eye-witness—the account of events given by Marco Guazzo in his *Historia di tutti i fatti degni di memoria nel mondo successi dal 1524 al 1549* (Venice: Giolito, 1549),[169] which is a shameless plagiarism of Martin Sanuto's *Spedizione di Carlo VIII*. He invokes the authority of Marco Antonio Sabellico—the great Venetian follower in the tradition of Florentine historiography, who conducted a lengthy polemic but eventually reconciled himself with Egnazio—in support of a comment he makes on Suetonius's life of Claudius.[170] And on the subject of curdled milk he cites "Crescentino,"[171] the ancient Palladius,[172] and other authors.[173]

Of the jurists, only a few names are mentioned: one at first sight rather obscure, "Pandolfo Colirasçio," jurisconsult in Pesaro;[174] and the more illustrious Bartolo da Sassoferrato[175] and "Barbacio," the latter "a doctor famous *in utroque iure,* who lectured in the city of Bologna,"[176] and who can almost certainly be identified as Andrea Barbazza, who taught law at Bologna from 1442 to 1478 and whose works include "various *Repetitiones* on constitutions and fragments of civil and canon law."[177]

Of the moralists, on the other hand, he has read various works, today completely forgotten. He mentions, for instance, a treatise on prayer, "a pious and beneficial work" by "Cardinal Fregoso,"[178] most likely the philologist Federico Fregoso (cardinal in 1539, died 1541), who was a great friend of Bembo, Sadoleto, and Castiglione. He has also read the *Espejo de la Fe* of "Ruberto de Leche,"[179] in other words, the sermons in the vernacular by the famous preacher Fra Roberto Caracciolo da Lecce (1425–1495), who was summoned to Naples by Ferrante I of Aragon and there made some illustrious friends, including various men of letters, became a member of the "Accademia Pontaniana,"[180] and published a number of collections of sermons in Latin and one in Italian, with the title *Specchio della fede cristiana* ("Mirror of the Christian Faith"). He also refers to two dialogues, "De la

---

169. *Qu.*, p. 228.

170. Ibid., p. 459.

171. This must be the Bolognese agronomist Pietro Crescenzi (1230–1310), author of *Opus ruralium commodorum libri XII,* of which several editions were brought out, including some in Italian, as soon as printing was invented; for further references to "Crescentino" see *Hist.*, VI, 49: I, 252a; VII, 24: I, 310a.

172. Rutilius Taurus Emilianus Palladius, Latin agronomist (4th century), whose *De re rustica* enjoyed considerable popularity in the late middle ages.

173. *Qu.*, p. 306.

174. Ibid., p. 460. This will doubtless be the Pesaro jurist Pandolfo Collenuccio, better known as author of the very fine *Canzone alla Morte* and the *Compendio della storia del regno di Napoli* (Venice, 1539); the latter was translated into Spanish by Juan Vázquez del Mármol, and is probably the work from which Oviedo gets his information on the death of the Emperor Henry.

175. *Hist.*, IV, 8, and XVI, 15: PT, I, 108, and II, 107.

176. *Qu.*, p. 510.

177. *Enciclopedia Italiana,* s.v. "Barbazza."

178. *Qu.*, pp. 219–20.

179. Ibid., p. 542.

180. *Enciclopedia Italiana,* s.v.

brevedad de la vida" and "Del exilio e destierro,"[181] by "Antonio Bruciolo,"—no doubt the famous Protestant, translator of the Bible and Pliny and commentator on Petrarch, Antonio Brucioli, a Florentine who emigrated to Venice, where he published his *Dialoghi della morale filosofia* (1528) and *Dialoghi facete* (1535), and where he died in 1556. His works were quickly placed on the Index.

Brucioli is not in fact the only author later condemned by the church whom Oviedo read and used. More than once he cites Erasmus's treatise "on language" and the "institution of the Christian prince,"[182] and the dialogues on love by "Master Leon, the Hebrew philosopher"[183] which, being written in Italian and given the absence of any Castilian translation before 1568, must be included among the "Italian sources" of Oviedo, who also composed Petrarchan sonnets "in the Italian style," which are, alas, almost indecipherable in the transcription available to us.[184]

We can therefore conclude that from earliest youth to advanced old age Oviedo was a tireless reader of Italian poets and historians, pamphleteers and moralists; his curiosity, aroused in some cases by personal events, extended in others to their lives and careers; his intellectual gaze was firmly fixed, beyond the remote Iberian peninsula, on the yet remoter lands of Italy, and more precisely on that busy center of literary activity, Venice, with its galaxy of publishers, refugee scholars, and professional writers. It was to Florentine humanist historiography and Venetian scholarship that Oviedo was constantly turning for formal and substantial elements of his descriptive technique and vision of the world.[185]

11. LEXICAL ECHOES AND RECOLLECTIONS

But this is not all. In both the *Historia* and the *Quinquagenas* the traces and memories of Italy go beyond mere literary references and connections. Despite Oviedo's exaltation of Castilian above every other tongue—and his boast of

181. *Qu.*, p. 543. On Brucioli, cf. Giorgio Spini, *Tra Rinascimento e Riforma: Antonio Brucioli* (Florence, 1940); on the particular dialogues mentioned, pp. 169, 191–92. The devoutly Catholic Oviedo has also read the Protestant historian Johannes Carion and speaks very highly of him (*Hist.*, XXXIII, 54: PT, IV, 257).

182. Oviedo mentions the treatise on language also in the *Qu.*, pp. 12–13 and 229–30 (in connection with the boastful soldier) and the "institution" (i.e., the *Institutio Principis Christiani*, 1516), pp. 307 and 312. On Oviedo's Erasmianism, see below, chap. XIX, sec. 17, and Bataillon, *Erasmo y España*, II, 247–48; Palm, *Monumentos arquitectónicos*, I, 105; Pérez de Tudela, "Rasgos," p. 408; *Hist.*, XXXIII, Proh.: PT, II, 350; XXIV, 8: PT, II, 412; XXXII, 4: PT, III, 408.

183. *Qu.*, p. 526.

184. See examples in Pérez de Tudela, "Rasgos," p. 400; idem, "Vida," p. xxxi.

185. Oviedo's biographers have always made vague references to the Italian influence. B. Moses, for example, in *Spanish Colonial Literature in South America* (London and New York, 1922), p. 42, summarizing Amador de los Ríos, "Vida," pp. xvii–xix, notes that "the art and literature of that country exercised a powerful influence on his intellectual development"; cf. Farinelli, *Divagazioni erudite*, p. 267, and Bataillon, *Erasmo y España*, II, 247–48. It is also worth noting that the Italian reminiscences are considerably more frequent in the *Historia* (1535–48) than in the *Sumario* (1526): in the former, written in the Indies, his memory turns back toward the Old World; in the latter, written without notes in Toledo, the effort of memory is concentrated on the New World.

speaking it extremely well[186]—he quite frequently finds Italian words springing to mind, and particularly the military terms he had learned in his adventurous and vagabond youth as he wandered from court to court and camp to camp. *Hacer alto* is an Italian or French expression,[187] but it just slips out; and he goes on to correct himself, noting that in Castilian it would be more correct to say *parar*.[188] The guns of Hispaniola are *de bronzo*.[189] When Hierónimo Dortal captures Capitán Bautista's soldiers and relieves them of everything, their booty and their horses, some "went off to Cubagua *desbalixados,* as they say in Italy, or stripped, with sticks in their hands instead of the gold they were seeking."[190] The Tamemes Indians take the field "in so many squadrons, beating drums, as if in Italy."[191] The gold of Cajamarca is assayed "on trust, like soldiers in Italy eating off other people's cloaks."[192] At one point in his campaign Cortés asks his allies for sappers and pioneers, or *"zapadores* and *gastadores,* as they call them in Italy."[193] *Rehenes* is an Arabic word, "and in Italy instead of *rehenes* they talk about *stagia* [ostaggi], and amongst Frenchmen *talla* [tailles?]: and all these words mean *hostage."*[194] But the boastful soldiers who transform every skirmish in which they have taken part into a pitched battle Oviedo stamps as *"charlatanes,* as they call those big talkers in Italy."[195]

A little further on Oviedo gives the definition of real "charlatans": "the romancers, who are those that in Italy they call charlatans, or persons who tell tales to the people in song," that is, *cantastorie* or *cantafavole* (balladmongers).[196] Of the vampire bats of Darien he observes: "In my opinion they must be the same as those that in Spain they call *bruxas* and in Italy *extrias* [streghe]."[197] And in Mexico there are public porters "that in Castile they call *ganapanes* and elsewhere

---

186. *Hist.,* I: PT, I, 10b.
187. According to Oviedo. But according to Littré, the French word *halte* comes from the Spanish or Italian *alto,* which in its turn derives from the German *halten.* The Oxford English Dictionary gives the same etymology. Italianisms in general, both lexical and orthographical, are abundant in Oviedo. But I am unable to say which are proper to him and which are due to the pervasive Italian influence on the Spanish language and literature of that epoch. J. Cejador y Frauca gives a long list of Italianisms in his *Historia de la lengua y literatura castellana* (Madrid, 1915), II, 34–37 (to which could probably be added, from Oviedo: *passatiempo, uvas moscateles,* etc.). Cf. also R. Menéndez Pidal, "El lenguaje del siglo XVI," in *Los romances de América y otros estudios* (Buenos Aires, 1939), pp. 148–53.
188. Cf. below, n. 199.
189. *Hist.,* XLIX, 14: IV, 450a. Later on he catches himself referring to lavish hospitality using the French term *banquetes,* but hastily corrects the error, saying that he should have spoken, in correct Castilian, of *convites* or *fiestas* (L, 10, 27: PT, V, 344b).
190. *Hist.,* XXIV, 9: II, 245b.
191. Ibid., XVII, 27: I, 571b. On the diminutive cache-sexe worn by the Venezuelan Indian women, consisting of no more than a couple of bits of twisted cotton crossed over the stomach, "the way one would fasten on a drum or tambourine," see *Hist.,* XXV, 9: PT, III, 34b.
192. Ibid., XLVI, 13: IV, 201b.
193. Ibid., XXXIII, 28: III, 408a.
194. *Qu.,* p. 178.
195. Ibid., p. 188.
196. Ibid., p. 233; see also the description of the madmen, almost animals, that "are usually called *selváticos* [wild men] in Italy" (ibid., p. 455).
197. *Hist.,* XXIX, 32: III, 159–60.

bastages [bastagi]."[198] The Spaniards newly arrived in the Indies are called *chapetones,* "just as in Italy they call the new soldiers *visoños.*"[199] And "soldiering in Italy" is a common term of comparison to indicate a hard and dangerous life.[200]

Without any precise reference to Italy, but with obvious recollection of his military experience, Oviedo observes that the caparisoned and armored mounted knights look as though they have imitated the integument with which nature endowed the armadillo;[201] and on the flat round bottom of the crater of Masaya he imagines how more than a hundred knights could joust, and more than a thousand people watch them.[202]

The bold captains of those times, just like the soldiers, are never far from his mind. In tones of deep respect he recalls "Ector Aferramosca" and his victorious challenge, and together with him the herculean Diego García de Paredes, familiar to D'Azeglio's readers.[203] Among Charles V's warriors he recalls, together with Mingo Val, "Master of the Horse and Viceroy of Naples," "the valorous marquis of Pescara, Don Fernando de Ávalos e de Aquino, and his nephew the marquis of Guasto."[204]

From Cortés he borrows the parallel between the confederations of the Mexican cities that came to each other's aid in time of war and the Italian cities' alliances for the same purpose; and the comparison between the Mexican governments and those of Venice, Genoa, and Pisa (though with a very cautious and sensible reservation: "However in this I defer to him, because I do not know what statutes they have nor how the seignories that he is comparing them with are gov-

---

198. Ibid., XXXIII, 10: III, 300a. Note that Cortés only used the term *ganapanes* (Cortés, op. cit., 1940 ed., I, 102).

199. *Hist.*, XXXIII, 36: III, 454b; XXIII, 3: II, 175b. On "those newly recruited soldiers known as *visoños,* and called *bisogni* by the Italians," cf. the colorful quotations in Croce, *La Spagna,* pp. 225–26, and idem, *Uomini e cose della vecchia Italia* (Bari, 1927), I, 129. Other examples in Giannini, op. cit., pp. 58*n3,* 74, 91. Oviedo himself recalls that when Gonzalo de Ayora had to train fifty halberdiers, he sent for "some expert soldiers from Italy, who were in due course welcomed to turn the novices into skilled soldiers" (*Libro de la cámara real,* p. 170). In the seventeenth century the term *visoño* was in common use (cf. Engel Sluiter, "Francisco Lopez de Caravantes' Historical Sketch of Fiscal Administration in Colonial Peru, 1533–1618," *HAHR,* 25 [1945], 238; Sverker Arnoldsson, *La leyenda negra: Estudios sobre sus orígines* [Gothenburg, 1960], p. 89). According to Cejador y Frauca, however, (op. cit., II, 37) *visoño* comes not from the Italian but from the French *béjaune* or *bec-jaune,* "fledgling, youngster, then newly recruited soldier." This word too, then, like *alto,* although learned and used in Italy, is apparently of non-Italian origin. Oviedo's curious illusion is due to the invasion and "acclimatization" in Italy, around the year 1500, of foreign armies and foreign military terms.

200. E.g., *Hist.*, XXXII, 2: III, 224b. For other echoes of the soldier's life in Italy, see below, sec. 15. Almagro's small but richly equipped army is described by Ordóñez (who is in turn quoted verbatim by Oviedo) as "the most splendid troops that I ever saw in my life. And so say others that have seen more soldiers than I have in Italy" (XLVII, 5: PT, V, 227a). Cf. also the "five trumpets, or rather fifes" of the cacique Diriajén (XXIX, 21: III, 103b).

201. *Hist.*, XLII, 5: PT, IV, 395b.

202. *Sum.*, chap. XXII, pp. 156–57; *Hist.*, XII, 23: PT, II, 47–48. Cf. Díez del Corral, op. cit., p. 165.

203. *Qu.*, pp. 353–55. On a lucky skirmish of his in the war of 1501, when Oviedo was in Naples, cf. Volpicella, op. cit., p. 62.

204. *Hist.*, V, 1: PT, I, 115. "Guasto" is the famous Alfonso d'Avalos, marquis of Vasto. The "nephew," Iñigo de Avalos, must have been known to Oviedo, as it was to him that King Frederick had entrusted (1501) the defence of the island of Ischia (see above, sec. 1; Volpicella, op. cit., pp. 87–91), but like all his family he remained "totally Spanish in mind and habit" (Croce, *La Spagna,* p. 123).

erned");[205] and he recalls having seen that "it was once the custom in Italy" that the person challenged to single combat had the right to choice of weapons and not to say what he had chosen until the time of the duel.[206]

12. GAMES, PASTIMES, AND REVERSES OF FORTUNE

Of Rome in the year 1500, under the pontificate of the Spanish pope Borgia (Alexander VI), Oviedo draws an indelible portrait of corruption and licentiousness. His enduring concern at the venality of the senior clergy and the greed of the lower, his persistent accusations, recommendations, and laments, can doubtless be traced back to that well-remembered Roman sojourn. Well over half a century had elapsed since his visit to the capital of Christianity when the almost octogenarian Oviedo wrote: "I have also seen friars and clerics and prelates as familiar with dice and playing cards as with their psalter and breviary. I could say plenty about this, and as an eye-witness, because I am old, and I have seen great personages with miters on their heads, and even the cardinal's scarlet, and as skilled and dedicated gamblers as any layman or man of the world. I mean in Italy, where everything goes, and this was quite customary when I saw it in Pope Alexander VI's time." [207]

In "Rome the Holy" he saw clerics "dealing and working mischief" in so many ways that if he once started recounting them he would never end, and so wickedly that he could only think "that it must be the true relics kept there that prevent that Holy City [he repeats the heavy irony], the capital of the world, from being swallowed up with the clergy and everything else." [208]

But that same city of Rome, with its unique guarantee against divine retribution, was also the setting for various races that Oviedo watched, in 1500, with undisguised delight. One of these, the old-timers' race, is described very vividly: one can still feel him rocking with mirth as he recalls the grotesque event involving some fifty seventy-year-olds, from the Campo dei Fiori, through the Banchi, and over the Castel Sant' Angelo bridge to St. Peter's Square and the Vatican. Some are in shirttails, others in breeches, and a good many of them keel over within a hundred paces of the start. The winner is so tired by the time he reaches the winning post that a three-year-old child could have knocked him over. His friends support him with the banner he has won, and while the losers

---

205. *Hist.*, XXXIII, 3: III, 272b; XXXIII, 45: III, 496b. Oviedo had a profound admiration, as did indeed many people, for the wise and prudent government of Venice, the "rich and wealthy city and republic, amongst the most noble known to the world, and one of the best governed," the city and state "that seems to me to contain all human learning and wisdom within it" (*Hist.*, XXXIII, 23: PT, IV, 120, and the unpublished passage in the *Batallas* quoted by Pérez de Tudela, "Rasgos," p. 411, and "Vida," p. lxxn2l2).

206. *Qu.*, p. 380.

207. Ibid., p. 382, and the unpublished passages cited by Pérez de Tudela, "Vida," p. xxvii, and "Rasgos," p. 407. When in a position of authority in Darien in 1521 Oviedo strictly prohibited cards and gambling games (*Hist.*, XXIX, 14: III, 71). Against gambling, see also *Qu.*, pp. 421–22, and below, chap. XVII, sec. 26, end.

208. *Qu.*, p. 494.

withdraw "limping . . . tired and dissatisfied . . . the victor, in fits and starts, to the sound of trumpets and helped by a few gulps of wine, celebrates his victory." [209]

His interest in games and pastimes also took him to quail fights[210] and numerous football matches, the real football, as he himself stresses, to distinguish it from the game played by the Indians. After a detailed description of the American version of the game, played with heavy, solid, rubber balls he recalls: "When I was in Italy I saw a game being played with a very heavy ball, as big as a four-gallon pitcher or bigger, which they call *balón* or *palón*. And in particular I often saw it being played in Lombardy and Naples by gentlemen; they kicked the ball with their feet, and in appearance the game is very similar to the one described above that the Indians play, except that here, as they strike the ball with the shoulder or knee or hip, the ball does not go as high as it does in the *balón* I described." [211] So both gentlemen and savages play ball. Oviedo watches them both, carefully noting how high the ball bounces, the rules of the game, and the common passion for sport bridging the vast gap in space and social conditions.

But when he thinks back to the princes and great lords he knew in his eventful youth, Oviedo's favorite memory is that of the alternating vicissitudes, personally observed, of glory and misfortune. "I saw his serene Highness Frederick of Naples in his prosperity and in his kingdom, and I saw him leave it and lose it, and go out into the world with his wife and sons. . . . I saw just the same happen to señor Ludovico, duke of Milan, who was one of the leading princes of Christendom, and I saw him toppled and driven out of the State. . . . I saw Don Cesare Borgia, Duke Valentino, when prosperous, and I was in Italy when he conquered numerous cities and towns and castles in Romagna; and I saw him later a prisoner in Medina del Campo in La Mota, whence he managed to escape."

And the conclusion he draws from these instances of "the mighty fallen" [212] is a stark historical pessimism, which he extends to the Peruvian wars. "Those that I saw were wise men, and this did not stop fortune performing its office and the changes I mentioned: fortune had somewhat less to do in bringing down Almagro and Pizarro, for although they had more gold and silver than those mentioned, they had little capacity and prudence as compared with those of which I have reminded the reader." [213] The Renaissance princes were endowed with virtue and wisdom,

---

209. Ibid., pp. 454–55. Cf. Dante, *Purgatorio*, VI, 1–6.

210. "I saw them gambling in Italy in this way on quails and partridges, when the birds fight to the death" (*Hist.*, XX, 16: II, 61b).

211. Ibid., VI, 2: I, 166b. On the version of football practiced by the Indians, who played without touching the ball with their hands or their feet, cf. also the account by Navagero, given by A. López de Meneses, "Andrea de Navagero," pp. 68–69.

212. Boccaccio's expression (*De casibus virorum illustrium*) that became almost proverbial in Spain (Farinelli, *Italia e Spagna*, I, 144–45).

213. *Hist.*, LXVIII, 2: IV, 364. The passage reoccurs, in shorter form, in the *Qu.*, p. 224. And elsewhere too: "I once saw King Don Federico of Naples prosperous . . . and he died exiled and poor. . . . I saw Lodovico duke of Milan prosperous and rich in his estate, and later he was taken prisoner and carried off to France, and put in a cage,

and the conquistadors of Peru possessed immeasurable riches; but Fortune,—the allegorical disguise of the enigmatic rationality of history and symptom of a dissatisfaction with vaguely providential explanations,—perfidious, capricious Fortune brought low both rulers and adventurers. From the courts of Italy to the valleys of the Andes it rules and destroys, equally indifferent to the refined arts of government and the treasure hoards of precious metals. Machiavelli, in the penultimate chapter of the *Prince,* had confined Fortune's sway to the half of man's actions and with sardonic humor had observed that "Fortune is a woman, and if one wishes to subjugate her she must be beaten and struck." For the Florentine politician Fortune could be tamed. But its mystery still disturbs Oviedo when he comes face to face with the unburied or half-buried body of Pizarro; and the words of the Gospel with which he seeks to set his mind at rest are mere formality.[214]

13. INTEREST IN PAINTING

There was, however, another aspect of the Italian experience that did even more, I think, to shape Oviedo's mental outlook than his personal observance of the exploits and misfortunes of the mighty: his contact with the limpid and robust art of the high Renaissance, a contact rendered even more fruitful by his lively, personal (and unusual) interest in the plastic arts, especially painting.

Oviedo learned to draw while still very young, no more than fifteen years old, and indeed, according to his biographer, "already had a reputation as an expert in the art of drawing."[215]

---

where he died" (*Qu.*, p. 55). In another passage, when talking about Lucas Vázquez de Ayllón, a good commandant, but lacking military experience, Oviedo recalls that he met his brother, "Perálvarez de Ayllón, whom I saw in Italy, soldiering in the service of the duke of Valentinois, Don Cesare Borgia, and held in high esteem by the gentlemen of his army. . . . I know very well, that this man would have been able to command soldiers, because he was a soldier and experienced in military discipline" (*Hist.*, XXXVII, Proh.: III, 624–25). And apparently he also witnessed the encounters between Valentino's Switzers and the pope's Spanish guard (Amador de los Ríos, "Vida," p. xviii, citing *Qu.*, pt. III, est. 45, fol. 74). In the first part of the same *Quinquagenas* Oviedo alludes vaguely to the time when "I saw certain uprisings that occurred in Italy, in the kingdom of Naples and the duchy of Milan," and he sides with the loyalists against the rebels (*Qu.*, p. 41). Elsewhere he recalls that he knew Duke Valentino, Ludovico il Moro, and Louis XII of France (*Qu.*, pp. 205–06). For reports—though perhaps not eyewitness ones—of challenges and duels and feats of arms by Spaniards in Italy, see *Qu.*, pp. 352–57; and for a duel fought in Marino (near Rome) between Ferrer di Lorca and the castellan of Arche (Arce?), who was defeated and surrendered, see *Qu.*, p. 380.

214. "And there was not even earth enough to finish covering his grave" (*Hist.*, XLVIII, 1: PT, V, 216: cf. *Qu.*, p. 101). On the link between the downfalls or violent deaths of princes and the stock phrases on the fickleness of fortune, a link made more conspicuous precisely by the events in the kingdom of Naples at the beginning of the sixteenth century, cf. C. Tutini, *Della varietà della fortuna* (Naples, 1754), and Croce, "Un poemetto popolare del Quattrocento sulle morti dei condottieri," *La Critica,* 36 (1938), 296–302. See also G. Procacci, "La 'fortuna' nella realtà politica e sociale del primo Cinquecento," *Belfagor,* 6, no. 4 (1951), 407–21. And on the ambiguous duality of the term *Fortune* in medieval historiography, where it sometimes symbolizes the irrationality of history and other times the mysterious working of Providence, see F. P. Pickering, *Augustinus oder Boethius* (Berlin, 1967). Oviedo picks up this same argument, taking his cue from the tragic ends met by almost all the conquistadors. See below, chap. XIX, sec. 5.

215. Amador de los Ríos, "Vida," p. xvii. He himself tells us how much he enjoyed painting with watercolors (*Hist.*, X, I: I, 363a). On the link between his aesthetic sensitivity and the powers of description he displays in the *Historia,* cf. Pérez de Tudela, "Vida," pp. cxli–ii.

Later on, when describing the Indies, whenever he finds words inadequate to give an exact idea of the form of an animal or an instrument, he resorts to drawing.[216] Sometimes a certain painting is recalled to make his description clearer. A splendidly feathered bird would make a fine polychrome plume on Charles V's helmet, resembling the sort one sees on the "tiara-shaped sallet with four golden crowns and rich pearls and stones" in certain portraits that Oviedo has seen of "Suluman Otoman, king of the Turks."[217] The houses of the people of Bogotá are so ingeniously surrounded "with many walls both outside and inside, and so artfully, that they call to mind the painting that is commonly called the labyrinth."[218]

The clothes of some Indians were "painted, in the manner of Spanish painters, with arabesques and florets and other paintings."[219] And a big wooden mask of the Indians of Yucatán is described as being gilded "in just the same way they gild an altarpiece in Castile, with size."[220] Some other Indians represent the devil, carved in wood or modeled in gold, "very fearsome and ugly, and very different from the way he is customarily painted by our painters at the feet of Saint Michael the Archangel or the Apostle Saint Bartholemew, or anywhere else where they want to

216. "A drawing . . . is a very suitable way for the author to be better understood" (*Hist.*, XLII, 13: IV, 112b). The engravings that adorn the 1547 edition of the *Historia* are certainly no masterpieces (see the reproductions of some of them in Winsor, op. cit., II, 11, 15, 16, 17). They are certainly finer and more detailed than those appearing in the 1535 edition, but they still retain a certain documentary quality and naivety of feature that are altogether lacking in the refashioned versions, complete with conventional "embellishments" and arbitrary variations, that appear in the Ramusio editions and the plates at the end of the Amador de los Ríos edition. On Oviedo as a poor draughtsman, on the contrary, cf. E. Alvarez López, "La historia natural en Fernández de Oviedo," *Ri*, 17, nos. 69–70 (1957), 573, 590.

217. *Hist.*, VI, 15: I, 203a. This could be a portrait of Suleiman the Great, a contemporary of Oviedo, though perhaps more likely of Sultan Mehmet II, who was painted by various other artists as well as Gentile Bellini, and always with three golden crowns. Cf. A. Venturi, *Storia dell'arte italiana*, vol. 7, pt. 4, *La pittura del Quattrocento* (Milan, 1915), pp. 226–27 and n. On this subject Giuseppe Billanovich told me that it could well be Mehmet II, and recommended looking at a whole series of studies by Babinger: e.g., "Zwei Bildnisse Mehmeds II von Gentile Bellini," *Institut für Auslandsbeziehungen, Stuttgart, Zeitschrift für Kulturaustausch*, offprint from vol. 12, nos. 2–3 (1962), 176–82; a recent article in *Arte Veneta*; and, for various references, "Ein vorgeblicher Gnadenbrief Mehmeds II für Gentile Bellini," *Italia medievale e umanistica*, 5 (1962), 85–101. But I must confess that I have not seen these articles.

The *pájaro mosquito*, with its beak as thin and pointed as a pin, and its feathers of gold and green and other beautiful colors, reminded Oviedo very much "in the delicacy of its legs and claws, of the tiny birds that illuminators often include in the margins of Books of Hours" (*Sum.*, chap. 47, p. 186; cf. Lowes, op. cit., p. 317). In the same way the *cangrejo* is made "in the same manner as the sign of Cancer is painted" (*Sum.*, chap. 60, p. 201).

218. *Hist.*, XXVI, 23: II, 389a.

219. Ibid., XXIV, 11: II, 251a. He is probably alluding to the decorative arabesques with which the primitives of the Castilian school covered the garments of saints and donors. A typical example of this is the picture of the Catholic Kings worshiping the Virgin Mary with the infant Jesus, painted around 1490 by a "Castilian master" and now in the Prado (reproduced in A. L. Mayer, *Meisterwerke der Gemäldesammlung des Prado in Madrid* [Munich, 1922], plate 95), which Oviedo could well have seen. Even Berruguete, whom Oviedo mentions as an excellent painter (*Hist.*, X, Proh.: I, 362a) and who worked in Italy (1477–83: influence of Piero della Francesca and Mellozzo), often goes overboard with damasked floral decorations on his drapery. The Italian influence on the plastic arts in Spain "from the fourteenth century to the Catholic Kings" is discussed by De Bosque; on Berruguete in particular, op. cit., pp. 157–58, 161–62, 296–98, 326–32.

220. *Hist.*, XVII, 13: I, 520a. Oviedo saw these and other treasures from the Yucatán, sent by Diego Velázquez to Charles V, in Barcelona, in 1519 (XVII, 19: I, 538).

paint him as a more fearsome figure." [221] Nor is there any lack of excellent materials for these artisans: the markets of Mexico are stocked with just as many colors for painters as can be found in Spain, and of equally excellent shades and finish." [222]

14. LEONARDO, MANTEGNA, AND THE SCISSORS

Traveling around the courts and cities of Italy at the end of the fifteenth century, Oviedo must have felt in a veritable spiritual paradise. We can hardly repress a twinge of envy and excitement when we hear him mention "Leonardo de Vince, or Andrea Manteña, famous painters that I met in Italy. . . ." [223]

But how did he come to meet them? What brought them together? In 1500 Oviedo was twenty-two, Leonardo forty-eight, and Mantegna almost seventy. What could the Spanish youth have had to say to those two masters at the peak of their glory? A fragment of the unpublished *Batallas* provides the somewhat disappointing answer. A fashion had developed in Spain for the "art" of cutting out minuscule designs. Oviedo took some lessons from the famous teachers of this frivolous art and by dint of study, tiring his eyes and wasting a considerable amount of time that he was later to regret, became extremely skilled—or so he says himself—at this ingenuous and delicate technique, done freehand, as he boasts, without any previous sketch or auxiliary instruments.

Capital letters, the symbols of the Passion, royal and princely crests were cut out by Oviedo from pieces of paper no bigger than a coin. As an old man he still remembered and prided himself on this manual dexterity. Thus we should not be

---

221. *Sum.*, chap. 10, p. 130; *Hist.*, XXIX, 31: II, 155a. Oviedo uses almost exactly the same words in reference to some other Indians, painters rather than sculptors, who "in their paintings usually depict the devil as being just as ugly and full of tails and horns and mouths and other faces, as when our painters paint him at the feet of the archangel St. Michael or the apostle St. Bartholomew" (*Hist.*, XLII, 5: IV, 75a; also V, 3: I, 138b). Among so many, suffice it to recall a *St. Bartholomew with His Foot on the Devil* by the Neapolitan Nicola da Credensa, who lived in Barcelona, which has since 1499 adorned the high altar of the parish church of Sitges (De Bosque, op. cit., pp. 339–40) and the *St. Michael and the Dragon* that appears on the Borgia seal (De Bosque, pp. 355, 360). Another more florid description of the horrible demons painted or sculpted or carved by the Indians or tattooed on their skins: *Hist.*, V, 1: I, 125–26. On masks with turquoise and gold mosaics (Yucatán), cf. *Hist.*, XVII, 13: I, 520b; XVII, 15: I, 526a, 528a.

222. *Hist.*, XXXIII, 10: III, 300b. This passage in fact comes from one of Cortés's letters: "They sell just as many colors for painters as can be found in Spain, and their hues are as excellent as can be" (Cortés, op. cit., I, 100). But the image of the Indian women grinding corn "by hand (like painters grind colors for their needs)" is Oviedo's own (Hist., VII, 1: I, 266b; *Sum.*, chap. IV, p. 94).

On the origins of painting, at first limited to outlining the human form, and later polychrome, right up to the famous masters, cf. *Hist.*, XXXIII, 44: III, 487–88. Oviedo's source is indubitably Pliny's *Natural History,* XXXV, 5 (*Historia Naturale,* trans. C. Landino [Venice, 1534], p. dccxlii; trans. Littré [Paris, 1883], II, 466–67). In the *Quinquagenas* Oviedo writes hyperbolically that "of all the famous painters the world has ever known" not one could pick up his brushes and paint the complexions on his "female images" the way natural skin really is (*Qu.*, p. 131).

223. *Hist.*, X, Proh.: I, 362a. Amador de los Ríos says that Oviedo was personally acquainted with Titian, Michelangelo, and Raphael too ("Vida," p. xvii), which I find unlikely for a variety of reasons of time and place, and suggested solely by Oviedo's general emphasis. The admiration of the Spaniards for Leonardo's art, and their frequent imitations, are well known. It is curious to note that the two famous painters mentioned by Oviedo are the first two mentioned by Ariosto among "those of our own times that were or are, Leonardo, Andrea Mantegna," etc. (*Orlando Furioso,* XXXIII, 2).

surprised that he used it to make the acquaintance of Ludovico il Moro, for whom he cut out "a polyphonic motet arranged for four voices" and decorated with the Sforza coat of arms, and then everything else he was asked for, with the result that the duke was led to show Leonardo these minute and fragile masterpieces; the great painter, Oviedo reports, was filled with admiration and amazement at such manual virtuosity, and the duke exclaimed that in Roman times the young Spaniard would have been proclaimed "the God of the Scissors."[224]

Oviedo had the same success shortly afterward at Mantua (Leonardo too went to Mantua, apparently in the company of Luca Pacioli, after the flight of Ludovico il Moro), at the court of Isabella d'Este (the daughter of Eleanor of Aragon) and with "that excellent painter" living in that city called Andrea Mantegna, and even greater success at the court of King Frederick,[225] where Oviedo found grace and favor with his unfailing scissors, then apparently reaching their peak of perfection. With great dash and aplomb the deft young Spaniard succeeded in splitting a hair that the sovereign "plucked from his royal head," and this at night, by candlelight; he then proceeded to make such microscopic little holes in a sheet of paper that not even the slenderest hair (we are not told whether from the "royal head" or some less venerable cranium) could pass through them.[226]

Oviedo took up his scissors for the last time, two pairs of excellent little scissors that Margherita of Austria, the daughter of Maximilian and widow of the prince Don Juan, had had made for him specially, when he was in Brussels in 1516 and the princess reminded him (a curious and pathetic reminder) of his skill of almost twenty years earlier; and once again, although by now completely out of practice, the thirty-eight-year-old Oviedo acquitted himself honorably: "I cut out two or three things with which Her Highness was very pleased." But it was his swan song, and on returning to Spain he gave away the scissors to rid himself of the temptation to waste any more time in such idle pastimes.[227]

The occasion of those meetings with Leonardo and Mantegna was therefore, as Oviedo himself indirectly and belatedly admits, totally trivial and accidental. But the fact remains that his words echo a universal admiration that Oviedo has made his own and cultivated with grateful and jealous faithfulness. He wishes there were a master like them (or Berruguete) to portray certain natural features of the Antilles or Nicaragua: a naive wish, and typical of a didactic approach to the arts, but

224. Pérez de Tudela, "Vida," pp. xx–xxi, xxiv–xxv; M. Ballesteros Gaibrois, *Vida del madrileño Gonzalo Fernández de Oviedo y Valdés* (Madrid, 1958), pp. 13–14. There was a considerable revival of the vogue for making paper cut-outs in France in the time of Louis XV, and alongside the fashion for silhouettes and Chinese shadows it lasted right up to the beginning of the nineteenth century: cf. J. Grand-Carteret, *Vieux papiers, vieilles images* (Paris, 1896), pp. 302–03; E. Littré, *Dictionnaire de la langue française,* s.v. "découpage"; and G. Maugras, *La Cour de Lunéville* (Paris, 1904), p. 111. It also flourished in England between the end of the eighteenth century and Victorian times: see "The Fine Art of Cutting Paper," by a Collector, *The Times,* 15 January 1966.

225. *Batallas,* quoted by Pérez de Tudela, "Vida," p. xxiv; "Rasgos," p. 414.

226. *Batallas,* quoted by Pérez de Tudela, "Vida," p. xxix; "Rasgos," pp. 413–15.

227. *Batallas,* quoted by Pérez de Tudela, "Vida," p. lxi; "Rasgos," p. 415.

betraying an implicit conviction that perfection in the arts and the discovery of a New World are parallel and concurrent phenomena in a single and unprecedented historical process.

15. ITALY PAIRED WITH SPAIN

The monuments, cities, and landscapes of Italy are ever present in Oviedo's mind, even after decades spent an ocean away, even after numerous journeys across Spain and one to Flanders. His partial Italianness, in an age when Italy was a synonym for civil perfection, compensates in his mind for his lack of a more refined and complete culture. Oviedo knows little Latin and less Greek and feels the lack keenly. But he is familiar with the things, books, people, and places of the peninsula.

Whenever he mentions some European luxury or refinement, Italy and Spain, jointly, are his terms of reference, his shorthand formula for western civilization. Although Spanish and proud of it, and although he never again saw Italy after setting sail from Palermo in May 1502, the memory does not fade with the long slow passage of the years. Italy and Sicily always remain—as he says in passing, almost as if it were an established fact, taken for granted—"the center of the world, or the best of it."[228]

Sicily in particular, situated between the two—Italian and Iberian—peninsulas and his point of departure when he left the former to return to the latter, always remains for him "the heart of the world." And whether he is referring to the makeup used by the women "in Italy and Valencia or Spain" to try to improve on the faces God gave them,[229] extolling the fertility of the Cordovan countryside and the island of Sicily,[230] or praising the musical skills of the young Mexicans (writing that "in Spain and Italy and wherever music is appreciated these Indians would be esteemed"),[231] admiring their dramatic arts (repeating that "in Italy or Castile no better could be done by the Italian or Spanish natives"),[232] or comparing the *areytos* of the West Indian savages with the popular songs to be heard "in Spain and Italy,"[233] or the tides of the Ocean with those of the Mediterranean "in Valencia, Barcelona, and Italy,"[234] or recommending hammocks as highly useful to armies on the march "in Spain, Italy, and

---

228. *Hist.*, VI, 9: PT, I, 169; cf. ibid., III, 11: PT, I, 82 ("the heart of Europe"), and V, 3: PT, I, 122. See also below, chap. XVI, sec. 8.

229. *Hist.*, X, 1: I, 363a.

230. *Hist.*, XXXIII, 40: III, 463b. Oviedo also says that Hispaniola is potentially richer than Sicily or England (*Sum.*, chap. 2, p. 85; *Hist.*, II, 11: I, 84a); like Las Casas, come to that, who compared it advantageously with the three most famous islands of the Old World, England, Sicily, and Crete (*Apologética historia*, chap. 20).

231. *Hist.*, XXXIII, 51: III, 537b. In the *Quinquagenas* (p. 24) Oviedo relates how in Naples, and later in Palermo and later still in Spain, he saw and heard the famous lutenist Jacobo Mirtheo on numerous occasions.

232. *Hist.*, XXXIII, 51: III, 538a.

233. Ibid., V, 1: I, 128b.

234. Ibid., II, 10: PT, I, 40b.

elsewhere,"[235] or comparing the centerposts of the Indians' huts to the supports for pavilions or tents "such as are used in the armies and encampments in Spain and Italy,"[236] or recalling that the salutary, scorching *ají* (chili) "is taken to Spain and Italy and elsewhere as a very good spice,"[237] or doubting that the perfection of the Mexican goldwork could be matched by anyone "in Spain or Italy,[238] or concluding that "any silversmith of Spain or Italy, or wherever they are most expert," would be very happy to discover the secret of the way the Indians gild copper and base gold[239]—the motherland and Italy remain mentally conjoined, fused in a single image of perfection, doubtless facilitated and made more spontaneous by the political ties that linked the two peninsulas and the current stylistic usage of "vocabulary pairs."[240]

Italy's particular preeminence in the textile arts, however, meant that Oviedo's praise for the "very rich crimsons" of Venice could not be matched by any corresponding eulogy of Spanish cloth of any color,[241] nor could he find any twin point of reference to accompany the velvet of Genoa, the "purple crimson silk" and "black" silk of Lucca,[242] the Florentine merchants' brocades and gold-embroidered fabrics,[243] the rich hangings and silver and gold brocades used for festive adornment of the rooms of the apostolic palace and other princely residences,[244] or the leather trappings "for the horses of gentlemen-at-arms" that were made in Naples "or wherever they are best made."[245]

On the other hand the excellence of the Atlantic countries' privateer ships, which as commandant of Santo Domingo he had good reason to know and fear, prompts him to note that "few masters in Italy and Spain and France, and even in all Europe," would know how to build ships like the Carthaginians' quin-

---

235. Ibid., V, 2: I, 132b. The first description of a hammock occurs in the pseudo-Vespucci: "They are in the habit of sleeping in certain large nets made out of silk and suspended in the air"; the author already recommends it as quite comfortable and pleasant (Navarrete, op. cit., III, 216; cf. A. Reyes, *Ultima Tule*, p. 86, and above, chap. VI, sec. 7.

236. *Hist.*, V, 1: I, 164. Further examples from military life, above, sec. 11.

237. *Hist.*, VII, 7: I, 275b.

238. Ibid., XXXIII, 11: III, 305b.

239. *Sum.*, chap. 82, p. 254. Spain and Italy are also coupled elsewhere, as for instance in *Hist.*, XIV, 2: I, 442a, and XLIX, 3: IV, 387a; on Cordova and Sicily (fertile lands), *Hist.*, XXXII, 40: III, 463b.

240. R. Menéndez Pidal, "El lenguaje," p. 160. Elsewhere, however (*Los españoles en la historia* [Buenos Aires and Mexico, 1951], p. 128), the same author says that Juan de Valdés and Garcilaso "were the first to teach Spaniards to admire Italy with deep Hispanic feeling."

The linking of Italy and Spain is already frequent in the Italo-Spaniard Peter Martyr. In the kingdom of Comogro, in Darien, there was a well-stocked cellar, "after the Spanish or Italian fashion" (*Dec.*, II, 3 [Buenos Aires, 1944], p. 148). Cf. also the reference to: "In Italy or in Spain" (*Dec.*, III, 2, p. 225); "Spain and Italy" (*Dec.*, II, 7 [Buenos Aires, 1944], p. 282; further examples are found in *Dec.*, III, 2 [Buenos Aires, 1944], p. 183, and V, 7, p. 435, etc.).

Quite often Oviedo translates the Latin words into Spanish *and* Italian. Referring to a statement by the lying Don García, in Ruiz de Alarcón's *Verdad sospechosa* (1624), Henríquez Ureña notes: "During the sixteenth century and right up to the beginning of the seventeenth century Italy was considered the most refined country of all. Spain represented rather more the qualities of brilliance and splendor" (*La cultura*, p. 48n). But sometimes, curiously enough, the couple is split: see below, chap. XVIII, sec. 20.

241. *Hist.*, XXXIII, 40: III, 463b.

242. *Libro de la Cámara Real*, p. 36.

243. *Hist.*, VIII, 24: PT, I, 363b; cf. above, n. 142.

244. *Hist.*, XLVI, 17: IV, 227.

245. Ibid., XII, 11: I, 406a.

quiremes.[246] Precision instruments too were better made in northern Europe than in Italy or Spain: Oviedo owned "one of those sundials that come from France and Flanders, with a little mirror and an ivory case, that could be worth three or four silver *reales* in Spain,"[247] and of which there are still (we might add) so many examples in museums. Likewise the fact that meat is an everyday food in France prompts Oviedo's observation that for the cannibals it was just as normal to eat human flesh "as in France, Spain, and Italy to eat mutton and beef."[248]

16. ITALIAN DELICACIES

Even the culinary delicacies of the two countries are linked in a nostalgically imagined banquet when Oviedo relates how Cortés and his companions were reduced to eating a horse killed by the Indians, "and even the innards tasted as good as the barbecued meat of Naples, or the delicate roast kid of Ávila, or the tender veal of Sorrento and Saragossa."[249]

There are in fact frequent gastronomic and culinary reminiscences of one or other country. One West Indian root (*romeracha*) reminds him—he tells us with a sigh—of the delicious radishes "which I ate in Rome and Naples and other parts of Italy."[250] In the Florida savannahs there can be found certain berries "that exist in Italy, growing on certain plants close to the ground, resembling tasty and fragrant *madroños*," strawberries in fact. "In the Kingdom of Naples these fruits are called 'fraoles' (*fragole*), and they are a delicate and a fine thing and highly thought of."[251] The four affectionate adjectives tell us how Oviedo's mouth watered at the memory of this succulent fruit. On the River Plate there are little partridges "like the *estarnas* in Italy,"[252] and no less memorable are the "*moscarela* pears of Sicily or Naples."[253] Even in the *Quinquagenas* of his later years there reappear, in verse and prose, "the carp of Lake Garda . . . much prized fish, and no less good than trout," that are caught in the Mincio, four inches thick or even a little bigger, "such as I ate in the city of Mantua in Italy."[254]

On the subject of the frogs eaten by the Indians, Oviedo recalls that in 1524 the Lord Chancellor Mercurio[255] gave them to Charles V (a notorious glutton) to try,

---

246. Ibid., XXXIV, Proh.: III, 558a.
247. Ibid., XLII, 11: IV, 95b.
248. Ibid., V, 3: I, 138a.
249. Ibid., XXXIII, 14: III, 328a. Villalón too mentions (ca. 1553–56) the excellent Neapolitan veal and other delicacies (Giannini, op. cit., pp. 94–95).
250. *Hist.*, XI, 1: I, 374b.
251. Ibid., XVII, 25: I, 559b.
252. Ibid., XXIII, 5: PT, II, 361a.
253. *Sum.*, chap. 76, p. 223.
254. *Qu.*, pp. 479–80.
255. In other words the Piedmontese Mercurio Arborio, marquis of Gattinara (1465–1530), Charles V's lord chancellor from 1518 onward; it was Mercurio who dreamed up the imperial scheme for a universal monarchy (cf. the article by C. Bornate in the *Enciclopedia Italiana*, and R. Menéndez Pidal, *La idea imperial de Carlos V* [Buenos Aires, 1941], pp. 9, 35; cf. *Qu.*, p. 378), which Charles rejected, entirely wrapped up as he was in a medieval fantasy of an "empire of Christian peace," although Oviedo himself continued to dream about his acquiring the "universal monarchy" (*Hist.*, VI, 8, par. 4: I, 180a; and cf. below, chap. XX, sec. 4). It is not perhaps entirely superfluous to point out that the "Mercurio" of the frogs also died of gout. On Oviedo's gluttony, cf. below, Appendix C.

which came as no surprise to Oviedo "since he was Italian, where it has long been a custom to eat frogs, and they make good eating. And many years ago I ate them in Mantua and Rome and Naples and other parts of Italy; and they are sold publicly in the market places as a healthy food, easy to digest and tasty."[256] At Mantua again, in the palace of the Marquis Francesco Gonzaga, Oviedo tasted the "hands" of certain young bears that the marquis used to raise and fatten and serve at table "as a much valued item"; Oviedo too found them "not unpleasant," but not as good as the "hands" of the American *tapir*.[257]

Finally, extolling the goodness of the pineapple, Oviedo describes it as better than the Sicilian *milleruelos,* the *moscarela* pears and other excellent fruit that Ferdinand I of Naples "collected in his gardens of the Park and the Paradise and Pujo Real," better even than the fruit cultivated by Ercole duke of Ferrara "in the Esquiva Noya . . . on the island in the Po," and superior even to the fruit grown by Lord Ludovico Sforza, duke of Milan, in his "transportable garden, from which the fruit-laden trees were wheeled in barrows right up to the table and to his bedchamber."[258]

17. CITIES AND LANDSCAPES OF SPAIN AND ITALY

The *Historia* and the *Quinquagenas* are of course teeming with images of the cities and towns of Spain and Flanders, often portrayed in graphically evocative sketches. There spring to mind, for example, Cordova in its fertile valley,[259]

---

256. *Hist.*, XIII, 10: I, 437b. One of his fellow dinner-guests on this occasion was "His Excellency Don Fernando of Aragon, Duke of Calabria." In Vitoria, one Friday in 1524, Oviedo ate "a dish of cooked frogs" (ibid., XIII, 10: I, 437a). But he declined the "large roast toads" which his Indian porters ate and offered him "amidst much laughter . . . saying they were very good" (ibid., IX, 25: I, 355b).

This habit of eating frogs made such a deep impression on the English that they disparagingly applied the term "frog-eaters" or "frogs" to the French and in general to all continentals, provoking the protests of the French even at the end of the eighteenth century (1781). See G. Chinard, *Les réfugiés huguenots en Amérique* (Paris, 1925), p. 201. The epithet has now fallen into disuse, writes D. W. Brogan, *The English People* (New York, 1943), p. 251n.

257. *Hist.*, XII, 11: I, 406.

258. Ibid., VII, 14: I, 280a. "Fernando I" is Ferrante of Aragon (Ferdinand I, 1431–94), who fostered agriculture in the kingdom (Croce, *Regno di Napoli,* pp. 79–80).

Naples: on the villa of Poggio Reale ("Pujo Real") near Naples, admired in verse by Charles VIII's court poet, Andrea della Vigna (and in prose by another comrade-in-arms of Charles VIII), cf. E. Müntz, *L'arte italiana nel Quattrocento* (Milan, 1894), p. 113 and n. 424; idem., *L'età aurea dell'arte italiana* (Milan, 1895), pp. 291–92; and S. Di Giacomo, *La prostituzione a Napoli* (Naples, 1899), pp. 25–29. J. Burckhardt, *Geschichte der Renaissance in Italien* (Stuttgart, 1891), pp. 240, 252, mentions that it contained "every sort of fruit tree that the climate would allow." Cristóbal Suárez de Figueroa, at the beginning of the seventeenth century, extolled it as a place of delight (Giannini, op. cit., p. 96). Galiani described it as "the first pleasure-palace built by any European monarch" (*Il pensiero dell'abate Galiani,* ed. F. Nicolini [Bari, 1909], pp. 385–86, with bibliography).

Ferrara: Oviedo seems to have confused, in his memory, the famous Schifanoia palace ("Esquiva Noya") built by Borso and enriched by Ercole d'Este, but which is *not* on an island in the Po, with the villa that Alfonso I (who came to the throne in 1505, after Oviedo left Italy) had built for himself on the little island of the Belvedere "formed by the splitting of the Po at Ferrara near Castel Tedaldo," and which he embellished with rare and exotic animals and graceful plants, making it "the most joyous island . . . ever surrounded by sea, lake, or stream" (*Orlando Furioso,* XLIII, 57; cf. XXV, 6; see G. Agnelli, *Ferrara e Pomposa* [Bergamo, 1902], pp. 62–63; Burckhardt, *Geschichte,* p. 241; G. Pazzi, *Il "Belvedere" ferrarese nei versi d'Ariosto e di Balbo* [Rome, 1933]). But perhaps Oviedo was thinking not about the Belvedere but about the palace garden that Ercole d'Este had created around 1480–90, that lacked "no beautiful or fruitful tree" (Burckhardt, *Geschichte,* pp. 252–53).

259. *Hist.*, XXXIII, 40: III, 463b.

Toledo on the fast-flowing Tagus,[260] and Miranda on the swift Ebro;[261] Seville on the broad Guadalquivir,[262] with the "melon-filled" boats,[263] the "Moorish slaves" with chains on their feet "pounding esparto-grass at the port of Triana in Seville,"[264] with the Giralda and its curious acoustic phenomena[265] and the Mexican treasures that Oviedo saw in the Casa de la Contratación[266] and the Casa de la Moneda, the mint that could not keep pace with the enormous quantities of silver being unloaded by the treasure fleets;[267] Salamanca, with its great square "all surrounded by arcades";[268] the freezing winds and snows of Burgos;[269] Valladolid with its somewhat uncatholic epitaph on the tomb of Don Pedro Niago outside the Church of St. Stephen;[270] Segovia with its miraculous, soaring, and ancient aqueduct-bridge, onto which the adolescent Oviedo had once ventured out, risking life and limb;[271] Medina del Campo with its fair and timber market;[272] the first[273] fields of maize near Ávila and Madrid,[274] the rows of vines in Catalonia, Toledo, and Madrid;[275] the rows of single houses in Galicia, Biscay, and elsewhere, contrasted to those in Managua, which "were strung out like a rope,"[276] foreshadowing—in Oviedo's simile too—the much-lamented "ribbon developments" of a later age; the streams in Castile, in which the local people steep the flax, weighting it down with stones, like the Indians do with the fibrous leaves of the *henequen;*[277] the mead of the Basque country[278] and the fattened capons of Aranda de Duero;[279] the "oxhide wineskins . . . used for carting and transporting the must in Medina del Campo and Arévalo and those parts'[280] the "very broad wagons with extra staves added at the sides, like

260. *Qu.*, p. 305; *Hist.*, VIII, 41: PT, I, 277; IX, 8: PT, I, 287; IX, 11: PT, I, 289–90.

261. *Hist.*, XLI, 3: IV, 30a. Elsewhere too Oviedo recalls "the tides in the Guadalquivir and the Tagus and other Spanish rivers that debouch into the sea" (*Hist.*, VI, 53: I, 261–62, and see XXIX, 2: III, 7b).

262. Ibid., XXV, 14: PT, III, 43a; XXV, 5: III, 604a.

263. Ibid., L, 20, par. 10: IV, 530.

264. Ibid., XXVIII, 3: PT, III, 181.

265. Ibid., XXXII, 4: III, 238–39; XXXIII, 10: III, 302b.

266. Ibid., VI, 8: I, 180b; XXXIII, 1: III, 259b.

267. Ibid., XXXIII, 41: III, 468B; XXXIII, 48: III, 521b. Seville and Cordova are also mentioned in XXXIII, 10: III, 299b. The earthquakes of Almería, Muxácar, and Vera are recalled in XLI, 3: III, 32–33.

268. Ibid., XXXIII, 10: III, 299b.

269. Ibid., XVII, 27: I, 571a.

270. Ibid., VI, 49: I, 250–51.

271. *Qu.*, pp. 500–01.

272. *Hist.*, III, 11: I, 85b; XXIX, 5: III, 19b; XLVI, 8: PT, V, 59b; *Qu.*, p. 256. The fair at Medina fell into decline after 1520 when the city refused to help Charles V in the war against the *comuneros* and was then burned and sacked.

273. Not actually the very first. Columbus wrote in 1498 that "there is now a lot of it [maize] in Castile" (*Relaciones y cartas*, p. 279). And in 1493 Peter Martyr had written that the West Indians "produce, without much trouble, a bread made from a grain that is a sort of millet, similar to that found in great abundance around Milan and in Andalusia" (*Dec.*, I, 1, p. 7). On maize, see Messedaglia, "Aspetti," p. 257, under "granoturco."

274. *Hist.*, VII, 1 and 14: I, 268b and 284. In Avila, Oviedo offered the empress a small jar of cocoa butter (*Hist.*, VIII, 30: I, 320b).

275. Ibid., VIII, 24: I, 309; VII, 2: I, 269a.

276. Ibid., XLII, 5: IV, 67; XXIX, 27: PT, III, 317–18.

277. Ibid., VII, 10: I, 277a.

278. Ibid., VIII, 20: I, 307a.

279. Ibid., XXIV, 3: II, 220a.

280. Ibid., XIII, 8: I, 433a; *Sum.*, chap. 83, p. 258.

they do in the kingdom of Toledo when they are harvesting the wheat";[281] and
the Holy Week ceremonies, with the crosses erected at the stations of the Via
Crucis.[282] In another more surprising image the sheltered countryside "that
stands at the foot of this city of Toledo" reminds him of the dense swarms of
cormorants congregating over the sardine-banks in the South Sea, so tightly
packed that they look like a piece of jet-black velvet laid over the waters.[283]

These striking images are interspersed with countless other less obvious
details, held in Oviedo's watchful gaze and implanted in his memory. With such
a wealth of material one can attempt no more than a rather clumsy enumeration,
which might include the drinking-troughs found in the Sierras of Segovia, which
the Indian canoes resemble;[284] the "spirited bulls of the banks of the Jarama" that
send the "laborers in my land" scattering in all directions, like the Indians when
they see horses;[285] the multicolored mantillas of the gypsies wandering across
Spain;[286] the merry peasant dances;[287] the great baskets "filled with sea-bream"
that are brought from La Montaña and Biscay to Burgos and Castile;[288] the
fearsome swordfish saws hung up as ex-votos in Spanish churches;[289] the fierce-
looking heads of boars and bears hung on the doors "of the gentlemen hunts-
men's houses";[290] the wizards and witches and the heretics of "Peña de Amboto"
in Biscay, where Oviedo was in 1504, and the "condemned sect of fray Alonso
de Mella";[291] the choir stalls in the cathedrals of Toledo and Seville;[292] the
wooden chairs and stools of Granada, and the ceremonious obeisances of the
Moors in that city;[293] the carts and brooms of Toledo;[294] the razor-sharp lance-
tips of Aspe in Biscay;[295] the high mountains near Segovia and the "easy, safe,
and level" highway from Valladolid to Medina;[296] not to mention the fragrant
little bread-rolls (molletes) of Zaratán and Barba[297] and other fruits of land and

---

281. *Sum.*, chap. 78, pp. 226–27.
282. *Hist.*, XXVIII, 3: PT, III, 181.
283. *Sum.*, chap. 38, pp. 177–78. They sound like flocks of guanay cormorants (and one is inevitably reminded of El Greco's moist and velvety shadows in the celebrated view of Toledo). The tall tower of San Román, in Toledo, is also mentioned in *Sum.*, chap. 78, p. 227, and *Hist.*, IX, 11: PT, I, 290a.
284. *Hist.*, XXXII, 4: III, 239b.
285. Ibid., XXIX, 21, par. 5: III, 105b. Elsewhere he recalls the contrasting fauna that he saw on the banks of the river Xarama, (or Jarama), as it wends its way down from the Sierra Guadarrama to the vicinity of Madrid, where it is joined by the Manzanares and debouches into the Tagus: "You will find there both very fierce bulls and vast numbers of good rabbits" (*Qu.*, p. 496).
286. *Hist.*, XVII, 25: I, 556–57.
287. Ibid., XVII, 27: PT, II, 173b.
288. *Sum.*, chap. 81, p. 247; *Hist.*, XXIX, 7: III, 33b; XXIX, 28: III, 140a.
289. *Hist.*, XII, 3: I, 426b.
290. Ibid., XVII, 28: I, 573b.
291. Ibid., XII, 13: PT, II, 44a; XXXIII, 46: PT, IV, 221b. On the obscure heresy of Alonso de Mella, who apparently preached (1442) the common ownership of goods and women, see Menéndez Pelayo, *Heterodoxos españoles*, III, 320–24.
292. *Hist.*, IX, 8: PT, I, 287A.
293. Ibid., IX, 1: PT, I, 279; XXXIII, 47: PT, IV, 220a.
294. Ibid., IX, 11: PT, I, 289b; LXII, 12: PT, IV, 425b.
295. Ibid., XXXIII, 13: PT, IV, 63b.
296. Ibid., XXII, 2: PT, II, 344a; XXV, 11: PT, III, 37b.
297. Ibid., XXV, 6: PT, III, 24a.

sea; or the architectural features of the grandees' palaces or the excellent hot springs.

On occasion this same gaze summons up a broader image that is strangely "modern" in its sensitivity. He notes, for instance, how the cities clinging to mountainsides, Granada, Toledo, Cuenca, and Burgos, are much more picturesque than the cities of the plain, when seen from a certain distance, beautiful by day and even more beautiful by night "because as some of the houses are higher than others one can see a large number of lights at dusk, and the sight of such towns is very beautiful." The cities of the plain, on the other hand, like Seville in Spain, Milan in Italy, or Ghent in Flanders, should be viewed from the top of some tall tower.[298]

Oviedo derived few other images from his short trip to the Low Countries in 1516: a fierce old lion in the emperor's palace in Ghent;[299] the crowd and the orderliness of the market in Antwerp;[300] the "Flemish-style marketplaces" where the citizens might practice archery on feast days, with the most skillful winning cash and other prizes;[301] the dyke and the salt flats of Zeeland near Middelbourg;[302] the wretched dwellings of the Flemish peasants, with thatched roofs, that are worse than the Indian huts in the Antilles;[303] and also pleasanter memories, the well-filled "pandas" (variety stores) of Flanders,[304] the singing and dancing when the peasants and villagers, men and women together, gather at the rustic summer "kermesses,"[305] and the ritual toasts of the drinkers;[306] the merchants' chests, well protected with iron bars;[307] the typical pewter plates that are put under the dishes containing hot food "to prevent them burning the tablecloths," whereas in the Indies they use disks of woven palm;[308] and more

---

298. Ibid., XXXIII, 4: III, 277b. There are also, of course, as one might expect, numerous comparisons between plants of the Indies and plants of Spain. Examples might include: the large *peras vinosas* (IX, 23: PT, I, 297a); the holm-oaks (IX, 14: PT, I, 292b); the sour cucumbers of Castile (IX, 11: PT, I, 290b); the large and fleshy olives of Seville (VIII, 34: PT, I, 275a; IX, 4: PT, I, 280a); the figs, also of Seville (VIII, 33: PT, I, 274a); the vineyards of Toledo (VIII, 41: PT, I, 277a) and the cool, white wine of Castile (XXIV, 3: PT, II, 396a; XXIX, 28: PT, III, 322); the beverage known to the Indians as *mazato*, a sort of gruel, like the Spanish *puches, poleadas,* or *zahinas* (XXV, 9: PT, III, 31); the ash trees that are used for lance shafts in Biscay (XLVI, 17: PT, V, 106a) and the willows lining the rivers in Castile (XLVI, 17: PT, V, 105a).

The animals mentioned include the good "Spanish turkeys" (XLII, 3: PT, IV, 375b); the pigs of Castile that are fattened in wooden cages (XLV, 3: PT, V, 30a); the tasty Spanish partridges (XXVI, 31: PT, III, 130b; XLII, 12: PT, IV, 423b); the beehives (XXXIV, 2: PT, IV, 270b); and the great quantities of sheep in Soria (XLVI, 9: PT, V, 61b; XLVI, 20: PT, V, 115b).

299. Ibid., XII, 13: I, 407a.

300. Ibid., XXXIII, 3: III, 272a. Cf. XLVI, 8: PT, V, 59b.

301. See Pérez de Tudela, "Vida," p. cxxxv.

302. *Sum.*, chap. 81, p. 245; *Hist.*, XXIX, 28: III, 139b.

303. *Sum.*, chap. 10, p. 133; *Hist.*, V, 1: I, 164b.

304. *Qu.*, p. 461; and in the *Historia*, the brothels and their madams (XLII, 12: PT, IV, 421).

305. *Sum.*, chap. 10, p. 133.

306. *Hist.*, XX, 25: II, 79b. On the beer drunk in Flanders and in England, ibid., XXIX, 28: PT, III, 322b.

307. Ibid., XLVI, 8: PT, IV, 59; XLVIII, 6: PT, IV, 231. On other "Flemish chests" sent to the Indies at this time, see J. Torre Revello, "Merchandise Brought to America by the Spaniards, 1534–86," *HAHR*, 23, no. 4 (1943), 776, 781.

308. *Hist.*, VIII, 30: I, 319. On other "German-type cloths," ibid., XX, 34: PT, II, 299b.

generally "those things of Flanders" so much appreciated in the Spice Islands, "like knives, mirrors, scissors, ivory objects, beads, and corals."[309]

But the Italian reminiscences are almost as frequent as the Iberian and considerably more numerous than the Flemish. Although it is sometimes difficult to establish whether they come from Oviedo's reading or from direct and personal impressions, they show an extraordinary and affectionate familiarity with the regions and cities of Italy and their characteristic sights.

Amid the long and jumbled pages of the *Historia* compiled in the Western Indies these glimpses of Italy stand out with the obviousness of "things seen," with the clarity and simplicity of woodcuts. We see flat Milan and Bologna with its Garisenda tower;[310] the Po at Ferrara and the Tiber at Rome, swift and muddy rivers;[311] the menageries of the Italian princes and the leopards of Louis XII's Lombard hunting expeditions;[312] Venice in the midst of its lagoons, like the cities of Mexico and Stockholm,[313] and the nearby "town of Murano, where they make the glass that is more precious than any other";[314] Pozzuoli with its earthquakes and volcanic phenomena ("I myself have seen a

---

309. Ibid., XX, 34: PT, II, 297a. Cf. above, n. 247.

310. "You will see the Garisenda tower in Bologna standing straight before you see my pen turning or departing from the truth" (*Hist.*, XXXI, Proh.: III, 186a). Cf. Dante, *Inferno*, XXXI, 136.

311. *Hist.*, XLI, 3: III, 30a.

312. "I have seen . . . a lot of royal lions in Spain and Italy and Flanders" (ibid., XII, 13: I, 406–07); "I have seen leopards taken hunting by King Louis of France and other princes in Italy" (XII, 14: I, 407a). On the "leopard that Caesar [Charles V] had, and hunted with," XII, 10: I, 403b, and XII, 14: I, 407a. Oviedo himself went hunting, for stags at least: in Tierra Firme he pursued and killed some with dogs and even bagged some with his crossbow (*Sum.*, chap. 17, p. 151).

On the vogue for menageries in the Renaissance, see J. Burckhardt, *La civiltà del Rinascimento* (Florence, 1921), II, 13–16, 306, and on hunting with leopards, ibid., II, 14*n3*. To Burckhardt's citations one might add F. Sacchetti, *Novelle* (Florence, 1860–61), II, 408; on Philip, duke of Burgundy, C. Reade, *The Cloister and the Hearth* (London, 1939), pp. 22 and 65–66 (chaps. 1 and 8); Müntz, *Il Quattrocento*, p. 315*n;* and M. Borsa, op. cit., pp. 167–68, 180, 209.

Borsa himself, op. cit., pp. 124–26, provides some curious details on the leopard hunts in which Louis XII took part in Lombardy, and which he introduced into France; and in particular on the hunt that he held to celebrate his marriage to Anne of Brittany and its somewhat disastrous conclusion. Marco Polo had already reported that the Great Khan kept numerous lions and leopards, "all good for hunting and catching animals" (*I Viaggi*, chap. 78, ed. cit., p. 130). See also L. Messedaglia, "Il pardo da caccia nella poesia, nella storia, nell'arte," *Atti dell'Accademia di Agricoltura, Scienze e Lettere di Verona*, 18 (1939–40), 27–104.

313. Oviedo got his information on Stockholm from the work by Olaus Magnus (*Hist.*, XXXIII, 23: III, 186; see above, n. 134) and on Mexico from Cortés's letters and other sources and reporters. But one is struck by the total absence of any reference, even the most fleeting, to other European cities, however illustrious. This could be taken as indirect confirmation of the fact that Oviedo, remaining true to the first of his historical principles, does not write about anything unless he has seen it with his own eyes. It is therefore highly likely that he saw at least the Spanish and Italian cities that he mentions. In point of fact Constantinople is mentioned at second hand (*Hist.*, XXXII, 4: III, 239b), and the school of Paris is mentioned in passing, together with those of Padua, Bologna, and Salamanca (XXIX, 30: III, 152a). For a parallel passage (without Padua) see II, 9: I, 40a. Salamanca, Alcalá, Paris, and Bologna are named in *Qu.*, p. 317; Paris, Salamanca, and Alcalá in *Qu.*, p. 482; Paris, Salamanca, Alcalá, Osuna, Lérida, Valladolid, Bologna, Louvain, etc., in *Qu.*, p. 498. "Bologna, which is a city in Italy where there is a university and general schools of various sciences, and colleges of scholars," is mentioned a little before Salamanca, in *Qu.*, p. 510 (the editor observes that Oviedo gives some curious information about the Spanish College in Bologna in the unpublished part of the *Quinquagenas*, pt. III, est. 20).

314. *Hist.*, XXXIII, 23: III, 386b. Oviedo compares the lava from a volcano with "molten glass, when it is being heated," ibid., XLII, 5: IV, 75b. Cups and goblets of Venetian glass are also mentioned in the *Libro de la cámara real*, p. 55.

lot of this");[315] Naples with its houses on the seashore "as close to the ships" as those on the Tiber harbor in Rome or the Guadalquivir in Seville or Triana,[316] and with its castles,—Castel Nuovo, Castello di Porta Capuana, the Castello dell'Ovo, and St. Vincent's tower—flaunting five hundred or more banners and standards;[317] and the expanses of excellent vineyards covering the whole of Monte Somma, once known as Vesuvius,[318] and the Greek wine vineyards in Campania and Lombardy, where the vines hang down from the willows and other trees supporting them;[319] and Mongibello (Etna) of which he heard "many people talk" when he was in Sicily,[320] and the stupendous and terrifying Stromboli,[321] and with particular frequency the little island of Vulcano that he visited and studied with great care and curiosity in 1501 ("I saw it and was in it")[322] and which he is always ready to compare with the volcanoes of Central America.

Less distinct, but no less certainly drawn from personal recollection, is the comparison between the harsh mountains of Hispaniola (an island whose mountain configuration would be represented by a bit of paper crumpled in one's fist) and the sierras of Spain, the passes in the Pyrenees, "the Alps as one crosses into Italy, or the German Alps leading down into Lombardy, or the mountains of Abruzzo or Tagliacozzo in the Kingdom of Naples,"[323] all places that Oviedo must have traversed in the days of his youthful adventures and services. In the same reminiscent and allusive spirit he compares the Inca's crimson wool headband to the headwear of the dukes of Milan, the doges of Venice, and the members of the college of cardinals (such as that sent by Paul III to Pietro Bembo), to kings' crowns and popes' tiaras—equal emblems of sovereignty "from the Appenines to the Andes."[324]

We know for a fact that Oviedo visited Virgil's presumed tomb with particular interest: "I was once in Naples," he writes about half a century later, "and on the way from there to Pozzuoli one passes that grotto or cave standing under that mountain on which there is a small place called Basilipo" (Posillipo). And with

---

315. *Hist.*, XXXIII, 53: III, 543a; LXI, 3: IV, 32b; XLII, 5: IV, 68b and 69a (earthquakes at Pozzuoli, "which I once saw almost destroyed by them"). He therefore advises against founding cities in the seismic zones of Nicaragua and Guatemala (XLI, 3: PT, IV, 361–62).

316. Ibid., III, 10: I, 84a.

317. "Cartas del Gran Capitán," in Rodríguez Villa, op. cit., LXX, 2.

318. *Hist.*, XXXIX, 2: IV, 10b.

319. Ibid., VIII, 24: PT, I, 262b. On the famous Greek wines of Mount Somma, highly prized by the Spaniards, see Giannini, op. cit., pp. 65, 94.

320. *Hist.*, XLII, 5: IV, 69b; cf. ibid., XXXIII, 16: III, 339a; XXXVIII, sole chap.: III, 637b.

321. "Estróngol," ibid., I, sole chap.: I, 2a. The same passage also refers to Etna and Vulcano (cf. XXXIII, 5: III, 278n). Oviedo's interest in volcanoes, also evident in his visit to the volcano Masaya in 1529, can perhaps be seen as yet another aspect of his devoted emulation of Pliny.

322. Ibid., XXXVIII, sole chap.: III, 637b. Cf. ibid., XXXIII, 16, 33, 41 and 53: PT, IV, 79, 162, 188 and 255; XLI, 3: PT, IV, 356; XLII, 5: PT, IV, 393, etc.

323. Ibid., V, 8: I, 151b.

324. Ibid., XLVI, 17: PT, V, 102b; XLVII, 9: PT, V, 160a. For Bembo, see above, sec. 8.

great exactitude he describes the fork in the main road leading to Rome and the minor road leading off to the left toward Pozzuoli, and the tavern or hostelry at the fork, "and there they say lay the body or bones of Virgil. It is certainly true that the publican or innkeeper that I found there, in the year 1500, said that the bones of Virgil of Mantua lay buried in that inn, but [and here we feel we can catch on the young Oviedo's face, as he studies his Neapolitan host, that same slightly skeptical smile that he always wore as he nosed about among the Indians and animals and marvels of America] I saw no letters nor other vestige to give credit to what he said."[325]

There can be no doubting the way Oviedo delights in and lingers over these glowing images and happy memories, as if recalling a pilgrimage. But in his remote West Indian island the captain of the fort also enjoyed showing off his perfect military knowledge of Italy, the European gem in Charles's world empire: and not only in writing, in the pages of his histories, but in his conversations and comments on the affairs of the day, chatting perhaps with the officials of the Audiencia and other notables of Santo Domingo, as the setting sun bathed the tropical port with its shimmering and ruddy glow. We really seem to see and hear him, the old *alcaide,* on that day when there arrived "in the Indies . . . news and letters from friends and trustworthy persons" announcing that the king of France and the emperor had signed a treaty handing over the duchy of Milan to the duke of Orleans. The duchy of Milan? No, come now, that's impossible: the expert in Italian geopolitics, a strategist in the Indies on the basis of his soldiering in Italy, gives his opinion, asked or unasked, announcing that the news is neither likely or credible: "And I said publicly that I was certain we would never see it; and if the emperor were to give away the duchy of Milan, you can believe that he would give with it Naples and all the rest, because I know Italy very well [a knowing wink to his listeners] and I saw it myself [the additional argument that reduces them to silence], and I know what I must believe about it" (the matter is not even open to discussion)—and the emperor knows it too and has good advisers, and they will all, like Oviedo, state emphatically, "Milan is the gateway to Italy!"[326]

---

325. *Qu.*, p. 338.

326. Ibid., pp. 144–45; for the snake on the coat of arms of Milan, see p. 146. The strategic importance of Milan as the "gateway to Italy" was apparently recognized by Cardinal Wolsey. On successive developments, see F. Chabod, "Milano o i Paesi Bassi? Le discussioni in Spagna sulla 'alternativa' del 1544," *Rivista Storica Italiana,* 70 (1958), 508–32. Oviedo was however absolutely right: under the terms of the Treaty of Crépy (18 September 1544) the parties agreed, though not necessarily with any intention of keeping the agreement, that if Francis I's second son, the duke of Orleans, married the Archduchess Anna, Charles's niece, he would be given in fief the state of Milan. But the duke promptly died (9 September 1545), Charles heaved a sigh of relief that he had done so "just in time," and everything remained as before. Again in 1626 Don Carlos Coloma, writing to the king of Spain from Florence, began his report with the words: "The state of Milan can very justly be called the heart and center of Your Majesty's monarchy" (O. Turner, "Il rapporto di D. Carlos Coloma dal Ducato di Milano, nel 1626, a Filippo IV di Spagna," *Rivista Storica Italiana,* 64 [1952], 584). And in Fénelon's *Dialogues des morts* (1712) Francis I and the duke of Burgundy learn from the mouth of Charles V himself that if he had surrendered Milan "all Italy would thereby have been forever enslaved" (Lutetia ed., pp. 408–09). Even the merchant in Manzoni's *I promessi sposi,* chap. XVI, knows that Richelieu "thinks

18. THE *HISTORY* ADDRESSED TO THE PEOPLE OF ITALY

It was to Italy, then, to its countryside and castles, however remote by now in time and space, that Oviedo's memory turned fondly back. And it was in Italy, the homeland of those learned men with whom he kept up a regular correspondence, that Oviedo hoped his reports from the Indies would find an audience. Possibly from Italy, and Italy alone, from Italian readers, Oviedo expected to gain the fame that the work deserved, as Oviedo well knew, and indeed still deserves, since he doubted—and with good reason—that the Spaniards of the sixteenth century or succeeding generations would ever recognize its merit.[327]

Although he prides himself on his position as Emperor Charles V's official historian and although he gives as his first reason for writing in Castilian the fact that Castilian is the language most widely known among his potential readers, the language of the actual protagonists of his history,[328] there is a less guarded passage in which Oviedo betrays his secret hope. It is a passage jingling with coins, as rapid as a bookkeeper totting up a row of figures, as revealing as a flash of lightning. In Santo Domingo beef costs two *maravedis* the *arrelde*. But nobody will know what a *maravedí* or an *arrelde* is, "unless the reader were Spanish." And Oviedo hastens to explain for the non-Spanish reader: "And so that this should be understood, I should say that a *dinero* or *jacques* of Aragon, or an Italian *dinero* is one and a half *maravedis,* and a Roman *quatrin* equals one *maravedí* and four Neapolitan *cavaluchos* are worth one *maravedí;* and an *arrelde* is a four-pound weight, and each pound weighs sixteen ounces. And like this I shall be understood by the Italians and many other peoples."[329]

---

up something new every day to spite the crown of Spain. But mainly he has his eye on Milan, because he is astute enough to see that this is where the king's strength lies."

The port of Santo Domingo, whose fortress Oviedo commanded, was likewise described as "the key to the Indies" (Pérez de Tudela, "Vida," p. cxxvi) and Nombre de Dios "the gateway to Peru and the Tierra Firme" ("Vida," p. cxxxviii). The anecdote however confirms that Oviedo's experiences in Italy left him with "a deepseated sense of superiority" ("Vida," p. xxvii).

327. One must pardon the extravagant conjecture of an Italian reader who, four centuries later, would like to offer Oviedo a little of the admiration that he has so long deserved and so long been denied. Early sixteenth-century Italy was even more interested than Spain in the discoveries (cf. A. Gerbi, "Vale un Perù: Le origini di un mito," in *Perù* [Milan, 1961], pp. 101–03; and among the Italians, the humanists, philosophers, and cosmographers were even more interested than the businessmen (cf. Humboldt, *Examen critique,* IV, 68–70, for the years around 1500, citing various curious observers, all from the Veneto). Only Palm, *Monumentos arquitectónicos,* I, 300, mentions Oviedo's "explicit references to his Italian public."

328. *Hist.,* L, 30: IV, 589b. A little earlier he had written with firm but totally fanciful conviction that his *Historia* had been translated into seven different languages, both living and dead, of both Christian West and Muslim East (XXXIII, 54: III, 552b; cf. below, chap. XIX, n. 243).

329. *Hist.,* III, 11: I, 87. "Tuscan" is named by Oviedo as the first of the foreign languages into which his *Historia* has supposedly been translated, and Italy as the first of the countries reached by his "treatises" (XXXIII, 54: III, 552b; L, 30: IV, 590b). In point of fact all cultured Italians of the sixteenth century were quite familiar with Castilian. Certain other Italian measures do however give Oviedo some difficulty. Surprisingly he is unacquainted with the very common *staio* (bushel). He reads that the Emperor Maximinus one day drank an amphora of wine, and then adds, probably copying from a marginal note, "an amphora is a measure of 48 staia"; this information is however immediately followed by the frank but embarrassed avowal: "I do not know what measure this is; I saw this written in Tuscan, and some people tell me that a *staio* equals an *azumbre,* and others say it is bigger" (*Qu.,* p. 255). An *azumbre* is one eighth of an *arroba,* and the old *arroba* used to be eighteen pounds. So an *azumbre* would be two and a quarter pounds.

To some very small extent his hopes were fulfilled. The only fragment of the parts subsequent to the first to be printed in Oviedo's lifetime was his summary of the chapters on the discovery of the Marañon (books XLIV–L), the summary that Oviedo sent Bembo in 1543 (see above, sec. 8). This was printed in Italian (there is even some doubt about the existence of a Spanish version) in Venice in 1556, in Ramusio's *Raccolta*. The following year Oviedo's death interrupted the printing in Valladolid of book XX, the first book of the second part. And for three centuries a fragment—a small but important fragment—of Oviedo's work was known solely in Italian.

19. THE ITALIANS IN THE INDIES

There is, finally, a human aspect that rounds off Oviedo's links with Italy and provides further proof of his long-lasting affection for the country. Oviedo looked askance at the foreigners who wormed their way into the Indies.[330] We know, however, that over many years (1523–1535) he maintained close business ties with the Genoese Franco Leardo ("my good friend") and Battista de Brive, who traded with the New Indies out of Seville,[331] and his pleasure at meeting an Italian seems to override his general aversion for the "foreigner," as he invariably mentions such encounters, often making no secret of his delight. He admiringly recalls the prowess of the Genoese Andrea de la Roca, a powerful and fearless swimmer, who in 1521, near Panama, succeeded—with the help of the Blessed Virgin—in escaping from a ray he had harpooned that dragged him along under water, some fifty fathoms down, for several nautical leagues.[332]

At another point the litany of the miraculous properties of the cacao plant is suddenly broken off and out of the depths of the Nicaraguan forest steps an Italian cook, probably from Apulia. "And I remember that in the place they call Manbacho there was an Italian, a good companion and a friend of mine, called Nicola . . . and he fed me very well, giving me and my men a lot of fish and eggs, and all cooked in this oil [cocoa oil]; and when I asked him where the fat came from he told me it was not fat [one can just see Nicola airily explaining how cunning he has been] but this cocoa oil, that it was excellent for wounds and he

---

330. This point is dealt with elsewhere in this study (see below, chap. XIX, sec. 15); cf. however Pérez de Tudela, "Vida," p. cxlvii*n491*, and the passage in the *Historia* (XLV, 2: IV, 141) in which Oviedo bewails the infiltration of "African and Levantine barbarians of various races and Italians of all parts and provinces of Italy, and Germans and French and English and people of as many other nations again" who pretend to be Spaniards, speak Spanish well, and meanwhile create turmoil and mischief.

331. Oviedo empowers them, for example, "to collect in Santo Domingo" sums due to him from the king (Otte, "Aspiraciones y actividades" p. 46; see also p. 33*n66*). Silvestro de Brive was a partner of Leardo. The Genoese Agostino Vivaldi and Nicola Grimaldi had permission to send factors to the Indies, but in 1520 the permission was rescinded (E. Otte, "Oviedo y los genoveses: El primer registro de Tierra Firme," *RI*, 22, nos. 89–90 [1962], 515–17). Cf. *Hist.*, xxxiii, 53: PT, IV, 254.

332. *Hist.*, VI, 38: PT, I, 196–97; Otte, "Oviedo y los genoveses," p. 516. For further studies by Otte on Genoese in the Indies in the early sixteenth century see his "Empresarios españoles y genoveses en los comienzos del comercio trasatlántico: La avería de 1507," *RI*, 23, nos. 93–94 (1963), 519–30, and "La flota de Diego Colón: Españoles y Genoveses en el comercio trasatlántico de 1509" *RI*, 24, nos. 97–98 (1964), 475–503.

himself had tried it a number of times when he was wounded and whatever the illness or pain or ulcers or swellings or tumors, it took care of everything; which I can well believe, from what I saw on my foot."[333] And in fact—praise be to the cook Nicola!—"cocoa butter" is still today the pharmaceutical basis of innumerable medicinal unguents and salves.

Expert craftsmen, hardworking farmers, and intrepid sailors—there was no lack of Italians in the Indies, nor did they lack recognition on the part of the historian. Out of a huge emerald that Oviedo received from Peru "an Italian jeweler called Roco" cut various "pieces of great perfection and greenness," to the customer's great delight.[334] From "Genoese and Italian and Greek merchants" who had been in Egypt and the East Oviedo learned—in response to his specific requests—that bananas existed in India and were common in Alexandria.[335] And from compatriots of Columbus, "men of his nation," questioned expressly, he gleaned various biographical details about the Admiral.[336]

Oviedo also mentions other examples of tireless diligence, especially on the part of Genoese. At one point he recalls that on the island of Chios in the Aegean archipelago, "the main possession of the Genoese," cotton is one of the greatest riches, while on Hispaniola, the historian laments, nobody can be bothered to grow it.[337] In the West Indies, however, the Genoese make their fortunes with sugar. On the island of San Juan (now Puerto Rico) a Genoese, Thomas de Castellón, built a "sugar mill," and although quarrels and lawsuits broke out among his heirs, whoever eventually got it, "they say that it is quite an inheritance."[338] And another Genoese, Juan Baptista Justinian, renovates an old sugar mill on Hispaniola that has fallen into disrepair after the death of one of its founders and turns it into a going concern again.[339] The second bishop of Santo

---

333. *Hist.*, VIII, 30: I, 320b. Oviedo had hurt his foot, jumping from one rock to another, to avoid a huge wave (ibid., pp. 319–20). Peter Martyr describes the cacao tree and the use of the seeds as money and for making the beverage, but says nothing about the therapeutic value of cocoa butter (*Dec.*, V, 4, pp. 393–94, and VIII, 4, p. 587).

334. *Hist.*, VI, 27: I, 213b.

335. Ibid., VIII, 1: I, 292a.

336. Ibid., II, 2: I, 12a. One of these was Pedro de Umbria, the pilot on the fourth voyage (III, 9: PT, I, 72b; XXI, 7: PT, II, 325b; XXVIII, 1: PT, III, 177b), on whom see also Harrisse, *Christophe Colomb*, p. 105n2.

Also perhaps Italian, despite their Spanish Christian names and the fact that they were related to the governor Diego Gutiérrez, were the brothers Captain Alonso and Lieutenant Diego de Pisa (*Hist.*, XXVIII, 4–5: PT, III, 190–92; XXX, 2: PT, III, 360a); and the paymaster Bernal de Pisa (II, 13: PT, I, 52a); and certainly Balboa's companion, the Sicilian Francesco da Lentini (XXIX, 3: PT, III, 213b); and perhaps also the bloodthirsty magistrate "who was known as Martín de Secilia . . . a great friend of Pizarro and a thoroughgoing rogue" (XLIX, 10: PT, V, 279b).

337. *Hist.*, III, 11: I, 85a. On the commercial activities of the Genoese on Chios, which was apparently also visited by Columbus together with other Savona "weavers", cf. Morison, *Admiral of the Ocean Sea*, I, 30–31; and Columbus's *Journal* for 12 November 1492. On the lasting "Genoeseness" of Chios, whose main families were called Muneses (?), Grimaldos (Grimaldi) and Garribaldos (Garibaldi), see the *Viaje de Turquia* (ca. 1557) attributed to Cristóbal de Villalón (Buenos Aires, 1942), pp. 162–66.

338. *Hist.*, XVI, 16: I, 489a. A certain Jácome de Castellón, whose nationality is not indicated but who was probably Spanish, established a prosperous sugar mill in Santo Domingo (ibid., IV, 8: I, 121b).

339. "Estevan Justinián, of Genoa" (*Hist.*, IV, 8: I, 120b). On these Giustiniani cf. Palm, *Monumentos arquitectónicos*, I, 102–03, and II, 53, 109. Another mill belonged in part to the heirs of "Agostín de Binaldo, of Genoa" (*Hist.*, IV, 8: I, 120a). The existence of twenty-eight sugar "presses" in Hispaniola had been mentioned by Peter Martyr (ca. 1520–22), *De insulis*, p. 364.

Domingo "was Master Alexander Geraldino. He was a Roman and a good prelate and a well-meaning man."[340] In a chapter that was later lost[341] Oviedo also recounted the "astonishing case" of two sailors, one Genoese and the other Venetian, who were shipwrecked on an island and remained there alone for several years, until "God freed them from this hardship."

20. The Venetian Codro

But the most conspicuous portrait of an Italian in the *Historia* is that of the Venetian Codro,[342] the doctor and "great Italian philosopher, who came to these parts in 1515" and discovered the properties of the balsam tree (*goaconax*). Oviedo knew him personally and has the highest praise for him, "a man in truth well versed in the humane letters and ideas, very wise and experienced in the natural sciences, a man who had traveled the greater part of the world and whose desire to see the Indies brought him to die there."[343]

---

340. *Hist.*, III, 10: I, 82b. The learned Geraldino (1455–1524), summoned to Spain by Queen Isabella to educate the *infantas*, was a friend of Columbus and, having died as bishop of Santo Domingo, "lies in that cathedral, the church primatial of America, in a splendid Renaissance sarcophagus" (Lozoya, op. cit., p. 185; cf. pp. 186–87, and Palm, *Monumentos arquitectónicos*, II, 46–47 and fig. 82). He laid the foundation stone of the cathedral of Santo Domingo, had the church decorated in the Florentine style and the Medici arms carved on it, and sang its praises in a Latin poem (M. Picón Salas, *De la conquista a la independencia* [Mexico, 1944], p. 56). He was the author of an *Itinerarium ad regiones sub aequinoctiali plaga constitutas* (1522), published by a great-nephew in Rome, 1631; and apparently sent Leo X, together with other gifts, the first specimens of turkeys—though it is not known how they came to be in the Antilles (Humboldt, *Examen critique*, III, 219–21).

Oviedo also recalls how this "Roman and very devout prelate" succeeded in averting a plague of ants, placing Santo Domingo under the protection of another Roman, the martyr St. Saturninus (*Hist.*, XV, 1: I, 451–52). Oviedo possibly knew the humanist prelate; and he certainly worshiped in the Italianistic cathedral that the bishop built, and was buried there near the altar of St. Lucy. Further details and bibliography on Geraldini can be found in Henríquez Ureña, *La cultura*, pp. 13, 43–44, 46–47; cf. also E. Rodríguez Demorizi, ed., *Relaciones históricas de Santo Domingo* (Ciudad Trujillo, 1942), I, 174–78, 225, 254 (reports by G. González Dávila and L. J. Alcocer); Mons. Belisario Conte Geraldini, *Cristoforo Colombo e il primo vescovo di Santo Domingo, mons. Alessandro Geraldini d'Amelia* (Amelia, 1892); G. Tiraboschi, *Storia della letteratura italiana*, VI, 2, p. 285 (cited by E. W. Palm, "Plateresque and Renaissance Monuments of the Island of Hispaniola," *Journal of the Society of Architectural Historians*, 5 [1946], 12*n*75); B. M. Biermann, "Alessandro Geraldini, Bischof von San Domingo, 1517–25," *Zeitschrift für Missions- und Religionswissenschaft*, 34 (1950), 195–206.

341. *Hist.*, L, 14: IV, 523. Only the summary title has survived.

342. I have not managed to establish whether he has anything more than the name (or sobriquet) in common with the Hellenist Antonio Urceo (1446–1500), who had no children or nephews (C. Malagola, *Della vita e delle opere di Antonio Urceo* [Bologna, 1878], p. 182). The humanist was born in Rubiera, but his family came from Brescia, and was thus from the Veneto; he was of somewhat unpredictable and irritable nature, like the American Codro: he despised the common herd of his contemporaries who "thought they knew everything," and bore his poverty proudly.

The sobriquet Codro seems to have come not from the heroic last king of Athens, but from the good Latin poet spoken of by Virgil (*Eclogues*, VII, 22, 26), or more probably the bad Latin poet mentioned by Juvenal (*Satires*, I, 2). The *Enciclopedia Italiana*, s.v., says that Urceo took the name from Horace's "Codro pauperior." Horace mentions only the Athenian Codrus, "not afraid to die for the fatherland" (*Carmina*, III, 19, 2), but the expression "Codro pauperior" is used by Peter Martyr: "Diego Velázquez, governor of Fernandina, in other words Cuba, who had more possessions than the wealthy Crassus, died more wretched than Codrus and poorer than a pauper" (*Opus Epistolarum*, epist. 806, Madrid, 22 February 1525, in *Raccolta Colombiana*, pt. III, vol. II, p. 72). It remains to be seen whether there is any connection with *Codrus . . . assertio inclitissimi Arturii regis Britanniae*, etc. (London, 1544), of the learned antiquary and chronicler John Leland (1506–1552). Cf. Malagola, op. cit., esp. pp. 144–46; L. Geiger, *Rinascimento e umanesimo in Italia e in Germania* (Milan, 1891), pp. 235–36; E. Raimondi, *Codro e l'umanesimo a Bologna* (Bologna, 1950), pp. 35–37. I have not seen Amadio Ronchini, *Del soprannome di Codro assunto da A. Urceo* (Brera Library, XC, VIII, 86, 3, but not there). In the *Quinquagenas* (pp. 322–23) Oviedo mentions the Codrus who was king of Athens, together with Leonidas, but without referring to his own contemporary with the same name. On Oviedo's Codro, see the note in R. Porras Barrenechea, *Los viajeros italianos en el Perú* (Lima, 1957), pp. 19–20.

343. *Hist.*, X, 3: I, 366b; XI, 4: I, 376a.

Elsewhere the name "Doctor Miçer Codro, a Venetian" crops up among the experts in medicine and "learned gentlemen" who went to the Indies and studied the simples and herbs of the region.[344] His death was in fact a great loss, since he would have been better qualified than anyone to describe animals like the iguana. "Codro, the Italian philosopher, would have been able to describe these matters, as he came to see these things and ended his life in that undertaking and was a very learned man."[345] Unfortunately Codro's comments were limited to the "great lizards of Tierra Firme," in other words the caymans or alligators, and Oviedo was thus unable to appeal to Codro in his argument with Peter Martyr, who claimed that the iguana resembled the Nile crocodile, while Oviedo considered it a snake and on the strength of descriptions given in Saint Isidore and Pliny ridiculed the notion that a small brown animal like the iguana could be related to the vicious creatures of the Nile, so huge and powerful, and yellow in color.[346] After Codro's death an aura of magic and legend quickly grew up around his name. In a land that was still so primitive the man of science was rapidly transformed into a being with supernatural powers, into something between dowser and wizard. It was said that Codro could locate islands and fresh-water springs and safe harbors where the pilot knew of nothing but "rough terrain." It was said of "Miçer Codro, the astrologer . . . who had come to these parts to see the world," that he had warned Vasco Núñez de Balboa that his life would be in great danger when a certain star was in a certain part of the heavens; and that Vasco scorned the prophecy and laughed at Codro and such "fortune-tellers"; but his death rapidly confirmed the doleful accuracy of the Italian's words.[347]

It was also related that Codro, a day or two before his death, "summonsed

---

344. Ibid., VIII, 2: I, 294. Peter Martyr in fact confirms that "a certain Italian scholar called Codro, who in order to investigate the properties of things betook himself to those places, having secured permission (since without it no foreigner can go there), persuaded the Spaniards that that liquid ['a sort of oily liquid, called mahate, obtained from certain trees,'] has the property of balsam" (*Dec.*, VII, 8, p. 542). This, or more probably Oviedo himself, is the source of the passage in Jerome Cardan: "It is said that the Italian doctor Codrus found some real balsam; this Codrus was so zealous and diligent in seeking out new things, that although he was very rich, he died in the southern part of the New World, near the port of Pumida, and the Zorobaros Islands (*De la subtilité* [Paris, 1556], bk. VII, 167ᵛ–168ʳ).

345. *Hist.*, XII, 7: I, 395–96. Oviedo was so interested in the iguana that he tried to send Ramusio a specimen (see above, n. 137) and also refers to it elsewhere as a snake, e.g., ibid., II, 13: I, 50a. Redi, as we said, notes that Oviedo makes no reference to the diuretic stone that according to other naturalists is generated in the brain or stomach of those "huge and loathsome great lizards, or aquatic reptiles called Iguanas" (*Esperienze*, p. 57).

346. See below, Appendix D.

347. Las Casas, *Historia de las Indias*, III, chap. 76 (ed. cit., III, 49). The anecdote is also reported by Washington Irving in his life of Vasco Núñez de Balboa (op. cit., V, 31–34), but without any indication of source; by Quintana, in his life of Balboa, in *Obras*, II, 309, 760; by M. Pagador, "Miçer Codro," in *La Floresta Española Americana*, 2d ed., 3 vols. (Lima, 1892), II, 683–84, with a number of pointless literary variations; and finally by Medina, *El descubrimiento*, pp. 202n60, 242n27. Codro's sad end is also recounted by Irving (op. cit., V, 62–64), using Oviedo's words. Note that Irving—and following in his footsteps the Spanish-American authors—follow Las Casas and always refer to Codro as "the astrologer," "the poor astrologer," "the unfortunate astrologer" (or, with more general sympathy, "the poor vagabond"), while Oviedo honors him with the solemn titles of cosmographer, philosopher, doctor, and scientist.

A posthumous reflection of his fame can perhaps be seen in the mythical Cudragni, mentioned by Thevet (*Cosmographie universelle*, 1575), who is said to have foretold the collapse of the Aztec empire. A great doctor and expert in the properties of herbs, he was a man "endowed with the gift of prophecy" and owned books full of mysterious signs. After leading an extremely simple life he eventually succumbed, at the age of 137(!), in 1523 (B. Keen, *The Aztec Image in Western Thought* [New Brunswick, N.J., 1971], p. 151).

Captain Gerónimo de Valençuela, who had maltreated him; and Codro's words were as follows: Captain, you will be the cause of my death, with the evil treatment you have meted out to me; I call you to judgment that you may stand before God to be judged with me within a year, as my life is forfeit because of your ill-treatment.'" The captain, who was a hidalgo "of few words and little piety," replied jestingly that as for his summons to appear in heaven, he would grant power of attorney to his father and uncle and others among the deceased, to act for him, and they would give Codro the reply he deserved. Codro died a good Catholic. But within a year the captain had joined him in the next world.[348]

The eccentric and mettlesome doctor, who died "in the performance of his work, like Pliny in his, investigating and looking into the secrets of nature throughout the world," was buried in accordance with his wishes on the Panamanian island of Cebaco,[349] at the foot of a tree in whose bark a cross was carved.

One day Oviedo went to visit Codro's simple sepulcher, guided and accompanied by the pilot who had buried Codro and still grieved at his death, "praising him as a good person." And surely the Castilian, as he bent his brow in Christian reverence over his friend's grave, called to mind their learned conversations on the nature of the iguana and the longing they shared to learn the things of the New Indies, and the strange destiny of the Italian. And perhaps, as one recollection gave way to another, some other distant islands and islets then swam up from the depths of his memory, islands treeless but bristling with marble palaces and golden churches; without springs, streams, or brooks,[350] but glittering with fires and incandescent liquids frozen by a puff of air into delicate crystal, and crowded and groaning with presses spreading abroad the wisdom of the ancients — other little islands enclosed and magically surrounded within a motionless lagoon, silent and so, so much smaller than that vast and empty Ocean, whose interminable roar accompanied the final and endless rest of the restless Venetian philosopher.

---

348. *Hist.*, XXXIX, 2: IV, 9–10; XXIX, 33, par. 28: III, 166b.

349. In the Pacific, not far from Panama. The island now belongs to the Republic of Panama. The port of Ponuba, discovered by Codro, is probably the nearby Bahia Honda, into which the River Panago flows.

350. The Cebaco Islands, are, as Codro had divined, "full of good springs and rivers or streams" (*Hist.*, XXXIX, 2: PT, IV, 343b). On the burial place of "the cosmographer Codro, a Venetian," see also XXIX, 13: III, 63a.

❦ XVI ❦

The Claribalte

1. Oviedo's literary debut

I T was to Ferdinand, duke of Calabria, firstborn son of King Frederick of Aragon, that Oviedo dedicated—both in the frontispiece and in the woodcut embellishing it—the first printed work to bear his name, the chivalric romance entitled the *Claribalte*. Unfortunately the *Claribalte* is one of those irritating works that pose more problems, arouse more hopes, and leave the reader with more doubts than their intrinsic merit can possibly justify.

The *Claribalte* was formally repudiated by its author and is in fact a somewhat sorry work. It was written, however, in 1519 and therefore deserves a certain attention as the first work to be published by Oviedo, who was then over forty and had written a fair amount, both as secretary to various eminent personages and on his own account, since he had started collecting material for a history of Spain from 1490 onward before he was out of his teens[1] and later during this first brief stay in America (from June 1514 to October 1515) had taken notes on his experiences in the New World.

There is another point too: the *Claribalte,* composed in the Indies, marks the ideological transition from Oviedo's life as courtier and military adventurer to that as observer, naturalist, and historian of the Americas. His immediately following work is the famous *Summary* of 1526, whose racy style and pictorial novelty of description make it perhaps his masterpiece, and at all events superior in every way to the *Claribalte,* which is so different in viewpoint, argument, and tone as to cast doubt on its being the work of the same author.

2. Authenticity in doubt

At one time this doubt appeared to be corroborated by the fact that the *Claribalte* is signed by Gonzalo Fernández de Oviedo "alias of Sobrepeña, householder of the noble town of Madrid," and not by Gonzalo Fernández de Oviedo

---

1. *Sum.*, "Dedication," pp. 77–78.

"alias de Valdés" as are all the chronicler's other works.[2] There are, however, a number of external and internal indicators that combine to remove this doubt and reinstate the future historian of the Indies as progenitor of the novel.

He himself, after resorting to the conventional fiction and announcing how he came across his story in the mysterious kingdom of Phirolt, had it translated by a Tartar interpreter,[3] and gave it Castilian form, adds that "then, while I was in India and the furthermost western part that is now known, where I went as inspector of the gold foundries . . . I expanded this chronicle without omitting anything of the substance of it, continuing the historical content of it in this style or manner of relating which is not as brief as its original form" (II^r).

This statement too must be taken with a pinch of salt, because in the second part of the novel there are so many geographical toponyms of localities visited by Oviedo in 1516 that is seems extremely likely that he wrote it after his visit to Flanders.[4] And yet one feels a certain reluctance to refuse to take this statement at face value, because if it were totally true it would make the *Claribalte* the first literary work composed in America (1514–1515), predating even that famous *Itinerarium ad regiones sub aequinoctiale plaga constitutas*, written by Alessandro Geraldini, bishop of Santo Domingo, in 1520 (and which was in fact published in Rome only in 1631).[5]

Unfortunately the text of the *Claribalte* reveals no "American" influence, no echo of that first sojourn of Oviedo's in the Indies, with the possible exception of the word *yerbas* as a synonym for poison;[6] there would therefore seem to be no solid basis for the statement by a recent scholar that Oviedo "translated" the

---

2. On this curious detail see Pérez de Tudela, "Vida," p. xiii. J. Uría Riu ("Nuevos datos y consideraciones sobre el linaje asturiano del historiador de las Indias, Gonzalo Fernández de Oviedo," *RI,* 20, nos. 81–82 [1960], 13–28) has ascertained that Oviedo's father was called Miguel de Sobrepeña and in passing (pp. 23–27) contests the "insinuation" of J. M. de la Peña y Cámara that Oviedo was of Jewish descent. De la Peña y Cámara, however, claims to be pro-Jewish and denies that his conjecture is intended to be derogatory in any way.

3. Although the *Claribalte,* which Oviedo repeatedly attributes to the "chronicler Listario" (fol. xiii^r, xlii^r, xliv^v, lvi^r, lxviii^v), is often cited as a translation on the basis of the frontispiece ("newly printed and put into this Castilian language") and the preface ("newly written and come to the notice of the Castilian language"), it is obviously in fact an original work. (The closing line, fol. lxxi^v, calls it "an elegant and new work.") References are to the 1519 edition of the *Claribalte.*

Amador de los Ríos, who still thought it was a translation when he was writing his biographical note on Oviedo (1851, "Vida," pp. lxii, lxv–vi), recognizes it as an original work in his *Literatura española,* VII, 386–87*n2.* Scholars more familiar than I am with the literature of the genre will have no difficulty in locating its sources and derivations. Despite the epigraphs, however, Oviedo certainly looks on it as his own original creation. It will be recalled that another of Oviedo's works, the *Regla de la Vida Espiritual y Secreta Theología* (1548), is always cited as a translation from the Italian, although no one has ever been able to determine with absolute certainty what its original text was (see, however, above, chap. XV, n. 104).

4. Amador de los Ríos too ("Vida," pp. xxix, lxxv) assigns the "translation" of the *Claribalte* to 1517, without giving any reason.

5. Henríquez Ureña, *Literary Currents,* pp. 12, 207, who calls Geraldini "probably the first man to write Latin verse and prose in the Americas."

6. "The emperor thought that he had been given poison" (fol. lxx^v). In the *Historia,* as in Oviedo's other works, *hierva* (grass) always mean the poison which the Indians used to make their arrows more lethal. Enciso also frequently uses the word *hierva* to signify poison and *flechas herboladas,* literally "grassed arrows," to indicate poisoned arrows. Other examples in M. A. Morínigo, *América en el teatro de Lope de Vega* (Buenos Aires, 1946), pp. 128–29.

Claribalte "when, under the influence of the military feats and his early view of the New World his mind was still filled with the chivalric inventions so much in vogue at the time."[7] No, Oviedo's enthusiastic reaction to the sight of America was to express itself shortly afterward in a more fitting and satisfactory manner. The *Claribalte* really seems to be a pure pastime, a not too arduous exercise for someone long familiar with letters, combined (as we saw and shall see) with discreet homage and expressions of goodwill to a prince in disgrace, whose faithful and devoted servant he proclaims himself.

3. THE AUTHOR'S REPUDIATION

Whether Oviedo later regretted this gesture of loyalty to a former master whom Charles V now kept in a gilded cage, or whether the disdainful pride he took in his noble calling as a historian made him deliberately choose to forget "the foolishness" of his chivalric tale, the fact remains that not only did he completely abstain from any further mention of the *Claribalte* (and he was not normally reticent about citing his own works, whether published or unpublished) but, as we know, at the slightest excuse and sometimes with no excuse at all, heaped abuse conjointly on both authors and readers of romances and chivalric epics, either as sources of deceitful lies or as the cause of waste of time that could be better spent.

The most surprising thing about the *Claribalte* is therefore its very existence. It is a straightforward chivalric romance, in the well-known tradition of the Amadis stories, and Oviedo's moralistic aversion not only for that particular genre—however popular it was with the Emperior Charles V and the plebs—but for all books of mere fantasy is notorious and abundantly documented.[8] To resolve this apparent contradiction it has been argued that Oviedo never really got over his taste for chivalric fiction, that this was why he wrote so many books on heraldry, genealogy, and feats of arms, and that even the *History* itself features numerous episodes containing "Amadis and Claribalte in the guise of conquistadors of the Indies."[9] But this excuse does not hold water: the stories of the paladins are "lies," and what Oviedo recounts is, as he so often boasts, the pure and simple truth. If anything, it would be more reasonable to say that the repudiated chivalric romances provide him with a yardstick for the deeds occur-

---

7. G. Otero Muñoz, "Galería de historiadores neogranadinos: Gonzalo Hernández de Oviedo," *Boletín de Historia y Antigüedades,* 21 (1943), 3, who oddly enough considers the *Quinquagenas* composed in Oviedo's old age to be "the first work of fiction composed in the New World."

8. Cf. Amador de los Ríos, "Vida," pp. xxix, lxxxv–lxxxvi; Pérez de Tudela, "Vida," p. cxlv*n480; Hist.,* VI, 8: I, 179a; VI, 49: I, 254; XVIII, Proh.: I, 578–79; XXV, 11: II, 304b; XXXII, 2: III, 223–24; XLVII, 6: IV, 280.

9. Edmundo O'Gorman, in the introduction to his selection from Oviedo, *Sucesos y diálogos de la Nueva España* (Mexico, 1946), p. x, cited by Salas, op. cit., p. 69*n23;* for a contrary view, ibid., p. 83. According to O'Gorman (*Cuatro historiadores de Indias* [Mexico, 1972], p. 50), even Oviedo's *Historia,* so sober and objective, is a book "of marvels, monsters, and portentous adventures"! I have not however seen Ida Rodríguez Prampolini, *Amadises de América: La hazaña de Indias como empresa caballeresca* (Mexico, 1948).

ring before his very eyes or reported directly to his ears, and perhaps that they prompt his boasts of the superiority and excellence of Spanish knights over all others.[10]

In fact his condemnation of that frivolous genre always remains explicit and fundamental. In the *Quinquagenas* of his declining years he repeats that they are wasting their time, these people "who read vanities and things that are made up and invented, departing from the truth and designed to attract persons of little learning, like Amadis, and Orlando, and Guerin Meschino and other suchlike tracts, with which their authors lose their souls, and so do those that heed them."[11] And there are seemingly endless outbursts against those "idle make-believe tracts, full of lies, concerned mainly with amours and lasciviousness and boastfulness, in which a single man slaughters and conquers many; and all the absurdities, however great, that come into the empty minds of those who compose them are solemnly recounted, so that the ignorant, who amuse themselves reading them, are driven raving mad, and they and weak-headed women are impelled into lustful errors."[12] Stanza XLIII opens with the lines "a blessed counsel it would be, / That we should never ever see, / nor even find put up for sale, / This wretched Amadis's tale," which are then expounded at length in the following pages, the knowledge of such books being defined as "gutter science." The stories of Amadis multiply like lies and Greek fables, but people buy them and spend their money on them rather than on "authentic and profitable books of fruitful and holy lessons."[13]

His dislike was therefore based not merely on moral considerations but on "scientific" grounds, too, given the falsehoods put out as history in the works of chivalry; and it was deepened and reinforced by his oft proclaimed intention of relating solely the truth, with neither fable nor fantasy. The point needed to be stressed: in the first half of the sixteenth century the distinction between histories and chronicles on the one hand and chivalric poems on the other was far from clearcut, and there was frequent confusion between the two.[14] Confusion, but not contamination. Schevill—who cites Oviedo several times—reached almost completely negative conclusions when studying this point,[15] finding no evidence

10. Salas, op. cit., pp. 82, 117–18.
11. *Qu.*, p. 191.
12. Ibid., p. 233.
13. Ibid., p. 484. Further outbursts on the subject of the *Libro del baladro del sabio Merlín* which Oviedo read, but which in the end left him "dissatisfied with the reading," because the book proved to be vain and untruthful, and which he therefore advises others not to read, ibid., p. 535; cf. above, chap. II, n. 158.
14. Leonard, op. cit., p. 576. Cf. Gibbon, at the end of the eighteenth century, on the hypotheses regarding accounts of the supposed journeys of fourteenth-century sailors: "The genuine or specious miracles of an Atlantic voyage would have been transcribed and read as eagerly *as a romance of Chivalry* or the legend of a Saint" (op. cit., p. 385, my italics).
15. R. Schevill, "La novela histórica, las crónicas de Indias y los libros de caballerías," *Revista de las Indias*, 59–60 (1944), 173–96.

of influence of the chronicles on the books of chivalry and only the merest traces of influence of the chivalric romances on the chroniclers.[16]

After the outbursts of Oviedo and many of his contemporaries,[17] the attacks, condemnations, and outpourings of combined moral and utilitarian scorn against books of imagination in general spread to various parts of Europe[18] and later, after Cervantes's immortal parody (1605) and the purely literary vogue for hero-icomic poems — an implicit satire of knightly prowess — were to emerge again in the fiery eloquence of Cotton Mather (1710).[19] Scarcely a year after the publication of his *Bonifacius* we come across it once more — turned inside out, so to speak, and in a form that would have pleased Oviedo — in Shaftesbury's sarcastic criticism of travelers' tales, then all the rage and corrupting the public taste: "Barbarian Customs, Savage Manners, Indian wars and Wonders of the Terra Incognita, employ our leisure Hours, and are the chief Materials to furnish out a Library. There are in our present Days, what Books of chivalry were in those of our Forefathers. . . . "[20] And following in his footsteps we find the "illuminato" Genovesi, an admirer of Shaftesbury, after a youthful infatuation ("I ran toward my ruin") having nothing but scorn and derision for the stories of knights errant that "are today laughed at by children."[21]

4. THE WORK'S MEAGER SUCCESS

It comes as no surprise, then, to learn that the extremely mediocre *Claribalte* should have remained almost unknown, except to bibliographers.[22] What is surprising, on the other hand, is that it should have been honored with a second edition during the author's lifetime when, as we know, of all Oviedo's other works only the first part of the *Natural and General History* was reprinted before his death.

No bibliographical listing mentions this second edition of the *Claribalte*, whose existence I learned of myself only from the catalogue of a secondhand bookseller. The title given in the catalogue is practically the same as that of the

---

16. Ibid., pp. 182–83.

17. Ticknor, op. cit., II, 163–65. The translator of the *Coloquio de las damas*, 1548 (see above, chap. XV, n. 167), also wonders "whether it is a sin to read books of profane stories, like the books of Amadís and Don Tristán and like this present dialogue" (ed. cit., fol. vii[r]). And shortly after the middle of the sixteenth century the Sieur de Gouberville, "when it rained, read Amadis de Gaule, in a Norman accent, to his assembled servants" (Emmanuel Le Roy Ladurie, "La verdeur du bocage," in *Le territoire de l'historien* [Paris, 1973], p. 218).

18. Arnoldsson, op. cit., p. 62 and n. 124.

19. Jones, *Strange New World*, p. 205. See also R. Bacchelli, *Non ti chiamerò più padre* (Milan, 1959), pp. 420–21, with reference to the early thirteenth century.

20. Anthony Ashley Cooper, earl of Shaftesbury, *Characteristics of Men, Manners, Opinions, Times* (1711; 6th ed., London, 1737), I, 344.

21. A. Genovesi, *Autobiografia, lettere e altri scritti* (Milan, 1962), pp. 9–10, 239–40, 513, 516–17, 525, etc.

22. The only persons, to my knowledge, that seem to have got beyond the title, counting the pages, and transcribing the colophon, are V. García Calderón, *Vale un Perú* (Paris, 1939), pp. 43–46 (cf. p. 34), and D. Turner, "Oviedo's *Claribalte*: The First American novel," *Romance Notes*, 6, no. 1 (1964), 65–68.

only edition known, the printing of which was completed in Valencia "on 30 May by Juan Viñao, MDXIX"; the colophon of the unknown edition, however, refers to completion of printing "in Seville in the house of Andrés de Burgos, the tenth day of December in the year 1545."[23] This particular printer's name does not figure on any other work of Oviedo's. And the author, who had returned to the Indies on 11 January 1536, only went back to Spain in the latter half of 1546. There is a further point: 1545 was the very year in which Oviedo began to draft his moralistic *Quinquagenas* which, as we have seen, contain particularly frequent outbursts against the "gutter literature" of the books of Amadis, the Orlandos, and Guerin Meschinos.[24] The 1545 edition of the *Claribalte* therefore represents one more of the many enigmas in Oviedo bibliography.

5. PLOT OF THE NOVEL

It is questionable whether the plot of the *Claribalte* merits even the briefest summary. Prince Don Felix quits his court of Albania incognito and betakes himself to London, where he participates in a tournament and wins the affection of the king's daughter, whose love he returns. He gives abundant and conspicuous proof of valor and wisdom, and the marriage is celebrated in secret. But the restless Claribalte (Don Felix) very soon learns that other tournaments are about to begin in Albania, and—in secret once again—he sets off once more for his own country, with the approval of his bride, his parents-in-law, and the "High Priest of Apollo," not however forgetting to send his wife various mementos during his journey, in the form of letters and defeated and captured knights.

In Albania, Don Felix, alias Claribalte, alias "The Knight of the Rose," performs miracles and carries off all the prizes: he reveals himself to his parents and then departs without taking his leave of anyone. In Sicily he meets four sorcerers, ranging in age from two hundred years upward. He is imprisoned and escapes in Messina, kills a giant, and under the assumed name of the "Knight of Fortune" challenges, defeats, and captures the wicked emperor of Constantinople and is proclaimed heir to the empire.

Once again he sets off, however, and while his wife in London is found to be with child and "is accused of betrayal," but victoriously defended by an unknown knight, Don Claribalte is shipwrecked, wanders lost over the oceans, and even-

---

23. The catalogue (The Dolphin Bookshop, Oxford, 1941, Catalogue of Old Spanish Books, no. 119) does not give the number of pages, nor does it give any other details that would enable one to establish whether the volume is a reprint, a new edition, or merely a new frontispiece prefacing an unsold copy of the first edition. It merely states that the book is "extremely rare . . . not mentioned in any bibliography," and asks the relatively modest sum of eight guineas. Even the 1519 edition is rare: it does not feature in the Union Catalogue, except for a photostat copy to be found in the Library of Congress, taken from a copy in the Bibliothèque Nationale de Paris, which obtained it from the Bibliothèque du Roi, which had in turn obtained it from Colbert's library. The copy I used was a photocopy taken from the Library of Congress's photocopy (1947), and subsequently donated to the Biblioteca Nacional de Lima. A facsimile reprint was published by the Real Academia Española in 1956. It was the Seville printer Andrés de Burgos who produced Enciso's *Suma de Geographía* in 1546.

24. *Qu.*, pp. 191, 233, 484, 535, etc. On the date of the beginning of the *Quinquagenas*, ibid., p. 96.

tually turns up dressed as a sailor. He then returns triumphantly to London, where public and solemn nuptials are finally celebrated.

A short military campaign against the king of France, who is also defeated and captured, and certain territorial and dynastic agreements with the emperor of Constantinople close this "first part of the Chronicle of the Knight of Fortune" or "First Book or Part of the History and Chronicle of the Emperor Don Felix" (LXXI^r and LXXI^v). The whole is spiced with the parallel activities of the confidants and followers, minor misunderstandings, carefully composed epistles and in fact all the regulation accouterments of this particular literary genre.

6. THE HERO'S CHARACTER AND OVIEDO'S HUMOR

The protagonist, Claribalte, is virtually indistinguishable from the conventional heroes of the chivalric romance. His rare individual characteristics do however betray some personal signs of the shortcomings Oviedo felt so keenly. While the historian has no skill in languages (see below, chap, IV, sec. 12), Claribalte is a polyglot—"he was very well versed in various languages including French, which he spoke as if he has been raised in Paris" (V^v2, V^v2); "Don Felix was as skilled in that language [English] as in Albanian (although, thinking he would have more need of it, he even sought to learn it better)" (VI^r2); "he was so marvellously fluent in various languages" (XXV^v2)—a realistic trait and typical of those times in which communications and journeys were more frequent than in the mythical Middle Ages of the Breton cycle.

Claribalte resorts to a somewhat unchivalrous strategem to effect his escape: "When he was on land he withdrew as if to take care of the needs that man cannot avoid" (LVII^r2). Like the idealized Almagro of Oviedo the chronicler, Claribalte "the Knight of the Rose never desired or requested treasure, unless to share it with others" (XLII^v2); and sure enough when he wins fifty-three thousand marks in a tournament he shares the money out with scrupulous fairness and painstaking exactitude, revealing the experience of Oviedo the bookkeeper (XLVII^v1).

The discreet and courtly humor that was to enliven the pages of Oviedo's major work also emerges occasionally in the *Claribalte,* relieving the otherwise stifling monotony. The knight dances with the king's daughter and of course dances "extremely well, although in truth if at some time it seemed they lost the tempo they immediately recovered it, since their new-found love at times made their steps exceed the timing of the dance, but not so inharmoniously as to look ungraceful, because they immediately regained the tempo, and indeed those who watched them thought that it was done purposely so that each could show what a good dancer he was" (XXII^v1).

Overcome by the same sort of amorous confusion, the princess finds herself unable to sleep, unbosoms herself to her confidant, and wants to write to the knight, "and many times took up her pen and paper in her hands to write to him, and as many times as she began, the same number of times she erased it and said that her happiness kept her so cheerful that she was quite unable to say anything of what she wished" (XXVIIIʳ1).[25]

After their secret marriage the two meet frequently "so that they might be no longer a betrothed couple but man and wife, or at least act as a married couple," with the result that while the confidants turn a blind eye, the princess "becomes heavy with child" (XXXIᵛ2; note also the allusion on p. XXXIIIʳ2). When she writes to the absent knight she then observes maliciously that the "reverend high priest does not write because his handwriting is like his age" (XXXVIIIʳ⁻ᵛ). And when the two are finally united, on the eve of the official and sumptuous nuptials, "Don Felix approached the Princess his wife that very night . . . the next day Don Felix did not much care to get up early nor yet the princess to wake him and make him get up" . . . (LXIVʳ⁻ᵛ).

7. FREQUENT ANACHRONISMS

An even more frequent cause of amusement than these deliberate and gentle little jibes is the series of fantastic anachronisms the story contains. The action is set in some vaguely pagan era. Venus, Apollo, and Jove are the gods worshiped by the priests, although they themselves are often described as "prelates."[26] In the same way the nuns are really Bacchantes: "Your father has a child that he had by a nun of the order of Bacchus" (XLIXᵛ1). At least once Oviedo indicates precisely that his story" occurred in the time of Laomedon, king of Troy, and some claim even earlier" (LXXᵛ1). However we are soon astonished to discover that in that mythological era there were regular coach services ("Don Felix and Laterio . . . left the kingdom by stagecoach"—Vʳ2) and postal services ("the postmen go faster than horses"—XXXIXʳ1; cf. LXXʳ1); that springals, crossbows, and even "very good artillery" were in use (LVʳ⁻ᵛ); that the king of England's palace window "had Venetian blinds in front of it" (XXIVᵛ1) and the English ladies went to the temple "veiled" (XXVIIIʳ2); that weddings were celebrated with "marvelous fireworks and illuminations" (LXIVʳ2); and even that payments were effected with sixty-day drafts on London! "He sent his drafts for that sum [5,000 marks] to be drawn from the monastery where it had been left and exchanged for London currency, and so it was done and within two months it was paid out in full in the city of London" (LXVIʳ2).

8. LITERARY AND GEOGRAPHICAL ECHOES

The literary and geographical reminiscences, and in particular the latter since the former are very rare, are normally precise and right on target. There can be

---

25. Other lightly humorous or ironic passages: fol. xxiiiʳ, xxviiiᵛ, liiᵛ, etc.

26. "An image of Venus" (fol. xxiiᵛ, xxiiiʳ); "for the venerable Venus or for some holy goddess to whom he was devoted" (fol. lxxᵛ); "High priest of Apollo" (fol. xxxʳ, lxxʳ); Milan, "which was in that time called the city of Jupiter" (fol. lxxᵛ). "Prelates," e.g., on fol. lviiiʳ, lxivᵛ, lxviiiᵛ, lxxʳ⁻ᵛ.

no doubt that they reflect works read and, at least in part, journeys made not very long before. Petrarch is cited in the prologue on the vanity of squabbling over kingdoms (II^v), and we seem to catch an echo of his famous hymn to Italy ("virtue shall take up arms against fury") in the description of a tournament in which "virtue and fury grew in the knights" (XLV^{r}l), just as one seems to catch an echo of Dante in the expression "no grief it seems to me can equal this . . ." (XII^{v}2).

Cristoforo Landino, author of the famous commentary on Dante, is named explicitly in connection with the chronology of Troy, Rome, and Christ (LXX^{v}2). And again on a question of chronology, the comparative antiquity of the Tartars and the Egyptians, Oviedo cites a classical author, the only one we come across in the *Claribalte,* Justin in his abridgment of Pompeius Trogus (II^v).[27]

With regard to geographical notions there is a clear distinction between the first part and the second part of the work: the former has very few precise place names, apart from Europe, England, Albania, France, Italy, and Calais. There is only an indirect reference to Milan ("Urial, son of the duke of Milan"—VII^{v}l); and he even quite simply omits the name of a city in Albania ("a monastery two miles or half a league from the city of . . . where the king resided"—XL^{r}l). There is a passing reference to the Greeks as "the most knowledgeable people in the world today and amongst the bravest" (XVI^{r}2) and to Italy as "the best [land] in the world" and "the most warlike and prosperous existing in the world at that time" (XL^{r}2).[28]

But from the middle of the book onward the toponyms become more frequent and more detailed and lend the narrative a spurious tone of realism and authenticity. Rome is always called Setorma (LXIX^{r}l, LXIX^{v}2), but various places are given their real names, including Milan (LXVIII^{r}l and LXX^{v}2), Venice (with a confused account of its origins—LXX^{r-v}),[29] Sicily ("the triangular island now known as Sicily"—XLIX^{r}l), and an "Arquinian" sea, "alias Ionian, today called the Adriatic" (ibid.), as well as various cities of the deep south of Italy such as Messina ("Lanteria, now called Messina"—LI^{r}2), Brindisi, Naples (LXIX^{r}l, LXIX^{v}2), and an improbable "port of Gallipoli, which is in the empire of Constantinople" (LII^{v}l).

The Italian reminiscences are accompanied by a number of Iberian recollections, or rather references to the maritime periphery of the peninsula, from

27. Certain ancient "emperors," Alexander the Great, Julius Caesar, Octavian, Diocletian, are mentioned in passing (fol. ii^r, lxx^v).

28. Further on, after Savoy and Milan, Claribalte receives the surrender of "all the rest of Italy, without a lance broken" (fol. lxix^r)—an expression that seems to contain an echo of Charles VIII's famous campaign and the well-known sayings to which it gave rise.

29. "Venice. Which was founded not on the water as it is now, but near the sea coast and no less powerful and populous than it is now. But it had another name, and was called La Pola" (Pola in Istria, captured by the Venetians in 1148? fol. lxx^{r-v}).

Narbonne, twenty leagues within the French borders, but taken and burned by the king of Spain (LXIX^{r}2), to Gibraltar, "the gateway and narrows of the great ocean sea, today called the Straits of Gibraltar" (LVII^{r}1), and from the "Western Cape, which is the one that is now called Finisterre in Spain" to that nearby "port that was called La Curna, which is the one today called La Coruña" (LVII^r).[30] Leaving the shores of Europe and following the path of the sun the traveler comes to the Canaries, "the island of dogs," dropping anchor "in the biggest of them, the one we now call Grand Canary" (LVIII^{r}1), and further on "one of the lost islands that are now called the Cape Verdes," reaching port "in the island of Fuego" (LVII^{v}2).

As we have already noted, however, place names of southern England and Flanders, which Oviedo visited in 1516, crop up with particular frequency in this latter part. Leaving aside Dover, which is mentioned at least half a dozen times,[31] the travels of one character or another take us to "the islands of Sorlinga near England" (XLIX^{r}2, LXXII^{r}2);[32] the Isle of Wight (the *ysla duyc* which is off the coast of England"—LVIII^{r}2), which protects the entry to the port of Southampton ("a port that was called 'Tona' that is now called Antona"— LVIII^{r}2, LXII^{r}2, LXIII^{r}2, LXIII^{v}1); the "Cornish" ports, Falmouth and Plymouth (LXII^{r}2) and the Channel ports, "the Dunas" near Dover (LVIII^{r}1) and Gravelines near Calais ("the plains of Gravelines, which is in the County of Flanders and two leagues from Calais"—LVII^{v}2), in addition to Calais itself, of course, mentioned many times,[33] and Boulogne and Guigne ("Guinez") and Hamez (Ham? Armentiéres?) and the illustrious city of Tournai (LXVIII^{r}1). The memories of his journey to Brussels, fresher in his mind that those of his sojourn in America and more in keeping with the chivalric material, leave an indelible impression on the poem of *Claribalte*.

9. DEDICATION TO THE DUKE OF CALABRIA

But the most interesting part of this fatuous and tedious prose poem is, in the last analysis, its dedication. Oviedo offers this, his first publication, "to his most serene lordship Don Fernando de Aragon, duke of Calabria," hoping it will serve him as a pastime and distraction and inspire him with hope and confidence

---

30. When he crossed in 1516 Oviedo landed at Corunna, whence he made a pilgrimage to the house of the Apostle St. James (*Hist.*, XXIX, 11: PT, III, 250a).

31. Fol. xxv^v ("strait of Dobra"), xxvii^r ("town of Dobra"); xxxviii^v, lxiii^{r-v}, lxviii^v ("castle of Dobra").

32. On the basis of Oviedo's account—that they were "driven back from the Flanders channel" and with great difficulty managed to land on an island in the archipelago of "Gorlinga," where they lived wretchedly for eight days, and from which they could see the coast of England and six or seven inhabited places; and from which, if they had not been able to reach the English coast, they would have had to go all the way round Ireland (*Hist.*, XIX, 11: PT, III, 250)—there can be no doubt that "Sorlinga" or "Gorlinga" was one of the Scilly Isles. Enciso's *Suma de Geographía*, which came out in the same year as the *Claribalte* (1519), mentions "the Sorlingas, which are some very dangerous shallows" (ed. cit., fol. xxx^r). The *Historia* (loc. cit.) also mentions Ushant ("Uxente").

33. At the very beginning: "Cales, which at that time was called Narrow Strait" (fol. vi^r); and then on xxxv^r and lxvii^v.

(II^{r-v}). These intentions are expressed so openly that the reader of the *Claribalte*
is often tempted to see the knight's adventure as alluding allegorically to Don
Fernando's many reverses and secretly nurtured ambitions (see above, chap,
XV, sec. 2).

The woodcut embellishing the frontispiece of the *Claribalte* carries the same
message in pictorial terms, showing the captive prince with proud and noble
features, a great sword at his side and a jewel-encrusted collar across his chest,
against a background of turreted and crenellated castles. Oviedo, anxious and
bearded, kneels in front of him, humbly offering him the poem, which then
immediately proceeds to exhort him not to lose faith, since God's goodness
brings great and surprising changes in human fortunes. Indeed, Oviedo assures
him, growing more specific, "He will determine your deeds with prosperity and
put it into the heart of the Catholic King our lord Don Carlos, that he should give
you the liberty that your servants desire" (II^v). We have already seen how vain
the dreams of the duke's restoration were to prove. But Charles V did eventually
at least allow him his personal freedom (4 February 1523),[34] while still keeping
him closely tied to his court. Later, the emperor wrote to him personally to
inform him of the capture of Tunis (25 July 1535),[35] and when Charles married
Isabel of Portugal the duke acted as sponsor for him.[36]

As we know, the book was later scornfully repudiated by its author, and only
in passing (or with studied indifference?) does Oviedo mention in the *History*
that the heir of Bogotá is called Chia, "as in Naples the firstborn or true successor
to the kingdom is called, before he is king, duke of Calabria, and in France
'Dauphin,' and in Castile 'Prince de Asturias de Oviedo.'"[37] But the Gothic
frontispiece of the folio is still resplendent with the great shield bearing the arms
of Aragon, covering the whole page with its pallets and crosses potent—"the
pallets of Aragon and the cross of Calabria" (De Marinis)—of that most famous
of dynasties, that was to die out in obscurity with our own Don Fernando.

The heraldic symbol, borne aloft and offered to the regal scion in exile as a
final act of homage from the knight and Spanish soldier who had faithfully served
the king his father, seems, for a fleeting second, to be meant as a token of
reparation and expiation for the treachery of which the young prince had been a
victim.

But when one scrutinizes it again, after reading the aspirations and hopes of
the dedication, the former vain and the latter frustrated, this martial and dynastic
image assumes a paler and a sadder look, suggesting more a funeral hatchment, a

---

34. On 3 February 1523 the duke arrived in Valladolid, where "His Majesty received and treated him very well"
(Foronda y Aguilera, op. cit., p. 214).

35. Ibid., p. 411.

36. Ibid., p. 270. Cf. *CDIE*, XXXVIII, 419. The duke went to receive the empress on 2 January 1526: ibid.,
pp. 431–32.

37. *Hist.*, XXVI, 29: PT, III, 122–23.

banner struck and fading, the emblem of a dream never to be fulfilled; or else, perhaps, a sort of graphic and solemn symbol of Oviedo's last farewell to his courtly and chivalric youth, his years in Italy and Naples, before turning to the furthest and most savage west, to recount ever more fabulous undertakings and describe the surprising lands of a still virgin world.

❧ XVII ❧

Historical Criteria and Geographical Setting

1. THE RENAISSANCE AND THE NEW WORLD

W H E N the thirty-six-year-old Oviedo stepped ashore in America for the first time and settled his gaze on the new lands his prompt and joyful reaction was an avid thirst for knowledge, just as it had been when, seventeen years earlier, he first greeted the lands, courts, and cities of Italy. Once again he felt the thrill of a sudden and vast expansion of his mental horizons. And just as his time in Italy had served to complete his own education, rounding out his own upbringing with the intellectual riches of humanism, so his immediate response on arriving in the Indies was not so much a feeling of the broadening of the known world—which meant the collapse of the old cosmographic schemes and which might have produced a certain bewilderment—as an awareness of the completion of the world, the reconquest of the terracqueous globe, the perfection of the sphere, with no more unknown regions or incalculable distances.

Humanism, leaping the centuries of the Middle Ages, had reembraced classical antiquity and given modern man a new self-confidence. The sailors and conquistadors, leaping the Atlantic, gave Spain and Europe a new mission and a new heritage, linking the circle of the continents and the oceans into a single vision and endowing the Indies—as yet fragmentary, no more than a blurred suggestive outline like an archipelago emerging in the morning mist—with the august title and fatal destiny of the West.

The concept of empire expanded, casting its aura of majesty over both New and Old World, spiritually united under the same purple mantle and golden scepter. In 1522 Cortés wrote to Charles V that he could assume the title of Emperor of New Spain "rightly and no less deservedly than that of Germany, that by the grace of God your sacred Majesty already possesses."[1]

This period of Oviedo's life is unrecorded, save in his later reminiscences, but

---

1. Cited and discussed by Menéndez Pidal, *La idea imperial*, p. 34.

there can be no doubt that almost from the day he arrived in the Indies the inspector of the gold foundries began to gather data and notes for the work that was to occupy the better part of his life. The quarrel with Las Casas (1518–1519) during his first return visit to Spain—the age-old quarrel between administrator and utopian, bureaucrat and idealist—and the bishop's temporary victory certainly made him more than ever convinced of the need for a realistic exposition of the things of America and the customs of the Indians, the violence of the Spaniards and the richness of the possessions that the monarch risked losing. At the end of 1519 the emperor ordered all senior officials of the Indies to provide Oviedo with an account of their doings, so that he might include it in the *History* that he had begun.[2]

2. THE *SUMMARY* OF 1525

On returning to Darien he continued to observe, note, and write, undeterred by the attempts on his life, the death of his second wife, the guerrilla wars, and the continual denunciations. In 1523 he returned to Spain for the second time, to accuse Pedrarias Dávila, and it was on this occasion that Charles V—whose interest in America had been rekindled with the arrival at Seville of more of Cortés's treasures and his victory over his European adversary at Pavia—asked him for a report on the Indies. Oviedo was now in a position to satisfy the request and on the eve of his departure rapidly wrote out, from memory, the *Sumario de la natural historia de las Indias* (1525), that was printed in Toledo the following year on the emperor's orders.[3]

The *Summary* is therefore not, as is too often said, either a précis of the *History*, of which only a small part had been written, not yet totally independent of the *History*, since it is based on the material in the form of documents and reports already collected by Oviedo and subsequently utilized more fully in the *History*. Many passages from the *Summary* were simply copied out in the corresponding places in the *History*. Some were developed and altered;[4] a few others

---

2. *Hist.*, I, sole chap.: I, 10a. Cf. Amador de los Ríos, "Vida," pp. xxxi–xxxii; Harrisse, *Christophe Colomb*, p. 101; Pérez de Tudela, "Vida," p. cxvi.

3. The relevant texts are transcribed, or cited, by Amador de los Ríos, "Vida," pp. lii, lxxxviii. To them should be added the significant comment in the *Sumario* (chap. 82, p. 254) regarding Mexican silver: "I shall say nothing at all about this province at present; I have, however, set down and written out everything in my *General Historia de las Indias*," which would seem to indicate that the *Historia* was thus already partly written around 1525, or indeed in 1523, when Oviedo sailed from the port of Acla in Darien (cf. Amador de los Ríos, "Vida," p. xii). As previously stated, references to the *Sumario* in the present work relate to the Miranda edition. In the *Sumario* there are frequent other references to the *Historia General* "that I am writing." And the *Sumario* is cited and corrected a number of times in the *Historia*, e.g., III, 10: PT, I, 77b; IX, 4: PT, I, 284; IX, 11: PT, I, 289b; IX, 23: PT, I, 297b; XIV, 7: PT, II, 73b; XV, 3: PT, II, 81a; XXIX, Proh.: PT, III, 205a; and esp. XXIX, 26: PT, III, 315.

4. Oviedo himself states at the beginning of the first part of his *Historia* that the *Sumario* is only "a summary account of part of what is here contained," and that everything that was in the *Sumario* will be found in the three parts of the work, "better and more copiously stated" (I, Proh.: I, 5a), which is not quite exact. The relationship between the two works is even more clearly defined in XXIV, 26: III, 128: when he wrote the *Sumario*, "not in as ordered a manner or as free from other concerns as I would have wished," the *General Historia* was in part already written, in part planned, "although not transcribed properly in the rough drafts and memoranda that I kept on these things," and the *Sumario* was by way of being a "messenger or harbinger of these treatises." The *Sumario* was written from memory,

omitted altogether. The *Summary*—a less ambitious composition than the *History;* undertaken with less "official" considerations in mind (Oviedo was appointed "General Chronicler of the Indies" only in 1532); devoted almost entirely to zoological, botanical, and ethnographical information, with brief excursions into day-to-day administrative matters, the Indians, the gold mines, or the route to the Spice Islands; aimed above all at providing the sovereign with "some relaxation"—is as swift, lively, and one might almost say (given a certain slight tendency toward the sensational) "journalistic" as the *History* is serious, heavy, diffuse, and encyclopedic. Finally while in the *Summary,* dashed off almost without notes in Toledo, the effort of memory is addressed to the Indies, in the *History,* drafted at leisure in Santo Domingo, the author's recollections are often turned back toward the Old World, and there is a greater and more obvious pleasure taken in recalling those memories and displaying other signs of a familiarity with European civilization.

In point of fact there is no real divergence of ideas between the minor and the major work. Some attitudes barely sketched out in the *Summary* are developed as fully as could be wished—and repeated even more than could be wished—in the *History.* Thus one can outline Oviedo's thought without lingering over analysis of its "phases of development" between 1525 and 1535.

3. The *History* of 1535–1549

It is equally impossible, without a painstaking preliminary study yet to be carried out, to fix a precise date for the various books and chapters of the major work, which was written over several decades, continually enriched with the addition of new details, and published in its entirety only in 1851–1855.

The first part, published in 1535, had grown by a third by 1542[5] and was reprinted, possibly without the author's agreement,[6] in 1547. The second part would appear, from various passages, to have been written between 1541 and 1548.[7] The third was dated 1549[8] but probably terminated only some years

---

the *Historia* from copious documentation to hand. The *Sumario*—except on the reverse of the title page, where it is called the "Summary of the natural and *general* history of the Indies"—is always called simply the "Summary of the *natural* history of the Indies." Thus it is inexact to state, as does Harrisse (*Bibliotheca Americana,* pp. 257, 338) that the *Sumario* is "a totally different work" from the *Historia,* and untrue to say, as does Medina (*Biblioteca,* I, 148), that the *Historia* "bears no relation" to the *Sumario.* See below, chap. V, n. 199, and the very sound comments by Salas, op. cit., pp. 14350.

5. *Hist.,* XXXIII, 53: III, 542a.

6. The 1547 edition does not, however, include the additional material that Oviedo had been gathering since the publication of the first edition. See Amador de los Ríos, "Vida," p. lxxiv*n35,* and his note at the end of *Hist.,* XXIII, 57: III, 556.

7. Some dates based on internal evidence: *1541:* XXXIII, 5: III, 537b; *1542:* XXXIII, 53: III, 541a; *1544:* XX, Proh.: II, 5b; *1548:* XXI, Proh.: II, 111b; XXVI, 2: II, 336b; XXXIII, 14: III, 326a; XXXIII, 55: III, 553a (Oviedo was in Spain throughout 1547 and 1548, devoting himself mainly to literary undertakings). In 1543 Oviedo can be found complaining about delays in the publication of the *Historia* due to his administrative duties and his being unable to leave the fort because of the war with France (letter of Cardinal Bembo, cited in Jos, "Centenario del Amazonas," p. 691). Since Oviedo had already expressed a desire to return to Spain in 1542 it seems probable that even then he intended to reprint at least the first part, expanded by a third.

8. *Hist.,* L, 30: IV, 592b.

later.[9] And we have Oviedo's own word for it that the work was not to be considered finished with the fifty books making up the three parts extant. There are various announcements of a fourth part, which Oviedo at first hoped to start in 1549[10] and then to write while the other three parts were being printed,[11] that was to cover the very latest discoveries and conquests, including those in the Spice Islands.[12]

Lastly, all the unpublished sections remained permanently "open" for further additions and corrections (cf. below, chap. XXI, n. 27). The best one can do, therefore, is to set out Oviedo's ideas as a whole, without drawing any distinction (however desirable this would be for a complete analysis) between his differing views on the various native tribes, or between the varying tones that can be detected in the work, going in general from the crude realism of his early years to the more mature and balanced vision of his later life. In other words we shall consider the *History* provisionally as a single unit, pointing out only, where opportune, certain shifts of accent or emphasis between the earliest and the final books.

4. LOFTY NOTION OF HIMSELF AS HIGH PRIEST OF TRUTH

The most important change is indubitably the one to which we have already alluded, in his notion of himself and his mission. Oviedo embarks on his study of the Indies in a spirit of eager curiosity, prompted by predominantly practical interests. But he soon begins to see his function as historian in quite a different and vastly more important light: it becomes a high priesthood of truth, calling for a religious dedication to exactness and fullness of information. The seriousness with which he tackles and pursues his task has been pointed out more than once.[13] If here and there it degenerates into the stubborn pride of a person convinced he is right and exulting in his privileged position, this is one more psychological affinity between Oviedo and those Renaissance Greek and Latin scholars whose devotion to the ancients was matched only by their professorial disdain toward the public their contemporaries.

Truth is Oviedo's supreme deity. But, as frequently with the high priests of any divinity, his worship contains no small measure of complacency at this exclusive position. Let the rabble approach the temple and learn from the "Chief Chronicler" what has been revealed to him over the long years of his initiation. Let him who

9. Amador de los Ríos "Vida," p. xcviii*n30*. In 1548, he wrote of the third part: "I shall not lack the will to finish it, because a large part of it is already written down in draft form" (IV, Proh.: I, 163b). Pérez de Tudela however considers the drafting of the *Historia* to have ended in early 1549 ("Vida," pp. cxxxix–cxl).

10. *Hist.*, L, 30: IV, 592b.

11. Amador de los Ríos, "Vida," p. xcviii*n30; Hist.,* IV, Proh.: I, 163b; XX, Proh.: II, 556b; XXXIII, 57: III, 556b; XLIX, 46: IV, 460a.

12. *Hist.*, VI, 15: I, 202b.

13. With particular emphasis by Carbia, *Crónica oficial,* pp. 27–28, 67–68, 270.

speaks from hearsay hold his tongue, and away with him who has not, like Oviedo, undergone endless tribulations, innumerable trials of mind and body.

The invoking of experience, including personal—indeed, extremely personal and even anecdotal experience—is so continuous that some commentators (Castro, Salas) have spoken of the "autobiographical" nature of the *History*. But perhaps it would be more accurate to refer to its "intimacy," spontaneity, or frankness, also because, despite his rhetorical claims (see below, n. 68), it was not revised, corrected, and polished; and so we come across Oviedo confidingly telling us about the room he slept in and how he would often stand by the window at night "stark naked, because of the heat," offering an easy target to anyone who might have wished to take a potshot at him with an arquebus.[14]

For Oviedo, as we saw when discussing his scorn for works of mere imagination, the investigation and apprehension of the truth possessed a higher moral value than artistic creation; and even the cherished art of painting he subordinated, as handmaiden of history, to the exact description of reality. This homage to truth is repeated time and again as a reminder to himself and the reader, like a sort of refrain to which in the end one no longer attaches much importance, however varied, energetic, and ingenious its variations. "Caesar wants no fables"[15] couples this reverence for the truth with reverence for the sovereign. The reverence for God, who is truth itself, while "the Devil is father of falsehoods,"[16] provides Oviedo's calling as historian with a firm foundation in the Faith. As he writes of the things of the Indies, of contemporary events, which everyone knows and can easily check,[17] Oviedo feels himself to be in the service of God and King,[18] but at the same time he also addresses the ignorant, the unlettered, the profane, the common herd who do not know who Heraclitus and Democritus are;[19] and his aim, as a "good historian," is to be "better understood"[20] by all. He does indeed observe the historical maxims of Diodorus

---

14. *Hist.*, XXIX, 19: PT, III, 292. Cf. Salas, op. cit., pp. 63–64, 107. Otte, on the other hand, as an insatiable seeker-out of biographical data both large and small, bewails the fact that "he tells us very little about his own life in his work" ("Oviedo y los genoveses," p. 516).

15. *Hist.*, X, Proh.: I, 361a. Oviedo also writes for Charles's brother, Don Fernando, later (1556) Emperor Ferdinand I, who expressly asked Oviedo so to do "in his letter" (ibid., XXII, Proh.: PT, II, 340b).

16. Ibid., XVII, Proh.: I, 579a.

17. Ibid., XLVI, 15: PT, V, 84a.

18. "The obedience and desire I have to serve God in this matter, and my king, at whose command I concern myself therewith" (XVIII, Proh.: I, 579a). Oviedo is "Their Majesties' chronicler of these histories of the Indies" (XVII, 26: PT, II, 167b). "I am writing these histories at Caesar's order . . . and if I pass over your works in silence," Oviedo warns the wicked governors, "I shall be failing in my duty . . . as I have God to my witness and you yourselves in this case, I dare to state the truth, without giving thanks to anyone for any bribe. . . . I ask favors from no one, and let no man give me any: for I have done nothing to earn them for what is seen here in favor of any particular person . . . my aim is to give nobody what is not rightly his, and not to deny anybody his just desert . . . for I have no intention of lying on anyone's behalf" (XXVII, 4: II, 476–80). "I am writing the chronicles of these countries at Your Majesties' command, and I find out about what happens here in any way I can" (letter to the sovereigns, 24 March 1537, *CDII*, I. 507).

19. Hist., VI, 8, par. 4: PT, I, 258b; cf. XXI, 4: PT, II, 315–16.

20. Ibid., XXXIII, 32: PT, IV, 157b.

Siculus, without having his learning or his elegance of style, but in compensation he writes at the prince's orders, and not as a mere pastime.[21]

Thus on the one hand he feels himself safe from the pangs of envy and the murmurings of the ignorant; on the other hand all Pizarro's and Almagro's gold would not suffice to make him write down one lie or omit one truth.[22] Lies kill the soul and rob men of their credit, "and this I shall maintain (through Jesus Christ) in such a way, that I shall give up my life sooner than the truth."[23] So that in the end, with a profession of faith that is less emphatic, less arrogant, less self-righteous, but for this very reason perhaps more sincere and credible, Oviedo comes close to Ranke's famous formula assigning the historian the task of simply narrating events "as they actually occurred": "my intention is principally none other than to write what actually happened."[24]

5. OTHER AIMS OF THE HISTORIAN

"Principally," says Oviedo; but onto this principal and strictly scientific aim he grafts others—juridical, moral, forensic, and revelatory. These accessory objectives cling like ivy to the massive trunk of his history. His work, as being true, will be an edifying hymn to the Lord: "Reading must not be for the pleasure of reading or hearing new things, but in order to praise and better know the Creator and cause of all things."[25]

His work will be the due reward to the great men forgotten: "At least, if their labors and merits remained unrewarded and unrequited, let their deeds not lack the remembrance they so richly deserved, and deserve, through any shortcoming of my pen or my sloth, because in truth this is a better satisfaction than any other."[26] There would seem to be an obvious classical derivation (Horace, *Carmina*, IV, ix, line 25, and *Orlando Furioso*, XXXV, 26) for this literary homage to the unsung heroes.

---

21. Ibid., XXXIII, 21: PT, IV, 108.
22. Ibid., XLVII, Proh.: Pt. V, 128b. The other promise he makes is even more picturesque: let no one think "that the rich tombs of this governorship [Cartagena: on the gold-filled tombs, see XXVII, 9: PT, III, 164–64], not the emeralds of the Alcázares, nor the gold of King Atabálipa, will prevent me speaking on these matters as freely as I always do" (XXVII, 13: II, 463b). See also the strongly worded professions of impartiality in XXVIII, 4: PT, III, 186–87; XLIX, Proh.: PT, V, 146b.
23. Ibid., XLVI, Proh.: PT, V, 233b.
24. Ibid., XLVII, 8: IV, 292b. "My aim is nothing more nor less . . . than to relate what actually happened" (XLIX, Proh.: PT, V, 233b). Again, when speaking to Johan Cano about his polemics with Las Casas, Oviedo repeated: "In truth I paid no heed nor respect, when I wrote that, to causing him pleasure or displeasure, but only to saying what happened" (XXXIII, 54: III, 552b). And in reference to Simón de Alcazaba he would relate "not what he thought he was doing or wanted to do, but what he did and what happened to him" (XXII, 1: II, 156a). A formula similar to Ranke's had already been used by Christian Wolff (G. Gusdorf, *L'avènement des sciences humaines au siècle des lumières* [Paris, 1973], p. 390n).
25. *Hist.*, XII, Proh.: I, 388b; cf. XII, Proh.: I, 433a.
26. Ibid., XVI, 7: I, 475a.

It will be a denunciation of the evildoers that have managed to conceal their crimes, "so that by my lines Caesar and his Royal Council may know that which others do not write to them" for fear, out of culpable negligence, complicity in the crimes "and even in some cases because they find it prudent not to take sides between the king and those he has to punish, and those who deserve to be punished," seeing that if one tells the truth one immediately attracts anathema, and few are rewarded for it.[27]

It will bring down infamy on the wrongdoer, however minor, and serve as an example to the waverer.

6. OVIEDO AND THE GALLOWS

To those who might object that it is not worth the trouble of reporting the petty larceny committed by two-bit conquistadors, since "every day numerous criminals are hung and quartered in different parts of the world, without earning a place in chronicles and suchlike histories," Oviedo replies firmly: "In truth, if I had my way I would certainly order that all punishments and major penalties inflicted on evildoers in any town must be written down and recorded; because now such punishments are only remembered by those who are to execute them, *and even they forget them.*"[28]

As a strict servant of the crown Oviedo has great respect for the gallows, which were ritually set up in the middle of the main square of all cities founded by the Spaniards: "The leader first ordered the erection of the gallows, and proclaimed that he had founded the town in the king's name."[29] And Oviedo goes on: "You should know that it was needful, and is needful, that there should be a gallows in the town, and a block, so that evildoers can be punished."[30] The Admiral, Christopher Columbus, was absolutely right to hang some troublemakers, whip others, and stop the rations of still others, because "without obedience there is no rule," especially "in these new lands."[31]

The Indians of Bogotá, too, are "straightforward people" in this respect, Oviedo hastens to assure us, as they are "strict in punishing crimes . . . and thus the body of a hanged man is no rarity, any more than in Spain or other areas of Christendom where there is good justice."[32] And the hangings must be carried out "in broad daylight," so that everyone can watch them with satisfaction.[33]

During his governorship in Darien, he tells us proudly, "I was a feared judge,"

27. *Hist.*, XXXI, 3: III, 195a. Cf. also XXII, 2: II, 160a; XXVIII, 4: II, 480a.
28. Ibid., XXVI, 6: III, 347, my italics.
29. Zavala, *Las instituciones jurídicas,* p. 184.
30. *Qu.,* p. 416.
31. *Hist.*, II, 13: PT, I, 51. Michele de Cuneo too planted "the cross and also the gallows" on the island given to him by the Admiral (cf. above, chap. V, sec. 4).
32. *Hist.*, XXVII, 28: II, 402b.
33. *Qu.,* p. 399.

leaving no crime unpunished,[34] and even—he says somewhat brazenly—"I was very soon hated."[35] It was there that he ordered the hanging of the rebel Indian Captain Gonzalo, despite the tears of the captain's wife who—a latter-day Sophronia—offered to take his place on the scaffold.[36] The woman who falsely accused her husband, on the other hand, he had soundly whipped and her teeth torn out.[37] And finally, of a pilot who refused to fulfil his function and "tendered his resignation" to his captain, Oviedo writes sarcastically that "he was lucky he didn't run into a captain who had him hanged from the yardarm."[38]

Years later, in a letter to the king, he deplores the want of sound justice in Santo Domingo, city and island: "What is owed is never paid and thieves go unpunished."[39] In his old age he admiringly reports the savage punishments meted out to thieves by the Tierra Firme Indians[40] and castigates as worse than a thief the person who fails to pay back the money lent him.[41] The bankrupt, are biggest thief of all, is worthy of the scaffold,[42] and the beggars and vagabonds, who should be chased out of the kingdom[43] or even sent to the galleys,[44] are little better than thieves.

But he has no sympathy for spies, whether paid police informers or voluntary spies conniving with corrupt judges,[45] nor does he approve of summary judgments, without due process (like those of certain captains, whose secretaries are reluctant "to waste ink where it will not bring in any money," and who are punished by heaven with equally summary deaths).[46] The *Quinquagenas* recount an exceptionally severe punishment inflicted by the Great Captain after a mutiny in Messina (Oviedo does not say whether he was present himself, and does not quote his source).[47] But he too—in just reprisal?—was robbed by his servants.[48]

There is another revealing sign of his unbending judgment in matters of punishment in his account of the doings of the hidalgo Álvar Núñez Cabeza de Vaca. I would not say that he actually "became friends"[49] with the "noble

---

34. *Hist.*, XXIX, 15: II, 72b.
35. Ibid., XXIX, 14: III, 71b.
36. Ibid., VI, 41: I, 232.
37. Ibid., XXIX, 19: III, 88a; and for this and two other occasions on which he abused or exceeded his powers he was condemned to pay a fine (ibid., pp. 87–88) and got into further legal trouble (ibid., p. 95b); Medina, *Descubrimiento*, I, 293.
38. *Hist.*, XVII, 10: I, 509b. On the just punishment for anyone who mutinies against his captain, whether Aragonese or Scottish or of any other nationality, cf. XXIV, 10: II, 248a.
39. Letter to the sovereigns, 2 May 1537, *CDII*, I, 506.
40. *Qu.*, p. 22.
41. Ibid., pp. 31–32.
42. Ibid., p. 73.
43. Ibid., pp. 389–90.
44. Ibid., p. 221.
45. Ibid., p. 258.
46. *Hist.*, XXIV, 9: II, 239b.
47. *Qu.*, pp. 350–51.
48. Ibid., p. 540.
49. Pérez de Tudela, "Vida," p. cxxxix–cxl.

gentlemen," but he certainly treats him with great respect and shows genuine compassion at his numerous reverses: "It is a great shame to hear it." Now Cabeza de Vaca, like Oviedo, was "unpopular" both with his own people and with the natives. Why? Oviedo supplies a detailed list of his "acts of justice." Two Indian women, "collaborators" with the Spaniards, are captured by their angry fellow tribesmen. Cabeza sends for the revenging kidnapers. The tribal chief has an eye ailment and sends the governor his two sons and other youths. Cabeza takes some of them and quite simply hands them over to the savage "Carib Indians, our friends, so that they could kill them and eat them, which they did." The others he orders to be publicly hanged. Some of these ask to be killed on the spot "so that the walls and floor might be painted and dyed with their blood, and they might be witnesses of their death, and all might know how the Christians treated their friends." A scuffle erupts, an Indian hangman is wounded, and Vaca immediately has all the prisoners massacred with arrows and daggers.

Another friendly Indian chief, Yacaré, is sent to explore the interior and comes back because he feels unwell. Cabeza de Vaca is "annoyed" and orders him to be hanged, which prompts a revolt that is bloodily suppressed. Later Vaca hears about certain presumed "Indian women archers," the same old phantom Amazons, and puts the whole region to fire and the sword, razes a village of nine hundred houses and sends the survivors off into slavery.

In the end Cabeza de Vaca is deposed and imprisoned; he escapes his jailers with a trick that is unworthy of a gentleman, but is recaptured, brought to judgment before the Council of the Indies and dismissed. Oviedo, visiting Spain in 1547, also heard Cabeza's and his friends' version of the events and acknowledges, or rather hints, that his accusers included certain persons who were notorious rivals and enemies of Cabeza; but "in the end, with regard to what eventually happened, things ended up as described."[50]

7. ACCESSORY AIMS OF THE *HISTORY*

But even this does not exhaust the tasks of the historian-cum-judge and on occasion cum-executioner. His *History* is to be the "mother of life," as Cicero put it.[51] It will serve as a guide to the ill-advised seekers after buried treasure[52] and a warning to unwary pearl buyers.[53] It will be helpful in providing notification for the relatives of Christians killed in the Indies—even if "low and

---

50. *Hist.*, XXIII, 16: PT, II, 383–86.
51. Ibid., XLIV, Proh.: IV, 126a.
52. "Here you have, gentle reader, the specific indications which will allow you, if you decide to go and seek this treasure, to find it, although I doubt that there will be any man so lacking in judgment as to be so greedy, after he has heard what I have to say" (ibid., XXV, 6: II, 289b).
53. Oviedo himself was cheated, and the chronicler is therefore "deserving of thanks" if he teaches how to distinguish good pearls from bad ones (ibid., XIX, 11: I, 610). Pearls, which are not born from the dew, as the ancients

plebeian" persons—for the purposes of allowing heirs to claim their due and widows to seek consolation by returning to the altar.[54] It will above all bring retribution and revenge for the mischief worked by his personal enemies. Diego del Corral, who insults Oviedo, fails to pay the dues he owes him, and turns as white as a ghost at Oviedo's rebukes, is portrayed with savage and implacable gusto as a coward, a lecher, and a master of hired ruffians: he left a relative of the valiant cacique Corobarí with child, keeps two local mistresses (although he has a wife in Spain), and in flight leaves his Christian fellow-soldiers to die in atrocious circumstances, while he provides transport, in comfortable hammocks, for his "Indian women when they got tired."[55]

8. ITS UNIVERSALITY

At the same time the work will be all-embracing. This determination to include everything in his account, to make it a "mirror of the New World," as if there were a danger of America disappearing the moment his description was completed, it not the only medievalistic trait of Oviedo's approach to history, but it is certainly the most general and formal. His *History* is not just the story of what happened, but simultaneously chronicle and cosmography, botany and ethnography, an animated bestiary and a book of prodigies. *Nihil Americani a me alienum puto.*

And in his unswerving homage to the truth Oviedo in fact rejects nothing, however obscene and repulsive. Anticipating Pierre Bayle's famous defense of his *Dictionary* against the charge of obscenity at the end of the following century,[56] Oviedo reports more than one Indian "abomination," "so as to make more manifest the fault for which God punishes these Indians, forgotten by His mercy so many centuries ago,"[57] in other words using a moralistic excuse. On

---

insisted, but from oysters (XIX, 2: PT, II, 194a; XIX, 8: PT, II, 204; Peter Martyr, *Dec.*, III, 2, pp. 218–19, had confessed his ignorance on many problems relating to pearls), must be bought fresh, because as they grow old they lose their luster and value: they are therefore not a good investment. Great care must also be taken to see that they are not mixed up with fragments of mother-of-pearl, and have no internal or hidden defects. They should also be washed from time to time and "treated very well" (XIX, 9–11: PT, II, 205–07; cf. above, chap. XIV, n. 65).

54. *Hist.*, XXIV, 12: II, 258b, making it clear that he does so "because these Indies of ours are a long way from our Spain," and with the curious justificatory codicil, "because in truth my aim is not to give anyone a bad reputation, but to do good to whomsoever I can." Elsewhere too Oviedo says that he gives the names of those who have died so that they will no longer be expected back in Spain, and that prayers might be said for their souls (XLI, 3: IV, 27b; L, 29:IV, 586a).

55. Ibid., XXIX, 16–18: PT, III, 271–80. But perhaps what really irks Oviedo most of all (cf. end of passage cited) is the fact that he was later fined twenty gold pesos for imprisoning Corral and deporting him to Spain.

56. Bayle feels himself justified in repeating indecent material from other authors, provided he does not approve it himself, and in fact "in several encounters" he takes it upon himself to fulminate against them and condemn the general laxity ("Eclaircissement sur les obscenitez," in his *Dictionnaire historique et critique* [Basel, 1741], IV, 637–54).

57. *Hist.*, XVII, 17: I, 533b. This particular instance concerned two obscene statuettes, which Oviedo describes very graphically. In 1514 he broke up another obscene gold statue with his own hands "on an anvil with a hammer, in the royal foundry in Darien" (V, 3: I, 221b; XXVI, 10: II, 355b).

Erotic artifices are described in XX, 35: III, 105b. But rather too often the eagle-eyed Oviedo is gratified to note that the native women's *cache-sexe* are too short and not properly tied, "so that as they move about or with a gust of wind,

other occasions certain repellent details gain entry into Oviedo's work on a theological passport, as examples and attestations of God's omnipotence in nature: "And although some of these things are loathsome or not so clean to hear as others, they are no less worthy of note, so that we may be aware of the differences and operations of nature through the dispensation of the Master thereof."[58]

The items he does suppress, sometimes, are those that tend to reflect discredit on himself,[59] and elsewhere, on occasion, instances of moral turpitude; he does, however, find a place for certain particulars that may be ethically instructive but are still trivial and indiscreet. Of the venerable treasurer Miguel de Pasamonte, praised as a cultured, knowledgeable, and virtuous man, he also reports— although it is difficult to see why, if not as an ambiguous way of extolling his continence—"and it is some people's opinion that he never knew a woman carnally. . . ."[60] Not even the great Cortés escapes his censoring scissors, Cortés, who, in a certain connection, "says other things that relate more to private passions than to honest history or to the pleasure of whoever might read them, and for this reason I am omitting them."[61] In the same way Oviedo abbreviates the account of the profanation of the body of Fra Dionisio, martyred by the Indians, leaving out "so many vile acts and obscenities . . . that are not for writing."[62]

In the pursuit of truth Oviedo recognizes no forbidden areas, nor does he spare himself any toil or danger. Remembering, particularly in his later years, that his history is written above all in praise of God and is broadcast "to the whole world" in accordance with the merciful will of the emperor and that, in short, it gives great pleasure to men "of whatever state they be, to hear new things which are— as these are—true,"[63] and that moreover the things he describes are so "great and strange" that "it is sufficient to relate them straightforwardly and without metaphors," so "singular and new and in keeping with the truth" that there is no need for "embellishment, or the accompaniment of fables,"[64] Oviedo does not hesitate to remind the reader, just in case he had forgotten, of the effort and risks

all is revealed; however this is the least of their cares" (XXIV, 3: II, 221b); or that this veil covers and uncovers "at the whim of the wind" (XXVII, 7: II, 446b; XXVI, 10: II, 356a, "however little wind there is"). Cf. also III, 5: I, 68b. He does however apologize for being unable to relate all the horrendous vices of the *indios*, as "it would not be possible to listen to them without much revulsion and shame, nor could I write them down, so numerous and disgusting are they" (III, 6: I, 72b).

58. Ibid., XXIX, 28: III, 139 .

59. For example the story of Vaca de Castro's rigorous inspection of the fortress under Oviedo's command; the story is deleted from both the text and the summary of chap. 3 of bk. XLVIII (PT, V, 222a). On this inspection (January 1541), see *CDII*, XI, 363–412, with numerous curious details of biographical interest. His hatred of the cruel, unjust, proud, and eventually incarcerated Vaca de Castro bursts out again in *Hist.*, XLIX, 6: PT, V. 246–49.

60. *Hist.*, III, 11: PT, I, 85a. Pasamonte's chasteness is also mentioned by Las Casas.

61. Ibid., XXXIII, 32; III, 432a. Cf. below, chap. XIX, sec. 6.

62. *Hist.*, XIX, 3: I, 596a.

63. Ibid., XXIX, 28: III, 141b.

64. Ibid., XXI, Proh.: III, 186a; cf. also XXXIII, Proh.: III, 257a.

and sufferings that went into the making of the monumental *History* offered to him.

There is absolutely no vainglory in all this, first of all because Oviedo can be modest when he needs to be and recognizes both what a paltry figure one solitary individual turns out to be when confronted with the enormous task he has set himself and the extent of his personal shortcomings from the literary and scientific point of view;[65] secondly because the hard life of the European in the Indies is one of his favorite themes and applies just as much to the historian as it does to the adventurers; and finally because he uses the concept to give greater dramatic relief to the basic canon, that one cannot recount the history of the Indies while remaining comfortably ensconced in Spain.

9. IMPORTANCE OF PRESENCE IN THE INDIES

Others may perhaps be able to write better, sitting back and relaxing in winter "hothouses" and summer gardens, "but a knowledge of the things of these parts can only be acquired with much thirst, much hunger and weariness, in war with the enemy and in war and peace with the elements, battling against many needs and dangers, wounded without surgeon, sick without doctor or medicine, hungering without having anything to eat, thirsting without finding water, tired without being able to take rest, wanting clothing and footwear, and he who could well ride going on foot, crossing numerous large rivers without being able to swim." And for many of those suffering these various trials it would be easy "to be brawling with the Turks . . . and dancing with the ladies . . . since although it is need that brings them to this remote place to live among savages, that same need makes them more worthy than others who were born more wealthy and live with their feet up, knowing no more than their neighbors, taking their ease and claiming to understand, without leaving their armchairs, what cannot be learned

---

65. "I know that I lack the memory and art that would be needed for the perfect completion of my work, which is not one of the smallest but one of the loftiest and most copious ever written by man, since the time of Adam, on such matters . . . in the matter of quality and quantity so abundant in itself that it exceeds the span of human life." Even Methuselah's life would have been too short "to be able to comprehend all the things to be said and to be known about these Indies" (XXII, Proh.: II, 154), and "however well these things are written, they will always be understood better by those who write after me, because time and experience will furnish other details" (VIII, 27: I, 312b). In the view of Schevill, "La novela," p. 181, "Fernández de Oviedo, reflecting on his *Historia General y Natural de las Indias,* concludes that God alone understands people, that he, as a historian, could very well have been mistaken, that between the reports of one person and another person ambiguities and falsehoods were bound to occur, and that he will continue to set right what has been said, whenever he can manage to distinguish between truth and falsehood": an unwarranted generalization, that makes Oviedo almost a Pyrrhonist.

In cosmographical matters he gives way in all humility to those who know more about the subject than he does (e.g., XXI, 9: II, 146a). And he does the same for astronomy ("in this celestial science I, sir, know much less than others, and as a man lacking such study . . ." etc., XXXIII, 53: III, 543b). Like Peter Martyr before him, he gladly stresses his own weakness as a writer (I, Proh.: I, 5b; XVII, Proh.: I, 579a; XXIX, 25: III, 142b), to some extent out of coyness, and to some degree to divert attention from the plainness of the form to the abundantly rich and wholly true material. "I confess," he writes in the closing lines of the *Historia,* "that my pen is not elegant enough to give me any deserved claim to good writing" (L, 30: PT, V, 416b). For a harsh verdict on his ignorance and bad syntax, etc., see Peña y Cámara, op. cit., p. 651*n86*.

without working, scoffing at those who being valiant people and neither usurers nor footpads, pass their days in these wanderings."[66]

The vehemence of this passage, with its unaccustomed outburst of abuse and sarcasm at the expense of the rich, the nobles, loansharks and brigands all lumped together, betrays its personal origin. Oviedo in fact boasts at the beginning of his work that it is not, like Pliny's, extracted "from two million volumes read," but "from two million labors and deprivations and dangers in the twenty-two years and more that I have been observing and experiencing these things in person."[67] And no little labor was involved in the final task of setting all those things down on paper, "all in my own hand . . . more than three thousand sheets of paper . . . that I have erased and amended and rewritten once, twice, and even more times."[68]

If in fact he were to set about relating everything he went through to learn what he recounts, his story would be twice as long; but he asks no further reward for his labors than to be able to narrate them just as, with God's help, he was able to bear them.[69]

At the age of sixty-nine, ignoring his gray hairs, Oviedo can still write with indomitable tenacity: "Not a day passes without my spending a few hours on this occupation, working with all my might and writing in my own hand," in the hope—that was to remain unfulfilled—of seeing all four parts of the work published.[70] In response to anyone who might find his information inadequate he begs that allowance be made for the toil "involved in investigating these things in new areas, living amongst savages, as we find ourselves here, scraping a living, and every day running into mortal dangers,"[71] without any of those conveniences and facilities, he repeats, "enjoyed by other authors writing in lands peopled by civilized and prudent peoples." In this combined excuse and boast one can glimpse an awareness of the novelty of his work, a realization that he is

---

66. *Hist.*, XVIII, Proh.: I, 579b. One is inevitably reminded of Hotspur's magnificent outburst, as he comes back exhausted from the battlefield and rails against a "certain lord, neat, trimly dressed, fresh as a bridegroom . . . perfumed like a milliner," who smiles and sniffs perfumes so as not to smell the pestilential odor of the corpses, makes free with his advice, and deplores the vulgarity of gunpowder and firearms (Shakespeare, Henry IV, Part 1, act I, sc. 3).

67. *Hist.*, I, Proh.: I, 6a. For a further criticism of the "great man . . . Pliny, to whom I am very partial," but who erred on various points, because "the ancient writers were unacquainted with the greater part of the world," see XXI, 5: II, 127.

68. Ibid., XXXII, 3: III, 229a.

69. Ibid, XII, 8: I, 398b.

70. Ibid., VI, Proh.: I, 162. And again, almost overwhelmed by the vastness of the material, he recalls his age and ailments and personal troubles, which will not however, prevent him—with God's help—"persisting, although weary, in the continuation of these histories" until death closes his eyes, those eyes which are already "so worn out in this undertaking, that only with difficulty can I now read certain authors that I quote for my purposes in certain places" (XXII, Proh.: II, 152b).

71. Ibid., VIII, Proh.: I, 288. Similar sentiments were expressed by a poor monk of Wessobrunn, who wrote pathetically of his labors, in the dark ages, when copying an ancient manuscript meant rendering civilization a service in no way inferior to that of a reporter on a new world: "The book which you now see was written in the outer seats of cloister. While I wrote I froze: and what I could not write by the beams of day I finished by candle-light" (quoted by A. Quiller-Couch, *On the Art of Reading* [New York and London, 1920], p. 235).

writing not as an academic historian but rather as a sort of special reporter or war correspondent, even willing to risk his life to get the latest on-the-spot news: a highly modern mission, often viewed today with a sort of feverish awe, but whose necessity, fascination, and demands for self-sacrifice were already familiar to Oviedo.

10. SATISFACTION WITH THE RESULT

With the result, as we have seen, Oviedo is quite satisfied. His offering to the emperor is the first true and faithful image of the richest and vastest of his dominions. And to the whole world—"it is only right that such records should be manifest in all the republics of the world"[72]—he offers, for the greater glory of Spain, a glowing description of Spain's overseas states, in a work of "very pleasant reading," not because of the style, but because it contains "so many secrets of nature"[73] and because the study of the things of the world and of nature gives "great delight and enjoyment to the intellectual spirit."

It is particularly notable how insistently Oviedo stresses the auspicious novelty of the information he has assembled, in perfect harmony with his concept of the New World rounding off the Old (see below, chap. XVIII, sec. 3). His intention is to recount new things, not to repeat the old familiar things: "My intention is not to relate the things . . . that have been written by other authors, but the notable things that come to my attention in these Indies of ours."[74] His scrupulous concern to relate only what he has seen with his own eyes thus fuses and merges with his anxiety to narrate and describe new and extraordinary things. And he will not even talk about the "new" things that are becoming commonplace and more familiar every day. "I shall not bother to say more than a few words about monkeys, because their arrival in Spain is a daily occurrence."[75] And on some other occasions he reluctantly suspends judgment because "as everything is new over here we do not know this by experience, only by reports from Indians."[76]

11. THINGS SEEN AND THINGS KNOWN

In one sense this pride in the wealth of material can be paralleled with the first conquistadors' enthusiasm for the metallic riches they plundered so freely. It

---

72. *Hist.*, I, Proh.: I, 5.

73. Ibid., Cf. also XXI, 2: II, 119a and the dedicatory letter to Cardinal García de Loaysa, president of the Council of the Indies. This delight in recounting the truth can be linked to his moralistic disapproval of those who write fables and adventures and made-up stories and tales, all of which he brands as "lies," condemning their perusal as a sinful activity. See above, chap, XVI, sec. 3, and *Qu.*, p. 82.

74. *Hist.*, V, 31: PT, I, 189b; cf. IX, 21: PT, I, 295b and passim.

75. Ibid., XII, 26: PT, II, 50a; cf. *Sum.*, chap. 25, p. 161.

76. *Hist.*, IX, 16: PT, I, 293b. When he comes to describe the strange houses with retractable stairways on the island of Guacea, in the Philippines, he produces a drawing, "these being a novel sort of building" (XX, 23: PT, II, 272–73). Prescott chides him for this "solicitude to tell what was new" (*History of the Conquest of Peru*, bk. IV, chap. 9, in *Mexico and Peru*, p. 1161).

may also remind us of the way successive generations of critics kept reiterating their futile laments at the fact that the glowing and glorious "nature of America" had not found its modeler and bard, either epic or lyric. In reality, however, it is closely bound up with the basic principle of Oviedo's historical method: the preeminence of the thing seen over the thing learned. It is not the literary form that interests Oviedo, but the meaty substance of items of information and secrets of nature.[77] He rarely transcribes documents in their original text,[78] and his endeavours are directed not toward the interpretation and elaboration of documentary facts, but toward the accumulation of the greatest possible quantity of directly apprehended facts. Information given by the most reliable witness is always considered less certain than something Oviedo has seen with his own eyes and heard with his own ears.[79]

He quotes Saint Gregory's maxim to back him up in this choice between skepticism and credulity: "He who speaks the thing he heard teaches with less authority than he who says what he saw."[80] And his contemporary and friend Sepúlveda also states his intention of recounting the deeds of Charles V "not only as a writer, but also as a witness," even if it means facing arduous toil and mortal dangers on the battlefield.[81]

Even when he does repeat information given him by other people, Oviedo never forgets his basic maxim: anything he has not himself seen is subject to confirmation, entailing a laborious investigation and repeated checks. I must leave it to scholars much more familiar than I am with the reports and chronicles used by Oviedo to assess the use and abuse that he made of them. But there can be no doubt that "source criticism" has a convinced and tenacious practitioner in Oviedo. It is his standard procedure to cite and evaluate every source he has

77. On one occasion he solemnly states that while all other writers found that the subject of their work, their material, was inferior to their narrative capacity ("no writer could find as much to say as he could relate") for him the opposite was true: "In the case of my history it is my tongue and ability that fall short."

But not exactly because of any implicit inability. The most famous poets, the most eloquent orators and "a thousand Ciceros" would not suffice to exhaust "the copiously abundant and almost infinite material of these marvels and riches to be found here and that I have in my hands to write about" (*Hist.*, VI, 8: I, 181a). One can almost hear the lucky author's greed and delight in those last few words. Here too Oviedo deviates sharply from Pliny who—even if only as a literary device—pours scorn on his material as sterile, sordid, neither surprising nor amusing, and endeavors to improve it with refinements of form (Praefatio, 9–11, ed. cit., I, 2–3).

78. Harrisse, *Christophe Colomb*, p. 97, "points out how rarely he [Oviedo] refers to original documents" (Winsor op. cit., II, 209*n*4). This failing, and the uncritical approach he adopts toward the reports and letters he receives, earn him a rebuke from Salas, op. cit., p. 103*n*. But, as we shall see more clearly in the following pages, this reproach too needs to be qualified.

79. But cf. below, chap., XXI, sec. 4. The extraordinary novelty of the phenomena of the Indies is a psychological justification of this empirical priority of the eye over the ear; Columbus, the first person to lay eyes on these wonders, was also the first to doubt that he would be believed: "If he who saw it himself was so amazed, how much more so will those who hear about it be, and nobody will be able to believe it without seeing it for themselves" (*Journal*, 25 November 1492). Oviedo professes to believe only in his own senses and observations—"the eyes are the chief factor in learning about these things" (VIII, 30: I, 316a)—an attitude reflected in the greater importance he attaches to content rather than to literary form.

80. *Hist.*, II, 7: PT, I, 29b.

81. Ca. 1536, in Morel-Fatio, *Historiographie*, pp. 46–47. But subsequently he had the good sense to modify this bold intention.

drawn on.[82] He exercises his criticism, for example, on a letter from "Fedreman" (Nicholas Federmann),[83] and then compares it with another by Jiménez de Quesada.[84] He is unsatisfied with the printed report of Cabeza de Vaca's expedition, for one thing because it talks about "little sacks of silver," though this must be "a printer's error," because it must have been a question of "little sacks of pearls," and for another because it is too brief and ambiguous on the subject of the metals: "I would like it to be clearer, and there to be a broader clarity in it."[85] Sometimes he refuses to accept a source, not because what it relates is intrinsically impossible, but because of the general unreliability of the reporter (see below, chap. XVII, sec. 19), as for instance when he tells us about the marsupial whose pouch opens and closes at will, as if it had a zipper: "These fastenings of the pouch I cannot accept"—the soldiers indubitably made the whole thing up.[86] At other times he proceeds to explain exactly what reasons and considerations accounted for the victory of the party that eventually succeeded in imposing its version of how things were.[87]

His habit of "superimposing" two or more accounts of the same event can sometimes be ascribed to the impartiality required of the historian. In other cases, however, it is obviously a literary expedient designed to give the facts greater dramatic relief, leaving the field open to the various parties, or possibly a prudent hint of skepticism ("audi et alteram partem, et chredi poco"—"I also heard the other side, and remained unconvinced"as the legend goes in the town hall of Certaldo), or else a scrupulous respect for documentary sources, akin to the naturalist's homage to the diversity and variety of the animal and vegetable species of America.

But Oviedo is a man of strong feelings and almost never remains really neutral.[88] In one way or another he lets us know his preferences and misgivings.

---

82. "In these matters I follow a rule . . . what you see, testify to it straightforwardly; whay you hear, say who you heard it from; and what you read, give the author of it. And thus I have always acted in these treatises" (*Hist.*, XLVII, 11: IV, 300a; cf. XLVII, 19: IV, 341a; XLVIII, 1: IV, 359, etc.). Pliny too was always scrupulous about citing the authors he used.

83. Ibid., XXV, 18: PT, III, 53a.

84. Ibid., XXVI, 11: PT, III, 83a.

85. Ibid., XXXV, 7: PT, IV, 317–18.

86. Ibid., XXVI, 31: PT, III, 130a.

87. Ibid., XLVII, 21: IV, 349–50; XLVIII, 4: IV, 369a.

88. "Oviedo is not . . . as ingenuous as people say" (Iglesia, *Cronistas y historiadores*, p. 86). "Oviedo's system was not as bad as had been said" (ibid., p. 201). He has also been rehabilitated by certain other modern authors of monographs dealing with points he covered, who have found that he is substantially reliable. See, for example, A. de Altolaguirre y Duvale, *Vasco Núñez de Balboa* (Madrid, 1914), p. clxxviii ("of the two accounts Oviedo's is, in our view, the correct one"), p. xlviin*l* ("when Oviedo is expounding [on things seen] he deserves special credit"), pp. 1–li, etc.: the frequent references in Lozoya, op. cit.; and the term "imponderable" twice used to describe him in the study by Ballesteros Beretta, "Muñoz," pp. 605, 630.

At the end of the last century the general opinion of historians, summed up by Winsor (op. cit., II, 345), was that Oviedo possessed "but scant scholarship, little power of discrimination—as shown in his giving at times as much weight to hearsay evidence as to established testimony—a curious and shrewd insight, which sometimes, with his industry, leads him to a better balance of authorities than might be expected from his deficient judgment," an extraordinary accumulation of contradictory qualities that supposedly explains how an ignoramus, a fool, and an idiot can, with patience and a little canny intuition, eventually uncover the truth. . . .

And even what he hears with his own ears from people of the Indies he accepts only provisionally, and subject to contradiction by some more reliable source: it is always wise, even when the event occurred nearby "to know the person who is speaking . . . and know what sort of person he is . . . and thus I have come across all sorts of people and I have heard things that I have listened to without either rejecting or accepting them, just jotting them down in my scratch pads, to remind myself; but I do not write them in my fair copy unless my eyes undeceive me or I find corroborating evidence that satisfies me."[89]

With this candid and straightforward account Oviedo shows us the whole process of elaboration of his "treatises": the collection of source material, the initial entries in his rough copy, the revision of his notes, the checking with his own eyes or against other testimony or subsequent reports, and finally the solemn transcription of his fair copy that gives his history its final form, lifts it above the controversies and errors of mortals, and submits it to the emperor's august scrutiny.

The fact remains, however, that if he has not seen something with his own eyes, he reserves judgment: he knows that sharks have double and powerful male members, but apologizes for being unable to tell us whether they use both in coitus, or each on its own account (?), or at different stages, "because this particular detail (I mean the exercise or coitus) I have neither seen or heard" (*sic*)![90]

This trust in his own senses and the implicitly critical attitude toward the evidence of witnesses can from one point of view be seen as perpetuating the attitude of the medieval chroniclers, for whom there was no real history apart from the history of what one had seen with one's own eyes and heard with one's own ears,[91] but from another angle it is typical of the enquiring mind that was gradually emerging with the Renaissance.

The theme is obviously inexhaustible. Need we really go back to Thucydides[92] or call to mind the classic examples of Leonardo da Vinci and Giordano Bruno? Perhaps we might settle for recalling the maxim of the Galician Orosius, for whom only eyewitnesses made history and the rest was mere compilation; or else what the Cordovan Pero Tafur related in his *Andanças e Viajes*

---

89. *Hist.*, XXXIV, Proh.: III, 558a. In fact by dint of this constant accumlation of information he has filled and revised and corrected the three thousand sheets of paper mentioned above, n. 68. In another passage Oviedo rejoices at the arrival of "information and intelligence that enabled me to polish up and perfect certain particular passages I had written down earlier, in accordance with information I received" (XXXIII, 54: III, 457a). But there are also grievous losses. When he has to cross a river on a cane raft which sinks under him, Oviedo takes off his socks and shoes, rolls up his shirt-sleeves, ties up his shirttails, and when he finally reaches the bank, finds that "everything I was carrying was soaked, including my papers and notes, which grieved me deeply" (XIII, 8: I, 398a).

90. Ibid., XII, 6: PT, II, 62a, with the delightful corollary that since the female shark has only one "nature," "one infers that it is more potent to receive than the male to operate. It is a common thing for such potency to be granted to the female sex. . . ." This is no more than an epigram, but cf. the ancient Chinese concept of sexuality, weak in the male, exuberant in the female (R. Van Gulik, *Le vie sexuelle dans la Chine ancienne* [Paris, 1971]).

91. F. Chabod, *Lezioni di metodo storico* (Bari, 1969), p. 37.

92. *History of the Peloponnesian War*, I, 22 (Oxford, 1881), I, 15.

(1435–1439): "I was given good information on the city of Damascus, but since I did not see it, I leave it for someone who did."[93] Likewise the Andalusian Francisco Delicado has his Lozana observe that anyone who lives a long time *hears* new things every day, but "he who moves about a lot, *sees* what there is to be *heard*."[94] Ariosto's Giocondo, in fact, finds the queen entwined with the dwarf—"he does not *hear* it from anyone else, but *sees* it for himself"[95]—and that's all he needs! In our own century Shaw's perceptive Elderly Gentleman reaffirms the superiority of the eye over the ear: "What the traveler observes must really exist, or he could not observe it. But what the natives tell him is invariably pure fiction."[96]

The spirit of the new age was turning away from the schoolmen toward empirical observation and abandoning the traditional teaching for nature rediscovered. In Oviedo the antithesis—which from the logical standpoint is totally inconsistent,[97] but which assures him of a marked superiority over his master Pliny the Elder[98]—assumes remarkable prominence, both because of the

93. Cited by R. Iglesia, "Bernal Díaz del Castillo y el popularismo en la historiografía española," in *El hombre Colón*, p. 62, who remarks, ibid., p. 265, that in Oviedo and Gómara "this attitude of confidence in one's own observation and experience, as compared with the opinions of authors considered to be 'authorities,' comes across very clearly."

94. F. Delicado, *La Lozana andaluza* (1524; Paris, 1888), II, 142–45, my italics.

95. *Orlando Furioso*, XXVIII, 33. Burke would exploit the same antithesis again at the end of the eighteenth century, loading it with heavy sarcasm: he "has *heard* a great deal concerning the modern lights; but he has not yet had the good fortune to *see* much of them" (*An Appeal from the New to the Old Whigs*, 1791, in *Works* [Oxford, 1928], V, 29).

96. "The Tragedy an Elderly Gentleman," act I, in *Back to Methuselah*. See *Collected Plays* (London, 1972), p. 522.

97. The argument, in fact, when carried through to its conclusion, destroys itself. Even Oviedo's reader knows what he learns from him because he is reading it in one of his "screeds," not because he has seen it with his own eyes. Oviedo's much vaunted immediate truth is already reduced to reported and indirectly learned truth, as soon as he attempts to communicate it to others. And he himself, for that matter, is continually obliged to report things that he knows only through the testimony of others (cf. the shrewd observations by Salas, op. cit., pp. 30–35, 39–41).

Thus I find the Oviedo-style hierarchy established by Porras Barrenechea, between chroniclers who "saw" and chroniclers who "heard it said," unacceptable; and likewise his distinction between chroniclers, as immediate witness, and historians, who "in calmer times" reconstruct the facts from a distance ("Los cronistas del Perú," *Mercurio Peruano*, 18, no.197 [August 1943], 367). Prescott, I think, comes closer to the truth when (talking, in fact, about Peter Martyr) he observes that his testimony is in a certain sense more reliable than that of the conquistadors who gave him the information, "since it is free from prejudice and passion, which a personal interest in events is apt to beget" (*Mexico and Peru*, p. 311). Las Casas turned Oviedo's argument against Oviedo himself: see Salas, op. cit., pp. 289, 291, and below, chap. XIX, sec. 31.

98. Pliny was a great scholar, not an original observer; his extremely valuable compilation cannot be equated, from the scientific point of view, with the evidence of Oviedo's own eyes. Experience, come what may, outweighs the authority of the ancient naturalist. Oviedo quotes him once and then immediately bursts out: "But why do I need Pliny or any other ancient author to prove the things that we see every day and are familiar to all men?" (*Hist.*, XV, 4: PT, II, 82a). On a number of occasions Oviedo, who professes the greatest reverence and a disciple's affection for Pliny (accepting, for example, his solution to the problem of why it is that the sea does not overflow, with all the water pouring into it from rivers and rains—ibid., XXIII, 2: PT, II, 354b), counters Pliny's outdated information with his own direct experience of the Indies: cf., for example, I, PT: I, 11b, and his criticism of Pliny's theory of tides in II, 10: PT, I, 41–42. See also the index of names in Pérez de Tudela's edition of the *Historia*, listing more than one hundred and thirty references to Pliny.

Vespucci, in his account of his third voyage, had already written: "Pliny, whose natural history embraces so many things, did not know a thousandth part of the products that we see here. If he had been acquainted with them he would have composed a much more imposing and more perfect work" (Humboldt, *Examen critique*, IV, 27). This is almost the program of Oviedo's *Historia:* see above, sec. 8, and below, chap. XXI, sec. 2.

polemical attitude Oviedo assumes toward Peter Martyr and because the principal domain of his historical study, American nature, had never been described before, was virgin territory as regards historiographical tradtion, and thus lent itself to a rigorous application of the empirical criterion.

12. THE POLEMIC WITH PETER MARTYR

With his *Decades* Peter Martyr d'Anghiera had produced the first history of the new world and its discoveries, and he had done so in Latin, thus rendering it immediately accessible to the scholars and educated public of all Europe. Oviedo either knew no Latin (according to the reproaches leveled at him by a number of his critics) or else did not want to burden himself with the task of putting his *History* into a language with which he was certainly not familiar.[99]

But Oviedo has been in the Indies, and Peter Martyr has not. So Peter Martyr is subjected to a constant barrage of criticism. Sometimes he is attacked directly, as ill-informed or incapable of assimilating his information ("Peter Martyr could not, from such a distance, portray those things the way they really are and the way the material really requires; and as for his informats, either they did not know how to describe things, or he could not understand them"),[100] sometimes with a casual and almost offhand little barb ("Peter Martyr says, mistakenly, that the manatee took its name from Lake Guainabó":[101] "Peter Martyr . . . who wrote of the things of the Indies without seeing them"),[102] or else with more than a hint of ridicule (the Indians of Cuba are terrible Christians, "although the chronicler Peter Martyr, getting his information from Bachiller Enciso, recounts

---

99. As for languages other than Castilian, Oviedo admits, "I did not study or devote myself to them" (*Hist.*, L, 30: IV, 590b), although, as we know, he was familiar at least with Italian. His "Latinity" falls far short of Bembo's, he tells us, and he mentions Latin, together with Greek, Hebrew, and Chaldean, as one of the four languages of excellence, being those of the Holy Scriptures (ibid.).

100. Ibid., XII, 7: I, 395b. In connection with the iguana, two pages further on, there is an allusion (relating to a 1515 incident) doubtlessly aimed at Peter Martyr: "The historians who write about the things of the Indies from Spain should know that they are as far from understanding them (or understanding themselves) as their eyes are removed from the sight of the things of these parts" (XII, 8: I, 392a). See also Amador de los Ríos, "Vida," p. xcix*n*32. Peter Martyr is also cited in passing in *Hist.*, II, 8: I, 34a; VIII, 1: I, 292a (citing *Dec.*, VII, 9; but see also *Dec.*, II, 1, p. 131, in reference to a species of fruit eaten in Alexandria); XXXVII, 1: III, 628a. Against certain biased historians who write in Spain about things they have not seen, cf. XXI, 5: II, 128b.

101. *Hist.*, XII, 9: I, 434b.

102. Ibid., XV, 4: I, 457b. Oviedo denies the existence in the Indies of an extremely bitter wood, proof against woodworms, as Peter Martyr had claimed (*Dec.*, III, 6, p. 275). But, quite apart from the fact that Martyr merely *repeats* what he was told by the cacique Careta, on this particular point the ill-informed Milanese was almost certainly right. Thus there is no mistaking the allusion in the Preface to the *Historia*: Oviedo may write with a poor style, but at least he will write "history that is true and far removed from all the fables that other writers have presumed to write on this matter, without seeing the country, without leaving Spain, and without getting their feet wet, composing elegant and elaborate letters in both Latin and the vernacular . . . compiling histories that have more to do with good style than the truth of what they relate," etc., (I, sole chap.: I, 4a), and even excusing themselves by saying "so I heard," but then daring "to write to the pope and foreign kings and princes" (II, 1: I, 10b, a clear allusion to Peter Martyr and his *Decades* and *Epistles;* for another unmistakeable allusion to authors that "in diverse epistles or decades and volumes have written from Spain," see VI, Proh.: I, 162a). It is thus strange that J. B. Muñoz (op. cit., XXIV, cited by Humboldt, *Examen critique*, II, 288) only mentions Oviedo's criticisms of Peter Martyr's style ("incorrectness and some affections").

marvels of the devotion and conversion of a Cuban cacique called the Comendador, and his people. I have heard nothing of all that, although I have been on
that island . . . I doubt it, because I have seen more Indians than that writer and
he who told him that" etc.).[103] On other occasions Oviedo's comments betray
sardonic irritation ("this island is, I believe, the one that chronicler Peter Martyr
chose to call Alpha, and other times he calls it Juana; however there is no island
with these names in these parts and Indies. I do not know what could have
prompted him to call it thus"),[104] a magisterial disdain ("Peter Martyr says that
these iguanas are similar to the crocodiles of the Nile, in which he was much
mistaken, and those who describe these things by hearsay are bound to commit
gross errors of this sort"),[105] or an almost imperceptible irony ("Libuqueyra,
which we Christians call Santa Cruz, and the historian Peter Martyr calls
Ayay").[106] And on still other occasions his observations are marked by an
exaggerated, sweeping, and radical condemnation ("as he [Peter Martyr] never
saw them [*hobos* or hogplums] nor ate them, nor came to these parts, so he was
deceived in this, as in many other things that he wrote, or rather those who told
him these things deceived him"),[107] or an affected sympathy, because no doubt
Martyr "wanted to write the truth, if he had been faithfully informed," but he
wrote what he did not see and it is therefore little wonder "that his decades suffer
from a lot of defects."[108]

In his irritation against the learned Latinist, Oviedo goes so far as to insinuate
(twice in the last chapter of the last book of the *History*—a doubly venomous
Parthian shot) that he wrote it in Latin so that his lies and inventions could not
easily be detected: "I consider it ridiculous what some Latin foreigners, writing
about things they have not seen, have said of these Indians of ours; and so it is
clear and apparent from their treatises that if they had been written in the
language of those of us who have seen them, they would have been discredited as
liars, as they recount many things the reverse of the way they are, and others that
never were, riddled with total impossibilities."[109] The allusion could hardly be
more explicit and the reticence is sheer hypocrisy. Here again there is an

103. *Hist.*, XVII, 4: I, 499a. The "Comendador's" Marian devotion and the miracles of the Virgin Mary on his
behalf are narrated by Martyr in *Dec.*, II, 6., pp. 170–75.

104. *Hist.*, II, 12: I, 49b; XVII, 2: I, 494b. Peter Martyr gives the name "Alpha ω" (not "Alpha α"), following
Columbus, not to the island of Cuba or Juana, but "to the first part of it . . . because he thought that our East finished
there, since the sun sets there, and he may think it the end of our West, when it rises there" (*Dec.*, I, 3, pp. 34–35; cf.
ibid., pp. 36 and 38. See Humboldt, *Examen critique*, IV, 192–93n). This is therefore one more misunderstanding on
Oviedo's part.

105. *Hist.*, XII, 7: I, 394b.

106. Ibid., II, 8: I, 34a. Here again Peter Martyr is right, citing the island "which is usually called Ay Ay *by the
natives*, but to which they [Columbus and his companions] gave the name of the Holy Cross" (*Dec.*, I, 2, p. 17).

107. *Hist.*, VIII, 2: I, 294a. Martyr writes of the *hobo*, "They consider this to be without doubt a myrabolan plum"
(*Dec.*, II, 9, p. 190; cf. III, 7, p. 283). Elsewhere he refers to the myrabolan without identifying it with the *hobo*: see,
for example, *Dec.*, I, 9, p. 104; III, 4, pp. 240, 242.

108. *Hist.*, XV, 4: I, 458b.

109. Ibid., L, 30: IV, 589–90.

unmistakably acid flavor in his references to those who can write (and find readers) in Latin.

13. OVIEDO'S IGNORANCE OF LATIN

Whether or not he knew Latin (and he could probably read at least the easier authors and the medieval chronicles), Oviedo was annoyed that he did not know it well enough. "Deep down," Iglesia justly remarks, "he feared that his education was inadequate."[110] In other words he suffered from a linguistic inferiority complex, not at all unnatural in someone who had earlier been in the service of Prince Don Juan—an excellent Latinist,[111] and who later become a follower of the Italian humanists. In the reproaches of Las Casas[112] and those (of which he was probably unaware) of Fernando Columbus, who refers in passing, as if it were an established fact, to "this Consalvo Fernández d'Oviedo's ignorance of the Latin language,"[113] he could perhaps have detected echoes of Lorenzo Valla's sarcastic comments about the barbarian and illiterate Spaniards "shunning the study of Latin literature" or Guicciardini's harsh conclusion: "they are not inclined to letters, and one does not find either in the nobility or in the others any notion, or only very little and in very few persons, of the Latin language."[114] One also seems to catch a hint of Oviedo's resentment in his vindictive and caustic observation that Ruy Falero "was a clever person and very devoted to his studies, and it was thus through them (or because God so permitted it) that he lost his wits and became quite mad."[115]

The charge of cultural inadequacy has remainded a blot on our author's reputation right into our own times. Humboldt observes that Oviedo and the other conquistador-historians make up for their "lack of learning" with their "amiable and naive directness."[116] Amador says that "although he was better educated than the general run of popular writers of his time, he cannot in any way be classed among the scholarly."[117] Icazbalceta writes that he made up with his experience of life for "what he lacked in the way of studies."[118] And Montoliu describes him quite simply "as a man without any intellectual culture."[119]

Henríquez Ureña confines himself to saying that Oviedo's "literary education"

---

110. "Bernal Díaz del Castillo," p. 66.
111. He kept up a literary correspondence with famous writers (Amador de los Ríos, *La literatura española*, VII, 196–97) and apparently prepared himself for death by reading the works of Aristotle (Peter Martyr, *Opus Epistolarum*, bk. X, epists. 174, 176, and 182, cited by Humboldt, *Examen critique*, III, 242n.).
112. Mentioned by Amador de los Ríos, "Vida," p. lxxxiii*n*, and by Fuente, op. cit., p. 336, note b.
113. *Vita de Cristoforo Colombo*, p. 38.
114. Cited by Cirot, op. cit., p. 79*n*2.
115. *Hist.*, XX, 1: II, 9a.
116. *Examen critique*, I, 134n.
117. Amador de los Ríos, "Vida," p. cv.
118. J. García Icazbalceta, "Historiadores de México," in his *Opúsculos y biografías* (Mexico, 1942), p. 12.
119. M. de Montoliu, *Literatura castellana* (Barcelona, 1937), p. 507.

was not extensive.[120] Even a carefree historian like Fueter can portray Oviedo—
a man imbued with Renaissance culture and philosophy—as "not in any way in
touch with humanism."[121] Ticknor comes closer to the truth in describing him as
"evidently a learned man,"[122] and Porras Barrenechea defines him more accurately as "a well-read hidalgo, a humanist courtier,"[123] while González sees him
as "a courtier by upbringing and taste."[124] "A learned man" was in fact the
qualification applied to Oviedo as early as 1524:[125] his education at the court of a
humanist prince and his subsequent wide reading certainly merited him that title.

14. Unfairness of the attacks on Peter Martyr

The basic injustice of Oviedo's attacks on Peter Marytr is obvious. The charge
of not having "seen" what he describes has been *seen* to be meaningless. And as
for the form and composition of the work, the pluridecennarial *History* is not
much of an improvement on the Milanese author's extemporaneous *Decades*.[126]
In some cases, such as that of the *manoatí,* Oviedo simply misunderstood Peter
Martyr's fairly undemanding Latin. The Milanese does not say that the manoati
took its name from Lake Guainabó (which does not make any sense anyway) but
that Lake Guainabó, in which the *manoatí* was found, "is hence called Lake of
the Manatee."[127] Looking at the text and the circumstances more closely, however, we find other grounds, both scientific and—alas—personal, that may have
given rise to Oviedo's resentment toward Peter Martyr.

One of Oviedo's pet theories is that the Hesperides can be identified with the
West Indies (see below, chap. XVIII, sec. 11). Peter Martyr unhesitatingly and
repeatedly identifies the Cape Verde Islands as the Hesperides.[128]

Oviedo's archenemy—never forgiven for that treacherous attack that almost
put an end to him—is Pedrarias. And Peter Martyr and Pedrarias were bosom
pals. Peter Martyr portrays his departure in a festive and almost triumphant scene
and does not hesitate to write that he will ask him for precise information on
pearls, knowing that Pedrarias will speedily give him an answer: "I know he
will make the effort, since he is a friend of mine." Of him and Gonzalo di

120. *La cultura*, p. 65.

121. Fuerter, op. cit., pp. 293–94; but Fueter has a limited concept of humanism, as adulation and imitation of classical antiquity; cf. ibid., p. 307.

122. Ticknor, op. cit., II, 40.

123. Porras Barrenechea, "Los cronistas de la conquista," p. 241.

124. Prologue to the reprint of the *Historia* (Asunción del Paraguay, 1944–45), p. 14.

125. Amador de los Ríos, "Vida," p. lxxxvii*nll.*

126. Salas, op. cit., p. 90; cf. pp. 95–96.

127. *Dec.*, III, 8, p. 292, Oviedo must have translated by ear: "from this lake the Manati is named"!

128. "We believe these isles [the Cape Verdes] to be the Hesperides" (*Dec.*, I, 9, p. 95). "Through the Hesperides, otherwise known as the Cape Verde Islands, which others call the Gorgon Medusas" (ibid.). In the first passage Peter Martyr adds, "these belong to the king of Portugal," while Oviedo claims the Hesperides for the kings of Spain. The Canaries are less firmly identified by Peter Martyr as the Fortunate Isles: "Some think that these are the Fortunate Isles, although others disagree" (ibid., III, 5, p. 256; cf. III, 7, p. 278; *De insulis*, p. 362).

Ayora he writes: "I am close to both of them, and indeed on terms of intimate friendship."[129]

On more than one occasion Oviedo bewails his precarious economic conditions and the strenuous difficulties facing a historian working in the Indies. The protonotary Peter Martyr, who never crossed the ocean, enjoyed—in addition to the title of Chronicler of the Indies and a seat on the Council of the Indies— lucrative ecclesiastical benefices in both Spain and the Indies: he was prior of the cathedral of Granada, was granted the archprebendship of Ocaña in New Castile[130] by Pope Hadrian VI and, as Oviedo himself tartly records, was titular of the abbey of Santiago in Seville the Golden in Jamaica, which in those days brought in "a goodly income."[131]

But there are other considerations too. In Peter Martyr's *Decades,* which were going the rounds of all Europe's scholars, Oviedo does not cut much of a figure. As soon as he got back from his first trip to the Indies, after a stay of little more than a year, Oviedo was quizzed, like so many other returning travelers, by the historian who had been busying himself with describing the new world for more than twenty years. From Peter Martyr's description of the meeting it is quite obvious that the elderly humanist looked down his nose at the inspector of mines, who was setting himself up as an expert on Indian affairs after such a short sojourn in the region. It also becomes clear that Oviedo had turned his attention to the study of the nature and customs of the peoples of America already on the occasion of that first contact with the Indies, and "boasted" of having a profound knowledge of the subject.

15. MUTUAL ACRIMONY

After one anonymous and fleeting—but almost certain[132]—reference to Oviedo, Peter Martyr refers specifically (and not without malice) to a "certain Gonzalo Fernández de Oviedo,"[133] and his stories of how he found a piece of

---

129. *Dec.,* III, 2, p. 219; III, 10, p. 319. Cf. *De insulis,* p. 362, where Pedrarias is said to have sailed with a ship "to explore the coastline: we do not yet know whether he has returned, but he does not lack luck." The following sentences, however, seem to prelude a judicious abandonment of the defence of Pedrarias, who had by then lost favor at the court. Of Pedrarias Dávila's replacement by Pedro de los Ríos, in response to constant pressure by Oviedo, Peter Martyr writes briefly that it was due to the former's voluntary resignation and makes no mention of the Asturian *veedor* (*Dec.,* VIII, 11, p. 639). It may also be recalled that Martyr makes no effort to disguise his skepticism regarding the scientific merits of Codro, Oviedo's great friend (see above, chap. XV, sec. 20; *Dec.,* VII, 8, p. 542).

130. Celotti, op. cit., p. 41.

131. *Hist.,* XVIII, 1: I, 528b. With the first year's income Peter Martyr was able to rebuild the abbey that had been destroyed in a fire (Celotti, op. cit., p. 43). He himself mentions his abbatial prelacy as the just reward of thirty-seven years' service to the crown (*Dec.,* VIII, 10, p. 624–25). On the titular abbacy of Jamaica, cf. Puente y Olea, op. cit., pp. 214–15.

132. "We have already described in its due place . . . what Pedrarias and his fellow-soldiers and *a certain royal official* found" (*Dec.,* III, 4, p. 255; cf. above, chap. VIII, n. 5). This "certain royal official" must be Oviedo, who is described shortly afterward as "the royal official that the Spaniards call the *Veedor*" (ibid., III, 5, p. 260).

133. Menéndez Pelayo may have had this passage in mind (although it is not cited by him nor, to my knowledge, by anybody else) or more probably the sarcastic prologue to the fourth Decade when he wrote that "Peter Martyr used his good judgment to try to sift the exaggeration and boasting out of their [the conquistadors'] reports" (*Historiadores,* p. 85). See above, chap. VIII, n. 5.

sapphire bigger than a goose's egg and saw lots of precious stones and big chunks of amber in the hills, and how the fleeing Caribs left jewel-encrusted fabrics of gold in their houses. The whole region is apparently overflowing with cochineal and gold, with nuggets lying about all along the beaches and banks. . . .

And after Oviedo the narrator of glowing marvels comes Oviedo the ethnographer, gently amused at the strange customs of the natives. "This Oviedo says" that in the area of Zenú, ninety miles east of Darien, "an unusual sort of trading" goes on: the inhabitants of the coast fill big baskets with cicadas, grasshoppers, crabs, periwinkles, and locusts, all well dried and salted, and take them to the inhabitants of the interior, "and by bartering these valuable little beasts [the irony is certainly Oviedo's] and salted fish, the inhabitants of these parts obtain the foreign products they want."[134]

16. The currents in the Gulf of Paria

Oviedo features once more in the *Decades,* appearing this time in his favorite role of investigator of the natural phenomena of the Indies. Columbus's observation that the waters of the Gulf of Paria flowed westward had posed a classic problem of cosmography and oceanography. How was it that this continuous current did not end up by emptying the ocean? Peter Martyr had already exercised his mind over this problem,[135] and one can imagine how absorbed he became in the argument sparked off on this subject between two old hands like Oviedo and the pilot Andrés Morales, Juan de la Cosa's friend and partner,[136] when they called on him at his house in Madrid; and how happily he sat down to write "of the new opinions on the westward-flowing current of the Gulf of Paria. . . . Andreas the pilot and Oviedo, whom I mentioned above, came to my house in Madrid, or, if you prefer, Mantua Carpetana. And an argument arose between them, in my presence, about the current."

---

134. *Dec.,* III, 5, p. 260–61. Peter Martyr goes on to give details (on the lands depopulated by the cannibals, on the cultivation of the *yucca* and its virtues and dangers, on *cazabi,* maize, and various trees and furnishings and funeral rites, on the goodness of the air and the orichalcum), many of which he undoubtedly got from Oviedo. This section of the *Decades* can therefore be seen as an embryonic version of the *Sumario* and the monumental *Historia.* Among other things, Peter Martyr tells how the Spaniards found irrigation canals in the valleys, "and in just the same way our own Milanese and Tuscans cultivate and irrigate their lands" (p. 261), which almost looks like a textual quote from Oviedo.

But Peter Martyr too exploits the techniques of comparative ethnography. Commenting on the absence of houses and persons in Paria, for example, he draws a comparison with the way "our own peasants often go a long way from their villages or the farms where they live to their arable land" (*Dec.,* I, 6, p. 73). Likewise the cellars of Comogro, in Darien, are compared to those filled with "earthenware jars or wooden barrels" in Spain or Italy (*Dec.,* II, 3, p. 148) and the wines stored in them, distilled from various fermented fruits and cereals, likened to the alcoholic beverages prepared by the northern Europeans or the mountain people of Spain, Switzerland, Sweden, etc. (ibid.). Similarly the black and hairy Ethiopians are contrasted with the white and smooth-skinned Indians, so different although they live in equally torrid zones (*Dec.,* I, 6, pp. 71–72).

135. "The time has come, Holy Father, to philosophize a little, to leave cosmography and reflect on the causes of the secrets of nature" (*Dec.,* III, 6, p. 266 [ca. 1515]).

136. "Andreas the pilot" of the passage cited is the "certain Andreas Morales, a pilot of those seas, a friend and companion of Juan de la Cosa" (*Dec.,* III, 4, p. 254), "the person who came to see me, as is the custom of those returning from the Ocean" (*Dec.,* III, 7, p. 277).

They agree that the land of Paria, beyond the islands, is all one and is connected with the lands to the north of the Gulf of Mexico (to give it its modern name). But the pilot holds that the water, following the broad curve of the land, is pushed northward and steered toward the ocean, which by its sheer bulk pushes it back and contains it, just as the waters of a millrace are lost and stilled when they fall into a lake. Peter Martyr recalls that Diego Columbus himself informed him that the return route from the Indies was difficult if one tried to follow the same path as the outward journey and easier if, before heading eastward (for Spain) one headed north; but he attributed the resistance to "the normal motion of ebb and flow" and was also convinced "that there must be a gateway whence these tempestuous waters escape to the west, because it is thus that the heavens have ordained that the waters shall circulate throughout the world."

Oviedo, on the other hand, agrees with Andreas that there is no opening, but he denies that the waters are pushed back by the hump of land sticking out into the sea. "In fact he says that he took particular care to notice that the waters flow westward from the open sea; whereas if one is sailing along the coast in a small ship, he claims, one falls in with a current flowing eastward, so that in the same place one can be carried two different directions," just as one often sees happening in rivers, with the whirlpools that form near the banks. Peter Martyr keeps an open mind. In fact one seems to detect a suggestion of a skeptical smile as he briefly sums up: "These are their opinions. I repeat them, although they differ. We shall refrain from adopting a firm opinion until we know the truth of the matter." And almost impatiently he concludes, "enough and more than enough of this ocean current."[137] Oviedo could hardly have felt flattered by this passage either.

It is of course true that Peter Martyr never went to the Indies, but he spent all the best years of his life in Castile precisely because it was here that he would have access to the most direct sources for the drafting of the work that he hoped would earn him immortality. In Castile he saw the savages, metals, and fruit arriving from the Indies and numerous other products of the New World.[138] As he himself wrote: "In the kingdom of Castile, where I have spent all the prime of my life, and where the material for my immortality was provided by the new worlds discovered by the Spaniards."[139] And Las Casas admitted that with his unremitting labors, "of those who wrote about those first things [the discovery

137. *Dec.*, III, 10, p. 326–27. On this problem, which remained unsolved until more was learned about the complex interplay of the equatorial currents and the Gulf Stream, see Humboldt, *Examen critique*, III, 99–110; Puente y Olea, op. cit., p. 8*n*3 (on Peter Martyr), pp. 280–82 (on Andreas de Morales) and 338–42 (on the problem in general).
138. Cf. Salas, op. cit., pp. 31, 34–36, 40–41.
139. *Opus Epistolarum*, epist, 757, 1670 ed., p. 437, cit. by Humboldt, *Examen critique*, II, 290*n*, who has the greatest respect for Martyr's truthfulness.

and Columbus's voyages] Peter Martyr is the most reliable," although in the following parts the *Decades* contain "some falsehoods."[140]

In reality, Oviedo's acid comments smack of professional rivalry, aggravated by a suspicion of linguistic inferiority and a firm conviction of twofold historical superiority, the superiority of the person who has himself been on the spot and of the person who— given the rapid expansion of geographical knowledge within the space of a couple of decades—can very easily spot instances of ignorance and error in the most famous author of the previous generation. When Peter Martyr was writing it was still universally believed that Cuba was part of the mainland.[141] When Oviedo is writing there are already doubts about the North American continent extending as far as Asia, and suspicions that it may be separated from it by another ocean. Advances in geography are exploited by the Asturian to point an accusing finger at the historical ignorance of the Lombard. But if in many cases Peter Martyr did not know what Oviedo knows, this is due not to any critical shortcomings nor to his having remained in Castile, nor to the unreliability of his sources—in fact to none of the causes of error imputed to him by Oviedo—but to the age in which he happened to live and write. It is in fact a question of time, not place.

17. Arguments with Lucio Marineo Siculo

Oviedo exhibits the same polemical acrimony in his attacks on another Italian humanist, Lucio Marineo Siculo. He too, like Peter Martyr, was honored by the court of Spain, enjoyed the title of official historian, wrote in Latin and took the liberty of describing the Indies "without seeing them," or rather, Oviedo goes on with somewhat farfetched irony, "he came to the Indies in a dream; and he spoke in a dream, because even if he had spoken in his sleep he could not have said so much the reverse of the truth as he did say, and this shows how necessary it is for anyone describing what he has not seen to take good care from who he gets his information"[142] Even in the *Quinquagenas* Oviedo is still persecuting

---

140. Menéndez Pelayo, "Historiadores," p. 83.

141. *Sic* Humboldt, *Examen critique*, IV, 129, possibly on the basis of *Dec.*, I, 3, pp. 35–36; but Peter Martyr is well aware of the fact that it is an island (e.g., *Dec.*, I, 10, p. 116).

142. *Hist.*, XXIX, 30: III, 145a. It is interesting to note that Oviedo showed dislike for only two Italians, and those two, Marineo and Martyr, were precisely the two humanists, summoned by the Catholic Queen to the court of Spain, who became official historians of the crown without setting foot outside Europe. Oviedo's usually spontaneous liking for Italians was obviously outweighed, in those two instances, by his resentment toward his two "competitors," foreigners and Latinists, describing the Indies from the safety and comfort of their own homes. On the two learned Italians, who were friends, see Amador de los Ríos, *Literatura española*, VII, 198ff.

In 1511 Marineo had Peter Martyr's first *Decade* published without the author's consent (Celotti, op. cit., p. 227). Marineo too, as a good humanist, was proud of his Latin which, after eighteen years in Spain, he even preferred to Italian; he reproached his new (Spanish) compatriots "for only one thing . . . their ignorance of Latin" (Cirot, op. cit., p. 78). By a curious twist of bibliographical irony the first edition of Oviedo's *Sumario*, translated by Andrea Navagero, was printed together with a summary of Peter Martyr's work (see Harrisse, *Bibliotheca Americana*, no. 190), and the English translation of part of his major work was published together with the translation of the Italian writer's *Decades*.

It is in fact quite possible that Oviedo, when still a youth and a member of the household of Prince Don Juan, met and

poor Lucio Marineo and "that tract of his that he wrote in praise of Spain, as it pleased him, and as he understood it, being a foreigner and not a native of it," allowing him, as a gourmet, the sole merit of having listed the good wines of Spain in learned fashion, a subject that "he treats . . . as a man who understood it."[143]

Finally the Milanese Peter Martyr and, if I am not mistaken, the Sicilian Lucio Marineo are the targets of Oviedo's indiscriminate sarcasm on a number of other occasions. He writes at one point, for instance, that it will be easier for him, even if endowed "with rude intellect," to learn the things of America being "in this land, rather than far removed from it in Milan or Sicily."[144] On another occasion he ridicules "certain Latin foreigners . . . authors of what they did not see," who wrote mendaciously of the Indies, "which authors [Oviedo adds with transparent malice] I saw and met and for their honor I will not name them, but refer anyone who should want to read them to their decades or Latin volumes."[145] Lastly one recalls the point where, in even more convoluted and urbane form, he observes that "the Sicilian and Lombard historians could not understand or investigate these matters from Spain . . . and although the protonotary Peter Martyr, who came from Milan, and Fray Bernardo Gentil, who was Sicilian, and both historians of his majesty, spoke about things of the Indies, I say that even though they wrote in Latin [the same sore point] and their treatises were not lacking in good style, one is forced to suspect that they lacked sound information in many of the things that they dealt with."[146]

18. ARMCHAIR HISTORIANS THE BUTT OF OVIEDO'S SARCASM

The sarcasm at the expense of armchair historians often becomes more general. At times Oviedo assumes a scandalized and scornful tone: "I am amazed how some persons (whose names it is better to pass over than to spell out) have proceeded to describe the things of these parts from Europe."[147] And when he is engaged on correcting certain points of cosmography and navigation he forcefully reminds his readers that he too has navigated, using the very best instruments — "I have held my astrolabes and quadrants and cross-staffs" — but above all he states what he states "because I have eyes, praise be to Him who gave them to me! And I have used them the way other free man can use theirs."[148]

Generally speaking, if he goes into so much detail, it is so that "historians who

---

listened to the humanist, who was one of the prince's tutors and who mentioned in that same year, 1492, how his house was filled with noble young gentlemen anxious to devote themselves to study and convinced that good letters, far from being an obstacle, were a help in the career of arms (passage cited in Lozoya, op. cit., p. 187).

143. *Qu.*, p. 538.
144. *Hist.*, XXXIV, Proh.: III, 558b.
145. Ibid., L, 30: IV, 589–90.
146. Ibid., XXXIV, 3: III, 562. On the Sicilian "Fray Bernardo Gentil," see above, chap. XV, n. 110.
147. *Hist.*, XXXIV, Proh.: III, 557b.
148. Ibid., XXI, 7:II, 137b.

write the things of the Indies from Spain might know that they are as far from understanding then (or understanding themselves) as their eyes are distant from seeing the things of over here."[149] Another time, having referred to a missionary who lost an eye to an arrow wound, he says that he will more willingly believe that one-eyed man "than those who see with two eyes and without understanding themselves or understanding what the Indies are or ever having come to the Indies, who from Europe tell and have written all sorts of stories, for which in truth I can find no more appropriate comparison than parrots' chatter, since although they talk, they do not understand a word of what they themselves are saying."[150] Even in the closing lines of the work Oviedo is warning the reader "against certain cunning historians, who talk of the Indies without seeing them," or report things in hearsay, or even steal "certain passages that I have written and these others amend, changing the words, so that it will appear that what they relate is their own."[151] The terms of the polemic remain unaltered but the angle of attack shifts, moving from criticism of his predecessors and claims of his own superior originality to denunciations of his plagiarists and a warning against repetition of the work of these deskbound chroniclers who casually cobble something together on the basis of Oviedo's labors.

19. EXPERIENCE AND TRADITION

It is this personal involvement that accounts for the vehemence with which Oviedo's maxim is expressed. Its theoretical implications, however, are considerably vaster. It means that personal experience takes precedence over tradition, both oral and written, that description of what the historian has seen with his own eyes has greater intrinsic value than reports of happenings, since no man can be present at more than a small proportion of events; that geography, in short, in its widest sense, absorbs within itself and overcomes history, in its narrowest sense.

It is therefore fair to say that Oviedo is greater as a naturalist than as a historian, as ethnographer and geographer than as chronicler of the conquests. But is should be added at once that the description of nature—nature seen and observed, whether by dint of trial and error in the botanical garden that he cultivates in Santo Domingo, or when he has a seven-and-a-half-foot serpent opened up and extracts "thirty and some eggs,"[152] or when, with great originality, he uses a rudimentary sounding device ("a well sealed gourd") to conduct experiments to test the existence of a hot spring that bubbles up from the bottom

---

149. Ibid., XII, 8: I, 399a. For further barbed comments about those who "write from Spain" and "speak without knowing what they are saying," always going by hearsay," see XLVIII, 3: IV, 368a.

150. Ibid., L, 24: IV, 574.

151. Ibid., L, 30: IV, 592b. A little later Bernal Díaz del Castillo was to make the same intuitive objections about Gómara's classical approach to history. Bernal Díaz chides Gómara for writing in fine style, which he Bernal cannot hope to do, while he never witnessed the facts he narrates, unlike Bernal who actually took part in them (cf., Iglesia, "Bernal Díaz del Castillo," pp. 144–45).

152. Hist., XII, 8: I, 399b. Cf. below, chap. XVIII, n. 247.

of a river of "fresh and good" water on the island of Dominica,[153] or even the post-mortem examination of two Siamese twins, which he witnesses and describes in minute anatomical detail[154]—this, for Oviedo, is the more real history, so that it is true to say that he brings a historical, comprehensive, discriminating, and particularizing spirit to the study of nature.

In considering the accounts of the feats of arms Oviedo adopts—as we have seen—a critical approach that is far from commonplace, but he makes almost no effort at reconstruction and interpretation. He receives the documents, scrutinizes them attentively, and then ranges them side by side or sometimes one on top of the other. But they are still, for Oviedo, *res inter alios actas,* tiles for his mosaic, not things of his own like personal observations. Far from passively accepting the sworn statements sent to him by eyewitnesses, however, Oviedo studies and sifts them. Sometimes he includes them without guaranteeing them. Other times he subjects them to his usual critical and moral censorship. In general, truth be told, he assesses them with almost legal precision, refusing to accept uncorroborated testimony,[155] or else apologizing when he can only produce one witness (but "he is a reliable man"),[156] in other words following a time-honored procedural maxim (*testis unus, testis nullus,* "a single witness is no witness at all") that counts rather than weighs the evidence, in response to practical needs rather than the pursuit of the truth.

But when a fact—the existence of mermen for instance—is attested to by *two* experienced sailors "located three hundred leagues from each other and at different times," one can indeed believe it.[157] When on the other hand *one* witness, even if it be a "hidalgo and reliable person," tells him how it rained red earth for two days on Alvarado's soldiers, he is loath to believe it—"I was somewhat incredulous about that report"—but then he meets Don Pedro de Alvarado in person, "and he himself assured me that it rained earth continuously for three days"; and, as if that were not enough, Livy too writes "that it rained earth in Italy before."[158] Two contemporary witnesses and one ancient make up a winning hand. The fact is proved. Usually, however, when the historian hears or sees something that seems to him incredible he settles for taking note of it, without believing it until either "my eyes disabuse me, if it is possible to see the things in question" or "I find someone that corroborates it to my satisfaction."[159] He prefers to wait and see, in fact. Even where there are irreconcilable discrepancies Oviedo is happy to wait for the truth to be revealed in the fullness of time or the second edition.[160]

153. *Hist.,* VI, 13: I, 199; cf. below, chap. XVIII, n. 224.
154. *Hist.,* VI, 11: I, 196.
155. Ibid., II, 1: I, 10a.
156. Ibid., XLIV, 3: PT, V, 22b.
157. Ibid., XXIII, 5: PT, II, 362b.
158. Ibid., XLVI, 17: PT, V, 98; cf. XLVI, 20: PT, V, 115a.
159. Ibid., XXXIV, Proh.: PT, IV, 267b.
160. Ibid., XXXIX, 4: PT, IV, 349b.

If, however, the evidence is provided by an unreliable source, whether individual or multiple, Oviedo at once denies it *a priori* any credibility. Pedrarias and his acolytes "dared" to write to the emperor (in 1525) that a city had been discovered in Nicaragua three leagues long, and other wild and shameless lies, which were even proclaimed from church pulpits "mixed up with readings from the Holy Gospel." "And I [Oviedo goes on] heard some of those sermons, and considered them fables, as indeed they were; not because I doubted them as impossible [anything is possible in the Indies, he seems to say] but because I was very well acquainted with the inventor of those stories and I knew how reliable his words were."[161]

All in all the accounts of other people's doings remain strictly "external" to his real interest, even if they sometimes arouse his patriotism or outrage his sense of morality.

To sum up, it could be said that Oviedo adopts a historicist approach to nature and a naturalist's approach to the history of the events of the New World. He is a chronicler of the adventurers and missionaries; but he is a historian of the plants, animals, and natives. Peter Martyr, with his delight in dramatic narration and his humanist's passion for all things human and only things human, had viewed the data on vegetable and zoological species (see above, chap. VIII, secs. 6 and 15) as mere interludes or accompaniment. Oviedo, on the other hand is first and foremost a devoted observer of the trees, plants, and animals.

It need hardly be added that since sixteenth-century America is almost a silent world as regards history, almost entirely lacking in any written past, but abundantly endowed with new forms and unknown creatures, it is immensely fortunate for Oviedo and for us that his mind was this way inclined.

20. The Southern Cross

When Charles V granted Oviedo an augmentation of arms in recognition of his "signal achievements and great services to Us," the device that the historian chose to add to the ancient bearings of the Valdés was not a helmet or sallet, not an arm brandishing a sword or some trophy from the battlefield, not indeed any other reminder of warlike deeds, but the marvel of the night sky of America, the Southern Cross, "four stars never before seen except by the first people,"[162] "four stars in the cross . . . that are a very notable feature in the sky."[163] Oviedo

161. Ibid., XLII, 5: PT, IV, 390–91.

162. Dante, *Purgatorio*, I, 23–24.

163. *Hist.*, II, 11: I, 46. Oviedo is extremely annoyed that Fray Blas del Castillo should have written that "Gonzalo Fernández de Oviedo, Their Majesties' chronicler of the Indies, merely because he saw the crater of Masaya asked His Majesty for it as his arms, etc. It absolutely never entered my head to ask for such arms or such a favor . . . and the friar said whatever he felt like saying about it" (XLII, 6: PT, IV, 398b). Cf. C. Miralles de Imperial y Gómez, "Del linaje y armas del primer cronista de Indias, el madrileño Gonzalo Fernández de Oviedo," *RI*, 18, no. 71 (1957), 73–126. The actual text of the imperial grant augmenting Oviedo's arms refers to "four stars or, or saffron-colored, arranged in the form of a cross, after the fashion of the four stars that rotate around the Southern Polestar; let these four

the naturalist with a passion for heraldry takes great pride in the sacred and celestial symbol. But Oviedo the man sighs wearily. Dante, in rapt ecstasy, had once sung of how "the sky seemed to rejoice in their sparkle" and envied those who drank in their light: "Oh widowed northern clime, Unable to admire these stars!" But Oviedo seals his book with the star-spangled arms and almost seems to place it under the mystical protection of the Sign, the book he wrote "in these parts, where men who see these stars suffer so many travails, and where I have consumed the better part of my life." [164]

But what did it really signify, that new antarctic constellation, that glittering repudiation of Aristotle's astronomy? From the time of the very first journeys beyond the tropics it had symbolized the mysterious wonder and Christian pre-destination of the New World. The Pinzóns already noticed that the new stars of the antarctic sky were very bright and very different from their own;[165] and the Portuguese, as they sailed to the Antipodes, admired, among radiant nebulas, "a notable star, similar to the star of ours which the common people believe to be the Pole" and which the Italians called the "Tramontana" and the Spanish the "North Star." [166]

Vespucci was the first[167] to be reminded of Dante's lines by the Southern Cross.[168] And indeed one seems to catch another echo of Dante in his letter from Lisbon (1502) describing his second voyage, where he talks about many new constellations in the southern sky, quite brilliant and beautiful, and ever invisible from the Northern Hemisphere.[169] Dante, approaching the summit of Mount Purgatory, sees the stars "brighter and bigger than usual." [170]

An engraving by Giovanni Stradanus, executed about 1522,[171] shows Vespucci looking at the Southern Cross, alongside a scroll bearing Dante's lines, in Tuscan and Latin, and a bust of the poet. Vespucci in fact says that those stars are "many more and much bigger and brighter than the stars of our Hemisphere." [172]

After Vespucci, the constellation was admired by Andrea Corsali (1517),[173]

---

stars testify and publish to posterity and future generations his illustrious deeds and great services to Ourselves, in that same New World of the Indies," and especially in Cartagena, which is almost on the equator (from Toledo, 10 October 1525, ibid., p. 122; cf. pp. 90–91).

164. *Hist.*, II, 11: I, 46.

165. Peter Martyr, *Dec.*, I, 9, p. 96.

166. Ibid., III, 1, p. 217.

167. Letter from Seville, 18 July 1500; see in Pohl, op. cit., p. 79. Cf. ibid., p. 56; above, chap. VI, nn. 9, 10, 30; and for the cross shining over the East Indies, Sassetti, op. cit., pp. 187, 328.

168. Humboldt, *Examen critique*, IV, 319, according to whom Dante knew of the constellation, ibid., pp. 323–25.

169. Pohl, op. cit., pp. 131, 135.

170. *Purgatorio*, XXVII, 89–90.

171. Reproduced in J. Díaz y Gil, *América y el Viejo Mundo* (Buenos Aires, 1942), fig. 144, and in Pohl, op. cit., pp. 64–65.

172. Navarrete, op. cit., III, 277; cf. p. 282: "We set our course by another star of the Southern Hemisphere."

173. "A marvellous cross . . . which I do not think can be compared with any celestial sign"; Da Mosto, in *Raccolta Colombiana*, pt. V, vol. III, p. 67n2 (referring to *Raccolta Colombiana*, pt. II, vol. III, p. 241); Humboldt, *Cosmos*, II, 266ff.; L. Hugues, *Ferdinando Magellano: Studio geografico* (Turin, 1879), pp. 21–23.

Pigafetta (1520),[174] an unnamed Portuguese pilot, and heaven knows how many other sailors. But only with the coming of Oviedo was the glittering celestial ornament elevated to the rank of heraldic and religious emblem.[175] After Oviedo the Southern Cross makes innumerable radiant appearances in French and other poetry.[176] Half a century after the Spanish historian, Tasso saw "the four clear and luminous stars" of the Southern Cross, which "our most blessed age descried sublime in the sky," as the very imprint of God Omnipotent;[177]and Tommaso Campanella wanted Spain to have the stars of the antarctic sky described, with "the Holy Cross appearing at the Pole," and therein inscribed the effigies of Charles V "and other Austrian gentlemen," as a way of uniting astrology with "local memory" and increasing the veneration due to illustrious men.[178]

In later times the Southern Cross was frequently called on to serve as a gnomon of the night hours,[179] or quite simply as a symbol of all the lands of the tropics[180] or Austral Spain.[181]

21. DESCRIPTIONS OF NATURE AND CHRONICLES OF CONQUEST

Oviedo began his history as a portrayal of American nature. The *Sumario* of 1525 is almost entirely devoted to nature,[182] and it is also interesting to note that in the dedication of that work the emphasis falls not so much—as in the *History*—on the contrast between his own immediate observation and the histories compiled at second hand, but on his special merit as a writer with an exclusive interest in historicoscientific enquiry. He admits that there have been "eyewitnesses" of the Indies and he often cites them in support and confirmation of his own assertions, but they were merchants or officials who failed to pay due attention to the things of American nature—unlike him, Oviedo, who "out of natural inclination . . . desired to know them, and for the sake of the work fixed his eyes on them."

174. "The Antarctic Pole is not as full of stars as the Arctic . . . . When we were in this gulf we saw a cross of five vividly bright stars, pointing to the West, and precisely in line with one another" (Manfroni, op. cit., p. 113).

175. Humboldt, *Examen critique*, IV, 332–35; *Cosmos*, II, 5, 286.

176. Jean Dorat: "a new star" (1575); Antoine de Baïf: "this cross . . . that holds the south enclosed" (1575); Pierre Ronsard: "its pole marked by four great stars" (1578), etc., in Le Moine, op. cit., pp. 44, 60, 215.

177. *Il mondo creato*, II, 524–33 (Florence, 1951), p. 43.

178. *Della monarchia de Spagna*, 1597, 1620, chaps. 10 and 22, in *Opere* (Turin, 1854), II, 117–18, 225.

179. "It is late, it is midnight; the Southern Cross is right on the horizon," Bernardin de Saint-Pierre, *Paul et Virginie* (Paris, 1873), p. 127.

180. Humboldt, *Reise in die Aequinoctial-Gegenden* (Stuttgart, 1859), I. 183–84.

181. E.g., in J. S. Chocano, "La Cruz del Sud," in *Poesias escogidas* (Paris, 1938), p. 88; cf. ibid., pp. 16, 258, 259.

182. In the early years of the conquest the investigations demanded by the monarchs from the persons occupying positions of authority in America or setting out to explore the territory were almost always limited to the natural resources, the fauna and flora. This was still true around 1518, until, with Las Casas's protests, the sovereign began (1525) to ask for details about the crimes committed in New Spain, and thus to shift his interest toward the political history of his dominions (cf. Carbia, *Crónica oficial*, pp. 74–75, and above, chap. XIII, sec. 1).

In the major work Oviedo finds it necessary to preface the description of nature with an account of the discovery, outlining Columbus's voyage that had unveiled the new lands. And only in a third stage, on the strength of his functions as Chief Chronicler and utilizing the sources of information made available to him by the sovereign,[183] does not set out to narrate the deeds of the Spanish adventurers. But the "political" history, even when it predominates in sheer bulk, remains ideologically secondary and supplementary to the "natural" history. The description of the discovery and conquest, "although not part of natural history, will be very necessary to it, to know the beginning and basis of everything."[184] But Oviedo takes every opportunity of reiterating that he would prefer to dwell on details and curiosities of natural history rather than on the conquistadors' bloody wrangles,[185] and as soon as he can he returns to the "more enjoyable matters,"[186] sometimes even bewailing the fact that his pen must "follow the form of a tragic story or *imitatio*."[187]

Thus to Oviedo more than to any other historian it would be fair to apply Romano's accurate general comment that the chronicle genre, on its last legs in Europe, takes a new lease on life in the Indies and rises to "real literary heights" particularly when it is recounting the struggles against an unfamiliar, indeed totally alien and outlandish nature, rather than wrangles between conquistadors.[188]

The illustration of the works and marvels of nature is an unceasing hymn to the Lord; but the account of the sufferings of the Spanish in the Indies sounds more like a funeral dirge than an epic.[189] While Oviedo's simple religosity found full satisfaction in contemplating the handiwork of God in the nature of the New World, his patriotism reacted with tones of grief and sorrow to the deeds of the Spaniards in the Indies. Oviedo, we must always remember, was not a conquistador, either major or minor (although he poses as such, writing of how he took part "in the conquest and pacification of some parts of that land by arms").[190] Oviedo was a *vecino,* a resident or householder, one of the first

---

183. "I have warrants and orders from His Imperial Majesty to the effect that all governors and justices and officials of all the Indies are to give me information and a true report of everything worthy of record, in reliable affidavits, signed with their names and sealed by public notaries, to prove their authenticity" (*Hist.,* II, 1: I, 10a). Even this was not always enough. Oviedo repeats, almost peevishly: "What I am saying is that I have royal warrants, ordering the governors to send me reports on anything relating to history in their governorships, for these histories." But Cortés, when asked for his report, merely sent Oviedo a copy of his famous letters to the emperor "and bothered himself no further" (XXXIII, Proh.: III, 258a; cf. below chap. XIX, n. 43). In a number of cases Oviedo summarizes the reports that come into his hands (e.g., *Hist.,* XXXIII, 43: III, 480, chapter title).
184. *Hist.,* I, sole chapter: I, 6b; cf. Pérez de Tudela, "Vida," p. cxlii, citing Alvarez López, "Historia natural," pp. 554–55.
185. E.g., *Hist.,* XLVI, 18: IV, 234a.
186. Ibid., XLVII, 21: IV, 350b.
187. Ibid., XXXVIII, sole chapter: III, 640b.
188. R. Romano, *Les mécanismes de la conquête coloniale: Les conquistadores* (Paris, 1972), pp. 65–66.
189. *Hist.,* XLIV, Proh.: IV, 124. This tragic vision of history will be analyzed in greater detail in chaps. XVIII and XIX below.
190. *Hist.,* I, Dedication: I, 46.

vecinos of the Indies, a tax official, administrator, local magistrate, a businessman, and not a military man. Although he held the rank of captain and his duties were not always peaceful nor entirely bloodless, Oviedo was a civilian rather than a soldier.

22. THE LAST (OR SHIPWRECK) BOOK

Oviedo can therefore observe the deeds of the Spanish soldiers and commanders with a certain detachment quite uncolored by any sense of personal involvemente.[191] Indeed, as the "chronicle" gradually prevails over the "physical description," or—by and large—as we slowly make our way from the earlier to the later books, from the enthusiasm at the discovery and the intoxication of the conquest to the colonists' daily grind, nature too becomes less friendly and the natives, more accurately and more humanly judged, turn out to be at heart more hostile and intractable. The sovereign himself, so grandiosely allegorized at the outset, ends up being accused of petty greed and almost of deceit.[192] And the fiftieth and last book closes the work with a grandiose and awe-inspiring flourish, a whole series of storms and shipwrecks and naval catastrophes, almost as if to conclude and circumscribe the New World with an ocean in turmoil, as if to bring home to us more clearly its perilous remoteness and to summon up the miraculous figures of the Virgin and Saints on the crests of the Atlantic waves.

One of Oviedo's purposes in composing his work is that men should know "how many dangers beset those that go to sea,"[193] and he certainly had the same literary-cum-didactic intention when already in the 1535 edition he followed up the first part of the *History*—by way of provisional conclusion—with eleven chapters of the thirty making up book L.[194] This arrangement—the story opening with Columbus's felicitous voyage and closing with a fortissimo chord of shattering timbers, screams, and desperate entreaties and whistling hurricanes— is perhaps the only deliberate attempt at "composition" to be found in the *History*. Oviedo was so pleased with this full-orchestra finale that he referred back to it at the beginning of his following work, the *Quinquagenas,* advising the reader that "in the book that I wrote on shipwrecks" he would find things so terrifying that "he would quite lose any desire to set sail."[195]

---

191. Thus I think it is incorrect to say, as do Fueter (op. cit., p. 293) and so many others, that Oviedo, like Gómara, writes from the practical or conquistador's viewpoint.

192. "I have noticed one thing, that nobody should forget, and it is that almost never do Their Majesties put their own property and money into these new discoveries, only paper and fine words, saying to these captains: if you do what you say, we shall do this or that or you will be rewarded," etc. (XXXV, 5: III, 527b). Cf. S. Zavala, *Los intereses particulares en la conquista de Nueva España* (Madrid, 1933), *Las instituciones jurídicas,* pp. 263–67, and *New Viewpoints on the Spanish Colonization of America* (Philadelphia, 1943), p. 69; R. Porras Barrenechea, *Cedularios del Perú* (Lima, 1944), p. xxii.

193. *Hist.,* L, Proh.: IV, 462a.

194. Cf. I, sole chapter: I, 6a; IV, 5: I, 112b; XXI, 8: II, 141b.

195. *Qu.,* p. 9.

Shipwreck stories were actually a fairly common literary form by that time.[196] Later, numerous utopias and imaginary discoveries and symbolic tragedies (such as Shakespeare's *Tempest*) were to open with a shipwreck and the resulting arrival at some unknown island or shore. The shipwreck is the catastrophe that destroys the prevailing economic and technical structure, without (by definition) taking the survivor's life. It annuls his historical and legal conditioning and turns him into a simple creature of nature. It thus forms the easiest passage from reality to utopia, from Society to Nature, from the Past to the Future. Oviedo's realism comes out clearly in the fact that he locates his shipwrecks at the end of his story, and not—like the utopians—at the beginning; at the outer edge of credibility, and not as a spur to flights of fancy.

I am not suggesting that Oviedo began or actually invented this particular literary genre (even if those eleven chapters were published as early as 1535). Certainly the genre was cultivated much more assiduously after Oviedo's *History*, possibly more assiduously in Portugal than in Spain, and with the same characteristics as in Oviedo. In each case his aim was not merely to provide a historical record in recounting stories of fatal and dramatic incidents, but to edify in a dual sense—in depicting the dangers facing the bold mariner and in "edifying" the mind of the reader with a demonstration of the miracle-working aid offered by the Celestial Powers—on occasion—to those unlucky men.

Suffice it here to recall, apart from the section in León Pinelo, the *Naufragios* (Zamora, 1542; Valladolid, 1555) by our old friend Alvar Núñez Cabeza de Vaca, about whom Oviedo tells us so much,[197] and those of the Portuguese soldier-poet Jerónimo de Corte-Real (died 1588), *O Naufragio y Lastimoso Suceso de Perdicão de Manuel de Souza de Sepúlveda* (Lisbon, 1594; translated into Spanish by Francisco de Contreras, *Nave Trágica de la India de Portugal*, 1624), and then the two volumes by Bernardo Gómes de Brito, *Relações de Naufrágios* (after 1580), published in Spanish as *Historia trágico-marítima* in 1735–1736.[198]

23. THE COMMANDANT OF THE FORTRESS OF SANTO DOMINGO

Oviedo was named Official Chronicler of the Indies and —since he wanted a "rest"—commandant of the fortress of Santo Domingo almost simultaneously.

196. See for example León Pinelo's *Epítome*, of which "title XIII" (pp. 50–51) deals with "shipwrecks in the Indies and the seas thereof."

197. Esp. *Hist.*, XXIII, 9–16: PT, II, 368–86, on his adventures on the River Plate (1542–44); and XXXV, 1–7: PT, IV, 287–318, on his incredible adventure following the disastrous expedition commanded by Pánfilo de Narváez (1527–36). Cf. above, chap. XVII, sec. 6.

198. Cf. F. Braudel, *La Méditerranée et le monde méditerranéen* (Paris, 1966), I, 514; H. Meier, "Letteratura portoghese," in *Storie letterarie di tutti i tempi e di tutti i paesi* (Milan, 1968), p. 307; *Neue Zürcher Zeitung*, 12 May 1974, p. 49. But specific mention should be made at least of the notorious *Relation d'infortunes sur mer* (1781), a collection that was republished by Deperthes under the title *Histoire des naufrages*, 3 vols. (1789), reprinted with notes in 1795 (5 vols.) and then again in 1816, 1818, 1821, 1825, etc.

Finding himself thus furnished with a sinecure and a pleasant and interminable occupation, he withdrew from the continuing upheavals and adventures of the mainland to the haven that was a required port of call for anyone going and coming between Europe and the Indies, the town that had reminded Geraldini— so much admired by Oviedo—of the fair cities of Italy.[199] And there, on the strength of his title "signed by His Majesty and sealed with a seal of red wax, and signed by some of the gentlemen of his Council of the Indies,"[200] as commander of a garrison of six men and a gunner (and even this meager complement not always up to strength), in a fortress with a tattered banner,[201] Oviedo set about interrogating each and every sailor and conquistador that stopped off at the island, devoting himself between ships to studying the plants, animals, and natural phenomena.

Santo Domingo was an ideal observatory. Strongly defended against the French and English pirates,[202] facing the Caribbean Sea precisely opposite the great northern curve of the continent, it represented the point of convergence, the geometrical target of the numerous rays bearing the light of information from throughout the mysterious south, from east to west, from the mouths of the Orinoco to the Gulf of Darien. Santo Domingo collected these concentrated rays and, like a magnifying lens, cast an exaggerated image into distant Europe. And in Santo Domingo, at the focal point of this vast optical apparatus, was Oviedo of the keen eye and enquiring mind. At the same time the city served as the nursery and breeding station for the new vegetable and animal species sent from Europe to America, many of which were acclimatized in the island before being dis-tributed, spread, and scattered throughout the lands of the continent, from one tropic to the other.[203]

It was not, however, solely from the geographical point of view that Santo Domingo enjoyed a privileged position. Its historical situation was also highly suggestive. When Oviedo arrived, Santo Domingo was already moving into decline, but it still kept traces of its past splendor, when it had been the main base and metropolis of the emerging empire of the Indies. "The capital and trade-mart," Peter Martyr had poetically called it, "of the whole bounty of the Ocean."[204] In Santo Domingo the past was still visible, visible as past, as recent, and living history. Although its almost half-century of splendor was drawing to a close, Santo Domingo still recalled that its Audiencia Real had been the first to

---

199. Biermann, "Geraldini," p. 200.
200. *CDII*, XI, 365.
201. Ibid., p. 390 (1541).
202. Oviedo boasts that "now," i.e., under his command, Santo Domingo is more impregnable then ever (*Hist.*, XIX, 13: PT, II, 209b; *CDII*, XI, 392 [1541]. But on the another occasion he reported to Madrid that Santo Domingo was so undefended that "any ordinary pirate could take it" (Archivo de Indias, Indiferente, legajo 1624); cf. below, chap. XIX, n. 254.
203. Puente y Olea, op. cit., p. 377. Cf. Díez del Corral, op. cit., pp. 156–68.
204. *Dec.*, III, 7, p. 277.

be established in the Indies, that its port had seen Cortés set sail toward the Aztec empire and Balboa toward the South Sea, and the first explorers and conquerors leave for Florida and Peru, that its stones had echoed the accusing and uncompromising voice of Bartolomé de Las Casas, and that galleons and caravels laden with gold, pearls, and silverware had sailed out of its harbor and into the sun heading for the eager welcome that awaited them in the Guadalquivir estuary.

In 1583 the University of St. Thomas was officially founded in Santo Domingo, the first University in the New World; but life was already moving away from this ocean crossroads and for more than twenty years the foundation remained a dead letter.[205] Santo Domingo was not yet a "dead city" or a "city of silence" (as Lozoya paints it with a degree of picturesque exaggeration),[206] but—perhaps a sadder spectacle still—a dying city, whose historical role was almost exhausted, and which the colonists were abandoning to seek more glittering objectives or to return to their native shores.

The Indians had been wiped out. The mining industry had died out by 1515–1520.[207] By 1548 there were less than six hundred householders left.[208] There were hordes of Negroes—treacherous, lascivious, thieving, and dirty, and so numerous in the sugar-cane plantations that Hispaniola seemed "an effigy or image of Ethiopia itself."[209]

24. THE NEGROES OF HAITI

The danger noted at that time by Oviedo and a little later by Benzoni during his eleven months' stay in Santo Domingo[210]—namely that the African Negroes

---

205. S. G. Inman, "Political Life in the Caribbean," in *The Carribean Area* (Washington, 1934), pp. 30–31; J. T. Lanning, "The Transplantation of the Scholastic University," in *University of Miami Hispanic-American Studies* (Coral Gables, 1939), p. 7.

206. Lozoya recalls that at the end of Ferdinand's reign Santo Domingo alone, on account of its cathedral and Audiencia Real, and because all expeditions were obliged to put in there, could be considered a real and obviously prosperous Spanish-type city. But this rapidly achieved apogee proved ephemeral, "and soon the Isabeline city of Santo Domingo, in the shadow of its Gothic cathedral and old fortresses, lapsed into a life of nostalgia and memories, a tropical counterpart to so many other cities in the heart of the Castiles" (op. cit., pp. 239–40).

Even in 1525 Oviedo noted that there were very few Indians left and that the Spaniards were "not as numerous as they should be," because being bachelors and impatient to make their fortunes, they emigrated to more promising lands and never bothered themselves with agricultural activities, because flour and wine were imported more cheaply from Spain (*Sum.*, chap. 2, p. 85). "By 1550 Santo Domingo had sunk into a state of definitive decay" (Henríquez Ureña, *La cultura*, p. 12).

207. Peter Martyr, *De insulis* (written about 1522), pp. 363–64, also mentions plagues in 1518; cf. W. Gerling, *Wirtschaftsentwicklung und Landschaftswandel auf den westindischen Inseln Jamaika, Haiti und Puerto Rico* (Freiburg, 1938), pp. 152, 154.

208. "And at one time the population was greater; but it was never so built up" (*Hist.*, VI, 26: I, 211a). On the depopulation of Hispaniola (Haiti), and possible remedies, see the abundant documentation (accusations by the Hieronymites, letters from royal officials, memoranda by colonists, etc.) in *CDII*, vols. I, III, and X. On the various categories of workers (Indian slaves, Caribs, "useless" natives, free natives, Europeans, and black slaves) see the well-documented study by S. Zavala, "Los trabajadores antillanos en el siglo XVI," *RHA*, nos. 2–4 (1938). 31–67, 60–88, 211–16 (without mention of Oviedo, however).

209. *Hist.*, V, 4: I, 141a. Further hostile references to the "evil breed" of Negroes, ibid., VII, 19: I, 286a; cf. *Qu.*, pp. 255–56, 469–70. Every day saw the arrival in Santo Domingo of more Negro slaves, invariably baptized within a day of their arrival; see below, chap., VI, n. 135.

210. 1544–45 (Henríquez Ureña, *La cultura*, p. 82).

would soon be masters of Santo Domingo[211]—has been a threat looming over the island throughout its history. The sharp rise in the Negro population at the western end of the island (Haiti) dramatically increased the threat.[212]

In 1794 the Spanish colony of Santo Domingo numbered a bare 35,000 whites, 38,000 mulattoes and freed slaves, and 30,000 Negro slaves.[213] But in 1789 the adjacent and prosperous French colony of Saint Domingue contained 30,000 whites, 275,000 mulattoes and freed slaves and no less than 465,400 Negro slaves. In 1804 the slaves of Haiti rebelled and occupied the whole island, which they held until 1844.

That same year (1844) saw the birth of the fragile and precarious independence of the Dominican Republic. The country was reoccupied by the Spanish for a few years (1861–1865), offered itself unsuccessfully to the United States in 1869— although it was actually garrisoned by American marines from 1916 to 1934— and has spent its existence in continual terror of the exuberant Negro population of Haiti, seeping through the feeble disphragm of the frontier and capable of splitting it wide open with its constant pressure—terror that has found alternating expression in acts of savagery like the massacre of some ten thousand Haitian Negroes (1937) and acts of apparent humanity like the offer of refuge to persecuted Spaniards and Jews to increase the demographic density of the white republic. The spatial localization of the Negroes in the western part of the island and the rupture of its political unity (as from 1697, when Spain ceded the western third of the island of Hispaniola to France) transformed the social problem noted by Oviedo into an acute international conflict.

25. THE CITY IN DECLINE

Almost as if to confirm the funereal character of the island and the role it played as graveyard of those first adventurous hopes, the most illustrious body of all, that of the Admiral of the Ocean Sea himself, was brought from Spain[214] to be buried in the chancel of the cathedral. The aged commandant thus witnessed the return to the shores of Santo Domingo—in a coffin—of the star-crossed

---

211. Benzoni, op. cit., bk. II, chaps. 1 and 17, ed. cit. (1965), pp. 71–78. Cf. also Humboldt, *Examen critique*, III, 305–09; and Rosenblat, op. cit., p. 174.

212. Document of Varinas (1677) in *CDIU*, XII, 42–43.

213. According to G. Timmenhauer, *Die Insel Haiti* (Leipzig, 1839), p. 425, cited by Gerling, op. cit., p. 166, the population fell to twenty thousand inhabitants in 1700, and six thousand in 1733.

214. "It is supposed" that the Admiral's bones were taken to the island in 1541, but the first mention of their presence in Santo Domingo dates from 1549 (Winsor, op. cit., II, 80). Humboldt, *Examen critique*, IV, 14, gives the date 1536; Morison, *Admiral of the Ocean Sea*, II, 423, plumps for "1541 or shortly after"; Rodríguez Demorizi, op, cit., I, 91, opts for 1544 (9 September). A warrant dated Valladolid, 2 June 1537, sets aside the "sanctuary of the Cathedral of Santo Domingo as pantheon for the Admiral and his descendants, and gives permission for his remains to be transferred from the monastery of Las Cuevas to Hispaniola." Oviedo makes no reference to the matter in *Hist.*, III, 9: PT, I, 75a, but he wanted his tomb to be close to the Discoverer's (L. J. Alcocer, *Relación sumaria de la Isla Española*, 1650, in Rodríguez Demorizi, op. cit., pp. 227–28).

Genoese whom he had first glimpsed in the days of his earliest youth, amid the splendors of the court and the victorious armies at the conquest of Granada.

Oviedo, who had a well-developed sense of the fickleness of all things,[215] who had met Columbus in Spain but who had himself stayed on in Europe another twenty-two years, who had seen Pizarro's and Almagro's galleons set sail from Panama, while himself never leaving Tierra Firme, and who was destined never to see with his own eyes (the only ones he trusted) the marvels of Mexico and Peru—Oviedo, forever left behind as the great waves of history swept on, must have felt fully in sympathy with the city that history was about to pass by, must have felt quite at home among the dilapidated bastions and towers of his "fortress," originally erected as a stockade and refuge against the Indians, then patched up to provide protection against the pirates, but lacking the halo of any great military feat, the glory of a siege withstood or an assault repelled.[216]

This locale, nurturing gloomy thoughts and bitter conclusions, can also no doubt partially explain the way truth itself, presented in such coldly scientific form in the early parts of the *History,* assumes a more judicial and polemical hue in the latter parts (see above, sec. 19), while a general tendency to preach and moralize becomes more evident. The quick little sketches based on his own observations give way to longwinded verbatim reports, and all too frequently the author gets bogged down in tediously monotonous detail.

26. ABUSES AND CORRUPTION IN 1554

But I am not sure that it is quite accurate to refer (as does Otte) to "senile importunings" and "angry resignation" in connection with the outburst contained in a very curious and melancholy document, one of the last of Oviedo's writings to come down to us, the very long letter that he wrote on 12 April 1554 to Prince Philip (the future Philip II),[217] and that gives us an extraordinarily vivid and

---

215. *Hist.,* XXVI, 2: II, 337; XXXI, 6: PT, III, 388b, with particular reference to prices.

216. See the long and affectionate description of Santo Domingo (though no longer as populous as in 1525, "because everything in this life has its ups and downs"), *Hist.,* III, 10: I, 82–84. In 1525 it had seven hundred "householders" (*Sum.,* chap. 2, p. 89). And Oviedo had prophesied: "This city is growing every day in size and nobility, and it will get better and better." In point of fact it was already on the downward path: see above, n. 206. On its demographic decline between 1494 and 1514, see Rosenblat, op. cit., pp. 96, 194–96.

On the excellence of its port, where the biggest ships could be unloaded "simply by throwing a plank across to the shore," see *Hist.,* VI, 174a, and on the rapid proliferation of buildings in this "very modern township," IX, 21: I, 352b. the city, founded in its present location after a hurricane had devastated the original site in 1504, was struck again, in 1508 and 1509, with hurricanes that Oviedo describes in splendidly forceful language. He also notes—endorsing the general opinion of the faithful and on the basis of his own experience—that from the time the Holy Sacrament was placed in the churches and monasteries of Santo Domingo "these hurricanes have ceased" (VI, 3: I, 168–69; cf. III, 10: I, 82a). On 3 December 1930, however, a hurricane completely destroyed Santo Domingo. For a time the name itself seemed destined to disappear, when the new capital of the Dominican Republic was christened Ciudad Trujillo.

217. Published by Otte, "Una carta inédita." Otte, who has a rather low opinion of Oviedo as a young man ("a resentful, eccentric and pugnacious man," fanatical and conceited), finds signs of dotage also in his final request for the governorship of Cartagena, which was ignominiously rejected by the Council of the Indies ("Aspiraciones y actividades," pp. 19, 49–50).

sordid picture of the once illustrious city in which Oviedo had lived for so many years.

In fifty-eight compact little chapters the commandant, who had been appointed perpetual *regidor* of the city of Santo Domingo in 1549, informs the young sovereign of the causes of the ruin of the island, "which is in a very poor state," causes that can be summed up as bad government, corruption, abuse, and pure and simple barefaced robbery. "This poor city is a prey of vultures."

Oviedo is now seventy-six, deaf as a post,[218] and up against the whole administration of the colony, led by the fearsome Diego Caballero, disturbed and angry at Oviedo's accusations.[219] But Oviedo's indictment is irrepressible and interminable, a veritable kaleidoscope of miseries, abuse, and ignominy, winding and unwinding like the coils of some great long snake, weaving together a thin stream of slander and a hefty list of despairing grievances.[220] Even *de minimis curat regidor*.

To begin with, or rather to put first things first, the fortress is not properly maintained and its commandant miserably paid. The church has no bishop and the clergy trade in soap, boots, and garlic (and the prices they charge!). The place is crawling with clerks, attorneys, pettifoggers of all sorts, "a swarming multitude of lawyers, etc. . . . greedy and quarrelsome and unworthy people," and all of them "stealing openly" (chap. 6 and 33). The property of the town council is squandered on gifts like gold chains, suede gloves, horses, slaves, Negroes, emeralds. The saltflats are contracted out to peculators, who spend their time, Oviedo says, playing "papasal," which is of course a children's game, but also means "eating up the salt." And when it was suggested that there should be a circuit of fortifications round the city, the people who owned land arranged for their "building plots" to be included within the circuit, even if it would have taken more than ten thousand armed men to defend such an extended line of walls.[221] Moreover three of the town councillors have already built their houses with lime mortar belonging to the town, which they acquired by cheating on the weight . . . (chap. 11).

There are swindles on cowhides and bricks, which are of very poor quality. Here Oviedo recognizes that he is actually arguing against his own interests, because his only daughter and son-in-law own the biggest herds on the whole island; but if the scandal goes on "this island will be lost" (chap. 13). The expected reward, promised to someone for capturing a highly dangerous Negro, was not paid, and the money in question—the property of His Majesty—was

---

218. Otte, "Una carta inédita," pars. 32, 52; Pérez de Tudela, "Vida," p. cxxxiii.

219. Letter of 29 August 1554, published by Otte, in "Kaiser Karl V."

220. A similar series of longwinded denunciations ("Oviedo shows no respect for anything") in a document of 1544 (Otte, "Aspiraciones y actividades," p. 48).

221. In 1543 Oviedo was the first to refuse to pay the *sisa* (levy) imposed for the construction of the ring of fortifications (Palm, *Monumentos arquitectónicos*, I, 156–59; Otte, "Aspiraciones y actividades," p. 48*n104*).

spent instead in building a convent for the daughters and daughters-in-law of the "bigshots" (chap. 14 and 15). A benefactor's will is disregarded and distorted—"I would like everybody to give alms out of his own pocket and not somebody else's" (chap. 16)—and even the wretched bones of the deceased were removed from the church and dumped in a classroom! (chap. 42).

The biscuit, flour, and sardines on board a caravel that had put into the harbor were "plundered" by the usual profiteers, who then had the effrontery to come and ask Oviedo himself to account for the stolen goods. And shortly afterward, while the populace was dying of hunger, they gave a splendid banquet, with excellent fresh bread, to fifteen guests and their consorts, followed by a bullfight and finally a tournament. It was hardly the moment to be partying, when French pirates had sacked and burned the township of Yaguana, while the naval expedition sent to fight the French, taking with it nine excellent bronze cannon ("de bronzo"—a significant Italianism), had been dashed to pieces by a violent storm, and one ship that went down was commanded by a youth of twenty, "completely inexperienced," whose father, in his determination to give him a command, thus succeeded in drowning his own son and his entire crew with him (chap. 20 to 22).

Other unnecessary works of defense and embellishment are denounced unrelentingly, as also the shameless nepotism in awarding offices and benefices, the fraudulent auctions, the culpable and criminal negligence in signing the town council's acts, the arrogance of having its books brought to one at home, and even open violence in the form of the stabbing of an "honest lawyer" (what a rarity!), one highly esteemed in the city (but at least in this case the guilty party was hanged!).

The sumptuary laws are not observed, despite the sky-high prices of silks and velvets. Likewise the nitre (saltpeter) indispensable for making gunpowder can in fact be found not far away, on the island of Margarita, off the Venezuelan coast, but it is imported at great trouble and expense from Tembleque near Toledo, via the Casa de Contratación in Seville.[222] A building belonging to the city is requisitioned for the lodging of certain officials and then when Diego Caballero—him again—is due to hand it back, he has it split in two and this un-Solomonic operation results in the destruction of no less than a brick staircase belonging to the Public Treasury!

On the other hand the life of a French pilot captured with his wife or concubine, apparently Andalusian (from Sanlúcar de Barrameda) is unjustifiably spared ("he should have been hanged or put permanently in the stocks"), and he is in fact lodged in the new house just referred to. In this house, only a few yards from Oviedo's fort, the wretched fellow—probably suffering from nostalgia—makes a habit of climbing up onto the roof terrace and gazing pensively out to

---

222. On another ingredient of the highly necessary gunpowder, see below, chap. XVIII, 232.

sea, for all the world like some sort of lookout. Eventually, some three or four months later, he learns that his French fellow-pirates are plundering the coast and flees during the night to join them, but then, in an excess of gallantry, comes back to collect "his wife and girlfriend" and twenty horsemen and six arquebusiers have to be sent out after him (chap. 43).

Another law to which a blind eye is turned, for reasons of gain, is the law very rightly forbidding the sale of wine to Negroes, both because they get drunk and because they steal without hindrance to be able to get drunk. The same applies to the law banning card games, and in fact there is gambling, and heavy gambling, in numerous houses and even on the doorsteps and in the doorways, out in the open, without the authorities lifting a finger; a barrel-load of playing cards is smuggled in as heaven knows what sort of merchandise and then illegally deposited in the arsenal as "lost property"! There are even lotteries for silverware and other things, "which is an honest manner of public robbery."

The jeremiad comes to an end. Oviedo's last hope, his ultimate remedy, is that Licentiate Alonso López Cerrato should be sent out with full powers to put things to rights. But the hope is voiced without conviction, half-heartedly, almost knowing that Prince Philip will do nothing about it. And in any case Oviedo had crossed swords with Cerrato more than once in the past, so that it is quite surprising that he should timidly and belatedly put forward his name.[223] Only three years later death came to assuage these long-standing grudges, cut short the denunciations, and cause the once proudly upheld accusing finger to fall back inert.

223. Otte, "Aspiraciones y actividades," p. 48n105; Pérez de Tudela, "Vida," pp. cxxxv, clix. In the *Historia* Oviedo can be found giving a cautious but harsh verdict on Cerrato (V, 12: Pt, I, 140), or else scoring out his name (XVII, 26: PT, II, 167) or reporting acts of severity on his part (XXVI, 17: PT, III, 99–100). On his relations with Oviedo, see W. L. Sherman, "Indian Slavery and the Cerrato reforms," *HAHR*, 51, no. 1 (1971), 28. On the ambiguous figure of Cerrato, "an old man of great guile and artfulness, and well able to use these gifts" (Bernal Díaz del Castillo in a letter of 22 February 1552), at first protected but later attacked by Las Casas (cf. MacLeod, op. cit., pp. 114–15), self-proclaimed as an incorruptible judge (refusing to take even so much as a chicken as a gift and refraining from paying court to the residents' wives), and subsequently accused of granting scandalously improper *repartimientos* of Indians to relatives and friends, see M. Bataillon, *Etudes sur Bartolomé de Las Casas* (Paris, 1965), pp. 200–01, 239–47, who, like Oviedo before him (V, 12: PT, I, 140), mentions his glowering features, his sarcasm, and his hectoring ways with anyone who appeared before him, reported with great gusto by Díaz del Castillo and by Sherman, op. cit., p. 33. Benzoni, ed. cit., (1965), pp. 44, 78, 196, who met Cerrato when he came to Santo Domingo to proclaim the freedom of the Indians, and again in Guatemala in 1553, pronounces a more generous verdict on him. MacLeod, op. cit., passim, esp. pp. 52–56, 109–16, 415n39, and 416n59, reaches a substantially positive conclusion on Cerrato's actions in Guatemala. But it is always possible that the elderly and embittered Oviedo only really meant to say: "What we need here is someone like Cerrato, who never cared a fig for anyone in Guatemala."

❦ XVIII ❦

View of the Historical and Natural World

1. PROVIDENTIAL OPTIMISM AND HISTORICAL PESSIMISM

F O R Oviedo, everything is material for history. But his view of the world of men is altogether different from his view of the realms of nature. Natural history and "general" history are coupled even in the title of his major work. In a certain sense, as we have already seen, one is the necessary complement of the other. But just as they are unequal in their degree of certainty and therefore in historical worthiness, so Oviedo's attitude of mind toward the two fields varies. Possibly as a reflection of the abovementioned gnoseological premises or more probably as a result of an accurate approximative intuition of the New World and its role in universal history — an intuition rooted in the spirit of the new times, which were eagerly apprehending the external world and manifesting a certain incipient disgust at the bloody vanity of war — Oviedo might be said, in a word, to be pessimistic about "history" and optimistic about "nature."

When he recalls his Christian faith Oviedo never fails to bow down before the inscrutable judgment of Divine Providence and sees the endless ups and downs of life as reflection of the avenging hand of supreme Justice;[1] but more often he openly expresses his bitterness at the way things go, at how easily the unworthy grow rich, while the deserving (including Oviedo) remain without "property," or lose what they have in the king's service.

We have already seen how he has to invoke irrational Fortune to explain the fall of the wisest and wealthiest princes, and we shall see further on how he takes a certain lugubrious and malicious delight in telling us of the catastrophes that smite the powerful. So that while human history sometimes strikes him as tragic (see above, chap. XVII, sec. 21), there are other times when he finds it "diaboli-

---

1. One example: "I find this business quite inscrutable or unintelligible once one tries to look into it closely, because it has not been within anyone's power to prevent things turning out the way they did. For myself, I think that the sins of some and the unworthiness of others lay at the root of their misfortunes," etc. (*Hist.*, XLVIII, Proh.: PT, V, 213).

cal": "The condition of the world is such that evil never lacks favor or supporters, through the industry of the common adversary of mankind."[2] The wise come to grief, and the flower of knighthood perishes. The gold flows into the hands of those who least deserve it, and the "honors" are so unevenly distributed that the historian has to intervene to bring about a little posthumous justice. And then one begins to wonder whether Oviedo might not have been more than a little influenced by the radical pessimism of Saint Augustine's disciple, the Spaniard Orosius, the doleful and widely read author of that *Moesta Mundi* that was also known as the *De miseria mundi,* or "museum of the horrors of history."[3] The powerful can always find someone to agree with them. And Oviedo, as we shall see, finds something to criticize about everybody: the Indians, Spaniards, captains, priests, lawyers, foreigners, and even—on rare occasions—the sovereign himself.

His chronic dissatisfaction often leads him into a sermonizing moralism, a moralism so universal that it achieves a certain negative impartiality, while at the same time making it impossible for him to understand the convergence of forces by which Spaniards and foreigners, sovereigns and soldiers, priests and Indians, willy-nilly and brawling with one another, succeeded in creating a new society in the land of America. The story of these endeavors, in which (for us at least) it is relatively easy to detect the arduous but triumphant march of civilization, a "manifest" if bloody destiny, a Vicoan "immanissima umanità," is however twisted in Oviedo's eyes into a meaningless series of adventures, sufferings, and slaughters. "I see that these changes of fortune and similar things of great importance do not always seem reasonable or what would seem just to men, but [the usual providential disclaimer] another higher definition and judgment of God that is beyond our understanding. . . . we cannot understand the ends for which things are done: and of God's providence it is not seemly that we should talk or think."[4]

2. NATURE MAGNIFIED

If the world of men is absurd and the observer can only find a rational explanation by invoking the higher authority of the Eternal Father, the world of nature is God's very reason unfolded and revealed in the phenomena. Divine omnipotence shines forth in the variety of the created world. This same creative omnipotence, that was to be exploited in various ways in the polemics of future centuries, becomes an argument to destroy the objections of theoretical and speculative naturalists. To those who maintain that the poles and tropics are

---

2. Ibid., XLIX, 8: IV, 398.
3. M. Niccoli, in *Enciclopedia Italiana,* s.v. "Orosio." Oviedo cites the *Ormesta Mundi* in the preface to the second part of the *Historia* (PT, II, 214b) and in XLI, 3: PT, IV, 354b.
4. *Hist.,* XXXIII, 12: III, 316b.

uninhabitable for man Oviedo retorts triumphantly not with the simple fact of the existence of natives between the tropics, but by insisting logically and firmly that God is not so impotent as to be unable to overcome these difficulties.[5]

The variety of creation and the delight in "peregrinations" through ever new lands are among the clearest motifs in Oviedo and are linked naturally and effortlessly with his faith in the Creator. His mission, joyfully accepted, is to see and narrate whatever exists in the wide world: "We should not be surprised at any people, clothed or naked, because the world is large and not all men can see it; and therefore God wishes that I and others should undertake these peregrinations and should see them [sic] and write of them, so that they should be known to everybody and God should be praised for everything."[6] "The world is a beautiful thing,"[7] and every part of it admirable. The Indies are its most stupendous part. As he tries to take in this world with a single glance, Oviedo is overcome with emotion and bewilderment: "What mortal mind can comprehend such diversity of languages, of clothing and customs in the men of these Indies? Such variety of animals . . .? Such an untellable multitude of trees . . . useful plants and herbs . . . innumerable others that are unknown to him . . . such variety of roses and flowers and sweet-smelling fragrance?" and so on, for one whole column and half the next, underlining the benign fecundity of nature, but not forgetting the wild animals, volcanoes, birds of prey, and mountains "so different and rugged."[8] As he sets out on the third part of the *History* Oviedo gloomily confesses his feeling of inadequacy before a world so vast and stupefying: "I well know that I am at the end of my life, and I find myself only just approaching the substance of the great and innumerable secrets about to be revealed in the second hemisphere. . . ."[9]

This commitment to exalting the greatness of the new lands robs Oviedo's detailed observations of any hint of denigration. He may find some animal or plant inferior to its counterpart in Spain, but he knows full well that taken overall American nature is so exuberant, richly diverse, and opulent that the emperor must be proud of these dominions of his, and God on high, if we can ascribe pride to Him, proud of these His creatures.

If Oviedo sometimes goes overboard, it is enthusiasm that carries him away.

---

5. Ibid., XXXVIII, sole chapter: III, 636a. And in similar vein elsewhere: "Understand then, gentle reader, that he who was able to make the world was capable of ordaining and creating within it everything of these parts that can be expressed by human voice, and incomparably more, in what remains to be said of these Indies" (XXXI, Proh.: III, 186b). On the tropics, see XXI, 6: II, 128a. The empirical proof of the Spaniards ("every day our Spaniards pass from the Tropic of Cancer to the Tropic of Capricorn and back") is advanced by Oviedo, together with other details on the inhabitability of the tropical regions, in XXXIX, Proh.: IV, 2a.

6. Ibid., XXVI, 10: II, 356b.

7. Ibid., XXXVIII, Proh.: III, 635a.

8. Ibid., I, sole chapter: I, 2–3.

9. Ibid., XXXIX, Proh.: IV, 1b. Pérez de Tudela writes that Oviedo was the first person fully to grasp the providential significance, the limitless natural exuberance and divine majesty of the New World ("Vision de la découverte," pp. 267, 275).

The providentiality of nature sometimes culminates in its appearing to be benevolently disposed toward man, whether native or European, or even Spanish soldier, a notion that curiously foreshadows the "harmonies" of Bernardin de Saint Pierre. Even the dried faeces of the Panamanian alligator serve to sharpen the Castilians' steel weapons: "They are better than pumice stone and emery to scrape and clean swords, and they do not scratch them; and when there were no swordsmiths the Spaniards cleaned their swords with these stones, or whatever they are."[10]

3. OLD WORLD AND NEW

This genuine sympathy for the New World helps Oviedo to pinpoint its position very accurately in relation to the Old. For the latter, as we have seen, Oviedo nourishes a filial affection and enduring interest. Only in one passage, written (in 1544) when the fortunes of war were turning in favor of Francis I, who was bombarding Nice, crossing the Alps, and winning at Ceresole while his barbarian allies were beating Charles V in Africa, does Oviedo, with obvious reluctance, abruptly turn his back on the Old World: "Let us leave this material of Asia, Africa, and Europe, that are so troubled in our time and in much danger, since here in the Indies we are so far from where these things are happening. . . . let us turn to the narration of this western empire of our Indies."[11]

But in general Oviedo sees the New World as the complement and not the antithesis of the Old. The two "worlds" are a single world, finally aware of its own oneness. Peter Martyr was, as usual, completely wrong in calling his decades the *Decades of the New World,* "because this world over here is neither newer nor older than Asia, Africa, and Europe." Merely because the great kingdoms of the Indies found no place in those three parts already known to the ancients "it seemed to the said author that he and his decades were dealing with a new world."[12]

4. PERILS AND PROBLEMS INHERENT IN THE ANTITHESIS

But here it must immediately be said that the term "New World," that we find so appropriate and natural, encountered considerable—and not altogether unrea-

---

10. *Hist.,* XLIII, 2: IV, 118b.

11. Ibid., XXXIII, 54: III, 546b. Oviedo takes his cue from the German historian Johannes Carion (on whom see Fueter, op. cit., pp. 186–87), consoling himself with Carion's prophecy that the German Empire (i.e., Charles V's) would last until the end of the world. I think it must be Carion's *Chronicle* (*Chronicarum ab initio mundi . . . ,* alias *Chronica teutonica*) that is cited with regard to Cain being killed by an arrow ("*Chronica Theutonica,* that deals with matters from the beginning of the world," III, 5: I, 68a), and in connection with Semiramis's tresses (XXIX, 21: IV, 118b) and the Apostles' abstinence (XXIX, 21: III, 103–04).

Johannes Carion's *Chronica* was published in Spanish (Medina del Campo, 1553; Antwerp, 1553) with the title *Suma y Compendio de todas las chrónicas del mundo, desde su principio hasta el año presente,* which translation was put on the index in 1583 (Bonilla y San Martín, "Erasmo," 498–99). But Oviedo appears to quote from a Latin translation of the original German (*Hist.,* III, 5: I, 68a; XXXIII, 54: III, 545a), on which see Turner, "Biblioteca Ovetense," p. 164, no. 27. Carion is also quoted in *Qu.,* pp. 102, 133, 136. In the same work Oviedo mentions other northern historians, though from an earlier epoch, Walafridus Strabone (*Qu.,* p. 298) and Helinandus (*Qu.,* p. 336).

12. *Hist.,* XVI, Proh.: I, 462–63.

sonable — psychological resistance before eventually being adopted. The inevitable contrast between Old World and New World lies at the root of all subsequent antitheses and polarizations, inappropriate comparisons and parallels. It is transformed too easily from an unarguable chronological relationship into a sophistical logical relationship, into an idealization or denigration of one or other world.

Oviedo is clearly reluctant to use the term "New World," that from its origins and right into our own times has always had a strongly emotional connotation, a polemical hue that could not have pleased the naturalist. He uses it almost exclusively in phrases where the courtier's voice is uppermost, to extol the greatness of the Catholic Kings, who "discovered this New World of these Indies,"[13] or the glory of Columbus, who "showed us this New World, so overflowing with gold,"[14] or the "magnificent, learned and noble gentlemen enrolled and delegated for the government of this New World,"[15] or to magnify his labor, "an account of a New World and a great sea."[16] The accolade awarded him by Humboldt for having "very sagely" discussed the question of whether the new lands merited the title of New World is thus richly deserved.[17]

The expression was probably born with Columbus himself, ever intent on magnifying his discovery. It is true that Peter Martyr uses it several times, as early as October and November 1493, if we can accept the dates that he puts on his letters, but he does it with a certain suspicious emphasis. When the letters were published for the first time, in 1530, Peter Martyr was already the author of the decades *De Orbe Novo* (1511, 1516) recalled sarcastically by Oviedo. Moreover, the letters would have been written when Columbus was not yet back from his second voyage.[18] Only on the third voyage, on first glimpsing (1498), to the south of Trinidad, the coastline of the mainland — which he still thought to be an island — did Columbus become convinced "that to the south there lay an infinite land, of which up until then nothing had been known": "so many [islands?], that are another world," as he then repeats several times.[19] And in the *Libro de Profecías* (1501–1502) the lines from Seneca's *Medea* (378–79) on the ocean, "let him discover new worlds; and let there not be any final limit to the lands," are translated by ear, but used with a view to magnifying the importance of the

---

13. Ibid., VI, 8, par. 4: I, 180a; but in the same sentence Charles is described as lord "of this other half of the world made up of his Indies."

14. Ibid., VI, 8, par. 11: I, 191b.

15. Ibid., VII, Proh.: I, 263b.

16. Ibid., L, 30: IV, 592a.

17. *Examen critique*, IV, 133–34.

18. Ibid., III, 179–81; Vignaud, *Histoire critique*, II, 290n52. On the dubious dates of various of Peter Martyr's letters see for example Humboldt, *Examen critique*, II, 291–93, and I. Bernays, *Peter Martyr von Angleria und sein "Opus epistolarum"* (Strasbourg, 1891). Morison (*Admiral of the Ocean Sea*, I, 71) says that the term "New World" was coined by Peter Martyr, and Luis H. Arocena says the same in his preface to the Buenos Aires reprint (1944) of the Spanish translation of the *Decades* (p. xiv).

19. Morison, *Admiral of the Ocean Sea*, II, 268–69 (abridged ed., pp. 383–84); *Relaciones y cartas*, pp. 271, 292, 320; Molinari, op. cit., p. 42.

discovery and applied to himself, Columbus: "a new sailor . . . will discover the new world."[20] Even the famous motto "Por Castilla y por León *nuevo mundo halló Colón*" ("For Castile and for Leon, a new world Columbus found"), although dated 1493 by Oviedo,[21] seems certain to be considerably later, probably from 1530 or thereabouts.[22] Contemporary writers were more guarded on the subject. And one of the most recent authorities is peremptory to the point of paradox: "Columbus did not discover the New World."[23]

Vespucci still hesitated in writing of the new lands, "which might legitimately be called New World, since amongst our ancestors nothing was known of it and it is a very new thing to everybody's ears." More boldly Fra Giovanni Giocondo actually gave the title *Mundus Novus* to the letter from "Albericus Vespucius" to Lorenzo di Pietro Francesco de' Medici (ca. 1502), in which the Florentine did indeed write that the newly discovered region "can legitimately be called the New World," the letter being circulated in various Latin editions and in German, French, and Dutch translations in the early years of the sixteenth century.[24] And even in our own day Vespucci and his 1502 reports (circulated in amplified form by the forgeries) are given exclusive credit by Pohl,[25] his most recent biographer, for having certified that the lands beyond the Atlantic were a real new world, a continent and not an archipelago; new, and not Asiatic. But the proud title still met resistance.

In the Vicenza edition (1507), entitled "The New World and countries newly found by the Florentine Alberico Vespuccio," the ample formula contained in the title is used generically, since the volume includes the journeys of Vasco da Gama and Cadamosto and, in the fourth of the six books, the *Libretto de tutta la navigazione de' re di Spagna* (first edition, Venice 1504) with Columbus's first three journeys and those of Pedro Alonzo "the Black" and Vicente Yáñez Pinzón.[26] Cadamosto himself, writing toward the middle of the fifteenth century, had called the west coast of Africa "another world." The term "New World," suggestively evocative of the expressions used by the early geographers (expressions which Humboldt has listed and annotated in very scholarly fashion),[27] was in fact a normal way of referring to any important discovery.

20. Vignaud, *Etudes critiques sur la vie de Colomb* (Paris, 1905), pp. 382, 415; Morison, *Admiral of the Ocean Sea*, I, 101.

21. *Hist.*, II, 7: I, 31b. In 1485 Columbus promised to discover "this New World," (ibid., II, 4: I, 19a, 20b), and later made the same promise to his sailors (II, 5: I, 23a). According to Reyes (*Ultima Tule*, p. 82) Columbus used the term "New World" to describe the lands discovered "without actually using the phrase in anything but a rhetorical sense," but the geographers realized "little by little that it was in fact a new world." For Columbus, Peter Martyr, etc., "New World" meant a land unknown to Ptolemy (Morison, *Southern Voyages*, pp. 98–99, 155).

22. Vignaud, *Etudes critiques*, pp. 83–93.

23. D. B. Quinn, "New Geographical Horizons: Literature," in *First Images of America: The Impact of the New World on the Old*, ed. F. Chiappelli (Berkeley and Los Angeles, 1976), p. 639.

24. Humboldt, *Examen critique*, III, 79: V, 10; Winsor, op. cit., II, 156–59, 169; Molinari, op. cit., p. 51.

25. Pohl, op. cit., pp. 140, 228.

26. Humboldt, *Examen critique*, IV, 77–81.

27. Ibid., I, 113–21; V, 182–84.

Cadamosto applies it to Africa, Peter Martyr to what he thought was Asia. Columbus uses it to glorify the vastness of the lands opened to Spain's dominion, to express the surprise, the wonder, the enchantment of the discovery, his own like any other discovery.

5. MESSIANISM OF THE TERM

Small wonder, then, that it was some time before this immensely promising formula came to be permanently attached to the group of islands and coastlines that were still far from revealing the profile of a continent. A possibly decisive factor in its adoption was the immediate burgeoning of hopes and utopian visions that resulted from the discovery of the lands across the sea; the prophetic dreams of European reformers proved more significant than mere chronological notation, endowing the formula with a messianic sense that dominated the imagination and imposed itself on the lexicon. In this sense the Americas were a new world, not because they were known *after* the old world, but because they were known by Renaissance Europe, avid for new worlds.[28]

A classical and Christian aspiration, rooted in the mists of time, found its fulfilment in this world beyond the seas, endowing it with an ideological and necessary newness to which the date of discovery served merely as an opportune pretext, as empirical justification. In this sense Vasco de Quiroga could write in 1535 that "this world over here is rightly called a New World, not because it was newly found, but because in its people and in almost everything it resembles the world of the first age, the golden age"[29]—new, therefore, because virgin, uncontaminated, pure, and sparkling.

The Latin translation (Milan, 1508) of the Vicenza collection (see above, sec. 4) actually abandons the title "New World" in favor of the more prosaic title *Itinerarium Portugallensium ex Ulisbona in Indiam* ("Of the Portuguese journeys from Lisbon to the Indies")—according to Humboldt, as a consequence of the "ever increasing interest in the sea-route to Calicut." Even in this the term "other world" refers to the part of equatorial Africa seen by Cadamosto. In the title of the coeval German translation, mention of the new world ("ein newe weldte")[30] is preceded by the lands discovered ("Unbekanthe Lande"), and another German edition, discovered by Humboldt in Dresden, talks even more vaguely about a "newly found nation that could well be called a world," miraculously discovered

---

28. Zavala, who made a detailed study of the attempts to create utopias in Mexico, comments that the efforts to build a world in America that was better than the European model led to its being "not a new world in the sense of geographical discovery, but in the sense of its promise for mankind" (*New Viewpoints*, p. 113). In the same line of thinking see the later examples (1564, 1594, 1645, 1682, 1690) of the highly evocative antithesis commented on by S. Landucci, *I filosofi e i selvaggi, 1580–1780* (Bari, 1972), pp. 39, 46, 164, 214, and those (dating from 1555, 1575, 1578, 1594) collected by Le Moine, op. cit.; cf. also above, chap. 1, sec. 5.

29. S. Zavala, *Ideario de Vasco de Quiroga* (Mexico, 1941), p. 40, citing *CDII*, X, 363.

30. Humboldt, *Examen critique*, IV, 84–87.

by the king of Portugal.[31] On a map dating from that same year, 1508, South America is baptized "Land of the Holy Cross or new world," but a note adds "this region is thought by many to be another world."[32]

Only when Pinzón's and Solís's voyages (1508) gave an idea of the extent of the Americas, and particularly after Balboa had discovered the Pacific Ocean (1513), did the Europeans realize, with growing wonderment, that the "Indies" were in reality, and not only on a provisional and rhetorical basis, a whole "world," and a new world. The subsequent revelations, enormously amplifying the horizon of the Antilles and the Caribbean, justified "more and more a name which had originally not been taken in a very precise geographical sense."[33]

6. ONENESS OF THE TERRAQUEOUS GLOBE

But in reality, Oviedo repeats, "the mainland of these Indies is another half of the world, as big as or perhaps bigger than Asia, Africa, and Europe: and . . . all the land of the universe is divided into two parts, and . . . one is the one the ancients called Asia and Africa and Europe . . . and the other part or half of the world is this one of our Indies." Only in this sense can one agree to Peter Martyr calling it the New World, on the basis of what the ancients were unaware of "and we can see."[34] The ancients knew the Hesperides, which Oviedo identifies with the Antilles. The mainland, however, is not the Hesperides, but "the half or greater part of the two main parts that the whole universe contains."[35]

Oviedo is so pleased at the notion of this ideological oneness of the world that he is delighted when he learns that there is also someone who affirms the physical oneness of all the land on the globe (Olaus Magnus, see above, chap. XV, sec. 8). He repeats the idea a number of times, scarcely varying the wording;[36] firmly rejects the ancient theories asserting the uninhabitability of one or other part of the terraqueous globe, the poles, tropics, or antipodes;[37] and uses it as the basis for his descriptive technique, relating to European things (and most often, as we have seen, to things of Spain and Italy) the unusual aspects of this new world which together with the *old* is *the* world.

The American continent completes the world. Discovered by the Old, it repays

---

31. Ibid., V, 6.

32. Ibid., II, 6.

33. Ibid., V, 184n; cf. Vignaud, *Etudes critiques*, p. 87.

34. The same idea of antiquity's necessary ignorance of the Indies reoccurs in *Hist.*, XVI, Proh.: I, 464b, and XXXIX, Proh.: IV, 1b. Alvarez López writes that for Oviedo the New World was no newer than the Old as creation, but new for the heirs of classical tradition, which had been unaware of it ("Historia natural," p. 547). On antiquity's ignorance of the extreme north too, see *Hist.*, XXI, Proh.: II, 112a; XXI, 5: II, 127b.

35. *Hist.*, XVI, Proh.: I, 463. On the Americas as "half the universal world, bigger than all those three parts, Asia, Africa and Europe, which in the imagination of the ancients made up the whole world": ibid., XXI, 7: II, 136a; cf. XX, Preface to the 2d pt.: II, 2a. "The Tierra Firme is another half of the world" (XVII, 7: I, 502b).

36. Ibid., XVI, Proh.: I, 462b, 463b, 464b; XXII, Proh.: II, 154b; XXXV, 4: III, 597b.

37. *Sum.*, chap. 10, pp. 118–19; *Hist.*, XXXIX, Proh.: PT, IV, 336–67; XXI, Proh.: PT, II, 306a; XXI, 5: PT, II, 319b.

it by bringing it to an awareness of the totality of the earth, in other words making it more conscious of itself. This lofty concept, implicit in Oviedo and still obscured by polemical considerations, but already more distinct in the naively resounding titles of contemporary geographical treatises like Sebastian Franck's *Weltbuch, Spiegel und Bildniss des gantzen Erdbodens* (Tübigen, 1534), Francesco Filopono's description of the *whole* earth (1557), and others,[38] was to become explicit only two centuries later, with Antonio de Ulloa's fulminations against the chronological or genealogical denigrations of the "new" world. "Who would have believed that those countries [America], not long ago unknown, were to be the medium and instrument through which one was to come to perfect knowledge and notice of the Old World; and that just as the New owed it its discovery, it was to repay this advantage by revealing to the Old World its own true shape, hitherto either unknown or denied."[39] And the message was to ring out loud and clear when Chocano sang Spain's praises by assuring it that "for you the Sphere was completed," and by telling the sovereigns that it was their dynastic boldness that had "rounded off the planet."[40]

7. OVIEDO AND ANTIQUITY

For Oviedo, as earlier for Vespucci, the Indies are "new" only inasmuch as they were unknown to the ancients. This may not be any special merit, but it is no defect either, no stigma of barbaric inferiority, no "eccentricity" as compared with the Europeocentric Graeco-Latin world. Oviedo's attitude to classical antiquity is complex and influenced by his anti-Roman patriotism, his much-regretted weakness in Latin, and his scorn for tradition when direct experience is possible.

Oviedo recalls that the extremely practical canoes used by almost all the Indians are like those "little boats made from a single log" that Pliny describes.[41] But when he cites Pliny in witness of the generation of worms and maggots in dead flesh he immediately burst out, "but why should I need Pliny or any other ancient author to prove the things that we see every day and that are well known to all men?"[42] In another place[43] Oviedo also answers his rhetorical question. If he quotes the ancients it is to make the things of the Indies more easily believable, to show that they are possible, that in fact they are in the nature of things, that they are not at all in contradiction with Pliny's science. In other words he quotes the Latin authors to prove the essential consubstantial oneness of the New World and the most ancient antiquity. The yearning of the Renaissance for

38. Rey Pastor, op. cit., p. 33*n*.
39. J. Juan and A. de Ulloa, *Relación histórica del viage a la América meridional,* bk. I, chap. 1 (Madrid, 1748), vol. I, p. 6.
40. Op. cit., pp. 13, 23.
41. *Hist.,* VI, 4: PT, I, 149a.
42. Ibid., XV, 4: I, 457a.
43. Ibid., XIII, 8: I, 432b, quoted below, chap. VI, n. 21.

totality and harmony is fully and clearly expressed in this immense embrace, linking phenomena separated by fifteen centuries of history and one hundred degrees of longitude.[44]

Oviedo asks himself the same question once again, after describing how the Indians make fire and recalling analogous examples in Pliny and Vitruvius: "But why should I want to produce ancient authorities for the things that I have seen, or those that nature teaches to everyone and can be seen any day?" Even carters know perfectly well that axles scorch and burn if a heavily laden cart goes too fast. Oviedo himself knows it and recalls that when (in 1538) "the very beautiful heavy artillery" was being unloaded from His Imperial Majesty's galleys for the fort in Oviedo's care and the seventy-quintal culverins, fifty-five-quintal cannons, and forty-quintal demiculverins were being dragged along at a run by the teams of Negroes, every fifty paces "the wheels caught fire" and he had to station men with cans of water alongside every team "to douse and put out the fires."[45] From the whirling of wooden spindles in the deft fingers of the natives to the spinning hubs bursting into flame under overloaded wagons and the fire-breathing bronzes being trundled along by African arms—the phenomenon is all one and the same in Oviedo's eyes: a rapid twisting motion produces fire.

Nature is all one, in Oviedo's Indies and Pliny's Rome. The whole world was created by God at a single stroke. The Indies are neither newer nor older than the rest; "it is no less old a land in its creation, nor more modern [in its] people than those inventors named above" (Diodorus Siculus, Pliny, Trogus Pompeius).[46] If anything, if a comparison must be made, America is greater in everything, in both good and bad. Many Jews were slaughtered during the siege and destruction of Jerusalem by Titus; but many more Indians perished in Cortés's conquest of Temistitán.[47]

Likewise Oviedo must reject Pliny's statement that Scythes invented the bow and arrow, Icarus sails, and Daedalus the masts and yards of ships. The Indians are only too familiar with both bow and arrow, and sails and masts, "without Icarus or his father Dacdalus having taught them."[48]

On the other hand numerous aspects and customs of the Indies will appear new, solely because the corresponding European ones fell into oblivion. Here again the Indies complete the science of the Old World, giving it back something

---

44. Thus the problem of a hypothetical "conflict" and "grave dilemma" between the rediscovery of antiquity (humanism) and the sum of the new geographical experiences (e.g., O'Gorman, above, chap. I, sec. 7, and Iglesia, *Cronistas e historiadores*, pp. 80–81) seems to me to be not so much a "fascinating study" as an artificial and misstated problem. The conflict between authority and empiricism is an ideological constant, not specific to the American discoveries. It was if anything the triumph of humanism that made it possible to reconcile the "conflict," despite the vast quantity of new experience, in a joyful and immediate satisfaction at the enrichment of the traditional schemes, that were in fact supplemented and strengthened rather than demolished.

45. *Hist.*, VI, 5: I, 172–73.

46. Ibid., VI, 45: I, 238b.

47. Ibid., XXXIII, 30: PT, IV, 151–52.

48. Ibid., VI, 45: PT, I, 205–06.

it had lost: they complete it in time, so to speak, showing it typical aspects of its own past. What a lot of things there are that "to those that have traveled over here appear new, and in Spain and in other kingdoms also would be held as such," but which are actually very similar to others described by the ancient historians and the Bible.[49] The maize of the Indies is the Indian millet written about by Pliny.[50]

The burial rites of the Indians, who have themselves interred with gold and jewels, are compared with those of the ancient Persians,[51] and their witch doctors and fortune-tellers with the Roman and Carthaginian soothsayers;[52] their tattoos are compared to those of the ancient "Britons or English," who, in the matter of vice (sexual promiscuity) were considerably worse than the Caribbean Indians;[53] and it is also true that the promiscuity of the native women can only be compared to that of "the Thracian people"![54]

The ceremonies used by the Indians to celebrate the cocoa harvest are paralleled with the feasts and sacrifices of the ancients after the crops were gathered in. Even more notably, Oviedo takes this point of comparative ethnography as a cue for a further analogical confirmation of the credibility of the Indian rite: "If such a custom was known to the ancients and among people of such reason, it is not so surprising that the Indians do the same."[55] Three hundred years later Humboldt was to note that all the writers of the sixteenth century, Vespucci, Fernando Columbus, Geraldini, Oviedo, and Peter Martyr, had a tendency "to rediscover amongst newly discovered peoples everything that the Greeks tell us about the earliest epoch of the world and of the customs of the barbarian Scythians and Africans."[56]

8. MUTUAL CORROBORATION

These cursory assimilations were obviously rendered easier and almost obligatory firstly by that error in historical perspective which allowed ancient and remote peoples to be characterized and frozen in paradigms — so that the Greeks, Romans, Scythians, Thracians, Germans, and Tartars were spoken of as though they had never changed in the course of time, as if the descriptions of some particular historian or traveler held true for all time[57] — and secondly by the error in geographical perspective by which the other term in the comparison, the "savage," was undifferentiated, always just simply "the savage," and the Carib,

---

49. Ibid., VI, 49: I, 251b; cf. ibid., p. 244a.
50. Ibid., VII, 1: PT, I, 228b.
51. Ibid., XXVII, 7, 9: II, 444a, 452a.
52. Ibid., XXIX, 26: III, 127–28.
53. Ibid., VIII, 6: I, 298b; XXV, 1: II, 272. On tattoos (without comparisons), XXIX, 7: III, 31a.
54. Ibid., V, 3: I, 135b, 137–38.
55. Ibid., XLII, 11: IV, 93a.
56. *Reise*, III, 397.
57. Hodgen, op. cit., pp. 34–35, 47–48, 137–38, 182.

Redskin, and Hottentot all revealed exactly the same traits, which at times even blurred over into the Aztec, the Peruvian, the Arab, or even the Chinese.

Later, as we know, these parallels became almost commonplace, a standard polemical device. Fontenelle claimed to be prepared to demonstrate "an astonishing conformity between the fables of the Americans and those of the Greeks," since fables were born from the ignorance of primitive peoples and not from a warmer climate or the livelier imagination of the Orientals.[58]

Elsewhere, after listing the various specialized deities of the inhabitants of Nicaragua, Oviedo adds: "So that it seems to me that they imitate the idolaters and gentiles of old, who made Ceres the goddess of abundance and Mars god of battle and Neptune of the sea and the waters, and Vulcan of fire, etc."[59] Likening the crude fetishes of the savages to the divine images of the classical poets, Oviedo boldly forges another link between Old and New World, robs Graeco-Roman antiquity of a little of its age-old prestige, and endows the Indians with an unarguable spiritual dignity.

The argument is so original and so powerful that there would be hardly a single apologist of the Indian who did not seize on it, frequently spoiling it by exaggeration and putting the Indians, whether baptized or innocent savages, above the skeptical and sanguinary pagans. Oviedo is considerably more shrewd and wary. He establishes no superiority on either side. Referring to the Mexicans' rites, he reports that the Romans were neither better nor worse than the Aztecs: "Those famous Romans . . . were neither more holy nor less holy than . . . these Indians. . . . if we look at the ways of the Gentiles in this case, we find them to be as profane and diabolical as those of our Indies."[60] The Indians of Nicaragua are a "very barbaric and ignorant" people, and therefore it comes as no surprise that they should also be idolaters and worship "images of stone and wood and clay, *which I have seen*," if the same is told of Prometheus and the Jews. And if these latter, so protected and favored by God, "were such, it does not seem to me that these other bestial Indians are so deserving of blame."[61]

In the same way, Pliny's description of tortoises is repeated to make what Oviedo says about the enormous West Indian turtles more easily believable to Europeans: "And should anyone doubt what I have said about these animals, let

58. Fontenelle, *"Sur l'historie,"* in *Oeuvres* (Paris, 1766), IX, 400–01; see also F. J. Teggart, *Theory and Processes of History* (Los Angeles, 1941), pp. 94–95.

59. *Hist.,* XLII, 11: IV, 99b.

60. Ibid., XXXIII, 46: III, 403b. With an almost Voltairian touch the legend of the birth of Montezuma's father is compared with the legend of Rhea, mother of Romulus and Remus: see above, chap. XV, n. 141. But Oviedo carefully refrains from the humanistic parallels of someone like Peter Martyr, for example, who seeks in the Indies the classical Amazons and the golden age of the poets: see above, chap. VIII, sec. 9. And when Oviedo refers to the Amazons encountered by Orellana—who also confines himself to saying that "they fought *like* Amazons"—Oviedo adds, "if one can really use the term Amazons," because they do not cut off their right breasts, and therefore "cannot be called Amazons" (*Hist.,* XLIX, 4: PT, V, 240a; cf. L, 24: PT, V, 392a, 394).

61. *Hist.,* XLII, 11: IV, 101–02.

him consult Pliny. . . ."[62] And the descriptions of monsters of old and Plinian prodigies serve to confirm the verisimilitude of the wonders of America.[63]

With the process reversed, American reality serves to illustrate the ancient texts and make them more credible and rational, to reinforce tradition with empirical observation. The savages drink blood to establish an indissoluble pact. So did Catilina's conspirators. "I am sure that Catilina did not know that these Indians form their confederations in this manner, not do they know who Catilina was; nevertheless the one we find written, and the other is here certain and verified."[64]

The common humanity of the savage is revealed and proved on the basis of the texts. What Oviedo *saw* in the Indies corresponds to what he *read* in the Bible. Empiricism and tradition enrich and reinforce one another. America and antiquity unite to give sixteenth-century Europe a new insight, one of the first overall views of the history of the human race.

It has been said of the Elizabethans that they realized that "if . . . the Red Indians could be referred to the men of the traditional Golden Age their novelty was tamed and they could be fitted into the old pattern and enrich it."[65] The same might be said of Oviedo, always provided one leaves aside this suggestion of an attenuation of reality. In him it is the scientific spirit that calls for unity, not some aesthetic yearning for modulated, restrained harmonies. Oviedo wants to "take in" or "comprehend" the New World, which literally means to "include" it in the categories of the known, to represent it as an organic stage in universal history.

9. IBERIAN NATIONALISM

Oviedo, however, does not develop this inspired intuition of his and fails to follow it through to the corollaries that to us seem so obvious. What prevents him setting the discovery and conquest of the Indies in the framework of the history of the whole world and thus limiting (but at the same time confirming) their value and significance—what prevents him considering the Spaniards' undertakings with the same cold objectivity with which he regards the natives' ceremonies is an accentuated Iberian "nationalism," somewhat curiously directed, for the purposes of his polemic, against the exploits and greatness of the ancients, and especially the Romans.

This attitude of scornful condescension has an obvious affinity both with the oft-vaunted superiority of the moderns over the ancients, of living experience over inherited wisdom and—in particular—with the arguments of the deter-

---

62. Ibid., XIII, 8: I, 432b.
63. Ibid., VI, 31: I, 219b.
64. Ibid., XXVII, 5: II, 434b; a similar expression is found in XXVII, 6: II, 435. The prime example of this attitude is Columbus, who *found* what was *written* in the texts: see above, chap. II, sec. 6 (end).
65. E. M. W. Tillyard, *The Elizabethan World Picture* (London, 1943), p. 93.

mined defenders of the new European states against the "barbarian" Romans. Pasquini would soon (1565) be reevaluating pre-Roman civilization at the expense of Rome; Hotman was actually girding himself up to reject Roman law, calling for its replacement with a French law;[66] and well ahead of these lawyers and historians, but certainly in line with the trend of the times (a typical case is his contemporary Ocampo, who saluted the Spanish as founders of *urbs,* the city)[67] Oviedo claimed for Spain an older and more glorious civilization than that of Rome. "Some impassioned modern Italian historians" believed that they were flattering Spain when they said that it received its civil arts and political life from the Romans. But this was completely false. Captains and consuls conquered Spain, but "they did not devote themselves so much to the virtues that they [i.e, the historians] profess, as to martyring Christians" and spreading idolatry. Oviedo gives a long list of Spanish saints martyred "for not wanting to follow or accept the Roman rites and idolatries. And afterward the people that threw these Romans out of Spain were Goths . . . so that Spain has far more reason to glory in its Goths and its own Spanish natives than in the benefits and industry of the Roman people."[68] This curiously romanticized Gothic and Christian nationalism is one of the most typical reflections in Oviedo of the Spanish Renaissance, with its mixture of medieval and modern elements. The dawning awareness of the concept of an Iberian nation and the imperial monarchy merged in strangely archaic forms, drew strength not from the recent example of the expulsion of the Moors, the wars of the Catholic Kings and Charles V, but from remote recollections of the first martyrs and the barbarian invasions.

For Oviedo the deeds of the Spaniards always remain something unique and unprecedented, marvelous and tragic adventures rather than historical fact. In recounting them with absolute simplicity, "without circumlocutions, with the rectitude of the man of religion testifying to what he saw," Oviedo compares himself to Livy and other historians, although they had "elegant letters and polished style."[69] Even when he presents himself as a continuer of Pliny, Oviedo notes: "And although I may not say it as well as he does, I shall speak at least in accordance with the truth, and as an eyewitness."[70] The fair *form* of the ancient Latins is balanced by the rich *substance* of the modern-day Castilian. Cortés is

---

66. On the "destruction of the Roman episode in the French past," see S. Bertelli, *Ribelli, libertini, e ortodossi nella storiografia barocca* (Florence, 1973), pp. 226–30, and cf. p. 294.

67. On Ocampo, see Cirot, op. cit., pp. 108–09, 120–23; Morel-Fatio, *Historiographie,* pp. 79–86.

68. *Hist.,* XX, "Ante-prohemio": II, 3–4. On "those famous Goths" and on the descent of Charles V "from that stock," see XXXVIII, Proh.: III, 634b. But in the *Quinquagenas* (pp. 491–92) Oviedo makes fun of those who claim descent from the Goths, as if this racial qualification was the equivalent of a patent of nobility. Elsewhere he boasts that the Spaniards are *all* valiant warriors, while in Italy, France, etc., only the nobles and knights devote themselves to the pursuit of arms, while the common people, the artisans, peasants, and plebs, neither indulge in warlike exercises nor show any admiration for them (*Hist.,* XVI, 7: I, 475b).

69. *Hist.,* L, 24: IV, 541a.

70. Ibid., XIII, Proh.: I, 423.

greater than Julius Caesar (and the Spaniard Viriathus) because he found himself having to fight in an unfamiliar and hostile terrain.[71]

On a more general level, the great deeds of the ancients cannot be compared even remotely with those of the Castilians. Columbus had launched this theme with his challenge; "Let those who have read the histories of Greeks and Romans tell me whether with so little they extended their sway so greatly, as now did your Majesty that of Spain with the Indies."[72] The chronicler Francisco de Jerez, whose manuscripts Oviedo had before him,[73] wrote in the prologue to his *True Account of the Conquest of Peru* (1534) that the exploits of the ancients and the moderns were eclipsed by the Iberian feats in the Indies, "and who can match those of Spain?"[74]

Oviedo, following here at least in Peter Martyr's footsteps (see above, chap. VIII, sec. 19), transfers the boast from the land conquered to the deed of the conqueror, from the prey to the hunt: "All the sailing that Ulysses did in his whole life is much less than the crossing from Spain to our Indies. . . . let the vessel of *Argo* stay silent, since we saw not long ago a vessel named the *Victoria,* that circumnavigated the world."[75]

10. JASON AND MAGELLAN

The superiority of the *Victoria* over the *Argo* is a notion already found in Transylvanus's *Relación.*[76] He in turn is followed and paraphrased by Ariosto ("but as the years pass I see emerging from the farthest West *New Argonauts* and new Tiphyses");[77] by Tasso (Magellan and his vessel "victorious and imitating the sun");[78] by Ronsard and an anonymous Frenchman of the early seventeenth century, for whom Jason's deeds are outshone by—need it be said—the Frenchmen André Thevet and Jean Alphonse;[79] and by Góngora, who has high praise for the pilots Tiphys and Palinurus "although both sailed a sea which the land had left as a pond," but higher praise still for the ships that furrowed not the enclosed Mediterranean but the broad ocean, including Magellan's, which "hangs, stranded in Neptune's watery temple, gaining immortal memory under the name of *Victoria.*"[80] The theme reoccurs in innumerable other poets, but if

---

71. Ibid., XXXIII, 20: III, 360; XXXIII, 29: III, 412. Almagro endured greater travails and dangers than the warriors of antiquity. Cf. below, chap. XIX, n. 13.
72. Letter of 1498, *Relaciones y cartas,* p. 262; cf. ibid., p. 271.
73. *Hist.,* XLVI, 14–15: PT, V, 84–85.
74. (Madrid, 1862), p. 319; Esteve Barba, op. cit., p. 398. Jerez also compares the Inca militia to disciplined Turkish troops, op. cit., p. 334b.
75. *Hist.,* XXXI, Proh.: III, 185.
76. In Navarrete, op. cit., IV, 284 (1522); and cf. Peter Martyr, *Dec.,* V, 7, p. 438; also see above, chap. VIII, n. 123.
77. *Orlando Furioso,* XV, 21.
78. *Gerusalemme Liberata,* XV, 30.
79. Le Moine, op. cit., pp. 204–05, 245.
80. *Soledad Primera,* lines 397–402, 466–80.

one name stands out it is that of Campanella, who in his verses *To The Italians Intent on Poetizing with the Greek Fables* (Madrigals 1, 2, and 3) ridicules Greece for having sailed "three spans of sea" in search of the Golden Fleece and then proceeding to "flatter the whole world with fables and extract unending praise from it," while Italy, that "acquired the whole Ocean" with Columbus and "a new world" with Vespucci, finds no one to magnify these deeds.[81] But the Italians are not the only ones forgetful of their glories: of the Castilians' discoveries and conquests too Campanella laments that the Spanish "took no trouble to see that these great deeds of theirs, far surpassing those of the Greeks and Macedonians, were described by persons competent to do so."[82]

Oviedo anticipates the "three spans of sea" of Campanella's Jason when he writes that if "Hercules sailed so little, just the distance from Greece to Cadiz, and for this the poets or historians say that he opened the door to the ocean," Columbus's glory is infinitely greater.[83] And in exactly the same way the labors of the Spanish are incomparably greater than the "fictions and metaphors" of Ulysses, Jason, and Hercules.[84] Jason and Medea are "lying stories," Theseus and the Minotaur "more like jokes and trifles" compared with what has been seen and is still seen in the Indies.[85] In similar vein, referring to the shipwreck of Alonso Zuazo, Oviedo observes that "not even in the stories of the fabled Greeks is there anything similar written, nor are all the metaphors of Ovid in his *Metamorphoses* an equal comparison."[86] And coming down from the men to the quadrupeds, Diego de Nicuesa's fearless greyhound is far superior to Jason's dog and other famous canines of antiquity.[87]

The story of Jason, as told by Ovid in *Metamorphoses* VI ("and here Ovid is gabbling sheer nonsense") seems particularly to have irritated the sailor Oviedo and becomes the target of his savage sarcasm. The poets insist on sublimating this Golden Fleece escapade, with its insomniac dragon and the pair of wild fire-snorting bulls "and other fictitious and pointless things, and the thing ends up with Medea's harlotry or witchcraft," in a fratricide and elopement[88] that bear no possible comparison with the Spanish voyages.[89]

This same sort of comparison is commonplace in López de Gómara. Solomon's fleets covered less water than Charles V's. "Jason's ship *Argo,* that has been praised to the skies, sailed very little in comparison with the ship *Victoria,* which should be preserved in the Seville dockyards as a memorial." And Ulysses

81. *Poesie,* pp. 85–86; *Opere,* II, 216–17; cf. above, chap. VIII, n. 123.
82. *Della monarchia di Spagna,* XXXII, in *Opere,* II, 225–26.
83. *Hist.,* XII, 10: I, 403a.
84. Ibid., XXXV, 3: III, 596b.
85. Ibid., pt. II, Proh.: PT, II, 212–13.
86. Ibid., L, 10: IV, 482b.
87. Ibid., XXVIII, 2: PT, III, 178a.
88. Ibid., XLVII, 6: IV, 280a.
89. Cf. also the favorable comparison of the *Victoria* with the *Argos* in *Hist.,* XX, 1: II, 21.

has nothing whatever to boast about compared with Juan Sebastián (De Elcano).[90] Even that famous writer Julius Caesar, Díaz del Castillo insists, did not fight as many battles as did he, Bernal: fifty-three the Roman, at least so it is said, one hundred and nineteen solidly proven the humble Spanish infantryman.[91]

Thus when Oviedo reads in Lucio Marineo that the Romans discovered America, the Romans and not the Spanish or Columbus, he flies, quite reasonably, right off the handle and retorts that the Spanish were acquainted with America before the Romans even existed. . . . Lucio Marineo "recounts this manifest nonsense, to snub the Spanish and Admiral Don Christopher Columbus, and wants to award the prize to the Romans, which is once again a load of poppycock or a misleading attempt at flattery. The Romans never knew these parts, nor did Siculo ever see it written that they did: the Spaniards on the other hand did, *before the Romans even existed,* because, as I have said, these islands are the Hesperides, so called from Hesperus, who was the twelfth king of Spain."[92]

11. The Indies and the Hesperides

The thesis that the Indies had been known to and owned by the ancient kings of Iberia had already been advanced by Oviedo when he was taking issue with the Portuguese;[93] he based his arguments on Berosus, in other words, on the forgeries of Annius of Viterbo which were of course accepted and warmly received in Spain.[94]

When, a few years before the publication of the *History,* Charles V was informed by Oviedo of the historico-constitutional-dynastic thesis that would be advanced therein, he was filled with curiosity and began to take a warm interest in the prospect. The identification of the Antilles with the Hesperides, and the Hesperides with the dominion of the mythical Hesperus, king of Spain, would be better than any bull or treaty, guaranteeing the crown's right to the Indies on the basis of diplomatic documents of insuperable antiquity.

Was Oviedo's thesis perhaps known to Solórzano, who upheld Spain's entitle-

---

90. *Historia general de las Indias,* ed. Vedia, p. 219a, quoted by Iglesia, *Cronistas e historiadores,* p. 113.

91. *The True History of the Conquest of Mexico* (1568; New York, 1927), pp. 560–62.

92. *Hist.,* XXIX, 30: III, 146a.

93. Ibid., II, 3: I, 14f; cf. Amador de los Ríos, "Vida," p. lix.

94. Fueter, op. cit., pp. 135f, 223–25; Cirot, op. cit., pp. 67–70, 109–10; see also the footnote by Amador de los Ríos, *Hist.,* I, 3: I, 15. Berosus is also quoted in the *Quinquagenas,* p. 305.

On the possible origins of Oviedo's theses, which took a myth based on a falsehood and twisted it around to make it serve the required legalistic purposes, see Humboldt, *Examen critique,* I, 133–35, and II, 146–48; and M. Mahn-Lot, *La découverte de l'Amérique* (Paris, 1970), pp. 88–89 (in which Agustín de Zaráte is made viceroy of Peru!). But the English too, some decades after Oviedo, latched onto similar claims to show that their fellow countrymen had discovered America before Columbus and Vespucci and therefore had prior rights over the Spaniards! (Keen, op. cit., pp. 170–71). A. Vivante and J. Imbelloni, *Libro de las Atlántidas* (Buenos Aires, ca. 1940), pp. 49–51, recall that the theory of the Hesperides was sometimes confused with that of Atlantis.

ment to the Indies independently of the papal bulls?[95] In any case, in reply to a letter of Oviedo's from Hispaniola, the Council of the Indies wrote that "it would like to see that proceeding."[96] And on 25 October 1533 the Emperor Charles wrote to Oviedo: "I also saw what you say you have in writing, and of which you plan to send proof from five authors, that these isles belonged to the twelfth king of Spain, counting from King Tubal, who held certain kingdoms after Hercules, in the year 1558 before the incarnation of our Redeemer, so that it is now three thousand and ninety-one years that those lands have belonged to the Royal Scepter of Spain; and that pursuing His mysterious way, after so many years, God returned them to the people whose they had been: and everything else that you say about this: and I should like to see the basis that you have for it: and therefore I command that if, when you receive this, you have not sent it, you send it by the first ship that departs for these kingdoms, and duplicated should you have already sent them."[97]

Such haste and precautions speak for themselves. But Oviedo's audacious theory had strange incidental repercussions. The more autonomous Spain's dynastic claim and ensuing right to the Indies became, the less it was obligated to Christopher Columbus and his heirs. The Admiral's son, when drafting the story of his father's life in the years immediately following the publication of Oviedo's history (1536–1539, but published only in 1571, in Venice, in the Italian version), therefore devoted chapter X to rebutting Oviedo's insidious thesis.

Fernando denies that the Hesperides of antiquity can be identified with the West Indies and that the Spanish held sway over the Hesperides. Thus bit by bit he demolishes Oviedo's argument, claiming that the Spaniard "not only seeks to invent new authorities for his writings, but bases himself on dubious material, either inadvertently or to please the person whom he is addressing."[98] And Vignaud, finally, utilized Oviedo's Hesperides invention to support his own theory that Columbus was not seeking Asia or the Indies, but new islands, or an altogether unknown territory.[99]

In its turn Fernando Columbus's reply came to be used, in times much closer

---

95. Zavala, *New Viewpoints*, p. 28.

96. Cf. Herrera, *Discursos morales . . . e históricos*, Disc. 15, cited by Amador de los Ríos, *Hist.*, I, 3: I, 15n.

97. Document transcribed in Jos, "Fernando Colón," pp. 18–19, and in idem, "Impugnaciones a la *Historia del Almirante* escrita por su hijo," *RI*, 3, no. 8 (1942), 204–05. Jos says that the letter is to be found in fragmentary form in Navarrete's *Biblioteca marítima*, and in more complete form in Herrera's abovementioned *Discursos* and in Díez de la Calle, *Memorial y Noticias . . . de las Indias Occidentales*. The affair is also mentioned (1650) by Alcocer, op. cit., pp. 227–28, who lists Oviedo's services to Charles V and adds, "and he also offered to give the emperor proof, based on five authors, that these Indies belonged to the crown of Spain one thousand five hundred and fifty eight years before the coming of Christ; this offer was never fulfilled, although there is a warrant from His Majesty charging Oviedo to expedite the work and forward the results to Spain."

98. Fernando Columbus, *Vita di Cristoforo Colombo*, pp. 36–45; idem, *Historia del Almirante*, I, 55. On the circumstances aggravating his annoyance and concern at Oviedo's thesis, see Jos, "Fernando Colón," pp. 17–18, who conjectures (p. 19) that Fernando knew about the thesis presented in the *Historia* before its publication; cf. above, chap. XV, sec. 3.

99. See esp. *Histoire critique*, II, 311–14.

to our own, first by Harrisse and then by Carbia, as an argument to refute the authenticity of the *Historia del Almirante* and (in Carbia's case) to attribute it, on the basis of its anti-Oviedoism, to Las Casas![100]

But to return to Oviedo's century, his audacious thesis was not quickly forgotten. In 1539 Fray Vicente Palatino de Curzola recalled that the Phoenicians, whose heirs were the Carthaginians, whose heirs were the Romans, whose heirs were the Spanish, were acquainted with the Hesperides, adding, "let no one doubt that these two islands of the Hesperides are those we call Hispaniola and Cuba or Fernandina, because the histories agree at all points"; and when some indecipherable inscriptions were found in "Ciçiniza" (Chichén Itzá) and Zacatlán (in Campeche, Yucatán) he concluded: "To my mind and judgment those letters were African, from the Carthaginians."[101]

Amid all the controversies the real implications of Oviedo's thesis—untenable as it was—went unnoticed. Fernando Columbus, Las Casas, and Herrera[102] were mistaken in seeing it as motivated by an intent to flatter. In fact, in a passage that is actually overtly adulatory, Oviedo forgets all about his thesis and writes that Charles is absolutely right to "bear as his device" the columns of Hercules, with the motto "Plus Ultra," since he placed them "in parts so distant from those reached by Hercules and thereafter reached by no other prince."[103]

Here again Oviedo was struggling to forge a mental link between the new lands and the classical world, seeking to discover in the texts of antiquity some supremely authoritative document that would legitimize the newly discovered lands historically as well as geographically, endowing them with a lineage of unarguable nobility.[104]

There is another factor too. Hoisting the banner of the kings of Spain, he found

---

100. See the interminable polemic between Carbia and Rinaldo Caddeo, defender of the authenticity of the *Historia* and, implicitly, of Oviedo, in: Carbia, "La supercheria en la historia del descubrimiento de América: Comunicación preliminar," *Humanidades,* 20 (1930), 169–85; Caddeo, "L'autenticità delle *Historie* di Colombo: Fernando Colombo, il padre Las Casas e un professore americano," *Le Opere e i Giorni,* 9, no. 3 (March 1930), 47–56, and "Polemica Colombiana," *Le Opere e i Giorni,* 9, no. 7 (July 1930), 48–51; Carbia, "F. Colón, el P. Las Casas, un señor Caddeo y yo," *Nosotros,* 68 (1930), 59–73; Caddeo, "Sobre F. Colón y el P. Las Casas," *Nosotros,* 69 (1930) 107–11; Carbia, "Fernández de Oviedo, Las Casas y el señor Caddeo," *Nosotros,* 70 (1930), 90–95; Carbia, *La nueva historia del descubrimiento de América* (Buenos Aires, 1936), esp. pp. 106–07. Carbia, in the abovementioned article in vol. 68 of *Nosotros* (pp. 63–65), claimed that a passage in one of Columbus's letters of 1498 ("I have never read of princes of Castile ever having won lands outside of it," etc.) was also a reply to Oviedo, and thus interpolated, or else an indication that the whole letter was a forgery, and that there were more anti-Oviedo alterations or insertions in the 1501 letter and Columbus's journal.

The polemic was taken up by Jos, "Supuestas falsificaciones del P. Las Casas en la historia de Colón," *Revista de Occidente,* 31 (February 1931), pp. 217–24, to which Carbia replied in "Los fraudes del P. Las Casas." For further developments, see the journal *Tierra Firme* (Madrid), 1 (1936), 47–71, and Jos, "Impugnaciones," pp. 189, 221. Las Casas in fact argued against Oviedo's thesis in his *Historia de las Indias,* chaps. 15 and 16 (ed. cit., I, 75–91). Cf. below, chap. XIX, n. 236, and Salas, op. cit., p. 228.

101. "Tratado del derecho y justicia de la guerra que tienen los reyes de España contra las naciones de la India Occidental," in *Cuerpo de documentos del siglo XVI,* pp. 29–30.

102. Jos, "Fernando Colón," p. 17.

103. *Hist.,* XII, 10: I, 403a. What about his famous Hesperus? . . . Parallel passage in the *Sumario,* chap. 11, p. 147.

104. For Rey Pastor, op. cit., p. 14, this "striving to bolster up the observed facts with the authority of the ancients," and the resulting creation of a "labored and imperfect science," is typical of this turning point in history.

himself part of a political trend affecting much of Europe, that was to find a warm welcome in Spain. Just as the French monarchs had claimed an ancestor of theirs in the mythical Trojan "Francus" and the Tudors had bolstered the throne of England with the fabled and equally threadbare Trojan "Brutus," or "Brut" (eponym of the "Britanni"!) so Oviedo summons from the depths of concocted chronicles a legendary Hesperus, lynchpin of the Spanish rule over those Hesperides which—as each passing day made clearer—were the best and brightest part of Charles's empire.[105] And if the French and English dynasties could boast of nothing less than "Trojan" heroes as founders of their families, Spain itself, Oviedo goes on, took its name from Hispán, nephew of the Libyan Hercules, "who lived, according to Berosus, before Troy was built," a good 223 years before.[106]

The new lands, in fact, were no more than a curious anomaly, a lucky accident, until a place could be found for them in the approved cosmographical system. Oviedo, who never tires of battling against those who consider Columbus's discoveries a stroke of luck, and repeating that the Admiral was looking for "what he found"—and who never suspected that his thesis would displease Columbus's heirs[107]—found immense speculative satisfaction in seeing the islands glimpsed in historical and mythical documents reemerge from the waters of the Caribbean. It was in line with his ideology, indeed its greatest confirmation, that the *whole* of the new world, empirically discovered, should coincide with what the textual authorities said: a thesis that was consistent and rigorous to the point of ingenuousness, and that was thus bound to stir up a hornet's nest of angry protest, accusation, and suspicion, still today not by any means assuaged or forgotten.

12. THE INDIANS AND THE TARTARS

A more fruitful example of the association of widely distant facts and situations is the parallel Oviedo draws between the Indians and the Tartars. The new American world could, as we have seen, be compared with the old world or classical antiquity, and Oviedo, as a cultivated and observant person, takes the opportunity of establishing some interesting points of contact and ideological links between the new Indies and Europe, between the Indians and the pagans. After Marco Polo, however, there was another world slowly coming to the surface of western consciousness, and, with the reports of the missionaries and

---

105. See F. A. Yates, *Astraea: The Imperial Theme in the Sixteenth Century* (London and Boston, 1975), p. 121.
106. *Hist.*, II, 3: PT, I, 17–20; the latter part reiterated, verbatim, in XXIX, 30: PT, III, 330, and XXIII, 9: PT, IV, 42.
107. Jos, "Fernando Colón," p. 22. These lands of America "he found written": *Hist.*, II, 3: I, 14a, 18b. Cf. Columbus's phrase (9 January 1493) quoted above, chap. II, sec. 6. For Oviedo "to find written" means to have the confirmation of authority: of the therapeutic use of leeches to draw off blood, in which he was loath to believe, Oviedo confesses that eventually "I found it written in Pliny" (*Hist.*, XV, 6: I, 459b).

Lodovico di Varthema, becoming steadily more obvious and concrete: the world of the eastern Indies.[108] Sepúlveda noted with satisfaction that "by dint of terror combined with doctrine" most of the Tartars, who would have rejected missionaries and preachers, had been converted to the Christian religion.[109] The inference for the Americans was obvious.

Oviedo has read about the customs of the Tartars in Saint Antoninus and is struck by the coincidence between what the archbishop reports about the inhabitants of the Far East and what he himself has seen of the inhabitants of the Far West,[110] "so much so that it seems that the Indians taught it to the Tartars, or that from Tartary the teachers of these vices came to the mainland."[111]

In war the Orientals are just as cruel as the Indians.[112] However, the death rate among the Spanish in the Indies is considerably higher than it was in the wars of Genghis Khan, when that "cruel first emperor of the Tartars" had one soldier in ten killed and fed to the other nine.[113]

No less pertinent are the comparisons between the Indians and the nomadic African Arabs, moving with their families from province to province.[114] The Indians paint and tattoo themselves, as do the dark-skinned women of Barbary "for show" or for display, and the warlike inhabitants of Mauretania, as an exhibitionistic display of their nobility and valor,[115] and as the ancient Britons used to do, though they are now a prosperous "Christian republic."[116] And, when they do not wash, they stink like the negroes of Guinea, with a stench "that is quite unbearable in some of them"![117] And the Inca's subjects wore "certain woollen caps, like Turks."[118]

---

108. Oviedo could not have been familiar with Ruy González de Clavijo's report on his embassy to the court of Tamerlane (1403–06), which was published only in 1582. But Vespucci, or rather the pseudo-Vespucci, had already described the first Americans as people with Tartar features (Humboldt, *Examen critique*, V, 24–25, 220; cf. above, chap. VII, sec. 5). And Pinzón described the nomadic Indians as living "like gypsies, or rather like Tartars" (Morison, *Southern Voyages*, p. 213). On Marco Polo and the Tartars, see Hodgen, op. cit., pp. 97–98.

109. Salas, op. cit., p. 273, quoting the *Democrates alter.*

110. For the mental outlook of a European (which is what Oviedo always remained), Tartary is the extreme East and America the extreme West.

111. *Hist.*, XXIX, 27: III, 134b. This curious parallel, which was trotted out again in the seventeenth century with the added twist that the Indians were then adjudged to be the most corrupt descendants of the Tartars (Hodgen, op. cit., pp. 315, 379), was taken up at the beginning of the nineteenth century by Volney: "There is a real analogy between the theological ideas of the savages of North America and those of the Tartars of Asia as they are described to us by the Russian scholars, who have been visiting them for the last thirty years" ("Eclaircissement sur les Sauvages," in *Tableau du climat et du sol des Etats-Unis* [1802; Paris, 1846], p. 727a).

112. *Hist.*, XXIX, 34: III, 175b.

113. Ibid., XXXII, 2: III, 224a; XXXII, 3: III, 232a.

114. Ibid., XXIX, 27: PT, IV, 318b. On the way many features of the *reconquista* of Spain from the Moors were transferred to the *conquista* of the American Indians, see Romano, op. cit., p. 41.

115. *Sum.*, pp. 140–41; *Hist.*, XX, 34: PT, II, 297; XXIV, 9: PT, II, 418a; XXV, 19: PT, III, 53b; XXV, 22: PT, III, 59–60; XXIX, 2: PT, III, 210b; XXIX, 28: PT, III, 324. "Alárabe" ("Arab") is used with the meaning "violent" in XLVII, 3: PT, V, 133b.

116. *Hist.*, XXV, 1: PT, III, 10a.

117. Ibid., XXIX, 27: PT, IV, 321b. On the large number of Negroes in Santo Domingo, see above, chap. XVII, sec. 24.

118. *Hist.*, XLVI, 17: PT, V, 150b.

These are no more than thumbnail sketches, fleeting comparisons, but here again Oviedo shows a broadness of historical perspective, a firm belief in the common nature of man in all latitudes and longitudes, a freedom from prejudice and a willingness to sweep the whole horizon in his search for features that will allow him to describe the way things really are as accurately as possible. Let us now see how he puts these same qualities to use in his favorite task, describing the natural history of the Indies.

13. NATURE IN THE INDIES

Menéndez Pelayo has noted with some justification that "it was an advantage for Oviedo that he had no connection with the official physics of his time, which was still so removed from reality, so formalistic and scholastic, or so superstitiously attached to the texts of the ancients."[119] But it must be added at once that in this respect Oviedo was certainly not behind the times and was indeed almost ahead of them. Precisely because he "depended solely on the resources of his prescientific observation" and was devoted to an "entirely empirical" method (the qualifying expressions are once again Menéndez Pelayo's) Oviedo took the natural sciences a great step forward.

Uncultured, perhaps, but not backward; indeed, when his restless spirit and all-pervading curiosity carry him along on the great tide of European progress to fix his gaze on the remote Americas, when he substitutes his own experience for the wornout schemes of scholastic philosophy, Oviedo is a standard-bearer, not some lucky ignoramus. At the same time Menéndez Pelayo's comment must be qualified in another way. In his form of exposition, Oviedo never gets much beyond the pattern of the medieval "bestiaries": he describes one animal (or plant) after another, without seeking any genetic affinities, and without any particular order—apart from a general adherence to Pliny's pattern of land animals, sea creatures, and then birds, with a sort of appendix for insects—but with a constant utilitarian concern and sometimes with a closing moral unmistakeably medieval in flavor.

In fact it seems that in this field, in contrast to the trend noted in the "general" history, the oldest parts are the most moralistic, while the later parts, composed by the administrator and colonist of the new lands, abandon the edifying flour-

---

119. "Historiadores," p. 88, and *Poesía hispano-americana*, I, 289. Less satisfactory is his remark, on the same page, that "his descriptions are not those of a naturalist, although the naturalists recognize them as being very accurate," an observation so ingenious as to be totally incomprehensible. It is also worth noting that Oviedo's age witnessed a marked revival in the natural sciences, with the work of Leonardo, Servet, and Vesalius, in keeping with the general trend of the times already manifest in another form in the geographical discoveries.

One early apologist of the Spaniards in America commented, with naive surprise, on the "happy combination" by which the discovery of the New World coincided with the "feeble dawn of the natural sciences" (B. María de Moxó, *Cartas mexicanas escritas . . . en 1805* [Genoa, ca. 1837–38], p. 10). But at least as far as the animals are concerned Oviedo is more "scientific" than the zoologists of his time, who stick to the Aristotelian classifications (e.g., Edward Wotton) or simply adopt an alphabetical order within those classifications (Konrad Gesner). A new and more rational classification of the species, particularly the plant species, had to await the coming of Ulisse Aldovrandi (1522–1605).

ishes in favor of practical information on the habits and customs of the animals and the therapeutic virtues of woods, leaves, and fruits. In the *Summary,* for example, still perhaps under the influence of the literary tradition of the bestiaries, the marvelous description of flying fish and seagulls culminates in a Christian parable. "I remember that one night, while the whole ship's crew were singing the *Salve,* kneeling on the highest deck of the ship, the poop, a certain band of these flying fish passed and it was quite rough weather, and many of them were left on the ship, and two or three fell by me, and I held them in my hands alive, and I could see them very well. . . . and while I was in those parts [near Bermuda] I saw a fight between these flying fish and dorados and seagulls, which was in truth, I think, the most entertaining thing to be seen at sea of this sort. The dorados swam along, occasionally breaking the surface, and they stirred up these flying fish, which they would chase in order to eat them, and the latter took to their wings to flee, and the dorados followed running behind them to catch them as they fell; on the other side, the seagulls took a lot of the flying fish in the air, so that they were not safe either above or below; and this same danger is encountered by men in the things of this mortal life, finding no safety in lofty or lowly estate of the earth, and this alone should be enough to make men remember that certain repose that God has prepared for those that love Him, and turn away from thoughts of this world, in which the dangers are so ever present, and turn them to eternal life, in which perpetual salvation lies."[120] Amen, one feels tempted to conclude.

In the *History,* on the other hand, there is indeed a chapter devoted to the "flying fish," but without that vivid sketch, without the tacked-on moral, but instead with the information that those fish can be seen only "coming from Spain to these Indies," and with a significant amendment to the few sentences that do correspond. In the *Summary,* Oviedo had referred to the flying fish "that I held alive in my hand, and could see very well. . . ." In the *History* he writes, "And I have held them alive in my hand and have eaten them"! In the *Summary* he had written that that spectacle was "the most entertaining thing to be seen at sea." In the *History* he twice refers to their edibility: "And they are very good fish to taste. . . . It is a very good fish to eat although they have a lot of bones."[121] Alimentary considerations outweigh the aesthetic.

14. Nutritional concerns

Preoccupations of this sort were only to be expected. The colonists had to eat, before all else. It was impossible to have their usual foods sent out from Spain.

120. *Sum.,* chap. 83 ("On fish and fisheries"), p.p. 261–63. Columbus noted in his journal, 29 January 1493, "fish called 'dorados' came aboard."

121. *Hist.,* XIII, 4: I, 427. In the preface to the same chapter Oviedo takes pleasure in reminding his reader that he has not only seen the fish he describes, but "eaten most of them, so that I can testify as to what I have been able to understand and consider of these things, both as regards the taste and as regards the shape of them" (*Hist.,* III, Proh.: I, 423b).

Their first investigations were therefore necessarily directed toward ascertaining whether it was possible to "live off the land," whether there were edible animals, whether cereals and vegetables grew there, whether the fruit was good, the game and fishing plentiful, stockbreeding and the raising of farmyard animals promising or impossible. The utilitarian-nutritional viewpoint was bound to take precedence over purely naturalistic research.[122] In one very moving passage Oviedo tells what befell the first Christians who stayed with Diego and Bartolomeo Columbus on the island of Isabella, where they ate everything, including dogs, snakes, and lizards, finding themselves driven by their hunger even "to eat those things so inimical to their health and so fearsome to the sight."[123] And a little further on, with more personal bitterness, our good glutton sighs, "In these regions we found no form of food resembling that which our fathers gave us."[124]

15. Scarcity of quadrupeds

One of the features that struck the Europeans when they came into contact with the Antilles for the very first time was the absence of edible quadrupeds in the islands. Columbus, commenting on the island of Cuba, noted that he and his companions "saw no four-footed beasts, apart from dogs that did not bark" (*Journal,* 6 November 1492). And as early as 1493 Alexander VI's bull characterized the inhabitants of the "far-off islands" discovered by Columbus as peace-loving, naked, "not flesh-eaters."[125] In the memorandum of 30 January 1494 addressed to the sovereigns from Isabella, the Admiral blamed the widespread illness among his men on the lack of "fresh meat," and begged them to send meat animals and draught animals "as there are no animals here that man can use to assist him."[126] When he came across large quadrupeds, deer, boar, and so on, on the Paria promontory, he immediately seized on the fact as an argument to prove that he had really touched terra firma, mainland Asia,[127] probably remembering Saint Augustine's uncertainty (in the famous passage in *De Civitate Dei,* XVI, 6–7) as to how the animals, and in particular the wild animals, could have reached the islands.[128] Twenty years later Giustiniani, in his life of Columbus

122. There is thus no reason for Cardoso's sarcastic reaction (op. cit., p. 332) to the fact that in their dealings with the batrachia the earliest conquistadors "mentioned as sole distinguishing feature their greater or lesser edibility"! On the other hand it has to be admitted that Oviedo sometimes dwells on dietary details that may be picturesque but are not exactly vital. He announces that the fruit of the *tambique* tree, found in Nicaragua and Tierra Firme, is tastier than the pine seeds of Castile, but he warns against eating too many of them "because they cause stomach flux, and stomach pains too; but if one eats a dozen or so of them, or eats them at the beginning of the meal, they do not provoke diarrhea" (*Hist.,* VIII, 32: I, 322b). On the tedium of an unchanging diet of coconuts and the powerful purgative qualities of coconut milk, see IX, 4: I, 337b.

123. *Hist.,* II, 13: I, 50a.

124. Ibid., V, 8: I, 151b.

125. 4 May 1493, in C. Mirbt, *Quellen zur Geschichte des Papsttums und des römischen Katholizismus* (Tübingen, 1924), p. 247; cf. Humboldt, *Examen critique,* III, 266.

126. *Relaciones y cartas,* pp. 208, 210; see also the undated memorandum on the provisioning of the Indies, ibid., p. 241.

127. See Humboldt, *Examen critique,* IV, 260–61.

128. Cf. Humboldt, *Kosmos* (Stuttgart, 1845), I, 489, and Gerbi, *Dispute,* pp. 567–68. See also Columbus's letter from Hispaniola (1498) in Las Casas, *Historia de las Indias,* I, 155, and in *Relaciones y cartas,* p. 260.

(1516), was to repeat that "no four-footed animals are encountered there [Hispaniola] apart from a few undersized dogs."[129] No less eloquent is the story Oviedo tells of the expedition of Juan de Grijalva, sent ahead by Diego Velázquez with a brigantine to wait for him at Cape Saint Anthony (Cuba). Velázquez duly arrived with the bulk of his forces but found nobody, and when some of his men leapt ashore they "found a gourd hanging on a tree and inside it a message that said 'those that came here with the brigantine went back with it, because they had nothing to eat.'"[130]

This bitter observation, dictated by obvious logistical considerations, was to hang like a millstone on the fauna of all America over the ensuing centuries. It seemed to point to some organic inferiority or deep-rooted poverty, and in some cases prompted the formulation of theories of physical decadence or immaturity, while in others—less extravagantly—it was explained in terms of a lack of food, a chronic hunger on the part of the Americans, who could therefore be pardoned for resorting to cannibalism.

16. Medicinal products

The culinary concern was closely followed by utilitarian and therapeutic considerations. In his expansive *Historia Animalium* (1551–1558) Konrad Gesner, looked on as the founder of modern zoology, takes the animals one by one and says what each single animal can be used for, whether it is good to eat and what its therapeutic uses are. As for the plants, they had of course been the basis of mankind's pharmacy since time began, and the Indies were packed with species and varieties never seen before.

It is in fact precisely on the subject of the plants—though expressing himself in terms so general as to be applicable to any physical element—that Oviedo declares the universal usefulness of everything to be found in the Indies; or, to put it another way, declares that all reality is friendly to man, the only limitation being man's own ignorance. If Oviedo's faith in the universal goodness of nature were not rooted in the opening lines of the Bible ("and God saw the things that he had made, and they were exceeding good," Genesis, I, 31) one might be tempted to detect a hint of Bruni or even Campanella in his memorable words; "And what is most surprising is that we never see any useless thing or anything unnecessary, only those things whose secrets and natural power are unknown to men, or else all those things with whose proper uses men are unfamiliar."[131]

Certain animal products, like bezoar (intestinal stones), were also reputed to

---

129. In Barros Arana, op. cit., VI, 10.

130. *Hist.*, XVII, 8: I, 503b. In the following century Bacon advised: "In a country of plantation, first look about what kind of victual the country yields of itself to hand" (*Essays*, XXXII, "Of Plantations," in *Works*, p. 88).

131. *Hist.*, IX, Proh.: I, 329b; cf. XIX, Proh.: I, 586a. Queen Isabella had already urged Columbus to bring her back from the Indies *all* the birds he could capture, both seabirds and woodland birds, because she wanted to *see* them all and acquaint herself with the curiosities of the new Indies (letter from Segovia, 16 August 1494, quoted in Humboldt, *Examen critique*, III, 148*n*).

be of great curative value.[132] It was recognized that certain basic items, such as milk, eggs, salt, and cooking fat, were indispensable in the diet. And the importance of skins and wool for clothing and timber for building houses and carts and ships produced a corresponding "scientific" interest in the natural products, particularly the animal and vegetable products. The minerals and metals, precious stones, and spices (although the latter were not actually found in the Indies) were the objects of trade, what we might somewhat inappropriately call "cash crops," in other words, articles for export, not for immediate local consumption.

In other words the Spaniards in America found themselves obliged to retrace, within the space of a few years (but with the help of several millennia of experience), the path that the human race had covered since it first began to exploit the products of nature and turn them to its own ends. The direction of their theoretical interests was dictated by those pressing needs, leaving them no choice but to follow the course marked out by that sum of inherited experience. Faced with a nature still unknown but indispensable, the Spaniard sought to tame it with the tools in his possession, sought to reduce it to his own norms, to comprehend it and compare it with the familiar nature of Europe so as to be able to make better use of it. The cognitive motive led to accentuation of the substantial affinities between American nature and the nature of the Old World. The practical motive led to study and emphasis of its strange, unusual, disconcerting, or miraculous aspects.

In the pictures presented by the polemical minds and schematic mentalities of ensuing centuries the New World frequently figured either as a uniform prolongation of the Old World or as its total antithesis; and in the second approach (which tended to predominate, given mankind's unfailing tendency to abstraction or impassioned ardor), the New World was sometimes pictured as inferior in every way to the Old, sometimes as so superior as to be held up against it as a paradigm or ideal (see above, chap. I, sec. 5). But Oviedo, as we saw, rejects the polarity of the two worlds and likewise avoids the unilaterality of those two mental stages in a single cognitive process. Without theorizing, because he is only a man of sound common sense, and no philosopher, Oviedo *knows* that nature is all one, in Europe and America, and knows that nature in America is different from European nature. Garcilaso was to say something similar, stating that American nature was like Europe's, and yet different from Europe's.[133]

17. DESCRIPTIVE TECHNIQUE

Oviedo's descriptive technique clearly reflects this dual conviction of his. For each animal and plant he begins by telling us how it resembles Spain's (if nothing

---

132. On the bezoar and its renowned medicinal properties, see Sassetti, op. cit., pp. 141–43 (letter of 1580); cf. ibid., p. 353 (letter of 1586).
133. *Comentarios reales,* VIII, 15, in *Páginas escogidas* (Paris, 1938), pp. 317–21.

else, giving it—at least provisionally—the name of the corresponding European creature); but then he goes straight on to tell us how it differs therefrom—and the stress usually falls on the differences, the peculiarities of the transatlantic creatures.[134]

Thus Oviedo might be said to follow a method of "successive approximations": first a rough assimilation, then a detailed differentiation—a method that was not only a highly effective way of whetting European curiosity (which had at first been slow to take an interest in the individual details of the New World, tending as it did to see everything *in toto*,[135] as virgin nature and prodigious opulence), not just the only possible way of representing the fauna and flora of such new lands to European minds, but an anticipation, it has been said, in crude and empirical form, of the more modern and rigorous methods of classification through generic affinities and specific differences.

Nature is one. The reader will bow down before the Master who made nature capable of "engendering and creating all the effects and properties that pleased him," and will see, "without misplaced suspicion, how capable this same nature is," and how far its truly infinite potential exceeds its present opulent achievement in America.[136] Strictly speaking, there is really no reason to be amazed at all, because nature is the work of the Almighty. But let Him be thanked, because the profusion of creatures, child's play for Him, offers the chronicler inexhaustible and marvelous material: "Without my pen departing from the path of truth never will it lack things to make men marvel."[137]

The first and most consistent of the marvels is that those plants and animals, similar to Europe's, are yet different.[138] No sooner has Oviedo neatly labeled an American creature with a familiar name than he has second thoughts and rushes to remove the label again. No sooner has he baptized an animal or a tree (and we use the term "baptized" advisedly, since in fact when Oviedo gives them European names he is bringing them within the common orbit of Christian civilization) than he is besieged by doubt as to whether the baptism might not be unlawful and almost fraudulent. It is as if he were already familiar with the

---

134. Cf. above, chap. I, sec. 3.

135. Henríquez Ureña, *Literary Currents*, p. 21. Discoverers, generally speaking, have no other course than to "make up for the unknown with the known or to measure and compare it with the known" (Blanke, op. cit., p. 5; cf. pp. 96–97).

136. *Hist.*, X, Proh.: I, 361. On the Europeans' disappointment (?) on discovering that the New World "despite its novelties, was not essentially different from the old," and that it had neither monsters nor fantastic creatures, see Rey Pastor, op. cit., p. 32.

137. *Hist.*, XV, Proh.: I, 450b; cf. XXXI, Proh.: III, 186a.

138. The prophetic Astarotte (in Pulci's *Morgante Maggiore* [1480], XXV, 231) had told Rinaldo that the Antipodeans worshiped the sun and the pagan gods, and that "they have animals and plants, like you, and often wage great battles with one another." Pulci may have got the idea from Paolo Toscanelli. The last two lines of the preceding stanza are of obvious Petrarchan derivation: "Look where the sun hastens on its way, / And over there, mark my words, it is awaited." Cf. Petrarch: "In the hour when the sun bends rapidly westward, / And our day flies to people perhaps awaiting it beyond" (*Rerum vulgarium fragmenta*, canzone 50). But Pulci drops the "perhaps," and underlines the statement ("mark my words").

axiom laid down by Vico in the *Scienza Nuova* to the effect that it is "a property of the human mind that whenever men cannot measure things far off and unknown they judge them by their own known and present things," a process Vico immediately identifies as a never-ending source of error and the root cause of the arrogance of nations and scholars.[139]

18. PLACE-NAMES

A specific example of this concern for exactitude is his constant carping at the place-names bestowed on localities in the Indies. While the animals might to some extent resemble those of Europe, the capes, gulfs, and mountains of America have personalities all their own, fully autonomous and in no way assimilable with the familiar "prototypes" of the Old World. The names with which they have been baptized are all wrong: "To ignore the original names is to sow confusion in everything,"[140] a statement which obviously adds further fuel to his unceasing criticism of the map-makers (see below, chap. XXI, sec. 4). But the Spanish soldiers and sailors, in their ignorance, did precisely this: they arbitrarily changed the native names, neglecting the most elementary geographical data—altitude, longitude, and latitude—and created an enormous muddle[141] that would require a long time and a lot more precise observation to unravel.

They were prompted by their devotion to the saints and madonnas or their wicked desires to pass themselves off as the first discoverers, thus stealing the glory of those who were really the first to reveal those lands, "which I do not intend to tolerate in my histories, nor deprive anyone of his just deserts."[142]

The local usage is thus always to be preferred; failing that, better the name given by the first person on the spot; as a third possibility it would be best to add at least some qualifying term to distinguish the place from others with the same name, as is the custom in Spain for the numerous Alcalàs and Villanuevas.[143] But the sailors of Pedro de Heredia, for instance, simply gave the name Cartagena to the city he founded, recalling the secure harbor of Cartagena in Spain; but this was "highly inappropriate," indeed "sailors' nonsense," because today one might be led to believe that the ancient Carthaginians had been in the Indies![144]

Oviedo also deplores the frequent repetition of place-names like Rio de Canoas, Cabo Blanco, Cabo de San Román, and others that give rise to this regrettable uncertainty; but that was often due to the multiplicity of discoverers at

139. Op. cit., I, 116. See also, along the same lines, Vico's criticism of false geographical designations, ibid., p. 681ff, which has numerous precedents in Oviedo, as will shortly be seen.
140. *Hist.*, XXI, 6: PT, II, 322b; XXI, 9: PT, II, 334a.
141. Ibid., XXIX, 21, par. 7: PT, III, 300a, 301a; XXXIII, 44: PT, IV, 207b; XLII, 12: PT, IV 424b.
142. Ibid., XX, 10: PT, II, 251–52; XXIX, 6: PT, III, 323b; XXXIX, 1: PT, IV, 338; XLIII, 1: PT, V, 8a. Cf. above, chap. XVII, sec. 5.
143. *Hist.*, XXI, 4: PT, II, 316a.
144. Ibid., XXVII, 8: PT, III, 160b.

different times, so that one has no choice but to accept it, although it is "a little annoying to the ear."

The numerous Jordans were also thus named, probably, because the conquistadors baptized a few natives there, "or for some other reason that I know not." In the same way the capes and gulfs named after saints probably owed the fact to their having been discovered on the respective saints' days, "so that looking at one of these navigators' charts, one gets the impression one is reading a jumbled-up calendar or catalogue of saints." [145] A chronological element imposed itself on a geographical location and so to speak historicized space. It was in any case much easier to "baptize" an estuary or a promontory than to instill the true faith into a native!

Even the familiar (and native) name of Peru becomes a target for Oviedo's criticism, and his discussion of the name closes with one more example of his favorite "contradiction" theme: "I wanted to say this here so that you might know, reader, that what is today called Peru and is so named, *is not Peru*." [146] "Peru is much more this way," and New Castile, "that the populace mistakenly call Peru . . . is the place where Señor Atabalipa was." [147] Thus "the name is inappropriate and the land that Pizarro and the Almagro conquered should not be called Peru." [148]

Oviedo's criticism was taken up by Fernando Columbus, [149] Father Acosta, and later, in the eighteenth century, by Buffon, who observed however that "names given by simple peoples [the native names dear to Oviedo!] relate to the properties of the thing named"; [150] and a picturesque and sarcastic echo can be caught in Father Mier, who blames the saints for these and other wrongs: their names "confuse the places, convert the geography of America into a litany or calendar, embarrass the prose and put beauty beyond the reach of the American muses"! [151]

19. ERRORS CAUSED BY OVER-HASTY ASSIMILATION

This concern for distinction is so automatic and so frequent in Oviedo that it soon acquires the fixed pattern of a refrain, with the same words recurring again and again like some sort of magic formula, a formula casting a spell of novelty over American nature, giving it an enchanted individuality.

---

145. Ibid., XXI, 9: II, 145–46. On the numerous "Cabos Blancos," in particular, see XXI, 4: PT, II, 316.
146. Ibid., XXXIX, 1: IV, 7b, my italics. Cf. XXXIII, 50: III, 534.
147. Ibid., VIII, 35: I, 325a.
148. Ibid., XXXIX, 1: PT, IV, 341a.
149. *Vita di Cristoforo Colombo*, pp. 83, 94, 137, 143, 153, 265, 313, 333.
150. Gerbi, *Dispute*, pp. 28–29; J. H. Pitman, *Goldsmith's Animated Nature* (New Haven, 1924), pp. 85–86.
151. *Historia*, II, 769n. And elsewhere: "The hypocrisy of the conquistadors, who gave saints' names to every place they came across, turned our geography into a calendar, and our muses cannot intone any song without it sounding like the Litany" (*Escritos inéditos*, pp. 312–13).

Oviedo knows "a fruit that here they call plantains but in truth they are not";[152] and "fruit that they call medlars, without their being so";[153] and trees called "quinces, although they are not";[154] and "birds that the Christians call pheasants—they are not, however";[155] and "this liquor that here they call balsam, although it is not";[156] and another liquor "that they also call balsam, without either actually being so";[157] and Mexican cherries "somewhat similar to those of Spain";[158] and "a certain sort of cucumbers, not like those of Castile, although they seem so from the outside,"[159] but then again they are not really so similar— "what the Christians call cucumbers are not cucumbers, although they gave them that name, nor do they look much like cucumbers."[160]

It remains to be seen how far Oviedo's formula is merely stylistic or literary in origin, or rather how far Oviedo endows a turn of phrase in current use with a new and critical thought. Columbus says he saw "a piece of land that has the appearance of an island, although it is not," instead of simply saying that he saw a peninsula. . . .[161]

There are numerous examples of these rectifications and retractions in Oviedo, revealing a chronic dissatisfaction over the definitions. At the end of one long chapter he adds this scrupulous postscript: "But just because I talked about cows above, the reader should not assume that they are like ours, but rather of the sort that the Spaniards call cows in some parts of the mainland, and some improperly call them *dantas*."[162] And in fact much earlier Oviedo had noted that "the Christians give this name *dantas* to those hides, not because they know that they are from *dantas*, for in truth they are not"[163] and that in Cueva (in present-day

152. *Hist.*, VIII, 1, par. 10: I, 290b. Oviedo quickly adds, "but they are struck with this incorrect name *plátanos*" (ibid.). On the marked similarity between the leaves of the "bihao" and "what they here call *plátanos* (although they are not)," see VII, 8: I, 276a. Thus Buffon's criticism about names confusing things can be traced back to Oviedo. Cf. also IX, 10: I, 342a: "And thus because of a single [feature] noted by those who are quite inexperienced in these matters, they give it the name, just as if it had all the parts and circumstances described by Pliny."

153. Ibid., VIII, 22: I, 308a.
154. Ibid., IX, 22: I, 352 (title).
155. Ibid., XXVI, 10: II, 354b.
156. Ibid., X, 3: I, 366a, 368a.
157. Ibid., XI, 4: I, 370a.

158. Ibid., XXXIII, 10: III, 310b, probably transcribed from Cortés's "cherries and plums similar to those of Spain" (*Cartas*, ed. Gayangos, p. 104, cited by Iglesia, *Cronistas e historiadores*, p. 26). But those Nicaraguan fruits "which our Spaniards call plums, although they are not," are solidly Oviedan (*Hist.*, VIII, 20: I, 306b; and the whole of the following chapter, I, 307–08); and likewise the cedars, which "I do not in fact consider to be cedars, but are nevertheless so called by our carpenters" (XXIX, 29: III, 143, and following note).

159. *Hist.*, XLVI, 16: IV, 215–16; and a little further on: "What the Christians call cucumbers are not cucumbers, although they gave them this name" (XLVI, 17: IV, 233b); and the walnuts of Hispaniola "are, at first sight, like the Spanish ones, except that the nuts from the trees of these parts are imperfect and do not release the fruit, and can only be eaten as a last resort" (IX, 3: I, 331–32); and "certain trees which, because they smell sweet, the Christians call cedars; but in truth I do not think that most of them are" (IX, 7: I, 339a; cf. preceding note).

160. Ibid., XLVI, 17: IV, 233b.
161. *Journal*, 14 October 1492.
162. *Hist.*, XXXV, 5: III, 608b.
163. Ibid., XX, 6: II, 40b.

Colombia) there are "cows of that sort that the Spanish call *dantas*, which they are not."[164]

Following the same strict approach Oviedo objects to tribes of fighting female savages being dubbed Amazons, as they were by "the first discoverers, in ignorance of what the term Amazon means";[165] and these savages are therefore called Amazons "improperly," and "cannot be called Amazons," even if in some of their customs it seems "they imitate those that the ancients called Amazons."[166]

20. THE PURSUIT OF ONOMASTIC ACCURACY

Thus whenever he is describing an animal the first reference, as we have seen, is to Spain (or, if the creature in question is some wild animal or other beast not found in Spain, to the Old World), the second to whatever is peculiar to and characteristic of the American animal. Sometimes the creature is bluntly defined as identical or totally different. The *tarucos* of New Castile are "after the fashion of the animals known in Italy as *mufros*" (*mufloni*, wild sheep) but "I do not think they exist in Spain,"[167] while in the kingdom of New Granada "there are a lot of bears alike in every way to those found in our own Spain."[168] But not even these bears are really identical to the Spanish ones. In describing the fauna of the kingdom of Bogotá, Oviedo repeats that "they are as big as Spanish bears" but— always that "but"—they have "rougher skins and very wide tails and big spines reaching down to the ground," and are known as anteating bears or anteaters "because they feed on ants."[169] In the same way, when he is getting ready to describe a whole series or species of animals—in the case in point the birds— Oviedo announces that he will deal first with those that resemble the Spanish and European ones, then with those that are different and proper to the Indies.[170]

---

164. Ibid., XXVII, 9: II, 452b. The *danta* is usually taken to be the tapir. But Cardoso, op. cit., XI, 345, insists that the animal which Oviedo and others call the *danta*, "met in Patagonia . . . is none other than the guanaco." In reference to a luminous animal known as the *carbunco*, Oviedo says tartly, "I can find no written trace of such an animal" (XX, 10: PT, II, 251).

165. *Hist.*, XXI, 8: II, 141a; XXVI, 29: II, 404a.

166. Ibid., L, 24: IV, 565b. See above, chap. X, no. 14. Of the supposed Amazons of Ciguatán, Nuño de Guzmán, freshly returned from that province, told him it was "a great big lie" (*Hist.*, XXXIV, 8: PT, IV, 284). One should note here too, as for the cucumbers (and the walnuts—VIII, 11: I, 300–01), that Oviedo does not deny the similarities, indeed explicitly recognizes them, but still firmly insists on the criterion of distinction.

Oviedo also distrusts the facile phonetic assimilations between the things of the New World and those of antiquity: he knows, for example, that Pliny refers to a place called "Améxico," but he is careful not to identify Pliny's city of the Troad with the Aztecs' capital (XXXIII, 49: III, 530). Referring to a certain West Indian archipelago, he says that the reader (who would actually have to be rather distracted) might take it to be the Aegean archipelago, "that famous group of islands written about by the ancients in Ptolemy's and Pliny's geography and other authors; however it is not" (XXI, 10: II, 147a). And in reference to a merchant called Johan Gutiérrez Pylo, who hanged himself in Santo Domingo in 1545, he notes that Pylos was an island contested between Athenians and Spartans, as Thucydides relates, "but this merchant, who hanged himself here, called Pylos, did not come from there, but from Seville" (*Qu.*, p. 393).

167. *Hist.*, XII, 32: I, 419a.

168. Ibid., XII, 37: I, 421.

169. Ibid., XXVI, 31: II, 411b.

170. E.g., *Sum.*, chaps. 28 and 29, pp. 167–68; *Hist.*, XIV, Proh.: I, 439a.

He always proceeds from the known to the unknown, or rather from the familiar to the surprising. Spain generally serves as the term of comparison, just as it serves to give an idea of the vastness of the main squares of Temistitán[171] or Cajamarca,[172] or the baskets that the Indians fill with cicadas, grasshoppers, "and *langostas,* the sort that jump" (e.g., locusts), baskets as big as those used for carrying fish from Biscay to Castile.[173] The wild cattle of northern Florida are bigger than the Spanish cattle, but carry their heads "somewhat lower than Spanish cows."[174] The pine seeds of those same regions are "as good as or better than those of Castile."[175] And the rabbits of Peru are "as perfect as those of Spain, except in their tails, which are long, like a mouse's."[176]

In general Spain is accepted as a quantitative term of reference, but the qualitative distinctiveness of the Indian species is promptly reaffirmed to avoid any possibility of misunderstanding. And as he goes along, comparing and discriminating, measuring and distinguishing, Oviedo is actually laying the foundations of the new science of nature: the mere "description" of the animals, characteristic of medieval science, gives way with Oviedo, under the mental stimulus of the strange creatures of America, to a rudimentary classification that immediately brings up the problems of species and genus, prototype and variety, essential qualities and secondary traits.[177]

171. "Twice the city of Salamanca," *Hist.,* XXXIII, 10: III, 299b.

172. "Bigger than any in Spain," *Hist.,* XLVI, 6: IV, 167b. This particular item obviously comes from the chronicle of Francisco López de Jerez, who says that Cajamarca's main square is "bigger than any in Spain" (op. cit., p. 330b). See also A. Pogo, ed., "The Anonymous *La conquista del Peru* (Seville, April 1534) and the *Libro ultimo del summario delle Indie Occidental* (Venice, October 1534)," *Proceedings of the American Academy of Arts and Sciences,* 64, no. 8 (July 1930), p. 232; cf. Sánchez Alonso, *Historiografía española,* I, 455–56; idem, *Fuentes,* no. 5262. Of Xauxa, Estete writes that "the village is made in the manner of those in Spain" (López de Jerez, op. cit., p. 262). Cortés says that Tlaxcala "is much bigger than Granada" (*Cartas,* ed. Gayangos, p. 67, quoted by Iglesia, *Cronistas e historiadores* p. 24), and Mexico Tenochtitlán had already been described as being "as big as . . . Seville and Cordova" (*Cartas,* ed. Gayangos, p. 103, quoted by Iglesia, *Cronistas e historiadores,* p. 26).

   This was of course a normal mode of expression and already common with Columbus, who was given to comparisons with the climates of Spain and references to the natives' bows being "as big as those of France or England" (Journal, 15 January 1493), etc. It is in any case a well-known fact that similarities are usually noticed before differences: I would almost be inclined to say that the recognition of a similarity belongs to the aesthetic phase, to expression using terms of comparison as familiar "words," while the recognition of differences is proper to a critical and judicatory attitude. Cattaneo, commenting in fact on the discovery of Mexico, observed that when the imagination is deeply moved it sees the generic, not the specific (*Opere* [Florence, 1881–92], III, 420). In the early chroniclers Spain is also frequently taken as a literary "basis" on which to extol the greater splendor of the Indies, without any real comparative intention. This is, for example (as Iglesia has pointed out, *Cronistas y historiadores,* p. 25), what happens with Cortés, who "whenever he draws a comparison, almost always does so to the advantage of Mexico rather than Spain."

173. *Hist.,* XXIX, 27: III, 140b.

174. Ibid., XXXVI, 1: III, 622a.

175. Ibid., XXXV, 5, 7: III, 618a.

176. Ibid., XLVI, 17: IV, 233a. But certain Florida pines "are perfect and as big as the biggest in Spain" (XVII, 24: I, 553b).

177. Cf. Rey Pastor, op. cit., p. 143.

21. MARVELS OF NATURE IN THE INDIES

It is not surprising that in this quest for the specific and typical Oviedo sometimes gives way to the temptation to depict nature in the West Indies as singular and portentous, outlandish and startling. When he stumbles across a real novelty, he is quite carried away with delight and amazement.

One such novelty, for instance, is rubber, and as Oviedo compares the Indian and European versions of *pelota* the very first rubber ball comes bouncing onto the stage of western history: "These balls bounce incomparably much more than the air-filled ones, because you only have to drop them on the ground from the hand and they rebound much higher, and keep bouncing over and over again, gradually decreasing, of their own accord."[178]

Another is kapok, of which Oviedo is the true and usually forgotten discoverer. "This wool," he writes of the flock contained in the fruits of the *ceyba,* or *Eriodendrum anfractuosum,* "seems to me to be a very notable thing." It flies away at a puff, "and then it looks like it has snowed wherever the wool has covered the ground"—and in fact the kapok fibers are *not* attached to the seeds.[179] "This wool is rather short-fibered and it seems to me that one could not spin it"—and true enough the main characteristic of kapok and the other less important silk cottons is that they are unsuitable for spinning.[180] "But for bed pillows or drawing-room cushions, provided it does not get wet, it is a wool unique in its softness and without any heaviness to the head, and for princely beds it is the most delicate and esteemed of all wools; it is a silk and more delicate than the finest silken fibers." And even today, in fact, the main use of kapok is for upholstery, for which purpose it is unrivaled. Oviedo concludes; "*I have tested all this out,* and provided this wool does not get wet there is nothing like it for cushions or pillows."[181] But the encyclopedias keep repeating that this vital fiber or bristle was imported into Europe "by the Dutch merchants who drew their supplies form Java."[182] Like *caucho* and *quina* the American plant was to have better luck in Asia. It is one of the most piquant ironies of history that the truest and richest treasures of the lands discovered by Columbus should have gone on to make the fortunes of the lands that Columbus was hoping to discover and thought he had discovered.

Then there is tobacco, glimpsed by Columbus among the Tainos and smoked by the Indians in a crude nose-pipe, "and they inhaled the smoke, once, twice,

---

178. *Hist.,* VI, 2: I, 166a. Oviedo does not seem to have had in mind Peter Martyr's description of the balls the Mexicans used, made from the juice from a tree, cooked, hardened, and kneaded, that "in some way, when they hit the ground, gather energy, so that if they are even struck softly they jump right up into the sky, with an incredible bounce" (*Dec.,* V, 10; p. 469). Cf. G. C. Vaillant, *The Aztecs of Mexico* (Harmondsworth, 1950), p. 198.
179. *Encyclopedia Britannica,* 11th ed., VII, 257a, s.v. "Cotton."
180. Ibid.
181. *Hist.,* IX, 11: I, 345.
182. *Encyclopedia Britannica,* 11th ed., X, 313a, s.v. "Fibres"; the same in *Enciclopedia Italiana,* s.v. "Kapok."

thrice, or more times, as much as they could manage," eventually getting intoxicated on it; and they consider it "a very precious thing," so that smoking was for them not only "something healthy, but also a very holy thing." Oviedo is somewhat at a loss: "I cannot imagine what pleasure one can derive from such an act," he proclaims sententiously, going on to add in almost scandalized tones, "I am aware that some Christians now use it"—apparently as an anesthetic, so as not to feel "the pain of swellings." But even this therapeutic or analgesic quality is insufficient to reconcile Oviedo to it, and he remains implacable, concluding harshly that the "cure" is no more than "a living death . . . in my opinion worse than the pain avoided, since it does not make one better."[183]

Yet another novelty is chewing *coca,* the basis of cocaine; Oviedo describes its method of use, identical to that still followed today by the Indians of Peru, with lime, little pouches, and rods, and the custom of swirling it about in the mouth from one side to the other ("from time to time they switch it from one cheek to the other"), its prodigious capacity for assuaging the pangs of thirst and fatigue and its pernicious effect of blackening and ruining the teeth.[184] There is even *barbasco,* the powerful vegetable poison that asphyxiates fish and that over the last half-century has begun to feature in the international insecticide trade because of its high rotenone content.[185]

More ambiguous, in the light at least of what hydrocarbons mean for us today, is his description of "petrol," of which "these Indies of ours" possess at least seven spontaneous springs, some of them abundant. It is mainly valued as pitch for caulking vessels, though Oviedo also tells us, repeating what he has been told by the natives and with a turn of phrase that strikes us as almost sinisterly prophetic, that "these spirits are appropriate for many passions"[186] and in particular—to clarify the verbal equivocation—for gout and cold illnesses "because this oil, or whatever it is [one can almost see Oviedo wrinkling his nose] is always said to be very hot."[187] These mushy poultices float on the surface of the sea in smelly patches, "great pools and stains, or quantities on top of the water,

183. *Hist.,* V, 3: I, 131; cf. XXV, 9: PT, III, 32b, where Oviedo also tells how the Negroes smoke tobacco after the day's work, to help them forget their weariness. For a detailed description of the technique of smoking, see XLII, 11: PT, IV, 416b. This harsh verdict was to be a source of surprise to J. J. Ampère, *Promenade en Amérique* (Paris, 1856), II, 210–14.

A century later the University of Paris rejected another great miracle-working novelty from the Americas, quinine, using an argument similar to Oviedo's, namely that "since quinine did nothing to relieve the noxious vapors in the blood, immediate benefits must necessarily be an 'artificial' cure or 'panacea' which left the patient worse off than before in spite of his own temporary delusion that he felt better" (T. W. Arnold, *The Folklore of Capitalism* [Garden City, 1941], pp. 56–57, 89–90). In each case it was not enough for Europe that the relief provided was *real;* it also had to prove itself to be *rational,* before it could be recognized and accepted. This restrictive reservation could sometimes result in quite ridiculous scruples, but it contained an uncompromising logical requirement, no different from that which illuminated the careful reasoning and "ridiculous" death of Don Ferrante in Manzoni's *Promessi sposi.*

184. *Hist.,* VI, 20: PT, I, 170–80; XXVI, 30: PT, III, 126a; XLVI, 17: PT, V, 105b.

185. Ibid., XIII, 1: PT, II, 56b; XIII, 9: PT, II, 66b. Barbasco is also mentioned by Father Cobo (*Historia del Nuevo Mundo,* 1653, bk. XIV, chap. 16, ed. Jiménez de la Espada [Seville, 1890–93], II, 227), again in 1668 and later by La Condamine (1745) and Juan and Ulloa (1748).

186. *Hist.,* I, 28: PT, I, 185–86; XVII, 7: PT, II, 117–18; XXV, 9: PT, III, 343; XXVI, 13: PT, III, 94a.

187. Ibid., XIX, 2: PT, II, 193b.

here and there, according to how the wind blows,"[188] so that it seems not altogether unreasonable that this "liquid that some call petrol" should be called by others *stercus demonis,* "devil's droppings,"[189] just as we might likewise be struck by the far-seeing accuracy of Carletti, who shortly afterward (1595) was to report that Peruvian pitch was being extracted "in huge quantities and making a handsome profit for its owners."[190]

But despite these occasional acerbic comments and failures of intuition (rubber, tobacco, and oil were to bring the Americas and the world more riches than the gold and silver mines), Oviedo is always quick to extol the plants and creatures of the western continent. His enthusiasm is held in check only with difficulty and carries him away completely when the peculiarity to be underlined serves to reinforce the notion of a nature generous and benign, or the image of a soft and peaceful world, not entirely free of snares, of course, but in which the wild beasts are less wild and the cries of animals muffled: a world of bright colors, languid breezes, solemn and tranquil landscapes, of an almost feminine softness, a world in which roaring and barking would strike a discordant note— the tropical and Caribbean world of the Antilles, Panama, and Nicaragua, which is the only one that Oviedo knew with his own voracious and astonished eyes. Not that this prevents Oviedo giving us—for Peru at least—an accurate diagnosis of what was later to be called climatic aggression: the difference in climate between coast and sierra brings about "such a change in the human body" that many people fall ill, and especially the Indians, because they are poor and undernourished; but the Spaniards too suffer from the change from the lowlands of Lima to the Andean valleys, and vice versa.[191]

22. THE CLIMATE AND THE COWS

In the blessed world of the tropics and the archipelagos, on the other hand, all magnificently green and gold like a vast tapestry adorning the throne room of Charles V, the climate is incomparably mellow and getting mellower with each passing day. "The region and its rigors are being tamed and softened, thanks to the rule of the Spaniards" and thanks particularly to the cows panting in the fields, "powerful animals, whose puffing and great numbers break up the air and do much to disperse the vapors."[192] The cattle brought to Hispaniola multiplied

---

188. *Sum.,* chap. 8, p. 103.

189. *Hist.,* XIX, 2: PT, I, 192–93. On Peruvian petroleum, see XLVI, 17: PT, V, 96a, 98b.

190. *Ragionamenti . . . sopra le cose da lui vedute nei suoi viaggi* (Florence, 1701), p. 63.

191. *Hist.,* XLVII, 20: PT, V, 207b; cf. Gerbi, *Dispute,* pp. 562–64.

192. *Hist.,* VI, 46: I, 239. The other animals, both domestic and wild, also make their contribution to this original form of air-conditioning. They are in fact, in the opinion of the experts, "a great cause of the vapors being thinned out and purified, and of the earth being tamed, as I said above" (ibid., p. 240a).

Oviedo's suggestions may well make us smile. But in the middle of the nineteenth century it was still believed that plagues could be brought under control by shifting the air, and in New Orleans, if the film *Jezebel* is to be believed, smoke and artillery salvoes were used to combat an outbreak of yellow fever. On man's efforts to improve the climate with agricultural works, see my *Dispute,* passim, and C. J. Glacken, *Traces on the Rhodian Shore* (Berkeley and Los Angeles, 1967).

enormously there. "There is an immense quantity of quadrupeds there," [193] Peter Martyr had written. And Oviedo: "The first cows having come from Spain to this island, there are now so many that the ships return laden with their hides," and more than once it has happened that their meat was "left to go to waste in the fields, so that the hides could be taken to Spain;" [194] and horses have been sold at three or four *castellanos,* a pregnant cow at one *castellano* and a ram one *real.* "I have sold them from my hacienda [sighs Oviedo] at this price and less."

Cotton, sugar, and canafistula thrive prodigiously there: "All the things that have been sown and cultivated in this island, of those that have come from Spain, most [note the abrupt, contradictory, but reasonable limitation] have taken and multiplied very well." [195] There are innumerable oranges and citrons, limes and lemons, both sweet and sour, "and everything is so good that the best of Cordova or Seville cannot match them, and they are always in season." [196]

23. PERPETUAL SPRINGTIME

This last feature is one that made a deep impression on Columbus, his companions, and the early settlers: the absence of clearly differentiated seasons, the unbroken productivity of the good earth. [197] One only has to recall the enormous importance of the seasonal cycle for the primitive mentality—the spring

193. *De insulis* (written ca. 1520–22), p. 364; cf. *Dec.,* III, 7, p. 283 (exporting of horses and hides from Haiti to Spain).

194. *Hist.,* III, 11: I, 85a; VI, 26: PT, I, 183a. The same was to occur two centuries later in the Argentine pampas. On the astonishing fertility and incredibly rapid multiplication of the cows on Cuba, see the report from 1578 in Carbia, *Crónica oficial,* p. 83n.

195. *Hist.,* III, 11: I, 85b. And if anything is lacking, like wine and bread, "it should not be thought that this is the fault of the land." The plants which fail to prosper are those that have been neglected or overlooked by people whose only concern is how to get rich quickly, and who therefore turn to trade, mining or pearl fishing; people impatient to make their fortunes and get back to Europe, rabble that look on "this land as stepmother, although it has treated many of them much better than their own mothers," jeers Oviedo, with subdued and pointed sarcasm, valid then, and no less valid now (III, 11: I, 86b; cf. V, 10: I, 156).

But Columbus had in fact already warned the sovereigns that the greed for gold would lure the settlers in Hispaniola away from farming (undated letter in *Relaciones y cartas,* p. 233). And his lament is echoed a number of times by Peter Martyr, for example, in reference to Hispaniola itself: "The raging thirst for gold has hitherto diverted the Spaniards from agriculture" (*De insulis,* p. 364). This optimistic view of the potential of the American soil was recalled at the end of the eighteenth century, at the time of the heated debates on the superiority or inferiority of America. Father Iturri reminded Muñoz: "Oviedo, who on this point is more valid than Your Honor, because he saw both worlds, and who was therefore qualified to comment, assures us that all the seeds that were brought from Spain did better in America" (*Carta crítica sobre la "Historia de América" del señor Juan Bautista Muñoz* [Madrid, 1798], p. 69).

196. *Sum.,* chap. 78, p. 229–30; *Hist.,* III, 11: I, 86a. Orange trees are extremely abundant (III, 11: PT, I, 79b; VIII, I: PT, I, 245b). Again in 1561 Licentiate Echagoian wrote from Hispaniola: "There are innumerable oranges and lemons of many sorts" (*CDII,* I, 13). But I can find no trace of the "delicious" orange marmalades mentioned in H. I. Priestley, *The Coming of the White Man* (New York, 1940), p. 24.

197. There are frequent references to plants that "never lose their leaves" in Columbus's journal and letters. And Peter Martyr recalls that "Columbus himself wrote, and all his companions agreed, that all the regions he traveled through were leafy, green, and pleasant throughout the year" (*Dec.,* III, 7, pp. 249–50); on Hispaniola, "all year long the trees are in leaf and the meadows covered with grass" (ibid., III, 7, p. 283; cf. III, 8, p. 295). On Cuzco's perennial grapes and the perpetual vineyards of the "islands of Jauja," see, among many possibilities, C. Gioda, *La vita e le opere di Giovanni Botero* (Milan, 1895), III, 322. Father Cobo also relates that in Peru "the vines keep their leaves throughout the year" (op. cit., bk. X, chap. 13; ed. cit., II, 381, quoted by Pereyra, *La obra de España en America* [Cartagena and Madrid, 1920], p. 164). Castile melons and figs, in greater or lesser quantity, and grapes ripen throughout the year (*Hist.,* IV, 2: PT, I, 93b).

blossoming, the summer harvest, the autumnal fall of the leaves, and the white sleep of winter—and the abundant residue that this elemental experience left in the myths, customs, legends, and religion of all Europe, indeed of all temperate climes, to understand the tone of absolute amazement in Oviedo's description: "There are very few trees[198] that lose their leaves in these parts." While in Asia, Africa, and Europe and all the rest of the world "outside these Indies of ours, there are very few trees that keep their leaves and have them continuously, here on the contrary they are never without them nor lose them at any time, except some and very few."[199] Even the savage, pictured in medieval fashion as hirsute rather than smooth-skinned as the travelers now reported, is said by one astonished versifier to be "hairy in body *in every season*"![200]

The same tone, in no way deprecatory as it would be in the eighteenth century, can be detected in the repeated, insistent assertion of the extreme humidity of the Indies[201]—a sign (even if it has a ruinous effect on leather and timber and causes weapons to rust) not of the continent's only recently having emerged from some flood or other, but of a dewy freshness, abundant vitality, and perennial, spontaneous fecundity.

24. VIRGIN FOREST AND TROPICAL FRUITS

This perpetual exuberance attains its supreme expression in the virgin forest, which Oviedo describes in terms of such florid and profuse vigor that his style seems to be trying to emulate the jungle. The multitude of trees is inconceivable and they are so different in height, trunk, branches, bark, leaves, and flowers that not even the Indians, let alone the Christians, know what their names are; the sky is blotted out by the thickly tangled leaves overhead, and at ground level the way is barred by the numerous other plants and greenery growing between the trees, "so matted and twisted and so full of thorns and creepers and other interwoven branches, that only with great labor and by dint of knives and axes can one clear a path."

198. For the fig tree, see *Hist.*, VII, 1, par. 3: PT, I, 245a; the *canafistola*, XIII, 1, par. 7: PT, I, 246b, and the hog plum, VIII, 2: PT, I, 251a, etc.

199. Ibid., II, 7: PT, I, 32a; IX, 21: I, 351a; cf. IX, Proh.: I, 329a. On 22 January 1518 Licentiate Alonso de Zuazo (uncle of the young man whose Boccaccesque adventure is recounted with great gusto in *Hist.*, L, 5: IV, 474–75) wrote from Hispaniola: "Your Majesty may be certain that this is the best land in the world . . . always green, and where the trees never lose their leaves" (in Jiménez de la Espada, *Relaciones geográficas*, I, xvii ff). On Alonso de Zuazo, see *Hist.*, IV, 2: I, 103b; XXXIII, 30: III, 423, XXXIII, 48: III, 518a; L, 10: 482a; and Carbia, *Crónica oficial*, p. 83n. After transcribing Zuazo's letter, Jiménez de la Espada goes on (p. xx): "And it should not be forgotten that shortly thereafter, in 1525, another man [our own Oviedo] as enthusiastic, learned, and industrious as the Licentiate and judge of Hispaniola, and likewise an office-holder on the island [not actually at that time, but later on, true enough] brought out his *Sumario de la Natural Historia de las Indias*, an excellent book considering the time when it was written, both for its intrinsic value, and even more as a genuine sample of that other more considered and complete work that the author of the *Sumario* wrote on the same subject." Cf. above, chap. IV, n. 4, and Bataillon, *Etudes*, p. 62.

200. François Deserpz (1564) in Le Moine, op. cit., p. 74. Cf. my *Dispute*, pp. 72–74.

201. "These Indies are a very wet land" (*Hist.*, VII, 1: PT, I, 230a; cf. VIII, 1: PT, 248b; XI, 9: PT, II, 24b; XV, 4: PT, II, 82b; XXIX, 18: PT, III, 278b; XXXII, 8: PT, III, 421a; XLIII, 2: PT, V, 9a).

The whole forms a *mare magnum* full of mystery. Some trees have pretty and sweet-smelling flowers and fragrant trunks, while others are so savage that only monkeys know what use they can be. There are those so thick with thorns that they cannot be touched with the bare hand, others covered with ivy and creepers, and yet others clothed from head to foot with a sort of filament, "so that they seem to be covered with spun wool, though they are not." And all grow in their own way and in their own time, so that "one sees everything together in one season and at any whatsoever time of year." Heaving another sigh at the secrets and still unknown properties of these marvelous ("to look at") forests and thickets, Oviedo brings to a close this veritable incunabulum of exoticism. Apart from those monkeys introduced half jokingly there is not a word about the animal life, although the forest is in fact teeming with creatures of one sort or another. Oviedo is completely absorbed in his utilitarian-botanical concerns and forgets the snakes, wild animals, and insects lurking in the depths. His virgin forest is part of nature benign, welcoming, and even perhaps at times a little suffocating, like a rather buxom and over-expansive aunt.

Where nature's benevolence reveals itself in its most quintessential and almost spiritual form, however, is in the excellence of certain tropical fruits. Oviedo, as we have already seen, was not without a certain sensual gluttony (see above, chap. XV, sec. 16 and below, Appendix C), and the pineapple has him drooling with ecstatic and baroque hyperboles.

25. OTHER PRODIGIES

One catches an echo of this same enthusiasm, though less lyrical in tone, whenever Oviedo is describing some new and unusual marvel of the Indies, from the freshwater springs emerging from the salt waters of the sea to the intermittent rivers and the winds that are sometimes healthy and sometimes harmful,[202] depending on what quarter they blow from; from the well-castrated cockerels that still manage to fecundate the hens, which "lay eggs without having seen anything of a rooster . . . from the mere conversation or company of the capons,"[203] to the amiable and docile bees that do not sting, indeed "if you take one and rub it between your fingers, it smells very nice";[204] from the "brown skunk," a cheerful and beautifully clean animal, that one of his caravels brought from Cartagena, where the "archer Indians" had bartered it for two fishhooks,[205] and from the famous Mexican turkeys, "better tasting and bigger than Spanish turkeys,"[206]

202. Ibid., XXVII, 7: PT, III, 153b; XXXII, 2: PT, III, 400b; XXXII, 4: PT, III, 409b; XXXIX, 32: PT, III, 343a.
203. Ibid., IV, 10: I, 194b.
204. Ibid., XXXII, 6; III, 246a; cf. also XXXIV, 2: III, 561b.
205. Ibid., XII, 25: PT, II, 49–50.
206. Ibid., XXXIII, 7: III, 291–92.

to the numerous vegetables that do as well in the Indies as "in any part of Spain," and indeed better, so that no other seeds need be brought over the ocean,[207] to the potatoes, "delicate and tasty," so good that they can be "presented to His Imperial Majesty as a very expensive dish"! "A salted potato," Oviedo assures us, his mouth watering, "is in no way inferior in taste to dainty marzipans."[208]

But what earns Oviedo's admiration more than anything else, whether useful or edible, fragrant or tasty, is a creature that has the sole merit of being extraordinarily beautiful. Aesthetic considerations once again take precedence over the utilitarian when Oviedo describes this animal prodigy, half cat and half bird, that sings as sweetly as a nightingale and belonged to an Indian princess related to Atahualpa. The creature was destined as a royal gift to Her Majesty the empress, but a careless servant, while larking about with other servants, "trod on the cat and killed it." Oviedo never actually set eyes on it either alive or dead. If he had seen it, even dead, he would willingly have given his cloak for a bit of salt to pickle it and preserve it. And he would rather have seen this miracle of nature alive than the innumerable priceless emeralds that passed through his hands.[209] To Oviedo this adorable little kitty (it was "very tame and domesticated and scarcely bigger than the palm of the hand") is a sign of the omnipotence of that God who in antiquity created gryphons, half lions and half eagles, and at the same time a token of the infinite number and magnitude of "the secrets of this great world of our Indies."[210]

26. Dumb cats and dogs

The land possesses another secret no less amazing. The Indies' singing cat has a partner in the silent cat. The tireless American cats mate all year round, but

---

207. Ibid., XI, 1: I, 373.

208. Ibid., VII, 4: I, 273–74.

209. In the same vein Oviedo refers to a certain bay in Peru where the water is fresh at high tide and salt at low tide, although a great river flows into it, and goes on to say how learning about such a curious phenomenon gave him "more pleasure and more contentment . . . than everything I have just mentioned," which was no less than a treasure hoard consisting of five large, absolutely perfect emeralds and some gold ingots, one of which weighed forty pounds, so that he could barely lift it with two hands! (*Hist.*, VI, 53: I, 261).

210. Ibid., VI, 52: I, 259–60. On the basis of this passage Alvarez López concludes that "for Oviedo the world is not the work of a Logos; nature is a perpetual miracle, in which there is no law, or if there is one, it is beyond our comprehension; contradictory beings are possible within it," etc., and that Oviedo is therefore much inferior to Acosta as a scientist and naturalist ("Acosta," pp. 309–10). Obviously Oviedo may have mistakenly believed in the existence of a natural prodigy, but this does not make him an irrationalist or pantheistic mystic. His openmindedness, recognizing that anything is possible in nature, is in its empiricism more "scientific" than Father Acosta's strict, sometimes finalistic, and often erroneous anthropocentric rationalism. Indeed it anticipates by several decades the Pyrrhonian theses of Francisco Sánchez, who—using that selfsame example of the Americas—denied that there were any eternal and incorruptible propositions, such as the notion that the parts of the world were three and three only, or that the tropics were uninhabitable, and continued: "Of the other species [other than that "miserable worm" man] the same can be said"; in the lands and the seas covering the globe there existed innumerable species "that seem to be distinct, and are so," even if it was not always easy to distinguish between them (*Quod nihil scitur*, ca. 1575–76 [1581; Buenos Aires, 1944], p. 83).

without disturbing the neighborhood with their caterwauling.[211] How many times, Oviedo recalls, "when I was studying at night in Spain, or reading for pleasure," he was distracted, annoyed, and exasperated by amorous cats! On the island of Hispaniola, at least, they pursue their pleasure "without shouts or cries."[212] Oviedo can study or read in peace. And of course cats that miaow do not even perform their proper task of catching mice: "A screeching cat will never catch a rat."[213] It is a nuisance to everyone and fulfils no useful function.

This feline dumbness, which would later be flung in America's face as one of the marks of its inferiority, is instead welcomed by Oviedo almost as a proof of the friendliness of American nature. From an anthropomorphic viewpoint, which is always the basic approach with Oviedo, the absence of an irritating attribute is a sign of providential predestination. In a climate of scientific objectivity (and of polemics on the subject of the New World) the voicelessness of the cats was to become a sign of organic deficiency and biological inferiority. An advance in method does not always lead directly to an advance in knowledge. Sometimes the obvious superiority of the new ideas beguiles the observer, takes him by the hand and blinds him with the dazzling brightness of the latest discovery, making him lose touch with humble empirical reality or inducing him to force the facts assembled in cruder and less expert enquiries into the deforming patterns of a brand new system. Oviedo, the innocent outsider, does not let himself be contaminated by such learned and impassioned aberrations. The taciturn and love-sick cat stalks noiselessly in and out, vanishing in the general image of a soft and sleepy nature. Its chivalric discretion gives it a dash of nobility and reserve that must have pleased the hidalgo Oviedo.

A cat's miaowing is simply a nuisance, but a dog's barking is not. It has a specific function linked to the animals' usefulness as a guard dog. A cat that is never heard is a supercat. A dog that cannot bark is a subdog. Roger Bacon had believed that dogs could not bark when they were under the evil influence of the

---

211. In Peru, on the other hand, there are "cats like those of Spain in the houses and the Indians set great store by them" (*Hist.*, XLVI, 17: IV, 233a). But those cats that sang in the middle of the night seem to hark back to Pliny's roosters: "They lie awake at night . . . and know the constellations, and they crow at intervals, every three hours" (*Natural History*, X, 24, trans. Littré, I, 399).

Oviedo's approval of silence is equally evident in his reference to the *coris* as "mute animals and not bothersome, and very tame; they move about the house and keep it clean, and they do not screech or make a noise or gnaw things and do damage" (*Hist.*, XII, 4: I, 390). And he tells us that the roosters never crow in the night hours, as they do "on the dot" in Europe, but only at dusk or a couple of hours after, and before daybreak or just as the sun is rising (IV, 10: I, 194).

Elsewhere however Oviedo seems to regret that in Hispaniola the swallow's song is "more raucous" than in Spain, and different, possibly because there have only recently been stone houses there, and in fact, "they are already beginning to breed in the parish church of this city and in the Dominican monastery" (XIV, 2: I, 442a). Attentive to nature's every voice, the historian hastens to note that first familiar chirruping of those highly civilized swallows, happy to be able to build their nests at last among the houses, churches, and monasteries of the first city in the New World.

212. *Hist.*, IV, 10: I, 195. Pliny too had heard them "in the leisure hours, in other words the night-time hours" (*Natural History*, Preface, 14, trans. Littré, I, 3b).

213. *Qu.*, p. 388.

shadow of a hyena.[214] And Oviedo, similarly, notes their dumbness as a curious shortcoming. Thus it is not with any sense of rejoicing at the goodness of nature but instead to express his dismay and concern at such a singular anomaly that he stops so frequently to tell us about the voicelessness of the mongrels of America. In many parts of the Indies "all the dogs that are native to the land do not bark (and I have seen many of them)."[215] And on Hispaniola the dogs that Columbus's companions ate were similar in color and coat to all the dogs known in Spain, but "all these dogs here and on the other islands were dumb, and even if they were beaten or killed they could not bark: some do whine or give a low growl when they are maltreated."[216] And how come? Why do these dogs not act like all the other dogs in the world? Oviedo lacks the sardonic and inspired imagination of the pedagogue Antonio Genovesi, who was to explain that the dogs of America obviously did not bark because nobody had taught them to![217]

Oviedo, as always, stresses the strangeness of the phenomenon: "As for the failure of these dogs to bark, it being such a natural thing for mongrels and dogs of all sorts, it is really remarkable, compared with those of Europe and most parts of the world." He tries to explain it to himself, or rather reassure himself, by repeating that nature is various, indeed that "by varying thus nature is beautiful" (see below, Appendix A). He recalls that Pliny talks about frogs that sing in one country and not in another. And prompted by his persistent curiosity he decides to conduct an experiment: "I wanted to test whether these dumb dogs, if removed from their country, would bark in another." So he takes a dog in Nicaragua and removes it to Panama, three hundred leagues away "and here too it remained dumb."

The result is negative. But Oviedo is not yet ready to give up, and with extraordinary scientific foresight he criticizes the method and conditions of his experiment. It was not surprising that the dog remained dumb in Panama, "because it is all one coast and mainland and, as I have said, in all of these parts and these islands the dogs that are native thereto are thus dumb." Perhaps if he

214. Perrier, op. cit., p. 2.

215. *Hist.*, VI, 31: I, 219a. Cf. *Sum.*, chap. 26, p. 163; *Hist.*, II, 13: I, 50a; V, 8: I, 151b; XII, 18: II, 408; XXIII, 12: II, 192b; XXV, 22: II, 331a; XXVI, 10: II, 355a ("even if they were beaten with sticks or cut with knives, they never whined, just emitted a certain low throttled growl, barely audible"); XLII, 2: IV, 49b; XLII, 12: IV, 108a; XLVI, 17: IV, 233a; XLIX, 4: IV, 388b, etc.

Columbus was the first to note those "dogs that never barked" (*Relaciones y cartas*, p. 48), and that they were the only quadrupeds on Cuba (ibid., p. 58). Las Casas too wrote that the dogs on Hispaniola "never bark, just growl in their gullets, and are like Spanish dogs, and only differ in that they do not bark" (*Historia de las Indias*, bk. I, chap. 42, ed. cit., I, 215). On the mute dogs of Santo Domingo, see Buffon, *Oeuvres complètes*, XV, 416–19, who cites Acosta, Charlevoix, and Jean de Laët, but *not* Oviedo. Morison explains that they were not "a special breed of canine, but common yellow 'hound dogs' that the Tainos domesticated largely for eating purposes," and that they only became extinct, or rather were wiped out, during the nineteenth century (*Admiral of the Ocean Sea*, I, 336–37; cf. also Cardoso, op. cit., X, 397–98 and note, who says that they were crab-eating raccoons). I have not seen Enrique Alvarez López's "El perro mudo americano (El problema del perro mudo de Fernández de Oviedo)," *Boletín de la Real Sociedad Española de Historia Natural*, 11 (1942), 411–17.

216. *Hist.*, XII, 5: I, 390b.

217. Op. cit., p. 497.

had taken the little mongrel off to Spain. . . . But unfortunately "when I left for Spain he was stolen from me [Oviedo affectionately sighs] and I had brought him up and he was very tame."[218] The gentle tone of these last few words can perhaps make us forgive those other savage "experiments," the recourse to sticks, stones, and knives to see if the dogs of those parts barked in pain like European dogs.[219]

27. METHODICAL EXPERIMENTS

But here it is worthwhile returning for a moment to Oviedo's constantly reiterated and reaffirmed faith in experimentation. An observer, however acute, is still passive before the spectacle of nature. But the scientific mind does not stop at description: it so to speak assaults natural reality, forcing it to yield its secrets. This attitude of Oviedo's is graphically and dramatically demonstrated in the way he tackles the anthills and termite mounds. "I had them broken open and flattened"; they are rock hard, in fact, and "very difficult to undo with picks and crowbars"; but the naturalist refuses to be beaten. "To understand this secret better, in my presence [a presence resplendent with the sovereign authority of science] I had it pulled down."[220]

Nor does he always confine himself to reporting what he saw with his own eyes. When the occasion calls he also reports what he has measured with his own hands, like the huge tree in Nicaragua, "which . . . I measured with my own hands with a piece of cord" and that proved to have a circumference at the base of thirty-three *varas* or 132 palms, without counting the trunk invisible near the roots, that must have been another three *varas*.[221] He scours the woods for Pliny's "terebinth," a source of the health-giving turpentine, convinced that it must be there somewhere, but alas, "what fits in with one characteristic, conflicts with others." The so-called terebinths of the Indies "have no more authority than having been thus called by whoever so desired"; perhaps they will turn up with time and experience.[222]

"I have tested it," "I have experimented with it," "from my own experience"

218. *Hist.*, XII, 5: I, 391b.

219. Very similar methods were sometimes used to convert the Indians, who were made to "bark" or "recite the creed" by application of exactly the same sort of violence as that used to try and persuade the American dogs to confess their substantial affinity with the dogs of Europe. The Inca Atahualpa, assaulted for his rejection of Valverde's religious injunctions, is the supreme and almost symbolic exponent of a conflict that at the other end of the scale includes the dogs kicked about by the Spaniards for being unable to bark the way Spanish dogs do. Oviedo, however, expressed his indignation at the incomprehensible *requerimientos* aimed at making the Indians play the role of rebels (e.g., against Valverde, i*Hist.*, XLVI, 7: IV, 173a; XLVII, 5–6: IV, 373b; cf. above, chap. IX, sec. 5, and below, chap. XIX, sec. 21).

220. *Sum.*, chap. 20. pp. 253–54; *Hist.*, XII, 47: PT, II, 46.

221. *Hist.*, IX, 11: PT, I, 289–90, cf. *Sum.*, chap. 78, pp. 225–28.

222. *Hist.*, IX, 10: PT, I, 277–78. The United States is today by far the world's largest producer of turpentine, which is derived from the longleaf pine.

are phrases that crop up all the time in Oviedo's prose.[223] And his experiments
are neither summary nor superficial. The Río Grande debouches into the Gulf of
Urabá and makes the gulf water fresh: "I have often lowered a silver jar, suspended by a cord, . . . from a ship anchored in eight fathoms . . . and brought
up water that is fresh and drinkable."[224] As for the science of navigation, he
admits that he could not hope to debate with the "scholars" and recognizes their
superior learning, but he feels sure that after the "many bad nights and days" he
has spent in "nautical exercise," he would be the winner in any practical test: "If
they were each to handle one ship and I another, I think I would get home
first."[225] He is also blessed with a good pair of eyes—"all praise to Him that
gave me them"—and he has used quadrant, astrolabe, and forestaff and taken his
measurements from on land and not while tossing and heaving about on the deck
of a ship![226] Nor, in so saying, does Oviedo exaggerate by one whit the perils
involved in taking astronomical observations from the poop deck of a caravel.[227]
When Columbus's disgruntled sailors were plotting to kill him their first idea was
that they could "judiciously throw him overboard and then announce that he had
been trying to look at the stars and the signs and had fallen inadvertently and
nobody would inquire into the truth of the whole matter. . . ."[228] Toward the
end of the sixteenth century Sassetti warned: "On board ship the observation of
the stars and the heavens . . . *does not speak the truth* because of the continual
bobbing about of the ship."[229] And a yachtsman of our own time has described
how, to take his readings, he had to balance himself against the surge of the
ship's deck and seek the right moment when the image of the sun's rim topped
the true horizon, "no easy combination when both deck and horizon are in
constant motion."[230]

But to return to the plants, Oviedo suffers one notable disappointment in his
orchard. Just like the terebinth, trees with pit-bearing fruit do not take in the
Indies, or if they take at all, manage to produce no fruit, only leaves. Oviedo
tries time and again with various types of peach, plum, and cherry pits, and
pine kernels too, and none of them take.[231] *Guazuma* bark, on the other hand,

223. E.g., *Hist.*, VI, 17: PT, I, 173a, with the account of another experiment. Salas recognizes that Oviedo has "an undeniable penchant for experimentation" (op. cit., pp. 114–15; see also p. 147).

224. *Hist.*, XXIX, 2: PT, III, 209b.

225. Ibid., XXI, 5: PT, II, 318. One of those with whom he is disinclined to argue is "the Florentine master" (Paolo Toscanelli?).

226. Ibid., XXI, 7: PT, II, 327a; XXIX, 21: PT, III, 301a; cf. above, chap. XVII, sec. 19.

227. On the problems inherent in taking reliable observations with an astrolabe on a rolling ship, see Pohl, op. cit., pp. 67 and 218n7. And it was in fact the astrolabe that Oviedo used on many occasions, in Panama (*Hist.*, XXXIX, 2: PT, IV, 343a) and Nicaragua (XXXIX, 2: PT, IV, 345a). Cf. Morison, *Southern Voyages*, p. 55.

228. Fernando Columbus, *Vita di Cristoforo Colombo*, p. 67. It should not be forgotten that modern biographers are inclined to think that the Admiral of the Ocean Sea could not swim.

229. Op. cit., p. 328.

230. Dougal Robertson, *Survive the Savage Sea* (London, 1973), p. 22.

231. *Hist.*, VII, 1, par. 9: PT, I, 247a.

is ideal for gunpowder: "I have tested it myself for the ammunition for this fort in the city of Santo Domingo," and artillery experts agree with him that it is better than German willow, vine trunks, or almond switches.[232] Equally excellent for manufacturing black powder, the most murderous invention of the human mind, is charcoal from *cigua;*[233] and there are certain round stones found in Cuba that would be just right for musket shot, in fact the bigger ones would do nicely for any artillery, even for "pieces of one quintal and two or more."[234]

Another item that Oviedo finds useful for the fortress entrusted to his care is the mighty *corbana,* out of whose rock-hard trunk he makes the axles of the gun-carriages for the culverins and other artillery pieces, as the wood never rots.[235] And after telling us about another culverin—seventy or more quintals of bronze—on its *cuya*-wood carriage, Oviedo adds that the mounting will last for an eternity, so that "the commandant that succeeds me will be able to understand what I shall not see, and make up his own mind."[236] Oviedo has no hesitation in conducting an experiment for the benefit and instruction of his successor. One cannot, on the other hand, quite see what useful purpose he hoped to serve in giving us the detailed prescription for the poison used by the Indians to "anoint" their deadly arrows.[237]

The local resources are not all exploited solely for warlike ends, however. With the black seeds of the *pitahaya* "I have made first quality ink and written with it, and it is of an excellent color between purple and bright crimson."[238] The fruit of certain Nicaraguan trees, dissolved in vitriol, "make very good ink," better than the usual type, very black and indelible: "I have written a lot of things in my notes" and after so many years "it seems that they are better now than when I wrote them."[239] Another magnificent coloring agent comes from certain scarlet-colored vegetable lozenges, used by the native men and women to paint themselves, that are better than the rouges used by Italian and Spanish women; Oviedo has tried out a lot of them "in sketches and paintings, to amuse myself, and to see if the color is lasting," and after six years the watercolors, without the tempera used by painters, have brighter and better colors than they

232. Ibid., VIII, 7: PT, I, 254b. On Oviedo's interest in gunpowder, cf. above, chap. XVII, n. 222.
233. *Hist.,* IX, 19: PT, I, 294b.
234. Ibid., XVII, 6: PT, II, 217a.
235. Ibid., IX, 16: PT, I, 293b.
236. Ibid., IX, 17: PT, I, 294a. On Oviedo's ideas about the defence of the city of Santo Domingo, which he felt should be effected not by building "expensive fortifications" but by training the soldiers in the use of arms, see Pérez de Tudela, "Vida," p. cxxxv.
237. *Hist.,* XXIV, 10: PT, II, 418–19.
238. Ibid., VIII, 26: PT, I, 246a.
239. Ibid., IX, 27: PT, I, 299.

did the first day.[240] On the other hand, the sunflower does not unfortunately produce the fruit "that is used for making the blue ink for illuminating capital letters usually made by those who write books in round hand with formed letters."[241]

Thus it is understandable that Oviedo gets irritated when despite repeated requests he fails to discover what use the natives make of certain *cardones.* Either they taste different to them or else serve "some other purpose that the Christians have not yet divined."[242]

The outcome of the experiments is not always positive, however. Oviedo tells us he tried the bitter-tasting *mangle* fruit, which the natives eat when they have nothing better, not because he was hungry but so that he could more accurately describe its taste as well as its looks: "So I tried this fruit. When all is said and done [we can almost picture him spitting it out], it is foul-tasting and only fit for savages."[243] On the subject of certain purgative almonds, a good nine of which apparently failed to move the stomach of a duenna ("so I heard it sworn by the lady herself . . ." Oviedo adds, forgetting that he only believes in the evidence of his own eyes), he tells the story of how Juan de la Vega, one of Columbus's companions on the second voyage, had taken some back to Spain and held them to be miraculous and offered them as a highly prized commodity; but when (in 1513) he administered half of one to a young nephew of his "it evacuated him in such a manner that he had no innards left in his belly," and in less than twenty hours the poor young man was dead; and Oviedo's own children almost expired as a result of stuffing themselves with them.[244] With the miracle-working *perebecenuc* herb, on the other hand, Oviedo was able to treat numerous Indians and black slaves and even some Christians in his own home; all recovered, without his having spent a penny on the treatment—obviously a factor of some importance to Oviedo, particularly as some of these wounds would have cost a packet if he had summoned a surgeon! In the event the treatment cost him not a penny nor a word of thanks, apart from the thanks due to Almighty God![245]

Another item that attracts Oviedo's curiosity is a certain paste, used by the natives to make combs, that looks like fried clay but is in reality bat droppings. Oviedo takes half a dozen of the crude combs back to Santo Domingo and puts

---

240. Ibid., X, 1: PT, II, 8b; cf. above, chap. XV, n. 222.
241. *Hist.*, XI, 2: PT, II, 18a.
242. Ibid., VII, 27: PT, I, 264–65. Mahn-Lot's comment (*La découverte*, p. 91) on experience opposed to the theories of antiquity, namely that it is "already noticeable in the observations of Columbus, Vespucci, and Oviedo," is therefore accurate, if too generic.
243. *Hist.*, IX, 6: PT, I, 286a. Oviedo is constantly trying things—meat, fish, snakes and fruit—to see what they taste like: the *coris* taste like young rabbits (ibid., XII, 4: PT, II, 30a).
244. Ibid., X, 4: PT, II, 13–14; cf. *Sum.*, chap. 80, pp. 233–34.
245. *Hist.*, XI, 5: PT, II, 21.

them in front of the fire: they melt like wax, but as they cool off become rock-hard again, and the teeth of the comb bite like iron.[246]

In 1530 a gunner in the fort finds a huge snake curled up on one of the guns and succeeds in decapitating it with a single swordstroke; "and I had it opened up and some thirty or more eggs were found in it,"[247] which passing comment would perhaps not be worth mentioning if the dissection of bodies for scientific pur-poses (even after Mondino and Leonardo) had been a current practice before Guillaume Rondelet (1507–1566) and Ulisse Aldrovandi (1522–1605).

On another occasion, in Panama, a Negro brings down a frigate bird with a well-aimed blow with a stick; Oviedo picks it up and notes that once it is plucked it is hardly bigger than a dove, although with its wings fully spread "good-sized men" cannot reach its wing-tips with their arms stretched out and hands open.[248] Equally astonishing is the *pájaro mosquito,* which together with its nest and feathers only just manages to tip a goldsmith's scale at two *tomines,* or twenty-four grains; in size it is smaller than the first joint of the thumb. And so on and so on.[249]

With his methodical attachment to experimentation, Oviedo is living disproof of the theories that accuse history, unlike the exact sciences, of being incapable of conducting experiments (or, what comes to the same thing, of "measuring"). Oviedo, as historian of the new material, describes and tests it. The experiment is a mental act, not a technique proper to this or that form of knowledge. It is proper to all of them. And to those who would quibble that Oviedo conducts experi-ments as a naturalist not as a historian, we would reply, first and foremost, that the objection begs the question. Oviedo's experiments are his questionings of things American: what logical difference is there between dissecting an iguana and firing questions at a returning conquistador?

But it should also be pointed out that not even the astronomer, for example, or the palaeontologist, conducts experiments in the strict sense of the term, yet nobody denies them the title of scientists. In fact in the founding of modern science, "it is not 'experience,' but it is 'experiments' which played a decisive role. Experimentation is the methodical interrogation of nature, an interrogation which presupposes and implies a *language* in which to formulate the questions, and a dictionary which enables us to interpret the answers."[250] And following the same line of thought Hadamard sees the founder of modern science not in Bacon or Descartes, but in Leonardo (and William Gilbert) because Leonardo

---

246. He also brought back to Santo Domingo from the island of Chira "some fine pieces" of majolica (ibid., XXIX, 21: PT, III, 298a, and LXII, 12: PT, IV, 424a).

247. Ibid., XII, 7: PT, II, 37b. Buffon too always said "I had a rabbit opened up," never "I opened . . ." (Gerbi, *Dispute,* p. 20). On a snake twenty feet long, see *Sum.,* chap. 55, p. 194.

248. *Hist.,* XIV, 1: PT, I, 69.

249. *Sum.,* chap. 47, p. 186; *Hist.,* XIV, 4: PT, II, 71b.

250. A. Koyré, "Galileo and Plato," *JHI,* 4, no. 4 (October 1943), 403.

did not confine himself to observing the principles of experience, like Bacon, but carried out experiments to test his speculations.[251]

But it is time we closed this somewhat rash digression and got back to the unbarking dogs and other "oddities" of the Indies.

28. OTHER ANIMAL CURIOSITIES

Oviedo has something apposite to say for almost all the other animals too, but when his natural curiosity is further stimulated by some genuine "phenomenon" of nature his tone becomes more lively and his words acquire a sharpness that has etched them into the memory of generations of subsequent chroniclers, polygraphs, and polemicists, and even the most casual readers.[252] Thus we need not dwell on the fleas, "much smaller, for the most part, than those of Castile; but they bite a lot more and are worse,"[253] nor on the tailless rats found in the Straits of Magellan, that Oviedo thinks must more likely have been *coris*,[254] nor on the notorious pigs with their navels on their backs.[255] We need not linger unduly over that fetid skunk killed by a Spaniard, whose posthumous stench alone sufficed to rout its assailants: the two dogs that had savaged it were seized with convulsions and vomiting, the horse brought up bile and "keeled over," and the horseman likewise threw up and dropped his lance ("because the foul smell and infection reached him along his lance"), and for days none of them could touch a bite of food.[256] We can pass quickly by that greedy Darien opossum that in the space of one night "slaughtered fourteen on my hens . . . and at a time when each one was worth three gold pieces or more";[257] and the ocean fish (presum-

---

251. J. Hadamard, "La science et le monde moderne," *Renaissance*, 1 (1943), 523–57, reviewed by Monelisa Lina Pérez Marchand, *RHA*, 17 (1944), 243.

On the difference between observation and experiment, with all that it implies as interrogative "activity," as hypothesis put to the test, as nature constrained and squeezed and even altered by the scientist's researches, it is well worth rereading the classic comments of Claude Bernard, *Introduction à l'étude de la médecine expérimentale* (Geneva, 1945), pp. 49–84, and the resulting savage attack on Bacon who "was no scholar and completely failed to understand the mechanism of the experimental method" (p. 125; cf. pp. 418–19). Bacon is defended and praised, on the other hand, by R. G. Collingwood, *The Idea of History* (Oxford, 1946), p. 269, and precisely because he put "Nature to the question . . . devising tortures under which she can no longer hold her tongue," in other words precisely because, in Collingwood's view, he possessed that inquisitorial spirit that is denied him by others, but is universally recognized as essential to the progress of knowledge. See also Dewey, for whom active experimentation replaced the contemplation of the ancients (G. De Ruggiero, "John Dewey," *La Critica*, 29 [1931], p. 343); and C. Lévi-Strauss, who accuses (*Tristes tropiques* [Paris, 1965], p. 60) the early explorers of America of having been "weak from the point of view of observation," whereas Oviedo, since we happen to be talking about him—and Lévi-Strauss himself invokes Oviedo's testimony a page earlier—both observes *and* experiments.

252. If, however, he is discussing an animal well known in Europe, Oviedo wastes no unnecessary time: "There is no need for me to dwell on this" (e.g., *Hist.*, XXXII, 4: III, 237a; XXXIII, 11: III, 350b). Cf. above, chap. XVII, sec. 10.

253. *Hist.*, XV, 3: I, 455b.

254. Ibid., XX, 6: II, 39b. On the *cori*: XII, 4: I, 390. Cardoso, op. cit., X, 405, writes that Oviedo "is precisely on target when he says that the *coris* are 'tail-less rats.'"

255. *Sum.*, chap. 19, p. 152; *Hist.*, XII, 20: I, 409a; XXV, 22: III, 331a.

256. *Hist.*, XLII, 15: IV, 114; cf. VI, 34: I, 224; XII, 17: I, 408; XX, 9: II, 46b; XXIII, 12: II, 193b; XXIV, 13: II, 259–60.

257. Ibid., XII, 27: I, 416a; cf. *Sum.*, chap. 27, pp. 164–65, where Oviedo however omits the number and unit price of his precious chickens. On the *churcha*, see Navarrete, op. cit., III, 22n.

ably a swordfish as it carried on its snout, "on the extremity of its upper jaw, that most ferocious sword full of razor-sharp tusks, along both edges, at regular intervals") that he found dead in a Nicaraguan lake, from which he deduced that the lake must have some subterranean connection with the sea;[258] and finally those voracious crickets that sang like the Spanish ones but gnawed things away worse than mice, as Oviedo learned by disastrous personal experience, when in Panama they ate his "smock" of "Valencia cloth . . . in one single night reducing it to such a state that I could not wear it the next day." . . .[259]

29. LIONS AND TIGERS

But we should not leave this subject without seeing what Oviedo has to say about the wild beasts, the lions and tigers, for one thing because of their popularity and the special attention they have always attracted, on the part of both the general public and the scientific community, and for another because Oviedo's acumen is in this case dazzlingly superior to that of many of his followers and copiers.

The lion, in the thinking of the time, was still truly the king of beasts. Not just any old *felis leo,* but a symbol of unflinching aggressive courage and sovereign scornful ferocity. On coats of arms or in the form of heraldic symbols like the winged lion of Saint Mark or the watchful Marzocco of Florence, it represented authority, the supreme political power of baron, city, or state. Its claws held the Sacred Tables of the Law or the Red Flower of the Lily. It was *leo rugiens quaerens quem devoret,* "the roaring lion seeking who it might devour." It was the richest ornament of the princely menageries. When a lion failed to display the valor and fierceness proper to it, it was taken as an evil omen, almost a disturbing disorder of nature, like a comet or some other monstrosity or upset in the regular course of the spheres and creatures.[260]

The Spaniards were therefore no little taken aback to find that the lions of America were not fierce, did not attack man and often, if attacked, turned tail and

---

258. *Hist.,* XLII, 4: PT, IV, 387b.
259. Ibid., XLIII, 2: IV, 119b.
260. See Burckhardt, *La civiltà,* II, 13–14, 306; Müntz, *Quattrocento,* p. 315 and note; Borsa, op. cit., p. 168. Michael Rostovzeff, in his *History of the Ancient World* (Oxford, 1936), I, 165–66, points out that the Babylonians already looked on any animal anomaly or monstrosity as a "sign," and the same is true of Aristotle: cf. Perrier, op. cit., p. 13.

By the beginning of the seventeenth century this prejudice had already disappeared, and a tame lion could be admired for its imperturbability. In the Medici menagerie Figueroa saw little boys putting their hands between the jaws of the lion Perino, a savage-looking animal, and noted that "this noble animal was as pampered as a pet puppy"; and it was in the same menagerie that Rabelais's rascally friar Bernard Lardon saw the unwelcome sight of "the lions and the Africans (I believe this is what you called the creatures they name tigers)" (*Le Quart Livre de Pantagruel,* chap. XI); here that Montaigne (in 1580) observed a beast the size of a mastiff, with the form of a cat, speckled with black and white, "which they call a tiger"; and here, according to the account of Anhalt-Köthen (1598), that the angry and agitated lions roared most alarmingly (A. D'Ancona, *L'Italia alla fine del secolo XVI: Giornale del viaggio di M. de Montaigne* [Città di Castello, 1895], p. 167 and n. 2).

ran. These "cowardly" lions struck them as one of the most extraordinary signs of a "topsy-turvy world," and one can understand that even centuries later, even to Buffon's "scientific" eye, they caused considerable surprise and some anxious questioning on the part of the observer. Oviedo writes that on the mainland there are "real" lions, but they are "smooth skinned" so that they almost seem like overgrown greyhounds; he notes that they "are cowardly and flee," and swiftly takes comfort in the authority of Pliny, who says that lions do no harm if they are not attacked. A few lines further on, however, he contradicts himself and draws greater comfort from an experience that precisely contradicts Pliny's authority: ". . . and they kill the Indians, when they find them alone."[261] Thus he is almost jubilant when he discovers that in Venezuela there are "certain animals" that they call brown lions that "in fact resemble lions, in their ferocity and weapons, as also in their size," although they are smooth-skinned and do not have "those long manes that African lions have."[262] However neither the "brown" lions nor the smooth-skinned lions of the mainland are really fierce, or not toward the white men at least: "I do not know of them having harmed Christians or attempting to do so, like the tigers."[263]

The lion shares the meek and gentle nature of the New Indies, but the tiger does not. The American tigers, "beautiful and ferocious animals, russet-colored with black spots (i.e., leopards or panthers or something of that ilk) leave Oviedo perplexed. Tigers? "I do not claim that they are, because they do not have the speed attributed to the tiger."[264] The ancients in fact wrote that the tiger "is the fastest of the land animals."[265] Now, these American tigers do indeed eat lots of Indians, "but I cannot make up my mind whether they are tigers, in view of what has been written of the litheness of the tiger and the evident clumsiness of the animals we call tigers in the Indies."[266]

He repeats this dubious reasoning in much the same terms in the *History* and

---

261. *Hist.*, XII, 12: I, 406.
262. Ibid., XXV, 22: II, 331a; cf. XXIX, 10: III, 44b.
263. Ibid., XII, 14: I, 407b. Even the large "brownish-colored" lion which he was brought from Peru was a "very meek" animal (XII, 36; I, 420b), a comment which, incidentally, gives the lie to the criticism made by de Pauw who, forgetting Oviedo's long years on the mainland, stated that "Oviedo could not, on the island of Santo Domingo, have seen these animals that have been called the lions of America, because there were none on that island" (*Défense*, p. 84). The lion's mane, whose absence made such a deep impression on Oviedo and the other chroniclers, was held to be an indication and almost a symbol of indomitable courage. "A lion's nobility is most excellent when a mane clothes its neck and shoulders" (Pliny, *Natural History*, VIII, 17, trans. Littré, I, 325a: "nobility" (the Latin word *generositas*) here signifies courage, as is clear from the following page, where he notes that "its nobility can be seen particularly when it is facing danger," ibid., VII, 19, trans. Littré, I, 326b). And Oviedo: "The crowned lion is not just any lion, but a lion that has reached adulthood and is bolder than others" (*Qu.*, p. 253). A lion without a mane was *bound* to be a cowardly lion.
264. *Hist.*, XXIX, 10: PT, III, 242a.
265. "An animal of tremendous speed," Pliny says in fact (*Natural History*, VIII, 25, trans. Littré, I, 329a); but "it seems doubtful that Pliny was familiar with the tiger, and Bontius [the author of the *Historia Naturalis Indiae Orientalis*] accuses him of being manifestly mistaken when he states that this animal is fleet of foot: the real tiger does not run fast" (de Pauw, *Défense*, p. 92n).
266. *Sum.*, XI, 487, p. 144.

one can almost see him, his head swimming with learned evidence, his gaze trained on the torpid creature, stroking his beard and weighing the pros and cons. Rarely had scientific reasoning expressed itself so nakedly, with such auto-biographical sincerity. "I would not hold them to be tigers," the *History* finally says, and yet, and yet . . . , on the other hand, why should there not be slow tigers, just as there are fast tigers? Nature is varied, plants that are beneficial in one region are lethal in another, birds that are delicacies in one place are considered not worth tasting elsewhere, "men are black in one place and as white as snow in other provinces, and both lots are men."[267] "Indeed it could be that tigers likewise were agile in one area, as has been written, while in Your Majesty's Indies [*sic* in the *Summary:* "on the mainland," the *History* says, more prosaically and more accurately] . . . they are clumsy and heavy." In conclusion, therefore, "this animal could be a tiger."

But the researcher's conclusions are never final; and Oviedo resumes his reasonings and cogitations and reconcludes that he must leave the question open: "As for my opinion, I cannot give any definite verdict as to whether these creatures are tigers or not, or panthers or some other animal that is described as having a spotted skin or perchance some new animal that likewise has a spotted skin and has not yet been described; because many of the animals of these parts . . . were completely unknown to the writers of ancient times."[268] Such careful scientific scrupulousness, such common sense and discretion would not be found again, after Oviedo, until Buffon; and in the eighteenth-century naturalist it was to be tainted by qualitative considerations and systematic concern unknown—fortunately—to Oviedo. What Oviedo knows for sure is that this "tiger" is a dangerous beast. "These animals are not suited to being among people,"[269] and when attempts were made to tame one in Spain it had eventually to be "helped to die";[270] and another that was caught in a trap died solely from loss of blood from an earlier wound, because subsequently attempts to dispatch it with crossbow bolts and arrows left its skin completely ungrazed.[271]

---

267. Ibid. In the *Historia,* with typical stylistic attenuation, he says "white" rather than "as white as snow" (XII, 10: I, 402a). Possibly in the *Sumario* Oviedo still had in mind not so much the swarthy Spaniards as the "white as snow" Northern Europeans, the Flemish and Germans. These were always Oviedo's models of pallidness of skin: he tells us that some Indians taken to Spain by Cortés were "paler than Germans" (XXXIII, 49: III, 528a). "The Germans were remarked on by the Spaniards, as being 'white' or 'blond'" (A. Morel-Fatio, "Les Allemands en Espagne du XVème au XVIIIème siécle," *Revista de Filología Española,* 9 [1922], 284, with a number of quotes).

268. *Sum.,* chap. 11, p. 146. The corresponding passage in the *Historia* is more longwinded and less effective, but substantially the same. Oviedo refers to other tigers in *Hist.,* XXIX, 10: III, 44b, "although I do not assert that they are so, because they do not have the swiftness ascribed to the tiger."

269. *Sum.,* chap. 11, p. 148.

270. For further details on this animal, the Lombard liontamer's tiger, see below, chap. XXI, sec. 14.

271. Oviedo hesitates as to whether the "lizards of the River Plate," that move their upper jaws like the crocodiles described by Isidore but do not have the saffron color of crocodiles and are smaller, are true crocodiles, but he concludes that they are, since compared with an anatomical characteristic as important as a mobile upper jaw, color and size cease to be significant features (*Hist.,* XXIII, 5: II, 177–78; cf. XXIV, 3: II, 218a, 221a): a singular classificatory insight that reminds us of his preoccupation over the iguana, on which see Appendix D, below.

30. ZOOLOGICAL ATOMISM

The limitations of this approach are a lack of coordination or a zoological atomism. Every animal is considered in and for itself, as an absolute type. The discussion on the nature of the iguana is really an exception. The sole point of reference is usually geographical, either to underline in what way the animal of the Indies is like or unlike its European counterpart, or to assign to each zone and region of the Indies its own fauna (and flora).[272] Oviedo insists, moreover, on his objectivity as narrator, making no attempt to astound the reader, quite unworried if the reader remains unmoved, refusing to lose himself in philosophical conjecturings on hidden causes, unconcerned with constructing systems. At the beginning of the book in which he deals with the insects Oviedo, with unusual solemnity, makes this programmatic announcement: "I state that my intention is to say what I know and not to cease saying what is true so that some distant listener or reader of my lines may marvel or cease to marvel; nor do I wish to conjecture about the source of the novelties that I recount—because I am neither enough of a philosopher to understand them, nor do I wish to waste my time in arguments—but rather in accordance with what I have seen, I shall say what I have been able to comprehend or have heard in these matters."[273]

The tone is still a little ingenuous and somewhat overemphatic, but there is an overtone of sincerity that cuts through the decades and the centuries, resurfacing with the irrepressible force of truth in Galileo's dialogues, in Francesco Redi's experiments and observations and, in other fields, in Spinoza's methodical impassivity and Isaac Newton's peremptory "I form no hypotheses."[274]

272. The *Sumario* and Part One of the *Historia* contain descriptions of the fauna of the Tierra Firme (Panama) and the various West Indian islands. For the fauna of the River Plate, see *Hist.*, XXIII, 5: II, 178, 183, 192–93; of Venezuela, XXV, 22: II, 330–31; of Santa Marta XXVI, 10: II, 354–55; of Bogotá, XXVI, 23: II, 389; XXVI, 31: II, 412; of Honduras, XXXI, 11: III, 220; of Mexico, XXXIII, passim: PT, IV, 7–266; of Gualdape, XXXVII, 3: III, 630; of Nicaragua, XLII, 12: IV, 104b; of Quimbaya and Poço, XLV, 3: IV, 143; of Peru, XLVI, 17: IV, 218, 224, 233, etc.; of Quito, XLIX, 3: IV, 388b, etc. Oviedo even tells us something of the fauna of the seven mythical cities of Cibola, XL, 1: IV, 19a. The passages dealing with the local flora are generally not far from those on the fauna. There is also one curious passage in which Oviedo, after describing the flora of the Tierra Firme, refers to the earlier books on Hispaniola and the other islands for the fauna: XXIX, 29: III, 143–44.

273. *Hist.*, XV, 1: I, 451a.

274. "But I have not yet been able to deduce the reason of these properties of gravity from the phenomena, and I form no hypotheses (*Philosophiae Naturalis Principia Mathematica* [Amsterdam, 1723], p. 484). Even closer to Oviedo's words is the critical maxim adopted by the Benedictines of Saint Maur, who, applying the new scientific spirit to philology, proclaimed (1686): "We determined that this should be our inviolable law, that we would never admit any conjecture into the text" (preface to the Benedictine ed. of St. Ambrose, Paris, 1686, cited by C. Dejob, *De l'influence du Concile de Trente sur la littérature et les beaux-arts chez les peuples catholiques* [Paris, 1884], p. 89n).

❧ XIX ❧

Relics of Medievalism and Dawn of a New Society

1. LINGERING MEDIEVALISM AND ITS POSITIVE ASPECT

THE above claims, however, are not intended to present Oviedo as being more "modern" than he really is. Oviedo is a typical Renaissance Spaniard, and the Spanish Renaissance is notorious for the way certain medieval elements stubbornly survived alongside the innovatory and progressive tendencies.[1] This association of long outdated cultural forms with the fruitful seeds of the new era tends at first sight to be rather disconcerting and sometimes, on closer examination, proves to have that alluring and ambiguous fascination that all hybrids have. Sixteenth-century Spanish literature, art, and political institutions are often found to contain features and elements which elsewhere had already dissolved in a higher synthesis, while there they persist alongside one another, mutually unaware of their reciprocal incompatibility, spanning distances of centuries with their jarring anachronism and thus furnishing the clear if crude documentary proof of a slow, complex, and labored process of historical formation.

From the *romance* to the *encomienda,* from the imperial dream of Charles V to the philosophy of Suárez, the most typical creations of the Middle Ages—feudalism, chivalry, the universal monarchy, scholasticism—come to life and bloom again in sixteenth-century Spain. Their exotic appearance—a chronological exoticism or, to put it more bluntly, outdatedness—in some miraculous way manages to merge with the new national forms of political life, with the startling offerings from the new lands across the sea, and with the first sporadic or

---

1. Lozoya, for example, remarks on the fact that in the Spanish Renaissance "medieval culture continues to develop unhindered, while in other areas its development was interrupted" (op. cit., p. 184), and Menéndez Pidal allegorizes the Spanish Renaissance as "that great tree with its roots sunk deep in the medieval earth, already sterile throughout Europe" (*La idea imperial,* p. 31). In point of fact the tree bore late fruits of somewhat antiquated flavor: books of chivalry at a time when they were already forgotten or—worse still—being lampooned in the rest of Europe, works of mysticism and theology when the science of nature and the philosophy of immanence were already advancing triumphant. Oviedo, studying the flora and fauna of America, was really considerably more "modern" than his lord, Charles V, the obsessed heir of the Holy Roman Empire. For all his lofty professions of faith, Oviedo's point of reference is rational, not providential.

embryonic manifestations of the modern spirit of observation and criticism. From this angle too Columbus turns out to be a symbolic figure, his mind still crammed with medieval science and superstition, and yet serving as Spain's and Europe's pilot marking out the route toward the New World and the new times.

This lingering medievalism is evident in Oviedo. We have already mentioned the absence of humanist principles and the lack of any sign of influence of the new classicism in the literary form of his major work. As for the content, there are three clearly discernible categories of medieval relic: the first consists of relics that are quite obvious but not vital, like the suggestiveness of certain numbers, the insistence on certain edifying formulas and superstitious prejudices—relics so innocent that they would perhaps be better described as intrusions, and which we mention mainly as picturesque curiosities.

The second category comprises certain attitudes that are still typical of a medievalistic mentality, but by now drained of their traditional content and corrupted in form: typical are the lip service paid to the sacred texts, the reverence for the authority of the ancients, the idolizing of Pliny the Elder—traits that are certainly far from modern, but in reality external and not restrictive of Oviedo's scientific horizon, indeed utilized by him to support some of his boldest theories—and when they prove unusable even for this purpose, simply discarded. We mention them only lest it be thought that our claims for Oviedo's humanism are based on his much flaunted and no less questionable familiarity with the Greek and Latin authors.

The third category comprises the typically medieval feelings and reactions, in other words those that are in obvious conflict with the spirit of the new times. Oviedo, we need hardly repeat, is a firm Catholic believer, a *hidalgo* and a Spaniard with all the haughtiness and arrogance of his nation and his rank, an official whose loyalty to the emperor still has much of the personal devotion of the vassal to his lord. This combination, as consistent as it is outdated—the *History* is contemporaneous with Gargantua and Pantagruel, Guicciardini and La Boétie—has a rigidifying and distorting effect on certain aspects of Oviedo's approach to history, but is particularly interesting in the way it begins to come apart the moment it collides with the social and political realities of America.

Oviedo's reaction to Indians and Spaniards, soldiers and captains, clerics and notaries, treasures and massacres, betrays a troubling of the conscience that never becomes a real spiritual crisis, indeed that often remains hidden behind a facile moralism, but is nonetheless a first clear sign of the disintegration of his mental and ethical system, no longer able to cope with the new and formidable problems of conquest and colonization, relations with the natives, and the conflicting claims of political power, apostolic mission, and economic interest.

When he is describing how the first political communities in the Indies were organized or recounting the problems arising in the relations between the aborigines and the Europeans and the deep-rooted conflicts between the various "waves" of the Europeans themselves, Oviedo is revealed to us as the first "sociologist" of America. He was already predisposed toward this scientific mission by his mental interests and the naturalist's instincts that predominated in his character. His "social types"—the adventurer, the cacique, the priest, the captain, and so on—are forcefully delineated, almost as if they were so many zoological species. There is certainly no lack of narration—or rather chronicling—of individual deeds and misdeeds. But these episodes obviously function as examples, illustrations, and Oviedo is clearly concerned mainly with outlining the "forces" at play, telling us how they should be regulated and manipulated, how the militia should be recruited, how immigration should be controlled, how to treat the Indians, or how to curb the greed of the clergy. Here too a practical concern prevails over the purely cognitive aim. The pure historian narrates impassively. The sociologist is irreparably drawn into playing the reformer.

Between the opposing dogmatisms of a Las Casas and a Sepúlveda (with regard to the Indians), Oviedo's empiricism may look like plain common sense, the golden mean; and in fact the alcaide was repeatedly attacked and slandered by the bishop, just as he has conversely been accused by more recent advocates of Spain's innocence of yielding to "Lascasian statistics" of slaughters. In reality, his attitude derives from ethical premises. Its basic inspiration is a consistent (if shallow) and quite usual (if purely verbal) "moralism," whereby he is moved to sadness at the facts, filled with pity at the sufferings, looks longingly to a divine justice to set things to rights, and remains as skeptical about the present reality as he is confident of the existence of means to correct and improve it.

Time and again Oviedo deplores the captains' savage acts of cruelty, especially if the captain in question is someone like Pedrarias Dávila, Hernando de Soto, or Francisco Pizarro. But when he is relating how Cortés's thirteen brigantines were greased and caulked "with the fat of the enemy Indians that the Christians killed, which was a great quantity," he permits himself to defend the gruesome expedient almost jokingly: if "it was commonplace for the Indians to dine off each other," why not use their fat for such a necessary tarring operation. And anyway, Christians had been known to use human fat for medicinal purposes, and surely victory over the enemy was more important than the curing of an illness?[2]

2. NUMERICAL QUIRKS: THE NUMBER FIVE

The black humor of this therapeutic-military cynicism takes us back to the vestiges of medievalism in Oviedo.[3] As we said, the most obvious features are

---

2. *Hist.*, XXXIII, 30: III, 423–24.

3. From a more general viewpoint parallels can be found for the Spaniards' action and Oviedo's comment in much earlier times than the Middle Ages, and in very modern times too, come to that. From the cannibal devoutly devouring his slaughtered enemy as a religious rite (the *fat* of his slaughtered enemy, presumably) in order to absorb his victim's strength and thus win further victories, to the accusation leveled against the Germans in the First World War that they

also the most innocuous. There is more literary whimsicality than cabalistic musing in his fantasy on the *five*[4] most famous ships in the world, a strange fleet—consisting of Noah's Ark, Jason's bark, a Pharaoh's bucentaur, Columbus's caravel,[5] and Magellan's ship—that calls to mind those colored plates on the progress of navigation found in popular encyclopedias.[6] The same is true of the story of Licentiate Zuazo's adventures on the island of the Alacranes, where *five* Negro slaves were sent off on an unsuccessful expedition to seek provisions from a nearby island: *five* great birds of prey alighted peacefully on the island to preen themselves, spread their wings, and serve as a good omen to Zuazo and his companions; and a later expedition returned with *five* turtles for the team that would set out on the rescue mission and *five* turtles to sustain those that would be left behind. But the really crucial quintet had been the *five* enormous turtles that had been caught in the nick of time ("when those people were so afflicted, weak, and harassed with raging hunger and thirst . . . not having drunk anything for *five* days") and which were offered by Zuazo to the *five* wounds of Jesus Christ: "I offer them to the *five* wounds of our Redeemer, whence came our redemption and true salvation and full satisfaction." And it was in fact from the wounds made in one of the giant turtles turned upside down on his shell that there issued forth the salvation of the shipwrecked sailors, in the form of a jet of blood.[7]

Licentiate Zuazo, who knew his Pliny by heart and was familiar with the singular healthiness and antitoxic virtues of turtles' blood,[8] to the horror and terror of his companions "drank a great draught of that blood before anyone

---

used the bodies of the fallen to make good the shortage of glycerine for explosives, our most noble human race has never ceased to seek new ways of exploiting the lipids of the slaughtered dead to help it wage war. Need one mention the methodical exploitation of the corpses in the Nazi concentration camps?

4. On the persistence, even in late Renaissance times, of the mystique of numbers, and particularly the number five, as a symbol of the universe (the four cardinal points, plus the center), see E. Cassirer, *Philosophie der symbolischen Formen* (Berlin, 1925), II, 178–82, and, for ensuing generations, B. Croce, "Libri sui misteri dei numeri," in *Nuovi saggi sulla letteratura italiana del Seicento* (Bari, 1931), pp. 115–23. The mystics fixed their gaze on the five wounds of Christ. Ben Jonson extols the number five, "for five the special number is Whence hallow'd union claims her bliss," being the sum of two and three, "which male and female numbers we do style" (*The Masque of Hymen,* quoted in Tillyard, op. cit., p. 78).

5. Which Oviedo ("wrongly" according to Humboldt, *Examen critique,* III, 159) calls the *Gallega* and not, in keeping with the current tradition, *Santa Maria*. But the *Gallega* was the ship provided by Juan de la Cosa, "that was later known as the *Santa Maria,*" as is explained by Reyes, *Ultima Tule,* p. 73. He too calls the other two ships the *Niña* and the *Pinta* (*Hist.,* II, 5: I, 25). On the names of the caravels, see Molinari, op. cit., p. 30.

6. *Hist.,* VI, 40: I, 230–31; XX, 5: II, 34–35. On Jason and Magellan, see above, chap. XVIII, sec. 10.

7. *Hist.,* L, 10, pars. 17–19: IV, 498–500. The birds were frigate birds, on which see XIV, 1: I, 440–41.

8. "Their [the tortoises'] blood gives clarity of sight and takes away suffusions of the eyes. And it helps against the poison of all snakes and spiders and suchlike. . . ." It also cures baldness, dandruff, and "all ulcers of the head." It is good for earache, helps asthmatics, and cures epileptics, administered either orally or by clyster. But what is even more extraordinary, and truly worthy of some of the publicity claims for today's toothpastes, is the statement that "if the teeth are rinsed three times a year in tortoise blood, they become immune from pain" (*Natural History,* XXXII, 14, trans. Littré, II, 376–77).

The blood of another species of turtle "instilled onto the brain [i.e., poured onto the head, drop by drop, as in the famous Chinese water torture] calms headaches, and the same goes for scrofula." But perhaps Zuazo remembered in particular the last detail given: that for their blood to be really health-giving the turtles must be flipped over on their backs and decapitated with a copper knife.

else," after which everyone "flung themselves one after another on the same turtle, as if a tavern of fine wine had suddenly appeared before them or those wholesome banks of the River Tagus, which is one of the best waters of Spain."

The gentle irony throws the gory scene into stark relief, as Oviedo goes on to describe it with quite unusual forcefulness. In a fervor of devotion mingled with innocent blasphemy, the thirst-crazed Spaniards celebrate this wild eucharist. Each of them, as he gets up after sucking at the stomach of the reptile, his face still smeared with blood and fat, "before he cleaned himself, raised his hands and his eyes to Heaven to give thanks to God for his help and mercy, that he had shown to all of them in providing them with blood to drink in memory of his most sacred passion, to whose wounds the *licenciado* had offered these turtles."[9]

The sanguinary episode was exactly repeated only a few years ago (1972). Fourteen days after being wrecked off the Galapagos, the six exhausted survivors of the *Lucette* caught a turtle and greedily gulped down the blood that came bubbling out of it, before it could coagulate. "The sight of me, my moustache dripping blood, was quite revolting."[10] The "orgy" (p. 98) was repeated several times and the "vampires" (p. 116) drank their fill of the life-giving vital liquid.

3. NUMERICAL QUIRKS: THE NUMBERS SEVEN AND TWELVE

For Oviedo the number seven is not as suggestive as the number five. A brief digression on the *seven* wonders of the ancient world,[11] the *seven* peculiarities "found in the yucca,"[12] the list, taken from Pedro Mejía, of the seven great one-eyed captains (Hannibal, Philip, Antigonus, Sertorius, Viriathus, Federigo d'Urbino, plus Lycurgus), to which Oviedo would like to add as "seventh," but really eighth, Diego de Almagro, greater and braver than all those ancients,[13] and the list of the *seven* most signal services rendered to the crown of Spain (three by discoverers, Columbus, Balboa, and Magellan, three by conquistadores, Cortés, Pizarro with Almagro, and Quesada; and one by the pacifier of Peru, Pedro de la Gasca)[14] prove nothing—even if one takes the trouble to note that this second passage concludes the forty-ninth and last book of the

---

9. *Hist.*, L, 10, par. 6: IV, 487–88. On the turtles of Hispaniola, see XIII, 8: I, 432–33.

10. D. Robertson, op. cit., p. 89, who among "prior instances of castaways drinking turtle blood," recalls the entry in Captain Cook's journal (1777) describing how one of his sailors killed a turtle and drank its blood, "which gave him great reliefe."

11. *Hist.*, XXXII, 4: III, 237–38.

12. Ibid., VII, 2: I, 272b.

13. Ibid., VI, 44: PT, I, 204. Oviedo could have updated his catalogue today by adding the names of Nelson, Moshe Dayan, and maybe even the "One-eyed Seer," as D'Annunzio was apt to call himself after losing an eye in the war.

14. *Hist.*, XLIX, 16: IV, 459–61.

History.[15] Oviedo himself, however, is at pains to tell us elsewhere that if Pliny, for his own reasons, chose the land animals as subject for his eighth book, he, Oviedo, attaches no importance to the number: "To my mind there is no particular importance to be attached to the number eight or nine or any other figure in the book, for the historical purpose and intention that I am pursuing."[16] And he boldly announces that he will describe the land animals in book XII.

This particular type of numbers game, however, proves to be catching, and after half-jokingly contrasting the eight principal winds of the globe—a possible justification for Pliny—with the eight passengers on the Ark (Noah, his wife, and their three sons with their wives), Oviedo forgets he has only just got through saying that numbers are not important for the purposes of historical discussion and launches into a litany or apologia of the number *twelve,* a number which can be considered excellent, "beautiful and holy and deserving to be remembered by any Catholic, and fitting for the book of animals."[17] And why on earth? Because of the twelve apostles, the twelve articles of faith, the twelve signs of the zodiac, the twelve months, the twelve patriarchs, the twelve tribes, and innumerable other round dozens and twelvesomes drawn from the Holy Scriptures and the history of Octavian Augustus.[18]

It is likewise unnecessary to detain ourselves with Oviedo's stubborn belief in antiquated biological theories such as the notion—destined to survive long after him—of animals being born spontaneously from the rain-soaked earth or sodden timbers,[19] or the idea of trees whose shade, if it did not actually blind or kill people sleeping below, at the very least gave them a splitting headache.[20] We need not really linger over the edifying anecdotes of blasphemers punished with thunderbolts and miraculously saved,[21] nor over the trees with leaves in the

15. $49 = 7 \times 7$. And book L is almost an appendix, given over entirely to accidents and shipwrecks (cf. above, chap. XVII, sec. 20). The number fifty, however, seems to possess a sort of organizational suggestiveness for Oviedo. The books of the *Historia* number fifty, and the sections within the elastic book VI, the "depository" book (VI, 50: I, 254a), were also to have totaled fifty; and the works of his old age are arranged in *Quinquagenas,* with and without *Batallas.*

16. *Hist.,* XII, Proh.: I, 386a.

17. Ibid., p. 388a.

18. Ibid., pp. 387–88. Cf. the astrological qualities of the twelve constellations, pp. 405–06. And see Salas, op. cit., pp. 115–16.

19. *Hist.,* XV, 4: I, 457a. On the turtles' eggs, that ripen "to putrefaction, and are turned into so many more turtles," see XIII, 8: I, 432a. Father Cobo refers to mice born "from the putrefaction of the earth," from the moisture from the rain and the heat of the sun (Cardoso, op. cit., X, 402–03). Cf. Gerbi, *Dispute,* pp. 8–10.

20. *Sum.,* chap. 75, p. 218; *Hist.,* VII, 2: PT, I, 250. Cf. Enciso, above, chap. IX, sec. 7, and C. H. Millevoye, "Le Poète mourant," in *Oeuvres* (Paris, 1880), I, 78.

21. Three times Oviedo tells the story of Captain Andrés de Garabito, who dressed up as a Moor for a fête, "spurred his horse toward where some Spanish ladies were watching the festivities, and when he got near to them, shouted out, 'Become Moors, ladies,' and other idiocies. And praising the sect of Mahomet, he dropped dead, without speaking another word" (*Hist.,* XXIX, 12: III, 61b; XXIX, 33, par. 12: III, 163b; XLII, 3: IV, 59b). He also tells the story of a pious lady, in her fifties, Cataline Sánchez, who was on board a ship that caught fire and was miraculously saved and offered hospitality in Oviedo's house when the ship docked at Santo Domingo; Oviedo stubbornly insists that he is convinced that in the midst of this fearful calamity there appeared to Catalina Our Lady of Guadalupe,

mystical shape of the cross,[22] nor the associated belief in the devil's active participation in human affairs and his probable accessibility through the craters of volcanoes.

4. SCARCITY OF PRODIGIES

If anything, it is worth making the point here once and for all that just as in questions of natural history Oviedo differs from his contemporaries mainly in what he does *not* say, in the paucity of his stories of animal prodigies or miracle-working plants, in fact in his healthy scientific diffidence, in the same way as regards mystico-religious topics Oviedo is set apart by a reserve that verges on incredulity. There are certain hot springs, he says, on which it is possible to cook meat or fish, "and they take no longer to cook than it takes to say the Creed twice; and eggs are done before you can get half way through the Ave Maria," using the expressions undoubtedly in a proverbial rather than any pious sense.[23] And when he visits the volcano of Masaya in Nicaragua he gives a picturesque description of the crater in eruption and adds that there will certainly not be a single Christian "who, recalling the existence of Hell, does not see this and become afraid and repent of his sins. . . ." But as for Oviedo, who never misses a chance of reminding the reader that he is a good Christian, he busies himself making a

---

although the pious lady denies it, "saying that she was not worthy of such a great blessing as to see the Mother of God" (L, 7: IV, 478b).

Miracles of the Holy Virgin and St. James the Apostle are reported in XXXII, 7: III, 250, and in XXXIII, 47: III, 510–11, where Oviedo replies to the skeptics that although he has not himself seen such miracles, he considers them quite believable, "since the Gentiles and heathen and idolaters write that there were great mysteries and miracles in their times, and those we know to have been caused and brought about by the Devil." So why should the Immaculate Virgin or the glorious apostle St. James have had any problem whatsoever? Particularly when the beneficiaries of the miracles were Spaniards and Christians, and at least some of them devout, and one was even a Knight of the Order of the Sword of that same apostle St James? For numerous other "acts of grace" and prodigies on behalf of the believer, see L, Proh.: IV, 464a; L, 1: IV, 466b, etc. Oviedo, in the Catholic tradition, avails himself of the ancient miracles to demonstrate the possibility of Christian miracles, just as, extending that particular demonstrative technique to another field, he avails himself of the authority of the ancient writers to make the marvels of the Indies more credible ("for this purpose I sometimes seek witnesses in the ancient authors, so that I may be believed as a modern author, speaking as an eye-witness"—XIII, 8: I, 432b; cf. above, chap. VIII, sec. 10, and chap. XVIII, sec. 7).

The validity of the argument is shown by the fact that when belief in (modern) miracles came under attack, the critics' chosen methodology was to begin by subjecting the ancient miracles to a rigorous skepsis. Fontenelle, when he wanted to demolish belief in the Christian prodigies, began (1687, *Histoire des Oracles*) by attempting to destroy the notion that the ancient oracles and miracles were the work of the devil.

22. *Hist.*, VIII, 4: I, 296b.

23. He admits, for example, the existence of mermaids and mermen, because Pliny and Eusebio Avilano (el Tostado) say they exist, and because they were described to him by "two trustworthy men," whose names and details he gives, in Panama in 1527 and Nicaragua in 1529; and also by a "man of honor" like Alonso de Santa Cruz and other veterans of Cabot's expedition to the River Plate (1526), who were questioned separately and whose testimony was in full agreement. After this whole rigorous procedure, however, his conclusion turns out to be somewhat reserved: "And given everything that has been said on this matter, it seems to be true that they exist" (*Hist.*, XXIII, 5: II, 179–80).

In point of fact the belief in male and female sirens lasted well into the eighteenth century, even among scientists (see examples in Lovejoy, op. cit., pp. 271–72, 368n57a; but of the examples given there the reference to the *Délices de la Hollande* should be deleted, both because it refers to the year 1430 and because the anonymous author recounts the event with obvious skepticism—see *Les Délices de la Hollande* [Amsterdam, 1685], pp. 197–98). Oviedo, like everyone else, accepts the Patagonian giants (e.g., XX, 6–8: II, 39–45), always "as witnessed by" the cleric Juan Aréizaga.

detailed sketch of "the shape of this mountain on paper," and jestingly identifies the devil in the old witch who—so a cacique reports—used to come up out of the "well" of the volcano to counsel the Indians, "a very old woman, naked . . . very old and wrinkled, and her teats hung down to her navel, and her hair was thin and standing up, and her teeth long and sharp, like a dog's, and her color darker and blacker than the Indians' and her eyes sunken and fiery; and in short he depicted her in his words just as the Devil must be. And she must have been the Devil in person, and if he was telling the truth one cannot deny that the Indians communicate with the Devil. . . ."[24]

Later on, repeating Alonso de Montemayor's stories of miraculous apparitions among the clouds in the sky over Quito after a sudden eclipse of the sun at midday, of armies in battle and lions devouring one another and mysterious cries of "long live the king" and drops of blood raining down on the earth and people dying of fright in the city, he coldly and rationally observes that vain and empty-headed people can easily find themselves seeing such shadowy and evanescent shapes in the clouds "if they fail to realize that they are the natural effect of the wind, and with it, they soon pass," but—he adds, with incongruous, recurrent, and vindictive moralism—the odious crimes of Gonzalo Pizarro may well have provoked "human and divine justice" into giving such signs of horror and warning.[25]

5. The military commanders and their inevitable fate

As regards, finally, his superstitious conviction that all *adelantados* come to a sticky end, this fits in with the general pattern of his historical pessimism and carries on a tradition well established in popular literature,[26] though it cannot be denied that within that pattern it introduces a note of fatalism, with the suggestion of a "jinx" on the name itself. "In truth, in the Indies this honor and title is a bad omen," begins Oviedo (who was never an *adelantado* and perhaps would have been inclined to run that risk); and he goes on to recount the stories of some twenty of them, assassinated, drowned, or ruined, before he finally comes across one, Alonso Luis de Lugo, who returned to Spain laden down with gold and emeralds; he did of course leave behind him in the Indies a reputation for

24. *Hist.*, XLII, 5: IV, 74–75. Anyone doubting that these last words are spoken ironically has only to read what follows: "The Indians are endlessly talking of these and other foolishnesses . . . ." (ibid.). Of the age-old belief, lasting well into the eighteenth century, that volcanoes were "mouths of hell," see León Pinelo, *El Paraíso*, I, 328, 348. Elsewhere Oviedo writes somewhat curiously on the subject of hell: "However, although Pliny denies or doubts hell, we Catholics in fact know and believe that it exists" (XLVII, 5: IV, 274a). In the course of one of his most eloquent tirades on the fatal greed for riches, Pliny wrote: "If there were any underworld, truly the burrowers of avarice and wantonness would already have dug it up" (*Natural History*, II, 63, trans. Littré, I, 129b). It is a passage that Oviedo must have wholeheartedly endorsed every time he read it. On other prodigies of the devil, see *Hist.*, VI, 50: PT, I, 220.

25. *Hist.*, XLIX, 10: PT, V, 283–84.

26. See Croce, "Poemetto," where these generalized laments are linked on the one hand with the various manifestations of the "dance of Death" and on the other with the frequently treated theme of reversals of Fortune (see above, chap. XV, sec. 12).

tyranny: "Nevertheless, he is successful; how will he end up? The Lord only knows. . . ."

He adds one more name to the sad procession, and then concludes that he has said enough "for any man of understanding not to seek such a title in these parts."[27]

But the title of governor is no better (Oviedo was "governor elect" of Cartagena but never took up the office): "most of the governors of the Indies met . . . such bad ends"[28] that "their stories seem veritable tragedies."[29] Nor is the rank of the "individual and subordinate captains" any more desirable: "How few are those that did not die a bad death"![30] Of the fifteen hundred Spaniards of all ranks that set out on Columbus's second expedition "very few are now left."[31] Of the two thousand five hundred in the Indies in 1513, barely forty were still alive in 1535.[32]

Only in the preface to book XXXVI, recalling the misfortunes of so many captains, does Oviedo console himself with the pious hope "that God will not have permitted their labors to have been in vain," as they fought for the propagation of the true faith. It is also possible that they sought the riches that led to their ruin for praiseworthy and even holy ends, "for charity" or "to visit the holy house of Jerusalem and other catholic and holy places of pilgrimage. And thus with diverse and good intentions they may well have ended well in God's eyes, although to men it seems otherwise."[33] Oviedo ironically makes a token bow to orthodoxy, but he cannot resist letting us know what his real views are. Elsewhere, in similar vein, he says that they would be worthy of the title of "martyrs" *if* they bore their sufferings without complaint, and *if* God accepted them in expiation of their sins![34]

---

27. *Hist.*, XXIII, 11: II, 189–90. "This title is . . . ill-fated" (XLI, 3: IV, 25b); it would be better for them "to call themselves *rezagados*" (stragglers) (XLI, 3: IV, 32b); see also, incidentally, XXIX, 9: III, 43a, and XLVIII, Proh.: IV, 355a.

Peter Martyr had already—to show how lucky Cortés was—noted "that many conquistadors came to a sticky end" (Iglesia, *Cronistas e historiadores*, p. 74). Mier (*Historia*, II, 769n) recalls that "Casas produced a book to prove that all the discoverers met an unhappy end: Remesal has kept us an analysis of it in his *History of Chiapa*, book 4 chapter 21"; and Porras, to underline how fortunate an exception Pizarro was, notes that "almost all the conquistadors were dispossessed by the crown of the fruits of their conquest, and sooner or later their authority slipped from their fingers (R. Porras Barrenechea, "Francisco Pizarro," *RI*, 3, no. 7 [1942], 33). C. H. Haring, in *The Spanish Empire in America* (New York, 1947), p. 25, confirms Oviedo's judgment: "Most of them survived but a few years, and their career was often a short and violent one." Cf. also R. R. Hill, "The Office of *Adelantado*," *Political Science Quarterly*, 28 (1913), 654–55. Morison too notes that they usually came to a miserable or tragic end (*Southern Voyages*, p. 184). On the institution of *adelantado*, which was already on the decline in Spain when it was transferred to the Indies and took on a new lease of life, see C. F. Barraza, "La institución de los adelantados in América: Aportación al estudio de las magistraduras indianas," in *Humanidades*, 28 (1940), 519–45, with bibliography and quotations from Oviedo, pp. 538–40.

28. *Hist.*, XLVIII, Proh.: IV, 353a.

29. Ibid., XXVIII, 4: II, 478a.

30. Ibid., XXIX, 32: III, 161b.

31. Ibid., II, 8: PT, I, 34a. And indeed those that had returned, rather than being "satisfied and well provided for," showed signs of the sufferings they had undergone and seemed "reduced to indigence" (Almagià, op. cit., p. 155).

32. *Hist.*, I: PT, I, 10a.

33. Ibid., XXXVI, Proh.: III, 619–21.

34. Ibid., XXI, 1: II, 156b.

6. THE GREAT CORTÉS

Oviedo's notorious antipathy for Francisco Pizarro, that has brought him into disfavor with Peruvian nationalists, is only partially offset by his admiration for the noble Almagro. Among other things, Oviedo is scandalized at the way the Pizarros cheated the emperor of his rightful share of the ransom collected for Atahualpa,[35] who was then treacherously murdered anyway, after atrocious tortures, because Pizarro "felt like it" and because of the cowardice and vengeful ingratitude of his acolytes.[36] But he displays an equally obvious antipathy for the great Cortés, the luckiest of the conquistadors. It is no surprise that Las Casas treats Cortés as a thief, a liar, and a usurper, "ending up as the marqués del Valle."[37] But Oviedo? Likewise. In the *Summary* Cortés is already mentioned somewhat peevishly and disdainfully as only the *third* Spaniard, not the first, dear me no, to enter New Spain. The first was Francisco Hernández de Córdoba, the second Juan de Grijalva, while "the said captain Hernando Cortés" was only the third—and even then he was acting on the orders of Diego Velázquez. This same Cortés described Mexico "as it appeared to him" in his *Cartas*. But he, Oviedo, will speak of it on the evidence of innumerable witnesses, "as a man who wanted to enquire and know the truth."[38]

Of Cortés, in fact, he cannot say what he says a hundred times for Peter Martyr and so many others—that he never saw what he described. He saw it and indeed *did* it. But Oviedo still tries to undermine his credibility. When Cortés tells how he was attacked by one hundred and forty thousand of the enemy, "that covered the ground as far as the eye could see," Oviedo notes ironically and skeptically: "I say there were exactly one hundred and forty thousand of them because this is what Hernando Cortés wrote to His Majesty."[39]

As for the actual enterprise of the conquest of Mexico, Cortés did not really play such a great part; he merely "took steps to come to an arrangement, without Diego de Velázquez, with His Imperial Majesty," in other words went over the head of his immediate superior and then maneuvered so cunningly and cleverly that he succeeded in getting himself appointed "governor and captain-general" of those lands, and later marqués del Valle, "and ended up a great lord," the disappointed and envious Oviedo concludes spitefully.[40] Poor old Diego Velázquez, on the other hand, "wasted his time and lost the property he had gained, all just to bring riches and good fortune to the marqués del Valle, Don Hernando Cortés."[41] And can we not catch a hint of mockery also in the oft-repeated

35. Ibid., XLVI, 18: PT, V, 109–10.
36. Ibid., XLVI, 22: PT, V, 121–22.
37. Salas, op. cit., p. 276.
38. *Sum.*, chap. 9, p. 109; *Hist.*, XXXIII, 54: PT, IV, 261a.
39. *Hist.*, XXXIII, 3: PT, IV, 17a.
40. Ibid., XVII, 19: PT, II, 147–52; XVIII, 1: PT, II, 185b; XXI, 8: PT, II, 329; XXXIII, 1: PT, IV, 9a.
41. Ibid., XVII, 3: PT, II, 115a; cf. also XXIX, 21, par. 8: PT, III, 301–02. Oviedo was in 1523 the "much fêted" guest of Velázquez, whose side he always takes (Pérez de Tudela, "Vida," pp. lxxi*n213*, xcii).

assertion that Cortés's followers are deservedly known by the noble and honorable epithet *cortesanos?*[42]

There is another point too. Oviedo, on the basis of the royal warrants that authorized him to ask governors and conquistadors for detailed reports, also addressed his request to Cortés: "I wrote and notified Don Hernando Cortés, marqués del Valle, that he should send me his"; but Cortés, obviously irritated at the request, merely sent back his *Cartas,* in fact "some missives that he had written to His Majesty . . . and bothered himself no further"![43]

It is therefore only natural that whenever Oviedo finds contradictions or ambiguities in these "missives" he jumps on them: Pánfilo de Narváez was sent by Diego de Velázquez to revoke Cortés's powers, but Cortés, after a scuffle in which Narváez lost an eye and was almost burned alive, promptly had him arrested and then deported. Oviedo says with transparent hypocrisy that he would not want to say which of the two was in the right, "so as not to be unfair to either side," but he tells how in Toledo, in 1525, he saw Narváez, "and he was saying openly that Cortés was a traitor . . . and a liar, and many other ugly words, calling him treacherous and tyrannical," ungrateful and disloyal toward Diego Velázquez, "and many other things that made a very bad impression."[44] Oviedo obviously listened to these slanders with slyly attentive delight—just as there is no mistaking his pointed indifference when he comes to describing Cortés's passionate outbursts against Velázquez as "more a matter for the court cases and petitions in which they got involved . . . than for our history."[45] Cortés must also have got carried away with the same sort of outburst when he said that all the colonists of Santo Domingo could not have raised a thousand pesos among them; "nor do I know what he could have been thinking of when he said that."[46] His final judgment, grudgingly delivered, is that Cortés was a lot better condottiere than historian or geographer or, as one said then, "cosmographer," expert in lands and straits.[47]

---

42. *Hist.,* XXXIII, 20: PT, IV, 98a; XXXIII, 21: PT, IV, 107b, 108b, etc.

43. Ibid., XXXIII, Proh.: PT, IV, 8b. In the same way he wrote to Pizarro, urging him to come to a peaceful agreement with Almagro, on the strength of his having known both of them when "very poor" and having seen them later "much exalted in titles and lordship and great riches," but Marquis Don Francisco Pizarro did not even deign to acknowledge receipt of Oviedo's letter: "If he ever received my letters he certainly never replied" (*Hist.,* XLVIII, 6: PT, V, 229b; XLIX, 1: PT, V, 235a); cf. the letter to the sovereigns dated 9 December 1537, in *CDII,* I, 529–42, and III, 70–82.

44. *Hist.,* XXXIII, 12: PT, IV, 58a. A young follower of Pánfilo de Narváez, Juan Cano, was to make the same and even more serious accusations against Cortés (ibid., XXXIII, 54: PT, IV, 259–61). In defence of Cortés, of course, and against Pánfilo and his public accusations, voiced with his normal pomposity and bombast, but occasioning the emperor's amusement, see Bernal Díaz del Castillo, op. cit., pp. 416–22, 540–41. See also F. Goodwyn, "Pánfilo de Narváez: A Character Study of the First Spanish Leader to Land an Expedition to Texas," *HAHR,* 29, no. 1 (1949), pp. 150–56.

45. *Hist.,* XXXIII, 33: PT, IV, 162a. See XXXIII, 41: PT, IV, 194, for further sarcasm: "Hernando Cortés was so mistaken in this case . . . and had his eyes so blindfolded."

46. *Hist.,* XXXIII, 41: PT, IV. 194b.

47. Ibid., p. 189. A more explicit eulogy occurs in XXXIII, 21: PT, IV, 108b.

7. THE WOES OF THE LESSER OFFICIALS

The sufferings of lesser officials and simple soldiers are also the object of Oviedo's concern and compassion, but they do not prompt him to the same sort of cataclysmic generalizations as the stories of the mighty fallen, evoking moralistic images of Capitol and Tarpeian Rock, blows of fortune reversing mens' destinies, and Providence working the ruin of those who would set themselves up on high. The *Schadenfreude* evident in his portrayal of the final undoing of the world's great leaders is not however solely the bitter residue of his own thwarted ambitions. It also marks a first step toward that shift in the object of history from ruler to populace, from general to humble foot soldier, from sovereign to subject, that was to be taken up in metaphysical vein by Giordano Bruno and that would lead, with slow and labored steps, to the recognition—a good two centuries after Machiavelli's *Prince*—of Vico's "nations."

Not of course that Oviedo in any way idealizes the "proletariat" of the expeditions. Only when the victim is a *hidalgo* does one detect a note of special sympathy. Oviedo, who filled the *Quinquagenas* with heraldic and genealogical disquisitions, and has no objection to "men of good breeding who were not brought up behind the plough"[48] seeking their fortunes in the Indies, laughs bitterly at the misfortunes that overtook one of them, "a gentleman called Don Antonio Osorio, brother of the lord marquis of Astorga," of whom he paints a portrait that calls to mind simultaneously the famished nobles of the *Lazarillo* and Don Quixote after one of his unlucky adventures. The illustrious Don Antonio, who followed Soto into Florida, was seen (in 1540) by eye-witnesses "with a garment of coarse cloth of that land, torn at the sides, bare flesh showing, bareheaded, bald patch revealed, legs bare of either socks or shoes, a buckler on his back, a sword with no scabbard, amidst the tremendous frost and cold; and

---

48. Ibid., XXIV, 4: II, 228a. The phrase does not imply contempt for agricultural labor, but merely reflects its standing. A man like Oviedo, so interested in nature and especially in plants, would certainly not be one to disparage rustic pursuits. One has only to note how he praises the successful Genoese farmers (above, chap. XV, n. 337), how he inveighs against the greedy colonists who neglect agriculture (above, chap. XVII, n. 206), how, foreshadowing Mussolini's "grain battles," he suggested a sizeable reward for the first person to harvest a hundred *fanegas* (about 160 bushels) of wheat (letter from Juan Ramos, 31 May 1537, cited by Amador de los Ríos, "Vida," p. lxivn3), how he writes that the "blame" for the lack of vineyards in Santo Domingo "lies not with the plant, nor with any defect of the soil, but with human industry, and the weakness of men" (VIII, 24: I, 310a), and how he longs for the tranquillity of the hard life in the fields: "Oh disasters and dangers of this human existence. . . . How much safer it is to toil with the hoe!" (L, 29: IV, 587b).

In 1533, in the early days of its government, the crown had shipped sixty farmers and their families out to Santo Domingo, and in these years the agricultural colonization of the West Indies received constant official encouragement (Zavala, *New Viewpoints*, p. 110). Toward the end of his life, in the *Quinquagenas,* Oviedo still refers on a number of occasions in sympathetic if fairly conventional terms to the workers in the field, chiding them with pennypinching moralism for their frivolous hairstyles: "In the days when the rustics had neither the knowledge nor the desire to comb their hair, agriculture and work in the field went better, and bread cost less" (*Qu.*, p. 425). Notice however that the sentiment expressed is still one of sympathy for work in the fields, rather than any attachment to the earth as a source of riches. Oviedo, like his contemporaries, prefers riches in the form of metals, and gems to real estate. And when he refers to his "property" he is normally talking about his monetary, liquid patrimony. (This thesis is developed by P. Corominas, as regards post-Cid Spain, in his *El sentimiento de la riqueza en Castilla* [Madrid, 1917]).

being of such illustrious blood made him bear his work and not complain, like many others, although there was no one to help him, being who he was and having held in Spain two thousand ducats of income from the church. And on the particular day that this gentleman saw him like that, he believed that he had not swallowed a mouthful, and he had to scratch for food with his fingernails, if he wanted to sup."[49]

This passage, like so many others, has an admonitory intent: to discourage the ingenuous and the greedy from deserting Spain or the older overseas colonies, like Santo Domingo, in vain pursuit of fabulous riches or what they imagine to be easy plunder. Thus if it is not actually exaggerated it is doubtless somewhat "touched up," with a view to frightening the reader into thinking matters over. But the portrait painted is so strikingly realistic that it acts as an extremely salutary and opportune corrective to certain impressions of easy conquest that were by then widespread in Spain and Europe and were reflected—to give just one splendid example—in Ariosto's ringing lines (1532), where Andronica celebrates the expeditions and the wars as a phantasmagoria of scenic dances and inevitable victories: "I see the Holy Cross and I see the imperial insignia set up on the green shore; I see some guarding the storm-tossed boats, others chosen to win the country; I see a thousand chased away by ten, and the kingdoms beyond India under Aragon's subjection; and I see the captains of Charles V, wherever they go, carrying all before them."[50]

The picture of these "captains of Charles V" painted by the emperor's official historian could hardly be more different. Oviedo sees them as possessed by some heroic folly, a frenzy compared with which the paladin Roland's madness is no more than a lover's whim. "I am often amazed at the recklessness or stubbornness or pertinacity or constant belief that the future held something better for these scoffed-at conquistadors, from one labor to the next, and from the next to another even greater, and from one danger to others and others, losing one companion here and three there, and there again more and from bad to worse, without learning their lesson."[51]

There are those who have boldly usurped the name of captain, without ever having seen a battle by land or sea; and because of their ignorance of the art of

49. *Hist.*, XVII, 27: I, 570–71. Oviedo also recalls his opposition to Las Casas, when the latter wanted to make knights with Calatrava-type crosses out of people with no nobility of blood, "being ploughmen and of other mixtures and kinds of lowborn people" (XXXIII, 54: III, 552b). On this incident, see Amador de Los Ríos, "Vida," pp. xxix–xxx, who also gives Las Casas's version, namely that he wanted to have "new people and different people from the past" to pacify and protect the Indians.

50. *Orlando Furioso*, XV, 23. A little further on Andronica refers to "Ernando Cortese," who "brought new cities under Caesar's rule, and kingdoms so remote in the East that to us, in India, they are unknown" (XV, 27). Note the gentle irony—typical of Ariosto—in the last line; and also how, in a spherical geography of the world, the Far East and the Far West coincide. It should not be forgotten that Ariosto offered his poem, in its definitive form, to none other than Charles V, in Mantua (1532), and that it was acutally in that year that "this addition appears to have been written" (comment by L. Caretti [Milan and Naples, 1954], II, 935).

51. *Hist.*, XVII, 25: I, 558a.

war, through being accustomed to a safe and easy life, "in winter gathered round the brazier and all tucked up, and in summer covered with taffetas and drinking cool drinks," they lead themselves and their followers to certain ruin. Tropical undergrowth and jungle, "dense woodland, thickets, thorns, plants, and grasses," where one needs a sword to cut a path and anyone who grows weary and falls behind "is never seen again," hunger, frost, burning heat, suffocating thirst, "all these and whatever else befalls them, these poor soldiers have to bear." They have been told that they would return to Spain loaded down with "oro y plata," gold and silver, but before they can lay their hands on it they are burdened down "de lloro e de planto," with weeping and wailing.

For every one that goes home rich, a hundred leave their bones to rot there: unburied, in the ocean depths or in fishes' bellies, or on sandy deserts or a prey to crows, wild animals, cannibals, snakes, or crocodiles. A soldier should take more vows than the three taken by friars—poverty, chastity, and obedience—and he would not have to put himself out to keep them, because he will have no choice but to observe them, save that of chastity (Oviedo cannot resist tempering his gloomy description with a passing jest) because "in many areas the women are in the habit of going around naked, and even if they go about dressed, they never let their admirers down. . . ."[52]

8. ORGANIZATION OF THE EXPEDITIONS

How are they organized, these expeditions destined to inevitable failure? Oviedo gives us a vivid picture of the first steps taken by one captain, who has not received a single *maravedí* from the sovereigns, just a signature, and the "title of *adelantado* or governor" with a license and powers to sign people on. These easy and seemingly lucrative concessions are ruinous for the king, for the Spaniards enlisted, and for the natives.[53]

The royal official paints a savage portrait of the adventurer, clutching his papers, marching out of the court and off to Seville,[54] with only a few pennies to

---

52. Ibid., XXIII, 3: II, 174–75. On the soldier's life, considerably harder than the Carthusians' and other friars' mode of existence, see XLIV, Proh.: IV, 125a. The vision of unburied bodies is possibly to some extent an echo of Pliny: "Although we sprinkle the earth with our blood, and cover the ground with our unburied bones" (*Natural History*, II, 63, trans. Littré, I, 129b); but in another way it seems to anticipate those Leopardian dead, "down in the depths of the sea, under the snow or the sand, or under the open sky," etc. (*Dialogo di F. Ruysch e delle sue mummie,* in *Opere* [Milan, 1935], p. 216).

53. *Hist.,* XLVII, 1: PT, V, 129–30. On this point cf. Salas, op. cit., pp. 130–32.

54. The cathedral in Seville was the place where contracts of all sorts were entered into, including those for taking on men for overseas expeditions (see note in Amador de los Ríos's edition of the *Historia,* II, 225*nl,* and Bataillon, *Etudes sur Las Casas,* p. 143). The soldiers waited outside, on the steps of the church, still today thronged with eager shoeshine men. Fernández de Lugo, one of the conquerors of the Canaries, is said by an early chronicler to have gone to the steps of the cathedral when he lacked funds for the expedition and to have been greeted by a shower of gold rained down on him by an angel, enough to satisfy all his needs. But J. D. Wölfel, in his article "Alonso de Lugo y Compañía," *Investigación y Progreso,* 8, nos 7–8 (July–August 1934), claims that the angel was a group of merchants with whom Lugo drew up a company contract (Zavala, *New Viewpoints,* p. 69). The legend shows the mutual contagion of sacred and profane elements, of religious and commercial interests, typical of a deal struck at the threshold of a temple.

his name; "and while over here a drum beats and over there a couple of friars and some clerics come rushing up on the pretext of converting the Indians, turning people's heads and promising the riches of those [the Indians?] that know nothing, the captain devotes himself to taking bills of exchange and buying weary old ships, that only reach here by the mercy of God and the power of doubled bilge-pumps, or are such that they are incapable of returning or taking back to Castile any news or account of the cargo they brought."

As "secretary" they sign up some boy "who never knew the meaning of the word 'secret,'" try to borrow money from the companions they have taken on and to get people to sign joint obligations with them;[55] and thus, with a bit of illusion and a lot of deceit, with a gambler's sleight of hand and a master usurer's cunning, they weigh anchor for the Indies. They set sail without any precise idea in mind, without a goal: "These captains have no idea where they are going."[56] "Oh captains," Oviedo berates them, "you go about preaching of the lands you are going to populate or assault and destroy, proclaiming conversion and baptism, but in reality bringing destruction to both the country and its natives, killing the Christians that have followed you, bewitched and bewildered by your promises . . . , sad unlucky wretches that hear you and believe you, without knowing where you are going."[57] This dismal procession of ignoramuses and dupes, all heading for certain ruin, almost seems to anticipate the Parable of the Blind that Peter Breughel was to paint a few years later (1568), with such crude bitterness and aching sorrow. For that matter it was already over a century since Gómez Manrique had issued his prophetically accurate warning: "When the blind lead, woe to those who follow!"[58]

9. DISSUASION OF WOULD-BE RECRUITS

But Oviedo refuses to give in. Oviedo is determined to open the eyes of the blind and the dazzled. Oviedo deliberately forgets the words of adulation and complacent optimism he had used in dedicating (30 September 1535) the first edition of the *History* to Cardinal García de Loaysa, president of the Council of the Indies, words that must have sounded almost ridiculous, or worse still, ironic, when their author reread them.[59] By now Oviedo considered it part of his historian's duty to prevent other simpletons being taken in. He provides a foretaste of the "dissuasions" addressed to the deluded and tempted immigrants that were to be so common from the middle of the eighteenth century through to the

---

55. *Hist.*, XXXV, 4: III, 597–98.
56. Ibid., XXXVII, 3: III, 632.
57. Ibid.
58. Cited by Menéndez Pidal, *Los españoles en la historia*, p. 51.
59. "The service of God flourishes in the Indies: the republics of Christians that exist there are growing more noble; the kingdoms of Spain are growing richer, and everything is getting better and better; and it is bound to be so and that every day so many benefits are multiplied, since Your Lordship governs these parts" . . . (*Hist.*, Dedicatory Letter, I, cxi).

early 1800s. The imaginary speech that he addresses to the soldier about to sign on for the Indies is, right from its first captivating words, "compañero amigo" (my good comrade friend), one long invitation to distrust and almost to insubordination. The arguments and oratory of the alcaide of Santo Domingo are worthy of a pacifist or a "subversive" agitator. Remember, "compañero amigo," that "many of these captains promise what they do not have, nor know nor understand, and in payment for your person they buy you with words that are less than feathers." Remember, "amigo compañero," not to believe "what is said by a captain coming to the Indies to discover what he never saw, as ignorant of its very existence as a new-born babe." Remember (a potent insinuation) that even if everything goes well for him, "he will not recognize or reward you, nor if you fall ill will he care for you, and even if you die he will not bury you"; and if things turn out badly for him, it will be you that gets the blame. . . . The rewards are aleatory. The riches, precursors of ruin. In short, "amigo compañero"—the orator concludes, with a gesture of grand eloquence—"if you have understood me I tell you that you should not take one step to follow the captain whose experience is still unproved and who is devoted to pomp and these vain undertakings."[60]

Oviedo perceives that the real cause of the failure of so many expeditions is not the curse attaching to the title of *adelantado* or governor, nor some hypothetically mighty power of nature and the natives (both of which, on countless other occasions, had been overcome by the valor of the Spaniards and European technology), nor an insufficiency of means, nor the essential injustice of the "aggression." All these factors, eloquently illustrated by historians old and new, and in passing by Oviedo himself, fade into the background and beyond when compared with the bad organization of the expeditions, bad organization due to the marriage of convenience between the fraudulent cunning of the leaders and the gilded illusions of the followers. Anyone seeking quick booty and treasure is himself an easy prey for anyone who—just to have one more sword to fight for him—is prepared to promise the applicant he will have them without running any risk. And the leader in turn, completing a vicious circle that will eventually be the ruin of them all when they reach the Indies, is none too scrupulous or shrewd in his choice of soldiers just as long as he can find someone to lead into conquest.

10. Qualities needed in the recruits

The expedition is doomed before it sets out. Oviedo, in fact, while advising the soldier to pick his captain carefully, is equally emphatic in his warnings to the

---

60. *Hist.*, XXIV, 4: II, 227–28. Much less realistic, even if partly complementing and correcting Oviedo's account, is G. Arciniegas's convenient and optimistic thesis on the "anonymity" of the conquest: "From these human dregs that filled the minor offices in the expeditions there arose the great men of the conquest. No Cortés, no Pizarro ever set forth from Cadiz as leader of anything. . . . the conquistadors emerged from the ranks of the common soldiers," etc. ("América, obra del Pueblo," *CA*, 22, no. 4 (July–August 1945), p. 115).

captains about the soldiers they are enrolling. "Hearken to me, my lord captain, and take heed for yourself": pay no heed to whether the recruit has a fine feather in his hat, if he has a clean arquebus or perforated hose and "taffeta frills and silk linings and brocade cloth";[61] do not believe him when he says what country he is from because lots of them, just to get permission to come to the Indies, even lie about their names, heedless of the holy place in which they perjure themselves; do not let yourself be attracted by tall stature or a well-combed beard; do not even consider anyone under twenty-five or over fifty.

The vital qualities are not physical but moral. "You must enquire secretly into their skills, and how they live, and what they can do." A soldier must above all be "virtuous and of good family," simple and not presumptuous. Charlatans and braggarts abound, one saying "that he was at the battle of Ravenna, another at the battle of Pavia or the sack of Genoa or Rome."

Such boasting was commonplace; suspicion of these glorious warriors of the Italian campaigns had reached the point where it was proverbial in the Indies to say, "Get away with your twenty years in Italy."[62] But Oviedo waxes even more ironic, gleefully ridiculing these supposed veterans of the Italian wars: "If he tells you that he was at the battle of Ravenna, pay no attention, if he is Spanish, since he came out of it alive and was not taken prisoner; and if he was at the battle of Pavia, likewise; or at the sack of Genoa or Rome, even less, since he did not get rich; and if he was he gambled it away, so do not trust him."[63] And if he really did fight in Italy, he will still find quite different travails and perils awaiting him in the Indies: "The soldier in Italy does not have to fight every day, but only a minority of the time; and besides earning his pay and other adventures with which they pass their time and make up for the travails of war . . . they eat as much as they like."[64] What counts, in any case, is not the courage in battle of either the captains (to whom the passage refers) or the soldiers (to whom it can equally well apply): "Fighting is the least part, because it is very rare to find a

---

61. "These slashed hose and shoes are useless for lands so overgrown and thick with trees and thorns as these Indies, and where so many rivers must be swum and so many swamps and marshes crossed" (*Hist.*, XXIV, 4: II, 226a). For further criticism of "these heavily slashed doublets and hose and soldierly puffs . . . these silk and crimson shoes, that I see on the feet of men who have nothing to eat," and which are ridiculously unsuitable in a land that is all woods and mountains and watercourses, all thorny jungles and sodden swamps, see XXVIII, 6: II, 493a. This must surely be one of the very first references to the need for special uniforms for colonial troops. The belligerents in World War II still made lots of mistakes of the sort for which Oviedo chides the captains of his day.

62. Pereyra, *Los conquistadores*, p. 111, with unidentified quote. Alonso del Valle is described as "a soldier of Italy" (*Hits.*, XLVII, 16: PT, V, 189a). Bernal Díaz del Castillo refers to a certain De Barrios, who was looked on as a brave soldier, and who had fought in Italy (op. cit., p. 495). Picatoste (op. cit.) recalls that if you said someone "had been in Italy," that meant he was a learned man, just as "he was in America" meant he was an adventurer (quoted by Giannini, op. cit., p. 64, who explains with the help of other quotations how Italy was coveted by soldiers mainly for its hostelries and the good life). Against "bragging" soldiers, see also p. 13. On boasting in general, see *Qu.*, p. 25, and more especially on the swaggering boastfulness of "big-mouthed" soldiers, *Qu.*, pp. 188, 347–48, 457. Against the soldiers who boasted of having been at the rout of "los Gerbes" (i.e., Los Gelves, or Djerba, 1510) or the battle of Ravenna, *Qu.*, p. 246. Against sailors' lies and boasting, *Qu.*, p. 317.

63. *Hist.*, XXIV, 4: II, 226a.

64. Ibid., XXXII, 2: II, 224b.

man of dignity who will not fight, when his honor is at stake."[65] What really makes a good soldier is loyalty and faithfulness to his captain; if these are lacking, my lord captain, you know what is in store for you: "As long as there is gold, or if they suspect that they will get it through your hand, you will be served by them very diligently; take care, however, because as soon as things do not turn out the way they want, you will either be killed or sold by them, or abandoned."

But when you do find a loyal soldier, do not drive him to crime or mutiny with your extortions. And if you want to keep your self-respect, the basis for the respect of others, examine yourself carefully, and treat the Indians as men, without reducing them to slavery "for no good reason," without massacring them, robbing them, or driving them out "from the place where they were created by God, who did not give them life or human existence to carry out your evil intention and will, but so that they should be saved."

Carried away by his own eloquence, the official historian points an accusing finger at those captains to whom he had originally been giving sound and practical advice for the selection of recruits; and after warning them against the deceitfulness of the soldiers he closes with a resounding condemnation of their own hypocrisy. "Do not say that you came to the Indies to serve the king and to make good use of your person and your time, as a valorous person and hidalgo, since you know that the opposite is true: that you did not come for any other reason than your desire to have more property than your father or your neighbors."[66]

11. CATASTROPHIC RESULTS

When these ambitious and inexpert captains and these soldiers dazzled with false promises arrive in the Indies, one can easily imagine what happens: they very soon come to grief, often taking whole sections of the native population with them. The Spaniards suffer, not infrequently with admirable fortitude, and the unhappy inhabitants of the country suffer too, to the point of destruction. The organic weakness of the expeditions, and not the individual wickedness of the conquistador (with a few signal and grim exceptions: Pedrarias Davila, Hernando de Soto, Carvajal, the Pizarros), is held responsible for the slaughters and catastrophes. With a true historian's eye Oviedo goes beyond the accidental qualities

---

65. Ibid., XXXV, 1: III, 586b.

66. Ibid., XXIV, 4: II, 226. The simple words "property," "father," and "neighbor" have a much more effective oratorical effect than the numerous tirades on man's "infernal greed" and his lust for "accursed riches." Oviedo's taunts are far more successful than his righteous indignation. It will also be remembered that he frequently complains about having lost "most of my property" in the service of the state (XXIX, 14: III, 68a) and having paid for certain peacekeeping operations out of his own pocket ("for some of them I had to contribute more than just words," XXIX, 15: III, 72a) without a word of thanks from anyone. Equally frequent is his bitter realization that riches do not come to those who most deserve them (e.g., XXIV, 4: II, 227b; XXXIII, 14: III, 328b), in line with his general view that things in this world are not what they ought to be.

of the individuals and reveals the radical flaw in the system. His portraits therefore have little depth, taken one by one, and an aura of moral disapproval spreads
like an artist's glaze over the savage features of the warriors that were in fact so
very different. But his overall judgment is firm and uncompromising, cutting to
the point of sarcasm: "Most of those that come here do so because at home they
do not have what they would need in such abundance as to satisfy their nice
desires and the merits of their persons."[67]

Greed and inexperience are what caused so many deaths, among both Indians
and Christians. The emperor-king is too far removed from these insatiable and
presumptuous captains.[68] Not even prudence, loyalty, and valor, however, provide a sufficient guarantee against ruin and death: only God can protect man,
Oviedo concludes, with his customary resigned pessimism.[69]

The courage and tenacity of many of the Spaniards are beyond question. Many
times Oviedo pays homage to the "boldness and spirit"[70] of the Castilians, and
not only in warlike enterprises,[71] but also in deeds of exploration, such as the
descent into the volcano of Masaya. Their capacity to confront and put up with
murderous sufferings is admired time and again and in many cases held up, in
truly Christian fashion, as initial expiation on earth for their greed and violence.[72] But their warlike temperament is not admired for itself, is indeed
mocked: "Our Spaniards . . . are such friends of war, that the first people they
wage it against is their reckless selves."[73] And, most notably of all, his sympathy never takes the form of indulgence. Oviedo condemns the crimes and savage
cruelty without mincing words, without any lawyers' quibbles, without pleading
"extenuating circumstances" in the difficulty of the situation or seeking acquittal

67. Ibid., XXX, Proh.: III, 177a. And elsewhere: "Most of the men that come to the Indies are motivated by their
own greed, and not, as those in holy orders would have us believe, by their professed zeal to serve God, and others to
serve the king. . . . both the former and the latter, with all the other people, of whatever quality they be, sail over here
for their own profit" (XXXII, 2: III, 223a).
68. Ibid., XXVIII, 4: II, 478–79; XXV, 1: III, 586 and passim. In 1543 Oviedo actually landed up in prison as a
result of his outspoken criticism of the way the Santo Domingo armadas were organized (Otte, "Aspiraciones y
actividades," pp. 47–48; Pérez de Tudela, "Vida," p. cxxxiii).
69. Hist., XX, 35: II, 109.
70. E.g., ibid., XLII, 11: IV, 100b.
71. Ibid., XLII, 10: IV, 87b.
72. A few examples: the sufferings in the Indies are worse and more varied and manifold than anywhere else
(Hist., XXVI, 18: II, 381a); the Indies' misfortune in being discovered by the grasping hordes that are punished there
(XXVIII, 6: II, 492–93); the fearful lack of food, clothing, and medicines and anything else useful—"a sheet of paper
cost one gold castellano, and a needle the same; without doctor or surgeon or medicaments, but not without many
illnesses" (XXXI, 6: III, 213b); the soaring death rate among the Spaniards in the Indies (XXXII, 2: III, 223–24); the
Spaniard's life in the Indies is worse than a laborer's or shepherd's in Spain, or a soldier's life anywhere at all (XXXII,
2: III, 224–25); and the "poor gentleman or needy nobleman," the dissatisfied craftsman, or peasant behind his
plough would have done better to stay where they were, rather than come to the Indies (XXXV, 3: III, 596a); what a
wretched and accursed life it is, this life of the "poor soldier" (XLIV, Proh.: IV, 124–25!). Similar lamentations in
XLVII, 6: IV, 280 and passim.
73. Ibid., XXVIII, 4: II, 484a, accompanied by criticisms of the emperor for failing to support his vassals, who
cannot therefore be blamed for being no more realistic than the king and thinking only about their own gain.

by shifting the blame onto "accomplices" in the form of foreigners who have wormed their way into the Indies, or criminals deported to the New World.

12. THE DOGS OF WAR

The *monteria*, the practice of hunting down the Indians with savage dogs, so much beloved of Hernando de Soto (the same Hernando de Soto that Garcilaso was to idealize in his *Florida del Inca*),[74] comes in for an unforgettable tongue-lashing from Oviedo. But de Soto was not the only one "much given to this custom of hunting down and killing Indians. . . . The reader must understand [Oviedo explains, with philological urbanity] that the term *aperrear*, 'setting the dogs on them,' means that dogs ate them or killed them, tearing the Indians to pieces, because [the "definition" is followed by the "historical example"] the conquistadors in the Indies have always had the habit, in war, of bringing greyhounds and fierce and fearless dogs with them; and thus [Oviedo concludes, as if he had not already made his point with abundant clarity] we used the phrase 'hunting down the Indians' above."[75] Nor, as conscientious chronicler, does he fail to give us gory details on the sadistic refinements adopted by Pedrarias Dávila when he had some Indian malefactors executed by his killer dogs ("trained greyhounds and wolfhounds")[76]—"they skinned them and disemboweled them and ate what they wanted";[77] nor on that vicious and "diabolical" greyhound—implacable defender of the catholic faith and of sexual morality—that had torn to pieces more than two hundred Indians "for being idolaters and sodomites and for other abominable crimes," and that had thus become particularly partial to human flesh.[78] The first example of dogs being used in war, with its implication that the Indians were animals to be *hunted* rather than to be *fought*, can be traced back to Columbus's companions on the second voyage.[79]

---

74. De Soto is also fiercely criticized in *Hist.*, XVII, 26: I, 567, and XVII, 27: I, 570–71.

75. Ibid., XVII, 23: I, 547b. Columbus himself, and indeed even before him the conquerors of the Canaries, knew that when fighting savages, one dog was worth ten men. And Balboa had forty members of the cacique Quaraquá's male harem torn to pieces by his dogs, although this was an official execution rather than an act of war (Morison, *Southern Voyages*, pp. 126, 203).

76. *Hist.*, XLII, 11: PT, IV, 419b.

77. Cf. ibid., XLIV, 3: PT, V, 22b.

78. Ibid., L, 10, par. 31: PT, V, 349–50. Other champions included Becerillo and his offspring Leoncico, whose amply detailed biographies in the chroniclers and historians (Herrera, Charlevoix) prompted Humboldt to complain that more was known about the life of the bold Becerillo than about Christopher Columbus's (*Examen critique*, III, 373–74, 399n). On Becerillo and Leoncico, see *Hist.*, XVI, 11: I, 483–85; on Leoncico, XXIX, 3: III, 9–10. On Becerillo again, J. J. Arrom, "'Becerrillo': Comentarios a un pasaje narrativo del Padre Las Casas" in *Libro de Homenaje a L. A. Sánchez* (Lima, 1967), pp. 41–44.

On other dogs (Bruto, Capitán, Amadís, Calisto, Amigo) used by the conquistadors, see Peter Martyr ("in the wars against . . . the naked inhabitants large numbers of dogs were used," *Dec.*, II, 10, p. 203; and, more fully, III, 1, pp. 208–09; III, 2, pp. 223–24); Las Casas, *Historia de las Indias*, bk. II, chap. 55, ed. cit., II, 325; Pereyra, *Los conquistadores*, pp. 162–63.

79. See Gerbi, *Dispute*, p. 194n170; Humboldt, *Examen critique*, III, 373–74; Morison, *Admiral of the Ocean Sea*, II, 124–25; Romano, op. cit., p. 19.

And the terrifying and haunting image of Cortés's hounds as seen by the natives—enormous dogs, with ears folded back, long drooling tongues, a fiery glint in their burning yellow eyes, hollow bellies, long straight flanks, tireless, enormously powerful, panting with open jaws, snapping left and right[80]—is indelibly branded on our memories. Alas, this cruel habit, sometimes deplored and sometimes recommended, continued to be practiced for a long time; it was still current in the eighteenth century and has indeed survived right into our own times, with the worldwide use of police dogs.

Oviedo, however, cannot forgive those "impassive and ruthless" captains, who would refuse a glass of water to a man dying of thirst, and treat the sick "as if they were stones";[81] nor those conquistadors who—anticipating Persigny and his satisfied announcement that "peace reigns in Warsaw"—"pacified" the countryside, and "what they called pacifying meant laying waste and ravaging and killing and destroying the land in many ways, robbing and killing the native inhabitants";[82] nor can he forgive the soldiers who forget the sacrifice of Jesus Christ and his precious blood and spill the blood of others with no motive at all: "Because I say unto you," Oviedo solemnly declaims, "that those who . . . here spill the blood of these savage peoples, although they are our fellow-men," will be punished by God with ruin and death.[83]

And worse still are those leaders like Pizarro and Almagro who unleashed bloody civil wars, "so that lions and tigers and wild beasts seem more sociable and merciful and less cruel than the men we have seen here."[84]

13. THE NATURAL RIGHTS OF THE NATIVES AND THE RESPONSIBILITIES OF SPAIN

Oviedo—who more than once betook himself from the Indies to Spain to bring abuses and outrages to the attention of the sovereign and whose major work was, as we have seen, intended at least in part as a grandiose supreme appeal to the justice of the emperor and the verdict of history—knows that crimes are committed in America by men of all nations, but he also knows, as a public official and proud patriot, that Spain's prime responsibility, preceding even its duty as protector of the undefended, is the maintenance of law and order, and he lays squarely at Spain's door, with a sort of romantic political fanaticism, the blame and infamy for all the crimes committed in its domains.

"Let not the reader think that they are all Spaniards, those who were guilty of these disturbances and acts of villainy and ugly deeds . . . betrayals and disloyalty and fickleness; for no tongue is lacking here of all those parts of the world where there are Christians, whether Italy or Germany, Scotland or England, and

80. Sahagun, cited by Keen, op. cit., p. 52; cf. ibid., p. 187.
81. *Hist.*, XXIX, 2: III, 7a.
82. Ibid., XXIX, 15: III, 73a; cf. XXVIII, 4: II, 478–79; XXXVII, 3: III, 632a.
83. Ibid., XXX, Proh.: PT, III, 357b.
84. Ibid., XLVIII, Proh.: PT, V, 212a.

there are Frenchmen and Hungarians and Poles and Greeks and Portuguese and men of all other nations of Asia and Africa and Europe . . . and although not all the malefactors are Spaniards . . . everything that looks bad is attributed to those of our nation: and this is just, since justice and punishment are in Spain's hands."[85]

Elsewhere, Oviedo asserts that there are not only Christians of all countries in the Indies, as mentioned in the passage just transcribed, but also unbelievers, "because the call of these riches attracts African barbarians and Levantines of many races, and Italians of all parts and provinces of Italy, and Germans and Frenchmen and Englishmen and people of numerous other nations," many of whom are so good at speaking Castilian that only God can recognize them as foreigners, and who have invariably played a part in the turmoil, providing a necessary separate flavor, "like vinegar in a meat sauce"; but "the blame for the tumults and escapades and quarrels is always laid at the door of the Spaniards, as is only right, since the leaders and those that command are from Spain."[86] And in yet another place he says that although they all call themselves Spaniards, many of the conquistadors were foreigners, indeed "many of them are enemies of our nation, and all the blame on either side is attributed to the Spaniards, and it is just that this should be so, since they tolerate it and take no action to remedy matters."[87]

The originality of Oviedo's attitude in this respect can best be measured by comparison with the almost contemporary theses expounded in Sepúlveda's *Democrates Alter* (1547). The proponent of the legitimacy of waging war on the Indians was in fact familiar with Oviedo's work (even if he did not, as has been claimed, make a summary of it)[88] and utilized it in his polemics with Las Casas, provoking the Dominican's savage response (and possibly posthumous revenge and editorial censoring) in respect of himself and his source Oviedo. And the learned jurist and Aristotelian philosopher Juan Ginés de Sepúlveda denies that Spain or its government can be held responsible for the misdeeds even of its own Spanish officials in the Indies, let alone those perpetrated by foreigners! His interlocutor Leopoldo points out that the war in the Indies is conducted "with all the outrage and cruelty of barbarians and in the fashion of robbers," so that the

---

85. Ibid., XXIV, 4: II, 224–25; cf. XXIX, 34: PT, III, 355a.
86. Ibid., XLV, 2: IV, 14a. This passage, which was written in Spain, is quoted, without reference, by Pereyra (*Los conquistadores*, p. 269), who goes on to remark, in scrupulous defence of the foreigners—strange in the mouth of a Hispanophile like Pereyra—that "what Oviedo says about the foreigners is blatant exaggeration, because amongst them there were a considerable number, from all backgrounds, who distinguished themselves by their natural goodness and law-abiding behavior" (p. 270). Pereyra obviously failed to understand that Oviedo, in the passage quoted, far from accusing foreigners en masse, is in fact absolving them en masse, shifting all the blame onto the Spaniards. Equally irrelevant is Díez del Corral's conjecture (op. cit., p. 245) that Oviedo's personal experiences should have made him "more open-minded in dealing with the peoples of Europe."
87. *Hist.*, XLVII, 21: IV, 349a.
88. *De rebus Hispanorum gestis ad Novum Orbem libri septem*, which, according to Fueter, op. cit., p. 234, cover the years 1492 to 1524 (but see Appendix E, below).

Spaniards should at least give back what was unjustly taken. But the subtle Democrates retorts that the legitimacy of the sovereign rule over a people does not imply approval of all the acts of ministers and prefects; and, reciprocally, if these latter commit misdeeds, they do not invalidate the just claims of their lord (unless he is an accomplice, or negligent): "If some act is carried out avariciously, cruelly, and flagrantly, by unjust and worthless men, as I have heard many deeds to be, it does not make the cause of the prince and of good men any the worse." The crimes of the conquistadors are not coessential with the war against the Indians. If this war is just in itself, individual excesses cannot alter its essential legitimacy. And there is no obligation, absolutely not, to give back what has been wrongly taken! Even if it was seized "as booty, with wicked intent, and not fairly," what's taken is taken; and great theologians (Saint Thomas) deny that the wrong committed obliges the *miles* or the *praefectus* to give back the "booty otherwise lawfully taken from a legitimate enemy."[89]

Compared with such specious indulgence toward the government's own agents, such careful separation of political and moral responsibilities, Oviedo's readiness to pin the entire blame on Spain for every single crime committed, even by foreigners, is typical of the historian and moralist in him, an aspect of his character for which we can only be thankful and which here again forced the hand of the official and courtier.

14. THE FOREIGNERS IN THE INDIES

This judicial impassivity is that much more remarkable when we remember that Oviedo holds no brief for these foreigners. He looks on them as dangerous interlopers, and one is almost tempted to suspect that he deliberately blames the foreigners' crimes on the Spaniards as a way of persuading the Madrid government to take more vigorous action against these undesirable adventurers. He certainly deplores the increasing liberality of Spain's immigration policy, even if he never comes out with it in so many words. While the saintly Queen Isabella was still alive the only persons permitted to go to the Indies were the Castilians, "in keeping with the fact that it was they who discovered the Indies and not Aragonese, nor Catalans, nor Valencians nor vassals of the royal patrimony of the Catholic Kings." After the death of Her Most Serene and Catholic Majesty in 1504 "the Catholic King . . . gave leave to the Aragonese and all his vassals to cross to these parts with offices and however it pleased him." And Charles V,

89. *Democrates Alter* (1547), ed. cit., pp. 96–98. And, further on, regarding the vices existing in all nations, as Leopold objects in defence of the Indians: "The public cause should not be judged in individual men, but in public customs and institutions." Adulterers, murderers, and other criminals are certainly to be found in all the Christian nations, but this is no reason to draw "rash" deductions (ibid., p. 122). In the final summary, moreover, Leopold, with Democrates's approval, stresses the positive side of the argument, namely the responsibility of the rulers for the crimes of the soldiers and captains, "if they do not take all possible measures and do their utmost to ensure that such crimes are not committed by men who have no sense of justice" (ibid., p. 156). The difference is only one of emphasis, but nonetheless significant.

finally, "further extended this leave, and now they come from all his domains and from all those parts and subjects under his monarchy."[90]

This thesis of Oviedo's (the exclusion of the Aragonese in the early years) has, after prolonged uncertainty,[91] been recognized as exact by the most recent student of the problem, Ciriaco Pérez Bustamante.[92]

Oviedo also mentions the squabbles in the Indies among the Spaniards themselves, between Basques and Catalans, between Andalusians and Valencians, Perpignanese and Cordovans, "and the Aragonese with the Guipuzcoano and the Galician with the Castilian (suspecting that he is Portuguese), and the Asturian and Montañés with the Navarrese," due principally to the fact that in the beginning for every noble and well-bred person "there came ten ruffians and people of other obscure and base lineage";[93] and he also recalls that in those early times, before the Indies gained their reputation for fabulous riches, the Catholic Kings had to arrange for them to be populated with criminals, ordering all the judges of Castile to "banish to these Indies those that they intended to sentence to death, or to the loss of a hand or a foot or to some other corporal and infamous punishment."[94]

That was in 1508; but in 1548, the year in which Oviedo was writing, anyone wishing to go to the Indies had to be expressly licensed by the emperor and his council, be of sound faith, and so on.[95] There had therefore been a drastic change. It is worth noting in this connection how Oviedo repeatedly stresses the fact that the Indies do not belong to "the Caesarean Empire" but to the "crown and royal scepter of Castile." They belong to Queen Juana, Charles's mother. And Charles administers them and governs them on behalf of his mother, Juana the Mad. He signs the orders and patents for the Indies, all alone, certainly, because the queen lives in pious retreat, but he signs them "I, king of Spain" not "Carolus."[96]

Ferdinand of Aragon's subtle and possibly crafty motives for assigning the Indies to the crown of Castile are still much discussed.[97] And Porras Barre-

90. *Hist.*, III, 7: I, 74 (also quoted by Pereyra, *Los conquistadores*, p. 265); cf. *Hist.*, II, 13: PT, I, 525; XLV, 2: IV, 141b.

91. See examples in Vignaud, *Histoire critique*, II, 131–34.

92. "Las regiones españolas y la población de América (1509–1534)," *RI*, 2, no. 6 (1941), 81–120, esp. pp. 86–87. Cf. also J. Martínez Cardós, "Las Indias y las Cortes de Castilla durante los siglos XVI y XVII," *RI*, 16, no. 64 (1956), 207–65, 357–411. See also Angel de Altolaguirre's "Epílogo" to the *Gobernación espiritual y temporal de las Indias*, in *CDIU*, 2d ser., XXV, 301–03, claiming that as from 1509 emigration was restricted to Castilians, and from 1525 passage to the Indies was opened to "the subjects of his majesty and natives of the empire and Genoese just like the natives of Castile and Leon." On this whole question see the subtle and well-documented study by R. Konetzke, "La legislación sobre inmigración de extranjeros en América durante el reinado de Carlos V," in *Charles quint et son temps*, pp. 93–111.

93. *Hist.*, II, 13: I, 54b.

94. Ibid., XXVI, 2: II, 335b.

95. Ibid., p. 336b.

96. Ibid., XXXIII, 21: III, 367a; cf. III, 7: I, 74.

97. See J. Manzano y Manzano, *¿Por qué se incorporaron las Indias a la corona de Castilla?* (Madrid, 1942), reviewed in *RI*, 3, no. 9 (1942), 561–63 (and his *Incorporación de las Indias a la Corona de Castilla* [Madrid, 1948]). Cf. also F. Pérez Embid, "El problema de la incorporación de las Indias a la corona de Castilla," *RI*, 8, nos. 33–34 (1948), 795–836.

nechea calls the regency of Juana the Mad "a pretense."[98] But on the arms of Lima, the City of the Kings, the J for Juana and K for Karolus solemnly testify, still today, to the accuracy of Oviedo's constitutional thesis.

In the passages transcribed the criticism of the current practice is subdued and is in fact almost unnoticeable apart from the term "leave"; elsewhere, however, Oviedo speaks out clearly and explicitly. She was quite right, "that most Catholic and serene Queen Doña Isabel, of immortal memory," when she allowed access to the Indies solely to her Castilian vassals and even among those, only to those who "were not of suspect faith, nor sons or grandsons of people who had been convicted by the Holy Inquisition, nor foreigners." Would that the practice had continued! But "later, because of the fault of the times and negligence of he who ought to have known better, many things have been done the reverse of the way they should have been: so that now that land is incomparably worse than Noah's Ark."

There is no nation that is not represented in the Indies by believers and heathen, with pagans and criminals all speaking Castilian, often to the detriment of God, the king, and the loyal vassals of the crown of Castile. And those among them that cannot manage to speak some sort of Castilian pretend to be subjects of one of the many lands of Charles's empire, and if "they are Portuguese, they call themselves Galicians, and the French call themselves Flemings, and the Swiss Germans, while the Italians say they are Sicilians or Neapolitans." Nor is that all, "since there are innumerable Greeks and Levanters and persons of other nations."[99] Their very presence gravely endangers "the good and virtuous *hidalgos* and the proper Spaniards or people of honor that are in these parts."[100] Just as Caracalla's extension of Roman citizenship to all the inhabitants of the

---

98. *Cedulario del Perú,* I, xxi.

99. *Hist.,* XXIX, 34: III, 174. On the Greeks and Levanters, many of whom were sailors and who were numerous among the followers of Gonzalo Pizarro, but to be viewed with suspicion because of their long and unprotesting subjection to the Grand Turk, see XLIX, 15: IV, 455b, 459a. In general, on the foreigners "of different races" passing themselves off as Christians and Spaniards, see XXXV, 6: III, 613a; and on the "mixed races of Levanters and foreigners," XXIX, 25: III, 124a, and *Qu.,* p. 430. On the French corsairs, mainly Normans and Bretons, see VI, 8: I, 182a; XIX, 12: PT, II, 208a; XIX, 13: PT, II, 209a; XXXIII, 37: PT, IV, 180–81; XXXIII, 48: PT, IV, 233b. On a French missionary, XIX, 3: PT, II, 194b.

It is curious that Oviedo never refers to Jews, save an armorer and blacksmith called Guzmán, "a native of Seville and son of a Jew," in a chapter transcribed from a report by Fray Diego de Loaysa of the Order of Preachers (XXXIII, 49: III, 525b). There is only one fleeting reference to the 1492 expulsion (II, 7: I, 28–29) and repetition of Pliny's comments on the Essenes as "chaste Jews" (VI, 33: I, 223b). This is even more surprising (unless one accepts the view propounded by José de la Peña y Cámara and rejected by J. Uría Rui, op. cit., p. 23, that he himself was a *converso*) in that he mentions the pretentious Christian names that the *conversos* are given by their baptismal sponsors (XLIX, 5: PT, V, 242–43) and also passes on some echo of Spanish anti-Semitism when he reports that the Spaniards called the Nicaraguan province of Barecla "Judea, because the people there are very base, despicable, and worthless" (XLII, 12: PT, IV, 426a), and when he attributes the causes of the Reformation to the Jews (see below, chap. XX, n. 12).

The Germans are mentioned a number of times as a yardstick for tall stature (*Sum.,* chap. 10, p. 116; *Hist.,* XXI, 2: PT, II, 312b; XXI, 3: PT, II, 356b; XXII, 3: PT, II, 351a) or for whiteness of skin (XXXIII, 49: PT, IV, 242b).

100. *Hist.,* XXIX, 34: III, 174a.

empire (*Constitutio Antoniniana*, 212 A.D.) strengthened the resentment of those who had previously been privileged,[101] the broadening of the Caroline monarchy to take in remote and non-Spanish-speaking parts of Europe gave rise to abuses that provoked the ire of the Madrid-born official.

15. THE SPANISH IN AMERICA

But if the foreigners in the Indies collectively irritate Oviedo, the Spaniards in America too, class by class and profession by profession, come in for their fair share of criticism and abuse. His skepticism on the subject of medicines and the ironies directed at the doctors and surgeons who set up in public practice without any sort of qualification, or else claim that they have "forgotten" to bring their diplomas from Spain,[102] can perhaps be overlooked, as conventional and almost proverbial expressions, but Oviedo's sarcasms at the expense of scribes, judges, and notaries, priests and preachers, are like a series of sharply drawn sketches of colonial life, acutely and bitterly critical of the basic elements of the new society taking shape in the Indies.

16. THE SPANISH IN AMERICA: PENPUSHERS AND PETTIFOGGERS

In respect of the legal profession—which was just then being banned from the utopias of Thomas More and Rabelais,[103] and whose entry into Mexico was forbidden by the emperor (1522) at Cortés's prompting, "to avoid having the people torn apart with litigation"[104]—Oviedo poses as the man of action, the soldier impatient at their hair-splitting. In the Indies these "alchemists" earn more than the royal officials, more than the greediest and luckiest merchant, but these alchemists do not toil away blowing on furnaces or mixing up mysterious formulas and do not lay themselves open to the just punishment awaiting the practitioners of that reprehensible art. "The alchemy that I say is practiced here in the Indies . . . is a permitted and much practiced art, and it takes no more than paper and ink. I saw a scribe in Darien swear that with a *real*'s worth of copperas and oak gall, and a ream of paper, that together cost him half a ducat in Seville, he had earned more than two thousand gold pesos," and he was not the only one, for indeed those "ink alchemists" are particularly abundant in the Indies,

---

101. M. Rostovzeff, *The Social and Economic History of the Roman Empire* (Oxford, 1926), pp. 367–71, which makes the point (p. 370) that when everybody was a Roman citizen "this meant in plain fact that nobody was such any more." Later in the same work (p. 605n37) one is reminded of a further parallel between the Roman Empire of the third century and the Spanish Empire of Charles V, with his subjects who could not even speak Spanish (the emperor himself, of course, knew not a word of Spanish when he was eighteen, and still at the age of twenty-four mixed it up with French—R. Menéndez Pidal, "El lenguaje," p. 162), in the fact that when Severus Alexander gave permission for Roman citizens to draw up their wills in Greek "a Roman citizen was no longer supposed to know Latin."

102. *Hist.*, X, 3: PT, II, 13a. Cf. the document in the *Archivo General de Indias* (Justicia 62, new numbering) given by E. W. Palm, "Hospitales antiguos de la Española," *Multa Paucis Medica*, 3, no. 5 (September–October 1946), 63; and the "doctor who never took any examination" in Otte, "Una carta inédita," par. 34.

103. *Utopia*, 1516; *Gargantua*, 1535, chaps. 52–57.

104. Botero, *Relationi universali*, pt. I, bk. V ("Messico"), ed. cit., p. 211.

"because it is the land of least truth." [105] The self-serving lies that the butchering captains dictate for their reports to the emperor and "that you cause to be signed by some crazy scribe you are in league with" [106] do not deceive God, nor in the end do they deceive the sovereign. They may give a false and corrupt idea of the new environment of the Indies, where His Majesty's orders, although written in good Castilian, "are no more heeded than if the king had dictated them in Chaldean," and where those in power have no difficulty in twisting them to serve their own ends. But although "the court's cosmography does not yet coincide with the cosmography of these parts," when the king is properly informed justice will finally triumph. [107]

Here again Oviedo, noting the glaring discrepancy between the monarch's intentions and the reality of the Indies, tries to reconcile the deference due to the sovereign with his duty as a truthful historian, claiming that the emperor is ill-informed, that because of the distance his orders are misunderstood or unheeded, that the factions lord it over everyone and violate the law with the complicity of those who should be concerned with ensuring that the laws are obeyed and letting Madrid know how things really stand. Judges and governors were of course subject to the *residencia,* during which efforts were made to force them to produce accounts: but "it is one of the things that is very frequent amongst governors and judges in these parts, when their term of office is finishing, that

---

105. *Hist.,* XXVIII, 6: II, 493, and cf. Otte, "Una carta inédita," par. 6. Oviedo's disapproval of alchemy (on which see also *Qu.,* pp. 10–11) can be seen as a straightforward endorsement of the church's harsh condemnations, or an echo of Erasmus's sarcasms (see *In Praise of Folly,* chap. 39), but it may also reflect the jealousy felt by a senior official of the authority owning the richest gold mines in the world toward those whose aim is to manufacture the metal artificially—the same jealousy as that felt by present-day owners of raw material deposits toward the inventors, whether individuals or peoples, of substitutes or surrogates.

Thus one cannot claim that Oviedo appreciated the importance of alchemy as the precursor of the science of chemistry. But one can make the general observation that—unlike Pliny, for once—Oviedo shows no more than a meager and occasional interest in inanimate nature (gold and precious stones, volcanoes, the more "animated" aspects of inanimate nature), while exhibiting a lively and untiring interest in animals and plants; his goddess is Life rather than Nature (to which it would be legitimate to riposte that alchemy did in fact treat minerals as living things, and should therefore have exercised a certain attraction for Oviedo).

106. *Hist.,* XXVIII, 4: II, 479a.

107. Ibid., XLV, 2: IV, 139b. In a letter addressed to the king on 25 October 1537 (quoted by Molinari, op. cit., p. 97*n*), Oviedo describes the procedure followed by Licentiate Espinosa, who—acting on Pedrarias's orders—pronounced sentence on Balboa: since there were no lawyers in the Indies "he pleaded for both sides, and pronounced in favor of the side for which he had argued best in his pleading." In this passage Molinari endorses Oviedo's accusations, but shortly afterward (p. 153*n*) he seems to sympathise with the poor lawyers "against whom Oviedo was so wont to rave." There were no lawyers in the Indies because they were forbidden to go there: see for example the capitulations with Pizarro, signed in Toledo on 26 July 1529, making it clear that "in the said land there shall be none of the said lawyers or procurators" (Porras Barrenechea, *Cedularios del Perú,* p. 50).

Oviedo lays into the members of the legal profession again in the letter of 24 May 1537 (*CDII,* I, 507–08). For his views on the corrupt and greedy judges whose sole concern is to go home from the Indies to Spain as wealthy men, so as not to be ridiculed and despised, see *Qu.,* pp. 112–13; for his disapproval of those harsh judges whose looks can kill, like the basilisk's, and who take advantage of the remoteness of the Indies to reduce the rod of justice to the thickness of the quill in Oviedo's hand, making it so flexible that it is forever inclining or swinging to one side or the other, see *Qu.,* pp. 120–21, 215. Lawyers, advocates, and procurators are all cheats; conflicts could be resolved far better by arbitrators—"however bad their decisions, the litigation is ended" (*Qu.,* pp. 373–75; cf. p. 428).

they make off with the money before the accounting, or they wait for it, having hidden away the cash."[108]

As for ecclesiastics, Oviedo always sees them against the background of Pope Borgia's Rome (see above, chap. XIV, sec. 12). He had of course already treated these "doctors of the soul," to a series of savage puns in his *Reply to the Moral Epistle of the Admiral of Castile* (1525): "Their Avicenas are *aves y cenas* [birds and suppers], their Hippocrates hypocrisy, their Gallienus *gallinas* [hens]."[109] In his subsequent and ultimate attitude one can already see signs of the resentment and rivalry between civil and religious authorities that was to last throughout the centuries of the Spanish domination, in all the American viceroyalties and governerships.[110] The only "saints" that he recognizes are certain missionaries massacred by the Indians.[111]

But unless we are mistaken in our interpretation of certain undertones of irony and heavily affected tokens of respect, Oviedo was also possessed of a goodly measure of humanist—and perhaps even more than humanist, Erasmian—anticlericalism.

17. OVIEDO AND ERASMUS

Spanish Erasmianism was at its most active in the years 1520 to 1535,[112] precisely the time when Oviedo was collecting the material for his *History* and drafting the first part (Seville, 1535). Oviedo cites "that notable and famous modern doctor, Erasmus of Rotterdam, in the beneficial tract that he drew up on the Christian's provision and preparation for death, and how he should make ready,"[113] and in connection with the temple of Diana he comments, "which the very learned gentleman Erasmus mentions in that book of his on language."[114]

108. *Hist.*, XXIX, 14: III, 67a. "The further the distance, the greater the danger," he had already written in 1535, in the albeit optimistic Dedicatory Letter, which recommended that the Council of the Indies exercise particular care to choose good ecclesiastics, judges, and administrators to send to the Indies. Cortés too, for that matter, fills his letters with pleas that the churchmen sent to Mexico should be "friars of austere life and not worldly prelates" (Iglesia, *Cronistas e historiadores*, p. 59, citing *Cartas*, pp. 319–20).

109. Pérez de Tudela, "Vida," pp. xxviii, xcviii.

110. Cf. especially J. A. García, *La ciudad indiana* (Buenos Aires, 1900), pp. 38, 96, 319–20; E. de Gandía, *Francisco de Alfaro y la condición social de los Indios* (Buenos Aires, 1939), p. 165; M. André, *La fin de l'empire espagnol d'Amérique* (Paris, 1922), p. 107; J. L. Mecham, "The Church in Colonial Spanish America," in *Colonial Hispanic America* (Washington, 1936), p. 230; J. P. de Oliveira Martins, "La política económica de la metrópoli," *Revista Universitaria*, 10 (1915), 2ff.

111. *Hist.*, XIX, 3: I, 594–96, confirmed with XXIX, 34: III, 174a. On the venality of the bishops, XLVI, 20: PT, V, 206a.

112. A. Valbuena Prat, *Historia de la literatura española* (Barcelona, 1950), I, 364–67.

113. *Hist.*, XXII, 3: II, 165b, i.e., the treatise *De praeparatione ad mortem*, 1533, which ran into a number of editions in Spanish: Valencia, 1535 (*Apercibimiento de la muerte*); Burgos, 1535 (*Aparejo . . . para bien morir*); Antwerp, 1549 (*Aparejo de bien morir*); Seville, 1551 (*Preparación y aparejo para bien morir*, also called, on folio 5, *Tractado cattólico muy provechoso del apercebimiento y aparejo para la muerte*, a title that comes rather closer to that cited by Oviedo). See Bonilla y San Martín, "Erasmo," pp. 480–82, whose study renders superfluous the notes by Menéndez Pelayo, *Heterodoxos españoles*, IV, 59–60, 128–34.

114. *Hist.*, XXXII, 4: III, 237. He is alluding to the treatise *Lingua, sive de linguae usu et abusu*, 1525, of which

Thus Oviedo recalls some of the humanist's ascetic and moral writings. But he is also familiar with his famous *Colloquies,* and it is in fact this work that he mentions in connection with the corruption of the clergy: "I do not wish to either believe or disbelieve Erasmus and his colloquies; however in these Indies things have been seen amongst the licentious clergy that it is better to pass over in silence, rather than stir up the matter any more."[115] Oviedo also mentions, as "an honorable and reliable man,"[116] Lazaro Bejarano, one of the most noted Erasmians of the New World.[117]

Oviedo does not figure on the long list of Spanish Erasmians,[118] and Fuente does not feel "that he can be counted amongst the Erasmians of that time, of which there were a good number in Spain."[119] Bataillon, on the other hand, writes unhesitatingly that Oviedo "was visibly touched by Erasmianism"[120] after having been "in fairly close contact with Italian humanism" in his youth;[121] and O'Gorman actually attributes Oviedo's repudiation of the chivalric romances, after his publication of the *Claribalte,* to the influence of Erasmus.[122]

Another figure demanding at least passing mention is the valorous Diego Méndez de Segura, Columbus's companion on the fourth voyage, a protégé of the Admiral and King Ferdinand, and a person well known to Oviedo,[123] who when he made his will in Valladolid in 1536 left among his books, the sole bequest to his children, five tracts of Erasmus, "whose satirical features can hardly have pleased the clergy in the peninsula."[124] But it is not known whether these tracts ever reached the Indies.

One thing that is certain is Oviedo's lasting aversion for clerics and prelates, missionaries that skimp their work, and fat friars intent only on filling their stomachs. In conversation with Johan Cano (1544) Oviedo is less circumspect in his mockery: "As for this load of friars everywhere, it seems to me in truth that these lands gush with friars or rain friars; however, since they are all without

various Spanish editions exist: one from 1528 or 1529; Toledo, 1533; further ones in 1533 and 1535; Seville, 1544; Antwerp, 1550. See Bonilla y San Martín, "Erasmo," pp. 471–79.

115. *Hist.,* XXIV, 8: II, 238a. On the numerous Spanish editions of the *Colloquia,* see Bonilla y San Martín, "Erasmo," pp. 433–59.

116. *Hist.,* VI, 19: I, 206b.

117. On whom see Henríquez Ureña, "La cultura," pp. 66–68, 79–80, Picón Salas, op. cit., p. 58, etc.; Bataillon, *Erasmo y España,* II, 441–43.

118. In Bonilla y San Martín, "Erasmo," pp. 385–87, where it is also stated that all educated persons in Spain in the first half of the sixteenth century were more or less Erasmians.

119. *Qu.,* p. xxx.

120. *Erasmo y España,* II, 247–48; cf. p. 295.

121. On Erasmianism in the Indies, see Alfonso Reyes's study "El Erasmismo en América," *Boletín del Instituto de Cultura Latino-Americana,* 2 (1938), 63–65; and the appendix on "Erasmo y el Nuevo Mundo," in Bataillon, *Erasmo y España,* II, 435–54.

122. In the introduction to his Oviedo anthology, printed in *Cuatro historiadores,* pp. 48, 51, 60, 65.

123. *Hist.,* III, 9: PT, I, 73–74: "A gentleman, a man of honor and householder of this city, and living to this day." Cf. *Hist.,* XXVIII, 3: PT, III, 188. He had a copy of Dante in Santo Domingo.

124. Humboldt, *Examen critique,* II, 352–53; Bataillon, *Erasmo y España,* II, 436–37. On Oviedo's acquaintance with the Erasmian Vives see above, chap. XV, n. 158, and on his approval of Aretino's attacks on the Roman curia, above, chap. XV, n. 168

white hairs and under thirty years, may it please God that they all manage to serve Him. I have seen them coming into the city, two by two, up to thirty of them, each with his staff and their skirts and scapularies and sombreros and no capes, and the bishop following them. It looked like some sort of pious masquerade. . . ."[125]

18. THE GREED OF THE CLERGY

Oviedo's reproaches, however, are generally aimed not so much at the vices branded by Erasmus, at the sensuality of the younger clergy, despite that reference to the "under thirties" and elsewhere the denouncing of certain "Greek-style" public marriages (*Quinquagenas,* p. 382), nor at that sin of gluttony of which he must have known himself to be guilty, nor at the chronic and recurring monkish squabbles between Franciscans and Dominicans, of which in the last analysis the Indians were the victims;[126] Oviedo's target is none of these, but instead the eternal and universal covetousness, the unrestrained and unscrupulous greed for riches, the simoniacal cheating and straightforward theft. Oviedo himself was a victim: "I would not wish to name prelate or priest, although some have robbed me and others, lest it should seem that I have a particular prejudice in this." But just as in the case of the attempt on his life (see above, chap. XIV, sec. 8), his partiality shows through at the very moment he is doing his best to suppress it and turn it into a moral lesson, explaining that the thief robs himself more than the person robbed, "because while I might lose part of my cloak, the person who takes it from me loses his whole soul."[127]

In truth, there are very few churchmen who are not on the make. The accusation was to be repeated a little later (1619) by a blunt-speaking Dominican, Fray Antonio de Remesal, Las Casas's first biographer and hagiographer: even the *domini canes,* in the tainted atmosphere of the Indies, have became so many *perros mudos,* while the secular clergy are for the most part "poor and ignorant creatures . . . moved by their worldly interests," who, when they find themselves without their pot of gold, go straight back to Spain or sign on as chaplains in the ranks of some ragtaggle conquistador, as rough and simple soldiers.[128]

At one point Oviedo comments drily that "these fathers, under the cloak of their habit, usually manage to do very well in various other transactions."[129] At

---

125. *Hist.,* XXXIII, 54: III, 553a. Cf. Pérez de Tudela, "Vida," p. cxxxiv. On the "devotional plays and presentations" put on by the Mexican child converts, and in general on the good results achieved by the missions, both Dominican and Franciscan, in Mexico, see XXXIII, 51: III, 537–38. On the "holy and learned persons" to be found in certain monasteries in Santo Domingo, Mexico, and other parts of the Indies, see III, 11: I, 87b; XXIV, 8: II, 238b; cf. *Qu.,* pp. 49, 385.

126. See the eloquent passage in VI, 6: PT, I, 68–69.

127. Ibid., XXIX, 31: III, 159a.

128. See the passages quoted in Bataillon, *Etudes sur Las Casas,* pp. xiv, 3*n,* etc. For Las Casas himself, ibid., p. 79.

129. *Hist.,* XXIX, 11: III, 52a; cf. XXIV, 14: II, 261–62.

another point he dwells on this scurrilous topic: "Very few of these fathers have I seen without covetousness, and less inclined to gold than me or any other soldier, and with less diligence seeking it, though they are cleverer and quieter about keeping it, because they hold it as piety that everyone should give to them for love of God, under pretext of some pious works and masses that they claim to say, and that they cannot perform." They mix with the laity, poke their noses everywhere, and are at pains to find out "which lands are the richest and contain least threat to life." And mingling with them there are sometimes "foreign and French friars, or spies disguised as friars." It may well be, Oviedo concludes, that their aims are good and holy and that they plan to spend these ill-gotten gains on ransoming prisoners or in other work pleasing to God; but even if this were the case it should not be done "to the prejudice of third parties" . . . Of course, Oviedo prudently admits, it is up to their prelates to correct them, and not a layman. But—he has to have the last word—"but I would like us all to be good, and not to content ourselves with seeming so." [130]

19. Failure to convert the Indians

What is the most serious consequence of the poor quality of clergy? Oviedo puts his finger on it unhesitatingly: the failure to convert the Indians. Just as the shortcomings of the captains lead to the slaughter and physical destruction of the natives, so the wordly interests of the ecclesiastics result in the loss of millions of souls, in the complete vanity of the spiritual conquest of the Indies. Christ's apostles preached and observed contempt of riches, "nor did they carry knives, nor gunpowder, nor horses, nor those other instruments for waging war and spilling blood." Our converters and baptizers, on the other hand, seized their converts' gold, and their wives and children and other goods, "and left them nominally baptized, but without any understanding of the benefit of the lofty sacrament they had received. I would to God that for each thousand of them baptized there were ten that really knew it." [131] One percent would already be

---

130. Ibid., XXIV, 8: II, 238–39. In a letter to the sovereign dated 31 May 1537 (*CDII*, I, 519), Oviedo reports that the clerics of the cathedral of Santo Domingo object vociferously—"jumping up and down and yelling"—to the establishment of further parish churches, "because they want to devour everything themselves." And in the *Quinquagenas,* the pious couplet "And do no disservice / To the religious" receives the following rather surprising commentary: "And this is right and proper, because they have the habit of going to law without a penny and no more than a *Deo gracias,* and also because they are expert and persistent, and they never die if the case is a monastery matter" (pp. 36–37).

See also, against the single wandering friars, but excepting those of the three monasteries in Santo Domingo, *Qu.,* pp. 49–52 (the three monasteries and the sole convent are also praised in *Qu.,* p. 385); and after telling the exemplary story of a blatant theft, which was not the first, Oviedo remarks, "nor will it be the last that they commit, under the pretext of coming to preach and convert, while they only really come for these things and similar ones" (*Qu.,* p. 51; cf. ibid., pp. 174, 415–16).

On the widespread greed of the clergy, both junior and senior, as a consequence of the enrichment of the church and the ambitions of disinherited younger brothers, who opt for ecclesiastical careers in an effort to compensate for their misfortune in not happening to have been firstborn sons, see Lozoya, op. cit., pp. 77–78, where the authorities quoted include Oviedo. See below, chap. XXI, n. 79.

131. *Hist.,* XXIX, 21: III, 103–04; cf. XXIX, 34: III, 174–75; on two converts who rejoin the savages, see the sarcastic comments in XVII, 16: I, 531a.

quite a lot. Elsewhere Oviedo drops the percentage to zero: "I have now seen a great number of these Indians in the thirty-five years that I have been acquainted with these parts and have seen these people, and not one perfect Christian have I found among them of those that have had dealings and acquaintance with the Christians (being of age)."[132] Truly, "one is beating one's head against a wall trying to make Christians out of these people."[133]

Their imperfect Christianization can, in fact, be traced back to Columbus, who, in the telling phrase of Fernández Armesto (op. cit., p. 147) was "religious, not human." Which is to say that his and many of his followers' unquestionable religiosity was devoid of charity and love, in fact was un-Christian. Moreover, as we have seen, the instruments and artisans of the Christianizing process were incurably corrupt. The end was debatable, the means foul.

Being convinced, as we are, that the imperfect Christianization of the natives lies at the root of the most of the ills still affecting the South American republics with a high proportion of native population, we cannot but join in Oviedo's ceaseless lament at those baptisms without conversion, at the way the Indians were deprived of their traditional religion without being offered another in its place, let alone a better one. In Cuba, for example, "they no more want to be Christians than all the others, although the chronicler Peter Martyr, on the strength of what he learned from the bachelor Enciso, speaks marvels of the devotion and conversion of a cacique of Cuba. . . . I have heard nothing of this although I have been in that island . . . however I doubt it, because I have seen more Indians than the man who wrote it or he who told him; and on the basis of my experience of these people, I believe that none or very few of them are Christians of their own will, and when one becomes a Christian, who is a mature man, it is more out of caprice than as a stamp of faith; because all he is left with is the name, and even that he swiftly forgets. It is possible that there are some faithful Indians, but I believe that they are very rare."[134]

So rare, in fact, or downright exceptional, that Oviedo suggests a singular wager: "Take those that have been baptized in the course of time by all the governors and captains that have entered that land [Nicaragua] since Captain Gil Gonçález Dávila, and for each one of those that have been baptized that can

132. Ibid., XXIX, 31: III, 157a, i.e., excluding the children brought up in the Christian faith, on whom see above, n. 125; II, 6: I, 72b; V, 3: I, 139b; VI, 9: I, 193b; XXIX, 34: III, 174a; XLII, 2: PT, IV, 366b; XLII, 3: IV, 59a. But as soon as they reach puberty, "the moment they know women," the sons of the Indians, whether baptized or not, immediately become wicked and polymorphous sinners. While the medieval view saw the baptized child, unacquainted with sin, as a symbol of perfect Christianity, Oviedo's verdict expresses a sort of naive and practical Beverlandism: sin enters into the world with lust. See the unpublished document in Pérez de Tudela, "Vida," pp. cxviii, cxxiii, and in "Rasgos," pp. 424–25.

The contrast between the relative Christianity of the young Indians and the recidivist, pagan, and brutish nature of the adults is pointed out by numerous authors: Romeo, op. cit., p. 341; for Canada in the early seventeenth century, S. Marion, *Relations des voyageurs français en Nouvelle France au XVIIème siècle* (Paris, 1923), p. 46. See L. Hanke, *All Mankind is One* (De Kalb, 1974), p. 105.

133. *Hist.*, V. Proh.: I, 125a. On Oviedo's skepticism and the consequences of his belief that the natives are enslaved to the devil, see Blanke, op. cit., p. 202.

134. *Hist.*, XVII, 4: I, 499. Cf. XXIII, 7: II, 438b; XLII, 14: IV, 113b.

remember his name and knows the Paternoster or the Ave Maria, or can give an account of himself as a Christian, I will pay one gold piece; and for each that cannot, give me just a *maravedí*. And with that arrangement, I think I shall earn a lot of money. . . ."[135]

Oviedo says quite straightforwardly that he dislikes this system of wholesale baptisms, whose sole aim is to allow the celebrant to boast of his statistics and claim some recompense or reward, or hang on to the benefices already obtained.[136] He repeats that one true Christian would be better than a thousand baptisms. It could even be that they end up by becoming Christians, but only "after a great lapse of time."[137]

All in all there is no mistaking his repugnance for this shameful trafficking in sacraments and souls. More than once he coolly and sarcastically takes the Indians' side, laughingly repeating, for example, the story of the Venezuelan Indian who, when the bishop reproved him for his lies and misdeeds—"tell me, you rogue, why you do these things"—replies: "Do you not see, my lord, that I am becoming a Christian," as if to say, Oviedo interprets, "I am becoming a rogue, like you Christians," adding that this should give the Christians food for thought, as "this reply on the Indian's part is no little shameful thing for them."[138] And in other places, almost in passing, he recalls that the Indians of Nicaragua call their gods *teot,* "and also call the Devil *teot,* and call the Christians *teotes* too." The Cueva Indians apply the name *tuyra* (or devil) to "the Christians, because they consider them cleverer and as such like the devil, thinking that in calling them *tuyras* they honor and praise them much."[139]

---

135. *Hist.*, XLII, 3: IV, 59a. On the following page Oviedo denounces the formal baptism of the black slaves disembarking in Santo Domingo, whose masters are charged half a peso or one peso by the priests for every Negro whom they "license" to eat meat during Lent "because there is a lack of fish," although of course the Negro has no idea "what Lent is"; and then the priests claim that the money is being collected "for a monstrance that is to be made, in God's good time, for the Holy Sacrament." On 22 May 1540 the Royal Audiencia of Santo Domingo begged the emperor, among other things "to request a Bull allowing Negroes and Indians to eat meat during Lent and on the sabbath" (*CDII*, I, 567; cf. above, chap. XVII, sec. 24).

136. For Mexico, Bataillon refers to a "precipitate rate" of conversions, without any preparatory instruction. See "Les Indes Occidentales, découverte d'un monde humain," in *La découverte de l'Amérique*, p. 8.

137. *Hist.*, V, Proh.: I, 125a. With a picturesque and possibly proverbial image he notes that they are incapable of persevering in the faith, "and instead simply slide away from it, like hail sliding off the tip of a lance" (II, 7: I, 30a).

138. Ibid., XXV, 22: II, 329. This must be one of the earliest examples—after those reported by Peter Martyr, above, chap. VIII, sec. 5—of the Indian pictured in the act of teaching the European a salutary lesson. Oviedo's Venezuelan is the ancestor of innumerable "innocents," Huron sages and savages voicing noble sentiments. Las Casas refers to the Indian who, when asked if he was a Christian, replied: "Yes, sir: I am already a bit of a Christian, because I can already lie a bit: one of these days I shall be able to lie a lot and I shall be very much a Christian" (*Historia de las Indias*, bk. III, chap. 145, ed. cit., III, 310, also quoted by Amador de los Ríos, "Vida," p. ciin35).

Oviedo also emphasizes that the Indians, lustful as they may be, strictly avoid incest, while Jews and Romans and Christians and even Spaniards, and even "a friar of the Military Order of Calatrava" committed incest or acts coming very close to that unholy union (*Hist.*, V, 3: I, 136–37); but he immediately goes on to point out that the savages refrain therefrom not out of virtue but out of superstitious fear, because they believe that they would die an evil death if they committed incest (which, Oviedo adds somewhat curiously on the following page, "one must conclude they have learned from experience").

139. *Hist.*, XXIX, 26: III, 127b; cf. XLII, 11: IV, 100a. I am not sure that Oviedo means to be sarcastic here. But from the general trend of his ideas, it would appear that he does. In another passage, speaking of the theft and plunder committed by the Indians who were accompanying certain Christians, believed to be magicians, he observes: "And

Thus the Indians are candid and ignorant; they are not, however, invariably good and docile, as Las Casas would have it, nor are they endowed with any natural innocence and wisdom, as so many subsequent panegyrists would claim. Oviedo describes them with total realism, making no attempt to conceal their vices (sodomy seems to be one of his principal preoccupations) but without declaring them guilty of nonexistent sins or shortcomings. They are totally hairless, both men and women, but this is because they are shaved as soon as they are born and then smeared with depilatory herbs. For Oviedo, however, this is not a cue for any pejorative corollaries regarding their sexuality; indeed he describes the women as unrestrainedly lascivious and the men as inveterate sodomites, libidinous and ready to forget all Christian virtue as soon as they reach the age for carnal knowledge of women (see above, n. 132).[140] Nor does he ever speak of race to judge them collectively: just as Homer never calls non-Greeks "barbarians," the term "race" is used by Oviedo solely for a species of Spanish pig.[141]

20. THEIR RIGHT TO INDEPENDENCE

In response to the accusation normally used to justify the punitive expeditions and massacres, namely that the Indians (in this case those on the island of Puna) are "rebellious," Oviedo coldly observes that "this rebellion, if you look at it carefully, is no such thing,[142] because one cannot call people subjects or say that they are duty bound to be loyal if they are under compulsion, robbed of their wives and children and property and deprived of their liberty, calling them friends and using them as slaves."[143] The terms are almost identical to those used by Father Las Casas to defend the just and indeed "holy" war waged by the Indians against their Spanish oppressors.[144]

There is thus a sort of bitter satisfaction (not unlike the sentiment lurking below the surface in the story of the foolhardy lion-tamer, below, chap. XXI,

---

apparently the dispossessed owners were delighted, thinking that this new sanctity was so ordained in heaven, whence they thought these Christians came" (XXXV, 5: III, 604–05). For the curious expedient adopted by the Indians of the island of Boriquén (San Juan) to ascertain whether the Christians were mortal or not, see the piquant account in XVI, 8: I, 479.

140. *Sum.*, pp. 91, 140; *Historia,* passim; cf. Vázquez, op. cit., pp. 490–92. On sodomy before and after Cortés, and the Mexicans' chronic attachment to that vice, see Keen, op. cit., pp. 62, 63, 101, 117, 140, 149, 153, 156, 171–72, 222, 245, 260, etc.

141. *Hist.*, XIX, 2: PT, II, 193–94. Cf. F. Ortiz, "*Raza,* voz de mala cuna y de mala vida," *CA,* 5 (1945), p. 90. It need hardly be recalled that in the sixteenth century "racialism . . . was all but nonexistent," and the term was used only for animals (Hodgen, op. cit., pp. 213–14).

142. Note that the same turn of phrase is used to distinguish between the animals and plants of America and those of the Old World. It is as inappropriate to apply the European legal term "rebellion" to the Indians as to apply the European zoological and botanical names to the animals and plants of the Indies. In the same way the so-called Christian Indians are *not* real Christians. Neither Christians nor rebels: neither the rites nor the legal judgments of the West can properly be applied to the primitive peoples of America.

143. *Hist.*, XLVIII, 6: IV, 374a. Shortly before that, Oviedo refers to the Indians "having very good reason to revolt" (XLVII, 20: PT, V, 207a).

144. Salas, op. cit., p. 274.

sec. 14) in Oviedo's account of the fate that befell Martín de Murga, the unwary Biscayan captain who refused to heed his warnings and left with an escort to collect a ransom of one thousand gold pesos from the cacique of Bea. He was treacherously killed with all his followers, and the bloodthirsty cacique, having donned a belt and collar of gold, had him dragged along by his feet for a quarter of a mile, through a crowd of singing and jeering men, women, and children, "and then they left him there for the birds to feast on." The cruel massacre is highlighted by one telling, grotesque, and macabre episode. The cacique, grasping his gold-tipped club, struck the body on the mouth, mocking it with the words, "eat gold, eat gold, eat gold."[145]

The tragic and perpetual law of talion binding gold and blood once again takes its toll, and we shall see other examples (below, secs. 36–37), but curiously enough the episode is not recalled when Oviedo is relating the story of Queen Tomiris, who had Cyrus's head cut off and plunged in a wineskin full of blood: "You thirsted for blood; now drink your fill."[146]

21. THE *REQUERIMIENTO:* ITS INCOMPREHENSIBILITY

In 1516 Oviedo asked the learned doctor Palacios Rubios[147] if the Christians' conscience could at least be clear if the ritual *requerimiento* had been made before war was waged on the Indians. The response he received was in fact in the affirmative and accompanied with much cynical laughter; but "I could laugh much more at him and his literary works (he being held to be a great man, and as such occupying a seat on the Royal Council of Castile) if I thought that what this *requerimiento* said could be understood by the Indians."[148] And eight years later (1524) he reported to the king that the *requerimiento,* far from being understood by the Indians,[149] "was not even understood by those who read it out." Between Palacios's raucous laughter and Oviedo's biting irony the vacuous formula is shown up for what it is: a fragile bubble of frothy legalistic hypocrisy.[150]

---

145. *Hist.,* XXIX, 15: PT, III, 267–68. In de Bry's famous engravings Indians can be seen pouring molten gold down the throats of Spaniards stretched out on the ground.

146. Ibid., XLI, 3: PT, IV, 354b.

147. The venerable Palacios Rubios, a close friend of Las Casas and drafter of the *requerimiento* (cf. *Historia de las Indias,* bk. III, chap. 57, ed. cit., II, 580; cf. above, chap. IX, sec. 5) is considered a true friend of the Indians and a sincere humanitarian. Las Casas recognizes him as such, although, in line with his own ideas, he disapproves of the text of the *requerimiento,* and criticizes it as hypocritical and formalistic (*Historia de las Indias,* bk. III, chap. 58, ed. cit., II, 581–84; cf. Salas, op. cit., pp. 247, 260–63). Las Casas waxes indignant, but Oviedo joins in D. Palacios Rubios's sarcastic laughter, just as he had been amused—on the strength of his own experience and its obvious and total superiority to the voice of authority—at Peter Martyr, shown up to be ignorant and almost foolish.

148. *Hist.,* XXIX, 7: III, 31–32. Cf. Terán, op. cit., pp. 133–34. Oviedo also uses the word *requerimiento* simply as a synonym for "summons," for example addressed by Spaniards to Portuguese and vice versa (*Hist.,* XX, 25: PT, II, 275a).

149. *Memorial,* given in Altolaguirre, op. cit., p. 211. Thus Chaunu is mistaken when he says in *L'Amérique et les Amériques* (Paris, 1964), p. 100, that the *requerimiento* was "approved by Oviedo."

150. Hollow formalities of a similar sort were still current in the nineteenth century, and indeed in our own century, being used for example to rob the Peruvian Indians of their lands (see Fr. Chevalier, "Témoignages littéraires et disparité de croissance: L'expansion de la grande propriété dans le haut Pérou au XXème siècle," *Annales,* 21, no. 4

Oviedo's basic argument is that the Indians do not and cannot understand the *requerimiento*. The inspector of mines found the document thrust into his hands in the harbor of Santa María, with orders to land and announce it to the Indians, "as if I could understand the Indians, for the purpose of reading it out to them, or as if we had someone there who could explain it to them, assuming they were willing to listen," because it had to be admitted that simply showing them the piece of paper "was rather beside the point." And Oviedo, being unable to communicate it to the natives, copies out the entire text for his readers instead, with a sort of conspiratorial wink, as if to say, see for yourselves what sort of a document it was!

In essence it is the same text as Enciso's (see above, chap. IX, sec. 6) and Palacios Rubios's (Palacios was one of the signatories), but rising to a crescendo of harshness in the last paragraph, with its threats of what will happen to the natives if they fail to accept it without delay: "I shall enter powerfully against you, and I shall wage war on you in every place and manner that I can," and I shall bind you into slavery, you, your women and your children, I shall sell them and do what I please with them, and I shall take away your goods, and shall do to you all the harm that I can, as is fitting with disobedient and rebellious subjects; and all of this [a truly amazing final shaft] will be your fault, not that of the sovereigns of Spain, "nor of those knights that came with me." [151]

The missionary friars announced in the *requerimiento* remain prudently on board "until they can see how things turn out." And Oviedo, with three hundred well-armed companions, takes part in a skirmish, kills three Indians with his musket, captures ten women and a female cacique, loses one man wounded by a poisoned arrow ("on the third day he died raving mad") but then, when a number of Spanish officers and officials are gathered in the presence of Pedrarias Dávila, Oviedo sarcastically informs the "general" of the expedition: " 'My lord, it seems to me that these Indians have no wish to listen to the theology of this *requerimiento,* nor do you have anyone who can explain it to them; will your honor order it to be kept, until we have one of these Indians safely locked up, so that he can gradually learn it, and my lord bishop can explain it to him.' And I gave him the *requerimiento* and he took it, amidst much laughter on the part of himself and all those listening to me." [152] Receipt declined, explicitly and categorically.

[1966], 828). For examples of *requerimientos ante litteram* (1509), or postdating the repeal order of 1573 (1598, 1680, 1697), see B. M. Biermann, "Das Requerimiento in der spanischen Conquista," *Neue Zeitschrift für Missionswissenschaft,* 6 (1970), 94–114.

151. *Hist.,* XXIX, 7: PT, III, 227–28. Another identical text, taken from M. Serrano y Sanz, *Orígenes de la dominación española en América* (Madrid, 1918), is given in Zavala, *Las instituciones jurídicas,* pp. 286–88. See also pp. 90–95 of this latter work, and the same author's *New Viewpoints,* pp. 6–7, 10–11. For other versions see Porras Barrenechea, *Cedularios del Perú,* pp. xxvi–xxvii; L. Hanke, "The Development of Regulations for Conquistadores," in *Contribuciones para el estudio de la historia de América: Homenaje al doctor Emilio Ravignani* (Buenos Aires, 1941), pp. 74–78. Hanke also states, in *Mankind,* p. 118, that Oviedo was the first to use it.

152. *Hist.,* XXIX, 7: PT, III, 229–30.

Oviedo's action was that much more opportune and necessary in that in practice, he repeats, instead of giving the natives time to study the *requerimiento*
properly and think about it, as was prescribed, what actually happened was that
the captains first attacked them, then chained them up, then read out to them
"that whole recapitulation of the *requerimiento*";[153] and they would read it to the
"wretched Indians" in Castilian, "without intermediary or interpreter and with
neither the reader nor the Indians understanding"; and the latter, even if they had
understood it through an interpreter, "were not at liberty to reply to what was
read out to them"; and they were at times obliged to walk forward on foot, and
cudgeled if they moved too slowly, and tortured in other ways, while their
women, as "women foreign to and set apart from the faith," were happily "forced
and violated," without one of the Spaniards ever being punished or reproved—
indeed, all outrages were invariably sanctioned.[154]

Oviedo is so nauseated that he decides on the spot to go back to Spain (1515) to
report to the king and seek a post in some land "safer for my conscience and my
life," claiming by way of excuse for the journey that the climate does not suit him
and he wants to be with his wife.[155]

Oviedo's criticism, against the background of the laughter of Palacios
Rubios—who was in fact an Indiophile—thus dramatizes the collision between
down-to-earth common sense and the legalistic and diplomatic formula, between
the rough and ready directness of America and complicated European tradi-
tionalism, the *reductio ad absurdum,* the chemical precipitation, in the natural
test tube of the Indies, of Old World ideologies, myths, and conventions. If
Palacios Rubios was amused rather than scandalized when Oviedo told him what
he had done with the *requerimiento* this meant that he too recognized it as
nothing more than the cynical verbal homage that everyone, at the outbreak of
war, feels duty-bound to render to the cause of peace.[156]

22. ITS IDEOLOGICAL PRECEDENTS

Among all this carping and quibbling, among all the precedents for the
requerimiento sought—and found—in the Ostiense[157] and in numerous other
authors, no one, as far as I know, has ever seen an immediate factual precedent

---

153. Ibid., pp. 230–31.
154. Ibid., XXIX, 9: PT, III, 237–39; XXIX, 34: PT, III, 353a. On the need for good interpreters see XXVI, 21:
III, 107b; and especially for the *requerimiento,* XXIX, 6: PT, III, 225. Same need stressed by Las Casas (Hanke,
Mankind, pp. 92–93).
155. *Hist.,* XXIX, 9: PT, III, 239–40. He left in October, in fact, having eventually overcome all the bureaucratic
obstacles placed in his way, and it was April 1520 before he sailed from Seville with his wife and two small children to
return to the Indies.
156. Bullón, op. cit., p. 141. In the centuries of the viceroyalties a similar conflict was expressed in the notorious
"obedience without execution," the standard response of the colonial official faced with a royal edict emanating from
Madrid that he could neither refuse nor carry out. Oviedo is well aware of the difficulty and often the uselessness of
issuing instructions for the Indies from far-off Spain (*Hist.,* XLVIII, 4: PT, V, 224–25).
157. On the theories of Enrico Bartolomei, Cardinale Ostiense, followed by Palacios Rubios and Sepúlveda, see
Höffner, op. cit., pp. 48–49, and Biermann, "Das Requerimiento," pp. 104–05.

in the enforced and totalitarian conversion of the Moors after 1492,[158] nor a remote source in the ritual "challenge" issued by the knight of the medieval romances, with its scorn of the adversary, the solemn and provocatory glorification of a lady or damsel (not necessarily of a holy religion, although in an allegory staged at the court of the duke of Burgundy there was also "a captive lady, representing religion"),[159] and the accompanying offer of peace of war.[160] In the modern duel, too, for that matter, the "offense" must be retracted or redeemed with blood (and there is also, perhaps, something of the medieval trial by combat in that ceremonial and bellicose challenge hurled at the natives). It was the same sort of logic, the same notion of "rustic chivalry," that prompted the murderer in Renato Fucini's *La 'olte dell' Assisi* to protest absurdly that his crime had not been premeditated "because I warned him about it first"![161] Homicide is legitimized by the giving of due warning!

There is another point too. The *requerimiento* was also a formal taking of possession in the presence of the native inhabitants of the land. When Columbus and Balboa declared that islands and oceans belonged to Spain, the event was witnessed solely by the heavens and their unfurled banners. But the Admiral had already postponed the legal occupation of the peninsula of Paria until a certain number of Indians could be found to join the monkeys as witnesses of the event.[162] "Form" is always a good protection for "substance." Thus the *requerimiento* obviously represented some advance over the habit of "hunting" the Indians like game. Becerillo and Leoncico had addressed no solemn injunctions to the natives: they just tore them to pieces. Nor have the Spaniards' methods of conquest been rejected or abhorred by later conquerors; indeed they have been adopted, adapted, and perfected. When the English conquerors of India met a new race, whether dark or pale of countenance, they happily—so Brecht said—used them for their "Beefsteak-Tartar."[163]

23. HANKE'S THESIS

I would not, on the other hand, agree with Hanke that the *requerimiento* can be traced back to the ritual formulas of the Romans, with their fetial priests setting a seal of legitimacy on the wars undertaken by the state.[164] Those ceremonies had

---

158. At the time there were those who suggested that the Moors "might justly be required to submit without exception to instant baptism, or to sell their estates and remove to Africa," thus obtaining spectacular mass conversions (Prescott, *Ferdinand and Isabella,* II, 407–09, 421; Menéndez Pidal, *Los españoles en la historia,* pp. 118–19).

159. J. B. La Curne de Sainte Palaye, *Mémoires sur l'ancienne chevalerie* (Paris, 1759), I, 190.

160. Ibid., pp. 259–63.

161. *Poesie* (Florence, 1876), p. 49.

162. Morison, *Southern Voyages,* p. 151.

163. The "Cannon Song," in Brecht's *Threepenny Opera,* act I.

164. L. Hanke, "España en las Indias y en las Filipinas," *Revista de las Indias,* 19 (1943), citing G. Salvioli, *Le concept de la guerre juste d' après les écrivains antérieurs à Grotius* (Paris, 1918), pp. 15–16, and Colman Philipson, *International Law and Custom of Ancient Greece and Rome* (London, 1911). Cf. also H. Kelsen, *Derecho y paz en las relaciones internacionales* (Mexico, 1943), pp. 67–68, and Sereni, op. cit., pp. 85–86. On the value of the legal fiction in general see H. S. Maine, *Ancient Law* (London, 1906), pp. 29–32.

a propitiatory character, in other words ensured, so it was hoped, the gods' agreement. But they established no relation with the enemy. The *requerimiento,* on the other hand, imposed an alternative, forced a choice: either admit that Dulcinea is the most beautiful princess in the world, that Christ—either in person or through his vicar on earth—gave the Indies to Ferdinand and Charles, or else perish for your stubborn impiety, your persistent heresy, for so obstinately and wickedly daring to deny such obvious truths. The "feudal" residue in fact leaps to the eye in the ninth paragraph, that qualifies those who reject the message as insubordinate "vassals," in accordance with the constitutional thesis that saw the subjugated kingdoms and peoples as "vassals" of the crown of Spain.

Inasmuch as a war was held to be "unjust" if there were no initiative by the enemy, without some act of aggression to repel, without a *justa causa* in the form of a wrong suffered, the *requerimiento* was a veritable incitement to commit a wrong, an expedient to create a ready-made *casus belli,* an act of provocation designed to produce an offense artificially and thus provide a fully just, legitimate, satisfying, reassuring, and comforting cause to move with fire and the sword against the naked and ignorant natives.[165]

To a man of practical common sense and antilegalistic mentality like Oviedo, all this labored legal fiction could only seem both grotesque and hypocritical. At bottom, that semijuridical semireligious liturgy must have struck him as hardly more serious than the incense that the natives (like the Romans in this respect) offered up to their idols to secure their partiality in the coming battle, the battle on which they embarked as soon as the fire went out. And in fact, Oviedo quickly adds, these people, as savage as you could wish, become enraged when they find themselves being invaded, and indeed "one cannot criticize their anger, only praise their tolerance."[166] *Cet animal n'est pas méchant, lorsqu'on l'attaque il se défend. . . .*

24. VERDICTS ON THE *REQUERIMIENTO*

The "provision of Granada" of 15 November 1526 had already decreed "that the text be made clear to the Indians," but apparently the order had had little effect.[167] To our eyes, Zavala says, "the captain reading out the *requerimiento* to

---

165. Magellan addressed a purely political *requerimiento* to the Philippine chieftain Lapu Lapu: if his subjects were willing to obey the king of Spain and recognize him as their lord, and pay tribute, he would be their friend; otherwise they would feel the steel of their lances. Lapu Lapu gave a defiant response, and in the ensuing skirmish Magellan was killed (Morison, *Southern Voyages,* pp. 428–29).

166. *Hist.,* XVII, 11: PT, II, 129a; see below, sec. 25 (end).

167. Zavala, "Palacios Rubios y Matías de Paz," pp. 156–57. Cf. Porras Barrenechea, *Cedularios del Perú,* p. xviii, giving the *requerimiento* to be addressed (1533) to the Peruvians (pp. 131–33), which was to be read out by skilled and faithful interpreters (p. 123). On Cortés's summons to Montezuma, see Bernal Díaz del Castillo, op. cit., pp. 168–69; cf. Oviedo, *Hist.,* XXXIII, 10: PT, IV, 43; on Valverde's historic and fateful injunction to Atahualpa, see Prescott, *Mexico and Peru,* p. 939. More *requerimientos* in Peru: *Hist.,* XLVI, 1–2: PT, V, 34, 36. Valverde would not perhaps have been killed by the Peruvian Indians "if the bishop had taught [the Indians] to believe and understand the Bible that he handed to Atahualpa when they took him prisoner" (XLVIII, 6: PT, V, 228a).

the Indians looks like . . . a fraud or a lunatic," but it is necessary to know the origins of the procedure and the theologicolegal context in which it had come into being.[168] Palacios Rubios's biographer, Eloy Bullón, maintains that the *requerimiento* was not really addressed to the Indians but to the governments of the European states, with a view to rendering Spain's conquests legally legitimate and formally irreproachable.[169] And Porras, while recognizing the formula as a "naive hotchpotch . . . evidence of theoreticism," find that it does have "a breath of humanity."[170]—perhaps because of that opening sentence announcing that all men are descended from Adam? Menéndez Pidal and Madariaga likewise applaud its "human brotherhood," in other words the fact that it recognizes the common humanity of the "savages" and the Europeans.[171] Even Zavala winds up seeing it as the basis of a just hegemony.[172]

Equally significant are the exertions of the learned Dominican Biermann. Beginning with his translation of the word *requerimiento,* which means "injunction" and not "official proclamation or interrogation,"[173] his whole article is an attempt to make light of the conquistadors' hypocritical procedure and to underline its gradual attenuation between its earliest and its final "application." From the point of view of missionary activity the real "significance" of the *requerimiento* consisted, he says, not in the violence done to men's consciences, since the state certainly has the duty to foster good and limit evil, but in the "fatal equation of state and church" (p. 113), that is to say a "defect in the system" (a criticism also made in his article on Geraldini) whereby evangelization was in reality subordinated to acceptance of the Spanish system of government, and was therefore actually obstructed by the *requerimiento!* Worse still: according to the erudite Jesuit Constantino Bayle the real drawback with the *requerimiento* lay in the fact that it had been drafted for men but was then read out to animals *(medio bestias)!*[174] But other scholars have differed. Pérez de Tudela describes it as a "curious expedient,"[175] Bataillon a "legal comedy," and Konetzke "pure farce."[176] Ramón Carande finds the *requerimiento* a document of "cabbalistic" subtlety, unrivaled as an expression of professional distortion.[177]

In point of fact the scandalized reactions of so many of our contemporaries (and indeed the would-be justifications of others) had already been voiced in

---

168. Zavala, "Palacios Rubios y Matías de Paz," p. 159.
169. Bullón, op. cit., pp. 138–39, followed by Höffner, op. cit., p. 168.
170. "El pensamiento de Vitoria," p. 475.
171. Menéndez Pidal, *Los españoles en la historia,* pp. 23–24; S. de Madariaga, *Cuadro histórico de las Indias* (Buenos Aires, 1950), pp. 43–44, and esp. p. 919.
172. *La filosofía política en la conquista de México* (Mexico, 1947), pp. 30–31.
173. Even the erudite theologian Höffner, op. cit., pp. 120, 126n73, 129n88, 166, always refers to this "curious document" simply as a "proclamation"!
174. Hanke, *Mankind,* p. 37.
175. Cf. "Vida," p. cliii, and "Rasgos" pp. 433–34.
176. Bataillon, *Etudes sur Las Casas,* p. xxvi; R. Konetzke, *Süd- und Mittelamerika* (Frankfurt, am Main, 1965), I, 168.
177. *Carlos V y sus banqueros* (Madrid, 1965), I, 478–79.

identical form at the time, in the early sixteenth century. The absurdity of the injunction was already glaringly apparent to Enciso, to Oviedo, to a Dominican of San Juan de Puerto Rico,[178] to a missionary mercenary (Pedro Ruiz Navarro), and to numerous other laymen and churchmen.[179] Particularly robust and substantial are the criticisms or rather sledgehammer blows delivered by Las Casas, who starkly revealed its internal contradictions and the way it begged the question, aggravated by the absurd demand for supine and immediate acceptance.[180]

At the beginning of the 1600s Campanella was suggesting that instead of imposing their will by violence the Spaniards should have catechized the natives; he sketches out a sort of *requerimiento* (without the fearful closing threats, of course) and concludes: "This preamble is what should have been addressed to these people."[181]

The *requerimiento*[182] was confirmed by the decree of 17 September 1527, "although with more rigorous requirements regarding its correct application," but after the matter had been discussed with Enciso[183] it disappeared to all intents and purposes with the promulgation of the New Laws (1542), influenced by Las Casas. It was only specifically eliminated, however, by the *Ordinances of His Majesty Made for the New Discoveries, Conquests, and Pacifications*, of 13 July 1573.[184]

25. ATTENTIVENESS TO THE INDIAN

Although he had first-hand experience only of the semisavage Indians of the Greater Antilles and certain areas of Central America, and not of the relatively civilized natives of Mexico and Peru, Oviedo displays such an understanding and sympathetic spirit that he has rightly been described[185] as being even more of an ethnographer (and naturalist) than a historian.[186] Since the time of Tacitus no

178. Quoted by Zavala, *Las instituciones jurídicas*, p. 93–94.
179. L. Hanke, "The Requerimiento and Its Interpreters," *RHA*, 1, no. 1 (1938), 25–34.
180. Salas, op. cit., pp. 247, 255–56, 260–63; Bataillon, *Etudes sur Las Casas*, pp. 178, 183–84.
181. *Della monarchia di Spagna*, XXXI, ed. cit., II, 217–20.
182. Examples from 1526, 1527, 1529, 1532, 1534–37, in Hanke, "The Development of Regulations," p. 78*n*; from 1541 in R. Ricard, *La conquête spirituelle du Mexique* (Paris, 1933), p. 105.
183. J. Pérez de Tudela, "La gran reforma carolina de las Indias en 1542," *RI*, 17, nos. 73–74 (1957), 463–509, esp. p. 470*n16*.
184. Hanke, "The Development of Regulations," pp. 79–80, quoting *CDII*, XVI, 142–87. But Höffner, op. cit., pp. 167–68, shrewdly recalls a very similar summons addressed by the Turks to the Viennese (1683)!
185. Ballesteros Gaibrois, "Oviedo etnólogo," pp. 445–67, including copious references, a recognition that Oviedo's feeling for nature is akin to Petrarch's and acknowledgment of his humanistic culture. Pérez de Tudela too admires him because far from limiting himself to "exotic curiosities" he paved the way for anthropology, the natural history of man ("Vision de la découverte," p. 276).
186. One significant example: the theory that Oviedo expounds on the origins of the magic arts, namely their derivation from medicine, with "the force of religion" added to that science's promises and flatteries, and finally "the mathematical art," in other words the divining of the future (*Hist.*, V, 1: I, 126b; cf. XXIV, 12: II, 255b; XXV, 9: II, 299b) comes directly from Pliny, as Oviedo himself admits. But it is interesting to see Pliny's theory of the proud art of magic, which "rose to such an exalted position that it is now paramount among most nations of the earth and in the East governs the actions of the most mighty kings," extended to the savages and witch doctors of Haiti. In the *Quinquagenas* (pp. 168–69), even more curiously, Oviedo draws a parallel between the magic arts of Zoroaster and the heresy of Luther, citing the passage in Pliny and his own personal experience of "Indians learned" in the arts of magic and necromancy.

historian belonging to the world of western civilization had devoted such careful attention to a people of a completely different civilization and in more than one sense backward. But while Tacitus had poetically idealized his Germans, Oviedo, more of a naturalist and less of a moralist than the Latin author, views the Indians almost as a semianimal species, with practices and customs, good and bad qualities but not, strictly speaking, vices and virtues.

The extraordinary novelty and abundance of the material act as a constant stimulus to his interest. And he is quite unworried by the enormous problems — ethnic, religious, and legal — arising out of the contacts with these peoples. Either he does not feel them as problems, or he leaves them to be dealt with by others, given to more subtle or more fanatical reasoning. He never doubts for a moment, however, even in the early years of relatively unalloyed severity, that the Indians are human. If just a moment ago we said that he considers the Indians almost as a sort of animal species, we were of course referring to his naturalistic, descriptive, generic, and dispassionate method, certainly not to any sympathy on his part for the point of view of certain Dominicans, who equated the Indians with the animals.[187] The Indians are "a savage people, but our brothers," and forgotten children of God.[188] Oviedo does not reach the point of saying expressly that they too were redeemed with Christ's blood, but he warns that "in memory of that precious blood" one must not spill the blood of any other creature.[189] The Indians are to be treated "as fellow-men," and for his part he cannot forgive the Christians that have grown rich by maltreating them.[190]

---

187. See Gerbi, *Dispute*, p. 63f. Oviedo mentions that he twice (at Toledo in 1525 and Medina del Campo in 1532) made sworn depositions before the Royal Council of the Indies on the Indians' capacities and recalls how learned and religious men indulged in lengthy discussion on how they should be treated, with numerous laws being passed to protect them; "but I can see that nothing has availed to prevent this unhappy people wasting away in these islands," a situation which he himself ascribes above all to the unceasing and savage quarrels between Franciscans and Dominicans, with each permitting what the other bans, thus sowing untold confusion in the minds of the natives (*Hist.*, III, 6: I, 72–73). In much the same way he observes elsewhere that there were "great legal altercations between famous lawyers, canonists and theologians and monks and prelates of much learning and moral worthiness . . . but as they were of widely differing opinions in this dispute, no profit has accrued therefrom to the land or the Indians" (IV, 2: I, 104b).

188. *Hist.*, III, 6: I, 72a; XVII, 17: I, 533b.

189. Ibid., XXX, Proh.: III, 177b.

190. Ibid., III, 6: I, 73b. When he goes on to discuss the civilized rather than savage natives of America, Oviedo warns that the Spanish robbed the Mexican Indians of "the liberty that they had always enjoyed," without heed to the natural resentment of those subjected to a "new yoke and slavery," and insisted on forcing the Mexicans to adopt new customs completely different from those in which they and their ancestors had always lived, customs and beliefs which had been handed down from far-off times and could not "be eradicated or removed so summarily and easily as to make the old men forget them; for as long as those old men are still alive, their inherited vices must perforce live on." Thus the Christians would do well to keep a wary eye open (XXXIII, 37: III, 456b). I fail to see why this passage, so full of good sense and human feeling, should have led Iglesia (*Cronistas e historiadores,* p. 90) to conclude that Oviedo "did not understand the Indians, and treats them with a mixture of distrust and disdain, thinking them always about to rebel."

Vázquez, op. cit., arrives at the same conclusion, defending Oviedo against Las Casas and praising his constant humanity, and indeed humanism, that grew out of his contact with the American world. Oviedo's verdict on the Indian improves over the years. The native is a victim of his own history, but he will progress, from the aesthetic point of view too, when Christianized. All of which justifies the Conquest and enslavement: even turning the Indian into a slave means "helping him to emerge from his condition as a slave of the devil."

26. HIS BALANCED JUDGMENT

Oviedo knows that the Indians are lazy, indolent, and slothful; he knows that before the arrival of the Spaniards "their main concerns were eating, drinking, idling, lusting, and idolatry, and the exercise of much other bestial filthiness";[191] he knows, or he thinks he knows, that "many of them, for their amusement, poisoned themselves so as not to have to work,"[192] and that "the men go off and get drunk and send their women to dig and sow and reap."[193] But it is not right for the Spaniards to imitate the Indians or take advantage of the docility of their women; it is not right—and Oviedo banned the practice in Darien in 1521, though for these and similar measures, he confesses, "I was soon hated"—to utilize them as beasts of burden: "And I forbade that the Indian women should be loaded down, that the Christians should use them like donkeys."[194]

The conclusion is what one might expect from a moralist: he finds it difficult to say which are worse, the natives or Spaniards. "The Indians did not dare to trust the Christians and the Christians distrusted them, and I think that they were both quite right, given the things that have happened on that coast."[195] And after relating that the Indians of Pelapia, Pelucho, and Capanapo handed over gold, "although little," Oviedo explains acidly: "This 'although little' can be taken in two ways—in one sense that the Indians could have given much more, and in the other that however much they gave, it would still seem little to the Christians."[196]

Oviedo has made a careful study of the Indians. He has explored their historical traditions and collected their songs (which he compares with those of the Spanish and Flemish peasants, with the traditional Spanish *romances,* and with the autobiographical verses composed by Frederick of Naples, in 1501, and King Francis I of France, in 1525)[197] he has interpreted their dances, compared their naive beliefs with those of the ancients, tirelessly observed their practices and customs, their vocabulary and marriage rites, laws of inheritance and funeral ceremonies, their feelings and reactions, physical gifts and artistic capacities; and he has admired the costumes they don for their dances in Nicaragua, with

191. *Hist.,* IV, 2: I, 105b. Salas is, I think, too harsh in concluding that Oviedo felt "no sympathy" for any native (op. cit., pp. 119–20), indeed experienced only antipathy and revulsion, without any Lascasian spirit of Christian charity (op. cit., p. 124); Hanke's judgment too, *Mankind,* pp. 40–45, is unwarrantably severe.

192. *Hist.,* III, 6: I, 71b.

193. Ibid., XXXIII, 51: III, 536b.

194. Ibid., XXIX, 14: III, 71b.

195. Ibid., XXVII, 5: II, 431b.

196. Ibid., XXVII, 8: II, 449; cf. XXVIII, 5: II, 487a.

197. Ibid., V, 1: I, 128–29a. Oviedo recognizes the historiographical role ("this form of history") of both the savages' songs ("and those songs remain in their memories in the place of books, to remind them of their history") and the verses used by his illiterate contemporaries to perpetuate the memory of great feats of arms, "without their being able to read what they are singing or reciting" (ibid.). Two centuries and more were to pass before Genovesi pronounced his Vico-style panegyrics of the songs of the Mexicans and Peruvians, nations without letters, both the heroic compositions in which "they celebrated the deeds of their ancestors" and the love songs and burlesques they used "like our own plebeians and rustics in their amorous pursuits or in their games" (letter to Giambattista Sanseverino, 25 December 1763, op. cit., pp. 159–60).

multicolored stockings and jackets, gorgeous plumes, and uniform tattoos like liveries, that make them "as well-dressed as the most elegantly decked-out German soldiers [Landsknechts?]," indeed, "elegant and extremely respectable men . . . who would look very well in Spain and France and Italy and Germany, and in any part of the world."[198] So Oviedo knows very well that their intellect is limited, or actually "brutish and evilly inclined,"[199] that however much one does for them they refuse to teach the Christians the virtues of the medicinal plants, "because that sort of knowledge is part of their dominion."[200] He knows there are some that try to avoid work by inflicting wounds on themselves or swallowing harmful drugs, who have to be "cured" first with medicine and then with a good dozen lashes;[201] and he knows that they are cruel and cunning, cowardly and idolatrous, many of them addicted to sodomy and some to cannibalism.

But they are still men, even these wretches that "are so savage that they think everything is common property."[202] and they are so little inhuman or brutish that they prove to be resolutely attached to their liberty, their beliefs, and traditions. And it is here, with remarkable anticipation of twentieth-century theories on native civilizations, that Oviedo formulates his universally valid maxim on the importance and durability of long-established tribal customs and beliefs.[203]

In Oviedo's portrait of the Indian, in short—a portrait to which he is constantly coming back to add fresh touches—the main features are perceived and rendered sympathetically and almost, I would say, with gratitude for the wealth of material that the Indians offer the historian. Almost all the features mentioned by Oviedo are so accurate that they have been repeated by a hundred other authors, to the point that they have become proverbial. Even today they can often be recognized either in reality or in certain conventional representations of the savage.

If we take, for example, a work of such pure and straightforward poetry as Pascarella's *La Scoperta de l'America,* we discover that the description of the virgin forest (sonnets 26–27) already recalls Oviedo's glowing lines (see above, chap. XVIII, sec. 24). And the half-naked "silly idiot" who gives the Spaniards the immortal response, "What's that to do with me? I'm just a savage" (sonnet 29), has a precursor in the Indian who replied with pride, when asked where he was from, "Where should I be from? . . . I am an Apalache Indian."[204]

The gleeful and highly profitable exchanges of little mirrors, "handfuls of

---

198. *Hist.*, XLII, 11: PT, IV, 413–14.
199. Ibid., V, Proh.: I, 125b.
200. Ibid., XI, 5: I, 378a.
201. Ibid., p. 379b.
202. Ibid., XX, 8: II, 44b. Cf. Ballesteros Gaibrois, "Oviedo etnólogo," p. 459; Vázquez, op. cit., pp. 483–519, with accurate remarks but excessively slavish adherence to O'Gorman's thesis.
203. *Hist.*, XXXIII, 37: PT, IV, 180b, cited above, n. 190.
204. *Hist.*, XVII, 24: I, 554b. But Pascarella's image of the "silly idiot with his head / Painted like some plaything, / Half-naked when dressed, with a crest / All formed of bird's feathers" (sonnet 29) would seem to come straight out of Columbus: "One of them . . . had his face all smudged with charcoal. . . . he wore all his hair . . . gathered into a little net of parrot's feathers, and he was as naked as all the others" (*Journal*, 13 January 1493).

baubles," and boxes of matches for brooches and earrings and baskets of gold, and the Indians' general willingness to "barter the things away" (sonnets xxxii–xxxiii), are extensively documented in Oviedo. The Indians "traded" everything "recklessly," giving "something worth a hundred for something not worth ten or even five," and if they were given a fine cloak they would very soon, "after a day or two trade it for a shoelace or a few pins; and in just the same way they bartered away everything else." [205]

27. SENSUALITY OF THE FEMALE SAVAGES

The fierce sensuality of the female savages and their marked preference for the white men is described by Oviedo a number of times. [206] "I mentioned above that the women of that island [Hispaniola] were restrained with the native men, but that they gladly gave themselves to the Christians," starting with Queen Anacaona herself, who was "very indecent in the venereal act with the Christians," so that she was reputed to be "the most dissolute woman of her rank or any other to be found in the island." [207]

There is even an episode that in Pascarella seems to be meant as jocular

205. *Hist.*, V, 3: I, 139. Even the "couple of bits of glass" (sonnet 32), colored of course, can be glimpsed in the hands of Columbus's companions, who offered the Indians "hawk-bells, pins, needles, and some glass beads of different colors" (*Hist.*, II, 6: I, 26a). On the Indians' propensity for barter (already observed and described with particular insistence by Columbus), see also VI, 22: I, 208b; XXVI, 4: II, 340b; XXIX, 28: III, 140a ("all these things and others are exchanged one for another, because they have no money"; cf. Pascarella "the savage . . . has no money . . . because commerce there is just like a spinning wheel" (sonnet 33). And the Spaniards exploit the situation, because when they pay the Indians "they give them a hawk-bell or a needle or a couple of pins in exchange for a mark or two of gold" (*Hist.*, XXXII, 2: III, 224a).

206. In Pascarella the Indians' revolt is explained in terms of the Christians' sexual indiscretion. The native growls threateningly, "Hands off our women" (sonnet 35). There is nothing of this in Oviedo. But in the instructions given to Pedrarias Dávila before he embarked, together with Oviedo, for the Tierra Firme, the Catholic King had said to him: "I have been informed that one of the things that has most unsettled them [the Indians] in the island of Hispaniola, and done most to turn them against the Christians, has been the habit of taking their wives and daughters against their wills, and using them as wives" (2 August 1513, in *CDII*, XXXIX, 291).

In his first *Decade* (first published in Seville in 1511), Peter Martyr had already lamented the fact that most of Columbus's companions "in carrying off the women of the islanders before the very eyes of their parents, their brothers, and their husbands, intent on rape and plunder, had deeply upset the natives" (*Dec.*, I, 4, p. 47).

207. *Hist.*, V, 3: I, 135b. In the tenth chapter of the *Sumario* ("On the Indians of Tierra Firme, their customs, rites and ceremonies," p. 121) Oviedo provides even more spicy details: "there are many [women] who willingly give themselves to any man who wants them, especially the chieftainesses, who themselves say that noblewomen and ladies should not deny anything that is requested of them, only low-born women"; and they happily give themselves even to common people, always provided these are Christians, because "they know that they are very manly, and they look on them all as noble, without distinction."

This salacious passage in the *Sumario* is considerably toned down in the parallel passage referring to these ladies in the *Historia*, where Oviedo says that "those who have had some conversation with the Christians are very friendly toward them because they say that they are good friends to brave men, and more inclined toward men of strength rather than cowards, and they know the advantage they have over the Indians" (XXIX, 27: III, 133b). So now it is no longer the vigor but the valor of the Christians that attracts the native women. . . .

At about the same time Peter Martyr was announcing — and illustrating with some highly suggestive examples — the fact that among the native women "the woman considered most generous and honorable is the one who, being capable, has accepted most men to lie with her" (*Dec.*, VII, 10. p. 563); and likewise "in accordance with the general nature of women, who prefer the things of others to things of their own, these women love the Christians most of all" (*Dec.*, VII, 8, p. 612). The Christians are preferred because they are different. . . .

It seems quite likely that these flattering references gave rise to the endlessly repeated thesis of the impotence and frigidity of the native men of America (see Gerbi, *Dispute*, passim).

exaggeration but which is reported in Oviedo as historical fact: "And they are such that an Indian woman took a bachelor called Herrera, who had fallen behind his companions and was left alone with her, and seized him by the genitals and made him very tired and exhausted, and if by chance other Christians had not passed that way to help him, the Indian woman would have killed him."[208]

Still on the subject of sex, Oviedo is frequently amused to note that the Indian men prefer wives who are *not* virgins and are delighted when they can exchange women and get an old woman instead of a young one, "because the old ones serve them better."[209] But here too he shows no sign of being shocked. There is at most a touch of mockery, or good-natured compassion. Oviedo is quick to recognize virtue and modesty even among the Indians, although on one occasion he says that they go about naked without "shame" because they have no idea what "shame" is. He draws lively thumbnail sketches of Indian women, both young and old,[210] such as his Indian servant-girl of fourteen or less, "a very clever girl who spoke Castilian as if she had been born and brought up in Castile," who was bitten by a viper and despite the prompt and attentive care bestowed on her—"everything was done for her that the surgeons ordered"— died before the third day was out.[211]

28. Portraits of Indian women

Equally sympathetic is the tale of the old Indian woman whom Diego de Salazar decided to feed to his savage dogs. The beldam was given a letter to take to the governor, a league away, and as she set off with the message, "going very happily along, because she thought that for delivering the letter they were setting

208. *Hist.*, XVII, 24: I, 554a; it would seem that in this case, however, the lady's main aim was to regain her liberty. Oviedo knows (see above, n. 132) that the native men, even if brought up from childhood as Christians, give way to the most unrestrained wantonness "as soon as they reach the age to know women, or for the women to know them, carnally"—note the latter half of the alternative (VI, 9; I, 193b).

209. On the first point see *Hist.*, XVII, 4: I, 499; XXIV, 3: II, 222b; XXIV, 12: II, 255b; XLII, 3: PT, IV, 375b ("many of the men prefer women already corrupted rather than virgins"); XLII, 11: IV, 97b; XLII, 12: IV, 103a.

Marco Polo had already spoken of husbands happy to have their wives belong to numerous strangers (*I Viaggi*, ed. cit., pp. 65, 171) and of Tibetans, among whom "no man would take a maid for a wife, for anything in the world; and they say that they are worthless, if she has not already had experience of many men. . . . the more men have laid with her, the sooner she marries" (p. 167), but also of Tartars that "hold the first wife to be the best and true wife, rather than any other" (p. 81). Diderot's Tahitian was to repeat the same theme five centuries later: "The more children our girls have, the more they are sought after" (op. cit., p. 773).

In the same lighthearted tone Oviedo goes on to relate how in the Islands of Thieves the bachelors are allowed to enter the houses of married couples, ask the husband to leave and lie with the wife as long as they please, while the poor "cuckold" can neither return until he is summoned, nor go and perform the same service in someone else's house! (*Hist.*, XX, 16: II, 61; cf. XXIV, 3: II, 222a).

On wife-swapping among the Indians, see *Sum.*, chap. LXXXI, p. 245; *Hist.*, XXIX, 27: III, 133b (where the motives given include the greater wisdom of the older women, and the fact that the natives "are less jealous of them"). In 1605 Fray Reginaldo de Lizárraga noted that the Indians of Peru "marry old women, so that they have someone to make their liquor and their clothed" (*Descripción colonial* [Buenos Aires, 1916], I, 295–96).

210. Rosenblat, op. cit., p. 235, is, however, going a bit too far when he says that Oviedo wrote an "apologia for the native woman, honest, pure, beautiful, and devoted to her husband."

211. *Sum.*, chap. 54, p. 193. Note also the reference to that "loquacious and brazen cacique's wife" who persuades her people not to resist (*Hist.*, XXVII, 7: II, 445a).

her free," he unleashed his mastiff after her. When the old lady saw that she was being followed she sat down on the ground and began to talk to the hound in her own language, "Good master dog, I am taking this letter to the governor"; and she showed it the letter or paper clutched in her hand and said to it, "Don't harm me, Mr. dog." And the dog in fact stopped, then approached her "and cocked a leg and piddled on her," as dogs do at the corners of houses, but otherwise left her unharmed. And the terrified old woman—Androcles reborn, in female garb—was spared her life by the Spaniards.[212]

On another occasion Oviedo himself took prisoner a beautiful female cacique, with a pride to match Tusnelda's, when one of his Negroes discovered her "hidden in the bush." This lady, "of fine appearance," died in his house in Darien a few days later, "and in my opinion she died of anger at finding herself a prisoner, although in truth she was always very well treated." Oviedo cannot however bring himself to go on without pronouncing a sort of nostalgic and pathetic funeral oration over her. "I said above that this Indian princess was beautiful, because in truth she looked like a woman of Castile in her whiteness; when one saw her naked her bearing and gravity were very admirable, without laughter or frivolity, but with a severe though modest appearance, although she could not have more than sixteen or seventeen."[213]

No less proud was that other Indian girl of seventeen or eighteen, who emerged alone from a hut besieged by the Spaniards "and attacked the Christians with her bow and arrows" and, like an Amazon reincarnate, injured four of them before they managed to capture her;[214] nor that mature armed virgin, who had been commanded by her dying father to preserve her chastity and fight with the men, and had scrupulously complied with these orders, to the point where she could handle a bow and arrow better than any Indian man.[215] In another

---

212. *Hist.*, XVI, 11: I, 484–85. There is also a fleeting glimpse of another poor little Indian girl sent by a chieftain as a gift to Captain Grijalva, together with some gold and precious stones offered for barter, "an Indian girl dressed in a delicate cotton gown, and he said that he did not want any reward or payment for the girl, and that she was a free gift" (ibid., XVII, 15: I, 528a).

213. On a number of other occasions Oviedo observes that some people go about naked and others clothed, without our being able to infer anything from this regarding their morals; and, with heavy satire at the expense of the Europeans, "In truth I have seen many naked Indians more modest than some fully-clothed Christian women" (*Hist.*, XXVI, 10: II, 356a). The simple little thread protecting the virginity of the Venezuelan maidens is more effective than "the cloister walls and doorkeepers that some highly respected women have in our own continent of Europe" (XXV, 22: II, 330b). And of some of the Indian women who apply caustic herbs to turn their skin pale, until they are as white "as if they had been born in Castile," he writes that neither they nor "the Christian Spanish ladies that waste corrosive sublimate and white lead in making themselves up" will ever manage "to be nuns or even to do anything honest whatsoever" (IX, 34: I, 360b). Shortly thereafter he refers again to the Spanish and Italian woman who "daub themselves in an effort to amend, or rather repair and ruin the image or face that God gave them" (X, 1: I, 363a).

214. *Hist.*, XXVII, 3: II, 422a. Cf. Sacchetti, op. cit., novella 136.

215. *Hist.*, XXVII, 6: II, 437. She too is held up as a model to the shameless Christian adulterers. There are also frequent, if conventional, satires in the *Quinquagenas* at the expense of the women of Spain and their levity (pp. 191–92, 329), their constant laughter as a sign of frivolity (pp. 24, 33), their elaborate coiffures (pp. 56–58, 131, 179, 235–36—an extensive and extremely sarcastic passage, 428), their clever quarrelsomeness (pp. 36–37), their ready lies and anger and hypocrisy (pp. 127–31), the dangers of matrimony (pp. 358–60, 402–03, 433–34), their aimless dawdling (pp. 308, 450), and frivolous songs (p. 339); "I, in my whole life, have never seen a woman singing without a lavish display of lewdness" (p. 425).

episode an Indian woman's pathetic conjugal love is movingly expressed as she offers herself as a latter-day Sophronia, asking to be executed in place of her husband, condemned to be hung by Oviedo. She proclaims herself responsible for his crime and begs that at the very least she be allowed to die with him on the same gallows, with her consort and her children only eight or nine years old; and when even this cruel favor is denied to her she "began to weep again."[216] Oviedo is also anxious not to "omit to praise" that other rough and ready Indian woman who took a club and struck a Spanish captain on the arm, almost breaking it and making him "give back what he was taking from her."[217]

29. LAS CASAS AND OVIEDO

There is thus no justification for Las Casas's repeated and inordinately vehement accusations that Oviedo "slandered" the Indians and maltreated and insulted them in his history in order to attenuate or even justify the fact of his having factually maltreated them as a conquistador. Las Casas's arguments[218] focus on his claims of the natives' exalted physical and moral qualities, a point that he felt to be crucial and on which he insisted for decades with all the monotonous insistence of a man possessed by an *idée fixe*. But there were deeper reasons for the quarrel with Oviedo and their mutual antipathy.[219]

Las Casas was a man of the middle ages, a man of erudite Latinity, a pugnacious and intransigent Christian, fanatical in his defense of the Indians and indifferent, or rather deaf, to the needs of the state and the political requirements of one of the first colonial empires; moved, certainly, by a spirit of charity and outrage at the abuses actually committed, but led by a spirit of accusation and denunciation and oratorical bullying into producing long lists of scandalous revelations and idealizing the pure, innocent, pathetic victims of these wicked excesses with all the rhetoric of a defending counsel. One of the most discerning of his apologists admits that he was "impassioned, violent, and reckless," vain,

---

216. *Hist.*, VI, 41: I, 363a. But Oviedo allowed her to be "allocated" together with her children to a "good householder" who would treat them well.

217. Ibid., XXVII, 5: II, 488b.

218. Las Casas's accusations still blacken Oviedo's name: one only has to look at the article devoted to him in Larousse, or to read the incredible verdict of one of his most recent editors and biographers: "On careful analysis his learned disquisitions reveal no glimmer of any real interest in the native peoples, whom he either fails to understand or despises" (González, op. cit., p. 14).

219. The reasons for Las Casas's hatred of Oviedo are still hotly debated. Caddeo, for instance, attributes them to Oviedo's being a "conquistador" of the sort detested by Las Casas ("Sobre F. Colón y el P. Las Casas," p. 109); but in reality the very least that can be said in Oviedo's defence is that, as a "conquistador" he was certainly not so typical and representative as to be able to serve as a favorite target for the barbs of the pugnacious bishop (cf. below, sec. 31).

According to Carbia the reasons for the dislike were entirely personal and amounted to a "maniacal passion" that prompted Las Casas to indulge in literary frauds and forgeries ("Oviedo, Las Casas, y Caddeo," p. 93; "Los fraudes," p. 151); but even this is insufficient explanation. See also Fueter, op. cit., p. 299 (they are both poor writers); Bataillon, *Études sur Las Casas*, pp. 70–73; Sánchez Alonso, *Historiografía española*, II, 98–99; A. Pincherle, in the introduction to his anthology of Las Casas entitled *La leggenda nera* (Milan, 1959), pp. xiv–xv; and Hanke, *Mankind*, passim.

incapable of practical action, and given to dogmatic statements with apocalyptic overtones.[220]

Oviedo, on the other hand, was a modern man, possessed of a critical and objective mind, an administrator conscious of his duties to the state, a Spaniard, ignorant of Latin possibly, but proud of his country and its overseas mission. Oviedo sees things as they are, Las Casas as he would like them to be or how they should be. He is therefore very close to Manzoni's Fra Cristoforo: "In my humble opinion there should be no challenges or carriers or beatings," to which the practical Count Attilio replies, "One can see that you don't know the world. . . . you would like to turn the world upside down."[221] The southerner Las Casas gives in all too easily to the heady wine of fine-sounding phrases, but in condemning the crimes and outrages committed by the Spaniards the Asturian Oviedo is as savage as the Sevilian.[222]

His emphasis is however different. It is not so much the crime against human-ity that grieves him but the offense against the interests of the sovereign; not politics prevailing over philanthropy, but a mistaken and shortsighted policy prevailing over a wise and farseeing policy. This aspect of Oviedo's attitude emerges so clearly that it should not have escaped Las Casas, even if the histo-rian had not expressed it with particular forcefulness in his criticism of Las Casas himself. The personal attack must have rekindled the smouldering resentment left by the court intrigues in Barcelona (1519) and transformed Oviedo, in the friar's inflamed imagination, into the prototype of the slanderer of the natives and one of their most typical oppressors. Even disregarding the chronological coinci-dence that Las Casas turned entirely to Indiophile preaching in the very year (1514) that Oviedo took up his post as an official in the Indies, it is a fact that Las Casas abandoned the scenario of the conquest at the very moment Oviedo made his entrance.

It has to be admitted that Oviedo enjoyed himself at the expense of the cleric who, before his famous debate with Sepúlveda and before the New Laws, could have been taken for just one more fanatic. The chapter in the *History* that pictures

---

220. Salas, op. cit., pp. 168–69, 205–06, 287–94.

221. Manzoni, *I promessi sposi,* chap. 5, which also refers to the fetial priests, on whom see above, sec. 23.

222. Moses writes (op. cit., p. 37) that Oviedo defended government policy, but goes on to say that he made "an attempt less radical than that of Las Casas to improve Spain's colonial administration" (p. 41). And this attempt, so he claims, consisted merely of Oviedo's well-known missions to Spain, to present his accusations and protests, and have governors replaced; while unlike Las Casas (the two descriptions are reproduced one after the other) he apparently remained quite unmoved as he recounted the highly dangerous practise of pearl fishing (pp. 50–54).

Henríquez Ureña gets closer to the truth when he says (in *Literary Currents,* p. 19) that all the charges contained in Las Casas's *Brevísima relación* were already present in Oviedo, although he was "completely and utterly the antithesis of Las Casas" (Salas, op. cit., p. 259). Bernal Díaz del Castillo too, for that matter, disagrees with Las Casas, and on the strength of Fray Toribio de Motolinía's authority reaffirms the need for severe punishments and reprisals, for the Indians to be "taught a lesson" if serious troubles are to be avoided and idolatry eradicated (op. cit., pp. 154–56). Thus I would be inclined to reverse the verdicts of Juan Natalicio González and Fernando Márquez Miranda, for whom Oviedo represents the Old World and Las Casas the young Americas: Oviedo stood for the reality of America, while Las Casas stood for Christian ideals that were outdated even in Europe and even if they could invoke the world to come; see Hanke, *Mankind,* p. 39.

him as the evangelizer of the "pacified" (in other words subjugated) cacique Don Enrique, without the knowledge or permission of the Audiencia and to its extreme displeasure and anxiety, as it "feared" that it might unsettle the very recently established peace—this chapter, though eulogistic in tone, already betrays a certain irony ("in the monastery of Santo Domingo . . . there was a friar called Fra Bartolomé de Las Casas. . . , who had not previously been in everyone's favor . . . because of a certain business . . . but . . . he may have meant well"),[223] but the further chapter devoted to his dealings is one long satire, muffled in tone but of exquisite insolence.

30. OVIEDO'S SATIRE

Oviedo narrates how in 1519 he was at court for the affairs of Tierra Firme "and there was a certain reverend father going about there, a priest, by name Licentiate Bartolomé de Las Casas."[224] Backed by "some Flemish gentlemen," promising "great things and much profit and increase in the royal income," vouching that he would convert all idolaters, so that "it seemed that his aim and intent was holy," accusing the experts of bad faith and corruption, "he was to be seen there day after day, submitting memoranda and petitions."

The accused experts put up a stout defence, the sovereign decided in their favor, and then the friar claimed that he had been misunderstood, that he had not wanted to take a band of savage soldiers or bloodthirsty warriors to the Indies, "but very peaceful and gentle working folk—and he would make these people nobles and knights with golden spurs." And the king in his generosity let him have his way, despite being advised to the contrary by various of his most authoritative counselors (among whom it is not difficult to make out Oviedo himself, modestly unnamed).[225] And the friar, "pursuing his flights of fancy," went off with his "peasants, his new knights with golden spurs" to Cumaná, that he imagined to be at peace and therefore easily convertible into an evangelical utopia. But the Indians had meanwhile revolted and massacred the Christians and made ready to do the same with Las Casas's followers, "all full of hope for the new knighthood promised to them."

In Oviedo's description Las Casas figures as a sort of Don Quixote *avant-*

---

223. *Hist.*, V, 11: I, 157–58.

224. Ibid., XIX, 5: I, 599a. Note that reference to Las Casas "going about there," presenting Las Casas as a loafer, a vagabond, unlike Oviedo, who is all involved in weighty political negotiations. Las Casas himself was to admit that he had made "some money" from trading in provisions, indeed "quite a lot," enough for him to "stay at court" for a number of years, with no money worries (Bataillon, *Etudes sur Las Casas*, p. 29n; cf. p. 79).

225. According to Las Casas, Oviedo was in fact his main opponent, both because "he was very well spoken, loquacious, and . . . very good at presenting his case," and because he was quoted as a particular expert, having only recently arrived from the Indies. The bishop of Burgos, the ringleader of Las Casas's enemies, sent Oviedo to the lord chancellor (Gattinara) and entrusted one of Gattinara's men with the task of introducing Oviedo as the right man: "Tell the lord chancellor that this gentleman, a servant of the king, and just come from the Indies, will give him very accurate information on the Tierra Firme" (Las Casas, *Historia de las Indias*, bk. III, chap. 139, ed. cit., III, 288–89). On the attempts that Oviedo himself then made to have Las Casas discredited, and the mutual rivalry, see Bataillon, *Etudes sur Las Casas*, pp. 77–72n.

lettre, without the ingenuous nobility of Cervantes's character. But his colonists, "those simple and greedy peasants that followed him at the mere whiff of the promised knighthood and his fables," are thoroughgoing quixoticized Sancho Panzas. The undertaking comes to grief, and Las Casas, lacking the wherewithal to settle the damages, has the bright idea "that by prayer and sacrifice . . . he would partially be able to satisfy the dead and would not have to contend any further with the living." He becomes a monk, shuts himself up in a monastery, and was "in truth considered a good religious," Oviedo admits, though maliciously going straight on to add, "and I can well believe that he will be a better monk than captain in Cumaná."[226]

Toward 1536 the turbulent friar was again severely condemned by another royal official, Rodrigo de Contreras of Segovia, Pedrarias's son-in-law and successor as governor of Nicaragua, and a good friend of Oviedo, who not only speaks favorably of him on a number of occasions but also invokes his testimony against that of, among others, Las Casas (on the dimensions of the volcano of Masaya). Contreras in fact described the cleric as "a very restless and harmful man," who mounted his pulpit to preach "whenever he had suffered some annoyance or setback," ignoring the maxims of the Gospel and scandalizing the faithful.[227]

There is also one final remark that betrays a certain professional jealousy on Oviedo's part, and perhaps some uneasiness at what the fiery apostle might write. "They say that he is writing about these things of the Indies as a pastime," but this pastime might not be altogether innocent "and it would be good that in due course it should be shown, so that those that are eyewitnesses can approve it or answer for themselves."[228] Las Casas did not show what he was writing either to his inquisitive colleague or to anyone else, but when the first part of Oviedo's

---

226. *Hist.,* XIX, 5: I, 601b. The editor of Sepúlveda's *Opera* (1780) described Oviedo's mockery as "quite humorous reading," and both A. M. Fabié (*Vida y escritos de Fray Bartolomé de Las Casas,* in *CDIE,* vols. LXX, LXXI), and Bataillon write that in his attack on Las Casas Oviedo resorts to "the invincible weapons of ridicule," showing a "scornful indulgence"; but they try to set the story straight, or rather the legend attested to by Oviedo and followed by Gómara (*Etudes sur Las Casas,* pp. 115–23). Salas too, op. cit., p. 175, follows and somewhat exaggerates Bataillon.

This account would appear to be the source of the similar stories in Girolamo Benzoni, who also concludes that Las Casas took the right step in becoming a monk rather than going back to Cubagua to fish for pearls (ed. cit., pp. 37–40; trans. W. H. Smyth [London, 1857], pp. 48–50), and in the "awesome great book" by Oviedo's friend and in part rival, Juan de Castellanos, *Elegías de varones ilustres de Indias* (Madrid, 1847), p. 147; see Menéndez Pelayo, *Poesía hispano-americana,* I, 414–22.

227. Salas, op. cit., p. 184, with no indication of source. Cf. *Hist.,* XLII, 5, 6, 11, 14, 16: PT, IV, 395, 400, 409–13, 430–32. For further insults and affronts suffered by Las Casas as bishop ("get that madman out of here") and from the mouth of Motolinía (who uses the same words as Contreras), see Salas, op. cit., pp. 190, 192, 202.

228. *Hist.,* XIX, 5: I, 602a. Cf. Salas, op. cit., p. 208. The rest of the chapter rounds off the satire on the subject of good intentions combined with military inexperince. Las Casas embarked on his history in 1527, took it up again in 1552, finished it, or rather left it broken off in 1561, and ordered it to be kept secret for forty years after his death. It was published for the first time in 1875–76. But in 1552 he had already brought out the notorious *Brevísima destrucción de las Indias,* to which Oviedo never makes the least allusion, just as he totally ignores López de Gómara's *Historia de las Indias* (1552), unless a couple of vague passages in the *Historia* (XXXIII, 56: PT, IV, 265; L. 30: PT, V, 417) are taken to be alluding to Gómara. See Salas, op. cit., pp. 80, 95.

History was published in 1535 he read what Oviedo had written about his enterprise. He was no little annoyed at the historian's sarcasms and when he was appointed bishop of Chiapa complained bitterly about Oviedo to the bishop of San Juan, Don Rodrigo di Bastidas, and asked him to bring his remonstrations to Oviedo's attention, "so that he would tell me [Oviedo writes] and so he did."[229]

Oviedo replied—as he himself told the story, as he was chatting one September evening in 1544 with the Mexican Juan Cano, a little before the Ave Maria, when Cano was on the point of embarking—equally impertinently. "The reply that I gave to his complaint was not given to satisfy the bishop of Chiapa, but the authority and goodness of the lord bishop of San Juan and his pious wish; and in reply I begged him to tell him that in truth it was not my concern or interest, when I wrote that, to bring him pain or pleasure, but simply to say what happened"; and would he also tell him that the book had been printed and translated and was available for anyone to read; and if the bishop of Chiapa "went ahead with further enterprises," he, Oviedo, as His Majesty's historian, would recount them, and he hoped they would be more successful than the first, "and then in future he would like my pen better." A regular telling-off, laced with all the chronicler's customary self-assurance.

The "noble" bishop of San Juan professed himself satisfied. And the bishop of Chiapa too "remained satisfied"—so Oviedo assures us, forgetting that only a moment earlier he had said that he could not discuss matters with Las Casas because "he and I are not on very good terms"; but still he cannot resist a parting shot: "He remained satisfied, although I do not make it my business to satisfy his palate or any other, but to accomplish what I must."[230]

Having thus clarified the "personal angle" Oviedo proceeds to give free rein to his satirical inventiveness, in a passage that we have already quoted (above, end of sec. 17), but whose biting and subtle savagery we can now more fully appreciate.

At the opening of book XXVI Oviedo again harks back to the events of 1519 and, without actually naming him, launches into an oblique attack on Las Casas. Three people asked His Majesty for governorships: one, Oviedo himself,[231]

---

229. *Hist.*, XXXIII, 54: III, 552b. Don Rodrigo de Bastidas, bishop of San Juan, was the son of the Rodrigo de Bastidas, governor of Santa Marta, who had (in 1527) invaded the governorship of Cartagena destined for Oviedo (who therefore declined the post); the son was a close friend of Oviedo, and it was Oviedo who put forward his name to the emperor in 1554 as successor to the archbishop and captain-general of Santo Domingo, Alonso de Fuenmayor, who had held these positions since 1549 and seemed to be on the point of death; even before that Oviedo had given one of his daughters in marriage to one of Bastidas's nephews, also called Rodrigo de Bastidas (Amador de los Ríos, "Vida," p. liv*n*28, pp. lxxviii–lxxix). Oviedo petitioned successfully for his office of *alcaide* of Santo Domingo to be transferred to this son-in-law (1556; Amador de los Ríos "Vida," p. lxxix).

230. *Hist.*, XXXIII, 54: III, 552–53. By 1544 Las Casas was already famous. In that very year he took up the post of bishop of Chiapa. Juan Cano says of him, with a certain irony, that "he was the mover and inventor of these changes [in the liberty of the Indians] and has a large number of young friars in his Order" (ibid.). On the quarrel, see also Amador de los Ríos, "Vida," pp. ci–ciii.

231. Cf. in fact *Hist.*, XXVI, 3: II, 337b.

asked for and got Santa Marta, although on certain conditions that he could not accept; another[232] asked for Trinidad, but "as he was a suspect person and there was some doubt as to whether he could accomplish what he promised," he was not granted his request; "the third only wanted simple peasants, and to turn them into knights and give them habits with a few crosses what would look something like the Order of Calatrava, and this person told all sorts of fables and promised numerous things and was more successful, eventually being granted the favor he requested, and he caused His Majesty to waste a lot of money. But he failed to carry out any of the things he had offered to do." Mistrusting, perhaps, the memory or perspicacity of his readers, and anxious to ensure that the transparent allusion is not missed, Oviedo hastily adds, "and it has already been said who this person was, when we were discussing the island of Cubagua in book XIX of the first part of these histories." Chapter and verse, as they say; and Las Casas is put in his place once again.[233]

How far Las Casas was from being satisfied, Oviedo's bold assertion notwithstanding, becomes abundantly clear in his *History of the Indies*.[234] Oviedo and Gómara are his *bêtes noires*, but Oviedo in particular because he was the source for Gómara,[235] and because he was guilty in both deed and written word. Las Casas starts out by refuting the recent theory ("a certain new idea") that the Indies belonged to Hesperus or can be identified with the Hesperides—a ridiculous and fallacious thesis, invented by Oviedo, "the first person to dream up this curious notion"[236]—and goes on to reproach him for having said that the Indians were "all sodomites," which must lie heavy on his conscience, and which he takes as grounds for demanding that Oviedo's "false history . . . should have a preface explaining how its author had been a conqueror, robber, and killer of Indians," to ensure that nobody believes what it says.[237] Then, to cap it all, he

---

232. Rodrigo de Bastidas? Cf. ibid., pp. 335–36.

233. Ibid., XXVI, 1: II, 333–34. Another probable allusion to Las Casas by Oviedo occurs in the passage in which he attacks "those vicious tracts, quite fantastic and without a shred of truth, that people have been composing and publishing here recently . . . as if they were true stories" (XXIX, 25: III, 124b). Oviedo was writing after 1542 (cf. ibid., p. 124a); and in 1542 Las Casas had written his *Veynte razones* and presented the emperor with his shocking *Brevísima relación* (printed only in 1552 however). The passage in Oviedo comes before a chapter dealing with the vices and idolatry of the Cueva Indians, but it remains deliberately vague, concluding: "I do not wish to name the books or the authors I am criticizing."

234. It will also be remembered that, according to Gómara (*Anales del Emperador Carlos V*, 1548), Las Casas tried to "obstruct the general and natural history of the Indies that Gonzalo Hernández de Oviedo showed the Council of Castile, with a view to publication" (cited in Rey, op. cit., p. 56). Cf. above, chap. XIV, n. 5; Salas, op. cit., pp. 199, 208, 288.

235. "A cleric called Gómara . . . took from Oviedo's history everything false about the cleric Casas" (Las Casas, *Historia de las Indias*, bk. III, chap. 142, ed. cit., III, 299); "he said everything Oviedo said, because he took it from Oviedo's book, and added some highly improper things" (bk. III, chap. 160, ed. cit., III, 364).

236. Ibid., bk. I, chaps. 15–16, ed. cit., I, 75–91. Oviedo's proof that the ancients used to name lands discovered or conquered after the discoverer is ridiculed as a dream or absurd guess. The polemic against Oviedo's cosmographic theories continues on p. 86, where Oviedo is accused of having misunderstood Julius Solinus's Latin. Cf. above, chap. XVIII, sec. 11.

237. Las Casas, *Historia de las Indias*, bk. III, chap. 24, ed. cit., II, 463–64. In his polemic against Sepúlveda, who had quoted Oviedo's *Historia* as an authority, Las Casas describes the work as "totally false and its author a tyrant

gives his own version of the quarrel of 1519, in which he relates that Oviedo was humiliated and disappointed (he must in fact have been among the counselors who sought to dissuade the emperor) and that was why in his account he had falsely portrayed Las Casas as greedy for power and command and had left out the greater part of the truth, mixing it with numerous lies detrimental to the Indians, "as he always did, being one of their chief enemies."[238]

31. LAS CASAS DEFENDS THE INDIANS

This is Las Casas's cue for five entire chapters devoted to defending the Indians and discrediting Oviedo.

The first part of this task commences with the charge of sodomy, which is simply dismissed as totally unfounded. As for the Indians' laziness, if they are disinclined to work this is because "they are by nature extremely delicate, like sons of princes," and anyway no one is "as idle, useless, or lazy" as the Spanish immigrants in the Indies.[239] As for their indulgence in savage internecine wars, "they do have the odd skirmish . . . but they are all like children's games and are soon settled." Their customs such as "urinating while seated and breaking wind in front of others" are minor peccadilloes, and their forgetfulness, untruthfulness, fickleness, and cruelty are likewise explained away.

As for Oviedo, indeed "Señor Oviedo" or "our good Oviedo," he is discredited first and foremost on the basis of his abysmal ignorance, "as he does not even know what Latin is."[240] Moreover he knows nothing about the Indians, having lived only five years in Darien, and has "never had anything to do with the Indians." He subsequently settles in Santo Domingo, "which is just the same as if

---

and enemy of the Indians" (*Colección de tratados, 1552–1553* [Buenos Aires, 1924], pp. 188–90, cited by Zavala, "Las Casas ante la doctrina de la servidumbre natural," *Revista de la Universidad de Buenos Aires,* 3d. ser., 2, no. 1 [1944], p. 48).

Sepúlveda had based himself on the passage in the *Historia* (III, 6: I, 72) in which Oviedo seeks an explanation for the destruction of the Indians on Hispaniola, who were reduced from the million or so that Columbus found there to less than five hundred by 1548 (the passage is therefore absent in the first edition, the only one known to Las Casas); and after listing the crimes of the Spaniards, and natural factors, such as epidemics, he adds that God in his justness must have permitted the slaughter because of the Indians' heinous sins, a generic and moralistic explanation rendered almost ridiculous by the addition that God had forgotten the Indians for a long time and when something jogged His memory and He suddenly remembered them—by a curious coincidence, apparently at the precise moment of the Spanish discovery and conquest of the Indies—He saw (as once before with the descendants of Adam, *Genesis,* VI, 5–6) that their wickedness was so great that He "allowed their lives to be ended. . . ."

238. *Historia de las Indias,* bk. III, chap. 142, ed. cit., III, 298.

239. Salas, op. cit., pp. 265–67.

240. Las Casas continues venomously, "although he quotes certain authorities in that language, which he persuaded certain clerics who were on their way through Santo Domingo to explain to him by dint of much begging and beseeching" (bk. III, chap. 143, ed. cit., III, 302). In another work, certainly unknown to Las Casas, Oviedo does in fact say that he consulted "a devout and scholarly churchman" on a point in the life of Trajan, and the "churchman" found the information sought in Saint Thomas! (*Qu.,* p. 336). Las Casas also claims (p. 304) that Oviedo's Pliny was "not in Latin but in Tuscan"; see however above, chap. XV, n. 63, and below, chap. XXI, n. 17. Another reflection of Las Casas's Latinity can be seen in the frequency with which he cites Peter Martyr, whom Oviedo, as we know, accused of knowing a lot of Latin and not much about the Indies: "No one is more reliable than Peter Martyr, who wrote his *Decades* in Latin" ("Prólogo" to the *Historia de las Indias,* ed. cit., I, 19; cf. bk. I, chap. 96, ed. cit., I', 400 and passim; but Martyr's authority is denied when he speaks ill of the Indians—bk. III, chap. 70, ed. cit., III, 29).

he had written his works while living in Seville," and he looks on the natives "exactly as if they were ants or bedbugs." Furthermore, Las Casas claims, ignoring the glaring contradiction, he enriched himself at the expense of the Indians. And even if one were to admit that he wrote in good faith, he let himself be taken in by false evidence, or trusted to conjectures and guesses. Lastly the reader is reminded that he was a cruel and bloodthirsty tyrant: "Here you have the conquistador Oviedo"![241]

To sum up, so great is the "falseness and lack of perception of this Oviedo" that in his whole writing "and in all his prattle" one can only believe what he writes about the trees and grasses of Santo Domingo and the Tierra Firme, "because he saw them and anybody who wants to see them can see them."[242] So extensive is the indictment that Las Casas himself seems to heave a sigh of relief when he reaches the end, when, as he writes with triple underlining of totalities, he has shown "that Oviedo slandered *all* these people of *all* this world and recklessly destroyed them before the *whole* world"[243]—and he can pick up the thread of his history again.

32. RELATIONS BETWEEN SPANIARDS AND INDIANS

We too might close our digression, then, and go on to see how Oviedo viewed relations between Spaniards and Indians, those relations that Las Casas saw unilaterally as savage oppression of the latter by the former. Oviedo, more balanced, and at heart more human, describes them as being in a state of per-

---

241. *Historia de las Indias,* bk. III, chap. 142, ed. cit., III, 299. According to Carbia, Las Casas's hatred of Oviedo is due not to the fact that Oviedo "had been a conquistador" but to his having "recounted details of his life that did him little credit" ("Oviedo, Las Casas y Caddeo," p. 93). See also Carbia, *La nueva historia,* p. 128n, citing other passages in Las Casas reviling Oviedo. There is some truth in those accusations and insinuations, but such a significant conflict cannot be reduced to the level of mere anecdote or tittle-tattle (see above, sec. 29). Nor can one accept Salas's conclusion that Las Casas's attacks on Oviedo had a "deadly accuracy" (op. cit., p. 120n).

242. *Historia de las Indias,* bk. III, chap. 142, ed. cit., III, 302. Thus despite all his resentment Las Casas recognizes Oviedo's importance as a describer of American nature. He also notes, snidely but quite justly, "how repeatedly, emphatically, and extremely arrogantly" Oviedo insists that he reports the whole truth and nothing but the truth. And he shrewdly turns against Oviedo his own oft-used argument that no faith should be attached to any evidence save that of eye-witnesses: see above, chap. XVII, sec. 11.

It need hardly be added that Oviedo is slandered almost every time he is named in the *Historia de las Indias.* Las Casas deplores his "ill-considered" choice of witnesses (bk. I, chap. 109, ed. cit., I, 200); his falsehoods, fables, and "embroideries" (bk. I, chap. 109, ed. cit., I, 440–41); his zeal "to excuse the Spaniards' acts of tyranny" (bk. II, chaps. 1 and 57, ed. cit., II, 330); an imagined error on his part ("I know that this is not true," but actually Oviedo does not say it is—bk. II, chap. 5, ed. cit., II, 151); the claims of "this gentleman" to love the Indians (bk. II, chap. 10, ed. cit., II, 167); his use of the term "pacify" to mean "conquer" (bk. II, chap. 55, ed. cit., II, 325); his custom of describing "a lot of things that he did not see" (bk. III, chap. 24, ed. cit., II, 467–68), as for example the fact that at the Indian weddings all the male guests "had to act improperly with the bride," and the version that he gives in "the so-called natural History" (XIX, 5) of Las Casas's expedition to Cumaná (bk. III, chap. 160, ed. cit., III, 363–67). The *Apologética historia* too seems to have been written with the prime aim of refuting Oviedo's calumnies (cf. its opening sentences, ed. cit., III, 395, with the similar statements directed at Oviedo, in the *Historia de las Indias,* bk. III, chap. 143, ed. cit., III, 304). Oviedo's misdeeds as foundry inspector and as man of action are denounced in the *Historia de las Indias* in bk. III, chap. 59 (II, 585), chap. 106 (III, 166), chap. 139 (III, 287–88), chap. 141 (III, 297) and chap. 162 (III, 372).

243. *Historia de las Indias,* bk. III, chap. 147, ed. cit., III, 315. Oviedo in fact boasted exaggeratedly to Juan Cano, and precisely when they were talking about Las Casas, that his *Historia* had been translated into Italian, French, German, Latin, Greek, Turkish, and Arabic, so that it was read in all languages! (*Hist.,* XXXIII, 54: III, 552b).

petual but reciprocal tension. When there is no actual open warfare there is mutual distrust, deceit, and trickery. Oviedo himself, whose imagination had been so stirred by those stories of pugnacious female savages, happily tells us how he "tricked" the Indians of Darien, palming off five hundred little hatchets on them in exchange for a goodly sum of gold. The hatchets were in fact made of tin and old iron, from the hoops of empty barrels, and, to add insult to injury, he charged them the same again three months later for making them new axes to replace those that had of course lost their edge and did not cut, but which were in fact the old ones secretly ground and sharpened by his men "out of sight" and given back to the unsuspecting Indians as new ones.[244]

And those same Indians, who are sometimes pictured as so naive as to be incapable of lying, are at other times "the biggest liars in the world, and the most accustomed to not telling the truth"; as soon as they see that the Christians are looking for gold they assure them that they will find it further on, *adelante*, "to remove them from their land and send them where they will get killed or lost." If they knew what the Earthly Paradise was, "they would have offered them that too, time and again, all over the place."[245] Bogotá uses a very similar ruse to "remove the Christians from his land and pass on the turmoil to his enemy's house";[246] and Oviedo's verdict on information supplied by other Indians about the famous mines of Cuyrcuyr, and on a hut made of parrot feathers, full of gold, and a house of the devil, half gold and half stone, is that it "was all a hoax,"[247] just as the story of the famous fountain of youth, desperately sought for more than six months by Juan Ponce de León and his caravels (who did however discover Florida) "was a huge hoax on the part of the Indians and a very great act of madness on the part of the Christians to believe it."[248] And in fact, Oviedo observes sarcastically a little further on,[249] it is absolutely true that the fountain

---

244. *Hist.*, XXVI, 4: II, 341; for certain details see Pérez de Tudela, "Vida," p. lxxxi. Oviedo calculates that he cleared one thousand five hundred *castellanos* in the first transaction and more than seven thousand in the second. This must be one of the first admitted cases of "colonials" being sold low-quality manufactured goods, with built-in obsolescence, so that they would very soon be forced to buy more of the same shoddy goods. Some recent biographers have been shocked at these commercial sharp practices, and generously conjectured that Oviedo passed on some of the profit to business partners in Seville (Peña y Cámara, op. cit., pp. 609–10; on other "deals" made by Oviedo, see above, chap. XIV, n. 65, chap. XV, sec. 9). But in fact Magellan had done just the same, loading up four hundred dozen German knives of "very poor quality" but still good enough to buy the favors (doubtless of acceptable quality) of the Guarani girls (Morison, *Southern Voyages*, pp. 343, 361).

Oviedo also tells of bartering glass beads and little bells for various precious objects, the Indians never having seen those things, "which gave them plenty to look at, and almost no benefit whatsoever" (*Hist.*, XXVI, 22: II, 338b). He also recounts the story of a Nicaraguan cacique who gave him, in exchange for a small pocket sundial, another made with a precious stone (a pearl) as big as a double ducat, set in a "stone of very excellent jasper or green porphyry" (XLII, 11: IV, 95b), and how three Christians set up as witch doctors or quacks, treating Indians (XXXV, 5: III, 604–06). But in these cases there is no precise intention of swindling on the part of the Spaniard.

245. Peter Martyr had already reported that the Indians, "to remove our people from their frontiers, enquired what it was they wanted, and when they discovered they were seeking gold or food, pointed to distant places," etc., *Dec.*, V, 10, pp. 465–66.

246. *Hist.*, XXVI, 24: II, 392b.

247. Ibid., XXVII, 11: II, 458a.

248. Ibid., XVI, 11: I, 482b.

249. Ibid., XVI, 13: I, 486a.

does restore extreme youth to the aged, but only "in the weakening of the brain, so that they become infants once again and of little understanding in their acts," leading them, in fact, not to their youth, but to a state of dotage, a second childhood.

33. DELUSION AND DEPOPULATION

The Indians got away with this simple little trick innumerable times, even when its very repetition should have made the Spaniards more suspicious; and it made a decisive contribution to the appearance and persistent reappearance of the myth of El Dorado.[250] The conquistador's avarice made him an easy victim for the conquered Indian's defensive guile. A proverb that Oviedo himself recalls teaches us that the "swindler" and the "grasper" soon come to terms.[251] But Oviedo, who knows how illusory these mirages are, who more than once deplores the fact that his Hispaniola is going to rack and ruin because the adventurers sail off to the Tierra Firme, Peru, and elsewhere,[252] that the islands of Cuba and Jamaica are becoming depopulated and decaying because the restless colonists are flocking to Mexico,[253] who even saw men leaving Panama for the dreamed-of riches of Peru, and who doubtless fears a similar fate for the stronghold entrusted to his care and constantly threatened by pirates[254]— Oviedo, who puts the colonist before the conquistador, and the farmer before the treasure-hunter,[255] who is well aware of the constant mobility of the mining centers and has a few sharp things to say about it,[256] remains stubbornly skeptical.

This restlessness, this unhealthy greed and impatience lead to certain ruin. El Dorado does not exist. In Santo Domingo, Oviedo questioned ten or more Spaniards returning from Quito. What they told him, he in turn reports to his

250. In W. N. Merryman's *Northern Caballero* (London, 1942) the Indians' age-old ruse, described as a "discovery," is actually given as the origin of the myth of El Dorado (see review in the *Times Literary Supplement*, 11 April 1942).

251. *Hist.*, XXII, 3: PT, 81, 347a; XXIV, 4: PT, II, 403a; XXIV, 9: II, 406b.

252. Ibid., III, 10: I, 84a; V, 10: I, 156. Some returned to Spain in their old age. Almost all the ships plying between Spain and what was effectually the archipelago of the Indies, both island and continental, called in at Santo Domingo. The city was therefore the strategic base for the whole of the early colonial empire: "Most of the Indies have always been discovered and populated and supplied from here, as it were from the head and nourisher of all the other parts of this empire" (ibid.). Cf. above, chap. XVII, n. 204.

253. The process is described in dramatic terms in *Hist.*, XXXIII, 41: III, 473, and deplored but at the same time justified in XVII, 2: I, 495b: the Spaniards that come to the Indies are "young men anxious to make their way in the world . . . valiant and needy" and therefore "not content to come to a halt in the parts already conquered."

254. F. A. Kirkpatrick, *The Spanish Conquistadores* (London, 1943), pp. 138–39. But Oviedo was not really so worried: indeed, he wrote that Hispaniola would lose nothing as a result of the conquest of Mexico, because in Santo Domingo alone "there are numerous householders and rich men, who have no need of New Spain or the Tierra Firme; in fact all those external establishments and foundations have been and are still sustained from here" (*Hist.*, XXXIII, 41: III, 473b).

255. See above, chap. XVII, n. 206.

256. *Hist.*, XXIX, 27: III, 132b: "The villages are created and abandoned, according to how the gold goes. . . . the miners move on from river to river . . . shifting their homes . . . like the Arabs of Africa," etc., with a shrewd characterization of the goldminers' nomadic existence.

readers, coloring the report with a subtle and almost mocking irony. This great prince, El Dorado, goes about covered in fine gold dust, like powdered sunlight. Any other garment he would find less beautiful. The vulgar habit of wearing "pieces or arms of gold worked with a hammer or stamped" is something that the proud and naked Indian chieftain leaves to other lords and princes, if they so desire. But "dusting oneself with gold is something unusual and new and more costly," because every blessed day he throws away the precious garment (or should we say tegument?). "I would rather have the sweepings of this prince's chamber"—mocks Oviedo—"than those of the great gold foundries that once existed in Peru. . . ."[257]

This mutual trickery, with the Spaniards intent on getting the Indians to barter away their gold and the Indians equally determined to get rid of the dangerous and insistent and importunate visitors—reflects a state of tension and latent hostility. The Spaniards always have the initiative, but the Indians are fighting for their very existence, and in their own country, so that they can to some extent make up for their inferiority in martial skills. They are unwittingly seconded in their resistance by the nature of America, with its wild beasts and varied perils, and by the errors of the Spaniards, with their vanity, ambition, and reckless greed. But all these factors can barely even slow down the invasion, and certainly not halt or repel it. The ideological forces and accidental incentives urging them on to the western shores of the Atlantic are much stronger than the Indians. The Spaniards are few in number, a long way from their bases, and driven onward, ever onward, by need and greed, by the very mechanism of the discoveries, each of which opened the way to others, and by the essential logic of the situation, by which they would have been lost the moment they abandoned the initiative or as soon as their offensive onrush had slowed down, in the midst of hostile peoples. Equilibrium could only be restored through the extermination of the more savage tribes and the subjugation of the meeker ones. With the failure of conversion, which would have put victors and vanquished on an equal footing in a new Christian society, there remained only slaughter and slavery as the basic elements of a new political society. In the islands and in Central America the Indians perished as if wafted away by the activity of the Europeans (to adopt Hegel's metaphor); in the Peruvian and Mexican ex-empires, they succeeded in adapting and forming the lowest stratum of the new state system.

34. Oviedo's easy acquiescence

Time and again we have seen that Oviedo abhors violence and massacre. But when faced with the *fait accompli* his conscience is all too easily calmed, as he

---

257. Ibid., XLIX, 2: IV, 383a. Cf. Pérez de Tudela, "Vision de la découverte," pp. 274–75. On the Spaniards' skepticism about El Dorado see Gandía, *Mitos,* pp. 113–14; Pereyra, *Los conquistadores,* pp. 39, 350; C. Bayle, op. cit., p. 416. For a contrary view, Kirkpatrick, op. cit., p. 230: "Oviedo's mockery was not shared by his countrymen."

recalls the sins and vices and idolatry of the vanquished and postulates, in providential justification of their destruction, other sins and vices known only to God.[258] Once they are dead, *Dieu choisira les siens.*

All too conveniently Oviedo lists the crushing labors, the shortage of food, the inclination to melancholy and inconstancy, the suicides and plagues, to explain how the Indians on Haiti were reduced from the million or so "counting children and adults" they totaled at the time of the discovery to barely five hundred all told in 1548.[259] All too lightly he mentions in passing that the death of a Christian is a considerably more serious thing than the death of a thousand Indians.[260] All too casually does he acquit the Christians who used the massacred Indians' fat instead of oil and tallow to caulk Cortés's brigantines (see above, end of sec. 1).

But this does not mean that he absolves the murderers, either the glorious captains or the "private soldiers, who like veritable hangmen or headsmen or executioners or ministers of Satan wielded their swords and arms more vengefully than the teeth and nature of tigers and wolves, with various and innumerable and cruel deaths that they perpetrated, as uncountable as the stars."[261] For Oviedo there is an obvious and unavoidable fate implacably awaiting all those who have soiled their hands with the Indians' blood, a fate they will meet in this world even before the judgment of the next.[262]

His verdict is in fact harsh but impartial. This comes out more clearly in certain anecdotes, perhaps, than in the bombastic tirades and streams of invective. There is, for instance, a tone of mockery toward the Indian, but at the same time of reproof for the brutality of the Spaniards, in the story of the two caciques, Suegro and Quemado: the reader might think—Oviedo breaks in—that those are not Indians' names, and truth to tell Suegro was really called Mahé, but the Christians took from him "three or four daughters that he had . . . and for this hospitality and the adulteries of the sons-in-law, which he had not wanted, they called him Suegro (father-in-law). . . . As for the other cacique, that they called Quemado (the Burnt One), this was because in fact and quite without cause they burned him, because he did not give them as much gold as they asked him for. But let us get back to our history."[263]

---

258. E.g., *Hist.*, XXIX, 25: III, 124a.

259. Ibid., III, 6: I, 71b. The passage, ascribed to "a serious and assiduous historian," was used by Sepúlveda (cf. Landucci, op. cit., p. 94*n5*). On the suicides to avoid work, cf. VII, 2: PT, I, 233a.

This must be an instance of the "Lascasian statistics" for which Pereyra rebukes Oviedo (*Los conquistadores*, p. 316). Another would be those two million Indians killed in Castilla del Oro between 1514 and 1542 (*Hist.*, XXIX, 25: III, 124), or the (same?) two million slaughtered at the instigation of Pedrarias Dávila between 1514 and 1530, "without their being given any understanding of the *requerimiento* which the Catholic King ordered to be brought to their attention before war was waged on them"; and the figure would be even higher than two million, Oviedo adds, if it included those that were carried off into slavery (*Hist.*, XXIX, 34: III, 172a). On Oviedo's contempt for the formality of the *requerimiento*, incomprehensible to the Indians, see also above, sec. 21. Cf. Kirkpatrick, op. cit., p. 319*nl*.

260. *Hist.*, XXVI, 24: PT, III, 112a.

261. Ibid., XXIX, 34: III, 173b. An exception is made for some few virtuous and temperate men.

262. Salas, op. cit., p. 129.

263. *Hist.*, XXIX, 10: III, 44.

35. His implacable severity

"Let us get back to our history." Oviedo's habitual phrase for closing a digression here assumes the value of a deliberate averting of the eyes from the pointless and bestial crime. More than once he tells the guilty that he cannot stay silent, that there are witnesses for what he recounts and denounces; with despairing insistence he cries out that they are things that he knows for himself. "In my presence all these treasures were melted down . . . the scribes placed themselves at my command . . . the accounts of their works and merits came into my possession, and I saw them, and read and saw most of their *residencias*." So let them be thankful for what he does *not* say: if they will respect his pen "they will see that I have treated them as friends, and completely impartially. . . ." But judgment is pronounced just the same. "I am required to give account of how this land came to be almost deserted, without Indians; and the foundation and principal cause is what I said."[264] The blame lies with the "conquistadors who would more accurately be called depopulaters or squanderers of the new lands."[265] Atahualpa was a savage and bloody tyrant, who on feast days drank out of his brother's carefully cleaned, highly polished and gold-rimmed skull; but his killing "was no small crime."[266]

The catastrophic consequences of the slaughters are already clear to Oviedo and perhaps sometimes fan the flames of his moral indignation. These rampaging adventurers are ruining the sovereign's patrimony. They are worse than poachers on the Royal Reserve of the Indies. When Oviedo bewailed the fact that "the Indians died out" in Hispaniola, he inaugurated a long lament that was to reappear on the lips of viceroys and governors, lawyers and theologians throughout the centuries of the Spanish domination, and that would be faintly echoed in today's recurrent complaints about the "labor shortage" or "poverty of human capital." Just as those "hard and merciless" captains should of course have known that "without people there is no office and no captaincy,"[267] so the captains in Peru that "took away peaceful Indians, three or four thousand at a time, as laborers," ought to have realized that "only by some miracle does an Indian return," while most die, "and thus that wretched people will very soon die out," and it will no longer be possible for such a rich and promising land to "sustain itself."[268]

---

264. Ibid., XXIX, 10: III, 51b.
265. Ibid., XXX, 1: III, 179b; VI, 22: PT, I, 191.
266. Ibid., VI, 22: PT, I, 191. Cunimondo "never had it so good": at least in Giovanni Prati's ballad ("Una cena d'Alboino re"), his skull is "unadorned."
267. *Hist.*, XXIX, 2: III, 7a.
268. Ibid., XLVII, 20: IV, 347.

36. Practical consequences of exploitation

The demands of production bring ruin and death to the selfsame basic factors of production. Unrestrained exploitation destroys itself and frustrates the greedy hopes of any further exploitation. The metal mined kills the miner and thus rules out any possibility of extracting more metals from the stratified bowels of the earth. This fearful antithesis, that was to torment the whole economy of the viceroyalties and to surface in protean variety of form in the timberyards, plantations, in the dry and dusty guano islands and in the forests oozing resins and gums, the antithesis between producer and product, between man and metal, between blood and gold, is hardly touched on by Oviedo.[269] But the anguish inherent in it, the mystery of its inexorable necessity, assails him ceaselessly.

The dull gleam of the accursed gold alternates, like the flashes of a lighthouse in the night, with the warm solar rays of the gold flowing from the Darien foundries into the holds of the galleons, into His Majesty's groaning coffers. Gold is power, and gold is damnation. It is gold that underpins Spain's political might, but it is also gold that destroys the prosperity of the colonies (the colonies first of all, and then the mother country, but Oviedo does not see that far ahead). Gold is the motive that lures everyone to the Indies, and gold is the surest factor in their ruin.[270] Yes, laymen and religious, "each and every one, and all other people, of whatever quality they are, cross the ocean for their own profit."[271]

37. The yellow of gold on the faces

And almost all are punished for their frenzied greed (the moral tone is almost always there); and all, more or less, are shown as resembling those Spaniards who, having come to the Indies to seek gold, go back to Spain with their faces the color of gold, "though not with the same luster"—Oviedo cruelly insists—"but looking like citrons, the color of saffron or jaundice, and so sick that they quickly succumb."[272]

269. In another small work I plan to develop certain typical aspects of this antithesis and its repercussions on the thinking of the mercantilists on the one hand and on the humanitarian tendencies on the other.

270. Oviedo's shudder of horror foreshadows the bewilderment that was so much later to grip the heart of Madame de Staël and lead her to condemn that heroic "greed for wealth" ("avidité de fortune," a precise translation of the Spanish *cobdiçia,* the term that Oviedo always uses), which "has something very somber about it when it leads men to risk their lives" (*Corinne,* I, 4 [Paris, 1858], II, 437).

271. *Hist.,* XXXII, 2: III, 223a. To describe his hero, Almagro, Oviedo knows no higher praise than to say that he is not driven by greed and only covets treasure so that he can share it out among his followers (XLVII, 19: IV, 341–42).

This covetousness remains Oviedo's *bête noire,* the vice from which he was not completely immune himself, but from which he never derived any appreciable profit, a fact that if anything increased his revulsion for it. In the *Quinquagenas* he repeats his all-embracing complaint: "The way things are today, covetousness very largely rules the world" (*Qu.,* p. 80; cf. pp. 90, 398–99, 435: most of these greedy adventurers are dead or ruined).

272. *Hist.,* II, 13: I, 50; cf. III, 4: I, 64a. The origins of this *topos* can be traced back to that tedious first-century Latin poet Silius Italicus (25–101 A.D., possibly Spanish), according to whom ". . . the greedy Asturian dives into the deepest entrails of the mutilated earth, and the unhappy wretch returns the same color as the gold he has dug out" (*Punica,* I [Paris, 1837], p. 218, col. 2; cf. H. Ellis, *The Soul of Spain* [London, 1937], p. 35). Silius's poem was rediscovered in the early fifteenth century. And Juan de Mena was already writing in one of his *coplas,* "Gold turns the goldminer yellow" (cited by Bataillon, "Montaigne et les conquérants de l'or," *Studi Francesi,* 9 [1959], p. 365, where Oviedo's *Historia,* XXX, 1, is also mentioned).

Death sets its imprint on those faces, with a mask as yellow as the metal itself.[273] The macabre fantasy, with its Holbeinesque hint of a fatal and indissoluble link between production and death, between gold and blood, with the blood becoming as pale as gold, was to be taken up and varied in countless metaphors, by Oviedo himself, by Las Casas, again in the seventeenth century, and even in our own times.

The gold of the Indies "is such a great amount that it cannot be comprehended in its infinity," but if one looks carefully "the gold here is more expensive than can be imagined by fools or wise men, or estimated by the covetous, because for one man to be rich, twenty and even a hundred men lose their lives."[274] With a sinisterly baroque image Oviedo warns that repentance comes too late to avoid the "palpable deaths that in these parts are set in mounts of gold and emeralds, the gold and emeralds that many seek and few enjoy."[275]

38. FUNDAMENTAL CONTRADICTION IN THE *HISTORY*

It is this agonizing realization—the knowledge that these lofty enterprises are inspired by the basest of motives, that it is vile greed driving the arms and banners of Castile on across the oceans and deserts to discover new worlds and lay low age-old empires, to destroy the natives and themselves in the awesome attrition of that first collision and fiery contact—that gives rise to the most strident contradiction in Oviedo's *History*. He is unwavering in his enthusiasm

---

This facile image spread rapidly among the early chroniclers of the Indies, who were already applying it to the veterans of Columbus's second voyage (1496). When Peter Martyr describes his guests Quicedo and Colmenares, freshly returned from the noxious land of Darien, he adds that "one has only to see their faces to realize how unfriendly the air of Darien is: they are yellow, as if they were jaundiced, and all swollen," which the gentlemen in question proudly ascribe to the "fearful deprivations" they suffered (*Dec.*, II, 7, p. 176, also quoted by Humboldt, *Examen critique*, V, 164*n*); and the settlers in Santa María del Antigua "are all pallid, like people with liver complaints" (*Dec.*, I, 6, p. 273). Of Juan de Quicedo, whom he succeeded (1513) as foundry inspector in Pedrarias's expedition, Oviedo writes that before he could reembark for the Indies in Seville "he died, swollen up, and as yellow as the gold he had gone to find" (*Hist.*, XXIX, 1: III, 4b). Oviedo could not of course resist such a moralistic image! But elsewhere he gives a rational explanation for their yellow skins: they ate the fruit of the *manaca* palm, having nothing else, "and it left their faces and their bodies very yellow; and those of them that returned to Spain had faces like this, the color of saffron or clay and worse" (*Hist.*, IX, 4: I, 332b).

273. Petrarch had already ascribed the yellowish and sickly complexion of many doctors to their insatiable thirst for gold and the time they spent staring at their patients' yellow urine! (*Invective contra medicum*, ed. P. G. Ricci [Rome, 1951], cited by A. Baldini in "Tastiera," *Corriere della Sera*, 17 May 1951). And another poet, closer to Oviedo's time, Ronsard, was to yearn (1555) for those blessed days "when sailors were not yet turning pale, on Tethys's back, seeking hoards of gold."

According to certain psychoanalysts the mental association between gold and feces (based mainly on objectively chromatic grounds, but with reflections of the pathological paleness of the miser) is typical of the desire for gain rooted in anal eroticism (examples and bibliography in Ernest Jones, *Traité théorique et pratique de psychanalyse* [Paris, 1925], pp. 879–81).

274. *Hist.*, XXXII, 2: III, 224.

275. Ibid., XXXII, 3: III, 232a. Nor are gold and jewels alone in being stained with blood. The valuable furs too cost sufferings and human lives: "Oh sable martens! I do believe that if those garments worn daily in winter by the princes and great lords of Europe were obtained at the price paid for that covering [i.e., privation and hunger to the point that the Spaniards "were food for each other"] they would prize them more highly; but the clothes are bought with money, and the furs with blood and lives" (ibid., XXXV, 3: III, 596b).

for gold, but indefatigable in his curse on riches. Addressing the sovereign, he extols the unlimited opulence of the royal possessions with adulatory eloquence. Addressing the Spaniards, he turns his oratorical skills to sermonizing on the fatal physical and moral consequences of this greed for treasure, the countless deaths and damnations it has caused. The contradiction is clear, and acutely felt, and finds no appeasement in some higher harmony. It is the aporia inherent in the pragmatic view of history, blind to the fact that the deed transcends the individual's intention, that history is act and process, not datum or result. It is in essence the mystery of political action that worries Oviedo, the mystery that two centuries later was to trouble the mind of Justus Möser.[276]

How can rapine produce an epic? How does the dim rapacity of the Westphalian peasant give rise to the firm and solemn tread of history? How can an empire be founded on covetousness? How can the actions of lowly individuals, driven by crude egoism—whether rustic German bumpkins or desperate Iberian adventurers—undergo transfiguration into the great undertakings that Clio engraves on the bronze tablets of the centuries? How do vices become great deeds? "How do deeds become history?"[277] Oviedo, one need hardly say, does not postulate the problem with the rigor and precision of the Romantics. But he has some inkling of it, and it grieves him.

In the same way, although he sees gold and the pursuit of riches as the mainspring of all Spain's political, civilizing, and evangelizing action, he cannot really be portrayed as a precursor of historical materialism. It is however true to say that when he finds himself face to face with one of the greatest manifestations of commercial enterprise and economic expansionism known to history, with the first great colonial experiment of modern times, Oviedo makes no attempt to evade the questions it raises, to worm his way out of it with facile formulas derived from a medieval theodicy. He frankly states the two irreconcilable extremes of the—to him—insoluble aporia and prefers to remain speared on the horns of the dilemma, rather than turning them over and burying them ostrich-fashion in the ground. He is no "historical materialist," then, but he is one of the very first historians to have taken the material instinct, the unceasing quest for terrestrial benefits, the Jeffersonian pursuit of happiness, as the protagonist of his history, indeed of all history.

Oviedo never voices his doubt in strictly historiographical terms, either, as he does, for instance, in contrasting things seen and things reported. But his preference for painting the world of nature, for telling the history of plants and animals, is undoubtedly linked in some degree to their greater scientific tran-

---

276. For more detailed treatment of the problems involved see A. Gerbi, *La politica del romanticismo* (Bari, 1932), pp. 23–24.

277. J. G. Droysen, *Historik* (Munich and Berlin, 1937), p. 322. Droysen sees this as a key problem and restates it in almost the same words on pp. 28, 394, and 421 of the same work; it was subsequently taken up by Simmel and later by Masur (see Meinecke, "J. G. Droysen" in *Staat und Persönlichkeit* [Berlin, 1933], p. 133).

quillity and reassuring ethical certainty. In those domains, doubt does not and cannot arise. The observer's mind finds perfect calm in portraying the physical world and full satisfaction in the richness and consistency of the material, instead of the nagging logical and moral torment provoked by the deeds of the conquistadors.

39. PRECIOUS METALS AND SPICES

Oviedo's enthusiasm for gold, for the extraordinary abundance of gold in the Indies and the fact that whole "potfuls" of precious metals can be collected with no trouble at all, is so well known and almost proverbial that specific examples would seem to be superfluous. But it may still be worthwhile stressing that during the years in which Oviedo was working on his *History,* precious metals emerged as the principal and almost only product sent from the Indies to Spain and thus as the very *raison d'être* of the colonies and empire.

The first voyages of exploration, including Columbus's, had been almost as much concerned with finding spices as with finding gold, the Moluccas as much as "Cipango." Between the 1200s and the end of the Middle Ages spices had once again, as in the first seven centuries of the Christian era,[278] become the most important commodity brought back from the East, being indispensable as an aid to digesting the undercooked meat that was then so widely consumed, appreciated for their aphrodisiac qualities and prized for their very rarity, high price, and unusual and surprising taste, three attributes which made them a typical luxury article (like today's truffles and caviar).[279] Spices—pepper, cloves, cinnamon, saffron, seasonings that mean no more to us than childhood memories of the pungent surprises that greeted us when we poked our noses into the neighborhood grocer's storeroom—then conjured up images of royal banquets, of gastronomic festive splendors, of precious cargoes borne with jealous care from the Sea of Sunda to Venetian and Portuguese warehouses. The diffusion of Arab medicine also contributed to the pharmaceutical prestige of the drugs of the Orient.

Little gold was found in the islands and lands discovered by Columbus, and no spices at all. Indeed Michele da Cuneo mentions that when the "blessed gold" was found he and his companions gave no further thought to spices. And in the

---

278. See the surprising statistics in H. Pirenne, *Mahomet et Charlemagne,* 2d ed. (Paris, 1937), pp. 71–73, 149–51. For more recent times see also G. D'Avenel, *Le nivellement des jouissances* (Paris, 1913), pp. 90–93; F. Braudel, *Civilisation matérielle et capitalisme* (Paris, 1967), pp. 162–65; Morison, *Southern Voyages,* pp. 447, 452; and the sound article by Gino Luzzato and Margherita Guarducci, in the *Enciclopedia Italiana,* s.v. "Spezie." The spice trade is picturesquely evoked, and its fabled aspects well brought out, in Zweig, op. cit., pp. 17–24. Even the austere *Mayflower* pilgrims "searched the Plymouth thicket for spices" (A. Nevins and H. Steele Commager, *America, The Story of a Free People* [Oxford, 1943], p. 27).

279. Among the secondary—though in certain periods at least by no means negligible—uses of spices one might mention their adoption in medications (whence the Italian term "speziale" (grocer), which originally meant "apothecary"), in cosmetics and salves (spikenard, etc.), and in religious services (the classic and portentous example here being of course the myrrh and frankincense offered by the Wise Men to the Infant Jesus).

end the expeditions by the Genoese left King Ferdinand with heavy debts. The thirst for gold remained largely unquenched until the treasures of Mexico began to arrive in Spain, followed by those of Peru. And Oviedo's paeans of praise for the limitless wealth of the gold seams of Hispaniola are obviously somewhat exaggerated and self-seeking: the first miners, he admits, found very little, but "subsequently many very rich mines were discovered and are now in operation, . . . and untold thousands of pesos of gold have been extracted, and never will it run out or finish until the end of the world."[280] An inexhaustible mine, no less! In reality, the mines were soon abandoned (see above, chap. XVII, sec. 23), and by the time of Adam Smith and Humboldt those fabulous and fabled deposits did not even merit a mention.

The urge to reach the Spice Islands was the motive for numerous other expeditions that ran along the southern coast of Brazil, sailed hopefully up the Rio de la Plata (Solís and Pinzón, 1515) and finally, with Magellan (1520) found the channel so tenaciously sought; found it, yes, but also found it to be so long and risky that from the commercial point of view the triumph was really a failure.

But if spices represented wealth, it was now becoming clear that wealth itself was a form and instrument of economic and political power. It was therefore preferable, if possible, to acquire it in the direct and immediate form of the metals representing ready cash. Demands of state easily prevailed over businessmen's calculations and commercial enterprises. With the king's agreement (1505) Vespucci had prepared (1506) his expedition to reach the "Spicery" by the westward route, across the lands of Central America. But Juan de la Cosa found gold in Haiti and on the mainland, so King Ferdinand changed his mind. The expedition to the "Spicery" was called off and the preparations diverted to the American gold mines (21 October 1507).[281] Already by the end of that year the ducats were flowing into the court in goodly quantities; and in the years immediately following the king's main concern was organizing and intensifying the extraction of gold from his transoceanic possessions.[282]

The spice archipelagoes remained in the shadows for some years while the gleaming West Indian gold stole the limelight, but they loomed up on the horizon once again when Vasco Núñez de Balboa learned from some Indians about a vast sea opening out beyond the mountains of the isthmus and passed on the information to the king (20 January 1513) together with the announcement that he had found the purest gold in the sand of the rivers and right on the surface of the

280. *Hist.*, XLIX, 3: PT, V, 240a. The meager quantities of gold gleaned by the Spaniards in the early days all came from alluvial deposits, from ransoms and ransacked tombs. But even in 1554 Oviedo wrote that "there is gold, and plenty of it" (Otte, "Una carta inédita," par. 48).

281. Molinari, op. cit., p. 62, under the title "Gold Pushes Spices into the Background." Cf. Humboldt, *Examen critique,* I, 318, V, 153, and F. Guerra, "La política imperial sobre las drogas de las Indias," *RI,* 26, nos. 103–04 (1966), 31–58.

282. Molinari, op. cit., pp. 70–71.

ground, as plentiful ("in very large pieces . . . the size of oranges and like one's fist") as it was easy to collect ("without any work").[283] The unknown sea might be the way to the Moluccas. King Ferdinand needed gold more than ever, what with the latest techniques of warfare calling for regular armies and enlisted soldiers instead of the old feudal bands, his unending wars in Italy (League of Cambrai against Venice, 1508, Holy League against France, 1511), in Africa (1509–1510) and in Navarre (1515–1514), and the huge bribes he needed to conduct his diplomacy. Balboa's assurances that the gold and riches of the newly discovered regions would allow him "to conquer most of the World"[284] consoled him and spurred him on. The lands announced by Balboa were rebaptized "Castile the Golden,"[285] and even before the news of the discovery of the Pacific Ocean (25 September 1513) reached Europe a great expedition, "the biggest of all those sent to America since the first discovery,"[286] its numbers swollen by numerous adventurers who had been about to follow the Great Captain to Italy, embarked under the orders of Pedrarias Dávila, the king's lieutenant general, on twenty-two ships and caravels. The Catholic King had paid everybody's passage, plus their keep during the crossing and for a month after disembarkation in Darien. In a state of high excitement and unbounded optimism the hordes set sail from Sanlúcar on 11 April 1514. Included in their number was Gonzalo Fernández de Oviedo, the newly appointed inspector of the gold foundries of Tierra Firme.[287]

After barely eighteen months' sojourn in the Indies, Oviedo went back to Europe to lay charges against Pedrarias, left again in 1520 and spent another three years in America. In November 1523 he was in Sanlúcar again. The following year, having presented himself at Charles's court, he was appointed governor and captain-general of Cartagena. Meanwhile Magellan had found the Tierra del Fuego passage and Cortés's treasures had been landed at Seville. Once again the greedy Europeans found themselves being offered spices and gold at the same time. On concluding his *Summary,* written for the emperor in 1525, Oviedo has no hesitation. The American dominions possess two great merits, but the first of the two is "the brevity of the way and preparation from the South Sea

283. Letter from Santa María del Antigua, in Darien, in *CDII*, XXXIX, 238–63, and esp. pp. 246–48.

284. Ibid., p. 253.

285. This is the name given to them in the act (of 27 July 1513) appointing Pedrarias Dávila captain general and governor of the province (*CDII*, XXXIX, 271) and in the instructions relating thereto (2 August 1513: "Castile the Auriferous," ibid., p. 280).

286. Bullón, op. cit., p. 130.

287. Amador de los Ríos, "Vida," p. xxii; Molinari, op. cit., pp. 74, 77–78. Both Oviedo (*Hist.,* XXIX, 1: III, 5a; XXIX, 6: III, 22b) and Las Casas give picturesque descriptions of the throng of noble gentlemen who had sold or pawned everything "to deck themselves out extravagantly in silks and brocades," in the hope of "despoiling the whole of France" (*Historia de las Indias,* bk. III, chap. 54, ed. cit., II, 566–67).

It has often been remarked how many of the people who sailed to the Indies on that expedition were later to become famous: Bernal Díaz del Castillo, Hernando de Soto, Pascual de Andagoya, Diego de Almagro, Francisco de Montejo, Benalcázar, etc., etc. Further details in Medina, *Descubrimiento,* I, 103–20.

to the trade of the Spice Islands, and the countless riches of the kingdoms and dominions adjacent thereto." Only as the second merit does Oviedo mention the wealth possessed by the New Indies themselves.[288]

40. THE WAY TO THE SPICE ISLANDS

These lines may conceivably represent one more attempt to score off the person who was the target of so many other attacks by Oviedo, Peter Martyr, who in July 1524, after reporting the efforts to find a "strait" (in other words, a channel) between the two oceans, had written (but his book was published only in 1530) that "if a passage were found from the southern to the northern sea, it would be easier to get to the islands that nurture the 'aromas' and pearls" and the disputes with the Portuguese would be avoided; "however there is little hope for the strait."[289]

In his turn Peter Martyr was echoing (though in the muted tones proper to a certain prudent skepticism) Cortés, who in his third letter (1522) had announced his discovery of a land path to the South Sea, and added that "all those who have some knowledge and experience of sailing in the Indies have considered it absolutely certain that if one could discover the way through to the South Sea by these paths one would find many islands rich in gold and pearls and precious stones and spices, and one would discover and find many other secrets and admirable things; and this has been affirmed and is still affirmed also by learned persons experienced in the science of cosmography."[290] Toward the end of the same letter the enthusiastic Cortés repeated: "Let your Majesty believe that this matter of the South Sea will be the greatest thing and the thing most beneficial to your Majesty since the Indies were discovered."[291] In the fourth letter (1524) Cortés is still talking about the "strait to the other sea" (the sea route) which is the "thing that in this world I most desire to locate";[292] and he goes on to say that he has a map in his possession leading him to believe that it debouches "very close" (!) to the archipelago discovered by Magellan.[293] In the last letter (1526), finally, Cortés goes back to the idea of a land passage, thus justifying the pessimism of Peter Martyr and coinciding by and large with the simultaneous hopes of Oviedo: "Seeing that no strait has been discovered, I am thinking about opening up a way through here to the Spice Islands. . . . by this route I offer to discover all the Spice Islands and other islands . . . and also to so arrange things that your

---

288. *Sum.*, chap. 76, "Conclusion," p. 273; *Hist.*, XXIX, 30: III, 151–52, where he cites the passage in his *Sumario* as being contained in the "eighty-ninth and penultimate chapter," with the rider that the figures he gives are accurate "unless we have been led astray by the details shown on these modern maps and the reports of the sailors; but even if they are wrong, it will only be by a slight amount."
289. *Dec.*, VII, 5, p. 526.
290. *Cartas*, II, 50.
291. Ibid., p. 62.
292. Ibid., p. 86.
293. Ibid., pp. 115–16.

Majesty does not hold the Spice Islands in pawn, as the king of Portugal does, but that you should hold them as a thing of your own."[294]

In 1529, in fact, as López de Gómara recounts, Charles V, wishing to attend "his glorious coronation in Bologna,"[295] pawned the Moluccas and the Spice Islands to the king of Portugal for the sum of 350,000 ducats that the latter had lent him on an indefinite loan; and in 1548 the Cortes were still suggesting to the sovereign that the Portuguese monarch be reimbursed and the Moluccas redeemed.[296] But the instructions given to Pedro de los Ríos, Pedrarias Dávila's successor, with whom Oviedo sailed to the Indies in 1526, already contain a very eloquent paragraph: "As I told you when I spoke to you," one of the best ways to the spice trade is across the South Sea, it being "such a short sail" from there to Moluccas. Until the passage is found two "houses" should therefore be established, one in Panama and one on the north coast, as near as possible to Panama; and the spices, landed in Panama, should be transported "by cart or on horseback" to the northern house; anyway, Pedro de los Ríos is to see to the organization of the whole traffic, opening up roads, checking whether they are usable by pack animals, and so forth.[297]

And even earlier than that, in fact as soon as the news of the discovery of the South Sea reached Europe, the Catholic King had sent Pedrarias Dávila more summary but urgent instructions to organize the path across the isthmus ("by the way that is shortest and least mountainous and best provided and supplied").[298]

It was gold that lured people to the newly discovered lands, but it was spices that enticed them to go on further, to discover new paths and new lands. For Oviedo the Indies, despite the Mexican gold, were to be prized above all as a way to the Moluccas, as a base for expeditions to the west, toward the magic solitude of the South Sea. Just as they would be later for Alvarado, the lands of America were still more "bridge" than "mine."

41. GOLD AND OTHER COMMODITIES

Twenty-three years later Oviedo had to admit that gold had once again got the edge over spices. "This [he recalls, having transcribed the passage from the *Summary*] I dealt with and wrote in the year 1526 [it was 1525 actually]; however, in those twenty-two years which have elapsed between then and the present, 1548, so many thousands of pieces of gold have been taken to Spain . . . because of Peru . . . that it is a thing beyond counting, and so stu-

---

294. Ibid., p. 244.
295. Oviedo, *Hist.*, IV, 7: PT, I, 104b.
296. López de Gómara, *Historia General de las Indias* (1552), in Vedia, op. cit. (vol. 22), pp. 222b, 257, cited by Iglesia, *Cronistas e historiadores*, p. 129; cf. K. Brandi, *The Emperor Charles V* (London, 1939), pp. 221, 463.
297. "This is what Pedro de los Ríos . . . is to do and let him comply with the orders sent to him, on His Majesty's command," Seville, 3 May 1526, in *CDII*, XXIII, 387–90.
298. "Capítulo de Carta," written in 1514, in *CDII*, XXXIX, 325–29.

pefying that neither pen nor time suffice to express this as carefully and properly as it really happens."[299]

Oviedo is, in truth, stupefied, but at heart not really satisfied. He has ceased to think, perhaps, about the "immobile fleet" of the aromatic isles,[300] but in the preface to the *History* he had already deplored the fact that hides, sugar, and canafistula, which the Spaniards introduced to the Indies, were not exported in greater quantities, and that numerous other extremely useful products native to the Indies were not exported at all, "Other things that are here forgotten and which these Indies, before they were ever discovered by the Spaniards, used to produce and still produce, like cotton, orchil, brazilwood, and alum and other commodities, that are sought after in many kingdoms of the world and would be of great utility to them, which our merchants do not want, because they only want to fill their ships with gold and silver and pearls."[301]

Even the abundant copper discovered in Haiti was neglected by the gold-hunters.[302] Gold, as an object of economic exploitation, led to the neglect — in the Indies just as it would later do in California and Australia — of other real sources of wealth. But gold is not only a commodity. And Oviedo, who for eighteen years (1514–1532), from his thirty-sixth to his fifty-fourth year, was "inspector of the gold foundries of Tierra Firme," and who feels and writes about gold — his focal interest during the greater part of his life — as an expert, already sees the metal in its political function, as a fluid, disruptive, overwhelming force. Falstaff too concurs, when he says to Ford: "Money is a good soldier, sir, and will on."[303] And Oviedo exalts gold particularly for the way it increases the emperor's power. Gold misspent, or stupidly hoarded by the miser, "is of no more profit than that gold hidden under the ground, that never saw the light of day."[304]

42. THE HISTORICAL ROLE OF GOLD

When it becomes an instrument of Charles's holy enterprises, however, when it serves to "complete the universal monarchy of our Caesar," gold is a token of God's aid, and thus a warning and a lesson to foreigners, "so that foreigners

---

299. *Hist.*, XXIX, 30: III, 152–53.

300. In the *Quinquagenas*, written in Oviedo's later years, the Indies are a source of gold, silver, and pearls, but not of spices, nor are they the path to the Spice Islands. Oviedo even goes so far as to make fun of the sailors who claim to be pilots and to be able to show "what route a fleet should take to go to the Moluccas . . . which are spice islands, the source of cloves, cinnamon, nutmeg, and other spices" (pp. 316–17).

301. *Hist.*, I, Proh.: I, 3a. At the end of the century Carletti was to observe that nothing could be got from Peru "but silver and gold, there being no other sort of merchandise there," and that "the merchants loading up the Spanish fleets bound for the Indies with a whole variety of goods would be out of their minds" if they thought they were going to sell them to the natives, who owned nothing at all ("Ragionamento Quarto," op. cit., pp. 70, 86).

302. *Hist.*, VI, 8, par. 2: I, 177a.

303. *The Merry Wives of Windsor*, act II, sc. 2, also reproduced faithfully in Boito's libretto for Verdi's *Falstaff.*

304. *Hist.*, VI, 8: I, 179a. When the miser croaks, "up come those hidden coins, that the wretch who hoarded them never dared to use," just as when the veins of the earth open, the blood-red streams of gold come bubbling up from its entrails.

should see and fully understand. . . ." The plunder from the sacking of Milan, Genoa, and Rome, Francis I's ransom, even Montezuma's treasure, are mere trifles beside "the riches of the South Sea." King "Athabalipa" was "so incredibly rich," and his people had such an abundance of gold, that in comparison "everything that has emerged or been called rich in the world" seems little. The gold can be used to punish the heathen, and it will also serve to check the turbulent Christians "if they fail to recognize as their superior, as they should and as God has ordained, our Caesar." [305] Oviedo never tires of extolling the possible and indeed morally obligatory *gesta Dei per aurum*. [306]

As we have mentioned before, however, he is equally quick to seize every chance of deploring the *gesta Diaboli per aurum*. Temporal goods are in reality evil and the treasures of gold and pearls hateful. [307] His heart grieves when he sees the "inhuman and unheard-of and abhorrent" things committed and suffered by the Spaniards who were not content with "a crust and their country." [308] "Cursed be wealth," [309] Oviedo bursts out at regular intervals, "Oh cursed gold! Oh treasures and profits of such danger! Oh sable martens!" [310] "Oh treasures of the Indies," [311] and umpteen other such sighs and lamentations.

We have already seen the general drift and certain typical forms of these complaints. Pliny, of course, had expressed himself in terms of almost "Oviedian" gloom, bitterness, and fatalism ("these effects of opulence all lead to crime, massacre and war")[312] and had added his voice enthusiastically to the agelong chorus damning the "accursèd hunger for gold": "Would that it could be wholly removed from life . . . rent by all sorts of constant clamor, and discovered to the ruination of life; how much happier the age" when gold was not yet known. [313] In short the point hardly needs to be stressed, and in any case such complaints were already quite common in the literature of the discoveries. The Admiral himself, despite his lofty and mystical view of the yellow metal, had warned that "in accordance with the lust for gold," everyone on Hispaniola would "want to busy himself more with that than in seeking any other profit";[314] and Peter Martyr and

305. Ibid., pp. 179–80.
306. Thus—quite accidentally—Oviedo makes the very novel and significant point that scientific progress was also furthered by the lust for gold: "In the pursuit of gold other secrets are daily revealed at the cost of the lives of these rapacious men, and also other things, which are a source of medicines and other benefits" (*Hist.*, XXVIII, 4: II, 482b). Góngora was to express it synthetically: "today covetousness shows the way" (*Soledad primera*, line 403). But all in all Oviedo thinks that the obsession with gold is an obstacle rather than a stimulus to an accurate knowledge of nature. In reference to an oceanographic phenomenon observed off the coast of Peru, he says it is little wonder that nobody noticed it before Baltasar García, "because every one goes past at speed and being filled with this ardent desire for gold, they fail to pay attention, or proper attention, to the other things . . . that most arouse the astonishment of persons with more judgment and sounder intellect" (*Hist.*, VI, 53: I, 261b).
307. *Hist.*, XXII, 1: II, 156b.
308. Ibid., XXV, 7: II, 291a; cf. XXVII, 8: II, 450b, etc.
309. Ibid., XXIV, 11: II, 252b.
310. Ibid., XXV, 3: III, 596b; cf. above, n. 275.
311. *Hist.*, XLVII, 5: IV, 274a.
312. *Natural History*, trans. Littré, II, 63, ed. cit., I, 129b.
313. Ibid., XXXIII, 3, ed. cit., II, 400a.
314. Letter to the sovereigns, undated, in *Relaciones y cartas*, p. 233.

Las Casas, to cite two authors whom Oviedo certainly did not take as models, had already bewailed the fatal lust for gold.[315]

43. CHARACTERISTICS OF THE INDIAN GOLD

It is however worth recalling that Oviedo, with his keen interest in practical and political matters, noted (and may even have been the first to do so) two characteristics of Indian gold that were to arouse the interest, astonishment, and vexation of later generations, two connected characteristics: its capacity for awakening envy and its uncontrollable transiency. Pizarro and Almagro obtained riches "in greater quantity than any man ever possessed before now, since the beginning of the world"; so that very soon "they aroused great envy in many kings and princes, because their kingdoms lacked gold and silver and pearls and emeralds."[316] And envy, of course, brings down on the person envied the fury of less fortunate rivals, whose one thought is how, by cunning or violence, they can lay their hands on his undeserved riches.[317]

The immediate consequence of this envy—but a consequence that is in any case the obligatory outcome of the play of economic laws whose effects may take a shorter or longer time to be seen, but are still ineluctable—is the smooth fluidity of gold, its miraculous quickness in passing from hand to hand, from one deluded owner to the next, until it disappears from sight like Angelica's veil. In the *Summary* Oviedo can already be found informing his "sacred, catholic, Caesarean, royal majesty" how rich the new transoceanic lands are in gold and precious stones, and he goes on as if flinging a handful of coins on the table, "These double ducats prove my point: your Majesty despatches them throughout the world, and once they leave these kingdoms they never return, because being the best currency circulating in the world today, once it falls into the hands of foreigners, there it stays [an embryonic formulation of Gresham's Law]; and if it does come back to Spain it is in disguised form, and debased, and with your royal insignia changed; if this danger did not exist, and this currency were not spoiled in other kingdoms for that reason I said, no prince in the world would have a greater quantity of gold coin, nor even as much, with a very great quantity and millions of gold like Your Majesty's."[318]

---

315. See Pereyra, *La obra de España*, p. 129. In his *De insulis* Peter Martyr had bewailed the fact that ever since he closed his *Decades* (with the third Decade), in Darien "nothing else had happened but destroying and being destroyed, slaughtering and being slaughtered" (p. 361). On the massacres, sufferings, deliberate abortions, etc., among the enslaved goldminers, who were reduced from 1,200,000 to a number he does not dare to repeat, see *Dec.*, III, 8, p. 295. Similar sentiments voiced by Oviedo himself (and repeated in more general terms in the *Quinquagenas*, pp. 45–46) are cited by García Icazbalceta, op. cit., p. 103.

316. *Hist.*, XLVIII, Proh.: IV, 354–56. What Oviedo does not see and cannot yet see is the curious process of compensation, the mercantile solution of the age-old alternative of gold or spices, by which the metals of the West Indies eventually served to pay for the spices from the East Indies. . . .

317. On the motto on which Potosí prided itself ("I am the envy of kings") and on some of the political and publicistic repercussions of that defiant statement, see my article, "Mito y fortuna del Perú," *Mercurio Peruano*, April 1943.

318. *Sum.*, chap. 86, "Conclusion," pp. 273–74. Oviedo voices the same idea thirty years later in *Qu.*, p. 441.

By the time he comes to the *History* the process is mentioned as a well-known fact, with the corollary that it is only right and proper that the foreigners who got the gold should also have got themselves syphilis! "Since so much of the gold of these Indies has landed up in Italy and France, and even in the possession of the Moors and enemies of Spain, and in all other parts of the world, it is only right that as they have enjoyed the fruits of our labors" they should also suffer our infirmities. "Many times in Italy I was much amused, hearing the Italians refer- ring to the *mal françes* and the French talk of the *mal de Nápoles,* when in truth both should more accurately have said the *mal de las Indias.*"[319] And how numerous were the Spaniards that found the gold "slipped through their fingers, like the dew or a shadow"![320]

The solid metal suddenly becomes impalpable. The inspiration of a thousand daring exploits, the diabolic instrument of the damnation of so many souls, melts away into so many droplets of dew. The flame of its splendor dies down and turns to ashes. The prize slips from their grasp. And the iron fist, all bloodied, reaches greedily out, and closes on air.

This passage already betrays a curious mixture of regret and pride. Those ducatoons which the king "scatters throughout the world" with sovereign generosity seem to echo those "big fat pearls" of Malabar that "are spread throughout the world, and this king has a great treasure of them" (Marco Polo, *I Viaggi,* chap. 151, ed. cit., pp. 255–56).

319. *Hist.,* II, 14: I, 55a. Cf. II, 13: PT, I, 49a, and below, chap. XXI, sec. 13. Ronsard, for instance (1553), refers to "the Neapolitan evil"—see Le Moine, op. cit., p. 192. But it is well known that "there is a natural desire to identify these things with some other nationality" (D. Loth, *The Erotic in Literature* [London, 1962], p. 177). It will be recalled (above, chap. XV, n. 130), that Oviedo knew and kept in touch with Fracastoro, the author of the poem entitled *Syphilis, seu de Morbo gallico* (1530).

320. And more generally: "Gold seems to stick to some people's fingers and slip through other people's, just as one sees happening in other property matters" (*Hist.,* VI, 8: I, 191b).

❧ XX ❧

The Quinquagenas

1. Tedious moralism

WE have already seen how the progression from the earlier to the later books of the *History* is accompanied by a steadily increasing occurrence of sermons, homilies, and edifying observations. It comes as no surprise, therefore, to find that the *Quinquagenas,* composed by Oviedo in his ripe but prolific old age (1546–1556), consist almost entirely of such elements. Perhaps we should really be glad that Oviedo had this moralistic work constantly to hand as a ready-made outlet for his banal reflections and puerile precepts, many of which therefore never found their way into the *History*.[1] What does surprise us, especially after the first of the three parts of the *Quinquagenas* appeared in a sumptuous edition in 1880, is that there should still be anyone who considers it a work of history. Whatever Oviedo's intentions were—and he apparently planned to draft biographical memoirs of famous Spaniards as a way of exalting virtue and branding vice, a sort of lay hagiography—the preaching totally stifles the narration. And the monumental and indigestible work choked with quotations from the Scriptures and the church fathers, lacking any sort of structure within the rigid format of the stylistic scheme adopted, and even, on occasion, downright irritating in its silliness and pedantry, turns out to be a twin to those *Rules of the Spiritual Life and Secret Theology* that Oviedo was translating from the Italian at about the same time for publication in Seville (1548), which, as we know (see above, chap.

---

1. The strictures on the subject of the "pestilence" of gambling (*Qu.*, p. 203) and the swindles posing as jewel lotteries (p. 197), the tirades against alchemists (pp. 10–11) and the extravagant dress, parties, funerals, etc., in the Indies, despite the high prices (p. 372), against the vices of the women (see above, chap. VI, n. 213) and the bawds (p. 403), all have parallels in the *Historia*.

More original are the diatribe against public bathhouses as haunts of vice (p. 446), the condemnation of foul language—exemplified in the noble little girl barely three and a half years old "so shameless and loose of tongue that the most wicked or dishonest woman in the world, even a brothel denizen or public whore, would not come out with the things she said" (p. 310–11)—and the denunciation of certain hypocritical devotional practices, such as that of the Genoese, "people who follow the merchant's art" and flagellate themselves on Fridays in Lent, which however does nothing to satisfy their creditors (p. 100).

Another notable point—among the whole jumble of sources—is the frequency with which Oviedo cites the moral works of St. Jerome (pp. 33, 66, 155, 213, 257, 290, 294, 323, 362, 417, 427, 433, 493, 502, 506, 516, 520, 523, 533) and St. Gregory (pp. 21, 124, 126, 166, 194, 222, 225, 264, 273–74, 278, 287–88, 292, 295–96, 444–45, 448–49, 453, 467, 478, 485, 492, 527, 531–32, 541); the editor notes (p. xxix) that these quotations are always in *Castilian,* and perhaps taken from various anthologies and thesauri.

XV, sec. 6) proved to be a singularly unsuccessful commercial venture. All in all, the *Quinquagenas* is a work almost totally alien to Oviedo's real personality, except where it goes back to themes already developed in the *History,* or lingers over reminiscences of his youth.

The editor of the 1880 version, the academician Don Vicente de la Fuente, was therefore being more clever than accurate when he wrote that "the work of the *Quinquagenas* stands in the same relationship to the *Batallas* as does World History to the particular History of Spain," and allowed himself to be similarly carried away in referring to the "historical and poetical *Quinquagenas.*" [2]

Oviedo himself gives the lie to this, making it immediately clear in the preface to his work that he had already composed the bulk of the *Quinquagenas* (borrowing the title from Saint Augustine and his three *quinquagenas* of commentary on the 150 psalms; from the grammarian Antonio de Nebrija, who composed certain *quinquagenas* on the difficulty and beauty of the Latin language; and from Admiral Don Fadrique Enríquez, author of some verse *quinquagenas*) [3] when he came across the work of Juan Sedeño, and then decided to "particularize" the general maxims by larding the moralistic text with examples of illustrious men, thus providing a more balanced mix of verse and prose, ethics and biography. [4]

2. EDITOR'S VERDICT AND FORMAL STRUCTURE

It becomes abundantly clear, on the other hand, that the editor has no illusions about the results of this hotchpotch, and with a candor unusual in the presenter of a previously unpublished work he sums up his verdict on the metrical pattern adopted in the *Quinquagenas,* namely that "its immediate effect is annoyingly distracting and its final effect soporifically enervating." If he labored over bringing these verses to the light of day, he adds—in terms of benevolent indulgence that make him sound like someone extolling the wifely qualities of a somewhat homely girl—it is because the work, "although less beautiful" than the *Batallas,* "does not lack gifts, graces, and good qualities." [5]

---

2. *Qu.,* pp. vii, xi; the *Batallas* are still unpublished. Oviedo, spurred on by the example of the contemporary compilations of Fernán Pérez de Guzmán (ca. 1466), Hernando del Pulgar (ca. 1499), and Juan Sedeño (*Qu.,* pp. 3–5), planned to compose a similar but broader and fuller work in the form of a dialogue between an *alcaide* (Oviedo himself, obviously) and a certain Sereno, who questions him and jogs his memory. When he came to Spain for the last time he brought a fair copy of the *Quinquagenas* to offer to Philip II and four bulging notebooks with the first draft of the *Batallas,* likewise divided into three parts. Of this enormous work "we have more than three hundred dialogues, although according to his plan they would have been as many as six hundred or maybe eight hundred, if he intended to write a fourth *batalla*" (*Qu.,* pp. vii, ix); and from it, on his own admission (p. xi), he drew some historical sections for the *Quinquagenas.*

3. On these dubious precedents, see A. Morel-Fatio, "Las Quinquagenas de la nobleza de España" (review of Fuente's edition of the *Quinquagenas*), *Revue Historique,* 21 (1883), p. 181.

4. See the Preface, *Qu.,* p. 4; "And I mixed in and inserted the famous lords and gentlemen of ancient and modern times," etc.

5. *Qu.,* pp. xix–xxi. A little further on, to justify the course adopted by the Academy, which decided to publish first the *Quinquagenas* and then the *Batallas* (and in fact failed to complete publication of the former and never got round to publishing the latter at all), Fuente recalls that Laban too chose to marry Leah first and Rachel afterward . . . (Oviedo's habit of copious biblical quotations seems to be catching). Menéndez Pelayo ("Historiadores," p. 87) was also surprised that it was "the indigestible and extremely tedious farrago of the *Quinquagenas*" that got

The first volume, the only one published, is apparently neither the best nor the worst. The worst is apparently the second, "resembling the first in its weighty and half-baked erudition, and possibly the least interesting of the three." The best is the third, because this is where Oviedo stuck almost exclusively to history; but—possibly because of this sober approach—it turned out to be much less bulky than the first two. Oviedo, with the concern for external balance so evident in the whole symmetrical architecture of the *Quinquagenas* therefore "elongated" it with a whole string of other items, unadorned with either verse or commentary, which appendages he then called *Acrescentados,* or "Augmentations" (pp. xxvi, xxviii).

Each of the three *Quinquagenas* is divided into fifty stanzas.[6] Each stanza consists of fifty eight-syllable lines, in rhyming couplets, with interruptions every two, four, six, or eight lines for a prose commentary. Sometimes the commentaries merely paraphrase the concept of the lines in question, and on other occasions wander off on long digressions, or get bogged down in almost autonomous notes, with their own headings. Although Oviedo fondly imagined that his "second rhymes" were something to set alongside Dante's and Petrarch's "terza rima,"[7] the interminable string of proverbs and judicious hints is actually even harder on the ear than the sort of doggerel chants that children endlessly repeat, which at least make no sense and do not pretend to. Only rarely do Oviedo's plaintive verses achieve a certain homespun felicity of expression, the pithiness of the proverb or popular refrain; most of the time, instead, the rustic form grates unpleasantly against the pedantry of the classical paradigms and biblical verses. As an example of their truly remarkable aphoristic banality, suffice it to quote the "verse" with which the work solemnly opens: "Years are considered good, if the wheat gives a good yield: He who has a good friend should keep him: He who goes by sea, has no sure hour. . . ." (p. 7). And suffice it to mention, as an example of absolute prosaicness, the verse in which Oviedo presents the basic rules of accounting in "second rhyme," that sound (in the original Spanish) for all the world like some sort of mnemonic doggerel made up by a student on the eve of his exam, and which literally translated provide the following enlightening information: "If the entries do not agree, with the debit on the receipt side the remainder remains in play, continuing to pay out, without anything on the account which has been carried over being subtracted." And somewhere among these sententious trivialities he finds room for trite notions of

---

published, rather than the *Batallas.* Even Morel-Fatio ("Las Quinquagenas," pp. 184–85) can find no satisfactory explanation for the Academy's illogical choice.

6. Every stanza and every verse of 2–8 lines open with a line that rhymes with the last of the preceding verse, and, by the same token, closes with a line that rhymes with the first of the following verse. The first line of the first stanza has no rhyme. The last of the last stanza rhymes with the fourth from last and fifth from last (while the penultimate and ante-penultimate have another rhyme), so that the stanza closes with a sort of strophic knot, a neatly tied little phonic bow.

7. *Qu.,* p. 54. Cf. Amador de los Ríos, "Vida," p. xcvii*n*27.

elementary psychology, soaring psalmodies in honor of Charles V, hymns to the Lord, and kitchen recipes.

3. SAVING GRACES

The *Quinquagenas* should not, however, be completely dismissed. The odd apposite observation,[8] the occasional spicy anecdote, various details of court etiquette, and glimpses of Madrid life make up for the tediousness of the long pages riddled with quotations, the irritatingly feeble puns,[9] the repetition, and the author's maddening habit of constantly invoking famous authors to support the most trivial little point, a habit that eventually tries the patience even of the long-suffering editor.[10]

The difference between the *Quinquagenas* and the *History* is already obvious from the fact that in the latter the most frequently quoted classical author, Oviedo's lord and master, is Pliny, the naturalist; in the *Quinquagenas,* it is Seneca, "Seneca the moralist," the illustrious "Spanish master" of whom Spain may rightly be proud.[11]

This brings us to what is possibly the most interesting aspect of the *Quinquagenas,* namely an accentuated Hispanicism under which Seneca is praised as a Spaniard, the emperor Trajan is "our Spaniard" (pp. 335–37, lengthy eulogy), and "the good patriot deserves much praise" (p. 346). And the accentuated religiosity of his old age, merging with this Spanish Catholic patriotism, is voiced in violent outbursts against the ally of the Turks, the "most Christian" king Francis I, and against Anabaptists, Lutherans, "Colampadarians" (pp. 132,

---

8. E.g., Oviedo's comments on the prejudice of nobility: all men are children of God, and it is "the senseless opinion of the common people" to view as noble someone who "is the son of a richer father, as if this nobility were not acquired by theft" (*Qu.,* p. 10). But even the authentic nobility of blood is subordinated to virtue: only if he has virtue must the noble be preferred to the plebeian (p. 502; cf. *Hist.,* XXX, 1: PT, III, 358b). Moreover *noblesse oblige:* the nobleman must feel himself honoured to be what he is and, without despising others, do his best to fulfil his role (pp. 70–71).

One notes however that his hatred of the Pizarros (e.g., p. 41 for Gonzalo) prompts him to add, the moment he names the greatest of them all, Francisco, "and this man was a bastard" (p. 431). In the same way he inveighs against the vanity of genealogical researches (pp. 523–24), but was himself obsessed with heraldry and genealogy (see Morel-Fatio, "Las Quinquagenas," p. 180) and praises the pre-Reformation Germans as great experts in lineages, arms, and blazons (p. 157). It is curious to note that de Pauw too, a good two centuries later, wrote: "It cannot be doubted that European arms originated in Germany," whose ancient customs were similar to the North Americans' and Scythians' (*Défense,* p. 162).

9. *Sic,* p. 458, with a longwinded panegyric. Seneca is also quoted on pp. 7, 9, 24, 28, 47, 66, 108, 125, 201, 207, 220, 221, 231, 234, 255, 326–27, 330, 359, 367, 387, 389, 391–92, 417, 454, 456, 467–68, 522, 532–34, 544, and no doubt elsewhere too. Pliny, unless other references have escaped me, only on pp. 86, 130, 160, 460, 519, 539.

10. "In truth," he burst out at one stage, "there was no need to quote Luis Vives to prove a banality of this sort" (p. 466), namely that a liar should not be believed!

11. *Sic,* p. 458, with a longwinded panegyric. Seneca is also quoted on pp. 7, 9, 24, 28, 47, 66, 108, 125, 201, 207, 220, 221, 231, 234, 255, 326–27, 330, 359, 367, 387, 389, 391–92, 417, 454, 456, 467–68, 522, 532–34, 544, and no doubt elsewhere too. Pliny, unless other references have escaped me, only on pp. 86, 130, 160, 460, 519, 539.

In the penultimate quotation Pliny, the author of the *Naturalis historia,* is mentioned, in connection with wine lees, as if he were Oviedo himself: "as you will find in Pliny's natural *and general* history"! The obvious lapse becomes more excusable when one notices that Fuente, in his preface (op. cit., p; xxxi), mentions among the commandant's books "The *Metamorphoses* of Oviedo"! Morel-Fatio points out other slips in the Fuente edition. Apart from the *Metamorphoses,* quoted on pp. 185, 202, 209, 329, 420–21, 433, 504–05, 508, Oviedo repeatedly cites Aristotle (pp. 306, 345), Vegetius (pp. 191, 480), and Sallust (p. 396).

273—followers of John Ecolampadio), and other heretics with which Germany must be swarming, Oviedo conjectures, since there are so many Jews there![12]

The threat of the Reformation, barely perceptible in the *History,* overshadows the whole of the *Quinquagenas.* Oviedo is worried about the wars in Germany and regrets that he is unable to write at greater length about them, but being so far away, in his fortress standing guard over the port of Santo Domingo, only "at very rare intervals do we have a letter that can be relied upon" (p. 98 and, analogously, pp. 101 and 133). He includes the text of the Statutes of Louvain, crudely translated from the Italian (1544, publshed 1545);[13] he knows about the savage wars of the Anabaptists (pp. 132, 135) and about the council convened in Trent (pp. 162, 265); and, noting the way the Lutheran heresy is spreading dangerously, he calls for the imperial election to cease being held in Germany, where so much good money has been squeezed out of his sovereign Charles, and to be held in Castile instead!

4. THE IMPERIAL ELECTION IN CASTILE

It was the church, he argues, that established the election in Germany, and the church could therefore "remove the said election from Germany" if it had reason so to do; and what better reason could there be than the Protestant heresy (p. 282)? Oviedo does not actually postulate the candidacy of Castile here, but merely mentions, with a certain obvious embarrassment, that "the Romans and other nations" are seeking the election, though not actually in so many words: "They do not ask for it verbally in fact. . . ." (p. 283). The Castilian claim is

---

12. After mentioning that a company of Germans seen in Genoa included ten or twelve Jews, he adds: "I say this, so that the reader will not be too amazed if Lutheran and Anabaptist heresies result and are formed from such a mixture" (*Qu.,* p. 164). Obviously, just as Charles V's old enemy had been in league with the Muslim heathen, so his more recent enemies "must" be hand in glove with the Jewish heathen.

Precisely at that time, in fact, his old French enemy was lending his support to the new Protestant enemy, so that Turks, Jews, Lutherans, Moors, Frenchmen, and Berbers made up the variegated host against which Charles unfurled his holy banners and God unleashed the gold of the Indies! Surrender, then, you motley band of unbelievers, "you see clearly from how far away, from how many thousands of leagues by sea and land God sends him money in abundance for his exchequer, to pay his armies" (p. 184). The French and the Turks are lumped together on p. 114 (see below, n. 18).

Oviedo, who more or less ignores the Jews in the *Historia,* (see above, chap. XIX, n. 99) considers them in the *Quinquagenas* to be as "stubborn" as unbelievers and "uncouth persons" (p. 37), approves their expulsion, and deplores the fact that Spaniards abroad are often called *marranos,* (meaning "converted Jews"), "without those using the term having any idea what *marrano* really means, merely wanting to dub them Jews" (*Qu.,* pp. 279–81). See A. Ballesteros Beretta, *Historia de España* [Barcelona, 1918—41], III, 793, and, on the old term of abuse being turned against the Spaniards themselves, A. Farinelli, *"Marrano": Storia di un vituperio* (Geneva, 1925), reviewed in *Revista de Filología Española,* 13 (1926), 306–08.

On the other hand the impartial Oviedo not only cites "Master León, the Jewish philosopher," and his *Dialogues on Love,* with apparent approval, but in the third (unpublished) *Quinquagena* recounts the bold feat of a "Jewess of Calahorra who [a latter-day Jael!] took a knife and killed all the Frenchmen lodging in her house" (*Qu.,* p. xxvii).

13. *Qu.,* pp. 266–73. The notes of the editor, a harsh critic of Oviedo's translation, reveal that he himself is even weaker in Italian: Ovideo's term *levar via,* for example, may well be an Italianism, but it is perfectly understandable as a synonym for "to root out," while the editor insists on translating it as "to bar the way, block the passage"! The note on Aretino (p. 373) and his ignorance of Pontano (p. 486), etc., confirm Fuente's unfamiliarity with the men and things of Italy in days gone by. For other gaps in Fuente's knowledge see Morel-Fatio, "Las Quinquagenas," p. 186n.

expressed in veiled form—thinly veiled—in an anagram that appears to have gone completely unnoticed, although Oviedo makes a clear allusion to it (p. 96). The first letters of the lines making up stanzas seven to twelve in fact form the following sentences: "Gonçalo Fernández de Oviedo composed these seven Quinquagenas. The emperor is the head and supreme lord of the Christians in temporal matters, and Germany is full of heretics. It is my belief that the election and electors should be removed and transferred to Castile, because it is insufferable for such a thing to remain among people suspect to the faith, nor ought the Catholic church to allow it and it would not be right for Germans to destroy more of the world." [14]

Obviously the idea of the universal empire of Spain would be lacking something if the emperors were not elected in the Castilian heart of that empire. And Oviedo is quite sure—if for no other reason because of the manifest preference shown by the Almighty in giving the Indies and their treasures to Spain—that "everything that the Sun measures Spain will command" (p. 105). [15] The fact that after so many years of exploitation the emperor is still in financial difficulty is due not to a decline in his income but to a rise in his military expenditure. [16]

14. The lines whose initial letters spell out the sentences in question appear on pp. 97–172. They were probably composed by Oviedo when the emperor's victory over the League of Schmalkalden (Mühlberg, 1547) seemed to have made it possible for Charles V to reorganize the empire on a new basis. One of the cities that surrendered to Charles before the battle of Mühlberg was Frankfurt, the traditional seat of the imperial election. In 1546 Oviedo had already begun the *Quinquagenas,* which were almost completely written by 1551 (*Qu.,* p. ix). In the *Historia* Oviedo dreamed of Charles's imminent establishment of a "universal monarchy . . . beneath his scepter" (VI, 8, par. 4: I, 180–81; cf. Pérez de Tudela, "Rasgos," p. 409) in a passage subsequent to the conquest of Peru, and later than 1538, thus probably written for the second edition, around 1547–48.
Was Oviedo's idea (of transferring the empire to Castile) original or quite commonplace among the publicists of the time? I must leave it for the specialists to define its place in the history of Charles V's imperial ideology, although according to Menéndez Pidal, *La idea imperial,* with the passing of time he became more and more Castilian and Christian and less and less of a "universal monarch." See also Sepúlveda, *Democrates alter,* ca. 1550. Is there perhaps some belated echo, in Oviedo's proposal, of the discontent of the Spaniards, and particularly the Castilians, when in 1519 Charles V decided to leave Spain to assume the burden of the imperial mantle (William Robertson, *History of Charles V* [Paris, 1835], pp. 182ff)? Or does it anticipate the discontent of the Germans, when they saw the empire's center of gravity shifting away from Germany to the Spain of Philip II and Philip III? (On the writings of German publicists, 1580–1635, against the Spanish universal monarchy, see H. Tiemann, *Das spanische Schrifttum in Deutschland* [Hamburg, 1936], pp. 32–38). Or could it have been a subtle manoeuvre of rather greater implication, aimed at mitigating Charles's notorious lack of interest in his American dominions (E. Otte, "El joven Carlos y América," *Homenaje a D. Ramón Carande* [Madrid, 1963], I, 162–63)? On the rumors rife in Peru, around 1567–71, that Charles V was already in 1542 on the point of abandoning his American possessions, see Bataillon, "Charles-Quint, Las Casas et Vitoria," in *Charles V et son temps,* pp. 77–92; cf. idem, *Etudes sur Las Casas,* p. 108, and Carande, "Viajes," p. 205. Charles's lack of interest is denied by Alexander von Randa, "Un aspecto poco conocido del ambiente histórico lascasiano," paper given at the Genoa Conference on Las Casas, 11–14 November 1974, pp. 3–9.
Campanella too was about to suggest that the Protestant electors should be deprived of their votes and that the pope should warn them that "unless they returned to the Church of Rome he would strip them of the honor of that election." The college should then be brought up to strength with Catholic princes, "and then the empire could easily be transferred to Spain" (*Della monarchia di Spagna,* II, 101–02).
15. See R. Konetzke, *Das spanische Weltreich, Grundlagen und Entstehung* (Munich, 1943), pp. 212–13.
16. "In this present year 1553 and in the year 1552 which preceded it, counting gold and silver alone, ten million gold ducats, or their value, have been taken out, in just the two metals I mentioned " (*Qu.,* p. 106). And somewhat more snappily: "Just think what this money is today. . . . early this year of 1555 we had certain news that General Bartholomé Carreño with the fleet of the emperor our lord is already sailing, and in Spain, with five and a half million gold pesos, in gold and silver" (*Qu.,* p. 183).

5. THE RICHNESS OF THE INDIES

God gave Spain "millions of gold pesos, thousands of quintals of silver, vast treasures and overflowing coffers . . . thousands of marks of pearls, and skeins of silk, produced in New Spain, and great abundance of cochineal seed, or to be more precise purpura, to give color to the silks and rich cloths."

What wonderful things, Oviedo sighs, could have been done with those riches! It would have been possible "with more facility and equipment and with well-paid people" to redeem the Holy Sepulcher and conquer Jerusalem (p. 106). Indeed, with those "other untold millions of gold and silver" existing in the Indies, the emperor will have no difficulty in conquering the "rest of the world" (p. 184). Even the little that has already reached Spain would have sufficed to clear the whole of the national floating debt ("all the government bonds could have been redeemed and settled" (p. 114). But unfortunately everything has been soaked up by the interminable wars and revolutions in Germany[17] and by the struggles on land and sea with the French and the Turks, "who seem to be one and the same thing" (p. 114).[18]

Same thing they may have been, but since the French were Christians and even more perhaps because at that particular time (1555) they were causing Oviedo considerable annoyance (he never has a moment's peace in his fort, he says, on p. 210, "because of the French pirates infesting the coasts"), he refers to the French in particularly scathing terms. And just as he is constantly harping on the treachery, the broken promises, and underhand cunning of the kings of France, from Louis XII to Francis I, so the humble coppersmiths and tinkers and lock-smiths that pour into Spain from the mountains of the Auvergne are described as being good for nothing but wrecking locks "and making bad keys, because everything they do is worthless, and they go off home to their lands loaded down with ill-gotten gains" (p. 244).

To sum up, and judging on the basis of the part published, it is fair to say that the *Quinquagenas* are of scant interest in themselves, but that in coming from the pen of the author of the *History* they deserve a certain consideration, in some ways as a complement to the major work and in other ways as a final development of it. With a little editorial fantasy one could imagine them—trimmed of all the borrowed erudition, the "second rhymes," the jeremiads and the rambling, and reduced to some seventy or eighty pages[19]—being printed at the end of the *History,* with the title, to which Oviedo could hardly object, of "Augmentations."

---

17. Charles V's tolerance, in leaving the seat of the empire in Germany, cost Spain "as many millions of gold ducats as have been obtained from these Indies of ours, and from his kindgoms, to deal with and pay for these wars and revolutions in Germany" (*Qu.,* p. 282).

18. Oviedo says that "they come from Urllac to Spain" (*Qu.,* p. 244). The editor conjectures that he is referring to Aurillac (*Qu.,* p. 554), capital of Cantal.

19. Morel-Fatio, "Las Quinquagenas," p. 185, also thought that "a slim collection of extracts" would have been more than enough.

❧ XXI ❧

Oviedo's Art and Humor

1. Negative verdicts on Oviedo's literary skills

O F Spanish literature, of the sixteenth or any other century, I must frankly admit
to a complete ignorance. But it seems obvious to me that Oviedo is not an
insignificant writer. The reader who has had the patience to stay with me thus far
should be as convinced of this as I am. I have quoted fairly abundantly, paying
little heed to the requirements of fluent exposition or the "beauty" of the printed
page, because I am persuaded that Oviedo's simple and colorful style can speak
for itself and gain the recognition it deserves.

To date, in fact, it has not received such recognition. Prescott, who can be
excused because he read Oviedo almost entirely in manuscript, condemns his
style and rejects his content: "His thoughts find themselves a vent in tedious,
interminable sentences, that may fill the reader with despair; and the thread of the
narrative is broken by impertinent episodes that lead to nothing."[1] Menéndez
Pelayo finds that Oviedo is not a "real writer."[2] Fueter judges him inferior to
Gómara in literary art.[3] Ticknor deplores his "loose, rambling style" and the
affectation of elegance.[4] Barnes qualifies or rather disqualifies him as "the least
artistic writer" of the early chroniclers of the Indies.[5] For Morel-Fatio there is
nothing "more awkward, more confused and even, at times, more grammatically
incorrect" than Oviedo's prose.[6] And the more modern historians of literature
spare him no more than a few lines, usually of a mildly condescending tone.
Valbuena Prat admits that "his comments on the native animals can be agreeable

---

1. *Conquest of Mexico*, bk. IV, chap. 8, in *Mexico and Peru*, p. 411; cf. *Conquest of Peru*, bk. IV, chap. 9, ibid.,
p. 1161.
2. "Historiadores," p. 87, and *Poesía hispano-americana*, I, 288. Menéndez Pelayo says that Las Casas "wrote as
badly as or worse than Oviedo" ("Historiadores," p. 94). Amador de los Ríos ("Vida," pp. civ–cv) is of much the same
opinion although he does find that Oviedo possesses some literary gifts, not always obscured by his "pedantry," "bad
taste," "bombast and obscurity," etc.; his overall conclusion, however, is that Oviedo's historical importance
"indubitably outweighs his literary importance."
3. *Op. cit.*, p. 293.
4. "Desirous to write in a good and eloquent style, in which he sometimes succeeded" (op. cit., II, 40). Cejador on
the other hand finds his style "flat and unpretentious" (op. cit., II, 44).
5. H. A. Barnes, *A History of Historical Writing* (Norman, Okla., 1937), p. 140.
6. "Las Quinquagenas," p. 185. For further negative verdicts see Salas, op. cit., p. 102*n*.

and—for today's reader—amusing," and he eventually concludes that his work has an "undeniable charm."[7] Montoliu dismisses him as a composer of works of "purely historical and scientific interest."[8] And Salcedo succeeds only in revealing his own impatience when he calls Oviedo's work "muddled and difficult to read."[9] The only full and explicit recognition has come from Ernesto Chinchilla Aguilar: "Oviedo is . . . one of the great Spanish prose writers of the sixteenth century,"[10] followed some way behind by Salas, who admits that he finds in Oviedo's descriptions "a delicate and poetic sensitivity."[11]

There is only one sense in which one can and must deny Oviedo any inkling of art and discipline: in the composition—one hesitates to say "structure"—of his major work Oviedo forgets the examples of humanism, loses all sense of measure and classical harmony, and lapses into the sort of turgid farrago typical of the medieval "summae." It is not all that easy to determine how much of this is due to imitation of his hero Pliny, the most farraginous and disorganized writer of the ancient world,[12] or the still worse example of his predecessor and despised rival Peter Martyr,[13] and to what extent the responsibility should be laid at the door of the prodigious and enormous novelty of the material, or blamed on the absence of historical canons or notions of classification, or, finally, on the Spaniard's natural exuberance, given free rein in the long empty hours in the colonies. Whatever the cause, the result is certainly deplorable and has done more harm to Oviedo's reputation than his prejudices and essential shortcomings.

2. PLINY AND OVIEDO

There are various other coincidences worth noting between Pliny and his successor. Pliny too was an official and later administrator of imperial revenues, and wrote in his free time.[14] Pliny too wrote numerous other works in addition to his major work, the *Natural History*, including one, subsequently lost, that seems to have been one of the principal sources of Tacitus's *Germania*, the greatest ethnographical work of classical antiquity. Pliny too was an insatiable gatherer of information, and so interested in volcanoes that he lost his life, of course, observing the eruption of Vesuvius in 79 A.D. Pliny's work too, drawn

---

7. Op. cit., I, 403, adducing as examples of this "agreeable" style Oviedo's descriptions of "the crab" and "the hurricane"!

8. Op. cit., p. 507.

9. *La literatura española* (Madrid, 1916), II, 458. Even the Dominican Henríquez Ureña, so jealously protective of the literary glories of his country, writes that "his gifts as a writer were limited" and ranks Las Casas above him for form (*La cultura*, p. 65). The chaotic structure of Díaz del Castillo's chronicle "was more or less the habit of such contemporary chroniclers as Gonzalo Fernández de Oviedo and Bartolomé de Las Casas" (H. R. Wagner, "Bernal Díaz del Castillo," *HAHR*, 25 [1945], 187).

10. "Algunos aspectos de la obra de Oviedo," *RHA*, 28 (1949), 323.

11. Op. cit., p. 83.

12. C. Marchesi, *Storia della letteratura latina* (Messina, 1929), II, 266–72.

13. Salas, op. cit., pp. 28–29.

14. Preface, 14, trans. Littré, I, 3b.

from more than two thousand volumes, is, as his nephew wrote, a "diffuse and erudite work, no less varied than nature itself." Pliny too had a great interest in and liking for painting. Pliny too hated to waste time (and Oviedo often writes that "there is no reason to waste time talking about" this or that subject). Pliny too is scrupulous about citing his sources and professes a firm attachment to truth, but reveals no critical turn of mind. Pliny too dedicates his work, as an absolute scientific novelty, to the emperor (Titus). Pliny too takes a utilitarian view of science and of his *History* (and the writers he admires are those in which "the usefulness of helping is given precedence over the charm of pleasing").[15] Pliny too prefaces each of his books with a "foreword" written in loftier and more passionate language (an idea which he in his turn took from the Spaniard Seneca). Both Pliny and Oviedo, finally, take pleasure and pride in the immensity of their empires, Roman and Spanish, each almost equal to an entire world, and as vast and varied as nature itself.[16]

Most of these "coincidences" are of course due to deliberate imitation on Oviedo's part (see above, chap. XVII, n. 98). Pliny could also easily have been the source, or at least the supporting authority, for certain aspects of Oviedo's "philosophy": his historical pessimism, his aversion for the magic arts combined with a belief in prodigies, the idea of nature as a multiple revelation of the single God, the moralistic deploring of riches (see above, chap. XIX, n. 312) and other elements of stoic origin.

Las Casas, it will be recalled, claims[17] that Oviedo's Pliny was in Tuscan and not Latin (see above, chap. XIX, n. 240); but Alvarez López[18] and Amador de los Ríos believe that Oviedo read Pliny in the original. The fact remains, however, that Pliny's *Natural History* was translated into Florentine by that same Cristoforo Landino whose commentary on *The Divine Comedy* and life of Dante are cited repeatedly by Oviedo, and that this work was published in a magnificent edition by Nicolao Jenson, in Venice, in 1476.[19]

In the introduction, in which he dedicates the work to King Ferdinand of Naples, Landino explains that "he found himself obliged to use non-Tuscan words for things which had no name in Florentine."[20] Oviedo, as we know, offers a similar justification for the American terms.[21] But Pliny himself had already apologized for having had to make use in his *History* of "either rustic words, or foreign words, even barbarian ones, and even terms that one has to preface with an apology."[22]

---

15. Ibid., 3a.

16. *Natural History,* III, 6, trans. Littré, I, 160, and XXVII, 1, ed. cit., II, 225.

17. *Historia de las Indias,* bk. III, chap. 143, ed. cit., III, 304, cited by Amador de los Rios, "Vida," p. lxxxiii*n.*

18. "Plinio y Fernández de Oviedo," *Anales de Ciencias Naturales,* 1 (1940), 43.

19. Reprinted and corrected, Venice, 1534; revised by A. Brucioli, Venice, 1543; new translation by A. Brucioli, Venice, 1548; new translation by L. Domenichi, Venice, 1561, reprinted 1573, 1580, and later.

20. Gamba, op. cit., nos. 980, 1344.

21. *Hist.,* I, sole chapter: I, 5b.

22. Preface, 10, ed. cit., I, 2–3.

3. Defects in composition

Oviedo's *History* is externally divided into three parts, the first two containing nineteen books each and the third twelve. The books themselves, however, are not even approximately equal units: some have a preface, others do not, and some, books I and XXXVIII, consist solely of the preface, or the preface plus a short summary. The books are in turn divided into chapters, varying in number from zero to fifty-seven (in book XXXIII), and the chapters sometimes subdivided into numerous paragraphs. The number of pages in each book is likewise arbitrary: book XL has only three pages, book XXXVI has five, XXXVIII has seven, four other books (I, XVIII, XXX and XLIII) each have eight; but several other books pass the hundred-page mark, and those fifty-seven chapters in book XXXIII total no less than two hundred and ninety-eight! Nine chapters of the last book[23] are missing entirely and chapter XX lacks five paragraphs out of fourteen.

The same sort of confusion reigns within these fictitious subdivisions. The only general principle followed in the arrangement of the material is a progression from south to north, from the Straits of Magellan to Greenland,[24] but with innumerable goings and comings, retracings of steps, digressions, and pure and simple repetition.

We have already come across Oviedo's conviction that almost everything he has seen is interesting and memorable, and his resulting tendency to accumulate rather than select, to repeat a thing even two or three times rather than risk forgetting it. He actually says that he hates to repeat himself—"I am not partial to relating things time and again,"[25] and he also explains how sometimes it may still be necessary to say the same things twice, for example when a number of witnesses are reporting on something he has not himself seen; in such cases the repetition "is not inappropriate since I myself have not been in that land." Elsewhere, however, he cites by name and surname a number of witnesses of something (an enormous fish that was not a whale) that he himself *had* observed.[26] But in point of fact he is always contradicting himself. He leaves all his books "open" so that he can incorporate the results of further findings as he goes along.[27] And he himself admits, as he crams the information in, that they are not ordered expositions, but "a medley or mixture of things,"[28] a "hotchpotch,"[29] or like that "conserve that is known as *compote*, which is a

---

23. *Hist.*, L, 11–19: PT, V, 357–58 (titles only).
24. Ibid., XXI, 11: PT, II, 339b; XXII, 1: PT, II, 342b.
25. Ibid., XII, 9: PT, II, 38b; XVI, Proh.: PT, II, 85–86.
26. Ibid., XIII, 2: PT, 58a; XXIII, 7: PT, II, 365b.
27. Between 1535 and 1542 the *Historia* (first part) grew by a third: XXXIII, 53: PT, IV, 254b. There are visible additions in XLII, 15: IV, 114a, for example, and in many other places. For further indication of a book left open-ended, pending the addition of further details, see XLIV, 3 (end): IV, 134. Cf. Ticknor, op. cit., II, 38–39n23.
28. *Hist.*, XLII, 12: IV, 106a.
29. Ibid., XLVI, 17: IV, 217 and 220b; XLVI, 18: IV, 234a. Oviedo also uses the term *hotchpotch*—even more justifiably—to describe his *Quinquagenas* (p. 367). On the real meaning and etymology of Oviedo's word *(pepitoria)*,

confection of different kinds of fruits all thrown into the same bowl," [30] or, more frequently and modestly, "repositories." [31]

The disorder, both in general and in the separate parts, is so obvious that it is difficult to understand how Ticknor could have found the *History* "not wholly without merit as a composition";[32] while only an excess of apologetic zeal can account for Amador de los Ríos's supposition that the lack of order was calculated and deliberate, designed to increase the reader's pleasure by variety;[33] and the same must hold true for the similar sophistical explanation provided by Menéndez Pelayo who, after telling us that Oviedo gave the drafting of his books "no more arrangement or order than he bestowed upon his everyday conversation," says that this very reason, the fact that he piles up "details without selection or discernment," explains how he wrote such an interesting book on America.[34]

In reality, the almost haphazard and undisciplined shape of Oviedo's work— Riva Agüero hit the nail on the head when he spoke of his pen "running away with him"[35]—is the reflection, or one of the reflections, of his total dedication to his material. He is so delighted with it that he never gives a thought to taming it: he happily allows himself to be smothered by it, reveling in the expanding bulk of the notes and chapters and books, watching the virgin forest spread across his desk and branch out among his pages. It has been said that the *History* is written after the fashion of a diary.[36] There is certainly some justification for this, not only because of the autobiographical element (see above, chap. XVII, sec. 4), but also because, like Columbus's diary, it defies the usual categories: it is not true history, and not mere chronicle. Day by day, over a huge span of years, Oviedo punctiliously reports not what he has *done* but what he has learned from here and there, which was, after all, what the official chronicler was required to *do*.

---

justifiably—to describe his *Quinquagenas* (p. 367). On the real meaning and etymology of Oviedo's word *(pepitoria)*, see a curious note by H. Schlayer, *Revista de Filología Española*, 18 (1931), 36–37.

30. *Hist.*, XLVI, 17: IV, 217; and with an even lengthier and more mouthwatering definition, XXIX, 26: III, 128b.

31. For example, the whole of book VI, which he uses as a dumping-ground for all sorts of details and curiosities, in order to make it easier for himself to get through everything else he wants to say in the following books. This book VI, which Oviedo also calls a "repository archive" (VI, 16: I, 203a), is thus an all-purpose storage space, which Oviedo hopes will save him from getting totally bogged down in his material.

32. Op. cit., II, 41. In the *Quinquagenas*, however, Oviedo advises the reader that "what appears to be disorder is in fact careful arrangement," and the jumping about from one subject to another is intentional, because "each thing serves in its time and place and proportion" (*Qu.*, p. 440), which smacks of an attempt to convince himself rather than the naive reader.

33. Amador de los Ríos, "Vida," p. lxxxv and n. 4.

34. "Historiadores," p. 87, and *Poesía hispano-americana*, I, 288. Barnes (op. cit., p. 140) comes closer to the truth when he comments, albeit in terms redolent of American publishing jargon, that he finds "the organization of material miserable" in the *Historia*.

35. In the famous essay on Garcilaso, reprinted in that writer's *Páginas escogidas*, p. 46.

36. Salas, op. cit., p. 106.

4. DESCRIPTIVE ACCURACY

This scrupulous respect for objective fact is also the inspiration for Oviedo's strenuous efforts to portray the things of the Indies, and their qualities and names, as accurately as he possibly can. Oviedo knows that he cannot hope to succeed in sorting out the umpteen cases of homonymy and the different words in the different dialects indicating the same thing,[37] but one has to admire his determined attempts to render the forms and sounds of the New World. When he feels his description is inadequate he helps himself out with a sketch, "with my bad drawing."[38] And if the drawing is not enough, as in the case of the cross-shaped leaves of the Nicaraguan fig, Oviedo seeks to convince the reader by reminding him that he picked some specimens "to show in Spain."[39] When he meets the empress in Avila in 1531 he offers her some dried and salted manatee meat, which tastes like very good tuna,[40] and "an Asturian gentleman, a relative of mine," is presented (in Madrid, 1547) with a sort of wild cat (cozumatle),[41] and so on in hundreds of other cases.

On certain other occasions, however, he admits that the drawing is not vital, but insists that the thing can be understood better if it is seen in "painting."[42] "I very much want painting in the things of history," he explains elsewhere, in a sort of anticipated recommendation of illustrated books, "because without a doubt the eyes play a great part in the information of these things, and given that they themselves cannot be seen or touched, the image of them is a great help to the pen."[43] And yet, even today, it is Gesner (*Historia Animalium*, 1551–1587) who is generally credited with having been the first person to illustrate his zoology with woodcuts.

Oviedo devotes the same exquisite care to rendering the sounds. When he transcribes an Indian word he gives the correct pronunciation: "they call it [a herb] *curi-á*. The *a* must be said very shortly after saying *curi*, if one wants to

---

37. "One thing has a lot of names, and also different things have the same name; and if one tried to get to the bottom of this one would never end" (*Hist.*, VII, 12: I, 279b).

38. Ibid., X, 1: I, 363b.

39. *Hist.*, VIII, 4: PT, I, 252. Likewise in 1532 he took to Spain "some plates or shells" of "armoured horses" (armadillos, XX, 9: PT, II, 250a).

40. Ibid., XIII, 9: PT, II, 64.

41. Ibid., XII, 39: PT, II, 55b.

42. Ibid., VI, 4: I, 172b; XXIV, 15: II, 265b.

43. The colors cannot be drawn, but Oviedo manages to convey them with remarkable accuracy. The skin of the *bivana*, for example, is of the color of "those patches that the fire makes on sheepskins, when the women who are singeing them are careless and the burnt part comes out a reddish yellow" (*Hist.*, XXIV, 13: II, 260b).

On the repeated requests for maps and paintings of the things of America (1533, 1536, 1539), until Francisco Hernández took along with him to Mexico a mapmaker, a "draughtsman," and a botanist, someone who would "seek out the plants for him," see Jiménez de la Espada, *Relaciones geográficas*, I, XXX–XXXI, XXXVIII, XLII, LXIII, LXXXVII. Oviedo is constantly poking fun "at what is depicted in these modern maps": *Hist.*, XX, 20: PT, II, 269a; XXI, Proh.: PT, II, 305a; XXIII, 2: PT, II, 355; XXIV, 8: PT, II, 414b; XXXIII, 52: PT, IV, 253 (Antonio de Mendoza); XXXIX, Proh.: PT, IV, 337b; XXIX, 3: PT, IV, 345, giving the peremptory warning that "in what I have seen with my own eyes, I prefer to believe myself"! In particular, "those lists [tables of longitude and latitude] that were made in Europe are absolutely worthless in the Indies" (L, 27: PT, V, 409b).

pronounce the word the way Indians do."[44] And one chapter is entitled "of a fruit called *names,* pronounced *nnames."*[45] The iguana "is called *yuana,* and is written with those five letters and is pronounced *y,* and with a very short interval *u,* and then the three final letters *ana,* joined or said quickly; so that in the whole name two pauses must be made, in the form stated."[46]

The voice of the *perico ligero* (sloth)[47] differs from that of any other animal: it sings by night and only by night "in a continuous song from moment to moment, or with measured pauses, singing six points each higher than the next, going continually down, so that the highest point is the first, and from that it drops, lowering the voice or rather sounding like someone singing *la . . . sol . . . fa . . . mi . . . re . . . do . . .* so this animal says *ha . . . ha . . . ha . . . ha . . . ha . . . ha . . .* "; whereupon Oviedo unfalteringly concludes that it was the *perico ligero,* and not Tubal-cain and not the Arcadians or Pythagoras, that invented music.[48]

Once he has pinned down the phonetics of a word he struggles to give its exact explanation: "I would like, when one comes across a name in some passage that is unknown to our Castilian tongue, to deal with it before going on, to satisfy the reader."[49] And there are in fact so many new words, Indian terms used for the first time in Oviedo's *Historia,* that the nineteenth-century editor added a glossary at the end of the fourth volume, a singularly incomplete one but still illustrating no less than 485 "American words used by Oviedo."[50]

5. CHOICE OF CASTILIAN

Many of those words eventually found their way into the Castilian language (and later the languages of all the world). That same Castilian, says Oviedo—as

---

44. *Hist.,* XI, 6: I, 380a.

45. Ibid., VII, 19: I, 289.

46. Ibid., XII, 7: I, 392a. And the Indians pronounce the word *Maria* differently from the Spaniards, "because after they have said *mari* they say the *a* with a short pause between the penultimate syllable and the last" (IX, 18: I, 349a). And Oviedo gives careful instructions on how to pronounce the word *higüero:* "the stress on the letter *u* must be long, or said slowly, so that those three letters *gue* are not pronounced quickly or combined, but with one lingering a short while between the *u* and the *e,* so as to say *hi . . . gue . . . ro.* I mention this so that the reader will not understand *higuero,* or *higuera de higos"* (VIII, 4: I, 295). In his pursuit of this unabashed linguistic pedantry he can sometimes be extremely—and delightfully—ingenuous.

47. Thus named by antiphrasis, in view of its slowness and laziness, just as in Spain "Negroes are often called Juan Blanco" i.e., John White (XII, 24: I, 412a; cf. *Qu.,* p. 199). Oviedo kept and studied one in his home, arriving at the conclusion that it lived on air ("and I found that a lot of people agreed with me") and was the ugliest and most useless creature that he had ever seen (*Sum.,* chap. 23, p. 157, and *Hist.,* XII, 24: I, 413–14). In the later *Quinquagenas,* on mentioning the chameleon and the popular belief that it "eats nothing at all and lives on air," he recalls that "in the Tierra Firme of these Indies there is another animal that does the same, that the Spaniards call the 'nimble parakeet,'" because it is extremely slow in its movements" (actually the sloth, *Qu.,* pp. 35–36).

48. *Hist.,* XII, 24: I, 413, with copious details. The same description features in the *Sumario,* chap. 23, p. 159, the only difference being that there the sloth's voice is represented in writing with six "ah's" rather than "ha's". Peter Martyr, too, had gone to great lengths to explain the correct way of pronouncing the *h* aspirate in the Indian languages (*Dec.,* III, 7, pp. 285–86).

49. *Hist.,* V, 3: I, 133–34; cf. I, sole chapter: I, 5b.

50. *Historia,* ed. Amador de los Ríos, IV, 593–608; cf. I, viii.

he outlines his reasons for adopting it for his history—is the best of the vernaculars and the closest to Latin, the language most widely used among the likely
readers of his chronicle,[51] and the language of the laws of Spain, given in the
name of that same emperor at whose command Oviedo is writing his *History*.
There were thus good reasons for his choice, even if it was customary at that time
to draft scientific texts and treatises in Latin,[52] and a good part of the *History*, the
better part, the part (one would say) that meant most to Oviedo, is natural
history, zoology, and botany, for which Latin was the normal vehicle of
expression.

There were other, less lofty motives too, admits the writer now within sight of
the end of his labors: he has written in Castilian, he confesses, because he studied
neither Latin nor Greek, neither Hebrew nor Chaldean, and because, he hopes,
the original will be translated into all languages of the Christians and heathen.[53]
The national vernacular—which Dante had already praised in Italy as "illustrious, cardinal, courtly, and curial,"[54] that Leonardo Bruni, mentioned several times by Oviedo, had defended against the claims of Latin (1436), affirming
that "each language has its own perfection and it is of no import to the greatness
of a poet whether he write in lettered style [Latin] or the vernacular,"[55] and
which had prompted Oviedo's contemporary Cardinal Bibbiena to write in the
prologue to the *Calandria* (1508) that "the language that God and nature gave us
must not be looked on by us with less esteem, as having less grace than Latin,
Greek, or Hebrew"—was emerging triumphant in Spain at precisely the time
Oviedo was composing his history. Nebrija, in the conviction that language
always followed dominion, drafted his *Gramática Castellana* (1492) "in certain
hope of the New World. . . . Spain dreams of an empire like the Roman Empire,
and Spanish will equal Latin."[56] And between 1492 and 1516 Castilian acquired
that degree of syntactic flexibility, lexical richness, magniloquence, and harmony that allowed it to accede to the rank of official language of the vastest
empire ever known, to become the supple instrument for the diplomatic maneu-
verings of the courts and chancelleries of Europe.[57]

A few years later (1536) Charles V could be found expounding the merits of
Castilian to Paul III, claiming the language was so noble that it should be

---

51. López de Gómara, who was in fact quite competent in Latin, gives an almost identical reason for writing his
Historia general de las Indias in Spanish: "I am now doing it in Castilian so that subsequently all of our Spaniards may
enjoy it" (Vedia, op. cit. [vol. 22], p. 156, cited by Iglesia, *Cronistas e historiadores*, p. 110). Cf. Salas, op. cit., p. 136.

52. G. Gusdorf, *Dieu, la nature, l'homme au siècle des lumières* (Paris, 1972), p. 257.

53. *Hist.*, L, 30: IV, 590–91. Oviedo's boast that the *Historia* had been translated into numerous Oriental
languages has turned out to be less illusory than was first thought. Thomas Day Goodrich, in his unpublished
Columbia University dissertation (1968), "Sixteenth-Century Ottoman Americana," mentions that parts of a sixteenth-century Turkish work (author unknown), the *Tarih-i Hind-i garbi*, are a précis or translation of chapters of the
Sumario. See also Elliott, op. cit., p. 88.

54. *De vulgari eloquentia*, I, 16–17.

55. *Enciclopedia Italiana*, XIX, 940a (article by Vittorio Rossi).

56. Menéndez Pidal, "El lenguaje," p. 140; cf. A. Alonso, "El descubrimiento de América y el idioma,"
Humanidades, 30 (1944–45), 119.

57. Lozoya, op. cit., p. 198.

understood by every faithful Christian, the language of diplomacy and politics.[58] Juan de Valdés, in his *Dialogue on Language* (1535–1536), had one of his Italian interlocutors saying that Castilian was the equal of Latin, and Cristóbal de Villalón repeated the same notion with words that are a precise translation of Bibbiena's: "The language that God and nature gave us must not be any less acceptable to us than Latin, Greek, and Hebrew."[59] In 1546 (not, as is usually said, 1585)[60] Ambrosio de Morales composed the famous preface to the works of his uncle Fernán Pérez de Oliva, with its proud and impetuous acclamation of the literary dignity of Castilian, that is also notable for its attack on the supporters of "natural" language, who make no distinction "between a man brought up since his earliest childhood amongst rustics, and another that grew up in a great city or at court,"[61] and for its deploring of the fact that Castilian has been debased in profane and frivolous writings: "Nothing has been written in Castilian but vain love stories or idle fables."[62]

There was perhaps no real need for Oviedo to waste so many words defending a choice that was in fact entirely consistent with the prevailing linguistic tendencies of his time, tendencies paralleling the dissolution of medieval unity and proving irresistible in the context of each of the new nation states. Equally in tune with the literary fashions of the age is Oviedo's formal homage to naturalness and simplicity of style. He has written, he assures us, in the language he learned in his cradle, "and that I know how to speak reasonably well" and not "in another more elevated style, that I lack"; he has written "without elegance or circumlocutions or affectation or rhetorical ornament, but plainly."[63] And Oviedo is in fact mentioned among the chroniclers of the Indies who began the reaction against the overblown prose of the books of chivalry, against the Latinizing neologisms and in favor of the simplicity of everyday speech "shared by all," although he too succumbs to the commonest stylistic vice of sixteenth-century Castilian, the tautologically coupled synonyms that slow the pace of the discourse and give it an artificial and monotonously measured tread.[64]

---

58. Ibid., p. 162; Menéndez Pidal, *La idea imperial*, pp. 30–31. Various studies on the glorification of Castilian in the Renaissance are cited in O. H. Green, "A Critical Survey of Scholarship in the Field of Spanish Renaissance Literature, 1914–1944," *Studies in Philology*, 44, no. 2 (April 1947), p. 241n55.

59. Menéndez Pidal, "El lenguaje," p. 165, who makes no mention however of the Italian source of Villalón's words. In France, King Francis I abolished the use of Latin in offices and courts (under the edict of Villers-Cotterets, 1539—Olschki, *Struttura spirituale*, p. 91); but it was only in 1549 that Joachim du Bellay published *La défense et illustration de la langue française* (especially as compared with Latin and Greek) and around 1579 that Henri Estienne wrote *De la précellence du langage françois* (particularly as compared with Italian). On Castilian's precocious and easy victory over Latin, see Olschki, *Struttura spirituale*, p. 20.

60. Bullón, op. cit., pp. 284–86.

61. H. Pérez de Oliva, *Diálogo de la dignidad del hombre* (Buenos Aires, 1943), p. 11.

62. Ibid., p. 19.

63. *Hist.*, L, 30: IV, 590a, 591b. When he set out on his history Oviedo had expressed himself with greater literary pride. He must not be blamed for using "barbarisms" because he is perfectly well aware of how the best Castilian is used, "and these words must not be laid to the account of my Spanish, because I was born in Madrid and grew up in the royal household and conversed with noble persons and I have read a fair amount, so that it can be imagined I will have understood my Castilian language . . . " (I, sole chapter: I, 5b).

64. Menéndez Pidal, "El lenguaje," pp. 160–61 and 185.

6. Oviedo's artistic originality

Oviedo's artistic originality lies elsewhere: not in the elevated or humble style, not in formal clauses or his penchant for popular sayings and the facile folk wisdom of proverbs,[65] but in a certain meticulous lucidity in his descriptions of nature, that sometimes remind us of those tensely expectant animals in Pisanello's frescoes (the hares, greyhounds, birds, and lions, all observed with such feeling for their nimbleness and strength), sometimes of the slimy and evil-looking serpents of Dante's *Inferno,*[66] and sometimes of those rabbits and monstrous great pigs, the stags and "hounds meager, keen, and dexterous," the rhinoceroses and sturdy white chargers that figure in the beautifully precise watercolors and picturesque engravings of Albrecht Dürer. Nor does Oviedo lack the occasional capacity to encapsulate a situation in a quickly drawn vignette, or the more frequent ability to catch the funny side of certain posturings and attitudes, revealing a satirical humor that may well, as the experts assure us, be "inborn and deepseated" in the Spanish people,[67] but which in Oviedo seems to me to be motivated and enlivened by a personal touch, even if it often betrays an ideological affinity with Erasmus's lively taste for caricature and the bitterness of the *beffa fiorentina,* the malicious practical joke so dear to Boccaccio and Machiavelli.

A fine example of his skill with these thumbnail sketches is the picture of Pizarro, after the unjust and cruel condemnation of Atahualpa, appearing to his lieutenants and "seeming deeply moved, with a great big felt hat on his head in mourning, pulled down over his eyes," looking just like Wagner's Wanderer, and sounding like the Wanderer too, groaning, making excuses, and complaining that he has been tricked. . . . [68]

Equally effective is the image of the proud Cortés, with his left hand wounded and his shield strapped to his arm, issuing forth from the fortress followed by a few bold spirits and scaling the tower occupied by five hundred Indians busily showering down stones and brandishing long needle-sharp lances, "despite which Cortés began to climb the tower with the Christians, and although they

65. Rather than giving a whole string of citations, which would be quite meaningless out of context, I prefer to mention some of the writers who have dealt with this subject: on the mania for proverbs between the end of the fifteenth and the middle of the sixteenth century, see R. Jente, "The Untilled Field of Proverbs," *Studies in Philology,* 42 (1945), 493–94, etc.; L. A. Acuña, "El refrán en Colombia," *Revista de las Indias,* 80 (1945), 224–25, quoting Oviedo; F. C. Hayes, "The Collecting cf Proverbs in Spain before 1650," *Hispania,* 20 (1937), 85–94; idem, "The Use of Proverbs as Titles and Motives in the *Siglo de Oro* Drama," *Hispanic Review,* 6 (1938), 305–23, 7 (1939), 310–23, and 15 (1947), 453–63; E. J. Gates, "Proverbs in the Plays of Calderón," *Romanic Review,* 38 (1947), 203–15.

66. See the graphic and highly colorful description of the snakes in the gulf that takes its name from them (*Hist.,* XXIX, 13: PT, III, 259b).

67. According to Olschki, *Struttura spirituale,* p. 153. On irony, skepticism, and humor in López de Gómara, see Iglesia, *Cronistas e historiadores,* pp. 172–73. Salas (op. cit., p. 138n) assures us that "the best and fairest eulogy" of Oviedo's prose is that written by Marcos Jiménez de la Espada, in his preface to the *Guerra de Quito* of Pedro Cieza de León (Madrid, 1877), pp. xxv–xxvii.

68. *Hist.,* XLVI, 22: IV, 249–50.

defended it stoutly and threw three or four Spaniards down, Cortés made it to the top."[69]

Another pitiless portrait shows the base and cruel Pedrarias capturing Vasco Núñez de Balboa and four of his followers by a trick and after a sham trial having them butchered in the plaza at Acla. "A post was erected, and on it was left the head of the *adelantado* [Balboa] for many days thereafter: and from a house, a dozen or so paces from the place where they had cut their throats (like sheep, one after the other) stood Pedrarias, peeping between the timbers of the wall of the house or hut."[70]

Or the proud Hernando Pizarro, "a tall thickset man, with fleshy tongue and lips and a bulbous glowing nose."[71] Or finally the greedy, vain, and cunning merchant García de Lerma, who got himself appointed governor of Santa Marta and immediately insisted on being addressed as "your Lordship" and being served "with great solemnity and ceremony," almost as if he were a grandee of Spain, "and equally deliberately he cleaned his teeth, after finishing eating, holding audience and transacting business after the customary manner of his Catholic Majesty King Ferdinand or some other great prince."[72]

7. HUMOR AND SATIRE

As for Oviedo's humor, his relish for anecdote and caricature, we have already seen numerous examples. Thus we need not dwell unduly on the countless targets of his more generalized satire, the greed of the tavern-keepers, who earn more from wine "than the Florentine merchants with their brocades and gold cloths,"[73] the impunity enjoyed by the doctors who slaughter their patients and who get off scot free, unlike tailors who have to pay for the cloth they ruin,[74] the

69. Ibid., XXXIII, 13: III, 321–32. As a result of the wounds received Cortés lost two fingers on his left hand (ibid., XXXIII, 15: III, 331b). One is reminded of the fiery Camillo in Machiavelli's *Commedia in versi:* "There is no Spaniard so bold in scaling castle walls as I am determined to be in launching my assault on her that I long for" (act IV, sc. 2). Cortés's own blunt description of the episode, in the second letter, has nothing of the lyrical fervor of Oviedo's account: "I emerged from the fortress, although without the use of my left hand . . . and with my shield tied on to my arm I went to the tower . . . and had it completely surrounded from the bottom . . . and I began to go up by the stairway of the said tower" (ed. cit., I, 135). Peter Martyr tells the same story in *Dec.*, V, 6, pp. 414–15.

70. *Hist.*, XXIX, 12: III, 60b; XXIX, 12: III, 60b. Note that Oviedo is rather hostile to Balboa in the *Historia*, while in his letters this hostility is outweighed by his hatred of Pedrarias (Medina, *Descubrimiento*, I, 153–54, 173). This secretive observation reminds one of Masolino's maidservant, shown covering her eyes with her hand, but peering out between half-opened fingers at the execution of John the Baptist, or Benozzo Gozzoli's famous *Vergognosa*, greedily spying on the drunken and uncovered Noah.

71. *Hist.*, XLVI, 1: IV, 148a.

72. Ibid., XXVI, 8: II, 350b. See also the scene played out between Almagro and Pedrarias, XXIX, 23: III, 119–20.

73. Ibid., VIII, 24: I, 310b. On the tavernkeepers' greed, see *Qu.*, p. 221.

74. *Hist.*, X, 3: PT, II, 129. Although attacks on the medical profession were commonplace at the time, and indeed have always been so, I think I can detect in these outbursts by Oviedo (who counted a number of doctors among his friends, and rated their skills very highly: for Codro, see above, chap. XV, sec. 20, and for Licentiate Barreda, a "great doctor" of Santo Domingo, see *Hist.*, VIII, 28: I, 314a) a distinct echo of Pliny: "They learn at our peril and keep experimenting until the patient dies; and a doctor can even kill a man with complete impunity," etc. (*Natural History*, XXIX, 8, trans. Littré, II, 300a). Against the "false apothecary" who "steals both property and life without any risk," see *Qu.*, p. 405, and against certain doctors that are like long-lasting plagues, see *Qu.*, p. 513. On the havoc wrought by doctors before they manage to effect a cure, see VIII, 2: I, 294b. Cf. also above, chap. XXIX, sec. 15.

efforts made to patch things up between him and his archenemy Diego del Corral (in an ironic phrase that anticipates Lesage's blistering satire—"because already they had made us friends, or at least we spoke to each other"),[75] or the stupidity of the captain who fell in love with a hideous old woman "possessed of all those four *f*'s that are usually attributed to such women, and he the fifth *f* of foolishness."[76] The same satirical vein surfaces in his scorn for the soldiers "who were not fit for war, but only for eating pies and cream puffs,"[77] and in the description of Diego Columbus's somnolent servant who slept and snored right through a tremendous storm (1523), "as relaxed as if he had been in Toledo, and the Admiral called him from time to time, saying 'Santa Cruz (because that was his name), can't you see that we are drowning? Why don't you wake up, traitor, and commend yourself to our Lord?' And the youth replied, saying, 'Yes, Captain, I see it.' And straightaway started snoring again."[78]

Humor and satire combine in the story of the useless precautions of certain prelates, who at the pope's and emperor's behest give orders to their vicars, and the latter pass them on to their curates, with no greater result that that obtained by the little old lady, "diligent but none too wise, who, to increase the safety of some chicks that were following the mother hen about, tied one to the next, and the next to the next, and so on for all ten or twelve, and the last to the mother hen, and the hen to the chair on which the old lady sat spinning; and the chick that was at the end of the thread, as it was furthest from the chair and the string was long, was seized by a kite; and except for one or two that were near the hen, where the thread broke, all the others were lifted away on the string, hanging from each other."[79]

Nor is Oviedo surprised that woodworms like cedar wood, that is so bitter to our palate, because "a woodworm's taste and a man's taste are not at all the same thing."[80] Nor does he omit to point an ironic finger at the contrast and simultaneous convergence between the natives' sumptuary vanity and the Spaniards' covetousness: the former "went out to fight . . . covered in gold armor, at the sight of which the Christians threw off their weariness and redoubled their efforts to disarm them."[81]

---

75. *Hist.*, XXIX, 20: PT, III, 286a.

76. Ibid., XXIX, 33, par. 31: III, 168a.

77. Ibid., XLVII, 13: PT, V, 178b.

78. Ibid., L, 4: IV, 472a; cf. Amador de los Ríos, "Vida," p. xliii*n*3.

79. *Hist.*, XXIX, 31: III, 158a, with the explanation that the old woman's chair is the seat of St. Peter, etc., but without the humor of Baron Münchausen, who took a bit of bacon and a piece of string, threaded five or six ducks together in a row, "like the beads of a rosary," and had himself flown home!

In an unpublished work of his early days Oviedo rails against the corruption and worldliness of the clergy and prelates, and refers to a similar "chain" in reverse: "The church serves them and they the flesh and the flesh the Devil" (quoted by Amador de los Ríos, "Vida," p. lxxxvii). And in a work of his extreme old age (*Qu.*, pp. 63–64) he comes back once again, with a rather muddled exposition, to the subject of prelates' duties. On the blame attaching to the clergy for the failure to convert the Indians, see also *Hist.*, II, 7: I, 30a.

80. *Hist.*, IX, 7: PT, I, 286b.

81. Ibid., XLV, 3: PT, V, 29b.

His irony is even more biting when he refers to contemporary events. Commenting on the custom followed by the ancient Britons whereby "six of them would marry a woman at the same time," he observes caustically: "That custom would not have been approved in these times of ours by King Henry VIII of England, in fact I think he would have commanded the opposite to be observed."[82] And in reference to the false virgins and adulteresses of the old world, he notes that "cloister and gatekeeper" are less protection and guarantee than the simple thread used to distinguish the true maids among "those savage people" of Venezuela.[83]

8. HIS IRONY GOOD-NATURED

This last comment brings us closer to the type of humor that is more typical and characteristic of Oviedo. When the Castilian sees how guileless the natives are he does not try to bring himself down to their level, nor does he idealize the simple savage, but instead reasserts his own mental agility and civilized experience in making good-natured fun of the Indian. There is no spleen, no relish for "slander," in the comic portrayal of the *indios* who wanted to explain that they had seen Licentiate Espinosa with a donkey—an animal utterly strange to them—and therefore "brayed or tried to say what they meant by braying like donkeys";[84] nor in the description of the other Indians who daubed their faces with cocoa and "thought that the more they daubed themselves the smarter they looked," and so went about their business, sucking a little of the grease "every now and then . . . taking it bit by bit with their fingers";[85] nor in the story of the "wild Indian" (but expert in the Castilian language) who had trained a sow and two piglets for hunting and was plunged into despair when the Spaniards, coming across "this native and his porcine company," slaughtered and ate the three pigs, prompting his anguished lament: "These pigs gave me my life and kept me, and I them; they were my friends and good company to me; one had such and such a name and another such and such, and the sow was called so and so," going on to recount how early in the morning "he would leave his hut and say to his companions the pigs, 'Come on then, my friends, let's go and find something to eat,'" and how they would then share the prey and the Indian would sleep "amongst this swinish company of his, scratching first one and then another, stroking them and the sow."[86] This curious symbiosis obviously amuses Oviedo, as if the Indian himself had been an animal and the whole episode was an Aesopian-Circeic fable alluding to captains and soldiers, a grotesque transposition to the rough world of

---

82. Ibid., V, 3: I, 137a. On the "improper marriages of King Henry VIII" see the broader treatment in *Qu.*, pp. 142–43, 465, and cf. (on Catherine of Aragon?) p. 72.

83. *Hist.*, XXV, 22: II, 330a; XXV, 5: II, 300–01.

84. Ibid., XXIX, 13: III, 61b.

85. Ibid., VIII, 30: I, 318a. Oviedo adds that Christians find this custom "very filthy, as indeed it is," but it is the way the Indians feed and protect their faces from the sun and air. . . .

86. Ibid., VI, 51: I, 257.

the native (savage and rebellious, but smart enough) of the cynegetic and military customs of Europe.

The same spirit—good-humored, indulgent, ironic, but understanding— illuminates the story of the Nicoya Indian's reply when he was asked why he kept his male member tightly bound (or infibulated?): "Because that was his custom, he said, and it was better to keep it so rather than loose, like the Indians of the island of Chira or like our horses." [87]

9. IRONY AT THE EXPENSE OF THE EUROPEANS

There is the same ambiguous smile, seemingly directed against the Indians but in reality against the Europeans, in the story of Francisco Martín, who lived for a year among the Pemenos Indians of Venezuela and was forced willy-nilly to learn their medical skills, as they refused to give him anything to eat if he refused to learn. In the end the Indians came to consider this *médecin malgré lui* their supreme physician, and none of them dared to attempt to cure himself without consulting him first. "Thus he became their leading doctor, and mayor, and chief examiner of the physicians that the devil kept in that province and of his herbalists and oculists and bonesetters. His medicines were to roar and puff and issue oaths; and fulfilling this office he survived among them and was held in much respect." [88]

But there is absolutely no sympathy for that other Indian chief, who came to the camp of Captain Badajoz, bringing his wife with him, who was cousin and sister to a great cacique, "and was a girl of gentle disposition; that same night a pious cleric who was accompanying the captain . . . had the chieftain thrown out of his hammock and took his wife into the hammock and slept with her, or to be more accurate did not let her sleep and made sure she knew about his adultery." The following morning "the prudent Indian said nothing about the offense . . . and with a gentle face, showing much pleasure, took leave of the captain, taking his horns and his wife with him," but headed straight to the cacique to demand vengeance, so that the brief and Boccaccesque tale ended in tragedy. [89]

But the pearl of these "Indian tales" is the story of the rich Mexican too clever by half, who saw a penitent heretic wearing his *sambenito,* the penitent's cloak betokening his disgrace, surrounded by a great throng of authorities and officials and citizens and converts. Noting how the solemn mass was followed by a great preacher addressing an impassioned speech to the condemned man, the Indian jumped to the conclusion that the *sambenito* was some high honor conferred at this festive ceremony; "and as he saw that amongst the Spanish Christians there were Knights Commander of the Orders of Santiago and Calatrava and Alcántara

---

87. Ibid., XXIX, 21: III, 110a.
88. Ibid., XXV, 7: II, 293–94, with this hazardous venture reaching a happy end.
89. Ibid., XXIX, 10: III, 48; cf. above, chap. XIX, sec. 18.

and of the Order of Montesa and St. John of Rhodes, with crosses on their chests of different sorts and colors, but they wore only one cross and that a small one, whereas the penitent was given two very big ones, one on the front and one on the back," he concluded that the Order of San Benito was the highest and most coveted of all. So as soon as he got home he set about making up three or four hundred *sambenitos* and took them to the market, "put them in a few heaps on a table, and at one corner of it stuck a stick or post, and thereon a *sambenito,* as a display or sign, so that people could see from afar what he was offering." A few Spaniards passed by and asked him the purpose of the penitential tunics, "and he replied that they were to turn people into knights, as they had done to the person mentioned." The Spaniards burst out laughing and walked off, "and the Indian kept crying out 'San Benito, San Benito.'" In the end, seeing that he was not getting any customers, he "asked where the man concerned lived, and took them all off to see if he wanted to buy them, and with great pleasure offered to make him a good price." But the other, "not being too happy with the new order, as the Indian thought, began to threaten him and swear at him," and the Indian had to take to his heels and seek police protection.[90]

The American's confusion when faced with the bewildering novelties from Europe, his naive astonishment and puerile efforts to turn them to his own advantage, are natural sources of humor; but Oviedo, serenely impartial, spares neither the parallel illusions of the Spaniards in America, with their perplexity at such an unexpected nature, nor the wild fancies of the Europeans left behind in Europe regarding the geographical and physical reality of the Americas. The ignorant Europeans "believe that the Indies must be like a kingdom of Portugal, or Navarre, or anyway some small and limited territory, where all the inhabitants know one another and can communicate with each other as easily as between Cordova and Granada and Seville, or at most from Castile to Biscay. And this is why some of the letters that come here from ignorant mothers and wives wanting to write to their sons and husbands, and others to their relatives, are addressed to my dear son Pedro Rodríguez, in the Indies,' which is like saying to my son Mohamet, in Africa, or Johan Martínez, in Europe.'"[91]

10. The Indies and the ignorant Europeans

Even at the end of the last century—so the Mexican Fray Servando Teresa de Mier relates—"in some parts [of Spain], when they heard that I came from

---

90. *Hist.,* XXXIII, 10: III, 301–02. On certain "painted *sambenitos,*" see *Qu.,* p. 491. The etymology of the term given in the Dictionary of the Academy refers to derivation from *saco bendito* (blessed cloak), while others have seen it as coming from *sabanito* (altar cloth), and Américo Castro traces it back to *San Benito* (St. Benedict), in other words the long scapular or apron worn by the Benedictines. Thus modern philology bears out the naive assumption of the Mexican native.

91. *Hist.,* XXXV, 4: III, 597a, cited also by Levene, op. cit., I, 81n. But Oviedo himself invalidates his own example when, to underline the mobility of the Spaniards in the boundless spaces of the Indies, he observes that "it is a matter of as little moment for our Spaniards to go from one part to another as from Andalusia to Castile, Navarre or Aragon" (*Hist.,* XXXIX, Proh.: PT, IV, 337a).

America they would ask me about such and such a person: of course you must know him, they said to me, because in such and such a year he went to the Indies. As if the Indies were simply some tiny little place."[92]

But how often, even today (so I found in Peru thirty years ago . . .) we would have friends writing to us from Europe asking whether we knew so and so who was in Buenos Aires, or if we ever came across old whatsisname who was working in Havana! The naive desire to re-create Spain in the Indies is ridiculed by Oviedo, when he tells how the Spaniards founded a village in the Yucatán "that was given the name Salamanca . . . though it has nothing of the science, nobility, and fertility of the other Salamanca."[93]

The misfortunes befalling the inexperienced Spaniards when they encounter American nature for the first time can also provoke Oviedo's derision. We shall shortly see (below, sec. 14) the classic and tragic instance of the lion and the Lombard lion-tamer. Almost as a comic and grotesque prelude to more mortal accidents we have "what I saw happen to one of these greenhorns or newcomers" who, having satisfied the call of nature, wanted to wipe himself and "came across, as luck would have it, certain branches thereabouts of the *guao* [a caustic grass] and he took a few leaves and wiped himself with them in such a way and was left in such a condition that throughout that night he could not sleep or even let others sleep, and the following day he was still suffering so painfully in that part that he was helpless."[94]

Ironic comments about other people's lack of expertise, sometimes sounding suspiciously like the know-all "specialist's" arrogant superiority,[95] are not in fact all that rare in Oviedo, even without the American background. In connection with Juan Díaz de Solís, a good sailor but less expert condottiere on land, he recalls how once in Spain he saw a pilot on horseback steering a very uneven course as he proceeded on his pilgrimage to the Madonna of Guadeloupe, in fact so inexpert that he soon got out of the saddle and switched places with his page and cabin boy, who proved to be an even less skillful horseman; and the horse took fright and the pilot took off after it, terrifying it even more, yelling to the rider, " 'Grab those lines, you devil.' And the cabin boy grasped one rein and let go of the other, and the pilot yelled to him, Not the port one, the starboard one.' "

92. *Memorias* (Madrid, ca. 1917), p. 282. And toward the middle of the same century (1849) a Melville character, Wellingborough Redburn, is highly amused at the Englishman who expresses surprise at Mr. Redburn not having met his brother, who had lived for a number of years on the banks of the Mississippi—but there are twenty million inhabitants, and who knows them all? (*Redburn*, chap. 43, in H. Melville, *Romances* [New York, 1931], p. 1597).

93. *Hist.*, XXXII, 2: III, 226b (with the point being further underlined by a play on words between *manca*—"defective, disabled"—and the name of the city).

94. Ibid., IX, 34: I, 359b. The year in which Oviedo's *Historia* came out (1535) also witnessed the appearance of the first certain edition of the *Gargantua* in Lyon. Like the greenhorn in the Indies, Rabelais's young giant too once availed himself of nettles and other stinging plants, "but it gave [him] the most terrible trots" (Rabelais, *Gargantua*, chap. 14).

95. Salas, op. cit., p. 103.

And when the lad finally managed to get down they continued on foot, the boy tugging the horse by the bit, and the pilot whipping it from behind with a stick.[96]

11. DELUSION AND DESPAIR AMONG THE IMMIGRANTS

An even more amusing example of deluded innocence is provided by the three Spanish peasants who arrived in Santo Domingo, set about looking for gold and, after a week or two without success, sat down under a tree "to snack, take a breather and get a little rest," and all began to bewail their lot, like the louts they were, incapable of bearing their sufferings and disappointments in silence. And one began to rue the day he sold his oxen in Castile, and the next to regret having parted with his wife's dowry and leaving his wife alone and penniless with their young children to look after, and the third, having cursed the day that ever he was born, began to abuse the art of navigation and its inventors, hurling imprecations at the inventor of the trireme and vituperating the Carthaginians for inventing the quinquireme and the Phoenicians for observing the course of the stars; "and most of all he called down curses on Columbus for teaching the way to the Indies."

But then, possibly because he was a man of a certain culture, he began to console his companions and exhort them to bear up; and the three were still sighing and weeping when through their tears "one of them saw a nugget of gold glittering in the sun more than twenty paces away from where they were, and he got up saying, we may yet get over our disappointment." The nugget weighed a good fifteen or twenty pesos, and the good fellow "began to jump about with pleasure, kissing it and giving thanks to God." The others found other nuggets, bigger and smaller, and they all began to scratch about on the ground, gathering gold and filling their shoes that they had taken off, "never ceasing to pray to God for the soul of Columbus, and blessing the mariner's art."[97]

The brusque alternation between hope and despair gives the story a striking parablelike quality. Another weakness common to the treasure-seeking Spaniards, the way they quarrel even before they can get their hands on the precious metal, is ridiculed just as dramatically and picturesquely in the tale of how Fray Blas and his partners attempted to go down into the Masaya volcano to extract the molten gold and silver that was boiling and gurgling in the crater, amid hellish smoke and flames; and how those who had been lowered into the abyss laid claim to this or that seam, threatening each other and quarreling among themselves, so that "every single calabash of water that was lowered to them got

---

96. *Hist.*, XXIII, 1: II, 168. A similar touch of nautical madness seems to have overtaken Capt. Shotover in Shaw's *Heartbreak House*, in *Collected Plays*, Bodley Head edition (London, 1971–74), V, 160.

97. *Hist.*, VI, 8: I, 189–90. The three sufferers from the alternating winds of fortune soon suffered a further disappointment, "because the mines were already earmarked for the King"!

broken with their squabbling." Meanwhile the friar up above, on the lip of the crater, beginning to get suspicious and sniffing a fraud, hastily declared, "You are my witnesses that I am not taking this seam or that, but this cauldron of metal boiling there, in the name of the king, our Lord, and my name and that of my companions'; at which they all burst out laughing."[98]

12. OVIEDO'S IRONY AT HIS OWN EXPENSE

Oviedo does not spare himself either and is quite prepared to laugh at his own naivety. He recalls, for instance, the time when the opossum attacked his chickens, slaughtering and sucking the blood of no less than fourteen of them in a single night, "at a time when each was worth three gold pesos and more," groans Oviedo, immediately following this economic lament with a culinary one: "And in truth I would not want so many birds for my plate all on one day."[99] And he ruefully remembers the time (in 1515) when he ate some *opuntias* (Indian figs) and his urine turned bright red, "no more nor less than actual blood. I was so worried about my health that I was quite stunned and petrified," thinking that he had managed to catch some unheard-of disease—so he says in the *Summary*—or burst all the veins in his body, from which all the blood was flowing into his bladder, according to the fuller version in the *History*.[100]

Oviedo adds another candid detail: "I did not even dare to produce as much [urine] as I could or as necessity urged me," for fear of bleeding himself dry; but he also relates the jibes of the knowing Andrés Niño, who comes up to Oviedo and says, "My lord, it seems to me that your color is not good. How do you feel? Is something hurting?" And Oviedo replies that he is fine, but he would give his horse and four more to be near a good doctor. . . .

The disquieting oddity of the *opuntia* is also described by Peter Martyr and the cleric Las Casas. The former writes: "There is another tree growing on the riverbanks that produces some apples which, when eaten, provoke the urine and foment it until they turn it blood-colored."[101] And the latter: "In the beginning, when we did not know what it was, some people ate it, not without great fear,

---

98. Ibid., XLII, 10: IV, 91b. One of Fray Blas's companions, Juan Sánchez Portero, wrote a "short account of the secrets existing in the volcano of Masaya, which the Indians call Hell, in the province of Nicaragua in the South Sea," though Medina, *Biblioteca,* VI, 534–35, is uncertain whether it was ever published. This is probably the report that Juan Sánchez Portero made to the king with a view to being authorized to continue his explorations, going halves on expenses and profits: see the "Capitulation made with Juan Sánchez Portero on the discovery of the volcano of Massaya," 28 September 1557 (headed "The King" and signed "The Princess"), in *CDII,* XXIII, 269–73. In the latter half of the eighteenth century Eusebio Llano Zapata confessed himself convinced "that the material constantly liquefying in that forge [of the volcanoes] is gold" (*Memorias histórico-físico-apologéticas de la América meridional* [Lima, 1904], p. 403; cf. A. Gerbi, *Viejas polémicas sobre el Nuevo Mundo* [Lima, 1946], p. 242).

99. *Hist.,* XII, 27: I, 416; XXVI, 31: II, 412b.

100. *Sum.,* chap. 80, p. 240; *Hist.,* VIII, 28: I, 313–14.

101. *Dec.,* VIII, 7, p. 601.

thinking it was blood that issued forth and that they must have burst all their veins."[102]

13. OVIEDO AND SYPHILIS

A misremembered recollection of this passage from Oviedo could possibly have been the starting point for the extraordinary legend repeated, according to de Pauw, by Falloppio (a contemporary of Oviedo, 1523–1562), to the effect that our distinguished chronicler contracted venereal disease in Naples, guessed that there must be a cure to be found in the Indies for the disease that came from the Indies, and for that reason undertook the journey to America. "The savages of Santo Domingo, just by looking at his face, knew that he was gangrened [some diagnosticians, these savages!] and showed him the gaiac tree" and thus—an even more amazing finale to this incredible string of "inspired inventions," a classic happy ending to this truly Boccaccesque tale, "Oviedo was fortunate through his misfortune and made a pile of money in Spain" by importing the savages' remedy for syphilis![103]

Another possible explanation is that de Pauw confused Oviedo's name with that of the Spaniard "Giovanni Consalvo" who, on his return from the Antilles, caught syphilis in Naples and decided to go back to America to find the remedy. "When he got there he found that gaiac wood was used there against syphilis and having tried it out and found it successful himself he had it brought to Europe, where it was sold in Genoa at no less that eleven gold *scudi* a pound. So Consalvo became extremely rich and when he died left a patrimony of three million gold florins."[104] But the story or fable seems to go back to the aforementioned Falloppio.[105]

One more even less plausible explanation of the origin of the legend is that in the same chapter in which Oviedo recounts the origin of the "French evil" or "Neapolitan evil" he refers to another ailment, *niguas* or chiggers, and says "I myself have had them in my feet."[106]

In the *Summary,* however, Oviedo had already asserted that syphilis "came

102. *Apologética historia,* chap. 12, ed. cit., III, 449, probably recalling Oviedo. On the use of *tunas* as a coloring agent (without any mention of Oviedo), see Yacovleff, op. cit., pp. 317–22. The *pitahaya* too "has the same effect on the urine as *tunas* does, but not so soon" (*Hist.,* VIII, 26: I, 311b). *Jagua* sprinkled on the skin produces black speckles that terrify women and "cause them to go rushing about seeking remedies, all of which are harmful," whereas in fact the color gradually fades away of its own accord (*Sum.,* chap. 76, p. 223).

103. *Les Américains,* I, 22. De Pauw invokes Oviedo as an authority on a number of occasions in this work (see I, 9), and in the *Défense* against Pernety, pp. 14*n,* 54–55, 66, 84, 91–92.

Another structurally similar legend is that Oviedo introduced the potato into Spain; but he himself only says that he took some all the way to Avila, and when he got there they were still edible (*Hist.,* VII, 4: PT, I, 235a); see P. Henríquez Ureña, *Para la historia de los indigenismos* (Buenos Aires, 1938), p. 73*nl,* quoting D. Bois, *Les plantes alimentaires chez tous les peuples et à travers les ages,* 4 vols. (Paris, 1927–37)), I, 317.

104. A. Benedicenti, *Malati, medici e farmacisti* (Milan, 1924), I, 721–22, quoting Corradi, "L'acqua del legno e le cure depurative nel '500," *Annali Universali di medicina,* 1884.

105. *De morbo gallico,* 1563. On the European renown of *guaiacum,* the "wood" *par excellence,* introduced into Spain in 1508 and into Italy in 1517, see Morinigo, op. cit., pp. 27–31, 50, 52, 71. Morison, *Southern Voyages,* p. 96, insists that it has "no therapeutic effect whatsoever."

106. *Hist.,* II, 14: I, 57b.

from the Indies," though it was in fact less dangerous there than in Europe. The Great Captain's troops introduced it into Italy. So the French call it the "Neapolitan evil" and the Italians "the French evil."[107] But in the nineteenth century the Mexican patriot Servando Teresa de Mier fiercely rejected the charge; America was blessed in possessing the sovereign remedy for syphilis, and Oviedo, "in his false and wicked history of the Indies, as Las Casas calls it and Herrera confirms," sophistically used this fact to argue that the foul disease came from America.[108]

In clear contrast with these explanations, Francisco Delicado, an expert in the field being a syphilitic himself and author of *Il mal francese* (1529), has his harlot Divicia say that the French evil originated among the troops of Charles VIII in 1488, which would be four years before the discovery of America, and specifically at "Rapolo" (Rapallo?), a seaport near Genoa. But Divicia and Lozana herself are optimistic (for professional reasons?), assuring us "that the wood provides a cure," and that the fearful calamity "is already beginning to be alleviated with the wood of the West Indies," thanks to which it will cease all together in 1548![109]

14. THE TIGER AND THE LOMBARD TAMER

The most complete of Oviedo's satires, however, is the story that features an American tiger and a European—in fact Lombard—tamer, and whose protagonists thus seem to represent Oviedo's whole history in microcosm, the Italianizing tendencies and the pride in the material offered by the Indies, the incredulity of the Old World and the surprising "novelty" of the new.

The *opuntia* was frightening but actually quite harmless. The precise opposite was true of the tiger (or *ochi*) that was brought to Toledo shortly after one of Charles V's leopards died. The Lombard lion-tamer, afraid of losing his job, suggested to the emperor that he train the American tiger for him, so that he could use it for hunting. He took it to a garden near the city where he kept it outside its cage, on a thin string, "and treated it so familiarly that I was astonished at what I saw."

The historian, as a specialist in such matters, hastened to explain to the tamer that he was dealing with a dangerous and treacherous animal, and "it was therefore all the more credit to him that he kept it peaceful and good-natured"; he should not trust it, however, should go warily and be constantly on his guard, because Oviedo felt he could already see him dead. "Then the lion-tamer, laughing and not thinking that I deserved any thanks for such counsel, approached the tiger and putting his hand on his back said: This is my boy, he is an absolute

---

107. *Sum.*, chap. 75, pp. 218–21.
108. Cf. also Mier, *Escritos inéditos*, p. 315.
109. Delicado, *La Lozana andaluza* (1524), ed. cit., I, 220–21; II, 160–61, 184–89, 200–01.

angel, I shall make him perform miracles; in fact I want to go to India and bring back five or six of these, only smaller, and I want Caesar to have a hunt worthy of an emperor, and I want him to give me a state."[110]

Some of the bystanders complimented him and others said nothing. Oviedo, unruffled by the sarcasm implicit in those scornful words, indeed filled with pity, again advised extreme caution, and suggested trimming the beast's claws, teeth, and fangs: "Don't think that God gave him them for you to feed him at fixed times, because never did any of his race eat out of a bowl or come to table summoned by a bell." And with a sudden change of tone, from the facetious to the very, very serious, and indeed almost threatening, he finishes: "I can promise you that if we live a year either you or the tiger will be dead; and forgive me, because in truth I pity you."

The tamer—who by this time seems to have become a little impressed— thanked him, but replied bravely that he knew his business. "As I had no obligation to teach him it, we went off laughing at his foolishness," not without having noticed with a certain anxiety that even when the tiger let itself be stroked "it seemed to be muttering something under its breath." This suppressed growl- ing obviously boded ill.

When Oviedo was drafting his *Summary* he was at pains to warn the emperor of the risk that the foolhardy tamer was taking. "This lion-tamer of your Maj- esty's, that has taken on the job of taming the tiger, might be an expert on something else more useful and profitable to him for his life, because this tiger is young, and each day it will become stronger and fiercer and twice as wicked."[111] But the warning came too late. The *Summary* had not yet come out, indeed only a week had passed since the visit, when "because of some disagreement or other over his lessons" the tiger almost killed his master," in fact would certainly have torn him to pieces if help had not arrived in time. "Shortly thereafter the tiger died, or his master helped him to die, which is more what I think. . . ." "No," Oviedo concludes, "in truth such animals are not suited to human company."[112]

---

110. The keeper's familiar and almost protective tone must have been in vogue, part of the required stock-in-trade of the court tamer. In a novel that once enjoyed considerable popularity, Charles Reade's *The Cloister and the Hearth* (1861), a huntsman-cum-keeper at the court of the duke of Burgundy (mid-fifteenth century) tells what befell the man who was unwise enough to throw a handful of dust at a leopard in the royal menagerie. The duke "shut him up in prison, in a cell under the ground, and the rats cleaned the flesh off his bones in a night. Served him right for molesting the poor thing" (chap. 7, ed. cit., p. 56). In the middle of the eighteenth century Oliver Goldsmith visited the wild animals on show in the Tower of London and was amazed to see the keeper of the ounce (or snow leopard) playing with the beast "without the smallest apprehension." And he goes on: "I own I was not a little uneasy, at first, for the man, when he put his hand through the bars, and called the animal by its name" ("Animated Nature," 1774, in *A History of the Earth and Animated Nature* [London and Edinburgh, n.d.], I, 377a). Cf. J. H. Pitman, op. cit., p. 55. But on that particular occasion the beast in question submitted peacefully.

111. *Sum.*, chap. 11, pp. 147–48.

112. *Hist.*, XII, 10: I, 403–04. The *Sumario* says that the sad event occurred "many days" after Oviedo had written his warning, obviously bearing out his prophetic wisdom. The *Historia* says that it came about "less than a week after" his visit, bearing out the timeliness and urgency of the advice given. The story is also told by F. Soler Jardón, "Tres 'tigres' para el Buen Retiro (1635)," *RI*, 8, nos. 28–29 (1947), 501–09.

Oviedo, a keenly interested and far from impassive onlooker, remains unwaveringly polite. Armed with his own personal experience and therefore torn between scorn and sympathy for this foolish braggart,[113]—although at heart quite glad to be able to witness the clash between the Lombard's arrogance and the snares of America's wildlife, which he confidently predicts must end in a fight to the death—he dominates the scene, staring down at the foolheardy tamer and the wild beast, mocking the one and warning against the other. A veritable *nuntius oceanicus* from the New World to the Old, he warns, instructs, advises, and softly smiles.

113. Oviedo tells a similar tale of fatal presumption on the part of an Italian in the third (unpublished) part of the *Quinquagenas*. A Spanish swordsman, after killing numerous adversaries with a secret thrust to the throat, retires from the world in penitence. An Italian soldier seeks him out, taking along two swords, and begs and beseeches the Spaniard to teach him the special thrust, adding that "he knew of a way of parrying it." The hermit sees no way out of it, grasps the sword and does such a good job of teaching the Italian his secret that the latter is killed on the spot (*Qu.*, p. xxvii).

In one of the published *Quinquagenas* Oviedo comments in verse, "No-one should test his strength / With beasts or mighty men," giving the example of a lion that breaks into a house and has to be killed as quickly as possible, and with the story of a presumptuous King Favila (who reigned from 732 to 734), torn to pieces by a bear that he insisted on challenging to single combat (*Qu.*, pp. 74–75: cf. p. 457). A wolf too is an inconvenient houseguest, and better killed! (*Qu.*, p. 259).

Appendix

Bibliography

Index

Appendix

A. THE FAMOUS LINE FROM SERAFINO DELL'AQUILA (see chap. XV, sec. 7)

THE two lines from Serafino dell'Aquila quoted by Oviedo belong to the same sonnet, number 48 in the first edition, which Serafino was suspected of having "cribbed" from a *comparation* by Cecco d'Ascoli. The full text of Serafino's sonnet is as follows (I have modernized the spelling):

> Io pur travaglio, e so ch'è 'l tempo gioco,
> Che se alcun stenta o vive oggi beato
> Non è viltà, non è virtù, ma fato
> Chè contra 'l ciel nostro operar val poco.
>
> Nascon due legni in un medesmo loco
> E de l'un fassi un Dio vago ed ornato
> Ch'ognun l'adora, e l'altro è sol dicato
> Ad esser forche, o destinato al foco.
>
> Così va il mondo, ognun segue sua stella,
> Ciascuno è in terra a qualche fin produtto
> E per tal variar natura è bella.
>
> Chi sparge il seme, e chi raccoglie il frutto.
> E cosi va persin che giunge quella
> Che con l'adunca falce adegua il tutto.

[I toil away, but I know that time is a game, for if someone is always in need, or today has everything he wants, this is not baseness, nor virtue, but fate, because our actions count for little against the heavens.

Two timbers are born in the same place, and one is fashioned into a god, gracious and ornate, worshiped by all the world, and the other is only destined to become a gallows, or firewood.

This is the way the world goes; everyone follows his star, each one of us is put here on earth for some end, and in this variation lies nature's beauty.

Some sow the seed, and some reap the harvest. And so it will go on, until death's curved scythe lays all things low.]

The line "Chi sparge il seme, e chi raccoglie il frutto" is quoted by Oviedo in support of his argument on the need for unprotesting acceptance of the differing destinies allotted by

409

God (*Hist.*, XVII, 19; I, 539a). The line "Per troppo variar natura è bella" (in which the "troppo" must be a copyist's error, because Oviedo translates the lines correctly into Spanish, and in the early editions, from 1535 to 1547, the line is quoted accurately) is recalled in connection with the nonbarking dogs, which are "a great novelty" compared with the European ones (XII, 5; I, 391). And without actually quoting the Italian line, Oviedo repeats that "nature's beauty lies in these varieties" after describing the torpedo fish (electric ray), the polecat, and the *bivana,* a creature remarkable for having fur that runs the wrong way (VI, 34; I, 225).

The same proverbial conceit crops up again in another passage. Oviedo recalls that all things in nature, including poisons, come from God and therefore have one and the same raison d'être, some evident or hidden usefulness; and he goes on, somewhat illogically, "and the more varied and different they are, the more beautiful nature is" (XIX, Proh; I, 586b).[1]

It may be worth noting that this same line, "Per troppo variar natura è bella," enjoyed an extraordinarily successful career in Spain.[2] It is used in an almost proverbial sense by Lope de Vega, Cervantes, Alarcón, Calderón, Tirso de Molina, and Gracián, and there is a whole bibliography on its vicissitudes:

a. Joaquim de Vasconcellos, note to his edition of Francisco de Holanda, *Vier Gespräche über die Malerei geführt zu Rom* (1518; Vienna, 1899), quoted in (f) below.

b. A. Morel-Fatio, edition of Lope de Vega's *Arte nuevo de hacer comedias en este tiempo,* note on line 174, *Bulletin Hispanique,* 3 (1901), 365–405.

c. A. Farinelli, review of the above in *Archiv für das Studium der neueren Sprachen und Literaturen,* 109 (1902), 467ff, reprinted in *Italia e Spagna,* II, 377–409.

d. R. Schevill and A. Bonilla, note in their edition of *La Galatea,* in *Obras completas de M. de Cervantes* (Madrid, 1914), II, 288–89.

e. A. Morel-Fatio, "La fortune en Espagne d'un vers italien," *Revista de Filologia Española,* 3 (1916), 63–66.

f. Enrique Díez Canedo, "Fortuna española de un verso italiano," *Revista de Filologia Española,* 3 (1916), 168–70. (Díez Canedo was the first to identify Serafino dell'Aquila as the source.)

g. A. R. (Alfonso Reyes), "Fortuna española de un verso italiano," in *Revista de Filologia Espanola,* 4 (1917), 208.

Farinelli, before he knew who its author was, wrote:

"'Per troppo variar natura è bella' is not actually a line of poetry but a proverbial expression. Whether the Spaniards were also aware of the obscene connotation of this very common saying (which is still current in Naples and elsewhere, so B. Croce tells me), I would not like to say. Lope, in the *Rimas de Burguillos* (the *canción* 'Ya pues que todo el mundo . . .') said 'pero siendo jüez naturaleza, / no es siempre agradecida la

---

1. Cf. also *Hist.*, VIII, 15: I, 302b ("Nature creates nothing superfluous or purposeless, and if certain things do not serve certain other purposes, it is because we do not know how to use them"), and XIII, Proh.: I, 423a.

2. In Italy the dictum reoccurs regularly through the ages, with only the most minimal variations in wording. The Rev. Don Callisto Placentino quotes it, without citing Serafino, in his *Expositione de Ageo Propheta* (Pavia, 1541), sheet C III.ʳ And Giordano Bruno gives it as a proverbial saying in his "Ars Memoriae," ca. 1582 (*Opere latine* [Naples and Florence, 1879–81], vol. II, pt. I, p. 83). A couple of centuries later Antonio Genovesi, to defend the diversity of tastes, appetites, feelings, and even opinions, invoked the same little maxim as a self-evident truth (op. cit., XIII, 528).

belleza / y la fé más sincera / quejarse de Aristoteles pudiera' ('but nature being the judge, beauty is not always grateful, and the most sincere faith could complain about Aristotle')" (*Italia e Spagna*, II, 395).

Nobody mentions Oviedo's precise citation, which possibly predates any of those given by the scholars—a further indication of the academics' limited familiarity with our chronicler. One notes how *tal* is almost always replaced by *troppo*, a substitution that accentuates the mannered and baroque tone of what is really a thoroughly trite little notion. It is also curious that almost everyone cites it as a well-known saying, of proverbial flavor, as "the Italian's rule" or the "common refrain," providing a further argument in support of Croce's thesis on the popular character of Spanish literature.

A. O. Lovejoy (in *The Great Chain of Being* [Cambridge, Mass., 1942], pp. 75–77) mentions certain Thomistic formulations of the thesis that nature attains perfection in variety, and some of its probable derivations in Leibniz. Jerome Cardan, an attentive reader of Oviedo, writes in his dedication to the *De subtilitate rerum:* "Nature rejoices in variety (as the saying goes)" and frequently repeats the notion in his *De rerum varietate* (Basel, 1557). Again at the end of the sixteenth century John Donne could be found speaking of "variety, for which the world is so delightfull" ("Paradoxes and Problems" in *Complete Poetry and Selected Poems* [London, 1939], p. 337). Méric Casaubon, son of Isaac, repeated (in 1638) "even herein nature delights in varietie" (quoted by Hodgen, op. cit., p. 209). And still in the middle of the eighteenth century Lope de Vega's couplet: "Buen exemplo nos da naturaleza / Que por tal variedad tiene belleza" ("A good example is given us by nature, that gains its beauty from such variety") was being discussed by Lessing.[3]

Some vestiges of the thesis can perhaps be detected in various of the romantics' eulogies of nature as variety or diversity,[4] for instance in Victor Hugo's preface to *Cromwell* (nature as divine variety, etc. [Paris, 1836], I, 57), or even in the words Leopardi puts into Columbus's mouth in the discoverer's *Dialogue* with Gutiérrez: "Nature is seen to be furnished with such power, and its effects to be so varied and manifold," and so forth (op. cit., p. 244). In truth, *habent sua fata versiculi.*

B. The contract between Oviedo, Gian Battista Ramusio, and Antonio Priuli
(see chap. XV, sec. 9)

In the name of Christ, Amen. In the year of His nativity 1538, in the eleventh indiction, on Saturday, 25 May, in Venice, in the house of Sire Antonio de Priuli, Procurator of St. Mark, situated within the district of St. Severus, in the presence of myself, a notary, and the witnesses mentioned below, a translation was made of a certain document written in the Castilian language (so it was asserted) in the hand of Don Consalvo Ferrando de Oviedo y Valdes, Castellan or Commandant of the Fort in the city of Santo Domingo on the island of Hispaniola, Historian of His Imperial Majesty. This document Messer Giovanni Battista Ramusio, Secretary of the Illustrious Seigniory of Venice, translated

---

3. *Hamburgische Dramaturgie*, LXIX, 29 December 1767, in G. E. Lessing, *Werke* (Leipzig and Vienna [1911]), V, 222–24; cf. the note by B. Matthews in his edition of Lope de Vega's *New Art of Writing Plays* (New York, 1914), p. 45.

4. E.g., Mme de Staël, *Corinne*, I, 4, ed. cit., II, 434: "all things natural are varied"; and "the fair inequalities produced by nature," ibid., IV, ed. cit., II, 489. I am deliberately ignoring the numerous generalized eulogies of "variety," from Euripides on.

word for word into the Italian language; the document is said to set out the arrangements relating to the setting up of a sort of company between the parties named below, i.e., Captain Don Consalvo Ferrando de Oviedo y Valdes, Castellan or Commandant of the royal fort of the city of Santo Domingo on the island of Hispaniola, Historian to his Sacred and Imperial Majesty, for one half, and Sire Antonio de Priuli, Procurator of St. Mark and Messer Giovanni Battista Ramusio, Secretary to the Illustrious Seigniory of Venice, for the other half of the said company. The document in question begins as follows.

The arrangement drawn up between the gentlemen Gian Battista Ramusio, Secretary of the Most Illustrious Seigniory of Venice and Antonio de Priuli, Procurator of St. Mark, of the one part, and of the other part Captain Consalvo Ferrando di Oviedo y Valdes, Commandant of the Fort in the City of Santo Domingo on the Island of Hispaniola, Chronicler of His Imperial Majesty, is as follows . . .

Firstly, the above named parties form a company for a period of six years, to run from the first day of January 1538 and closing at the end of 1543, for such profit and loss as God will give them, without limitation or interruption of any kind; and whereas the said Captain has written to the said gentlemen asking them to allow him to include in this company such person as he wishes; and whereas the capital is four hundred ducats of sterling gold and correct weight each of which is worth three hundred and seventy five *maravedis* in Spain, so that the four hundred ducats will in all amount to one hundred and fifty thousand (150,000) *maravedis;* and whereas the said Captain has not determined the person to whom he will give the fourth part of this company, half is to be charged to the name and risk of the said Captain, and the said Antonio di Priuli, as a concession to him and a favor to all parties involved will put up all four hundred ducats and lend them for the first shipment without any interest or exchange, on the condition that from the first proceeds deriving from the said cargo, before all else, he is first of all paid and reimbursed all four hundred ducats, and the surplus of the earnings will remain as capital of the said company, for trading between the Indies and Spain, through the said Captain, and to the other parts of the Indies, and the said gentlemen will take on cargoes in Italy, in Venice, and elsewhere, sending to the said Captain in the name of the said company whatever they find and deem to be appropriate for the profit of the company throughout the said time, and in accordance with the instructions of the said Commandant, and at the end of the time specified whatever God has given and increased will be divided up, and the Captain will be taken at his word on the basis of his sworn oath and signature, as regards the accounts that are kept showing the purchases and sales by the said company. And this is the arrangement that the said gentlemen will adopt in order to settle matters up with respect to the said one hundred ducats that each of them puts into the company, and the Captain as regards the other two hundred ducats for himself and the person he names to be included in the company; and if the said gentlemen feel that the principle should not be four hundred ducats but three hundred, as was the previous arrangement, so it shall be, if the said gentlemen so command, on the understanding that as a concession to the said Captain, they will be four hundred for the purposes he referred to in his letters.

The merchandise shall be shipped to Cadiz, and shall there be registered in the name of the said Captain, and his shall be the only name put on it, although in reality it must be divided into four equal parts, namely for the two said gentlemen, and the said Commandant and the person he names as the other two; and on behalf of the company there shall be a person in Cadiz designated by the said Secretary and Procurator of St. Mark, who shall receive the merchandise to be forwarded to the said Commandant in Santo Domingo, and the merchandise that the latter sends to the two gentlemen for the company, and who shall sell syrups and sugars, and do with what is sent to him whatever he is ordered by the said company, and shall follow their instructions.

The freight costs at Santo Domingo will be paid by the said Commandant, and the costs to be paid in Spain will be the responsibility of the two gentlemen, and in Venice of the company, and both the said parties will keep detailed ledgers and daily accounts containing all matters affecting the company, and as regards anything done in connection with company affairs, and entered in the accounts, the reasons must be clearly and accurately explained on a day-by-day and continual basis, for both income and expenditure, as is only right and proper between such persons; and the commercial formalities that have to be completed in Cadiz shall be the responsibility of the said gentlemen and not of the said Captain, and those in the Indies the responsibility of the said Captain.

It shall be left to each of these gentlemen, and shall be the responsibility of each of them, to insure whatever each person forwards at the highest price acceptable to God and his conscience either wholly or partially, as he deems fit.

Before the agreement reaches Venice the said gentlemen shall write that the three hundred ducats will be debited in the name of all three, the said gentlemen and the Commandant, and when it arrives the other remaining one hundred ducats will be put up, if it so pleases the said Signor Antonio Priuli, for the said company, and in the name of all, that the fourth person shall be the person designated by the said Captain; and these shall come at the risk of the said Commandant, and shall serve for the purpose of the things lacking or else it will be seen what the said Commandant requests, in addition to what the said gentlemen have sent.

Inasmuch as the coin current in the Indies is bad, and to make it good for the whole company, the Commandant is entrusted with the task of exchanging what he has of the comapny's money into whatever he thinks fit, or sending it to Spain if he thinks that is best, this being done at the risk, cost and damage of all the parties. At the end of the six-year period each party shall send the said accounts, right from the beginning, to Seville, signed and sworn to for his discharge, to close the accounts; on the basis of these documents and ledgers the accounts shall be checked by persons that the parties shall nominate for this purpose, and an equal division shall be made in accordance with what each should have, and the funds shall be deposited in a bank with the parties' agreement in order that they may be repaid everything that one party has advanced to another, and that party to another, and this shall constitute a conclusion, closure, and settlement for all parties, and for all persons, with the said third persons or accountants signing their names before a notary public.

If the said gentlemen and the said captain so wish they may increase the capital and prolong the term of this company, provided they are all in accord, and not one without the others, but all three in agreement, and in no other way. And I, the said Commandant, signify my agreement henceforth to the said company and send the same to the said gentlemen, and they too are to send, duly signed and sworn, another document similar to the present, in which I swear to God and St. Mary, and with the sign of the cross which I physically touched with my right hand, that I shall keep, and perform all the aforegoing, as regards my part of the agreement. And if it should be necessary I pledge my person, my possessions, both present and future, and I submit to the authority of any whatsoever court and jurisdiction and to the decisions thereof, that they may oblige me to abide by and comply with the aforegoing on pain of paying everything that I owe in respect of the above, plus two thousand ducats to the lawful party, in respect of which I renounce each and every privileged court, decree, and ordinance that may be to the contrary, and the law, if applicable, concerning the jurisdiction of all judges, and the article on penalties, together with all that which deals with and regulates that matter, and the law stating that no renunciation is valid, and as the person that I am henceforth. And I for myself pledge my faith and word, as a gentleman, that it will be observed by me, and all the above accomplished, and so I affirm before the witnesses. In the city of Santo Domingo, Hispaniola, 20 December 1537. Witnessed by Hernando Garzia, gunner, and Antonio Sanchez, custodian of the fort of Santo Domingo.

G. H. de Ov.

H. G.   A. S.

Sire Antonio di Priuli, Procurator of St. Mark, and Messer Giambattista Ramusio, Secretary of the Most Illustrious Seigniory of Venice, have, in the presence of myself, a Notary, subscribed to the abovementioned articles of the said company, which, on their order, I have registered in my protocol; the said Sire Antonio Priuli and Messer Giambattista Ramusio aforesaid, in the presence of myself, a notary, and the undermentioned witnesses, have sworn to these articles and confirmed the said agreement precisely as it stands, save that they declare that the capital put up by Messer Antonio di Priuli in the said company will be in ducats of 6 lire and 4 soldi, that is to say a total of four hundred Venetian ducats of 6 lire and 4 soldi. The same Venetian ducats of 6 lire and 4 soldi amount to three hundred and twenty and one half *maravedis* each, so that the four hundred ducats would be one hundred and twenty-eight thousand two hundred (128,200) *maravedis;* however, as it is not known how much the insurance came to, and the freight charges to be paid from Messina to Calais, and it is impossible to know exactly if the said Sire Antonio di Priuli will put up four hundred (400) ducats, (and not gold ducats as set out in the article of the said company), or more or less than that, the sum named will be entered in the books of the company with the stipulation that the said Sire Antonio di Priuli shall, from the stock sent here from Hispaniola by Captain Gonzalo Fernando de Oviedo, take out first the four hundred (400) ducats, that the said messer Antonio lent to the company, or that greater or lesser amount that he has lent, and the rest shall remain in the company, as explained in the above article, and the said Sire Antonio di Priuli and Messer Giambattista Ramusio are agreeable to allowing the said Signor Gonzalo half of the ensuing profit and loss that ensues in the said company on the said four hundred ducats, or more or less, that will be to the profit or loss of the said Signor Gonzalo de Oviedo, as he requests, he being empowered with his said half to nominate as partner one or more persons, as he wishes, in the said company for the time abovementioned, and the other half shall fall to Sire Antonio de Priuli for his profit or loss, and the other half to messer Giambattista Ramusio for his profit or loss, he being the fourth of the said company. And if perchance—God forbid—all or part of the said things purchased for the account of the said company, that have now been loaded here in Venice for Messina on my lord the duke of Ferrara's ship, with orders that these goods should be sent from Messina to Cadiz and from Cadiz to Hispaniola, to the city of San Domingo where Signor Gonzalo da Oviedo resides—if perchance, either on the way there, or in such goods as

Signor Gonzalo sends here to Venice, there were to occur some shipwreck, either total or partial, so that with the stock brought to Venice it were not possible to recoup the said four hundred (400) ducats that the said Messer Antonio di Priuli lent to the said company, or more or less, as it may have been, in this case let it be made clear that the same Messer Antonio di Priuli is to be reimbursed by each of the partners in the said company for the amount he lent to the said company, in other words one half shall be the responsibility of Signor Gonzalo da Oviedo, and a quarter the responsibility of Messer Giambattista Ramusio and the other quarter of the said Messer Antonio, all of whom undertake within one year in the event—God forbid—of the occurrence of that which is mentioned above, to repay to the same Messer Antonio the amount that he has lent, as is only honest, and if there were to be insurance on the said shipwreck it should be encashed at the risk of the partners, and Signor Gonzalo assigned his half and Sire Antonio his quarter and Messer Giambattista his quarter, as is only right.

Sire Antonio de Priuli, Procurator of St. Mark, and Messer Giovanni Battista Ramusio, Secretary of the Most Illustrious Seigniory of Venice, here in the presence of myself, a notary, and the undersigned witnesses, the sacred scriptures having been touched, and with the sign of the most holy cross, both promised and affirmed on oath, confirming all things, both the separate articles and the other things contained in the provisions relating to the company in question; and if necessary, and appropriate, the aforesaid gentlemen Antonio de Priuli, Procurator, and Giovanni Battista Ramusio, pledge their persons, with all their property, both present and future, submitting to the authority of any whatsoever court and jurisdiction, and to the decisions thereof, and undertake to pay the full amount that the said gentlemen Antonio de Priuli and Giovanni Battista Ramusio owe and in respect of which either one of them is a debtor, regarding the abovementioned provisions contained in the said document relating to the company, plus two thousand ducats to the lawful party, over which they renounce any whatsoever privileged court, statute, and decree that may be to the contrary, and the law, if applicable, concerning the jurisdiction of all judges and the article on penalties, to the effect that no renunciation shall be valid. Moreover the said gentlemen Antonio and Giovanni Battista promise to maintain, comply with and observe all and each of the things contained in the instrument setting up the company, including all and each of its separate articles and agreements, notwithstanding any conventions, laws, decrees, statutes, and any whatsoever rules and formulas and ordinances existing to the contrary. In respect of these separate aforegoing matters I, the notary named below, was summoned to draw up a public instrument, the charter containing the instrument of the company in question having been read out, as regarding its essentials, and ratified, confirmed, and approved.

I, Antonio de Priuli, Procurator of St. Mark, declare the above to be true.

I, Gian Battista Ramusio, Secretary, declare the above to be true.

Presbyter Caraccia, Chaplain of St. Proclus, Giorgio Ongaro, member of the household of the said Sire Antonio.

Signatures of witnesses.

I, the Reverend Pietro Caraccia chaplain of St. Proclus, swear that I was present with all the above witnesses, and signed with my own hand.

I, Giorgio Ongaro, residing in the district of Santa Maria Formosa, having been asked to serve as a witness, duly gave my oath.

Done in Venice, in the year, month, indiction, and place abovementioned, in the presence of the abovementioned witnesses.

Faithfully copied from the deeds, and the protocol of me, Presbyter Pietro de Bartolo, Chaplain of St. Severus, Imperial and Venetian Notary.

I, Presbyter Pietro Caraccia, Chaplain of St. Proclus, was a witness to all the above, and signed with my own hand.

I, Giorgio Ongaro, resident in the district of Santa Maria Formosa having been asked to serve as witness, duly gave my oath.

Faithfully copied from the deeds of me, Presbyter Pietro de Bartolo, public notary of Venice and the empire.

Agreement relating to the Company that messer Giovanni Battista Ramusio had with Sire Antonio de Priuli, the Procurator, and Signor Gonzalo di Oviedo.   1538

C. Oviedo's gluttony (see chap. XV, sec. 16)

Oviedo himself gives us convincing and autobiographical proof of his gluttony, although he strenuously denies being a gourmand (*Hist.*, VIII, 28: I, 314b) or even just a gourmet (VIII, 18: I, 304).[5] In the moralistic *Quinquagenas* of his declining years he can still be found denouncing the sin of gluttony as "very dangerous, and especially for women" because it is an incitement to lust . . . (pp. 47–48; cf. pp. 203–04, 422–23).

But he describes *chicha* (fermented maize) as better than the cider or apple wine made and drunk in Biscay, and "the beer or ale drunk by the English and in Flanders (both of which I myself have tried and drunk") (*Hist.*, XXIX, 28: III, 136–37). And as for food, one need look no further than the animal he fell upon with voracious delight—it was "very plump and very well-roasted and basted and larded and with garlic, and I found it not bad at all"—until his friends, seeing the gusto and enthusiasm with which he was attacking it, told him it was dogmeat . . . (XII, 5: I, 391a). But horsemeat is quite tasty too, when there is nothing else, "because this sauce of hunger . . . is the best cook of all" (XXXIII, 35: III, 444b).

His sensual appetite and delicacy of taste emerge again when he is holding forth on the oysters of the Indies, which are not as good as the Spanish ones, but tasteless and indigestible; in fact there is a considerable difference, "but everything gets eaten in the end" (XIX, 9: I, 606b; XIX, 10: I, 608a). On other occasions he remembers a certain "fat and tasty suckling pig" (III, 7: I, 75), extols (albeit at second hand) some partridges that are as delicious as those of Spain and twice as big (L, 24: PT, V, 380), indulges in a long digression on the various ways of cooking the sweet and very palatable banana (VIII, 1: I, 291) or gets altogether carried away with fervent rhapsodies in praise of the pineapple or the medlar.

His enthusiasm for the liberality of nature (of which we have already had much to say) is in fact seen in its most quintessential and almost, one might say, spiritual form when he is describing the succulence of certain tropical fruits that are beyond the wildest dreams of the Europeans. When he comes face to face with that remarkable novelty, the pineapple, Oviedo goes into raptures.

---

5. There is thus no cause to assume, as does Díez del Corral (op. cit., p. 166), that Oviedo had himself taken on as a page "because of the succulent food served in the kitchens of the Renaissance princes."

The hymn of praise that he sings in its honor is too long for us to quote in its entirety, but its very candor gives it a "flavor" all its own. After explaining how the *piña* is pleasing to the sight, smell, taste, and touch, Oviedo adds, with a flight of baroque fancy: "As for the fifth sense, which is hearing, the fruit can neither be heard nor listened to; but in place of that the reader may attend to my description of this fruit. . . ." Its perfume is a distillate of all the tastiest and most excellent fruit. To the palate "it is something so appetizing and sweet that there are no words to describe it properly; because no other fruit is remotely comparable with this one." Truth to tell, it is a bit rough and harsh to grasp: "The fruit itself seems to need to be picked carefully, with some cloth or kerchief; but once it is in the hand, no other gives such contentment." Words do not suffice to tell its virtues, nor does mere drawing; colors would be needed, and even these would not be really adequate. It can be cut any way one wants, with the greatest of ease. The goodness of its flavor exceeds that of any other fruit, as the feathers of the peacock outshine those of any other bird. And when, having admired it, handled it, smelled it, and popped it in one's mouth one finally swallows it, one is delighted to find that it stimulates the appetite, quenches the thirst and therefore helps dropsy sufferers; and its thorny fibers can only be harmful to the teeth and gums "when one continues to eat it very frequently." [6]

When he comes to the *mamey*, however, Oviedo forgets the prize he has just awarded to the *piña* and declares that the mammee, "is the best [fruit] there is on this island of Hispaniola" (VIII, 20: I, 305n), possessing an "exquisite and refreshing" taste. Likewise the medlar (or Nicaragua *munonçapot*) "is the best of all fruits, in my opinion . . . and I can find nothing to compare with it or match it" (VIII, 22: I, 308; cf. VII, 20: I, 306; VIII, 30: I, 316b). He then goes on to add a mouth-watering description of its taste and highly exclusive smell—"no one can catch or smell this fragrance except the actual person eating the fruit"—and the final comforting assurance that however much of it one eats "it never causes indigestion or discomfort." Then when he comes to sip the pellucid milk of the

6. *Hist.*, VII, 15: I, 280–84. Oviedo's panegyric, which is the development of a passage in the *Sumario*, chap. 80, pp. 235–36, is perhaps the first instance of idolization of a tropical fruit, although Peter Martyr had already praised that "scaly" fruit that "in aspect, form, and color resembled a pinecone, but was as soft as a melon, and tastier than any garden fruit." The pineapple was highly prized by King Ferdinand ("and the king himself awarded it the palm"), but poor Peter Martyr never even got to taste it, since all but one of the few brought to Spain turned out to be rotten on arrival (*Dec.*, II, 9, p. 191). Charles V, whose northerner's palate was less sensitive to those delicacies, only appreciated the smell of the fruit (Pereyra, *La obra de España*, p. 209, quoting Acosta; cf. also p. 135). At the end of the century (1583–86) Sassetti went into raptures over the East Indian pineapple, the best fruit in the world: "Its color is golden, tending a little towards copper . . . its flavor is like that of a strawberry or melon; it is juicy, and very agreeable to the taste"; it is healthy, diuretic, and costs only a few pennies (op. cit., pp. 254, 272, 323). An almost word-for-word echo of the passage in Oviedo ("a collection of different fine flavors," etc.) can be heard in B. Mandeville, *The Fable of the Bees* (Oxford, 1957), II, 194–95. There is no truth, at all events, in Paul Fénelon's claim that "the pineapple was discovered in Brazil in 1555, by Jean de Léry" ("Apports américains dans le domaine animal et végétal de l'ancien continent," in *La découverte de l'Amerique*, p. 262).

In later years similar panegyrics were pronounced in honor of cacao, *chicozapote*, and *chirimoya*. Even today one can hear the same sort of naive enthusiasm from the apologists of *quinea*, the banana, and the papaya. The Honduran José Cecilio del Valle (1780–1834), for example, extolled the banana in the following terms: "In the originality of its physiognomy [*sic*], in the beauty of its shape, in the glaze and size of its leaves, in the cheapness of its cultivation, in the short time it takes to fruit, in the bounty of its production, in the amount of nourishment in the fruit itself, in the flour it gives when it is unripe; in the dishes that can be made from it when it is in season; in all the features that make a plant valuable, the banana is outstanding, the glory of America, the wealth of its children, the beauty of its land" (J. C. del Valle, "Vegetales indígenas de América," 1821, in *Obras* [Guatemala, 1930], II, 106, cited also by R. H. Valle, "Un ilustre americano," in *Revista Mexicana de Sociologia*, 6 [1944], 16, who detects in this resounding litany "the radiant spirit of bucolic poetry"!).

coconut he feels marvellously conforted and contented *de planta pedis usque ad verticem,* from head to toe.[7] To the insatiable naturalist each fruit that he sinks his teeth into seems to be the best he has ever tasted.

In actual fact Oviedo willingly admits that he has a weakness for fruit: "It is absolutely true that I have felt more kindly disposed toward fruit than meat, or other food" (VIII, 18: I, 304b). But on the subject of the medlar he goes into details of an almost morbid refinement. "When one puts it into one's mouth, as soon as the tooth feels it, as soon as it begins to break up between one's jaws, a fragrance immediately rises to the nostrils and head, that even musk and civet cannot match" (VIII, 22: I, 308b, with a comparison involving two heady perfumes that our twentieth-century olfactory senses might well find somewhat repellent). One would have to await Paul Valéry's *Cimetière marin* to find such rapturous responses as Oviedo's: "Comme le fruit se fond en jouissance / Comme en délice il change son absence / Dans une bouche où sa forme se meurt" ("as the fruit melts in voluptuousness, As it changes its absence into delight, / In a mouth where its form dies").

But perhaps his preference for fruit is only the reflection of Oviedo's unholy terror of the filth and faithlessness of the cooks, "a danger facing those of us who live in these Indies" (*Qu.,* p. 370; cf. pp. 208, 243).

A final confirmation of his gastronomic interests can be seen in his insistent use of alimentary or culinary metaphors. Twice he approvingly recalls "the Italian proverb which says, It takes more than a white tablecloth to make a table" (*Qu.,* p. 230; cf. p. 245). And elsewhere he compares his opulent *History* with a princely feast of varied dishes (*Hist.,* VI, 49: I, 253b).

Finally, as an inducement to tackle great enterprises, "great and lofty things," in their right place and time, with the greatest probability of a successful outcome, Oviedo argues thus: "How many men have you seen that have swallowed a partridge or a capon at one bite? None, you will say; and you can point to many that, a mouthful at a time, have eaten this and more" (*Qu.,* p. 424). With regard to the Mexican cannibals, however, one can be sure that they have killed and devoured a number of the Christians that have fallen into their hands: with their greed for human flesh, "one is bound to suspect that they must treat it as gluttons do a good capon or pheasant or good partridges" (*Hist.,* XXXIII, 21: III, 375b).

D. THE IGUANA DISPUTE (see chap. XV, sec. 20).

The correct zoological classification of the iguanas and other lizards—the question that so mightily taxed Oviedo's mind and provided him with one more occasion for heaping scorn on Peter Martyr and his armchair history—seems to remain unresolved even today. Some naturalists put the order *lacertilia,* which includes the family *iguanidae,* together with the order *ophidia* (serpents) in the class *Squamata,* while assigning the various crocodiles and alligators to the class *Loricata* (thus endorsing Oviedo's view). Others tend to look on the lizard family as reptiles considerably closer to crocodiles than to snakes (thus supporting Peter Martyr). But the latest expert on crocodiles dissents categorically from this view: "The superficial resemblance between lizards and crocodiles is misleading, for the two

---

7. *Sum.,* chap. 65, p. 209; *Hist.,* IX, 4: I, 336b. The rhapsody over the coconut, which is fairly lengthy, but "needs no apology," is repeated in full by Lowes, op. cit., pp. 321–22.

groups have gone their separate ways since the end of the Paleozoic era."[8] The whole question is really one of the most obscure and difficult aspects of reptilian zoology, posing extremely complex problems for the large number of extinct species too.

The *Encyclopedia Britannica* (11th ed., s.v. "Lizard") admitted: "It is well-nigh impossible to find a diagnosis which should be absolutely sufficient for the distinction between lizards and snakes." In 1842 P. T. Barnum's museum of natural curiosities contained an exhibit that claimed to be, "the Siren, or Mud Iguana, a connecting link between the reptiles and fish" (Lovejoy, op. cit., p. 236, citing M. R. Werner, *Barnum*, 1923, p. 59). And a recent historian of pre-Columbian art calmly talks about "crocodiles" or caricatures of crocodiles when describing the realistic and obvious Central-American representations of iguanas (P. Kelemen, *Medieval American Art* [New York, 1943], I, 193, plate 144).

To Oviedo's contemporaries the strange beast represented an ambiguous and puzzling phenomenon, almost a symbol of the surprising novelty of the American species.

Columbus had simply called it a "serpent" (*Relación del primer viaje,* 21 October and 22 October 1492). But the author of the report on the second voyage, the Sevillian Dr. Chanca, almost certainly includes it among the "lizards" which "the Indians so much like to feast on . . . just as we would do in Spain with pheasants" (in Navarrete, op. cit., I, 358–59).

Peter Martyr, who dwells at some considerable length on the iguana, is more explicit, pointing to a certain morphological affinity with the Nile crocodile: "They say, in fact, that these snakes are in no way different from the crocodiles of the Nile, except in size. And indeed according to Pliny crocodiles have been found measuring up to eighteen cubits, while the biggest of these snakes was only eight feet" (*Dec.,* I, 3, pp. 36–37). Columbus's snake was seven palms long. Eight feet is extremely large for an iguana. And one is tempted to wonder whether they were not in fact caymans. But Peter Martyr's identification leaves no room for doubt. The only quadrupeds on Haiti are the nonbarking dogs "and the iguana snakes, that I described sufficiently in my first Decade; they resemble crocodiles, are eight feet long, live on land and are extremely tasty" (*Dec.,* III, 7, p. 281).

This excellence of the meat of the iguana is also mentioned by Peter Martyr elsewhere: "Of all edible things there is nothing which they so prize as those snakes; it is less permissible for their common people to eat those snakes than for ours to eat pheasants or peacocks (*Dec.,* I, 3, p. 37; and with even richer culinary details, I, 5, pp. 63–64).

A few pages after the first passage cited the historian again refers, with curious insistence, to "the snakes, those same that they look on as the greatest delicacy, that resemble crocodiles; we described them earlier on; they are called iguanas" (*Dec.,* I, 5, p. 63).[9] In

---

8. Review of C.A.W. Guggisberg's *Crocodiles* (London, 1972) in the *Times Literary Supplement,* 30 May 1972. Dougal Robertson, op. cit., p. 188, describes land iguanas as "large lizard-like creatures . . . slow-moving . . . quite unafraid" (while the black marine iguanas piled up in motionless heaps remind him, p. 189, of "hideous black spaghetti"!).

9. The existence of "crocodiles" in the New Indies is stated once again in *Dec.,* II, 9, p. 123; and in the *De Babylonica legatione,* III, p. 444, the crocodile is said to be "persimilis," very similar, to the lizard, which is common in the Indies: *Dec.,* II, 2, p. 135. For crocodiles that gave off "an odor . . . more sweet than musk or castor," see *Dec.,* III, 4, p. 246; for ferocious crocodiles, p. 248; for crocodiles on land, p. 253; for large crocodiles, pp. 257–74. All the rivers of America are teeming with crocodiles: *Dec.,* V, 9, p. 603. For a lengthy description of the habits and customs of Nile crocodiles see *De Babylonica legatione,* pp. 441–45. Oviedo takes issue with Peter Martyr, pointing out among other things that the dimensions he gives for the iguana are grossly exaggerated, in *Hist.,* XII, 7: I, 394b.

the last Decade, finally, he refers to the iguanas of Chiribichi as snakes with four paws and a repulsive appearance, but inoffensive and edible (*Dec.,* VIII, 7, p. 602).

Vespucci's description of the iguana is somewhat fanciful: he says it is roughly the size of a young goat and very much like a serpent, but without the wings.[10] When he said serpent, Vespucci may perhaps have meant a sort of winged dragon.[11] But he too insists that these hideous-looking but edible creatures "have snouts and features of real serpents and sort of bristles sticking up from their snouts all the way down their backs to the tips of their tails, so that we must proclaim these animals to be actual serpents" (Navarrete, op. cit., 2d. ed., III, 230–31; cf. ibid., p. viin2).

Enciso is already more accurate, when he refers to the lizards "that they call iguanas, which are large and like lizards, and these ones have round heads, and from their foreheads to their tails there runs a ridge of raised spines, very fierce looking; they are dark in color, and somewhat mottled; they live in the hills; they are fearsome to look at and not harmful, because they capture them live and kill them with sticks; they are good to eat, and their meat is much appreciated in those parts. The eggs of these creatures are very tasty" (op. cit., p. xxvii).

Cortés mentions the iguanas "which are some big lizards found in the islands" (fifth letter, 1526, ed. cit., II, 171). Las Casas on the other hand says that the iguana is a "snake, a real snake," but to explain himself better he qualifies his assertion, "almost after the fashion of a crocodile or like a lizard." The Indians and the Spaniards are enthusiastic about its meat which (as Peter Martyr had written) they find to be tastier than chicken breasts or pheasant; but Las Casas, even when famished, could never bring himself to try it (*Historia de las Indias,* I, 43, ed. cit., I, 217).

López de Gómara too called the iguana a snake, but immediately went on to add that "it looks like a lizard"; he praised its meat, which "tastes like rabbit, only better," and offered a curious liturgical confirmation of the ambiguity of its nature: "They eat it in Lent as fish, and outside Lent as meat, saying that it partakes of two elements, and consequently is suitable for both times" (*La conquista de México,* 1552, chap. 24 [Mexico, 1943], I, 100). This interpretative elasticity and the resulting permission to eat iguana on Fridays scandalized Bishop Las Casas—"I cannot imagine where they found that it was fish" (*Apologética Historia,* chap. 10, ed. cit., III, 438)—but perhaps it could have furnished a basis for negotiations and the source of an eventual amicable compromise, over a nice iguana roast, between the gourmandizing Spanish official and adventurous Venetian astrologer.

Oviedo's description of the iguana in the *Summary* (where he never actually names it) is a somewhat picturesque and terrifying portrait, accompanied by a warning that "it is a lot better to eat than to look at,"[12] because its meat "is as good as rabbit's or better," save for people who have had syphilis (chap. 6, p. 100, all features found again in Gómara). Later, however, he seems to have had a change of heart. Either he became more choosy and nostalgic in his tastes or iguana, "always the same old iguana," finally became too much for him. In the *Historia* he refers disdainfully to the meat of those animals "which when

10. For Herrera (*Historia general,* dec. IV, bk. x, chap. 12), the iguana becomes a winged dragon (Bayle, op. cit., p. 216).

11. There are of course plenty of classical and biblical precedents for winged serpents (e.g., Isaiah, XXX, 6); cf. D. C. Allen, "Milton's Winged Serpents," *Modern Language Notes,* 59 (1944), 537–38.

12. Fearsome to behold but very good to eat (when properly cooked), says Thomas Gage, *Travels in the New World* (1648) (Norman, Okla., 1958), pp. 224–25.

you look at them make you more afraid of them than desirous of them, if you do not know them, like those serpents that they call iguanas, snakes, or lizards" (V, 8: I, 151–52).

Bembo, repeating Oviedo's earlier version (see above, chap. XV, sec. 8), says that in the Indies "the snakes have an altogether new type and shape of body, and they are usually a foot and a half long, and live on water and land, and are looked on as very precious meat."[13] Oviedo, "the person who describes it best," is also the source for the description of the iguana given by Antonio de León Pinelo, who (on the basis of Peter Martyr) expands on its edibility (the female is better than the male) and on its essentially aquatic nature, which makes it legitimate food for Friday, although deep down he still has doubts "as to whether it should be viewed as a water creature or an ambiguous animal, or neutral," and goes on to describe another wonderful characteristic it possesses, its extraordinary "lightness," which enables it to walk on the water as if it were land, without swimming and without sinking, and to walk on the bottom as if there were no water,[14] twin marvels that ideally reflect the little animal's enigmatic nature.

Benzoni too (1565) is acquainted with "certain four-footed animals, called iguanas, similar in form to our lizards," and he also tells us that the females taste a lot better than the males, that "their eggs are a lot better-tasting than the meat," and that these creatures are amphibious.[15]

After him Botero (clumsily plagiarizing Acosta, as usual) remasticates the dithyrambs on the meat of the iguana, "an animal similar to the green lizard"; but he cannot make up his mind whether it is Lenten food or carnival food, "because it jumps from the trees into the rivers, and is obviously quite at home there, and is also found a long way away from water."[16]

The dispute on the edibility of the iguana has also flared up in times closer to our own. Cornelius de Pauw (*Recherches philosophiques sur les Américains* [Berlin, 1768], I, 16–17, 65n) wrote of its tastiness and health-giving qualities, though warning, like Oviedo and Gómara, that syphilis-sufferers should avoid it. He assured his readers, however, that this "strange animal" was "a true lizard" (p. 15). And on this point at least his archenemy Clavigero agreed with him, stating that "their meat and their eggs are edible, and praised by many authors, but their meat is harmful for those suffering from the French disease" (*Storia antica del Messico* [Cesena, 1780], I, 94).

In contradiction of Muñoz (op. cit., p. 268), who calls it "a dish reserved for the great lords," Father Iturri (op. cit., p. 29) claimed it was "everyday food for all the islanders."

---

13. *Della historia vinitiana* (Venice, 1552), p. 74n. Plants and animals that lived solely on air were a well-known phenomenon. Suffice it to mention here Pigafetta's self-propelled leaves (above, chap. XI, nn. 19–20), or the mythical chameleon, at least according to the Talmud and Leonardo (*Enciclopedia Italiana*, s.v. "Camaleonte"), "those animals that come from beyond the world, that feed on air," as Nanna says in Aretino's *Sei giornate*, p. 95, which Antonia then identifies precisely as chameleons. Don Ferrante too had an explanation for "how the chameleon feeds on air" (Manzoni, *I promessi sposi*, chap. XXVII, ed. cit., p. 428). Cf. above, chap. XXI, n. 47.

14. León Pinelo, *El paraíso*, II, 120–21. The tastiness of iguana meat was also extolled by Father Acosta and Sánchez Labrador (cf. Cardoso, op. cit., [1926], pp. 320–21).

15. Benzoni, op. cit., p. 113. The "Uvana" is also mentioned by Ubertino da Carrara, in his *Columbus* (1715): see M. Segre, *Un poema colombiano del Settecento* (Rome, 1925), p. 100.

16. Botero, op. cit., p. 221. Acosta preferred iguana to armadillo meat: "I have tried it [armadillo]: it did not seem anything very special to me. Much better eating is the iguana, although it is pretty repulsive in appearance, since they look just like the lizards in Spain; but these are an ambiguous species, because they go in the water, and come out on the land, and climb up the trees standing on the edge of the water, and as they launch themselves from there into the water, they can be caught by stationing a boat below" (op. cit., p. 288).

The most recent explorer of the West Indies assures us that "roast iguana is a delicious meat" (Morison, *Admiral of the Ocean Sea*, II, 121; cf. also P. Ghiglione, in a dispatch from Mexico to the *Corriere della Sera*, 21 August 1951).

Finally the contrast between the iguana's hideous appearance and its meek passivity, between its looks of an antediluvian monster and its stolid inertia, prompted some elegant elaborations on the part of Ortega y Gasset: "The two horrific iguanas, the sea one and the land one, representing the final degeneration of the proud heraldic race of dragons and saurians, . . . huge ancient lizards, bristling with serrated heads, moving stupidly . . . these iguanas, of fearsome armor and kindly gaze, are of an unusual meekness. There is no way of angering them. . . . To what end, then, their serrated crests, their claws, their powerful limbs, their size, that is sometimes as much as four foot."[17] The mysterious iguana seems to be destined to play the same role as the sphinx of the ancients, confronting the keenest and boldest minds with tormenting riddles.

E. Oviedo and Sepúlveda

We are constantly being told that the *De rebus gestis Hispanorum ad Novum Orbem libri septem*—written by Sepúlveda, it would seem, between 1560 and 1567, but not published until 1780, by the Academia de la Historia in Madrid, in the third of the four volumes of Sepúlveda's Works—are a summary or "Latin adaptation" (Fueter) of Oviedo's *History*.[18]

The truth of the matter is somewhat different. The title is broad and all-embracing,[19] but after two books devoted to Columbus and the early settlements, up to about 1519, taking up less than a quarter of the total, however, page 46 sees the arrival on the scene of Cortés and his letters, and all at once the subject is narrowed down to the conquest of Mexico up to the taking of the capital. Thus the other three-quarters or more of the book cover a mere couple of years.

But Oviedo, Sepúlveda's supposed source, had *not* dealt with Mexico in the *first* part of his *History*, published in 1535; instead, as we know, and as he himself announces, this subject would be covered in book XXXIII of the *second* part, the part that remained unpublished until 1851–1855, and was thus presumably unknown to Sepúlveda.

So where did Sepúlveda get the information on Cortés that fills the last five books of the *De rebus gestis?* The answer is easy, inasmuch as Sepúlveda himself tells us he used Cortés's "commentarii," which is a Latinized way of referring to the celebrated *Cartas de relación* to Charles V. He even seems to have drawn on the first letter, which was of course subsequently lost. He certainly paraphrases and translates Cortés continually, even using the same comparisons and metaphors; and it is precisely with regard to the legit-

17. J. Ortega y Gasset, "Galápagos, el fin del mundo" (article on W. Beebe's book on the Galapagos) in *Espíritu de la letra* (1927), in *Obras* (Madrid, 1943), II, 1067. Note also the symbolic meaning of the monstrous little animal in Tennessee Williams's *Night of the Iguana*.

18. See for example Fueter, op. cit., p. 234; Hurtado and Palencia, *Historia de la literatura española* (Madrid, 1943), p. 397; Esteve Barba, op. cit., pp. 93–94; Sánchez Alonso, *Historiografía española*, II, 104–05; idem, *Fuentes*, no. 3586; D. Turner, *Bibliography*, no. 321. Even the highly knowledgeable Morel-Fatio talks at length about Sepúlveda's work (*Historiographie*, pp. 69–72) without ever looking very closely at its content, let alone discussing it. Even Aubrey Bell, who has certainly read the *De rebus gestis hispanorum*, writes in his *Juan Ginés de Sepúlveda* (Oxford and New York, 1925), pp. 47, 53, that Sepúlveda "had to rely mainly" on Oviedo's *Historia*.

19. Could that very curious *ad* be a copyist's error? The Academy editors write more correctly that Sepúlveda recounted "de rebus Hispanorum *apud* novum Orbem gestis" (ed. cit., I, xcix–c).

imacy of the conquest of Mexico that López de Gómara refers explicitly to Sepúlveda.[20] But this obvious truth—which was in fact already clear to the publishers of the 1780 edition[21]—has only recently been recognized and proclaimed again,[22] and still does not seem to have been accepted by a lot of scholars.

Sepúlveda was a great admirer of Oviedo. He too, like Oviedo, had learned the ways of the world during his long sojourn in Italy (1515–1536) and always looked back on that time with fond memories;[23] he also shared with Oviedo the underlying hostility of and for Las Casas, whom he never deigns to mention in his writings, however. At the very beginning of the *De rebus gestis* he hastens to praise Oviedo as "a wise and careful man" who wrote, as an official task, "very lengthy commentaries," but only, unfortunately, in Spanish. He, Sepúlveda, therefore, intends to render them into Latin, "lest we should leave this part of history untouched," but for this noble end he chose possibly the most annalistic parts of the *History*,[24] which in his abridgment sound even more arid and coldly remote.

In Sepúlveda's summary, adorned here and there with classical and imaginary speeches, the most curious thing (for us at least) seems to be his embarrassment when he has to decide between the two conflicting versions of the relations between Hernan Cortés and Diego Velázquez. Cortés is certainly a great man, "both in soul and in counsel." But Oviedo is an extremely careful and reliable historian. Sepúlveda cannot bring himself to take sides and for a moment seems as nonplussed as Buridan's ass. After giving the condottiere's version however—namely that Velázquez was making difficulties for him on the sly, "quietly and secretly"—he eventually adds that among the common people prevailing opinion still favors Oviedo's version, namely that the two did indeed separate by mutual agreement, but then Cortés, whose fleet had been equipped at Velázquez's expense, "seeing a prospect of success, and worried lest his deeds and praise should be lessened by being shared, rejected his friend and companion. And this is the way Gonzalo Fernando,[25] a careful writer, who told this story in the Spanish language, seems to have recorded it,"[26] implying that he, Sepúlveda, is inclined to endorse Oviedo's malicious version.

20. "He wrote it [the "justification"] in Latin, in most learned fashion" (quoted in Esteve Barba, op. cit., pp. 95–98).

21. "Editorum praefatio" (anonymous, but by Francisco Cerdá y Rico), in *Opera,* I, cv–cvi: "It is generally considered that he copied a lot of things from the letters of Hernán Cortés, as will be seen if we compare each work with the other"—unless it is assumed that Sepúlveda was acquainted with the unpublished parts of Oviedo's *Historia.* There is a copy of the latter in the Bibliotheca Marchionis Truxillorum (the Cortés library) but it lacks books XXXI to XXXVI (i.e., including XXXIII, the chapter dealing with Mexico and Cortés). For a century and a half no one followed up these explicit indications. Not surprisingly, perhaps, because the reader who never gets beyond the title or the first few lines of a work is going to have no qualms about sparing himself the trouble of reading the 144 large pages of Latin dealing with the author's life and writings!

22. Angel Losada, "Una historia olvidada de nuestro descubrimiento de América (*De orbe novo* de Juan Ginés de Sepúlveda)," *RI,* 8 (1947), 509–20, and "Hernan Cortés," pp. 127–69. Losada has also written an article and a long book on Sepúlveda that I have not seen, the former in *Hispania* (Madrid), 8 (1948), 234–307, the latter entitled *J. G. de Sepúlveda a través de su Epistolario y nuevos documentos* (Madrid, 1949). Nor have I seen the Göttingen thesis written by one of Brandi's disciples, Count Looz-Corswaren, on Sepúlveda's historical works (see Losada, "Una historia olvidada," p. 514), nor T. A. Marcos, *Los imperialismos de J. G. de Sepúlveda* (Madrid, 1947).

23. Morel-Fatio, *Historiographie,* p. 51.

24. *De rebus gestis,* ed. cit., pp. 1–2. But "he did not follow Oviedo so slavishly that he failed to consult also the commentaries of the leaders" etc. (Praefatio, p. lvi). And in fact, as we have seen, his chief source is Cortés.

25. "Oviedo" is missing both here and in the index of names, which may be why the reference was missed by the compilers of the indexes and the commentators.

26. Op. cit., p. 61; cf. p. 83. Oviedo's version can be found in *Hist.,* XVII, 19: PT, II, 147–52.

Bibliography

Acosta, José de. *Historia natural y moral de las Indias*. Seville, 1590.

Acuña, L. A. "El refrán en Colombia." *Revista de las Indias* (Bogotá), 80 (1945), 221–34.

Agnelli, Giuseppe. *Ferrara e Pomposa*. Bergamo, 1902.

Aiton, Arthur. *Antonio de Mendoza*. Durham, N.C., 1927.

Alberi, Eugenio. See Contarini.

Alcocer, Luis Jerónimo. *Relación sumaria de la Isla Española* (1650). In Rodríguez Demorizi, ed., *Relaciones históricas de Santo Domingo*, q.v.

Alemán, Luis E. *Santo Domingo Ciudad Trujillo*. 2d ed. Santiago, Dominican Republic, 1943.

Allen, Don Cameron. "Milton's Winged Serpents." *Modern Language Notes*, 59 (1944), 537–38.

Almagià, Roberto. *Gli Italiani primi esploratori dell'America*. Rome, 1937.

Alonso, Amado. "El descubrimiento de América y el idioma." *Humanidades* (La Plata), 30 (1944–45), 117–27.

Altamira y Crevea, Rafael. *La huella de España en América*. Madrid, 1924.

Altolaguirre y Duvale, Angel de. *Vasco Núñez de Balboa*. Madrid, 1914.

Alvarez Baena, J. A. *Hijos de Madrid*. 4 vols. Madrid, 1789–91.

Alvarez López, Enrique. "El Dr. Francisco Hernández y sus comentarios a Plinio." *Revista de Indias*, 3, no. 8 (1942), 251–90.

————. "La filosofía natural en el P. José de Acosta." *Revista de Indias*, 4, no. 12 (1943), 305–22.

————. "La historia natural en Fernández de Oviedo." *Revista de Indias*, 17, nos. 69–70 (1957), 541–601.

————. "El perro mudo americano (El problema del perro mudo de Fernández de Oviedo)." *Boletín de la Real Sociedad Española de Historia Natural*, 11 (1942), 411–17.

————. "Plinio y Fernández de Oviedo." *Anales de Ciencias Naturales* (Madrid), 1 (1940), 40–61; 2 (1941), 13–35.

Amador de los Ríos, José. "Vida y escritos de Gonzalo Fernández de Oviedo." In vol. 1 (pp. ix–cvii) of his edition of the *Historia general* of Fernández de Oviedo, q.v.

————. *Historia crítica de la literatura española*. 7 vols. Madrid, 1861–65.

Amoretti, Carlo. Introduction to Pigafetta's *Primer viaje*, ed. Morcuende, q.v.

Ampère, Jean Jacques. *Promenade en Amérique*. 2 vols. Paris, 1856.

André, Marius. *La fin de l'empire espagnol d'Amérique*. Paris, 1922.

Anghiera, Pietro Martire d'. See chap. VIII, n. 1.

————. *De Babylonica legatione* (Alcalá, 1511). In Cologne edition of the *Decades*, below.

————. *Una embajada de los Reyes Católicos a Egipto*. Translation of preceding item into Spanish by Luis García y García. Valladolid, 1947.

————. *De insulis nuper inventis* (Alcalá, 1516). In Cologne edition of the *Decades*, below.

————. *Mondo Nuovo*. Partial translation into Italian of the *Decades* by Temistocle Celotti. Milan, 1930.

————. *Opus epistolarum* (Alcalá, 1530). Amsterdam, 1670.

————. *De Orbe Novo decades*. . . . Translated into Spanish by Joaquín Torres Asensio (1st ed., Madrid, 1892). Preface by Luis H. Arocena and bibliographical study by Joseph H. Sinclair. Buenos Aires, 1944.

————. *De Orbe Novo decades*. . . . Translated into French by Paul Gaffarel. Paris, 1907.

————. *De Orbe Novo decades*. . . . Translated into English by F. A. Macnutt. 2 vols. New York and London, 1912.

————. *De Orbe Novo decades*. . . . Translated into Spanish by Agustín Millares Carlo, with study and appendices by Edmundo O'Gorman. 2 vols. Mexico, 1964.

————. *De rebus oceanicis et Novo Orbe decades tres*. . . . Cologne, 1574.

Anónimo Sevillano. *La conquista del Perú* (1534). See Pogo.

Aquila, Serafino de' Ciminella dell'. *Rime*. Edited by Mario Menghini. Bologna, 1894.

Arana-Soto, S. "Puerto Rico rinde homenaje al Dr. Chanca." *Revista de Indias*, 27 (1967), 267–69.

425

Arciniegas, Germán. "América, obra del Pueblo." *Cuadernos Americanos,* 22, no. 4 (July–August 1945), 112–26.

Aretino, Pietro. *Coloquio de las damas.* Seville (?), 1548.

––––––. *Il secondo libro delle lettere.* Edited by Fausto Nicolini. 2 vols. Bari, 1916.

––––––. *Sei giornate.* Edited by G. Aquilecchia. Bari, 1969.

Arias-Larreta, Abraham. *Historia de la literatura indo-americana.* Kansas City, 1970.

Ariosto, Lodovico. *Le opere.* 2 vols. Milan and Naples, 1954. Vol. 1 contains the *Orlando Furioso* and vol. 2 the minor works, commentary on the *Orlando Furioso* by Lanfranco Caretti and commentary on the minor works by Cesare Segre.

Arnold, Thurman W. *The Folklore of Capitalism.* Garden City, 1941.

Arnoldsson, Sverker. *La leyenda negra: Estudios sobre sus orígenes.* Gothenburg, 1960.

Arocena, Luis H. Preface to Asensio's translation of the *De Orbe Novo* of Pietro Martire d'Anghiera, q.v.

Arrom, Juan José. "'Becerrillo': Comentarios a un pasaje narrativo del Padre Las Casas." In *Libro de Homenaje a Luis Alberto Sánchez,* pp. 41–44. Lima, 1967.

Asensio, Eugenio. "La carta de Gonzalo Fernández de Oviedo al cardenal Bembo sobre la navegación del Amazonas." *Revista de Indias,* 9, nos. 37–38 (1949), 569–78.

Atkinson, Geoffroy. *The Extraordinary Voyage in French Literature Before 1700.* New York, 1920.

––––––. *Les nouveaux horizons de la Renaissance française.* Paris, 1935.

Bacchelli, Riccardo. "L'Ammiraglio dell'Oceano." In *Nel fiume della storia.* Milan, 1945.

––––––. *Non ti chiamerò più padre.* Milan, 1959.

Bacon, Francis. *Works.* London, 1902.

Balbuena, Bernardo de. *El Bernardo.* Biblioteca de Autores Españoles, vol. 17. Madrid, 1851.

Ballesteros Beretta, Antonio. *Cristóbal Colón y el descubrimiento de América.* 2 vols. Barcelona, 1945.

––––––. "Don Juan Bautista Muñoz: La *Historia del Nuevo Mundo.*" *Revista de Indias,* 3, no. 10 (1942), 589–660.

––––––. *Historia de España y su influencia en la historia universal.* 10 vols. Barcelona, 1918–41.

Ballesteros Gaibrois, Manuel. "Fernández de Oviedo, etnólogo." *Revista de Indias,* 17, nos. 69–70 (1957), 445–67.

––––––. *Vida del madrileño Gonzalo Fernández de Oviedo y Valdés.* Madrid, 1958.

Bancroft, Hubert Howe. "Early California Literature." In vol. 38 of *Works.* 39 vols. San Francisco, 1882–90.

Bandello, Matteo. *Le Novelle.* Edited by Francesco Flora. 2 vols. Milan, 1934.

Bandini, Angelo Maria. *Vita e lettere di Amerigo Vespucci.* Florence, 1745.

Barlow, Nora, ed. *Charles Darwin and the Voyage of the Beagle.* New York, 1946.

Barnes, H. A. *A History of Historical Writing.* Norman, Okla. 1937.

Barraza, Carlos F. "La institución de los adelantados en América: Aportación al estudio de las magistraduras indianas." *Humanidades* (La Plata), 28 (1940), 519–45.

Barros Arana, Diego. *Obras.* 15 vols. Santiago de Chile, 1908–14.

Bartolozzi, Francesco. *Ricerche storico-critiche circa alle scoperte d'Amerigo Vespucci. . . .* Florence, 1789.

Bataillon, Marcel. "Charles-Quint, Las Casas et Vitoria." In *Charles-Quint et son temps,* q.v. (pp. 77–91), and in *Etudes sur Bartolomé de Las Casas,* below (pp. 291–307).

––––––. *Erasmo y España.* 2 vols. Mexico, 1950.

––––––. *Etudes sur Bartolomé de Las Casas.* Paris, 1965.

––––––. "Les Indes Occidentales, découverte d'un monde humain." In *La découverte de l'Amérique,* q.v. (pp. 7–10).

––––––. "Montaigne et les conquérants de l'or." *Studi Francesi,* 9 (1959), 353–67.

Bayle, Constantino. *El dorado fantasma.* Madrid, 1930.

Bayle, Pierre. *Dictionnaire historique et critique.* 6th ed. 4 vols. Basel, 1741.

––––––. "Réponse aux questions d'un provincial." In *Oeuvres diverses,* vol. 3. The Hague, 1737.

Bell, Aubrey F. G. *Juan Ginés de Sepúlveda.* Oxford and New York, 1925.

Bellonci, Maria. *Lucrezia Borgia; La sua vita e i suoi tempi.* Milan 1939.

Bembo, Pietro. *Della historia vinitiana.* Venice, 1552.

––––––. *Lettere inedite.* See Spezi.

Benedicenti, Alberico. *Malati, medici e farmacisti.* 2 vols. Milan, 1924.

Benzoni, Girolamo. *La historia del Mondo Nuovo* (Venice, 1565). Milan, 1965.

––––––. *The History of the New World.* Translated by W. H. Smyth. London, 1857.

Berchet, Guglielmo. See Scillacio.

Bernard, Claude. *Introduction à l'étude de la médecine expérimentale.* Geneva, 1945.

Bernays, I. *Peter Martyr von Angleria und sein "Opus epistolarum."* Strasbourg, 1891.

Bertelli, Sergio. *Ribelli, libertini e ortodossi nella storiografia barocca.* Florence 1973.

Biagi, Guido. *Fiorenza, fior che sempre rinnovella.* Florence, 1925.

Biermann, Benno M. "Alessandro Geraldini, Bischof von San Domingo, 1517–1525." *Zeitschrift für Missions- und Religionswissenschaft* (Münster), 34 (1950), 195–206.

––––––. "Das Requerimiento in der spanischen Conquista." *Neue Zeitschrift für Missionswissenschaft,* 6 (1950), 94–114.

Blanke, Gustav H. *Amerika im englischen Schrifttum des 16. und 17. Jahrhunderts.* Bochum, 1962.

Bonilla y San Martín, Adolfo. "Erasmo en España." *Revue Hispanique,* 17 (1907), 379–548.

————, ed. See Schevill.

Borsa, Mario. *La caccia nel milanese dalle origini ai giorni nostri.* Milan, [1924].

Bosch Gimpera, Pedro. "Para la comprensión de España." *Cuadernos Americanos,* 1 (1943), 153–74.

Bosque, A. de. *Artisti italiani in Spagna dal XIV secolo ai Re Cattolici.* Milan, 1968.

Botero, Giovanni. *Le relationi universali.* Venice, 1602.

Bourland, C. B. "Boccaccio and the Decameron in Castilian and Catalan Literature." *Revue Hispanique,* 12 (1905), 1–232.

Brandi, Karl. *The Emperor Charles V.* London, 1939.

Braudel, Fernand. *Civilisation matérielle et capitalisme.* Paris, 1967.

————. *La Méditerranée et le monde méditerranéen à l'époque de Philippe II.* 2 vols. Paris, 1966.

Bredner, Leicester. "Columbus in Sixteenth-Century Poetry." In *Essays Honoring L. C. Wroth,* pp. 15–30. Portland, Maine, 1951.

Brogan, Denis W. *The English People.* New York, 1943.

Brunetière, Ferdinand. *Manuel de l'histoire de la littérature française.* Paris, 1898.

Bruno, Giordano. "Ars Memoriae" (ca. 1582). In vol. 2, pt. 2 of *Opere latine,* edited by Fiorentino, Tocco et al. Naples and Florence, 1879–91.

Buffon, Georges-Louis Leclerc, comte de. *Histoire naturelle, générale et particulière, avec la description du Cabinet du Roi.* 44 vols. Paris, 1749–1804.

————. *Oeuvres complètes.* Edited by M. A. Richard. 32 vols. Paris, 1826–28.

Bullón, Eloy. *El Dr. Palacios Rubios.* Madrid, 1927.

Burckhardt, Jacob. *La civiltà del Rinascimento.* 2 vols. Florence, 1921.

————. *Geschichte der Renaissance in Italien.* Stuttgart, 1891.

Burdach, Konrad. *Reformation, Renaissance, Humanismus.* Berlin, 1918.

Burke, Edmund. "An Appeal from the New to the Old Whigs." In vol. 5 of *Works.* 6 vols. Oxford, 1928.

Burton, Robert. *The Anatomy of Melancholy.* New York, 1938.

Busson, Henri. *La pensée religieuse française de Charron à Pascal.* Paris, 1933.

Butler, Samuel. *Alps and Sanctuaries.* London and Toronto, 1931.

Caddeo, Rinaldo. "L'autenticità delle *Historie* di Colombo: Fernando Colombo, il padre Las Casas e un professore americano." *Le Opere e i Giorni* (Genoa), 9, no. 3 (March 1930), 47–56.

————. "Polemica Colombiana." *Le Opere e i Giorni* (Genoa), 9, no. 7 (July 1930), 48–51.

————. "Sobre F. Colón y el P. Las Casas." *Nosotros* (Buenos Aires), 69 (1930), 107–11.

————, ed. See Fernando Columbus.

Caillet-Bois, Julio. "Un olvidado erasmista de América: Diego Méndez de Segura." *Humanidades* (La Plata), 30 (1944–45), 59–66.

Calmeta, Vincenzo. "Vita del facondo poeta volgare Seraphino Aquilano" (1504). In Aquila, *Rime,* q.v.

Campanella, Tommaso. *Della monarchia di Spagna, 1597–1620.* In *Opere,* edited by Alessandro D'Ancona. 2 vols. Turin, 1854.

————. *Poesie.* Edited by Giovanni Gentile. Bari, 1915.

Capéran, Louis. *Le problème du salut des infidèles.* 2 vols. Toulouse, 1934.

Carande, Ramón. *Carlos V y sus banqueros.* 3 vols. Madrid, 1965.

————. "Carlos V: Viajes, cartas y deudas." *In Charles-Quint et son temps,* q.v.

Carbia, Rómulo D. *La crónica oficial de las Indias Occidentales.* La Plata, 1934.

————. "Fernández de Oviedo, Las Casas y el señor Caddeo." *Nosotros* (Buenos Aires), 70 (1930), 90–95.

————. "Fernando Colón, el P. Las Casas, un señor Caddeo y yo." *Nosotros* (Buenos Aires), 68 (1930), pp. 59–73.

————. *Historia de la leyenda negra hispano-americana.* Buenos Aires, 1943.

————. "La historia del descubrimiento y los fraudes del P. Las Casas." *Nosotros* (Buenos Aires), 72 (1931), 139–54.

————. *La nueva historia del descubrimiento de América.* Buenos Aires, 1936.

————. "La supercheria en la historia del descubrimiento de América: Comunicación preliminar." *Humanidades* (La Plata), 20 (1930), 169–85.

Cardan, Jerome. *De la subtilité.* Paris, 1556.

————. *De rerum varietate.* Basel, 1557.

Cardoso, Anibal. "Nuestros conocimientos in ciencias naturales durante la Época colonial." *Humanidades* (La Plata), 10 (1925), 371–407; 11 (1925), 339–76; 12 (1926), 315–61.

Carletti, Francesco. *Ragionamenti . . . sopra le cose da lui vedute nei suoi viaggi. . . .* Florence, 1701.

Cassirer, Ernst. *Philosophie der symbolischen Formen.* 3 vols. Berlin, 1925.

Castañeda, Vicente. "Don Fernando de Aragón, duque de Calabria; Apuntes biográficos." *Revista de Archivos, Bibliotecas, y Museos* (Madrid), 25 (1911), 268–86.

Castellani, C. "Pietro Bembo bibliotecario della libreria di San Marco in Venezia (1530–1543)." *Atti del Reale Istituto Veneto di Scienze, Lettere, ed Arti,* 7th ser., vol. 54 (1895–96), 862–98.

Castellanos, Juan de. *Elegías de varones ilustres de Indias* (1589 et seq.). Biblioteca de Autores Españoles, vol. 4. Madrid, 1847.

Castro, Américo. *La realidad histórica de España.* Mexico, 1954.

———. "Sambenito." *Revista de Filología Española*, 15 (1928), 179–81.
Cattaneo, Carlo. "Gli antichi messicani." In vol. 3, pp. 409–40, of *Opere*. 7 vols. Florence, 1881–92.
CDIE, CDII, CDIU. See *Colección . . .*
Cedularios del Peru, siglos XVI, XVII y XVIII. Edited by R. Porras Barrenechea. Lima, 1944.
Cejador y Frauca, Julio. *Historia de la lengua y literatura castellanas.* 14 vols. Madrid, 1915.
Celotti, Temistocle. See Anghiera.
Cervantes, Miguel de. See Schevill.
Chabod, Federico. *Lezioni di metodo storico.* Bari, 1969.
———. "Milano o i Paesi Bassi? Le discussioni in Spagna sulla 'alternativa' del 1544." *Rivista Storica Italiana*, 70, no. 4 (December 1958), 508–32.
Chariteo, Il (Benedetto Gareth). *Rime.* Edited by Erasmo Pércopo. Naples, 1892.
Charles-Quint et son temps. Colloques internationaux du Centre National de la Recherche Scientifique, Paris, 30 September–3 October 1958. Paris, 1959.
Chaunu, Pierre. *L'Amérique et les Amériques.* Paris, 1964.
Chevalier, François. "Témoignages littéraires et disparité de croissance: L'expansion de la grande propriété dans le Haut Pérou au XXème siècle." *Annales*, 21, no. 4 (1966), 815–31.
Chinard, Gilbert. *Les réfugiés huguenots en Amérique.* Paris, 1925.
Chinchilla Aguilar, Ernesto. "Algunos aspectos de la obra de Oviedo." *Revista de Historia de América*, 28 (1949), 303–30.
Chocano, José Santos. *Poesías escogidas.* Biblioteca de cultura peruana. Paris, 1938.
Chroust, Anton-Hermann. "Utrum Aristoteles sit salvatus." *Journal of the History of Ideas*, 6 (1945), 233–38.
Ciampi, Ignazio. "Le fonti storiche del rinascimento: Pietro Martire d'Anghiera." *Nuova Antologia*, yr. 10, vol. 30 (1875), 39–79, 717–44.
———. *Storia moderna dalla scoperta dell'America alla pace di Westfalia.* 3 vols. Imola, 1881–84.
Cian, Vittorio. "Pietro Bembo (Quarantun anni dopo)." *Giornale Storico della Letteratura Italiana*, 88 (1926), 225–55.
Cirot, Georges. *Les histoires générales d'Espagne entre Alphonse X et Philippe II, 1284–1556.* Paris and Bordeaux, 1904.
Clavigero, Francesco Saverio. *Storia antica del Messico.* 4 vols. Cesena, 1780.
Clemencín, Diego. "Illustraciones al elogio de la reina Isabel la Católica." *Memorias de la Real Academia de la Historia*, Vol. 6. Madrid, 1821.
Cline, Howard F. "The 'Relaciones Geográficas' of the Spanish Indies, 1577–1586." *Hispanic American Historical Review*, 44, no. 3 (August 1964), 341–74.
Cobo, Bernabé. *Historia del Nuevo Mundo* (1653). 4 vols. Seville, 1890–93.
Colección de documentos inéditos para la historia de España. Edited by Martín Fernández Navarrete, Miguel Salvá, Pedro Sainz de Baranda et al. 112 vols. Madrid, 1842–96. *(CDIE)*
Colección de documentos inéditos relativos al descubrimiento, conquista y colonización (organización) de las posesiones españolas en América y Oceania. Taken mainly from the Real Archivo de Indias and edited by Joaquín F. Pacheco, Francisco de Cárdenas, and Luis Torres de Mendoza. 42 vols. Madrid, 1864–84. *(CDII)*
Colección de documentos inéditos, relativos al descubrimiento, conquista y organización de las antiguas posesiones españolas de Ultramar. 25 vols. Madrid, 1884–1932. *(CDIU)*
Collingwood, R. G. *The Idea of History.* Oxford, 1946.
Columbus, Christopher. *Journal.* See Jane.
———. *Relaciones y cartas.* Madrid, 1892.
Columbus, Fernando. *Historia del Almirante.* 2 vols. Madrid, 1892.
———. *Historia della vita e dei fatti di Cristoforo Colombo.* Edited by Rinaldo Caddeo. 2 vols. Milan, 1930.
———. *Vita di Cristoforo Colombo.* London, 1867.
Comito, Terry. "Renaissance Gardens and the Discovery of Paradise." *Journal of the History of Ideas*, 32, no. 4 (1971), 483–506.
Comparetti, Domenico. *Virgilio nel Medio Evo.* 2 vols. Livorno, 1872.
Coniglione, Matteo Angelo. *Bernardo Gentile, O.P.: Umanista siciliano del secolo XVI, cronista di Carlo V, poi vescovo di Bosa, 1470–1537.* Catania, 1948.
Contarini, Gaspare. "Relazione." In *Relazioni degli ambasciatori veneti al Senato,* edited by Eugenio Alberi, 1st ser., vol. 2. Florence, 1840.
Contribuciones para el estudio de la historia de América: Homenaje al doctor Emilio Ravignani. Buenos Aires, 1941.
Corominas, Pedro. *El sentimiento de la riqueza en Castilla.* Madrid, 1917.
Coréal, François. *Voyages aux Indes Occidentales . . . depuis 1666 jusqu'en 1697.* 2 vols. Paris, 1722.
Cortés, Hernán. *Cartas de relación.* 2 vols. Madrid, 1940.
Costa, Gustavo. *La leggenda dei secoli d'oro nella letteratura italiana.* Bari, 1972.
Croce, Benedetto. "La corte delle Tristi Regine," *Archivio Storico per le Provincie Napoletane*, 19 (1894), 354–75.
———. "La grandiosa aneddotica storica di Paolo Giovio." *La Critica*, 40 (1942), 176–97. Also in *Poeti e scrittori,* below.
———. "Libri sui misteri dei numeri." In *Nuovi saggi sulla letteratura italiana del Seicento.* Bari, 1931.

_____. "Un poemetto popolare del Quattrocento sulle morti dei condottieri," *La Critica*, 36 (1938), 296–302. Also in *Aneddoti de varia letteratura*, vol. 1., Naples, 1942.

_____. *Poesia antica e moderna*. 2d ed. Bari, 1943.

_____. *Poeti e scrittori del pieno e del tardo Rinascimento*. Bari, 1945.

_____. "Serafino Aquilano." *Quaderni della Critica*, 17–18 (1950), 42–46.

_____. *La Spagna nella vita italiana durante la Rinascenza*. Bari, 1917.

_____. *Storia del regno di Napoli*. Bari, 1925.

_____. *Storie e leggende napoletane*. Bari, 1948.

_____. *Uomini e cose della vecchia Italia*. 2 vols. Bari, 1927.

Crónicas del Gran Capitán. See Rodríguez Villa.

Cuerpo de documentos del siglo XVI sobre los derechos de España en las Indias y las Filipinas. Edited by Lewis Hanke and Agustín Millares Carlo. Mexico, 1943.

Cutright, Paul Russell. *The Great Naturalists Explore South America*. New York, 1940.

Da Mosto, Andrea. "Vita di Antonio Pigafetta." In *Raccolta Colombiana*, q.v. (pt. 5, vol. 3, pp. 13–47).

D'Ancona, Alessandro. *L'Italia alla fine del secolo XVI: Giornale del viaggio di M. de Montaigne*. Città di Castello, 1895.

D'Annunzio, Gabriele. *Le Laudi*. 2 vols. Milan, 1904.

Darwin, Charles. *Voyage of a Naturalist Round the World*. 2 vols. New York, 1871.

D'Avenel, Georges. *Le nivellement des jouissances*. Paris, 1913.

D'Azeglio, Massimo. *La Disfida di Barletta*. Florence, 1850.

La découverte de l'Amérique: Esquisse d'une synthèse, conditions historiques et conséquences culturelles. Dixième stage international d'études humanistes, Tours, 1966. Paris, 1968.

Dejob, Charles. *De l'influence du Concile de Trente sur la littérature et les beaux-arts chez les peuples catholiques*. Paris, 1884.

Delicado, Francisco. *La Lozana andaluza* (1524). 2 vols. Paris 1888.

Délices de la Hollande. Amsterdam, 1685.

De Lollis, Cesare. *Cristoforo Colombo nella leggenda e nella storia*. 3d ed. Rome, 1923; definitive edition, Lanciano, 1931.

_____, ed. See *Raccolta Colombiana*.

De Marinis, Tammaro. *La biblioteca napoletana dei Re d'Aragona*. 6 vols. Milan and Verona, 1947–69.

De Pauw, Cornelius. *Défense des Recherches Philosophiques*. Berlin, 1770.

_____. *Recherches philosophiques sur les Américains*. 2 vols. Berlin, 1768–69.

Deperthes, J. L. H. S. *Histoire des naufrages*. 3 vols. Paris, 1789.

De Ruggiero, Guido. "John Dewey." *La Critica*, 29 (1931), 341–57.

Díaz del Castillo, Bernal. *The True History of the Conquest of Mexico*. New York, 1927.

Díaz y Gil, J. *América y el Viejo Mundo*. Buenos Aires, 1942.

Diderot, Denis. *Supplément au voyage de Bougainville* (1772). Pléiade edition. Paris, 1935.

Díez Canedo, Enrique. "Fortuna española de un verso italiano." *Revista de Filología Española*, 3 (1916), 168–70.

Díez del Corral, Luis. *Del viejo al nuevo mundo*. Madrid, 1963.

Di Giacomo, Salvatore. *La prostituzione a Napoli nei secoli XV, XVI, e XVII*. Naples, 1899.

Donne, John "Paradoxes and Problems." In *Complete Poetry and Selected Poems*, edited by John Hayward. London, 1939.

Droysen, Johann Gustav. *Historik*. Munich and Berlin, 1937.

Duchet, Michèle. "Monde civilisé et monde sauvage au siècle des Lumières: Les fondements de l'anthropologie des Philosophes." In *Au Siècle des Lumières*. Paris and Moscow, 1970.

Dudley, Edward, and Maximilian E. Novak, eds. *The Wild Man Within*. Pittsburgh, 1972.

Eguiara y Eguren, Juan José de. *Prólogos a la Biblioteca Mexicana*. Edited by Agustín Millares Carlo. Mexico, 1944.

Elliott, J. H. *The Old World and the New, 1492–1650*. Cambridge, 1970.

Ellis, George Edward. "Las Casas and the Relations of the Spaniards to the Indians." In Winsor, *The Narrative and Critical History of America*, q.v. (vol. 2, pp. 299–348).

Ellis, Henry Havelock. *The Soul of Spain*. London, 1937.

Enciso. See Fernández de Enciso.

Esteve Barba, Francisco. *Historiografía indiana*. Madrid, 1964.

Estienne, Henri. *De la précellence du langage françois* (1579). 2 vols. Paris, 1879.

Fabié, Antonio Maria. *Vida y escritos de Fray Bartolomé de Las Casas, obispo de Chiapa*. In *CDIE*, q.v. (vols. 70 and 71).

Farinelli, Arturo. "Appunti su Dante in Ispagna nell'età media." *Giornale Storico della Letteratura Italiana*, 45 (1905), suppl. 8, pp. 1–105.

_____. *Divagazioni erudite*. Turin, 1925.

_____. *Italia e Spagna*. 2 vols. Turin, 1929.

_____. "Marrano": *Storia di un vituperio*. Bibliothèque de L'Archivum Romanicum, 2d ser., vol. 10. Geneva, 1925.

_____. *Sulla fortuna del Petrarca in Ispagna nel Quattrocento*. Turin, 1904. Also in *Italia e Spagna*, above.

Fénelon, François de Salignac de la Mothe. *Dialogues des morts* (1712). Paris: Nelson, n.d.

Fénelon, Paul. "Apports américains dans le domaine animal et végétal de l'ancien continent." In *La découverte de l'Amérique*, q.v. (pp. 253–66).

Fernández-Armesto, Felipe. *Columbus and the Conquest of the Impossible*. London, 1974.

Fernández de Enciso, Martin. *Descripción de las Indias Occidentales*. See Medina. (For Enciso references in general, see chap. IX, n. 2).

———. *Suma de geographía, que trata de todas las partidas y provincias del mundo, en especial de las Indias. . . .* 3d ed. Seville, 1546.

Fernández de Navarrete, Martín, ed. *Colección de los viages y descubrimientos que hicieron por mar los españoles desde fines del siglo XV*. 5 vols. Madrid, 1825–37.

———. See *CDIE*.

Fernández de Oviedo, Gonzalo. *Historia general y natural de las Indias*. Edited by José Amador de los Ríos. Published by the Real Academia de la Historia. 4 vols. Madrid, 1851–55.

———. Reprint of the above edition, with a preface by Juan Natalicio González. 14 vols. Asunción del Paraguay, 1944–45.

———. *Historia general y natural de las Indias*. Edited by Juan Pérez de Tudela Bueso. Biblioteca de Autores Españoles, vols. 117–21. 5 vols. Madrid, 1955.

———. *Libro de la cámara real del príncipe D. Juan e officios de su casa e servicio ordinario*. Edited by Juan M. Escudero de la Peña. Colección "Bibliófilos españoles." Madrid, 1870.

———. *Libro del muy esforçado e invencible cavallero de la fortuna propiamente llamado Claribalte. . . .* Valencia, 1519; Seville, 1545.

———. *Las Quinquagenas de la nobleza de España*. Published by the Real Academia de la Historia under the direction of Vicente de la Fuente. Madrid, 1880.

———. *Regla de la vida spiritual y secreta theología*. Seville, 1548.

———. *Relación de lo sucedido en la prisión del rey de Francia. . . .* In *CDIE*, q.v. (vol. 38, Madrid, 1861).

———. *Sumario de la natural historia de las Indias*. In Vedia, ed., *Historiadores primitivos de Indias*, q.v.

———. The same. Edited by José Miranda. Mexico, 1950.

Fernández Duro, Cesáreo. *La mujer española en Indias*. Madrid, 1902.

Ferrando, Roberto. "Fernández de Oviedo y el conocimiento del Mar del Sur." *Revista de Indias*, 17, nos. 69–70 (1957), 469–82.

Fiorini, Matteo. "Qualche cenno sopra Girolamo Fracastoro." *Rivista Geografica Italiana* (Rome), 7, (1900), 433–49.

Firpo, Luigi, ed. *Prime relazioni di navigatori italiani sulla scoperta dell'America: Colombo, Vespucci, Verrazzano*. Turin, 1966.

Flourens, P. *Histoire des travaux et des idées de Buffon*. 2d ed. Paris, 1850.

Fontenelle, Bernard de. "Sur l'histoire." In *Oeuvres*. 11 vols. Paris, 1766.

Foronda y Aguilera, Manuel de. *Estancias y viajes de Carlos V, desde el día de su nacimiento hasta el de su muerte*. Madrid, 1914.

Friederich, Werner P. "The Unsolved Problem of Dante's Influence in Spain, 1515–1865." *Hispanic Review*, 14 (1946) 160–64.

Fucini, Renato. *Poesie*. Florence, 1876.

Fuente, Vicente de la. Introduction to the *Quinquagenas* of Fernández de Oviedo, q.v.

Fueter, Eduard. *Geschichte der neueren Historiographie*. Munich and Berlin, 1936.

Gaffarel, Paul. See Anghiera.

Gage, Thomas. *Travels in the New World* (1648). Edited by J. Eric S. Thompson. Norman, Okla., 1958.

Galiani, Ferdinando. *Della moneta* (1751). Edited by Fausto Nicolini. Bari, 1915.

Gamba, Bartolommeo. *Serie dei testi di lingua italiana e di altri esemplari del bene scrivere*. Venice, 1828.

Gandía, Enrique de. *Francisco de Alfaro y la condición social de los Indios*. Buenos Aires, 1939.

———. *Historia crítica de los mitos de la conquista americana*. Madrid, 1929.

García, Juan Agustín. *La ciudad indiana*. Buenos Aires, 1900.

García Calderón, Ventura. *Vale un Perú*. Paris, 1939.

García Icazbalceta, Joaquín. *Opúsculos y biografías*. Mexico, 1942.

García y García. See Anghiera.

Garcilaso de la Vega, el Inca. *Páginas escogidas*. With an essay by José de la Riva Agüero. Biblioteca de cultura peruana, vol. 3. Paris, 1938.

Gaspary, Adolfo. *Storia della letteratura italiana*. 2 vols. Turin, 1900–14.

Gates, Eunice J. "Proverbs in the Plays of Calderón." *Romanic Review* 38 (1947), 203–15.

Gatti, Sergio. "L'attività milanese del Cesariano dal 1512–13 al 1519." *Arte Lombarda*, 16 (1971), 219–30.

Gavira Martín, José. "Recientes investigaciones sobre el Mar de los Sargazos." *Boletín de la Real Sociedad Geográfica* (Madrid), 80, nos. 1–6 (1944), 441–47.

Gebhart, Emile. "L'histoire d'une bibliothèque espagnole." In *De Panurge à Sancho Pança*. Paris, 1911.

Geiger, Ludwig. *Rinascimento e umanesimo in Italia e in Germania*. Translated by D. Valbusa. Milan, 1891.

Genovesi, Antonio. *Autobiografia, lettere e altri scritti*. Edited by Gennaro Savarese. Milan, 1962.

George, Wilma. *Animals and Maps.* London, 1969.

Geraldini, Belisario. *Cristoforo Colombo e il primo vescovo di Santo Domingo, mons. Alessandro Geraldini d'Amelia.* Amelia, 1892.

Gerbi, Antonello. *The Dispute of the New World: The History of a Polemic, 1750–1900.* Translated by Jeremy Moyle. Pittsburgh, 1973.

––––––. "Mito y fortuna del Perú." *Mercurio Peruano* (Lima), 18, no. 193 (1943), 131–40.

––––––. *La politica del romanticismo.* Bari, 1932.

––––––. "Vale un Perù: Le origini di un mito." In *Peru,* ed. Centro di Azione Latina, pp. 99–119. Nazioni. Collana di monografie sui paesi dell'America Latina, no. 1. Milan, 1961.

––––––. *Viejas polémicas sobre el Nuevo Mundo.* Lima, 1946.

Gerling, W. *Wirtschaftsentwicklung und Landschaftswandel auf den westindischen Inseln Jamaika, Haiti und Puerto Rico.* Freiburg, 1938.

Giannini, A. "Impressioni italiane di viaggiatori nei secoli XVI e XVII." *Revue Hispanique,* 55 (1922), 50–160.

Giannone, Pietro. *Storia civile del regno di Napoli.* 5 vols. Milan, 1844–47.

Gibbon, Edward. *The English Essays.* Oxford, 1972.

Gioda, Carlo. *La vita e le opere di Giovanni Botero.* 3 vols. Milan, 1894–95.

Glacken, Clarence J. *Traces on the Rhodian Shore.* Berkeley and Los Angeles, 1967.

Goldsmith, Oliver. *A History of the Earth, and Animated Nature,* (1774). 2 vols. London and Edinburgh: Fullarton, 1856–57.

Gombrich, Ernst H. *Symbolic Images: Studies in the Art of the Renaissance.* London, 1972.

Gómez Canedo, Lino. *Los archivos de la historia de América: Período colonial español.* 2 vols. Mexico, 1961.

González, Juan Natalicio. Preface to his edition of the *Historia general y natural* of Fernández de Oviedo, q.v.

Goodwyn, Frank. "Pánfilo de Narváez: A Character Study of the First Spanish Leader to Land an Expedition to Texas." *Hispanic American Historical Review,* 29, no. 1 (February 1949), 150-56.

Gothein, Everardo. *Il Rinascimento nell'Italia meridionale.* Florence, 1915.

Grand-Carteret, John. *Vieux papiers, vieilles images.* Paris, 1896.

Grande, Stefano. *Le carte d'America di Giacomo Gastaldi.* Turin, 1905.

––––––. *Notizie sulla vita e sulle opere di Giacomo Gastaldi, cosmografo piemontese del secolo XVI.* Turin, 1902.

––––––. "Le relazioni geografiche fra P. Bembo, G. Fracastoro, G. B. Ramusio, G. Gastaldi." *Memorie della Società geografica italiana* (Rome), 12 (1905), 93–197.

Green, Otis H. "A Critical Survey of Scholarship in the Field of Spanish Renaissance Literature, 1914–1944." *Studies in Philology,* 44, no. 2 (April 1947), 228–62.

––––––. *Spain and the Western Tradition: The Castilian Mind from "El Cid" to Calderón.* 4 vols. Madison, Wis., 1963–66.

Guerra, Francisco. "La política imperial sobre las drogas de las Indias." *Revista de Indias,* 26, nos. 103–04 (1966), 31–58.

Guerra, José. See Mier.

Guggisberg, C. A. W. *Crocodiles: Their Natural History, Folklore and Conservation.* London, 1972.

Guicciardini, Francesco. *Storia d'Italia.* Florence, 1835.

Günther, Siegmund. "Il cardinal Pietro Bembo e la geografia." In *Atti del Congresso internazionale di scienze storiche* (1903), vol. 10, pp. 55–68. Rome, 1904.

Gusdorf, Georges. *L'avènement des sciences humaines au siècle des lumières.* Les sciences humaines et la pensée occidentale, vol. 6. Paris, 1973.

––––––. *Dieu, la nature, l'homme au siècle des lumières.* Les sciences humaines et la pensée occidentale, vol. 5. Paris, 1972.

––––––. *Les principes de la pensée au siècle des lumières.* Les sciences humaines et la pensée occidentale, vol. 4. Paris, 1971.

Habert, Jacques. "Jean de Verrazane: État de la question." In *La découverte de l'Amérique,* q.v. (pp. 51–59).

Hadamard, J. "La science et le monde moderne." *Renaissance,* 1 (1943), 523–57.

Hanke, Lewis. *All Mankind Is One.* De Kalb, Ill., 1974.

––––––. "The Development of Regulations for Conquistadores." In *Contribuciones para el estudio de la historia de América,* q.v. (pp. 71–87).

––––––. "España en las Indias y en las Filipinas." *Revista de las Indias* (Bogotá), 19 (1943), 51–89, and 197–238.

––––––. "The Requerimiento and Its Interpreters." *Revista de Historia de América,* 1, no. 1 (1938), 25–34.

––––––. "Viceroy Francisco de Toledo and the Just Titles of Spain to the Inca Empire." *The Americas* (Washington), 3 (1946–47), 3–19.

––––––, ed. See *Cuerpo de documentos del siglo XVI.*

Haring, Clarence H. *The Spanish Empire in America.* New York, 1947.

Harlow, V. T. See Raleigh.

Harrisse, Henry. *Bibliotheca Americana Vetustissima: A Description of Works Relating to America Published Between the Years 1492 and 1551.* New York and Paris, 1866.

––––––. *Bibliotheca Americana Vetustissima: Additions.* New York and Paris, 1872.

––––––. *Christophe Colomb.* Paris, 1884.

Hayes, F. C. "The Collecting of Proverbs in Spain before 1650." *Hispania*, 20 (1937), 85–94.
––––––. "The Use of Proverbs as Titles and Motives in the Siglo de Oro Drama." *Hispanic Review*, 6 (1938), 305–23; (1939), 310–23; 15 (1947), 453–63.
Heeren, Arnold Hermann Ludwig. *Ideen über die Politik, den Verkehr und den Handel der vernehmsten Völker der alten Welt*. 6 vols. Göttingen, 1824–26.
Henríquez Ureña, Pedro. *La cultura y las letras coloniales en Santo Domingo*. Buenos Aires, 1936.
––––––. *Literary Currents in Hispanic America*. Cambridge, Mass., 1945.
––––––. *Para la historia de los indigenismos*. Buenos Aires, 1938.
Herrera y Tordesillas, Antonio de. *Discursos Morales y Históricos*. Madrid, 1804.
––––––. *Historia general de los hechos de los castellanos*. 4 vols. Madrid, 1601–15.
Hill, Roscoe R. "The Office of Adelantado." *Political Science Quarterly*, 28 (1913), 646–68.
Historiadores primitivos de Indias. See Vedia.
Hodgen, Margaret Trabue. *Early Anthropology in the Sixteenth and Seventeenth Centuries*. Philadelphia, 1971.
Höffner, Joseph. *Christentum und Menschenwürde: Das Anliegen der spanischen Kolonialethik im goldenen Zeitalter*. Trier, 1947.
Hugo, Victor. *Cromwell*. Paris, 1836.
Hugues, Luigi. *Ferdinando Magellano: Studio geografico*. Turin, 1879.
––––––. *L'opera scientifica di Cristoforo Colombo*. Turin, 1892.
Humboldt, Alexander von. *Cosmos*. Spanish translation of the *Kosmos* (see below) by B. Giner and José de Fuentes. 4 vols. Madrid, 1874.
––––––. *Examen critique de l'histoire de la géographie du Nouveau Monde*. 5 vols. Paris, 1836–39.
––––––. *Kosmos*. Edited by J. G. Cotta. 5 vols. Stuttgart and Tübingen, 1845–62.
––––––. *Reise in die Aequinoctial-Gegenden des Neuen Continents*. 4 vols. Stuttgart, 1859–60.
Humboldt, Wilhelm von. *Über die Aufgaben des Geschichtschreibers*. Leipzig, 1821.
Hurtado, Juan, and Angel González Palencia. *Historia de la literatura española*. Madrid, 1943.
Iglesia, Ramón. "Bernal Díaz del Castillo y el popularismo en la historiografía española." In *El hombre Colón*, below.
––––––. *Cronistas e historiadores de la conquista de México: El Ciclo de Hernán Cortés*. Mexico, 1942.
––––––. *El hombre Colón y otros ensayos*. Mexico, 1944.
Inman, Samuel G. "Political Life in the Caribbean." In *The Caribbean Area*. Washington, 1934.
Irving, Washington. *The Life and Voyages of Christopher Columbus*. Nepperhan edition. 5 vols. New York and London: G. P. Putnam's Sons [ca. 1892]. The pagination of this edition corresponds to that of vols. 9–13 of the *Works of Washington Irving*, Holly edition, 40 vols., New York: G. P. Putnam's Sons, 1857–97.
Iturri, Francisco. *Carta crítica sobre la "Historia de América" del señor Juan Bautista Muñoz*. Madrid, 1798.
Jane, Cecil. *The Voyages of Christopher Columbus: Being the Journals of His First and Third, and the Letters Concerning His First and Last Voyages.* . . . Translated and edited, with an introduction and notes by Cecil Jane. London, 1930.
Jefferson, Thomas. *Notes on Virginia* (1784). New York: Modern Library, n.d. Also in *Works*, edited by P. L. Ford, vol. 3, pp. 349–517, New York and London, 1904–05.
Jente, Richard. "The Untilled Field of Proverbs." *Studies in Philology*, 42 (1945), 490–97.
Jerez, Francisco. See López de Jerez.
Jiménez de la Espada, Marcos. Preface to the *Guerra de Quito* by Cieza de León. Madrid, 1877.
––––––. *Relaciones geográficas de Indias*. Vol. 1: *Antecedentes*. Madrid, 1881.
Jones, Ernest. *Traité théorique et pratique de psychanalyse*. Paris, 1925.
Jones, Howard Mumford. *Ideas in America*. Cambridge, Mass., 1944.
––––––. *O Strange New World: American Culture, the Formative Years*. New York, 1964.
Jos, Emiliano. "Centenario del Amazonas: La expedición de Orellana y sus problemas históricos." *Revista de Indias*, 3, no. 10 (1942), 661–709; 4, no. 11 (1943), 5–42, 255–303, 479–526.
––––––. "Fernando Colón y la *Historia del Almirante*." *Revista de Historia de América*, 9 (1940), 5–29.
––––––. "La génesis colombina del descubrimiento." *Revista de Historia de América*, 14 (1942), 1–48.
––––––. "Impugnaciones a la *Historia del Almirante* escrita por su hijo." *Revista de Indias*, 3 (1942), 189–221.
––––––. "El libro del primer viaje: Algunas ediciones recientes." *Revista de Indias*, 10 (1950), 719–51.
––––––. "Supuestas falsificaciones del P. Las Casas en la historia de Colón." *Revista de Occidente* (Madrid), 31 (1931), 217–24.
Jowett, Benjamin. See Thucydides.
Juan, Jorge, and Antonio de Ulloa. *Relación histórica del viage a la América meridional*. 4 vols. Madrid, 1748.
Keen, Benjamin. *The Aztec Image in Western Thought*. New Brunswick, N.J., 1971.
Kelemen, Pál. *Medieval American Art*. 2 vols. New York, 1943.
Kelsen, Hans. *Derecho y paz en las relaciones internacionales*. Mexico, 1943.
Kirkpatrick, Frederick Alexander. *The Spanish Conquistadores*. London, 1943.
Konetzke, Richard. "La legislación sobre inmigración de extranjeros en América durante el reinado de Carlos V." In *Charles-Quint et son temps*, q.v. (pp. 93–112).
––––––. *Das spanische Weltreich, Grundlagen und Entstehung*. Munich, 1943.

———. *Süd- und Mittelamerika*. 2 vols. Frankfurt am Main, 1965.

Koyré, Alexandre. "Galileo and Plato." *Journal of the History of Ideas*, 4, no. 4 (1943), 400–28.

Krinsky, Carol Herselle. "Cesariano and the Renaissance Without Rome." *Arte Lombarda*, 16 (1971), 211–18.

La Curne de Sainte Palaye, Jean Baptiste. *Mémoires sur l'ancienne chevalerie*. 2 vols. Paris, 1759.

Ladurie, Emmanuel Le Roy. *Le territoire de l'historien*. Paris, 1973.

Lagomaggiore, Carlo. "L'*Istoria viniziana* di M. Pietro Bembo." *Nuovo Archivio Veneto*, new ser., yr. 4, vol. 7 (1904), 5–31, 334–72; 8 (1904), 162–80, 317–46; 9 (1905), 33–113, 308–40.

Landucci, Sergio. *I filosofi e i selvaggi, 1580–1780*. Bari, 1972.

Lanning, John Tate. "The Transplantation of the Scholastic University." In *University of Miami Hispanic-American Studies*. Coral Gables, 1939.

Las Casas, Bartolomé de. *Apologética historia de las Indias*. 2 vols. Madrid, 1909.

———. *Colección de tratados, 1552–1553*. With a foreword by Emilio Ravegnani. Buenos Aires, 1924.

———. *Historia de las Indias*. 3 vols. Madrid, 1875–76.

Le Moine, Roger. *L'Amérique et les poètes français de la Renaissance*. Ottawa, 1972.

Leonard, Irving A. "Conquerors and Amazons in Mexico." *Hispanic American Historical Review*, 24 (1944), 561–79. Reprinted in *Books of the Brave*, Cambridge, Mass., 1949.

Leoni, Francesca. "Il Cesariano e l'architettura del Rinascimento in Lombardia." *Arte Lombarda*, 1 (1955), 90–97.

León Pinelo, Antonio de. *Epítome de la biblioteca oriental y occidental, náutica y geográfica*. Madrid, 1629.

———. *El Paraíso en el Nuevo Mundo*. 2 vols. Lima, 1943.

Leopardi, Giacomo. *Opere*. Edited by Riccardo Bacchelli and Gino Scarpa. Milan: Officina Tipografica Gregoriana, 1935.

Le Sage, Alain René. *Le diable boiteux*. 2 vols. Paris, 1880.

Lessing, Gotthold Ephraim. *Hamburgische Dramaturgie*. In *Werke*, edited by Georg Witkowski. Leipzig and Vienna, [1911].

Leturia, Pedro de, S. J. "Ideales poltíco-religiosos de Colón en su carta institucional del mayorazgo." *Revista de Indias*, 11 (1951), 679–704.

Levene, Ricardo. *Investigaciones acerca de la historia económica del virreinato del Plata*. 2 vols. La Plata, 1927–28.

Lévi-Strauss, Claude. *Tristes tropiques*. Paris, 1965.

Libretto de tutta la navigatione de' re di Spagna, le isole et terreni nouamente trovati. Venice, 1504. A pirated edition of the first decade of Pietro Martire d'Anghiera's *De Orbe Novo decades*, translated into Venetian by Angelo Trevisan.

———. Facsimile edition of the above item, with an introduction by Lawrence C. Wroth. Paris, 1929.

Lizárraga, Reginaldo de. *Descripción colonial* (1605). Edited by Ricardo Rojas. 2 vols. Buenos Aires, 1916.

Llano Zapata, Eusebio. *Memorias histórico-físico-apologéticas de la América meridional*. Lima, 1904.

López de Gómara, Francisco. *Anales* (1548). Edited by Merriman. Oxford, 1912.

———. *La conquista de México* (1552). Edited by Joaquín Ramírez Cabañas. 2 vols. Mexico, 1943. Includes the "De rebus gestis Ferdinandi Cortesii."

———. *Historia general de las Indias*. Saragossa, 1552.

López de Jerez, Francisco. *Verdadera relación de la conquista del Peru* (1534). Madrid, 1862.

López de Meneses, Amada. "Andrea Navagero, traductor de G. F. de Oviedo." *Revista de Indias*, 18, no. 71 (1958), 63–71.

———. "Gonzalo Fernández de Oviedo, traductor del *Corbaccio*." *Revista de la Biblioteca, Archivo y Museo del Ayuntamiento de Madrid* (Madrid, 1933). Also in *Clio* (Ciudad Trujillo), 10 (1942).

Losada, Angel, "Hernan Cortés en la obra del cronista Sepúlveda." *Revista de Indias*, 9 (1948), 127–69.

———. "Una historia olvidada de nuestro descubrimiento de América (*De Orbe novo* de Juan Ginés de Sepúlveda)." *Revista de Indias*, 8 (1947), 509–20.

Loth, David. *The Erotic in Literature*. London, 1962.

Lovejoy, Arthur O. *The Great Chain of Being*. Cambridge, Mass., 1942.

Lowes, John Livingston. *The Road to Xanadu: A Study in the Ways of the Imagination*. Rev. ed. London, 1930.

Lozoya, Juan Contreras, marqués de. *Los orígenes del Imperio: La España de Ferdinando e Isabel*. Madrid, 1939.

Luengo Muñoz, Manuel. "Inventos para acrecentar la obtención de perlas en América durante el siglo XVI." *Anuario de Estudios Americanos* (Seville), 9 (1952), 51–72.

Lynn, Caro. *A College Professor of the Renaissance: Lucio Marineo Siculo Among the Spanish Humanists*. Chicago, 1937.

MacLeod, Murdo J. *Spanish Central America: A Socioeconomic History, 1520–1720*. Berkeley and Los Angeles, 1973.

Macnutt, F. A. See Anghiera.

Macrì, Oreste. "L'Ariosto e la letteratura spagnola." *Letterature Moderne*, 3, no. 5 (1952), 515–43.

Madariaga, Salvador de. *Cuadro histórico de las Indias*. Buenos Aires, 1950.

Magnaghi, Alberto. *Amerigo Vespucci*. 2 vols. Rome, 1924.

———. 2d ed. of the above. 1 vol. Rome, 1926.

———. "Antonio Pigafetta." In *Enciclopedia Italiana*, s.v.

Mahn-Lot, Marianne. *La découverte de l'Amérique.* Paris, 1970.
———. Review of "Le nouveau monde, l'autre monde et la pluralité des mondes," by W. G. L. Randles, q.v. *Annales,* 19, no. 6 (Nov.–Dec. 1964).
Maine, Henry Sumner. *Ancient Law.* London, 1906.
Malagola, C. *Della vita e delle opere di Antonio Urceo.* Bologna, 1878.
Mandeville, Bernard. *The Fable of the Bees.* Edited by F. B. Kaye. 2 vols. Oxford, 1957.
Manfroni, Camillo, ed. *Relazione del primo viaggio intorno al mondo (di Antonio Pigafetta).* Milan, 1929.
Manzano y Manzano, Juan. *¿Por qué se incorporaron las Indias a la corona de Castilla?* Madrid, 1942.
———. *Incorporación de las Indias a la Corona de Castilla.* Madrid, 1948.
Manzoni, Alessandro. *I promessi sposi.* Milan: Officina Tipografica Gregoriana, 1934.
Marchesi, Concetto. *Storia della letteratura latina.* 2 vols. Messina, 1929.
Mariéjol, J. H. *Pierre Martyr d'Anghiera: Sa vie et ses oeuvres.* Paris, 1887.
Marinelli, Giovanni. "Venezia nella storia della geografia cartografica ed esploratrice." *Atti del Reale Istituto Veneto de Scienze, Lettere ed Arti,* 6th ser., vol. 7, no. 7 (1888–89). 973–74.
Marion, Séraphin. *Relations des voyageurs français en Nouvelle France au XVIIème siècle.* Paris, 1923.
Marmontel, Jean François. *Les Incas.* Paris, 1777.
Martínez Cardós, José. "Las Indias y las Cortes de Castilla durante los siglos XVI y XVII." *Revista de Indias,* 16, no. 64 (1956), 207–65 and 357–411.
Martyr, Peter. See Anghiera, Pietro Martire d'.
Mateos, F. "Ecos de América en Trento." *Revista de Indias,* 22 (1945), 581–600.
Maticorena Estrada, Miguel. "Una traducción desconocida de Fernández de Oviedo." *Estudios Americanos* (Seville), 13, nos. 67–68 (1957), 299–300.
Matos, Luís de. "Un aspect de la question vespuccienne: L'auteur du *Mundus Novus.*" In *Charles Quint et son temps,* q.v. (pp. 157–65).
Matthews, Brander, ed. *The New Art of Writing Plays,* by Lope de Vega. New York, 1914.
Mattingly, Garrett. *Catherine of Aragon.* London, 1971.
Maugras, Gaston. *La Cour de Lunéville au XVIIIéme siècle.* Paris, 1904.
Mayer, August Liebmann. *Meisterwerke der Gemäldesammlung des Prado in Madrid.* Munich, 1922.
Means, Philip Ainsworth. *Biblioteca Andina.* Transactions of the Academy of Arts and Sciences. New Haven, Conn., 1928.
Mecham, J. Lloyd. "The Church in Colonial Spanish America." In *Colonial Hispanic America.* Washington, 1936.
Medina, José Toribio. *Biblioteca Hispano-Americana (1493–1810).* 7 vols. Santiago de Chile, 1898–1907.
———. *Colección de documentos inéditos para la historia de Chile,* 30 vols. Santiago de Chile, 1888–1902.
———, ed. *Descripción de las Indias Occidentales, por Martín Fernández de Enciso.* Taken from the *Suma de Geografía* of that author and reprinted with a bibliographical preface by J. T. Medina. Santiago de Chile, 1897.
———. *El Descubrimiento del Océano Pacífico: Vasco Núñez de Balboa, Fernando de Magellanes, y sus compañeros.* 2 vols. Santiago de Chile, 1913–14.
Meier, Harri. "Letteratura portoghese." In *Storie letterarie di tutti i tempi e di tutti i paesi.* Milan, 1968.
Meinecke, Friedrich. *Staat und Persönlichkeit.* Berlin, 1933.
Melón, Amando. "Del portulano de Juan de la Cosa a la carta plana de Martín Fernández de Enciso." *Revista de Indias,* 10 (1950), 811–15.
Melville, Herman. *Redburn.* In *Romances.* New York, 1931.
Menéndez Pelayo, Marcelino. *Historia de la poesía hispano-americana.* 2 vols. Santander, 1948.
———. *Historia de los heterodoxos españoles.* 8 vols. Buenos Aires, 1945.
———. "De los historiadores de Colón" (1892). In vol. 12 of *Obras completas.* 22 vols. Madrid, 1883–1908.
Menéndez Pidal, Ramón. *Los españoles en la historia y en la literatura.* Buenos Aires and Mexico, 1951.
———. *La idea imperial de Carlos V.* Buenos Aires, 1941.
———. "El lenguaje del siglo XVI." In *Los romances de América y otros estudios.* Buenos Aires, 1939.
Merkel, Carlo. *L'opuscolo "De Insulis nuper inventis" del messinese Niccolò Scillacio professore a Pavia, confrontato colle altre relazioni del secondo viaggio de Cristoforo Colombo in America: Memoria.* 2d ed. Milan, 1901.
Merryman, William N. *Northern Caballero.* London, 1942.
Messedaglia, Luigi. "Aspetti della realtà storica in Merlin Cocai." *Atto del R. Istituto Veneto di Scienze, Lettere, e Arti,* 93 (1939), pt. 2.
———. "Il pardo da caccia nella poesia, nella storia, nell'arte." *Atti dell'Accademia di Agricoltura, Scienze e Lettere di Verona,* 18 (1939–40), 27–104.
Mier Noriega y Guerra, José Servando Teresa de. *Escritos inéditos.* Edited by J. M. Miquel i Vergés and H. Díaz-Thomé. Mexico, 1944.
———. *Historia de la revolución de Nueva España.* 2 vols. London, 1813.
———. *Memorias.* Introduction by A. Reyes. Madrid, [ca. 1917].
Millares Carlo, Agustín. See *Cuerpo de documentos* and Eguiara y Eguren.
Millevoye, Charles Hubert. *Oeuvres.* 3 vols. Paris, 1880.

Miralles de Imperial y Gómez, Claudio. "Del linaje y armas del primer cronista de Indias, el madrileño Gonzalo Fernández de Oviedo." *Revista de Indias,* 18, no. 71 (1957), 73–126.
Mirbt, Carl. *Quellen zur Geschichte des Papsttums und des römischen Katholizismus.* Tübingen, 1924.
Molinari, Diego Luis. *El nacimiento del Nuevo Mundo.* Buenos Aires, 1942.
Mollat, Michel. "Soleil et navigation au temps des découvertes." In *Le Soleil à la Renaissance.* Institut Universitaire pour l'Etude de la Renaissance et de l'Humanisme, Colloque. Brussels, 1965.
Mongitore, Antonino. *Biblioteca Sicula.* 2 vols. Palermo, 1707–24.
Monnier, Philippe. *Le Quattrocento: Essai sur l'histoire littéraire du XVme siècle italien.* 2 vols. Paris, 1908.
Montaigne, Michel de. *Essais.* Bibliothèque de la Pléiade. Paris, 1933.
Montoliu, Manuel de. *Literatura castellana.* Barcelona, 1937.
Morales, Ambrosio de. See Pérez de Oliva.
Morcuende, Federico Ruiz, ed. *Primer viaje en torno del globo (de Antonio Pigafetta).* Translated into Spanish by Federico Ruiz Morcuende, with an introductory study by C. Amoretti. Madrid, 1922.
Morel-Fatio, Alfred. "Les Allemands en Espagne du XVème au XVIIIème siècle." *Revista de Filología Española,* 9 (1922), 277–97.
————. Edition of Lope de Vega's *Arte nuevo de hacer comedias en este tiempo. Bulletin Hispanique,* 3 (1901), 365–405.
————. "La fortune en Espagne d'un vers italien" *Revista de Filología Española,* 3 (1916) 63–66.
————. *Historiographie de Charles-Quint.* Paris, 1912.
————. "Las Quinquagenas de la nobleza de España." Review of Fuente's edition of Oviedo's *Quinquagenas. Revue Historique,* 21 (1883), 179–90.
Morínigo, Marcos A. *América en el teatro de Lope de Vega.* Buenos Aires, 1946.
Morison, Samuel Eliot. *Admiral of the Ocean Sea: A Life of Christopher Columbus.* 2 vols. Boston, 1942.
————. *The European Discovery of America: The Northern Voyages, A.D. 500–1600.* New York, 1971.
————. *The European Discovery of America: The Southern Voyages, 1492–1616.* New York, 1974.
————. "Texts and Translations of the Journal of Columbus's First Voyage." *Hispanic American Historical Review,* 19 (1939), 253–61.
Morse, Richard M. "Toward a Theory of Spanish American Government." *Journal of the History of Ideas,* 15, no. 1 (January 1954), 71–93.
Moses, Bernard. *Spanish Colonial Literature in South America.* London and New York, 1922.
Moxó, Benito María de. *Cartas mexicanas escritas . . . en 1805.* Genoa [1837–38].
Muñoz, Juan Bautista. *Historia del Nuevo Mundo.* Madrid, 1793.
Müntz, Eugenio, *L'arte italiana nel Quattrocento.* Milan, 1894.
————. *L'età aurea dell'arte italiana.* Milan, 1895.
Navagero, Andrea. *Lettere al Ramusio.* Venice, 1556.
Navarrete. See Fernández de Navarrete.
Nevins, Allan, and Henry Steele Commager. *America: The Story of a Free People.* Oxford, 1943.
Newton, Isaac. *Philosophiae Naturalis Principia Mathematica* (1686). Amsterdam, 1723.
Nicolini, Fausto. "Giambattista Vico e Ferdinando Galiani." *Giornale Storico della Letteratura Italiana,* 71 (1918), 137–207.
————, ed. *Il pensiero dell'abate Galiani.* Bari, 1909.
Nunn, G. E. *The Geographical Conceptions of Columbus.* New York, 1924.
O'Gorman, Edmundo. *Cuatro historiadores de Indias: Martir, Oviedo, Las Casas, Acosta.* Mexico, 1972.
————. "Trayectoria de América." In *Fundamentos de la historia de América.* Mexico, 1942.
————, ed. *Sucesos y diálogos de la Nueva España.* Selected from Oviedo and introduced by Edmundo O'Gorman. Mexico 1946.
Oliveira Martins, Joaquim Pedro de. "La política económica de la metrópoli." *Revista Universitaria* (Lima), 10 (1915), 226–54, 322–34, 410–31.
Olschki, Leonardo. "The Columbian Nomenclature of the Lesser Antilles." *The Geographical Review,* 33 (1943), 397–414.
————. "Hernán Pérez de Oliva's *Ystoria de Colon.*" *Hispanic American Historical Review,* 23 (1943), 165–96.
————. *Storia letteraria delle scoperte geografiche.* Florence, 1937.
————. *Struttura spirituale e linguistica del mondo neo-latino.* Bari, 1935.
————. "What Columbus Saw on Landing in the West Indies." *Proceedings of the American Philosophical Society,* 84, no. 5 (July 1941), 633–59.
Ortega y Gasset, José. "Galápagos, el fin del mundo." In *Espíritu de la letra* (1927) in *Orbas.* Madrid, 1943.
Ortiz, Fernando. "*Raza,* voz de mala cuna y de mala vida." *Cuadernos Americanos,* 5 (1945), 77–107.
Otero Muñoz, Gustavo. "Galería de historiadores neogranadinos: Gonzalo Hernández de Oviedo." *Boletín de Historia y Antigüedades* (Bogotá), 21 (1934).
Otte, Enrique, "Aspiraciones y actividades heterogéneas de Gonzalo Fernández de Oviedo, cronista." *Revista de Indias,* 18, no. 71 (1958), 9–62.
————. "Una carta inédita de Gonzalo Fernández de Oviedo." *Revista de Indias,* 16 (1956), 437–58.

———. "Documentos inéditos sobre la estancia de Gonzalo Fernández de Oviedo en Nicaragua." *Revista de Indias*, 18, nos. 73–74 (1958), 627–51.

———. "Empresarios españoles y genoveses en los comienzos del comercio trasatlántico: La avería de 1507." *Revista de Indias*, 23 (1963), 519–30.

———. "La flota de Diego Colón: Españoles y Genoveses en el comercio trasatlántico de 1509." *Revista de Indias*, 24 (1964), 475–503.

———. "Gonzalo Fernández de Oviedo an Kaiser Karl V über die Zustände in Santo Domingo." In *Spanische Forschungen der Görresgesellschaft*, 1st ser., vol. 2 (1928).

———. "Gonzalo Fernández de Oviedo y los genoveses: El primer registro de Tierra Firme." *Revista de Indias*, 22, nos. 89–90 (1962), 515–19.

———. "El joven Carlos y América." In *Homenaje a D. Ramón Carande*, vol. 1, pp. 155–71. Madrid, 1963.

Oviedo. See Fernández de Oviedo.

Pagador, Mariano. "Miçer Codro." In *La Floresta Española Americana*. 2d ed. 3 vols. Lima, 1892.

Palau y Dulcet. *Manual del librero hispano-americano*. 2d ed. 28 vols. Barcelona, 1948–77.

Palm, Erwin Walter. "Hospitales antiguos de la Española." *Multa Paucis Medica* (Mexico), 3, no. 5 (September–October 1946), 49–75.

———. *Los monumentos arquitectónicos de la Española*. 2 vols. Ciudad Trujillo, 1955.

———. "Plateresque and Renaissance Monuments of the Island of Hispaniola." *Journal of the Society of Architectural Historians*, 5 (1946), 1–14.

Palmieri, Ruggero. "Di una imitazione spagnuola del *Cortigiano* (*El Cortesano* di Luis Milán)." *Il Conciliatore* (Turin), 2 (1915), 471–93.

Papi, Fulvio. *Antropologia e civiltà nel pensiero di Giordano Bruno*. Florence, 1968.

Pascal, Blaise. *Lettres provinciales* (1656–57). Paris, 1926.

Pascarella, Cesare. *La scoperta de l'America*. Turin, 1926.

Pazzi, Gianna. *Il "Belvedere" ferrarese nei versi d'Ariosto e di Balbo*. Rome, 1933.

Peña y Cámera, José de la "Contribuciones documentales y críticas para una biografía de Gonzalo Fernández de Oviedo." *Revista de Indias*, 17, nos 69–70 (1957), 603–705.

Pennesi, Giuseppe. "Pietro Martire d'Anghiera e le sue relazioni sulle scoperte oceaniche." In *Raccolta Colombiana*, q.v. (pt. 5, vol. 2).

Penrose, Boies. *Travel and Discovery in the Renaissance*. Cambridge, Mass., 1925.

Pércopo, Erasmo. See Chariteo.

Pereyra, Carlos. *Historia de la América española*. 8 vols. Madrid, 1920.

———. *Las huellas de los Conquistadores*. Madrid, 1929.

———. *La obra de España en América*. Cartagena and Madrid, 1920.

Pérez Bustamante, Ciriaco. "Las regiones españolas y la población de América (1509–1534)." *Revista de Indias*, 2, no 6 (1941), 81–120.

Pérez de Oliva, Hernán. *Diálogo de la dignidad del hombre*. Preface by Ambrosio de Morales. Buenos Aires, 1943.

Pérez de Tudela Bueso, Juan. "La gran reforma carolina de las Indias en 1542." *Revista de Indias*, 17, nos. 73–74 (1957), 463–509.

———. "Rasgos del semblante espiritual de Gonzalo Fernández de Oviedo." *Revista de Indias*, 17, nos. 69–70 (1957), 391–443.

———. "Vida y escritos de Gonzalo Fernández de Oviedo." Preface to his edition of the *Historia general* of Fernández de Oviedo, q.v. (vol. 1, pp. vii–clxix).

———. "Vision de la découverte du Nouveau Monde chez les chroniqueurs espagnols." In *La découverte de l'Amerique*, q.v. (pp. 267–77).

———. Review of Edmundo O'Gorman's *La idea del descubrimiento de América* (Mexico, 1951). *Revista de Indias*, 12, no. 47 (1952), 147–50.

Pérez Embid, Florentino, "El problema de la incorporación de las Indias a la corona de Castilla." *Revista de Indias*, 8, nos. 33–34 (1948), pp. 795–836.

Perrier, Edmund. *La philosophie zoologique avant Darwin*. Paris, 1884.

Peschel, Oscar. *Geschichte der Erdkunde*. Munich, 1865.

Peter Martyr. See Anghiera.

Picatoste, Felipe. *Los españoles en Italia*. Madrid, 1887.

Pichardo, Bernardo. *Reliquias históricas de la Española*. 2d ed. Santiago, Dominican Republic, 1944.

Pickering, F. P. *Augustinus oder Boethius*. Berlin, 1967.

Picón Salas, Mariano. *De la conquista a la independencia*. Mexico, 1944.

Pigafetta, Antonio. See Manfroni; Morcuende.

Pincherle, Alberto. *La leggenda nera*. Milan, 1959.

Pirenne, Henri. *Mahomet et Charlemagne*. Paris. 1937.

Pitman, James Hall. *Goldsmith's Animated Nature: A Study of Goldsmith*. New Haven ,1924.

Pliny the Elder. *Histoire naturelle*. Translated into French by Emile Littré. 2 vols. Paris, 1883.

———. *Naturalis Historia*. Translated into Italian by Cristofaro Landino. Venice, 1534.

Pogo, Alexander, ed. "The Anonymous *La conquista del Peru* (Seville, April 1534) and the *Libro ultimo del summario delle Indie Occidental* (Venice, October 1534)." *Proceedings of the American Academy of Arts and Sciences*, 64, no. 8 (July 1930), 177–286.

Pohl, Frederick, J. *Amerigo Vespucci: Pilot Major*. New York, 1944.

Polo, Marco. *I Viaggi*. Edited by Adolfo Bartoli. Florence, 1863.

Poma de Ayala, Felipe Guamán. *Nueva corónica y buen gobierno*. . . . Paris, 1936.

Porcacchi, Tommaso, ed. *Lettere di XIII Huomini illustri*. Venice, 1560, 1584.

Porras Barrenechea, Raúl. *Cedularios del Perú, siglos XVI, XVII y XVIII*. Lima, 1944.

———. "Los cronistas de la conquista: Molina, Oviedo, Gómara y Las Casas." *Revista de la Universidad Católica* (Lima), 9 (1941), 235–52.

———. "Los cronistas del Perú." *Mercurio Peruano* (Lima), 18, no. 197 (August 1943), 361–78.

———. "Francisco Pizarro." *Revista de Indias*, 3, no. 7 (1942), 5–39.

———. "El pensamiento de Vitoria en el Perú." *Mercurio Peruano* (Lima), 27 (October 1946).

———. *Los viajeros italianos en el Perú*. Lima, 1957.

Prescott, William Hickling. *History of the Conquest of Mexico and History of the Conquest of Peru*. Modern Library. New York [1936].

———. *History of the Reign of Ferdinand and Isabella the Catholic*. Edited by J. Foster Kirk. 3 vols. Philadelphia, 1872.

Priestley, H. I. *The Coming of the White Man*. New York, 1940.

Procacci, G. "La 'fortuna' nella realtà politica e sociale del primo Cinquecento." *Belfagor* (Florence), 6, no. 4 (1951), 407–21.

Puente y Olea, Manuel de la. *Los trabajos geográficos de la Casa de Contratación*. Seville, 1900.

Quiller-Couch, Arthur. *On the Art of Reading*. New York and London, 1920.

Quinn, David Beers. *England and the Discovery of America, 1481–1620*. New York, 1974.

———. "New Geographical Horizons: Literature." In *First Images of America: The Impact of the New World on the Old*, edited by Fredi Chiappelli, vol. 2, pp. 635–58. Berkeley and Los Angeles, 1976.

Quintana, Manuel José. *Obras completas*. 3 vols. Madrid, 1897–98.

Raccolta Colombiana. See Reale Commissione Colombiana.

Raimondi, Ezio. *Codro e l'umanesimo a Bologna*. Bologna, 1950.

Raleigh, Walter. *The Discoverie of the large and bewtiful Empire of Guiana*. Edited by V. T. Harlow. London, 1928.

Ramusio, Giovan Battista. *Raccolta di navigationi et viaggi*. 3 vols. Venice, 1550–56.

Randles, W. G. L. "Le nouveau monde, l'autre monde et la pluralité des mondes." In *Actas do Congreso Internacional de História dos Descubrimentos*. Lisbon, 1961.

Ravegnani, Emilio. See *Contribuciones;* Las Casas.

Reade, Charles. *The Cloister and the Hearth* (1861). London, 1939.

Reale Commissione Colombiana. *Raccolta di documenti e studi*. Published on the fourth anniversary of the discovery of America. Edited by Cesare de Lollis. Rome, 1892–96.

Redi, Francesco. *Osservazioni intorno alle vipere*. Florence, 1686.

———. *Esperienze intorno a diverse cose naturali*. Florence, 1686.

Relación del último viage al estrecho de Magallanes de la fragata de S.M. "Santa María de la Cabeza" en los años de 1785 y 1786. . . . Madrid, 1788.

Relaciones y Cartas. See Columbus, Christopher.

Retz, Cardinal de. *Mémoires*. Pléiade edition. Paris, 1968.

Revelli, Paolo. *Terre d'America e archivi d'Italia*. Milan, 1926.

Rey, Agapito. "Book XX of Oviedo's *Historia Natural y General de las Indias*." *Romanic Review*, 18 (1927), 52–57.

Reyes, Alfonso. "El erasmismo en América." *Boletin del Instituto de Cultura Latino-Americana* (Buenos Aires), 2 (1938), 63–65. Reprinted in *Revista de Historia de América* (Mexico), 1 (1938), 53–55, and in *Ultima Tule*, below, pp. 147–52.

———. "Fortuna española de un verso italiano." *Revista de Filologia Española*, 4 (1917), 208.

———. "El presagio de América." In *Ultimo Tule*, below.

———. *Ultima Tule*. Mexico, 1942.

Rey Pastor, Julio. *La ciencia y la técnica en el descubrimiento de América*. Buenos Aires, 1942.

Ricard, Robert. *La "conquête spirituelle" du Mexique*. Paris, 1933.

———. "Reflexiones acerca de la evangelización de Méjico por los misioneros españoles en el siglo XVI." *Revista de Indias*, 5 (1944), 7–25.

Rich, Obadiah. *Bibliotheca Americana Nova*. London, 1835–46.

Rioja, Enrique. "Apostillas de un naturalista a la relación del primer viaje del Almirante de la Mar Océana." *Cuadernos Americanos*, 6 (1945). 137–48.

Riva Agüero, José de la. See Garcilaso de la Vega.

Robertson, Dougal. *Survive the Savage Sea*. London, 1973.

Robertson, William. *The History of America*, 2 vols. London, 1777.

———. *History of Charles V*. Paris, 1835.

Rodríguez Demorizi, Emilio, ed. *Relaciones históricas de Santo Domingo.* Ciudad Trujillo, 1942.
Rodríguez Villa, Antonio, ed. *Crónicas del Gran Capitán.* Madrid, 1908.
Romano, Ruggiero. *Les mécanismes de la conquête coloniale: Les conquistadores.* Paris, 1972.
Romeo, Rosario. *Le scoperte americane nella coscienza italiana del Cinquecento.* 2d ed. Milan and Naples, 1971.
Ronchini, Amadio. *Intorno a un rarissimo opuscolo di Nicolò Scillacio messinese sopra il secondo viaggio di Cristoforo Colombo alla scoperta dell'America.* Modena, 1846.
———. *Nicolò Scillacio e la sua relazione sulla scoperta del Nuovo Continente.* Modena, 1875.
Rosenblat, Angel. *La población indígena de América desde 1492 hasta la actualidad.* Buenos Aires, 1945.
Rossi, Giorgio. "Serafino Aquilano e i suoi sonetti: Un'edizione delle Rime di Serafino Aquilano sfuggita ai bibliografi." In *Varietà letterarie.* Bologna, 1912.
Rostovzeff, Michael. *A History of the Ancient World.* 2 vols. Oxford, 1936.
———. *The Social and Economic History of the Roman Empire.* Oxford, 1926.
Rousseau, Jean Jacques. *Oeuvres.* 4 vols. Pléaide edition. Paris, 1959–69.
Sacchetti, Franco. *Novelle.* 2 vols. Florence, 1860.
Saint-Pierre, Bernardin de. *Paul et Virginie* (1789). Paris, 1873.
Salas, Alberto M. *Tres cronistas de Indias.* Mexico and Buenos Aires, 1959.
Salcedo Ruiz, Angel. *La literatura española.* 2 vols. Madrid, 1916.
Sánchez Alonso, Benito. *Fuentes de la historia española e hispanoamericana.* 3d ed. 3 vols. Madrid, 1952.
———. *Historia de la historiografía española.* 3 vols. Madrid, 1941–50.
Sánchez de las Brozas, Francisco. *Quod nihil scitur* (1581). Translated into Spanish as *Que nada se sabe.* Buenos Aires, 1944.
Sanford, Charles L. *The Quest for Paradise.* Urbana, Ill., 1961.
Sardella, Pierre. *Nouvelles et spéculations à Venise au début de XVIème siècle.* Paris, 1948.
Sassetti, Filippo. *Lettere.* Edited by Ettore Marcucci. Florence, 1855.
Sbaraglia, Giacinto. *Supplementum et Castigatio ad Scriptores Trium Ordinum S. Francisci.* 3 vols. Rome, 1908–36.
Scherillo, Michele. *Le origini e lo svolgimento della letteratura italiana.* 2 vols. Milan, 1926.
Schevill, Rudolf. "La novela histórica, las crónicas de Indias y los libros de caballerías." *Revista de las Indias* (Bogotá), nos. 59–60 (1944), 173–96.
Schevill, Rudolf, and A. Bonilla y San Martín, eds. *La Galatea. In Obras Completas de M. de Cervantes.* Madrid, 1914.
Schlayer, Hilderose. "Pepitoria 'abatis.'" *Revista de Filología Española,* 18 (1931), 36–37.
Scillacio, Nicolò. *De insulis Meridiani atque Indici maris nuper inventis.* Reprint of the 1st ed., Pavia, 1494 or 1495, by M. J. Lenox, with English translation by the Rev. John Mulligan. New York, 1859.
———. "De insulis nuper inventis." Edited by G. Berchet. In *Raccolta Colombiana,* q.v. (pt. 3, vol. 2, pp. 83–94).
Segre, Mario, *Un poema colombiano del Settecento.* Rome, 1925.
Sepúlveda, Juan Ginés de. *Democrates alter* (1547). Translated into Spanish as *Tratado sobre las justas causas de la guerra contra los indios.* Mexico, 1941.
———. *Opera.* 4 vols. Madrid, 1780.
Sereni, Angelo Piero. *The Italian Conception of International Law.* New York, 1943.
Serrano y Sanz, Manuel. *Orígenes de la dominación española en América.* Madrid, 1918.
Shaftesbury, Anthony Ashley Cooper, earl of. *Characteristics of Men, Manners, Opinions, Times* (1711). 3 vols. 6th ed. London, 1737–38.
Shaw, George Bernard. *Collected Plays.* Bodley Head edition. 7 vols. London, 1971–74.
Sherman, William L. "Indian Slavery and the Cerrato Reforms." *Hispanic American Historical Review,* 51, no. 1 (1971), 25–50.
Silius Italicus. *Punica.* Paris, 1837.
Simón, Fray Pedro. *Noticias historiales de las conquistas de tierra firme en las Indias Occidentales 1626–27.* 3 vols. Bogotá, 1892.
Sinclair, Joseph H. See Anghiera.
Sluiter, Engel. "Francisco Lopez de Caravantes' Historical Sketch of Fiscal Administration in Colonial Peru, 1533–1618." *Hispanic American Historical Review,* 25 (1945), 224–56.
Smith, Bradley. *Columbus in the New World.* New York, 1962.
Soler Jardón, Fernando. "Tres 'tigres' para el Buen Retiro (1635)." *Revista de Indias,* 8, nos. 28–29 (1947), 501–09.
Solinus, Gaius Julius. *Collectanea rerum memorabilium.* In *Antiquitatum variarum Autores* (Lyons, 1560), pp. 252–454.
Spezi, Giuseppe, ed. *Lettere inedite del Cardinale Pietro Bembo e di scrittori del secolo XVI.* Rome, 1862.
Speziale, Giuseppe Carlo. *Storia militare di Taranto negli ultimi cinque secoli.* With a preface by Benedetto Croce. Bari, 1930.
Spini, Giorgio. *Tra Rinascimento e Riforma: Antonio Brucioli* (Florence, 1940).

Spivakosky, Erika. *Son of the Alhambra: Don Diego Hurtado y de Mendoza, 1504–1575.* Austin and London, 1970.
Staël, Germaine Necker, Madame de. *Corinne.* Paris, 1858.
Stegmann, André. "L'Amérique de Du Bartas et de De Thou." In *La découverte de l'Amérique,* q.v. (pp. 299–309).
Tasso, Torquato. *La Gerusalemme liberata.* Venice, 1580.
———. *Il mondo creato* (1592). Edited by Petrocchi. Florence, 1951.
Teggart, Frederick J. *Theory and Processes of History.* Los Angeles, 1941.
Terán, Juan Bautista. *La nascita dell'America spagnola.* Bari. 1931.
Thacher, John Boyd. *Christopher Columbus; His Life, His Work, His Remains.* 3 vols. New York and London, 1903–04.
Thucydides. *Thucydides Translated into English.* With an introduction by Benjamin Jowett. Oxford, 1881.
Ticknor, George. *History of Spanish Literature.* Boston and New York, 1891.
Tiemann, Hermann. *Das spanische Schrifttum in Deutschland von der Renaissance bis zur Romantik.* Hamburg, 1936.
Tillyard, E. M. W. *The Elizabethan World Picture.* London, 1943.
Tinland, Franck. *L'homme sauvage: Homo ferus et Homo sylvestris, de l'animal à l'homme.* Paris, 1968.
Torre Revello, José. "La expedición de don Pedro de Mendoza y las fuentes informativas de Herrera." In *Contribuciones . . . Ravignani,* q.v. (pp. 605–29).
———. "Merchandise Brought to America by the Spaniards (1534–86)." *Hispanic American Historical Review,* 23, no. 4 (1943), 773–81.
Torres Asensio, Joaquín. See Anghiera.
Transylvanus, Maximilianus. *Relación . . . de cómo y por quién y en qué tiempo fueron descubiertas y halladas las islas Molucas.* In Fernández de Navarrete, *Colección,* q.v. (vol. 4, pp. 249–84).
Trilussa. *Le Poesie.* Milan, 1951.
Turner, Daymond. "Biblioteca Ovetense: A Speculative Reconstruction of the Library of the First Chronicler of the Indies." *Papers of the Bibliographical Society of America,* vol. 57, 2d quarter (1963), 157–83. Reprinted, with amendments, in *Revista de Indias,* 31, nos. 124–25 (1971), 139–98.
———. *Gonzalo Fernández de Oviedo y Valdés: An Annotated Bibliography.* University of North Carolina Studies in the Romance Languages and Literatures, no. 66. Chapel Hill, N.C. 1966.
———. "Oviedo's *Claribalte:* The First American Novel." *Romance Notes,* 6, no. 1 (1964), 65–68.
Turner, Ernest S. *A History of Courting.* London, 1954.
Turner, Olga. "Il rapporto di D. Carlos Coloma dal Ducato di Milano, nel 1626, a Filippo IV di Spagna." *Rivista Storica Italiana,* 64 (1952), 581–95.
Tutini, Camillo. *Della varietà della fortuna.* Naples, 1754.
Ullmann, B. L. "Trends in Greek and Latin Studies." *Studies in Philology,* 42 (1945), 403–12.
Ulloa, Antonio de. See Juan, Jorge.
Uría Riu, Juan. "Nuevos datos y consideraciones sobre el linaje asturiano del historiador de las Indias, Gonzalo Fernández de Oviedo." *Revista de Indias,* 20, nos. 81–82 (1960), 13–29.
Vaillant, George Clapp. *The Aztecs of Mexico.* Harmondsworth, 1950.
Valbuena Prat, Angel. *Historia de la literatura española.* 3 vols. Barcelona, 1950.
Valéry, Paul. *Poésies.* Paris, 1930.
Valle, José Cecilio del. "Vegetales indígenas de América." In *Obras.* Guatemala, 1929–30.
Valle, Rafael Heliodoro. "Un ilustre americano." *Revista Mexicana de Sociología, 6 (1944),* 7–18.
Van Gulik, Robert. *La vie sexuelle dans la Chine ancienne.* Paris, 1971.
Vázquez, Josefina Zoraida. "El indio americano y su circunstancia en la obra de Fernández de Oviedo." *Revista de Indias.* 17, nos. 69–70 (1957) 483–519.
Vedia, Enrique de, ed. *Historiadores primitivos de Indias.* Biblioteca de Autores Españoles, vols. 22 and 26. Madrid, 1858. Vol. 22 contains Oviedo's *Sumario.*
Venturi, Adolfo. *L'architettura del Quattrocento.* 2 vols. Milan, 1924.
———. *Storia dell'arte italiana.* Vol. 7, pt. 4: *La pittura del Quattrocento.* Milan, 1915.
Verlinden, Charles. *Kolumbus: Vision und Ausdauer.* Göttingen, 1962.
———. *Origines de la civilisation atlantique.* Neuchâtel, 1966.
Verrua, Pietro. *Umanisti ed altri "studiosi viri" italiani e stranieri di qua e di là dalle Alpi e dal mare.* Geneva, 1924.
Verzone, Paolo. "Cesare Cesariano." *Arte Lombarda,* 16 (1971), 203–10.
Vico, Giambattista. *La Scienza Nuova.* Edited by Fausto Nicolini. 3 vols. Bari, 1911–16.
Vignaud, Henry. *Etudes critiques sur la vie de Colomb.* Paris, 1905.
———. *Histoire critique de la grande entreprise de Christophe Colomb.* 2 vols. Paris, 1911.
Villalón, Cristóbal de. *Viaje de Turquía* (ca. 1557). Buenos Aires, 1942.
Villoro, Luis. *Los grandes momentos del indigenismo en México.* Mexico, 1950.
Vivante, Armando, and José Imbelloni. *Libro de las Atlántidas.* Buenos Aires [ca. 1940].

Vocino, Michele. *Marinai italiani ed iberici sulle vie delle Indie*. Rome, 1955.

Voigt, Georg. *Il risorgimento dell'antichità classica*. 2 vols. Florence, 1888.

Volney, Constantin François, comte de. *Tableau du climat et du sol des Etats-Unis* (1802). Paris, 1846.

Volpicella, Luigi. *Federico d'Aragona e la fine del Regno di Napoli nel MDI*. Naples, 1908.

Voltaire. *Dictionnaire philosophique* (1764). Paris, 1879.

Wagner, Henry R. "Bernal Díaz del Castillo." *Hispanic American Historical Review*, 25 (1945), 155–211.

———. *The Rise of Hernán Cortés*. Los Angeles, 1944.

Wassermann, Jakob. *Christoph Columbus, der Don Quichote des Ozeans*. Berlin, 1930.

Weigert, H. A. *Generals and Geographers: The Twilight of Geopolitics*. New York, 1942.

White, Hayden V. "Foucault Decoded: Notes from Underground." *History and Theory*, 12 (1973), 23–54.

Winsor, Justin. *The Narrative and Critical History of America*. 8 vols. Boston and New York, 1886–89.

Wölfel, Dominik Josef. "Alonso de Lugo y Compañía." *Investigación y Progreso* (Madrid), 8, nos. 7–8 (July-August 1934), 244–48.

Wroth, Lawrence C., ed. See *Libretto de tutta la navigazione de' re di Spagna*.

Yacovleff, E., and F. L. Herrera. "El mundo vegetal de los antiguos peruanos." In *Revista del Museo Nacional* (Lima), 3, no. 3 (1934), 241–323.

Yates, Frances A. *Astraea: The Imperial Theme in the Sixteenth Century*. London and Boston, 1975.

Young, Filson. *Christopher Columbus and the New World of His Discovery*. London, 1911.

Zabughin, Vladimiro. *Storia del Rinascimento cristiano in Italia*. Milan, 1924.

Zavala, Silvio. *America en el espíritu francés del siglo XVIII*. Mexico, 1949.

———. "La doctrina del dr. Palacios Rubios sobre la conquista de América." In *La "Utopía" de Tomás Moro en la Nueva España y otros estudios*. Mexico, 1937.

———. "Las doctrinas de Palacios Rubios y Matías de Paz." *Memoria del Colegio Nacional* (Mexico), 5 (1951), 71–94, and 6 (1952), 67–159.

———. *La filosofía política en la conquista de México*. Mexico, 1947.

———. *Ideario de Vasco de Quiroga*. Mexico, 1941.

———. *Las instituciones jurídicas en la conquista de América*. Madrid, 1945.

———. *Los intereses particulares en la conquista de Nueva España*. Madrid, 1933.

———. "Las Casas ante la doctrina de la servidumbre natural." *Revista de la Universidad de Buenos Aires*, 3d ser., vol. 2, no. 1 (1944).

———. *New Viewpoints on the Spanish Colonization of America*. Philadelphia, 1943.

———. "Los trabajadores antillanos en el siglo XVI." *Revista de Historia de América*, nos. 2–4 (1938), 31–67, 60–88, 212–16.

Zweig, Stefan. *Magellano*. Translated by Lavinia Mazzucchetti. Milan, 1938.

Index

Abruzzi, 145, 193
Academia de la Historia, 132–33, 379, 422
Accademia dei Lincei, 132n
Accademia della Crusca, 162
Achemenides, 64
Acheron, 159n
Acla, 214n, 395
Acorns, 32, 33
Acosta, José de, 11, 24, 37n, 125, 132, 283, 293n, 295n, 417n, 421n
Acuña, L. A., 394n
Adam, 7, 13, 38, 72n, 78n, 81, 82
Adorno, Giovanni, 138
Adriatic, 115n
Aeneas, 62
Agathyrses, 62
Agnaneo, 63
Agnelli, Giuseppe, 188n
Aguilar, Isabel de, 142
Aiton, Arthur, 169n
Alacranes, 309
Alaminos, Antón de, 88
Alarcón, 410
Alberi, Eugenio, 57n
Albertus Magnus, 157n
Albizzi, Francisco, 47
Alcalá de Henares, 122n, 192n
Alcazaba, Simón de, 102n, 218n
Alchemy, 73n, 158, 331, 332n, 378n
Alcocer, Luis Jerónimo, 198n, 250n, 272n
Aldovrandi, Ulisse, 276n, 300
Alejo de Orrio, Father Francisco Xavier, 37n
Alemán, Luis E., 141n
Alexander the Great, 79, 209n
Alexander VI, Pope (Rodrigo Borgia), 138, 145, 166n, 179, 278, 333
Alexandria, 50n, 197, 231n
Alfonso d'Este, 149n, 188n
Alfonso the Wise, 78n
Allen, Don Cameron, 420n
Alligators, 69n, 86, 170, 199, 258
Almagià, Roberto, 50n, 115n, 116n, 173n, 314n
Almagro, Diego de, 142, 178, 180, 251, 269n, 283, 310, 315, 316n, 326, 366n, 371n, 376, 395n
Almería, 189n
Almonds, 299
Aloes, 24

Alonso, Amado, 392n
Alonzo, Pedro, 260
Alonzo of Aragon, 146
Alphaeus, 68
Alphonse, Jean, 269
Alps, 193
Altamira y Crevea, Rafael, 77n
Altolaguirre y Duvale, Angel de, 228n, 329n
Alvarado, Pedro de, 119, 120, 241, 373
Alvarez Baena, J. A., 162n
Alvarez López, Enrique, 132n, 135, 182n, 245n, 262n, 293n, 295n, 387
Amadis, 203, 204, 205n, 206
Amador de los Ríos, José, 103n, 129n, 130, 131n, 133, 136n, 137n, 140n, 141n, 143n, 156n, 162n, 164n, 165n, 176n, 181n, 182n, 183n, 202n, 213n, 214n, 216n, 231n, 233, 234n, 238n, 271n, 272n, 317n, 318n, 338n, 357n, 371n, 380n, 385n, 387, 389, 396n
Amalfi, 152
Amazon River, 39, 167. *See also* Marañón River
Amazons, 21, 61, 85, 96n, 105, 107, 221, 266n, 285
Amber, 236
America: absence of seasons in, 290–91; climate of, 13, 14, 18n, 24, 25, 71, 123, 289; degeneration of, 3; fertile soil of, 24, 28, 71, 72, 73, 96, 114, 290n; immaturity of, 3, 279; inferiority of, 3, 13; its lack of written history, 242; landscape of, 19, 96, 114, 289; as literary inspiration, 227, 283; naming of, 35, 46, 49; physiognomy of, 167, 237–38, 259, 278; propitious for livestock, 71, 72, 96, 123, 257, 289–90; and the Spanish government, 117–23; wetness of, 48, 291; youthfulness of, 7. *See also* Fauna, American; Flora, American; New World
American Indians (redskins), 112n, 113–15, 267, 275n, 338n
Amoretti, Carlo, 102, 107n, 109
Ampère, Jean Jacques, 288n
Anabaptists, 381, 382
Anacaona, 111n
Andagoya, Pascual de, 132n, 371n
André, Marius, 333n
Anghiera, Pietro Martire d': anti-Semitism of, 60n; on Amazons, 61; and antiquity, 53–54, 96, 265, 266; his benefices in the Indies, 235;